Language

An Invitation to Cognitive Science
Daniel N. Osherson, Series Editor

Volume 1: Language
Edited by Lila R. Gleitman and Mark Liberman

Volume 2: Visual Cognition
Edited by Stephen M. Kosslyn and Daniel N. Osherson

Volume 3: Thinking
Edited by Edward E. Smith and Daniel N. Osherson

Volume 4: Conceptual Foundations
Edited by Saul Sternberg and Donald Scarborough

Language

An Invitation to Cognitive Science
Second Edition

Volume 1

edited by Lila R. Gleitman and Mark Liberman

A Bradford Book
The MIT Press
Cambridge, Massachusetts
London, England

© 1995 Massachusetts Institute of Technology

This book was set in Palatino by Asco Trade Typesetting Ltd., Hong Kong and printed in the United States of America.

Library of Congress Cataloging-in-Publication Data

An invitation to cognitive science.—2nd ed.
    p.   cm.
  "A Bradford book."
  Includes bibliographical references and indexes.
  Contents: v. 1. Language / edited by Lila R. Gleitman and Mark
Liberman—v. 2. Visual cognition / edited by Stephen M. Kosslyn and
Daniel N. Osherson—v. 3. Thinking / edited by Edward E. Smith
and Daniel N. Osherson.
  ISBN 0-262-65045-2 (set).—ISBN 0-262-15044-1 (v. 1 : hardcover).
—ISBN 0-262-65044-4 (v. 1 : pbk.).
  1. Cognition. 2. Cognitive science. I. Gleitman, Lila R.
BF311.I68 1995
153—dc20   95-10924
                                          CIP

Contents

List of Contributors

Gary S. Dell
Department of Psychology
University of Illinois

Janet Dean Fodor
Linguistics Department at Graduate
Center
City University of New York

Lila R. Gleitman
Departments of Psychology and
Linguistics
University of Pennsylvania

James Higginbotham
Centre for Linguistics and
Philosophy
University of Oxford

William Labov
Department of Linguistics
University of Pennsylvania

Richard Larson
Department of Linguistics
State University of New York at
Stony Brook

Howard Lasnik
Department of Linguistics
University of Connecticut

Mark Liberman
Department of Linguistics
University of Pennsylvania

Elissa L. Newport
Department of Psychology
University of Rochester

Barbara H. Partee
Department of Linguistics and
Philosophy
University of Massachusetts at
Amherst

Steven Pinker
Department of Brain and Cognitive
Sciences
Massachusetts Institute of
Technology

Mark Steedman
Department of Computer and
Information Science
University of Pennsylvania

Janet F. Werker
Department of Psychology
University of British Columbia

Edgar B. Zurif
Department of Psychology
Brandeis University

Foreword

The book you are holding is the first of a four-volume introduction to contemporary cognitive science. The work includes more than forty chapters, written by linguists, psychologists, philosophers, computer scientists, biologists, and engineers. The topics range from muscle movement to human rationality, from acoustic phonetics to mental imagery, from the cerebral locus of language to the categories that people use to organize experience. Topics as diverse as these require distinctive kinds of theories, tested against distinctive kinds of data, and this diversity is reflected in the style and content of the chapters.

The authors of these volumes are united by their fascination with the mechanisms and structure of biological intelligence, especially human intelligence. Indeed, the principal goal of this introductory work is to reveal the vitality of cognitive science, to share the excitement of its pursuit, and to help you reflect upon its interest and importance. You may therefore think of these volumes as an invitation—namely, the authors' invitation to join the ongoing adventure of research into human cognition.

The topics we explore fall into four parts, each corresponding to a separate volume. The parts are: language, visual cognition, thinking, and conceptual foundations. Each volume is self-contained, so they can be read in any order. On the other hand, it is easiest to read the chapters of a given volume in the order indicated. Each chapter concludes with suggestions for further reading and a set of problems to test your understanding.

It remains only to wish you a pleasant and invigorating journey through cognitive science. May it lead to a life-long interest!

Istituto San Raffaele
July 1995

DANIEL N. OSHERSON
SERIES EDITOR

ix

The Study of Cognition

Daniel N. Osherson

Cognitive science is the study of human intelligence in all of its forms, from perception and action to language and reasoning. The exercise of intelligence is called cognition. Under the rubric of cognition fall such diverse activities as recognizing a friend's voice over the telephone, reading a novel, jumping from stone to stone in a creek, explaining an idea to a classmate, remembering the way home from work, and choosing a profession. Cognitive processes are essential to each of these activities; indeed, they are essential to everything we do.

Research on cognition has historical roots in antiquity and was already flourishing in the 1800s. The field drew new impetus in the 1950s from theoretical innovations in linguistics (Chomsky 1956, 1957) and computer science (Minsky 1956, 1961; Newell and Simon 1956). The rapid development of these fields raised the possibility of genuine insight into the structure of human cognition and exerted a magnetic attraction on other disciplines concerned with intelligence, both human and artificial. These disciplines included parts of neurophysiology, psychology, philosophy, anthropology, mathematics, and economics. The result has been a vigorous dialogue among scientists working within diverse traditions, employing different methodologies, and starting from different assumptions. By the mid-1970s it was becoming clear that the different approaches were complementary and that the next generation of scientists would need to have a distinctive kind of training, drawing from several established disciplines. In response, undergraduate and postgraduate programs in cognitive science were started in many universities in North America, Europe, and Japan.

The new programs have created a need for new textbooks, especially introductory textbooks that open cognitive science to the beginning student. Such is the purpose of these four volumes. They provide a glimpse of the topics treated within the discipline, the methods used, and the theories produced so far.

Why Study Human Cognition?

Before looking at the contents of the volumes in more detail, let us consider some reasons for the scientific investigation of human cognition.

The Fascination of Cognitive Science

Think about your last conversation with a friend. From a certain point of view it went this way. Your friend had an idea or thought that she wanted to convey to you. For this purpose she sent volleys of commands to scores of muscles in her abdomen, chest, throat, tongue, and lips. The resulting oral gymnastics had the effect of vibrating the air molecules around her. Ultimately, the vibrations in the air caused corresponding vibrations at your eardrum. These vibrations were passed along in attenuated form through bones, fluids, and tissues in your ear until they resulted in a volley of sensory discharges along the auditory nerve to your brain. The sensory discharges then acted in such a way as to cause some counterpart of your friend's idea to be formed in your brain. This idea gave rise to an idea of your own, so you sent volleys of commands to scores of muscles in your abdomen, chest, throat, tongue, and lips that had the effect ... and so forth. The intricacy of this process is astonishing. It allows the communication of ideas and thoughts of great originality and subtlety, yet operates at remarkable speed (producing comprehensible speech at several words per second) and requires no noticeable mental effort by the speaker and listener. This point is worth stressing. Speech and understanding are effortless and unconscious activities that go on while we think about the topic of the conversation (instead of having to think about the mechanism of communication). How does this marvelous communication system work? Such is the subject of volume I, *Language*.

Almost any human competence arouses the same sense of curiosity and wonder. Consider visual recognition. For you to know that it is your friend across the room, it suffices for light reflected from his face to flash across the retinas of your eyes for a fraction of a second. Within broad limits, it does not matter how much ambient light there is in the room, or whether the light reflected to the retinas comes from a profile or frontal view of your friend's face. Typically, the central area of only one retina is enough for the job, which amounts to no more than 10 square millimeters of retinal surface (about 3 percent the size of a fingernail). As in the case of language, the nervous system relies on unconscious processes to transform successive flashes of light on the retina (which typically jumps from position to position several times per second) into the seamless visual scenery we experience. These processes are the subject of volume 2, *Visual Cognition*.

In addition to the fascination engendered by their sheer intricacy and efficiency, human cognitive processes are of interest for another reason. To a large extent a person just *is* the ensemble of cognitive processes she harbors; the thoughts, perceptions, utterances, and actions created by these processes help define her as a person. As a result, cognitive science focuses on a fundamental question both for the individual and for the species, namely, What does it mean, from the cognitive point of view, to be human?

Technological Development

It is a commonplace that Western societies are being transformed by the introduction of computer technology. Every month brings news of faster computers and the development of software for new domains of modern life. It is easy to be dazzled by the pace of progress.

For this reason, it is important not to lose sight of a sobering fact about modern computers and the programs that make them run. Years of effort have not succeeded in endowing computerized systems with even rudimentary abilities in areas where humans excel. An example is tool use. No computer-driven, mechanical hand approaches the multipurpose dexterity of the human carpenter's hand, and no breakthroughs are in sight that will close the gap. The human advantage is even more pronounced with respect to perceptual-motor coordination. No existing computerized system rivals the effortless partnership between visual processing and motor planning that underlies the carpenter's ability to drive a nail just where it is needed.

The same can be said for other human competences. In the case of language, computerized translation lags far behind the skill of bilingual humans. Even within a single language, although automatic comprehension continues to improve, there is as yet nothing close to a computer program that can discuss airline reservations, for example, in normal speech. Even the elementary task of transcribing the continuous speech of an arbitrarily chosen, native speaker of English remains beyond current technology, whereas this ability amounts to little more than basic literacy in the human case.

These considerations suggest that the investigation of human intelligence can play a useful role in the search for artificially intelligent systems. Study of the human case might suggest new design principles to be incorporated into computerized systems. For example, investigating how the human visual system processes and interprets light might aid computer scientists in attempting to build automated systems with similar powers. Of course, there is no guarantee that investigating the human case will shed light on the artificial case. The human system might prove so difficult to understand that computer scientists would do better to look elsewhere for guidance. In addition, Nature may not have invented the only way to process visual information efficiently, to move a hand, to speak, and so on. Analogously, bird and insect flight—involving the deformation and agitation of wings—did not turn out to be the only mechanism available for air travel. Nonetheless, the tremendous powers of the human system provide good reason to study it, and collaboration between cognitive scientists and computer scientists has increased steadily over the years.

Preparation and Repair of the Cognitive System

The human cognitive apparatus may be thought of as a tool for interacting successfully with the environment. Like any complex instrument, this tool must be fine-tuned to the specific circumstances of its use and repaired if damaged. These activities correspond to education and medical treatment, respectively. Research in cognitive science can contribute to both domains.

Education. Designing a successful curriculum for a given field of knowledge (say, one of the sciences) requires two kinds of expertise on the part of the designer. First, she must be solidly competent in the field. Second, she must understand (if only implicitly) how the learner's cognitive apparatus is structured. The second kind of expertise guides the way lessons are built and organized, so as to maximize learning. It is reasonable to expect that progress in cognitive science will illuminate the cognitive structure of children and adults in such a way as to aid in the design of effective curricula. Research relevant to this theme is presented in chapter 4 of volume 3, *Thinking.*

Another kind of learning consists in better appreciating the strengths and weaknesses of one's cognitive apparatus. To illustrate the point, consider your ability to assign probabilities to chance outcomes. In what kinds of situations do you do this correctly, and in what kinds of situations are you subject to illusions and systematic error? Research in cognitive science raises and analyzes questions of this nature. It thus alerts us to potential pitfalls in our reasoning, and can ultimately aid our judgment. Some aspects of human judgment are discussed in these terms in chapters 2–3 of volume 3.

Medical treatment. The brain may lose its remarkable cognitive powers through traumatic injury, stroke, or diseases like schizophrenia or Alzheimer's syndrome. Advances in tissue grafts and in brain chemistry have brought treatment of such conditions into the realm of possibility. If, however, new treatments are to be effective in restoring lost or threatened functions, much information will be needed about the cognitive role played by different neural structures. This is a primary area of research in cognitive science, discussed in several of the chapters that follow.

Cognitive science is also central to advances in the diagnosis of neural disease and damage. In light of detailed knowledge of the relation between brain and cognition, the fine grain of a patient's perceptual, linguistic, or motor behavior may assume diagnostic significance. The attempt to correlate such behavior with the onset of neural disease is another area of active research in cognitive science (see Kosslyn 1988; Posner et al. 1988).

Social Choices

How people decide to organize themselves when they are free to choose, as well as what social structures they find tolerable when their choices are constrained, is determined in part by their conception of themselves as human beings. Consider the following opposing views:

View 1: People are basically lazy, moved to activity and inquiry only under the pressure of organic need.

View 2: People are innately curious and industrious, becoming lazy only from stifled ambition and training for passivity.

A community that shared view 1 might well be led to different political choices than would a community that shared view 2.

A scientifically sound theory of human cognition can be expected to throw light on questions such as these. It is not to be expected (or desired) that, by itself, information of this sort determines social choices; they are also governed by the values and aspirations of those concerned. Nonetheless, it may be hoped that greater understanding about this one component of human nature, namely, human cognition, can lead to more adaptive reflection on some of the choices that face contemporary society.

Organization

Let us now consider some of the principles that underlie the organization of the four volumes.

The Parts of Cognitive Science

Human cognition is so complicated that only small pieces of it can be investigated at a time. Unfortunately, it is not obvious how to divide up cognitive activity into parts that can be meaningfully studied in isolation. As an example, consider a conversation between friends over coffee. Numerous cognitive capacities are implicated in this commonplace activity, each interwoven with the others. Linguistic ability is exercised in formulating and understanding the sentences traded back and forth. Auditory perception is involved in interpreting the speech produced by each participant (and separating it from background noise). Visual perception is implicated both in registering the reaction caused by an utterance (in the form of smiling, head shaking, brow furrowing, and so on) and in "reading" features of the speech signal from the lips of the speaker. Motor control is presupposed in the act of talking, since each articulator in the mouth and throat must be sent into motion at just the right moment in order to create the desired speech sound. Finally, an underlying process of thinking and reasoning controls the selection and interpretation of the utterances produced. Thinking and reasoning of course embrace a multitude of cognitive capacities, from remembering old information and integrating new information to planning a course of action and anticipating its consequences. It is not immediately evident how to factor these cognitive prerequisites to a conversation in a way that favors understanding any one of them. Indeed, the factorization question can be theoretically controversial in its own right.

For this reason, the organization of these volumes does not represent a theory of the natural components of human cognition but instead reflects the informal understanding that most people have about their mental faculties. Among other abilities, people typically recognize competence in the areas of language, visual perception, and thinking. The first three volumes of this work are titled accordingly. The fourth volume includes a variety of supplementary topics that bear on conceptual foundations and methodology. In all, the chapters represent a selection of topics that are central to contemporary cognitive science and illustrate the kind of progress that has been made in the field as a whole. Although many topics are omitted, a healthy sample of contemporary concerns is represented.

Levels of Analysis for Cognitive Faculties

The choice of chapters for each part has also been influenced by an important methodological principle. Since the appearance of an influential monograph by David Marr (1982), it has been widely appreciated that a given cognitive competence can be investigated at three levels of analysis. The levels are often given these names:

1. implementation
2. representation and algorithm
3. computation

The following analogy explains these distinctions.

A computer engaged in a complex calculation may be approached at each of the three levels. At the level of implementation, the computer's hardware is described. At the level of representation and algorithm, a more abstract description of the computer is given, including a representational part and an algorithmic part. The representational part concerns both the form in which the computer stores data needed for its calculation and the form in which it writes its output and any intermediate results. The algorithmic part concerns the succession of decisions and operations carried out by the computer as it performs its calculations in real time (for instance, whether an input number is squared before it is added to some other input number, or whether the addition comes before the squaring). These kinds of facts about representation and algorithm are easily obscured at the level of implementation because the details of hardware do not allow the logic of the computer's behavior to shine through. This logic is captured at the middle level, which abstracts away from the physics of circuits and chips to describe how the hardware is being used. The third, computational, level abstracts away even further. At this level computational analysis of the computer provides a mathematically transparent description of what it is doing by providing, for example, an equation for the function being calculated. At this level as well, the efficiency of the computer is analyzed by characterizing the time and memory resources it requires to perform its calculation.

A central idea of modern cognitive science is that the human cognitive system can be understood as though it were a giant computer engaged in a complex calculation. As with the computer, it is assumed that we may approach human cognition at the three levels just described. In the case of language, for example, the level of implementation corresponds to neurological analysis of the structures and connections in the brain that underlie the use of language. The level of representation and algorithm focuses on the processing of information by the system and on the format of linguistic knowledge stored in memory. It is at this level that cognitive scientists attempt to describe the information flow required by language use, that is, the successive or simultaneous psychological steps required to interpret or produce speech. At the level of computation, language is analyzed grammatically and its structural properties are exposed. At this level an attempt is also made to understand the general properties of the procedures described at the second level, including their efficiency and reliability.

It is crucial for understanding contemporary cognitive science to see that the different levels of analysis are connected, in the sense that facts and principles discovered at one level contribute to analyses at other levels. For example, knowledge of the grammar of a language (described at the computational level) informs us about the kind of algorithm needed to recognize and understand its sentences. Grammatical knowledge thus constrains our hypotheses about the information processing that underlies language use, since an accurate theory of information processing must be consistent with the grammatical properties of language. Similarly, an implementational theory of the brain imposes requirements on theories at level 2, inasmuch as the information flow imputed to the brain must be capable of being implemented using neural hardware.

The organization of these volumes has been greatly influenced by the foregoing approach. Each volume includes chapters that focus on distinct levels of analysis: implementation, representation/algorithm, and computation. Where possible, information about theories at one level is brought to bear on theories at another.

A final comment will set the stage for all that follows. The authors of the present work hope that it will communicate our fascination with human cognition and our conviction that the abilities it comprises are among the great miracles of life. As much as an invitation to explore theories and data, these volumes are our invitation to you to share the intellectual excitement of cognitive science.

References

Chomsky, N. (1956). Three models for the description of language. *IRE Transactions on Information Theory* IT-2(3), 113–124.

Chomsky, N. (1957). *Syntactic Structures*. The Hague: Mouton.

Kosslyn, S. (1988). Aspects of a cognitive neuroscience of mental imagery. *Science* 240, 1621–1626.

Marr, D. (1982). *Vision: A computational investigation into the human representation and processing of visual information*. San Francisco: W. H. Freeman.

Minsky, M. (1956). *Heuristic aspects of artificial intelligence*, Lincoln Laboratory, Technical Report 34-57, MIT, December 1956.

Minsky, M. (1961). Steps towards artificial intelligence. *Proceedings of the IRE* 49, 8–29.

Newell, A., and H. Simon (1961). The logic theory machine: A complex information processing system. *IRE Transactions on Information Theory*, IT-2(3), 61–79.

Posner, M. I., S. E. Petersen, P. T. Fox, and M. E. Raichle (1988). Localization of cognitive operations in the human brain." *Science* 240, 1627–1631.

The Cognitive Science of Language: Introduction

Lila R. Gleitman and Mark Liberman

The essays in this volume are designed to reveal why language holds a special place in cognitive science. They do not do so, for the most part, by patiently surveying elementary background material on each subdiscipline that is part of the study of language. Instead, most authors raise a fundamental question and then try to answer it by carefully examining some detail of language use, design, or interpretation that is a microcosm of the larger system. Thus, in order to approach the grand question "What is the nature of language?" several authors in turn ask: What is the speech of infants, babies, children like? How do standard American English and African-American Vernacular English treat copular sentences? How do speakers of the West African language Mawu form their words? What scenario comes to your mind first when you hear "Horace saw the man with a telescope" or "Smoking volcanos can be dangerous"? Was Freud right about when we are likely to commit a slip of the tongue? What explains the symptoms of those afflicted with brain injury that damages or destroys the capacity to speak or to understand?

In this introduction we put the essays in context and try to show how, taken as a group, they introduce the fundamental conceptual questions of the cognitive science of language.

Perhaps the first of these questions should be: *What's so special about language?* Well, a first answer to this question is: Maybe nothing if you are a snail or a camphor tree. But language is paramount among the capacities that characterize humans, setting us off from even the most perfectly formed and functioning of the other beasts on earth; so, as a matter of species pride—if nothing else—we would hold up language as a marker of our humanity and thus a focus of our scientific interests. By understanding language, we understand something important about ourselves.

Human language is probably also the most intricately structured behavior to be found on our planet. This alone recommends it to us for careful study and defines another question: *What are linguistic structures like, and why?*

Linguistic structures also have the curious property of being meaningful, at least sometimes, and this makes language uniquely revealing of our mental and social life. Having said this much, the question immediately arises: *What is meaning, and how does language express it?*

This is a profound and difficult question, for which the best available answers are only partial ones. In the cases that can be modeled successfully, linguistic structures are intricate and abstract things, which tie sound and meaning together in complex and subtle ways. Two sentences can be almost identical in sound and yet mean quite different things, or they can be wholly different in sound yet nearly equivalent in meaning. The use of language thus requires rapid and intricate information processing to relate the meaning to its complex embedding in the sound wave. Usually, we just understand what we hear and say what we mean without thinking about manipulating a complex hierarchy of interlocking pieces. Yet the pieces are there and go together in too many ways for all the combinations to be memorized. *How do we produce linguistic messages? How do we understand them? What goes wrong when we fail in either task?*

Finally, because human languages differ widely and change constantly, each of us needs to learn the sounds, words, and structures of our native language(s). This requires perceiving and remembering an enormous amount of nonobvious stuff and figuring out how to put it together in even more nonobvious ways. *How do children learn language? What assumptions and special skills do they bring to the task?*

In chapter 1 Gleitman and Newport open the discussion from the perspective of this last question. They focus their attention on the irrepressibility of language learning under extraordinarily varying environmental circumstances. How can blind children come to understand even such "vision-related" words as *see?* When language is closed to the ears and tongue of deaf children, why does it dart out through the fingers? For Gleitman and Newport this stubborn sameness of successful learning in the face of enormous environmental variation shows that learning a language is something that biology builds children to do, just as bats are built to hang upside down, and termites to construct communal mounds.

Specifically, it is the brain status of the young human child that is the crucial factor explaining language learning. If this brain state differs from the usual (the learner is mentally handicapped, or of normal mentality but adult), then language learning becomes harder and sometimes impossible. Nearly all other handicaps or special circumstances can be overcome if this key factor is present; but even the best schooling, the highest motivation and intelligence, and decades of practice are usually not enough to give an adult second-language learner the native fluency of an average five-year-old, because the adult lacks this crucial factor—the brain of a child!—despite many other advantages.

This perspective frames the theory of language acquisition in terms of a linguistically tuned brain/mind that can acquire a language from ambient data (say, one's mother's speech in context) in a relatively short time (within about four years from birth). This is a very difficult problem to solve. Despite considerable progress in understanding and modeling the process, no one can yet provide a computer program that really learns a human language in anything close to the sense we are discussing here. The more closely we examine the language-learning problem, the more impressive the performance of ordinary children becomes. These special abilities of young human children suggest a significant biological substrate for language. Common sense, though, denies that language is "biologically given" at all—if language were built into the human genome, then the dispersal of peoples at the Tower of Babel should not have changed the way they talked, any more than it changed the way they walked or chewed or blinked.

Indeed, languages do differ from one another, shown most poignantly by noticing that the speakers of one cannot understand the speakers of the next. By this test there are perhaps four or five thousand languages on earth today, and ongoing changes continue to result in new ones. What, then, could be meant by the claim that language is built into our biology?

Gleitman and Newport defend the view that what biology provides is *the capacity to learn (human) language.* Is this capacity just an incredible amount of general learning ability? Well, human infants are certainly extraordinary creatures, and close scrutiny shows that any given human language is even more complex than it appears at first—but this same careful examination shows that different languages are much less different from one another than they first appear to be. These deeper similarities among languages presumably reflect the infants' learning capacities and inclinations; to put it another way, human children find language learning easy and natural because human languages, despite their many and sometimes bewildering surface differences, are all basically set up in the way that human biology expects them to be. This basic set-up, or at least its specifically linguistic aspects, has come to be called *universal grammar.*

In chapter 2 William Labov focuses on certain differences between Standard English (SE) and the African-American Vernacular English (AAVE) spoken in many inner-city and rural American communities. These two ways of talking are versions of English that are (usually) mutually intelligible, even though each has aspects that speakers of the other may miss, especially because most white speakers of SE do not learn AAVE. Because these two speech patterns are so close, it is not much of a stretch for universal grammar to encompass both of them. However, Labov's analysis presents two points that are crucial for the treatment of languages that differ much more widely.

First, vernacular languages—the ways that ordinary people ordinarily talk—are not "ungrammatical" or otherwise imperfect approximations to standard or literary linguistic norms. Such vernaculars have their own grammatical systems that are just as subtle, abstract, lawful, and complex as those of more prestigious dialects; indeed, they are often more coherent than the artificial standards imposed by copy editors and language columnists. For the purposes of this book we are concerned with the grammars implicit in everyday human linguistic behavior, not with the pronouncements of self-appointed (or even official) guardians of correct linguistic form.

Second, small changes in an abstract grammatical system may produce complex patterns of change on the surface of the language, magnifying the apparent differences. Labov focuses on the different treatments of the copula that have developed in SE and AAVE and shows that they are individually more complex, but jointly more similar, than they seem. According to Labov's analysis AAVE is (in this particular corner of the grammar) essentially like SE with one grammatical principle added, allowing forms of the verb *to be* to be omitted in certain circumstances. Thus SE can contract the copula *is* to *'s* in many circumstances ("She's leaving" as well as "She is leaving"); and in such cases AAVE, in addition to the full and contracted forms, also allows forms with the copula missing ("She leaving"). When SE (and AAVE) cannot contract ("He seems as nice as he says he is," not "as he says he's"), AAVE also cannot omit the copula (so that "He seems as nice as he says he" is not proper AAVE). In both speech communities the copula contracts or disappears in intricate patterns whose explanation requires considerable grammatical sophistication—and specifically requires the assumption that AAVE speakers know that the copula is an implicit part of their mental representation of the sentence, even when they do not express it.

In sufficiently isolated speech communities, the sorts of differences that SE and AAVE exhibit can develop over a few generations to the point that mutual intelligibility is lost; the two dialects become separate languages. How far apart can languages get? In one sense, separated languages can diverge without bound, so that after enough time (perhaps ten thousand years) it may be difficult or even impossible to determine whether there ever was a connection between them. This is because we determine the historical relationship between two languages on the basis of patterned similarities in the sound of pairs of words with similar meanings. When the stock of words that two languages once shared has dissipated—through independent borrowing and invention of new words, semantic drift in old ones, and many layers of change in sound—it will not return. The connection between the sound and meaning of a word is largely arbitrary; thus, there is no interesting limit to the set of sounds that might be the word for "head" in some particular language, and no expected connection between that and the sound of its words for "water" or "rock" or whatever.

However, the hypothesis of universal grammar suggests that variation in grammatical systems—unlike variation in the pronunciation of words used for a single concept—ought to be quite limited. At first sight this claim of universality seems difficult to maintain. For instance, the sound systems of the world's languages differ widely, encompassing not just easy and common sounds like the vowels we might write as *ee, ah,* and *oo,* but also rare and difficult sounds like the clicks of IsiXhosa or the initial consonant of English "thumb." In chapter 3 Mark Liberman presents a detailed picture of the sound system of Mawu, a language spoken by about 100,000 people in Guinea and the Ivory Coast. A number of characteristics make it seem "exotic" in the sense of being organized via principles and properties that are wildly different from those underlying English and other languages familiar to American readers. If languages from distant places and cultures really were organized on arbitrarily divergent principles, then the core idea of universal grammar would be untenable.

Liberman focuses specifically on two phonological properties of Mawu that seem typologically unusual and so are candidates for the charge of "exotic" or, at least, "not like us." He argues that in these cases the apparent peculiarity of Mawu is more bad analysis than good anthropology. The more carefully and deeply we examine it, the more clearly we see that the sound system of Mawu is built out of the same parts and fittings as the sound systems of more familiar languages. For example, the complex grammatical rules that determine the tone of Mawu compound nouns seem to be nearly identical to those that operate in the Osaka dialect of Japanese. Since other Manding languages (related to Mawu) and other Japanese dialects work differently, this similarity is not because of some previously unsuspected historical connection between the northwestern Ivory Coast and the Kansai area of Japan. Rather, it is because both languages have wandered by accident into the same corner of universal grammar.

Before leaving the discussion of these two chapters (Labov and Liberman) we should note that their interest does not lie solely in exposing the fact of the abstract unity among all human languages and dialects. Using the case-study format, each of the two articles introduces and describes in some detail several specific properties of all languages, thus beginning to put some flesh on the bones of universal grammar. Here we pause to note just one of these properties: the "zero" element in language design. Recall that Labov postulates that the speaker of English, regardless of dialect, mentally represents the copula *is* in such AAVE sentences as "He my man" and in such SE sentences as "He's my man." Thus *is* "was there" even though a listener hears only *'s* or nothing. Liberman observes that the "floating nasal element" at the end of Mawu words whose final vowel is also nasalized is "purely potential." It has no effect on pronunciation in isolation but will nasalize a nonnasal sound at the start of a following word. As Labov presents the overarching issue in his introductory remarks: "No part of cognitive science illustrates the problem of abstract inference better than the interpretation of *linguistic zeroes*."

The interpretation of zero elements is possible only because the abstract structures posited by linguistic analysis can make sense of the elements that are actually heard only by inferring elements or relationships that are not. As all the essayists in this volume are at pains to make clear, cognitive science is based on the hypothesis that these abstract structures are not (only) an elegant description of the theorist's subject matter, but also a key part of every human language user's implicit knowledge of language. Cognitive theory must explain the inferential processes that carry a listener who knows a language from the manifest sounds of a phrase to its form and meaning, including the things about it that are not directly and explicitly expressed. An even harder task is to explain how a child becomes a listener who knows a language. In chapter 4, Janet Werker considers the plight of an infant washed in a stream of sound whose analysis into discrete segments, syllables, and words is no more manifest acoustically than phrasal divisions in a long sentence are manifest in print—and whose sound system might be that of any language on earth, whether present, past, or potential future.

Werker describes the considerable evidence that evolution gives infant learners a big leg up in discovering the web of sound relations characterizing the language they happen to be hearing. Several kinds of learning and habituation studies show that even very young infants (1–4 months) can discriminate syllables of all kinds that appear in actual human languages, even those not used in their native language. Thus, in a realistic sense the infant is a "universal listener." The question Werker now pursues is how one gets from this initial open-minded (maybe we should say "open-eared") status to the phonetic rigidity of the adult state in which, to take a well-known example, Japanese adults (unlike their babies) cannot discriminate *la* from *ra* and cannot produce this distinction reliably.

A first finding is that by the age of 1 or so (just when real speech begins), the infant already shows decreased ability to differentiate among foreign sounds. Thus the universal capacity is of the appropriate sensitivity to linguistic stimulation across the full range of human languages, and infants can learn any language to which they are exposed, rapidly calibrating to their native tongue by loss of noncontingent discriminations. But the final mystery that Werker pursues is this: The laboratory demonstrations show loss of foreign discriminations by age 1, but the relevant language-learning literature concerning perception and production of foreign phonetic contrasts shows no deficit until about age 7 or later. Werker then sketches a hypothetical speech-perception mechanism that does not lose these hard-wired sensitivities, but rather acquires postperceptual processes essentially editing out phonetic information that plays no informational role in the language being learned.

Once children have figured out the sound system of their language and have begun learning words, how do they learn the different forms that a single word might have? In chapter 5 Steven Pinker inspects the acquisition of regular (*walk/walked*) and irregular (*run/ran*) forms of the past tense in English. The technical word for such variation in word form is *morphology*, and so Pinker is examining a case of the acquisition of morphology.

Simple as it is, we know that this aspect of learning English is not trivial, for even 5-year-olds will sometimes say "brang" or "goed," and Dizzy Dean was heard to remark that the fielder would have caught the ball but was "blound by the sun." Thus the past-tense feature of English is a good testing ground for modeling this part of the acquisition process. Pinker considers two general models that in principle might be able to perform this learning task. The first is a classical symbol-manipulating model that relies on the so-called *Blocking principle* for acquiring the irregular forms: hearing the irregular form "held" blocks the competing regular form "holded." The second is a connectionist (PDP, or neural network) model, which works by memorizing specific pairs (such as *walk/walked, hold/held*) and then generalizes these to new cases using partial analogies; for example, perhaps words ending with (the sound we write as) -*alk* add -*t* in the past tense, while words ending with -*old* substitute -*eld* in the past tense. Pinker shows how both models can provide respectable accounts of errorful early learning ("holded") and final attainment of knowledge, with roughly complementary areas of success and failure. In the end he concludes that "both approaches might be right, but for different parts of the mind."

Perhaps the most compelling aspect of this essay is the way that it brings several different sources of evidence to bear on the choice between the models. In pursuing this question Pinker introduces an important idea that will recur in other essays: we can learn a lot about how a process works by looking closely at how and when it fails.

The essays we have just described focus on several aspects of language (phonology, morphology, syntax) that children acquire in the first few years of life and also several aspects of their environments that may differ; particularly, Gleitman and Newport discuss effects (and non-effects!) of differences in adult correction of the learner, extralinguistic support in the ambient scene, and so forth. In the final essay on learning (chapter 6), Pinker pulls together a variety of such empirical findings and logical arguments from the structure of languages to ask very generally about the conditions (internal and external) that make language learning possible. Aside from the substantive interest of this essay, it also has the virtue of exposing the challenge this topic poses for computer science insofar as it seeks to provide a model of learning, reasoning, and communication; nowhere is there yet an explicit model that comes close to the accomplishment of the human 3-year-old who has inferred a language from adventitious encounters with a haphazard sample of its forms and meanings.

Young children still learning their language are not the only ones who make revealing mistakes. We have all had the experience of substituting one word for another, or switching words around, or misplacing sounds so that the result is no word at all. For example, a certain Oxford dean named Spooner is reputed to have erred often and creatively, producing such (perhaps apocryphal) gems as "Work is the curse of the drinking classes" and "Can I sew you to another sheet?" Such errors are called *spoonerisms* in his honor. In chapter 7 Gary Dell shows that these adult errors tell us a lot about language and its use.

Speech errors arise when, having mysteriously moved from a thought (what we want to mean) to a phrase or sentence in our language, we set out to produce a series of motor commands to move our vocal apparatus in the appropriate pattern. This is not a trivial thing to do: Pronouncing a sentence requires extraordinarily rapid and precise control and coordination of dozens of muscles in half a dozen functionally separate but physically interconnected organs. In its own way, it is as much a feat of skill and athleticism as playing a passage of Liszt or dropping a bunt down the line to third base. We know that we cannot account for this marvelous skill as a matter of retrieving fixed motor patterns for whole sentences, since we sometimes have something new to say. There must be some way to combine what we know about how to say individual words into an effective plan for saying phrases. As Dell explains, a good deal of what we know about how speech production works comes from the study of speech errors. When you say that Joe is a barn door—but *meant to say* that he is a darn bore—Dell and his fellow researchers begin to see how the mental wheels must be turning as they retrieve relevant aspects of the stored linguistic knowledge base and arrange them in some ordered representation, preparatory to the act of speaking.

Patterns of speech errors suggest that we create sentence pronunciations out of word pronunciations arranged in structures like those that syntacticians postulate, while word pronunciations are themselves assembled, as we speak, from constituent parts that look like the same hierarchical arrangement of sound elements into consonants and vowels, syllables, and stress patterns hypothesized by phonologists. Thus, when bits of "darn" and "bore" recombine into "barn" and "door," we see that words are not stored and retrieved from memory as units and executed as fixed motor acts, but rather must be stored in an internal phonological code and then assembled for the sake of talking in a form that allows phonologically coherent bits to be misplaced. As a result, large corpora of speech errors not only provide a basis for inferring the underlying procedures involved in talking, but also offer an unexpected source of converging evidence about what the basic categories and structures of human language are. This is a paradigm example of what the cognitive science of language can accomplish by uniting the formalisms and techniques of several relevant disciplines: linguistics, cognitive psychology, and computational modeling.

Speech errors teach us about how speakers put sentences together to express a meaningful proposition in the form of a complex motor gesture whose output is a sound wave. In chapter 8 Janet Fodor focuses on how listeners take sentences apart so as to recover their meaning. She starts out by making the point that word meanings are usually combined in a structure-directed way, not just in any way that makes sense. This idea is central to several of the essays in this volume, and so it is worth dwelling on here.

We can communicate a great deal without words, by the expressive use of eyes, face, hands, and posture. We can draw pictures and diagrams, we can imitate sounds and shapes, and we can reason pretty acutely about what somebody probably meant by something they did (or did not do). Despite this, we spend a lot of time talking. Much of the reason for this love of palaver is, no doubt, the advantage of sharing words; using the right word often shortcuts much gesticulating and guessing, and keeps life from being more like the game of charades than it is.

Given words, it is natural enough to want to put them together. What somebody means by combining several words should logically have something to do with what they would mean by using each of them alone. Multiple "keywords" in a library catalog listing can tell us something more about the contents of a book than a single keyword could. We can see this effect to some extent by calculating the words whose frequency in a particular book is greatest, relative to their frequency in lots of books; here are a few sample lists of the top-forty locally frequent words, with the titles of the books they came from:

College: The Undergraduate Experience: undergraduate faculty campus student college academic curriculum freshman classroom professor.

Earth and other Ethics: moral considerateness bison whale governance utilitarianism ethic entity preference utilitarian.

When Your Parents Grow Old: diabetes elderly appendix geriatric directory hospice arthritis parent dental rehabilitation.

Madhur Jaffrey's Cookbook: peel teaspoon tablespoon fry finely salt pepper cumin freshly ginger.

In understanding such lists, we are making a kind of semantic stew in which the meanings of all the words are stirred up together in a mental cauldron. Such a stew obviously provides a certain amount of intellectual nourishment, but it would be poor fare as a constant diet. The last word list gives us a pretty good clue that we are dealing with a cookbook, and maybe even what kind of cuisine is at issue, but it does not tell us how to make any particular dish. Adding more words, like the next ten in order from the same book

stir lemon chicken juice sesame garlic broth slice sauce chili

does not help. To understand a recipe, we need more exact information about how the words (and ingredients!) combine.

In fact, when people communicate with words, they just about always put the words together in a hierarchical or recursive way, making bigger units repeatedly out of smaller ones. The meanings combine in a way unlike the way that ingredients combine in a stew, but more like the combination of ingredients in an elaborate multilayered pastry, where things must go together in a very precise and specific way, or we get not a sachertorte but a funny sort of pudding.

This is the principle of *compositionality*, which is one of the major themes of these essays and indeed of cognitive science: Language is intricately structured and is interpreted compositionally in a way that depends on this structure. Fodor's chapter combines this theme with the question of "linguistic zeroes," and focuses specifically on how the structure of sentences guides the interpretation of *empty categories*—a particular kind of zero that we can think of as tying together the roles that noun phrases play in the different clauses of multiclausal sentences.

In chapter 9 Mark Steedman discusses compositionality from the point of view of computational linguistics. He argues that a strict form of compositionality constrains human languages in order to make their form-to-meaning relations easier to learn and simpler to compute. This strict sort of compositionality permits what is called "syntax-directed translation" in the terminology that computer scientists use to talk about compilers for computer languages. It means, for instance, that $(1 + 2) * 3$ can be understood by first adding 1 and 2 and then multiplying the result by 3, whereas to understand $1 + (2 * 3)$ we first multiply 2 and 3, and then add 1 to the result. In this way the interpretation of arbitrarily complex expressions can be computed layer by layer, combining the interpretations of simpler parts.

In order to do something similar in natural languages, we need to overcome the fact that we normally do not say the parentheses out loud (although sometimes we modulate pitch and time so as to make the structure plain). This lack of vocalized parentheses sometimes leads to uncertainty about exactly what the structures are: Thus a "stone traffic barrier" is probably a kind of traffic barrier and not a way of dealing with stone traffic, while "steel bar prices" are what you pay for steel bars. We know this only because we know what interpretations make sense: just the fact that we have three English nouns in a row does not specify either the structure (1 (2 3)) or the structure ((1 2) 3).

The number of logically possible alternative structures, assuming that each piece is made up of two elements, grows rapidly with phrase length. For instance, "Pennsylvania state highway department public relations director," which contains seven words, has 132 logically possible structures, each of which has many possible meaning relationships between its elements. We understand it fairly easily, all the same, because we are already familiar with phrases like "public relations," "state highway," and so on.

In contrast, consider "process control block base register value," taken from the technical manual for a once-popular minicomputer. To those familiar with the jargon, this clearly meant "the value of the base register for the block of memory dealing with process control," that is, a structure like

(((process control) block)((base register) value))

To most people, however, the structure of this compound is completely baffling. Manuals of style sensibly suggest that writers of English should avoid long noun compounds because they are a lot of work for readers, and may be misunderstood if the reader is not as familiar as the writer with the bits of jargon involved. English noun compounds also suffer from semantic vagueness in the relations between the words, even when we know the structure. Thus "peanut oil" is oil made from peanuts, but "hair oil" is not oil made from hair; a "snow shoe" is a shoe to walk on snow with, but a "horse shoe" is not a shoe to walk on horses with.

In order to limit this kind of uncertainty, languages provide all sorts of help to their users. For example, there are always special words or endings that make structural or semantic relationships among other words explicit. We just used words like "for" and "of" and "dealing with" to help clarify the form and meaning of the phrase from the computer manual. Languages also establish conventions about the interpretation of word order. For instance, even though English compound nouns are about as loose a system as language ever uses, English normally does insist at least that the head (or dominant element) of noun compounds should be on the right; thus, "dung beetle" is a kind of beetle, while "beetle dung" is a kind of dung. We can see that this is not logically necessary because Welsh and

Breton regularly make exactly the opposite assumption from English in this case. Thus Breton *kaoc'h kezeg* is literally the would for "manure" followed by the word for "horse," that is, "manure horse" in a word-by-word translation; but the Breton phase means "horse manure," that is, manure produced by a horse, not some kind of horse associated with manure.

This situation is common: Individual human languages often have regular patterns of word order in particular cases, even though these patterns may vary from language to language. Thus, English expects determiners (words like "the" and "a") to come at the beginning of noun phrases, and adjectives to precede nouns they modify; we say "the big cow" and not (for instance) "cow big the." As it happens, Mawu expects determiners to come at the end of noun phrases, and adjectives to follow nouns that they modify, and so the equivalent phrase in Mawu is "nisi ɓwo ∼ ŋo," which is literally "cow big the." Word order is more rigid in some languages than in others; or perhaps it is better to say that in some languages word order is more rigidly dependent on grammatical relations (roughly, the structures that specify who did what to whom), while in other languages the arrangement of information in the discourse can play a larger role. All languages do, however, impose some kinds of expectations about the correspondence between meaning and order.

Steedman shows us how to express a language's expectations about order in a simple and elegant formal system. This formal system, because it embodies such a strict correspondence between syntactic and semantic composition, can be used directly by a rather simple algorithm, of a kind that can be implemented on a digital computer, to "parse" (or "generate") sentences, in a way that keeps track of complex forms and the associated meanings at the same time. Steedman applies this system to a range of cases in English, including some subtle and difficult cases of the coordination of sentence fragments, and some examples in which the normal "intonational phrasing" of the utterance cuts across the constituents that standard syntactic analyses would specify. Steedman shows that it is possible (and even surprisingly easy) for a theory of strict compositionality to deal with such examples.

Steedman's main concern is with the implications of a computational theory of compositionality. In chapter 10 Howard Lasnik examines the problem of natural language syntax from a slightly different perspective. He focuses especially on the intricate patterns exhibited by English verbs, verbal endings, and auxiliary verbs (what grade school teachers used to call "helping verbs"). This is the larger context of Labov's copula problem, and it is a very complicated business indeed. This is a paradigm example of the kinds of linguistic phenomena that have motivated the idea of *syntactic transformations*. Since the list of possible interactions among verbal tense, aspect, mood, question formation, verb phrase ellipsis, and so on is finite, we can always express these facts of English as a rather long list of structural schemata showing how all the parts fit together in various cases. Depending on how we approach the problem, this list might have several hundred or even several thousand entries in it. Lasnik shows that such a list is uninsightful and unnecessary as well as tedious. If we adopt a simple and plausible idea about the nature of the basic syntactic structures involved, and postulate a couple of transformations that can rearrange words and endings, while assuming as usual that some elements are sometimes "zeroes," then presto! the whole complex array of facts appears as if by magic.

The only price that we pay for this triumph is the assumption that individual English sentences are considerably more complex than they appear at first; however, the overall pattern of English sentences becomes enormously simpler than it appears at first. Even better, the basic structures that we postulate for English now look a lot more like the basic structures that we postulate for other languages, as in the comparative analysis of English and French that Lasnik cites. As before, we see that a more careful analysis generally makes individual languages look more sensible and also makes different languages look more similar.

As Lasnik observes, the basic structure of the account that he gives for the English auxiliary system was first provided by Noam Chomsky in his monograph *Syntactic Structures*, published in 1957. The elegance of this account was no doubt one of the reasons why this book impressed its readers so strongly. Nearly forty years later, the story has stood up remarkably well.

The striking local rearrangement of formatives found in the English auxiliary system is not a ubiquitous property of syntactic phenomena, although some syntactic theories aim to achieve greater generality by moving things around in constructions where the superficial order is less obviously disturbed. For instance, English subjects normally precede the verb, but some syntacticians have experimented with theories in which subjects start out following the verb and then move. Whatever the extent of transformational rearrangement, it operates in the context of the basic assumption of compositionality: complex phrases are put together recursively out of simpler ones, and the interpretation of complex messages is a structured combination of the interpretation of their parts.

In chapter 11 Barbara Partee focuses her attention on the semantic aspects of compositionality. In order to approach the more general problem of the nature of meaning, and especially the nature of the meaning of words, she explores the way that word meanings combine in elementary structures. Partee explores many aspects of semantics; here we mention only her central example, which is one of the simplest ones imaginable: the combination of a modifier with a noun.

From the point of view of patterns of word order, this is not a terribly complicated business. In English, adjectives precede their nominal heads, while some other modifiers (such as prepositional phrases) normally follow them, so that we have "the large cow," "the cow in the cornfield," and so on. There is little problem in getting the word order right, or in establishing appropriate structures. Partee shows us, though, that it is not at all trivial to provide a rigorous model of the compositional interpretation of these simple phrases. Precisely because the structures in question are so simple, her discussion does not depend on any particular syntactic account. However we describe or derive the structure of a modified noun, at some point we must explain how to combine the meaning of a modifier and the meaning of a noun in order to give the meaning of a modified noun.

In pursuit of this goal Partee introduces a key concept that we have not yet mentioned: the idea of *intensionality*. Following in the footsteps of philosophers such as Frege, she rejects the idea that the meaning of the word "red" might be its *extension*, the *set of things* that happen to be red just now in this all-too-transitory and contingent world, in favor of the notion that the meaning of "red" is its *intension*, the *property of redness* that might apply to things that do not now exist, or are not now red, but might be as real and red as you please in some other state of affairs. Building on this foundation, she introduces concepts that enable her to model the effects of overall context (so that "giant" can take on a different range of meanings in a fairy tale and in ordinary life) and of linguistic context (so that a short college basketball player can really be short, even though she is much taller than the tallest first grader in the country).

Based on these ideas, Partee shows how we actually could construct a model of compositional semantics for natural language that is analogous to the recursive interpretation of arithmetic expressions like $((1 + 3) \times 4)$. While focusing on the core problem of adjective-noun interpretation, Partee's essay ranges widely through the varied and interesting landscape of semantic theory and allied areas of philosophy of language.

In chapter 12, Richard Larson approaches semantic compositionality from a different angle, centered on the interpretation of *determiners*, words like "some," "every," "any," and so on. The basic perspective is the same as Partee's, but a different set of semantic questions is highlighted. Partee's essay gives center stage to the problems of intensionality and contextual interpretation, whereas in Larson's essay the focus is on some properties of meaning that are manifest even in sentences that are interpreted entirely extensionally, that is, by checking how they refer to things and events in the real world—say, sentences about major league baseball statistics for the 1993 season.

Larson's notions of "downward entailing" and "upward entailing" environments can be perfectly defined on sentences like

(a) Every third baseman committed three or more errors.
(b) Every infielder committed three or more errors.

(c) No third baseman committed three or more errors.
(d) No infielder committed three or more errors.

(e) Some third baseman committed three or more errors.
(f) Some infielder committed three or more errors.

Those of us who are not deeply knowledgable about baseball will not be sure which of these sentences are true. But without knowing what happened in 1993, we do know that if (b) is true, then (a) is, and that if (d) is true, then (c) is, whereas if (f) is true, then nothing follows about (e). In fact, the implication goes in the other direction in this pair, so that if (e) is true, then (f) is. In Larson's terminology this means that "every" and "no" are downward entailing (with respect to the subject in these sentences), while "some" is upward entailing. It follows, for instance, that "every third baseman who ever played for the Red Sox ..." and "no third baseman who ever played for the Red Sox ..." are well-formed sentences, while "some third baseman who ever played for the Red Sox ..." is peculiar. None of this depends on intensional or contextually restricted meanings (although, of course, we could construct similar examples in intensional contexts).

Similarly, Larson's hypothesis of *conservativity* of determiners can be defined and checked in purely extensional cases. Exemplifying this hypothesis, Larson observes that there are no single determiner-words that mean things like "everyone except" or "all but." Imagine adding to English a word "blout" with such a meaning. Then we could say something like "Blout pitchers batted over .150," meaning "everybody except for pitchers batted over .150." We often want to say things like this, actually, but we always have to use a slight circumlocution like "everybody except ..."

For Larson, this is an example of a much more general hypothesis about determiner meanings that can be expressed in simple mathematical terms, once the basic structure of compositional semantics is adopted. This hypothesis appears to be true not only of English but of other languages as well. Since the meanings associated with the forbidden determiner meanings are perfectly reasonable and even common, this conservativity of determiners is a substantive hypothesis about universal grammar. However it is ultimately explained, it constrains the space of possible languages in a way that makes learning easier.

Larson's conservativity hypothesis deals mainly with semantic categories. It should apply equally well to languages like English, where the determiner starts the noun phrase, and to languages like Mawu, where the determiner comes last. The only claim made on the syntax and word stock of the language is that there must be a syntactic category of *determiner* that combines with nouns, with meanings roughly like those of English determiners. Likewise, Partee's account of the semantics of adjective-noun combination is not especially restricted to English. Something quite similar, perhaps almost identical, should apply in French or in Mawu, where adjectives typically follow rather than precede nouns.

Suppose that we knew what words mean and a great deal about how to put meanings together—everything that Partee and Larson explained to us, and a lot more besides—but we had no real clue about syntax. In this imaginary condition we do not know what order adjectives and nouns should come in, we do not know where verbs should go relative to their subjects and objects, and so on. There are some general principles that might help us, such as that semantically related words will probably tend to be closer together than semantically unrelated words are, but, otherwise, we are back with the "word stew" we imagined earlier. Under these circumstances we could still probably understand a lot of everyday language, because some ways of putting words together make more sense than others do, but some examples will confuse us.

We are in something like this condition when we try to read a word-for-word gloss of a passage in a language we do not know. Often, such glosses can be understood; thus, consider the following ancient Chinese proverb (tones have been omitted):

fu   ching hu   yu,   mo zhi zhi   zai;
luck light than feather, not it   know carry;

huo   zhong hu   di,   mo zhi zhi   bi.
misfortune heavy than earth, not it   know avoid.

This means something like "although luck is lighter than a feather, we don't know how to carry it; although misfortune is heavier than the earth, we don't know how to avoid bearing its weight." Most people can figure this out, at least approximately, despite the elliptical style that does not explicitly indicate the nature of the connections between clauses, and despite the un-English word order. The trickiest part may be recognizing that "know" can mean "know how to" when combined with a following verb. We also have to see that the subject of "know how to carry" or "know how to avoid" is omitted and is understood as something like "people in general." Few of us will have any trouble grasping that it is luck that is (not) being carried, and misfortune that is (not) being avoided, because that is the only connection that makes sense in this case.

A scholar will explain to us, if asked, that this proverb exemplifies a particular fact about ancient (pre-Qin) Chinese, namely that object pronouns ("it" in this case) precede the verb when it is negated. This syntactic fact would have helped us figure out that "it" is the object of "avoid" rather than the subject of "know"—but we guessed that, anyway, because things made more sense that way.

Sometimes the nature of the ideas expressed doesn't make clear who did what to whom, and we (or modern Chinese speakers), expecting objects to follow verbs, might get confused. Thus

er   wei shi   wo fei ye
but not ever I   criticize

means "but (they) did not ever criticize me," not "but I did not ever criticize (anyone)."

The task of trying to interpret glossed passages in a language we do not know may give us some appreciation for the situation of people whose ability to process syntactic structure is neurologically impaired, even though other aspects of their mental functioning, including their understanding of complex propositions, may be intact. In chapter 13 Edgar Zurif explores how some aspects of the sentence comprehension mechanism are neurologically organized, using evidence based on language disorders resulting from damage to particular places in the brain.

When the lesion is in the frontal lobe of the left cerebral hemisphere, the result is often a syndrome called *Broca's aphasia*. The most important symptom is an output problem: people with Broca's aphasia cannot speak fluently, tend to omit grammatical morphemes such as articles and verbal auxiliaries, and sometimes can hardly speak at all. Their comprehension, by comparison, seems relatively intact.

Careful study, though, shows that their ability to understand sentences turns out to be deficient in systematic ways. They always do well when the nouns and verbs in the sentence go together in a way that is much more plausible than any alternative: "It was the mice that the cat chased," "The postman was bitten by the dog," and so forth. If more than one semantic arrangement is equally plausible, such as "It was the baker that the butcher insulted," or if a syntactically wrong arrangement is more plausible than the syntactically correct one, such as "The dog was bitten by the policeman," then they do not do so well.

Over the years a number of hypotheses have been advanced to explain the error patterns that Broca's aphasics show in understanding such sentences. Perhaps the simplest idea is that they have no syntactic knowledge at all, and so they first try to guess the meaning that makes the most sense. If that strategy does not give a clear winner, they try to make the first noun phrase they hear into the *agent* (that is, the one who acts, usually an animate sentient entity). When research first began into the symptomatology of Broca's aphasia, this was the favored theory. Recent experiments, however, show that this theory is not adequate. Broca's aphasics are not entirely "agrammatical"—they continue to get some value from syntactic clues, even though their syntactic processing is indeed impaired. An active and ongoing body of research suggests that the deficit is crucially connected to the processing of a particular kind of syntactic "zero," namely the *traces* whose role in normal syntactic processing was discussed in Fodor's essay. Since the role of traces is precisely to define the connections between (nominal) arguments and (verbal) predicates—keeping track of who did what to whom despite within-clause and across-clause reorderings —it is not surprising that a problem in dealing with these zeroes would degrade the normal ability to interpret syntax, while leaving some aspects of the process intact. It remains to be learned how these subtle problems in processing traces are linked to the profound disruption of fluency that afflicts these patients.

The concluding essay by James Higginbotham brings together themes in language form and interpretation that are often separately studied in various disciplines or subfields; hence the dramatis personae for his synthesis are Logician, Syntactician, Semanticist, and Philosopher. Phonologist, Psychologist, and Computer Scientist are off playing darts at the pub, which is just as well since the four worthies who remain have adequate difficulties in communicating. They confront the same linguistic phenomena with such different preoccupations and explanatory goals in mind that they are sometimes reminiscent of the proverbial blind men touching various parts of an elephant, each hypothesizing its nature from his own parochial information sources. Higginbotham exposes the deficiencies of any one such perspective using the example of English verbs that accept sentencelike complements, such as "I see John eat," "I think that John eats," "I want John to eat." There are subtle syntactic differences among these, consequent on the choice of verb; for instance, it is anomalous to say "I think that John eat" or "I think John to eat."

Are these differences just arbitrary lexical facts? That is how they were traditionally treated in school grammar books, which presented lists of "irregularities" to memorize. Alternatively, could the differences systematically interrelate various aspects of language organization? Higginbotham's academic discussants answer the question in their own favorite terms— syntax, interpretation, inference, or communication—but the truth requires all four. We may even have to call Psychologist and the others back from the pub. Higginbotham implies that language is like the elephant palpated from different sides by blind men: too large and differentiated to understand by poking only at one end with the restricted tools of a single discipline.

Young children, who are not limited by the traditional disciplinary boundaries of academia, arrive at their own successful (if so far unpublished) analysis by the time they are 4 or 5 years old. Recall Gleitman and Newport's mention of blind babies who understand that *look* and *see* are perceptual terms. Of course they understand these terms haptically rather than visually, and thus will raise their hands rather than their eyes if told "Look up!" They do not confuse the terms with nonperceptual contact terms. For instance, if a blind child hears "You can touch the table but don't look at it!" she will give a little tap or bang on the tabletop. But if told "Now you can look at it," she will systematically explore the table's surface with her hands, sometimes replying "Now I see it."

Higginbotham's Syntactician and Semanticist wonder together whether certain verbs license specific kinds of sentence complement ("I saw/heard him fall") just because they are "about" spatial perception ("I thought him fall" and "I smelled him fall" are awkward in contrast). Turned on its head and used as data to construct a theory of child learning, one could ask: How did the blind child find out that *see* is a term of perception (haptic perception, to be sure)? Certainly not by visually seeing things. And, after all, every time the mother might have said "Do you see the pumpkin?" or "Look at this boot," though the blind child was usually then haptically perceiving the pumpkin or boot (it was in her hand), she was necessarily then also touching the pumpkin/boot.

If the situation observed is the only evidence that this learner will countenance, she should never come to differentiate—as she did as a mere babe—the meanings of *touch* and *look*. But the physically blind child, unlike the conceptually blind philosophers of legend, may not restrict herself to the evidence of the senses and the situations these reveal. Rather, learners appear to be greedy, gathering up crumbs of information from any and all sources. Here, one might conjecture, the blind child understands that the surface forms of sentences are projections based on the meanings of their predicates: If one's mother says "Did you see the pumpkin fall?" and if perceptual verbs are just the ones that can license tenseless sentence complements, then the blind learner—in addition to mapping the meanings "pumpkin," "fall," and "you" from their environmental contingencies—can entertain the idea that "seeing" may well have to do with the perception of this embedded event.

This book attempts to address an interrelated set of questions about language structure: its nature, acquisition, interpretation, use, and decay. We have omitted a number of important problems that in fact are deeply connected to the questions we do address, but that lead in different directions and would require too much space and time to cover adequately:

perception and production of speech signals, discourse structure, conversational interaction, and interpersonal communication in a broader sense. Cognitive Science purports to be the synthesizing interdiscipline that will succeed in developing a unified computational theory of language design, processing, acquisition, and use in context. Whether a unified science of language will be possible in the end is unknown at this early stage of investigation (which is why, for now, we must think of Cognitive Science as an "interdiscipline" rather than a "discipline"), but this book invites the cognitively minded to join in the quest to find out.

Language

Chapter 1

The Invention of Language by Children: Environmental and Biological Influences on the Acquisition of Language

Lila R. Gleitman and Elissa L. Newport

Human children grow up in cultural settings of enormous diversity. This differentiation sometimes leads us to overlook those aspects of development that are highly similar, even universal to our species. For example, under widely varying environmental circumstances, while learning different languages within different cultures and under different conditions of child rearing, with different motivations and talents, all normal children acquire their native tongue to a high level of proficiency within a narrow developmental time frame. Evidence from the study of the language learning process suggests that this constancy of outcome, despite variation in environment, has its explanation in biology. Language is universal in the species just because the capacity to learn it is innately given. In Descartes's (1662/1911) words: "It is a very remarkable fact that there are none ... without even excepting idiots, that they cannot arrange different words together, forming of them a statement by which they make known their thoughts; while on the other hand, there is no other animal, however perfect and fortunately circumstanced it may be, which can do the same."

In other words, some part of the capacity to learn languages must be "innate." At the same time, it is equally clear that language is "learned." There are about five thousand different languages now in use on the earth, and the speakers of one cannot understand the speakers of the next. Moreover, specific exposure conditions strikingly influence how each of these is acquired: there is a massive correlation between being born in England and coming to speak English and being born in France and speaking French. This immediately shows that the language function is heavily affected by specific environmental stimulation.

Acknowledgments: The writing of this paper and some of the research reported herein were supported in part by NIH grant DC00167 to E. Newport and T. Supalla, and by a NSF Science & Technology grant to the University of Pennsylvania. We are grateful to Steve Pinker for helpful suggestions on an earlier draft of this chapter.

1

How can both of these claims (language is innate, and it is learned from the environment) be true? Like many developmental processes that have been studied in animals, *language acquisition in humans seems to involve a type of learning that is heavily constrained, or predisposed to follow certain limited courses, by our biology*. Clearly, no specific language is innate; the particular languages we come to speak must be learned. Yet, the commonalities among human languages are, upon careful study, far more striking than the differences among them. Every human language is organized in terms of a hierarchy of structures, composed of speech sounds that lawfully combine into morphemes and words, which in turn combine into phrases and sentences. Every human language has the wherewithal to express approximately the same meanings (that is, they are intertranslatable). Apparently, human children are in some sense prepared by nature to learn only languages that have just these formal and substantive properties, and to learn such languages relatively effortlessly during the natural course of maturation.

This chapter reviews two kinds of evidence for the claim that there is an important biological endowment in humans that supports and shapes language acquisition: (1) language learning proceeds uniformly within and across linguistic communities despite extensive variability of the input provided to individuals; (2) the child acquires many linguistic generalizations that experience could not have made available.

1.1   Uniformity of Learning

1.1.1   Milestones of Normal Development

Language learning follows the same course in all of the many languages that have been investigated. Isolated words appear at about one year of age. These are mainly nouns that describe simple objects and a few social words such as "bye-bye". Sometime during the second year of life, there is a sudden spurt of vocabulary growth accompanied by the appearance of rudimentary sentences. At first these are limited to two or three words; for example, "Throw ball," "Kiss teddy," and the like. These early sentences display considerable structure despite their brevity. Roughly speaking, there is a place for the noun and a place for the verb; moreover, the subject and object noun are positioned differently within the sentence. Thus, though the young learner never says long sentences like "Mommy should promptly throw that ball," the distinction between subject and object will show up in such foreshortened attempts as "Mommy throw" (the subject precedes the verb) versus "Throw ball" (the direct object follows the verb). As soon as children begin to combine words at all, they reserve structurally determined positions for subjects and direct objects.

This ability to hone in on such a crucial and fundamentally linguistic distinction forms a kind of skeletal base of language learning; this shows up early and in much the same way in two-year-olds all over the world.

Language use by the child in normal learning settings undergoes considerable elaboration between the ages of 2 and 5. Complex (multiclausal) sentences appear, and the function morphemes (prepositions, articles, bound morphemes like -ed, and so forth) make their appearance. By age 5 or before, youngsters sound essentially adult.

Lenneberg (1967) argued that these uniformities in the course of learning for children exposed to different languages are indicators that language learning has a significant biological basis. Like the regularities of physical and motor development (the appearance of teeth, or of walking), they suggest that language learning is controlled, at least in part, by some underlying maturational timetable. He provided some normative evidence that the achievement of basic milestones in language learning can be predicted from the child's age and seem, in fact, to be intercalated tightly with the aspects of physical development that are known to be maturationally dependent. For instance, youngsters utter first words just when they stand, two-word sentences just when they walk, and elaborate sentence structures just when they jump.

These findings alone, however, cannot prove the position that Lenneberg proposed, for they are consistent as well with other quite different conjectures about the processes that underlie language learning. Possibly, children move from talking childishly to speaking with great sophistication because of the maturation of their brains; but, on the other hand, they may go through these regular stages because such stages are the only logical way to learn, through time and exposure, all the detailed facts about the language that they are hearing from adults around them. (After all, foreign adults first arriving in a new linguistic community will also say things like "Throw ball" and later speak in longer and more complex sentences; but this is surely not because they are biologically changing from a primitive to a more advanced maturational state.)

A stronger way to test this view is somehow to disentangle the environmental exposure from the maturation of the learner. We will therefore next consider these two aspects separately, looking first at how language learning proceeds when the learning environment is changed, and second at how language learning proceeds when the maturational status of the learners themselves is changed. As we will show, while languages are in some sense certainly learned from the environment, alterations in the environment over a very large range do not change the fundamental character of acquisition. In contrast, changing the learner's maturational status has substantial effects on the nature and success of acquisition.

1.1.2   Altering the Learning Environment

There are several ways in which one might examine alterations in the linguistic environment to observe the consequences for acquisition. We will consider three: first, the modest natural variations in the degree to which mothers adjust the complexity of their speech to children; second, a much more radical change, in the presence versus absence of any conventional linguistic input; and third, a similarly radical change, in the presence versus absence of the visual nonlinguistic world during language learning. In each case, we will argue, young children proceed on a remarkably stable course of early acquisition.

Variation in Motherese

It is obvious that mothers talk differently to their young children than they do to other adults. This natural simplification is clearly an adaptation both to the fact that children are cognitively immature and to the fact that their understanding of the language is primitive. But it has sometimes been asserted that this simple kind of speech does more than serve the immediate communicative needs of caretakers and infants. Simplified speech (often fondly called Motherese; Newport, Gleitman, and Gleitman 1977) may play a causal role in the language-learning process itself. The idea would be that the caretaker first teaches the child some easy structures and contents, and then moves on to more advanced lessons—essentially, provides smallest sentences to littlest ears. For instance, perhaps the fact that the child learns nouns before verbs and declarative sentences before interrogative sentences is a straightforward consequence of caretakers' natural behavior toward infants.

This hypothesis, though plausible, turns out to be false. By and large, mothers speak in whole sentences even to youngest learners. Nouns, verbs, prepositions, and so forth occur in speech even to the youngest learners, and yet the children all select the nouns as the first items to utter. Worse, contrary to intuition, maternal speech is not characterized by simple declarative sentences of the kind that children utter first, such as "Mommy throw ball." In fact, these apparently simplest declarative formats occur in speech to youngest learners only about 25 percent of the time. Instead, the mother's speech is replete with questions ("Where is your nose?") and commands ("Get your foot out of the laundry!"), while the child's own first sentences are mostly declaratives.

Most interestingly, variations in maternal speech forms have been investigated to see if they are predictive of the child's learning: perhaps some mothers know just how to talk to help their children learn; other mothers may not be inclined to speak in ways that facilitate the learning process, in which case their children should progress more slowly in language knowledge. One method for studying this (Newport et al. 1977) is to select a group of young children who are at the same stage of language knowledge (for example, 15-month-olds who speak only in single isolated words) and to collect samples of their caretakers' speech. If learning is a function of the caretaker's speech style, then variation among the mothers at this time should predict the further progress of these children. To study this, the children's speech was sampled again six months later. Analyzing the children's speech at these two times (ages 15 months, then 21 months), one can compute growth scores for each child on various linguistic dimensions (the length and structure of the sentences, the size of the vocabulary, and so forth). The question is whether properties of the mother's speech (in the first measurement, at age 15 months) predict the child's rate of growth on each measured dimension and explain the child's language status at the second measurement six months later.

The outcome of these studies was that, while the details of mothers' use of a few particular constructions of English predicted the children's rate of acquiring these same few constructions, the mothers' overall simplicity did not predict the rate at which their children progressed through the stages of acquisition. In this sense, then, the children's learning rate was largely unaffected by differences in their mothers' speech. Each child seemed to develop according to a maturational schedule that was essentially indifferent to maternal variation.

While such studies preclude certain strong versions of the view that language is learned just because it is taught, they also unfortunately leave almost all details unresolved. This is because the absence of measurable environmental effects may be attributable to threshold effects of various sorts. After all, though the mothers differed in their speech styles to some degree, presumably they all uttered speech that fell into some "normal range" for talking to children. This complaint is quite fair. To find out how the environment causes (or does not cause) a child to learn its native tongue, we would need to look at cases in which the environment is much more radically altered. The most straightforward technique would be to maroon some infants on a desert island, rearing them totally apart from adult language users. If they could and would invent a human language on their own hook, and if this invented language developed just as it developed in infants acquiring English or Urdu, this would constitute a stronger argument for a biological basis for language learning.

Classical cognoscenti will recall that, according to Herodotus (ca. 410 B.C./1942), this ultimate language-learning experiment has been performed. A certain Egyptian king, Psammetichus, placed two infants ("of the ordinary sort") in an isolated cabin. Herdsmen were assigned to feed them but were not to speak to them, on pain of death. Psammetichus's experimental intent was to resolve the question of which (Egyptian or

Phrygian!) was the first of all languages on earth. Appropriately enough for a king, he appears to have been a radical innatist, for he never considered the possibility that untutored children would fail to speak at all. Herodotus tells us that two years later ("after the indistinct babblings of infancy were over") these children began to speak Phrygian, whereupon "the Egyptians yielded their claims, and admitted the greater antiquity of the Phrygians."

In effect, if Herodotus is to be believed, these children reinvented Phrygian rather than merely learning it: though the children were isolated from input, Phrygian emerged as the pure reflection of the language of the soul, the original innate language.

Of course, modern scientists have reason to doubt the reliability of these particular findings, but the concept of Psammetichus's experiment (modified by our increased concern for the possibility that the children might require more kindly environments) is still highly pertinent to the questions of languages and language acquisition. While we would no longer conduct this experiment on purpose, it has been possible, surprisingly enough, to observe natural circumstances that reproduce some of the essentials of Psammetichus's experiment in modern times. In the sections below, we will discuss several examples of language learning in environmentally deprived circumstances. As we will see, the outcome is not Phrygian. All the same, we will apply the same reasoning to the findings as did Psammetichus: those aspects of language that appear in children without environmental stimulation or support must reflect preprogrammed tendencies of the human brain.

Language Invention by the Isolated Deaf Child

Extensive study over the past thirty years has shown that the sign languages used among the deaf differ but little from the spoken languages of the world (Klima, Bellugi et al. 1982; Supalla and Newport 1978). Their vocabularies are the same, and their organizational principles are the same; that is, they are composed of a small set of primitive gestural parts (analogous to speech sounds), organized into morphemes and words, which in turn are organized into meaningful phrases and sentences. Moreover, deaf or hearing children who acquire a sign language from their deaf parents follow the learning course typical of spoken-language learning (Newport and Meier 1985).

Most deaf infants, though, are born into hearing families in which the parents know no sign language. In many cases the parents make the decision not to allow the children access to sign language at all. They believe that the children can come to know a spoken language by formal "oralist" training in which the children are taught to lip-read and utter English. (This method has at best mixed results; few totally deaf children ever come to control spoken English adequately.) Because the children are not exposed to a sign language and, at the same time, are not able to hear a spoken language, they are effectively deprived of linguistic stimulation during their early years. They cannot learn the language around them (spoken English) just because they cannot hear it. And they cannot learn an alternative—one of the sign languages of the deaf—because they have not been exposed to it. The question is whether, like the Psammetichus children, these youngsters will invent a language in circumstances that provide no opportunity to learn one.

Goldin-Meadow and her colleagues (Feldman, Goldin-Meadow, and Gleitman 1978; Goldin-Meadow and Mylander 1984) have studied the development of language in ten of these language-isolated, congenitally deaf children, from the ages 1–4 years (the period during which they would ordinarily be acquiring an environmental language). The findings were quite startling. As mentioned earlier, normally circumstanced learners acquiring English or Urdu from their caretakers produce isolated words starting around their first birthday. The deaf isolates in this same time period began to produce single manual gestures, much like the single words of the youngsters next door who were learning English "from" their caretakers. These gestures were understandable because of their iconicity; for example, the deaf children would flutter their fingers for "snow," and they would cup their hands behind their ears to render "Mickey Mouse." The hearing parents much more rarely produced such gestures; instead, they more frequently simply pointed at objects or pantomimed an action using a nearby object, hoping that their oral speech would itself thereby be comprehensible enough. Nevertheless, the size and content of the children's gestural vocabulary approximated that of their hearing peers even though they had to invent their own "words."

At about age 2, again in common with their hearing peers, the deaf children began to sequence their gestures in rudimentary two- and three-sign sentences, with occasional examples of yet further complexity. For example, a child would point to a chicken on the table and then extend his open palm ("give"), or point at himself ("me") and then produce a gesture at his mouth ("eat"). Most surprising of all, when these signed sentences were analyzed like sentences of hearing children, it was discovered that they were structurally organized, with distinct structural positions assigned to the verb and nouns in each utterance. For instance, just like the youngest English speakers, the deaf children had structurally distinctive ways of expressing "Chicken eat" and "Eat chicken." This syntactic structuring of signed sentences was not observed in their hearing caretakers.

Evidently, where the environment provides no language samples, children have the internal wherewithal to invent their own forms to render the same meanings. What is more, the timing of language development—at least at the early stages investigated here—is approximately the same whether one is exposed to a fully elaborated natural language or not: first words at age 1, rudimentary sentences at age 2, and elaborations beginning to appear at age $2\frac{1}{2}$ to 3. The appearance of the skeletal base of a language is thus part of the biology of normally developing children; it appears on the maturationally appropriate timetable even when a normal linguistic environment is absent.

At the same time, it is important to point out that the development of this homemade system does not appear to advance to anywhere near the level of full natural languages, whether signed or spoken. In particular, the function morphemes, such as articles, verbal auxiliaries, and bound morphemes marking tense and case, are virtually nonexistent in these children's signing. As we stressed at the beginning, languages are not fully innate, but instead are acquired as a product of both linguistic input and biology. Many complex aspects of linguistic structure do not therefore appear in full without linguistic input; in a later section (see "Pidgins and Creoles") we will discuss more about the circumstances of input and maturation in which these more complex elements appear. The important point to notice for now is the rather remarkable achievement of the early parts of language development, which the isolated learners can produce without an environmental language at all.

Language Development in the Blind Child

The case just considered involved children who were cut off from opportunities to observe a language. Evidently, they could invent something like a skeletal human language all the same, demonstrating that there is something within the human child that makes it "natural" to develop a language of a certain type—one that has words, phrases, and so forth. But a little reflection reveals that, in some ways, language invention seems an easier task than ordinary language learning. After all, the inventors of a new language are free to choose their own instantiations of each item that is dictated by the internal predispositions for language. Those who want a word for Mickey Mouse can just make one up, say, by mimicking Mickey's big ears through an iconic gesture. The learners of English or Greek have no such freedom. They must learn just which sound (such as the sound "snow") is used to express the concept *snow* in the linguistic community around them.

How is this done? Clearly, learners observe the real world contexts in which words are uttered; thus, presumably, they will notice that "cup" is uttered in the presence of cups, "jump" is uttered in the presence of jumping, and so forth. But if this is the whole story of vocabulary learning, then we should expect delays and perhaps distortions in the language learning of the blind. After all, some words refer to things that are too large, distant, or gossamer for the blind child to apprehend through tactile means—such as mountains, birds, and clouds. Overall, the restrictions on blind children's access to contextual information ought to pose acquisitional problems. Yet study of their progress demonstrates that there is neither delay nor distortion in their language growth (Landau and Gleitman 1985). They acquire approximately the same words at the same maturational moments as do sighted children, and their syntactic development is unexceptional, with phrases and sentences occurring at the ordinary time.

A particularly surprising aspect of blind children's learning has to do with their acquisition of terms that (seem to) describe the visual experience in particular—words like *look* and *see* (Landau and Gleitman 1985). Because blind children cannot experience visual looking and seeing, one would think that these terms would be absent from their early spoken vocabularies. Yet, in fact, these are among the very first verbs to appear in blind (as well as sighted) children's spontaneous speech. And these words are meaningful to their blind users. For instance, sighted 3-year-olds (even if blindfolded) will tilt their faces upward in response to the command "Look up!", presumably because they understand that *look* has to do with visual-perceptual inspection. Blind children raise their hands instead, keeping the head immobile, as though they too realize that *look* has to do with perceptual inspection—but in the absence of a working visual system, this perceptual inspection must necessarily be by hand. This interpretation is reinforced by the finding that blind youngsters distinguish between the perceptual term *look* and the contact term *touch*. Thus, if told "You can touch that table but don't look at it!", the blind 3-year-old responds by gingerly tapping the table. And then if told "Now you can look at it," the child systematically explores all the surfaces of the table with her hands. Despite radical differences in the observational opportunities offered to blind and sighted babies, both populations come up with interpretations of quite abstract words in a way that is fitting to their own perceptual lives.

Let us now try to organize these facts. Clearly, learning a language is a matter of discovering the relations between the sounds (or gestures) and the meanings that language can express. Thus, the novice English speaker must learn that there is a relation between the sound "see" and the meaning *inspect by eye* (or *by hand*, if the learner is blind), while the Spanish novice must discover that the sound "see" means *yes*. The deaf isolates were deprived of the sound side of this equation. They neither heard sounds nor saw formal gestures; as a result, they could not learn any of the languages of the community around them. All the same, they were capable of inventing the rudiments of such a system, assigning distinct, spontaneously invented gestures to particular objects and events that they could observe in the world around them. In contrast, the blind children had access to all the sounds and structures of English, for they could hear. Their deprivation had to do with simultaneous observation of some of the things in the world to which their parents' speech referred, and which could provide the clues to the meanings of the various words. For instance, when the blind child's mother asks her to "look at the pumpkin," the child decidedly cannot look, in the visual sense of this term. All the same, blind learners come up with a perceptual interpretation of the word—a haptic-perceptual interpretation, to be sure—that is relevant to their perceptual functioning. In content as well as in form, properties of mind appear to legislate the development and character of human language.

To summarize the effects of altering the learning environment: While language may not be quite as innate as Psammetichus reported (none of the subjects of these studies spoke Phrygian), there is a remarkable range of environments in which the normal milestones of language structure and content appear. Apparently, then, significant aspects of language development are dictated by our biology. In the next section we will examine the opposite manipulation, in which normal environments are presented to learners who vary in their maturational status (that is, who vary in their biology). If what we have said thus far is correct, it should be the case that changes in the biology of learners have far more dramatic effects on the process of learning a language.

1.1.3   Changing the Learner's Mental Endowment

Deprivation of First Language Exposure Until Late in Life

Thus far, we have argued that language learning is the natural product of the developing human mind and brain, that linguistic-learning events in the child's life are the natural consequences of maturation rather than rote outcomes of what children hear and see in the world around them. After all, various children hear different sentences in different contexts, but they all learn the language of their communities in just the same way. But if maturation is a serious limiting factor in acquisition, learning should look different if it takes place later in life than in the usual case: Presentation of a full and complete environment for language learning, but at a time after the usual maturational sequence should have been completed, would on this view not result in normal acquisition. Where can one find cases in which learners are exposed to normal linguistic input only late in life?

One such case is the (fortunately) occasional situation in which children have been reared, like Romulus and Remus, by wolves or bears, and then attempts are made to rehabilitate them into human society. Unfortunately such "pure" cases of isolation defy interpretation, owing to the collateral physical, nutritional, and other deprivations that accompany such individuals' language deprivations (Brown 1958).

More interpretable cases involve children raised by humans under conditions that are almost unimaginably inhumane. "Isabelle" (a code name) was hidden away in an attic by a deranged mother, apparently never spoken to at all, and provided with only the minimal attention necessary to sustain her life. She was discovered at age 6. Unsurprisingly, she had learned no language, and her cognitive development was below that of a normal 2-year-old. But within a year Isabelle learned to speak at the level of her 7-year-old peers. Her tested intelligence was normal, and she took her place in an ordinary school (Davis 1947).

The first lesson from this case is that a 7-year-old child, with one year of language practice, can speak about as well as her second-grade peers, all of whom had seven years of practice. Relatedly, bilingual children (who presumably hear only half as much of each language they are learning as do monolingual children, unless they sleep less) acquire both languages in about the same time that it takes the monolingual child to learn one language. That is, bilinguals speak at the level appropriate to their age, not the level appropriate to their exposure time. Such findings argue that maturational level, not extent of opportunities for practice, is the chief limiting factor in language growth. But the second inference from Isabelle's case seems to be that learning can begin late in maturational time and yet have the normal outcome: native-level fluency.

However, any such conclusion would be premature. Rehabilitation from isolation does seem to depend on maturational state. A child, "Genie," discovered in California about twenty years ago, was 13 years old when she was removed from the hideous circumstances of her early life. From the age of about 20 months, she had lived tied to a chair in a darkened room, was frequently beaten, and never was spoken to—in fact, she was barked at because her deranged father said she was no more than a dog. But despite intensive long-term rehabilitation attempts by a team of sophisticated psychologists and linguists, Genie's language learning never approached normality (Fromkin et al. 1974; Curtiss 1977). She did rapidly pass through the stages we have discussed thus far and identified as the skeletal base of the language-learning capacity: she acquired vocabulary items and put them together in meaningful propositions much as 2-year-olds do—for example, "Another house have dog," "No more take wax." But she never progressed beyond this stage to complex sentences or acquisition of the function words that characterize normal 3- and 4-year-olds' speech.

Another case of late language learning, but without the extreme abuse suffered by Genie, has been reported in a study of a woman called "Chelsea" (Curtiss 1989). Born deaf, Chelsea was mistakenly diagnosed by a series of doctors as retarded or emotionally disturbed. Her family did not believe that she was retarded, but, because of these diagnoses, she was raised at home and never exposed to either sign language or speech training. She was, however, otherwise healthy and emotionally and neurologically normal. At age 31 she was referred to a neurologist, who recognized that she was merely deaf. When she was provided with hearing aids, her hearing tested at near-normal levels. Intensive rehabilitation, along with several years of this radically improved hearing, has led to her acquisition of a sizable vocabulary, as well the production of multiword utterances. However, her sentences do not have even the rudimentary aspects of grammatical structure found in Genie's. For example, Chelsea says such things as "Breakfast eating girl" and "Banana the eat."

Why did Genie and Chelsea not progress to full language knowledge while Isabelle did? The best guess is that the crucial factor is the age at which exposure to linguistic stimulation began. Age 6 (as in Isabelle's case) is late, but evidently not too late. Age 13 or 31 is too late by far. There appears to be a critical or sensitive period for language acquisition, a consequence of maturational changes in the developing human brain.

The notion of a critical period for learning has been studied primarily in animals. Acquisition of a number of important animal behavior patterns seems to be governed by the timing of environmental stimulation. One example is the attachment of the young of various species to their mothers, which generally can be formed only in early childhood (Hess 1973; Suomi and Harlow 1971). Another is bird song. Male birds of many species have a song that is characteristic of their own kind. In some species this song is entirely innate, but in other species the song is partially acquired or modified through exposure. They learn this song by listening to adult males of their own species. However, this exposure will be effective only if it occurs at a certain period in the fledgling's life. This has been documented for the white-crowned sparrow (Marler 1970). To learn the white-crowned sparrow song in all its glory (complete with special trills and grace notes), the baby birds must hear an adult song sometime between the seventh and sixtieth days of life. The next forty days are a marginal period. If the fledgling is exposed to an adult male's song during that period but not before, he will acquire only some skeletal basics of the sparrow song, without the full elaborations heard in normal adults. If the exposure comes still later, it has no effect at all: the bird will never sing normally.

It is tempting to extend such findings to the cases of Isabelle, Genie, and Chelsea. Though Isabelle's exposure to language was relatively late, it might have fallen full square within the critical period. Genie's later exposure might have been at the "marginal" time, allowing her to achieve only the skeletal base of a human language. Chelsea's even later exposure might have been entirely too late. But in order to draw any such grand conclusions, it is necessary to look beyond such complex and tragic individual cases at a more organized body of evidence to examine the effects of brain state on the capacity to learn a language.

Second Language Learning

Much of the literature on this topic has traditionally come from studies of second-language learning, for the obvious reason that it is hard to find adults who have not been exposed to a first language early in life. But individuals acquire second—and third, and fifth—languages throughout their life spans. Do they acquire these differently as a consequence of differences in their degree of brain maturation?

The facts are these. In the first stages of learning a second language, adults appear to be more efficient than children (Snow and Hoefnagel-Hohle 1978). The adult second-language learners produce primitive sentences almost immediately, whereas the young child displaced into a new language community is often shocked into total silence and emotional distress. But the long-range outcome is just the reverse. After a few years very young children speak the new language fluently and sound just like natives. This is highly uncommon in adults.

This point has been made by investigators who studied the long-run outcome of second-language learning as a function of the age at first exposure to it (Johnson and Newport 1989; Oyama 1978; Patkowski 1980). In the study by Johnson and Newport, the subjects were native Chinese and Korean speakers who came to the United States and were immersed in English at varying ages. The East Asian languages were chosen because they are maximally dissimilar to English. The subjects were tested for English-language knowledge after they had been in the United States for at least five years; therefore, they had ample exposure and practice time. Finally, all of them were students and faculty members at a large midwestern university, so they shared some social background and presumably were about equally motivated to learn the new language so as to succeed in their jobs and social roles.

These subjects listened to English sentences, half of which were clearly ungrammatical ("The farmer bought two pig at the market, The little boy is speak to a policeman"); the other half were the grammatical counterparts of the ungrammatical sentences. The task was to identify the grammatical and ungrammatical sentences. The results were clear-cut. Those learners who (like Isabelle) had been exposed to English before age 7 performed just like native speakers. Thereafter, there was an increasing decrement in performance as a function of age at first exposure. The later they were exposed to English, the worse they performed.

Late Exposure to a First Language

Immediate objections can be raised to the outcomes just described as bearing on the critical period hypothesis. The first is anecdotal. All of us know, or know of, individuals (such as Joseph Conrad or Vladimir Nabokov) who learned English late in life and controlled it extraordinarily well. But the point of the studies just mentioned has to do with population characteristics, not extraordinary individuals. Every child of normal mentality exposed to a (first or second) language before age 6 or 7 learns it at native level. It is a rarity, the subject of considerable admiration and awe, if anyone does as well when exposure begins in adulthood.

The second objection is more substantive. Perhaps the difficulties of the learners just discussed had to do specifically with second-language learning. Maybe older individuals are not worse at learning language but rather are troubled by their sophisticated knowledge of the first language. One body of language knowledge may interfere with the other.

For this reason, it is of interest to look at acquisition of a first language late in life. The best available line of evidence comes from work on the acquisition of sign language. As we saw earlier (see the section "Language Invention by the Isolated Deaf Child"), most deaf children are born into hearing families and are therefore not exposed to a gestural language from birth. These individuals invent a skeletal communication system that compares quite well with language in the normally circumstanced 2-year-old (Feldman et al. 1978; Goldin-Meadow and Mylander 1984). Yet they do not advance to an elaborate language system containing function morphemes and other very complex linguistic devices. In some ways their spontaneous development seems akin to Genie's; early in life these isolates control no elaborate linguistic system. At varying points in life, as accidents of personal history, most of these individuals do come in contact with a formal language of the deaf, such as American Sign Language (ASL), which they then learn and use for all their everyday communicative needs. Sometimes contact with a formal sign language comes relatively early in life but sometimes as late as 15 or 20 years of age. These individuals are essentially learning a first language at an unusually late point in maturational time.

Does this late start matter? Newport (1990) studied the production and comprehension of ASL in three groups of congenitally deaf people. All of them had been using ASL as their primary means of communication for at least thirty years, a virtual guarantee that they were as expert in this language as they would ever be. The only difference among them was the age at which they had first been exposed to ASL. The first group consisted of deaf children of deaf parents who had been exposed to ASL from birth. The second consisted of early learners, those who had been exposed to ASL between ages 4 and 6. The third group had come into contact with ASL after the age of 12. All subjects were at least 50 years of age when tested. The findings were dramatic. After thirty years or more of exposure and constant use, only those who had been exposed to ASL before age

6 showed native-level fluency. There were subtle defects in the middle group, and those whose exposure occurred after the age of 12 evinced significant deficits. Their particular problems (as usual) were with the ASL equivalents of the function morphemes and with complex sentences.

Pidgins and Creoles

A fascinating line of research concerns the process of language formation among linguistically heterogeneous adults who are thrown together for limited times or purposes (Bickerton 1975, 1981; Sankoff and LaBerge 1973). They may be occasional trading partners of different language backgrounds who have to communicate about the costs of fish and vegetables, or foreign coworkers who come to a new country to earn money and then return to their native land, or citizens of a region in which there are too many languages for everyone to learn them all. In order to communicate across language barriers, these individuals often develop a rough-and-ready contact language, a lingua franca, or *pidgin*. Not surprisingly from what we have discussed so far, these pidgin languages are rudimentary in form, perhaps because all their speakers are late learners. Thus, there are interesting overlaps between the pidgins and the first attempts of young children learning an elaborated natural language (Slobin 1977). For example, at the first stages of both, the sentences are one clause long and have a rigid simple structure and few if any function words.

Very often, a pidgin will develop into a full language. An example is Tok Pisin ("Talk Pidgin"), a language of Papua, New Guinea, with pidgin origins. When the speakers of different language groups began to marry, they used this pidgin as the only means of linguistic communication. Most important, they had babies whose only language input was the pidgin itself. Once a pidgin language has native speakers (and thus by definition is called a *creole*), it undergoes rapid change and expansion of just the sort one might expect based on the learning data we have presented so far: Multiclausal sentences and a variety of function morphemes appeared in the users who heard the pidgin from birth rather than acquiring it during adulthood. Sankoff and LaBerge 1973 (see also Bickerton 1975, 1981) showed that this elaboration of structure was carried out primarily by the child learners who, between the ages of about 4 and 7 years, refined and expanded upon the formal resources available in the pidgin.

Singleton and Newport (1994) have shown a related effect for the children of late learners of ASL. Recall that the late learners, even after thirty years of exposure and practice, have substantial problems with the complex parts of ASL: While they may have good control over the basic vocabulary and simple clauses of ASL, they use more complex structures of ASL inconsistently, and they often omit multiclausal sentences and function morphemes altogether. In this sense, then, their late-learned language is somewhat like a pidgin (see Schumann 1978 for a similar analogy between late-acquired second languages and pidgins). When two late learners marry, their children (learning ASL in the family home from their parents) are therefore like creole speakers. Singleton and Newport observed such a child, "Simon," from the time he was about 2 years old until he was 9, and recorded both his parents' and his own use of ASL. Simon's parents provided his only input to ASL; as is common for deaf children, no one at Simon's school knew ASL at all. His parents showed the characteristic restrictions of late learners of ASL described above. In contrast, however, Simon's own ASL surpassed his parents'. At the appropriate maturational time (ages 4 to 7), he refined, expanded, and grammaticized the resources of his input, creating an elaborated language complete with complex sentences and function elements.

In a nutshell, both for the spoken creole of Sankoff and LaBerge and the gestural creole of Singleton and Newport, the first language-learning situation, carried out at the correct maturational moment, creates new resources that are not properties of the input pidgin, are highly abstract, and are the very hallmarks of full natural languages.

1.2   Every Learner Is an Isolate

Most of our discussion so far has focused on language learning in unusual and apparently especially difficult conditions—when the learner was blocked from getting information of various kinds by accidents of nature or circumstance, or even when there was no full language out there in the world for the learner to observe. Rising above these inadequacies in the data provided, children learned language even so. These findings point to a human "linguistic nature" that rescues learners from inadequacies in relevant nurture.

In one sense, these populations provide the most solid and dramatic evidence for our understanding of language learning because they extensively remove or reduce the contributions from one of the components of the nature/nurture equation and thereby reveal the effects of the other. But in an important sense, it was not really necessary to look at special populations to conclude that language learning must be largely "from the inside out" rather than being "outside in." The special cases serve only to dramatize what are actually the ordinary conditions for language acquisition. For every learner of a human language, no matter how fortunately circumstanced, is really in the same boat as, say, the blind child or the learner exposed to a rudimentary contact language: isolated from much of the information required to learn a language from mere exposure. At best, the child's environment offers some fragmentary and inconclusive clues, with human nature left to fill in the rest. In short, children are able to acquire English or German or Tlingit just because in some sense they know, from their biological predispositions, the essence of language.

We can document this point with a few examples. Consider the information children are given for learning that the sound "dog" means *dog*. No one tells the child the meaning of the word (perhaps, *cute, furry, tame, four-legged, midsized mammal of the canine variety*). Instead, the child will see a few dogs—say, a chihuahua and a Great Dane—and in their presence the caretaker will utter, "That's a dog," "Be careful; that dog bites!", "I'm glad we don't have a dirty dog like that at home," or something of the sort. From such adventitious encounters with dogs along with sentences about dogs, rather than from any direct encounters with the meaning of *dog*, novices must deduce that there is a category *dog*, labeled "dog" in English, that can be applied to certain kinds of creatures in the world. Though their observations may include only the chihuahua and the Great Dane, they must be able to apply the word to future terriers and poodles as well, but not to cats or elephants. That is, the use of even the homeliest words is creative. Once learned, they are applicable to instances never previously observed, so long as they fit the category. But just what the appropriate extensions are, from the particular examples they have seen to new things in the world, is left to the children to figure out on their own.

Such are the real conditions for vocabulary acquisition. The category (or *concept*) is never directly encountered, for there are no categories indicated directly in the world; there are only individual things, complex events, and so forth. Learners are thrown upon their own internal resources to discover the category itself. Yet the most ordinary child by age 6 has acquired about ten thousand words, hardly any of them ever directly defined by the adult community.

To see the real dimensions of this vocabulary acquisition task, consider now the acquisition of *know*, a vocabulary item within the range of every self-respecting 4-year-old. In certain conversational contexts the novice will hear, "Do you know where your blocks are?", "I don't know what you're crying about," "You know Aunt Mary, don't you? You met her at Bobby's house last week." In consequence of such contacts with the world and the word, children come to understand the meaning of *know*. How do they manage to do this? What is the meaning of *know*, such that it refers truly and relevantly to the (infinitely many) new knowing situations but not to the infinitely many other new situations that involve no knowing? Just what are the situations that license uttering "know"?

All in all, it seems that the word learner is "isolated" from direct information about word meanings, even under optimal environmental conditions. The instances offered by experience are insufficient to warrant discovery of these meanings, but the child does so anyway, and for a formidably large set of words.

Lay observers are often impressed with the fact that very young children may sometimes overextend some term—for example, calling the dog in the street "Fido" if that is the name of the child's own dog, or calling the man in the street "Daddy." But these errors are quite rare, even in the toddler (perhaps that is why they are so treasured), and have largely disappeared by age 2. More important, the rare errors in applying a word are highly constrained: no child uses the word *dog* for an onion or jumping or redness. Even when toddlers are slightly off the mark in using first words, they are admirably close to correct, despite the fact that the information presented in the environment is ludicrously impoverished. It must be that the categories in which language traffics are lavishly prefigured in the human mind.

Similar arguments for the poverty of the stimulus information (and thus the need to look to nature to understand the emergence of language in children) can be made by looking at almost any property of syntactic structure. No mother explains English grammar to her child. One reason is that no one knows the grammar in any conscious way and so could not explain it if they tried. Another is that the babies would not understand the explanations. Just as in the case of vocabulary, acquisition of syntactic structure proceeds on the basis of examples rather than explanations. One can thus ask, for syntax as well as vocabulary, whether the example utterances that children hear are really sufficient to account for what they come to know about the structure of their language. The structures we will use for illustration come from a discussion by Chomsky (1975).

In simple English declarative sentences, the verb occurs after the subject noun phrase: for example, *The man is a fool.* To form the interrogative, the *is* "moves" into initial position preceding the subject (*Is the man a fool?*). But can any *is* in a declarative sentence be moved to form an interrogative? It is impossible to judge from one-clause sentences alone. The issue is resolved by looking at more complex sentences, which can contain more than one instance of *is*, for example:

(1)   The man who is a fool is amusing.

(2)   The man is a fool who is amusing.

Which of the two *is*'s in each of these sentences can move to initial position to form an interrogative? Suppose we say that it is the first of the two *is*'s that can move. This will yield:

(1')   Is the man who a fool is amusing?

(2')   Is the man a fool who is amusing?

Sentence (2') is fine, but (1') is clearly ungrammatical. No one talks that way. Therefore, the "rule" for forming an interrogative cannot be anything like "move the first *is*." But a new trouble results if we try to move the second *is* instead. This would yield:

(1")   Is the man who is a fool amusing?

(2")   Is the man is a fool who amusing?

Now sentence (2") has come out wrong. Thus *no* rule that alludes to the serial order of the two *is*'s will correctly account for what is and what is not a grammatical interrogative. The only generalization that will work is that the *is* in the *main clause* (rather than the subordinate clause, the one introduced by *who*) moves. The problem with (1') and with (2") is that we tried to move the *is* in the subordinate clause, a violation of English syntactic structure.

English speakers by age 4 are capable of uttering complex interrogatives like those we have just looked at. No one has ever observed a youngster to err along the way, producing sentences like (1') or (2"). But how could they have learned the appropriate generalization? No one whispers in a child's ear, "It's the *is* in the main clause that moves." And even such a whispered hint would be insufficient, for the task would still be to identify these clauses. Sentences uttered to children are not marked off into clauses such as:

(3)   The man [who is a fool] is amusing.

nor are clauses marked "main" and "subordinate" anywhere in the speech stream. No one hears sentences like:

(4)   beginning-of-main clause: "The man," subordinate clause: "who is a fool," end-of-main clause: "is amusing."

In short, the analysis of utterances required for forming the correct generalization is not offered in the language input that the child receives. Even so, every child forms this generalization, which operates in terms of structures (such as "the main clause") rather than according to the serial order of items (such as "the first *is*").

The distinction between main and subordinate clauses—or, in modern linguistic parlance, "higher" and "lower" clauses—is no arcane byway of English grammar. Consider as one more instance the interpretation of pronouns. Very often, pronouns follow their antecedent, as in:

(5)   When John arrived home, he ate dinner.

But we cannot account for the antecedent/pronoun relation simply by alluding to their serial order in the sentence (just as we could not account for the movement of *is* by alluding to its serial position in a sentence). This is because a pronoun can sometimes precede its antecedent noun as in:

(6)   When he arrived home, John ate dinner.

But this is not always possible, as shown by:

(7)   He arrived home when John ate dinner.

Sentence (7) is perfectly grammatical, but its *he* cannot be John, while the *he* in sentence (6) can be John.

What is the generalization that accounts for the distinction in the interpretation of (6) and (7)? It is (very roughly) that the pronoun in the main (higher) clause cannot corefer with a noun in the subordinate (lower) clause. Again, it is necessary to invoke structures within sentences, rather than the serial order of words (here, nouns and pronouns), to understand how to interpret the sentences.

How could a child learn that the principles of English syntax are— always, as it turns out—*structure-dependent* rather than serial-order-dependent? Why are errors not made on the way to this generalization? The problem is that sentences spoken and heard by children in no way transparently provide the structural information . The "stimulus information" (the utterances) is too impoverished—just a bunch of words strung in a row—to sustain the correct generalizations. And yet these generalizations are formed anyway.

The solution seems to be that learners are innately biased to assume that generalizations in natural languages will always be structure-dependent rather than serial-order-dependent. Indeed, extensive linguistic investigation shows this to be true of all languages, not just English. With this principle in hand, children have a crucial leg up in acquiring any natural language to which they are exposed.

To summarize this discussion, every real learner is isolated from many of the kinds of elaborate information that would be necessary for discovering the word meanings and grammatical forms of a human language. Children use neither dictionaries nor grammar texts to redress this paucity of the information base. It follows that innate principles must be guiding their linguistic development. Children can learn language because they are disposed by nature to represent and manipulate linguistic data in highly circumscribed ways.

1.3   Conclusions

In the preceding sections we have presented some of the complex facts about language and language learning. We have suggested that these facts support the notion that there are biologically given dispositions toward certain types of language structure and toward a particular maturationally based sequence in which these structures appear. We have given evidence that, to a surprising degree, language is the product of the young human brain, such that virtually any exposure conditions short of total isolation and vicious mistreatment will suffice to bring it forth in every child. In retrospect, this is scarcely surprising. It would be just as foolish for evolution to have created human bodies without human "programs" to run these bodies as to have created giraffe bodies without giraffe programs or white-crowned-sparrow bodies without white-crowned-sparrow programs. It is owing to such biological programming that language is universal in our species and utterly closed to other species—including even college-educated chimpanzees.

The universality of language is, moreover, no quirk or back corner of human mentality but rather one of the central cognitive properties whose possession makes us truly human. If we humans ever get to another planet and find organisms who speak like us, it is likely that we will feel some strong impetus to get to know them and understand them—rather than trying to herd them or milk them—even if they look like cows.

While we have emphasized the biological underpinnings of language acquisition, we must also repeat that part of the normal acquisition process clearly involves learning from the environment as well: English children learn English, not Greek or Urdu. The surface manifestations of human languages are marvelously variable, and children learn whichever of these manifestations they are presented with (as long as what they hear is organized in accord with the general principles of human language, and as long as it is presented at the proper maturational moment). Language acquisition is therefore a complex interaction between the child's innate capacities and the social, cognitive, and linguistic supports provided in the environment. What we have tried to emphasize, however, is that acknowledgment of significant environmentally caused variation should not blind us to the pervasive commonalities among all languages and among all their learners. Specific languages are apparently acquired within the constraints of a specialized and highly evolved biological endowment, which learns languages only in particular ways and only at particular moments of life.

Perhaps it would repay serious inquiry to investigate other complex human functions in ways similar to those that have been exploited in the study of language learning. There are vast differences in human artifacts and social functions in different times and places, with some humans riding on camels while others rocket to the moon. All the same, it may well be that—as is the case for language—human individuals and cultures do not differ from one another without limit. There may be more human universals than are visible to the naked eye. Beneath the kaleidoscopic variation in human behavior that we easily observe, there may be many universal organizing principles that constrain us and contribute to the definition of what it is to be a human.

Suggestions for Further Reading

Noam Chomsky (1959) initiated modern debate on the nature-nurture questions for language acquisition in a review article that contrasted his view with that of the great learning theorist B. F. Skinner. This classic article is still timely today, nearly forty years after its publication.

When considering problem 1.2, you may want further information on language learning and retardation that can be found in the following: Fowler, Gelman, and Gleitman 1994, Johnston 1988, and Nadel 1988.

The study of brain state and organization and how this affects language learning is in its infancy. Two entirely different approaches can be seen in Borer and Wexler 1992 and in Landau and Jackendoff 1993. The first article argues for a maturational schedule in language development by comparing formal properties of child and adult language organization. The second article relates differences in language categories (such as noun, preposition) to the storage of information concerning objects and places in the brain.

Some of the same kinds of empirical and logical evidence that have been adduced in favor of biological supports for language learning have also been raised for other abilities, for example, the acquisition of numerical abilities by young children. For this, see Starkey, Spelke, and Gelman 1990.

A view that is strongly opposed to the one taken by Gleitman and Newport in the present chapter is that language substantially affects how we think, rather than language being essentially the natural product of human thought. For this different view, see its original formulation in Whorf 1956.

The debate about whether specifics of a language truly affect thought has been carried out extensively by examining color terminology, to discover whether linguistic communities that have different color terminologies perceive hues in the world differently (the "Whorfian" position) or whether perception is independent of language. See, for example, Berlin and Kay 1969, Brown and Lenneberg 1954, and Heider and Oliver 1972.

Problems

1.1 As an example of examining language learning "with changed mental endowment," our article discussed learners of different ages. Mentally handicapped children (for instance, with Down Syndrome) offer another kind of opportunity to examine the effects of brain status on language learning. Describe a study you might do of language acquisition in Down Syndrome children, describing the factors that would have to be controlled or manipulated to understand their learning.

1.2 Suppose an adult and child human arrive on Mars and discover that there are Martians who seem to speak a language to one another. If the adult and child human stay on Mars for several years and try to learn this language, what do you think will be the outcome?

References

Berlin, B., and P. Kay (1969). *Basic color terms: Their universality and evolution.* Berkeley: University of California Press.

Bickerton, D. (1975). *Dynamics of a creole system*. Cambridge: Cambridge University Press.

Bickerton, D. (1981). *Roots of language*. Ann Arbor: Karoma Press.

Borer, H., and K. Wexler (1982). Bi-unique relations and the maturation of grammatical principles. *Natural Language and Linguistic Theory* 10, 147–189.

Brown, R. (1958). *Words and things*. New York: Free Press, Macmillan.

Brown, R., and E. Lenneberg (1954). A study in language and cognition. *Journal of Abnormal and Social Psychology* 49, 454–462.

Chomsky, N. (1959). A review of B. F. Skinner's *Verbal Behavior*. *Language* 35, 26–58.

Chomsky, N. (1975). *Reflections on language*. New York: Pantheon.

Curtiss, S. (1977). *Genie: A psycholinguistic study of a modern day "wild child."* New York: Academic Press.

Curtiss, S. (1989). The case of Chelsea: A new test case of the critical period for language acquisition. Manuscript, University of California, Los Angeles.

Davis, K. (1947). Final note on a case of extreme social isolation. *American Journal of Sociology* 52, 432–437.

Descartes, R. (1662). *Discours de la méthode*, part 5. In *Philosophical works*, translated by F. Haldane and G. Ross, 1911. Cambridge, England: Cambridge University Press.

Feldman, H., S. Goldin-Meadow, and L. R. Gleitman (1978). Beyond Herodotus: The creation of language by linguistically deprived deaf children. In A. Lock, ed., *Action, symbol, and gesture*. New York: Academic Press.

Fowler, E. E., R. Gelman, and L. R. Gleitman (1994). The course of language learning in children with Down Syndrome. In H. Tager-Flusberg, ed., *Constraints on language acquisition: Studies of atypical children*. Hillsdale, NJ: Erlbaum.

Fromkin, V., S. Krashen, S. Curtiss, D. Rigler, and M. Rigler (1974). The development of language in Genie: A case of language acquisition beyond the critical period. *Brain and Language* 1, 81–107.

Goldin-Meadow, S., and C. Mylander (1984). Gestural communication in deaf children: The non-effects of parental input on early language development. *Monographs of the Society for Research in Child Development* 49 (3–4), serial no. 207.

Heider, E. R., and D. C. Oliver (1972). The structure of the color space in naming and memory for two languages. *Cognitive Psychology* 3, 337–354.

Herodotus (ca. 410 B.C.). *The Persian wars*, book 2, chapter 2. New York: Rawlinson, 1942.

Hess, E. H. (1973). *Imprinting*. New York: Van Nostrand.

Johnson, J. S., and E. L. Newport (1989). Critical period effects in second-language learning: The influence of maturational state on the acquisition of English as a second language. *Cognitive Psychology* 21, 60–90.

Johnston, J. (1988). Specific language disorders in the child. In N. Lass, L. McReynolds, J. Northern, and D. Yoder, eds., *Handbook of speech-language pathology and audiology*. Philadelphia: Decker.

Klima, E. S., U. Bellugi, et al. (1979). *The signs of language*. Cambridge, MA: Harvard University Press.

Landau, B., and L. R. Gleitman (1985). *Language and experience: Evidence from the blind child*. Cambridge, MA: Harvard University Press.

Landau, B., and R. Jackendoff (1993). "What" and "where" in spatial language and spatial cognition. *Behavioral and Brain Sciences* 16, 217–266.

Lenneberg, E. (1967). *Biological foundations of language*. New York: Wiley.

Marler, P. (1970). A comparative approach to vocal learning: Song development in white crowned sparrows. *Journal of Comparative and Physiological Psychology*, monograph 7, 1–25.

Nadel, L. (1988). *The psychobiology of Down Syndrome*. Cambridge, MA: MIT Press.

Newport, E. L. (1990). Maturational constraints on language learning. *Cognitive Science* 14, 11–28.

Newport, E. L., H. Gleitman, and L. R. Gleitman (1977). Mother, I'd rather do it myself: Some effects and noneffects of maternal speech style. In C. Snow and C. Ferguson, eds., *Talking to children: Language input and acquisition*. Cambridge: Cambridge University Press.

Newport, E. L., and R. Meier (1985). The acquisition of American Sign Language. In D. I. Slobin (ed.), *The crosslinguistic study of language acquisition*. Hillsdale, NJ: Erlbaum.

Oyama, S. (1978). The sensitive period and comprehension of speech. *Working Papers on Bilingualism* 16, 1–17.

Patkowski, M. (1980). The sensitive period for the acquisition of syntax in a second language. *Language Learning* 30, 449–472.

Sankoff, G., and S. LaBerge (1973). On the acquisition of native speakers by a language. *Kivung* 6, 32–47.

Schumann, J. H. (1978). *The pidginization process: A model for second language acquisition*. Rowley, MA: Newbury House.

Singleton, J., and E. L. Newport (1994). When learners surpass their models: The acquisition of American Sign Language from impoverished input. Manuscript, University of Rochester.

Slobin, D. I. (1977). Language change in childhood and in history. In J. Macnamara, ed., *Language learning and thought*. New York: Academic Press.

Snow, C., and M. Hoefnagel-Hohle (1978). The critical period for language acquisition: Evidence from second language learning. *Child Development* 49, 1114–1128.

Starkey, P., E. S. Spelke, and R. Gelman (1990). Numerical abstraction by human infants. *Cognition* 36, 97–127.

Suomi, S., and H. Harlow (1971). Abnormal social behavior in young monkeys. In J. Helmuth, ed., *Exceptional infant: Studies in abnormalities*, Vol. 2, New York: Brunner/Mazel.

Supalla, T., and E. L. Newport (1978). How many seats in a chair? The derivation of nouns and verbs in American Sign Language. In P. Siple, ed., *Understanding language through sign language research*. New York: Academic Press.

Whorf, B. L. (1956). *Language, thought, and reality*. Cambridge, MA: MIT Press.

Chapter 2

The Case of the Missing Copula: The Interpretation of Zeroes in African-American English

William Labov

2.1 The General Problem of Cognitive Science: Extending Direct Perception by Inference

Most scientific work begins with the close observation of sense experience. But it is not long before every field develops inferences about invisible, inaudible, and intangible elements. Atoms, particles, chemical bonds, microbes, and longitudes may eventually become "visible" to us through new instruments of observation that extend our senses, but these objects were originally the abstract creations of inferential reasoning. More than any other field, cognitive science is involved with this process of inference, which is itself one of the main objects of study. We therefore find ourselves from the outset making inferences about inferences.

The observation of language provides one of the most concrete inputs to cognitive science, since what people say and write is audible and visible. But very quickly we discover that the essential cues to an understanding of language structure involve what is not said rather than what is said. No part of cognitive science illustrates the problem of abstract inference better than the interpretation of *linguistic zeroes*: the absence of the very behavior that we have come to observe.

This chapter will concern the interpretation of such linguistic zeroes. It will engage a particular problem that has been the center of much linguistic research: the absence of the verb *to be* in African-American Vernacular English and the search for the underlying grammar that produces this result. But before confronting this nonstandard variety of English, we need to consider how zeroes are identified in the analysis of the general English grammar.

2.1.1   The Surface of Language and What Lies Underneath

Linguistic zeroes are not immediately obvious to inspection: they are not features of the surface structure of language. When we use language in the normal unreflecting sense and are not engaged in the scientific examination of language, our omnipresent reality remains the everyday world of things seen and heard. That everyday language consists primarily of two things: the sounds and the words. These form the "surface structure" of language, which is directly accessible to sense experience: In every society that we know of, people are concerned with the sounds and words of their language; they give a great deal of attention to distinguishing between "proper" and "improper" uses, polite and impolite ways of saying things, and "correct" conformity to older uses as opposed to "incorrect" yielding to newer trends.

However, speakers of a language are not at all concerned with the cognitive processes that underlie these surface forms. Most people think of a language as a collection of words. If one does not understand a sentence, the answer is to be found by looking up the meanings of the words in a dictionary. Early efforts at mechanical translation from one language to another followed that strategy; engineers built computational dictionaries that would locate the corresponding words in each language. The near-total failure of such massively funded programs was one of the most striking results of computational linguistics in the 1960s. In one way this failure was a positive result, since it illustrated the validity of the fundamental principle of linguistics:

(1)   A sentence cannot be understood as a linear combination of individual words.

To put it another way, sentences have structure. The nature of that structure, its complexity and its underlying simplicity, is the focus of Howard Lasnik's chapter, "The Forms of Sentences," in this volume. Readers are strongly recommended to follow his exposition for a systematic understanding of the development and motivation of syntactic theory. Here we will explore sentential structure as it relates directly to the problem of understanding the absence of the copula in AAVE.

The first step in understanding a sentence is to combine words into small groups, or phrases, and to combine the meanings of words in these phrases to arrive at a meaning of the phrase. This process continues in the combination of small phrases into larger phrases, erecting a hierarchical tree structure for the whole sentence.

One reason for the failure to understand sentences by linking the semantic features of individual words is that most words have many meanings, so that a combination of twenty words, each with three or four meanings, can produce a bewilderingly large number of possible interpretations. But as words combine in phrases, they limit and select the possible meanings of other members of the phrase. Consider this sentence:

(2)   She is the first one who started us off.

One cannot understand this sentence by simply linking together the meanings of the words that refer to objects and events in the real world: *she, first, one, start, us, off*. The meaning of *first* or *one* does not combine with *us*, nor does *us* combine with *off* in any meaningful way. Instead, we must begin with our knowledge that *start* and *off*, though separated on the surface, go together to form the verbal phrase *start off*, and that *us* is the object of this phrase within the larger verb phrase as a whole.

(2a)

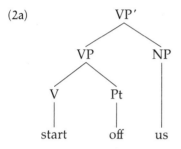

We now notice that there is no subject preceding this verb phrase: it is an empty position. We can record this observation by entering for the subject NP a node in the tree that terminates with the symbol "e" in (2b).

(2b)

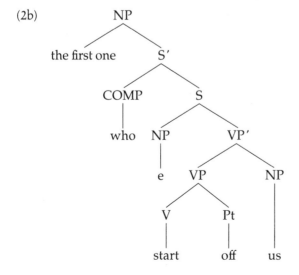

The major problem of interpreting this sentence, of knowing who did the starting off, is then equivalent to identifying the "e." The sentence doesn't do that directly, but inserts the relative pronoun *who* into the position of the complementizer of the lower sentence S' in (2b), which informs us that the small tree of (2a) is to be understood as a restrictive modifier of the immediately preceding noun phrase, *the first one*. This is an indefinite phrase: the indefinite word *one* lets us know that lots of people might have done the work of "starting us off," and we then realize that the sentence is about the *first* of these.

Finally, we understand that the main message of the sentence is to identify *she* as the person described by (2b): she is the *first* of this indefinite group of "people who started us off," through the connection of the copula verb, *is*, which links everything together:

(2c)

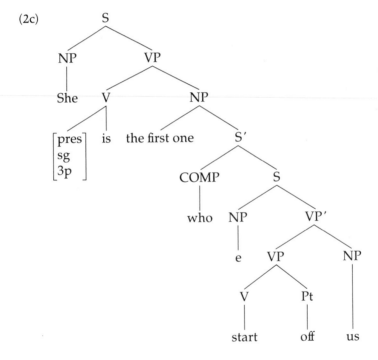

This is only a superficial account of the grammatical knowledge required to understand sentence (2). But this one example, which we will return to again, shows us two things about the work of interpreting sentences:

1. The interpretation of sentences relies on an understanding of small bits of sound that are often hard to hear. In many languages these are inflectional endings: single sounds or syllables attached to

the content words. In English the grammatical signals are most likely small unstressed words: *is, one, the*. For a nonnative speaker, they are just as hard to hear as the endings of German or Russian words are for an English speaker; in fast speech they all but disappear.

2. A good proportion of the problems of linguistic analysis depends upon the interpretation of *zeroes*: the complete absence of linguistic material in a place where we normally expect to hear something. In (2), the problematic zero is just before the verb *start*. The problem that still baffles computer programs for speech understanding (or mechanical translation) is to locate such a missing subject. Since this information is not given by any signal in the speech wave itself, it must be implicit in the order of words and the inferred relationships among them that we see in (2a–c).

2.1.2   A Sociolinguistic Approach to Linguistic Zeroes

The interpretation of linguistic zeroes is, therefore, a major interest of linguists. But, as we suggested above, it is not within the range of features that speakers of the language can normally focus on. Studies of language within the speech community show that almost everyone has a keen interest in the words and the sounds of the language that they speak and in the small differences among speakers and dialects. It is rare to find any social concern with grammatical particles, with relations between words, or with linguistic zeroes. The kinds of mental processing that allow people to interpret sentences like (2)—their linguistic intuitions—are summoned up swiftly and automatically, and they are not easily available for introspection. A great deal of linguistic analysis proceeds by asking speakers whether they might be able to say this or that sentence, or what the sentence means, but it is not useful to ask them why they can't say it or how they know what it means. People usually cannot be drawn into the study of abstract grammatical questions until they study a foreign language; there they unfortunately have no intuitions at all about whether the rules are right or wrong.

We can sometimes get more insight into the problem of figuring out the grammatical structure of a language when we consider differences among dialects. The standard English of the classroom is a well-known dialect; most of its grammatical structures have been intensively discussed for some time. The speech community also has a number of different dialects that we seem to understand fairly well. We seem to know what all the words mean—at least the content words—but as we learn more about these dialects we often discover that we have understood less than we thought. Closer attention to the sentences of these other dialects often shows sentence structures that can't be interpreted easily in terms of well-known grammatical rules. We are in the peculiar position of thinking that we understand what people are saying, but we don't know the system that they use to say it. This makes the study of nonstandard grammar particularly interesting for developing the general theory of language and the cognitive processing involved in the understanding of sentences.

This chapter will consider the interpretation of zeroes in the verbal auxiliary of the nonstandard vernacular of African-American Vernacular English (AAVE). The data will be taken from spontaneous speech recorded from members of the African-American communities in South Harlem, Philadelphia, East Palo Alto, and elsewhere. Because research over the past three decades has given us a great deal of information on how people actually speak this dialect of English, we can make a direct comparison between how speakers think they speak and what they actually say. We may also gain insights into the important question of when people can report reliably on their language and when they cannot.

2.2   The Case of the Missing Copula

The first problem in the interpretation of zeroes in AAVE arose with sentences like (3). It was spoken by Dolly R., a thirty-five-year-old black woman who had just returned from South Carolina to New York, as part of a long telephone conversation with her cousin about family affairs.

(3)   She the first one started us off.

It differs from the example sentence (2) by two additional zeroes: there is no subject relative pronoun *who*, so the complementizer position is a zero, and the copula *is* that links *she* to the rest of the sentence is absent. The zero subject relative is not uncommon in AAVE, but rare in standard English and other dialects.[1] A high frequency of zero subject relatives produces quite a few problems of interpretation and analysis, but the focus of this article will be on the first zero: the absence of the copula, which is one of the most common features of AAVE. It was the first problem of the interpretation of zeroes that was extensively investigated in the quantitative study of linguistic variation and change. In trying to interpret this zero, we will have to decide what it represents: a reduction to zero of the phonetic form of the word *is*, the absence of any concrete grammatical form for the copula in this position, the absence of the category of the copula in the grammar, and/or the absence of the semantic information that is carried by the copula.

---

1. In fact, an extensive treatment of the cognitive processing involved in relative pronouns by Bever and Langendoen (1973) asserted that the subject relative pronoun cannot be deleted in English, and for a long time this judgment was accepted.

The extremely common absence of the copula can be observed freely in any body of AAVE speech. Most of the following quotations are taken from one of the first studies of this subject: the recorded speech of boys in South Central Harlem age 10 to 17. The central speakers of AAVE were members of organized groups, or "clubs": the Jets, South Harlem, the Cobras, the Thunder-Birds—and their use is characteristic—but I have also included sentences taken from studies done in other parts of the country, from youth and adults, females and males. The grammar of AAVE described here is used throughout the United States in very much the same way by black people of all ages when dealing with other speakers of the same vernacular. We often observe a zero where the finite form of *to be* (*is, am, are, was,* or *were*) would be used as a main verb in other dialects.

(4)   He fast in everything he do.

[M, 16, Jets]

(5)   Michael Washington out here sellin' his rocks.

[F, 14, East Palo Alto]

The absence of the verb *to be* is not confined to the main verb, which is usually indicated by the term *copula*, but is also absent where other dialects use *to be* as an auxiliary in the progressive.

(6)   Boot always comin' over my house to eat, to ax for food.

[M, 10, T-Birds, South Harlem]

(7)   He just feel like he gettin' cripple up from arthritis.

[F, 48, North Carolina]

(8)   Y'all got her started now, she fixin' to give y'all a lecture!

[F, 14, East Palo Alto]

2.2.1   Inherent Variation of the Copula

In reading through these examples, one might get the impression that AAVE simply does not use the linking verb *is*. This would not pose a difficult problem for analysis, since many languages of the world show that pattern, such as Herbrew, Hungarian, Russian, and many creole languages of the Caribbean. Jamaican Creole English (Bailey 1966) shows no copula before predicate adjectives.

(9)   im sik bad   She is very sick.

(10) di tiicha gud   The teacher is good.

Furthermore, the sentences used generally by children learning English from 18 to 24 months show no copula, and there seems to be little basis for constructing one in the underlying phrase structure (Bloom 1970).

(11)   That a lamb.

(12)   That a bear book.

(13)   Tiny balls in there.

(14)   Mommy busy.

The suggestion that AAVE has no copula or auxiliary *be* is therefore plausible in that this is a very common pattern. In this analysis AAVE would differ from standard English in a high-level rule of grammar; however, a little more attention to the pattern of speech shows that the situation is not so simple. We find that the absence of the copula varies with its presence, in both full and contracted form.

(15)   We send Kenneth, 'cause Kenneth is tough.

[M, 12, T-Birds, South Harlem]

(16)   Now a girl will get out there Q I mean, she's not particularly tryin' to hurt you, but she'll put a hurtin' on you.

[M, 25, New York City]

(17)   I know it's the root of all evil, but I will fight over it.

[M, 15, Cobras, South Harlem]

(18)   I told you, I don't believe there's no God.

[M, 16, Jets, South Harlem]

(19)   About two is in jail, now.

[M, 29, New York City]

(20)   It ain't that much—you know—people out in Long Island you be around with than it is in New York.

[M, 13, Jets, South Harlem]

2.2.2   Variable Copula in Sounding

Extensive variation of this kind is always a problem for linguists—indeed, the aim of most linguistic analysis is to eliminate variation and give the rules for when and where each type of utterance is used. When this variation of the copula in AAVE was first pointed out, some linguists argued that it was due to a mixture of grammars: that whenever speakers used *is* or *'s*, they were borrowing these forms from standard English, and only the zero represented the true AAVE grammar. This would be particularly persuasive if *is* or *'s* were used whenever members of the black speech community were talking to outsiders, or speaking formally.

At this point the concept of the vernacular becomes important in the argument. The vernacular is defined as the form of speech that is learned early in life, that is used when the least attention is paid to speech, in close interaction with friends and family. It is the form of language that we know best, the most consistent form of the grammar, which is used with perfect linguistic security and shows no interference from the teacher's instructions about what is correct or incorrect. The main goal of sociolinguistic methods is to obtain access to this vernacular. By one means or another, the various field projects referred to above produced many spontaneous recordings of the vernacular: in loud and uncontrolled gatherings of adolescent youth in Harlem, or among core groups of young adults in Philadelphia, or among adults in California who rarely dealt with speakers of other dialects. In these recordings we find extensive variation of the full, contracted, and zero forms of *to be*. Typical examples of this inherent variation come from the observation of ritual insults: the speech event known as "sounding" in the New York City of the 1960s, but known under many other names as well—*signifying, cutting, joining, screaming, chopping, woofing, snapping, bus(t)ing*. Here the speakers of the language are engaged in intense interaction with each other, using their basic vernacular, and we observe the rapid alternation of zero, contracted, and full forms of the copula:

(21)   Your mama's a weight-lifter.

(22)   Your mother a applejack-eater.

(23)   Your mother is a Phil D. Basket.

(24)   Your mother's a diesel.

(25)   Your mother a ass, period.

(26)   Your mother IS a lizard.

(28)   Your mother a fleabag.

(29)   Your mother so white, she hafta use Mighty White.

(30)   Your mother's so skinny she could split through a needle's eye.

(31)   Your mother's so skinny, about that skinny, she can get in a Cheerioat and say, "Hula hoop! hula hoop!"

(32)   Because he old, he's old, that's why!

2.2.3   Searching for an Explanation

The inherent variation of the copula in the African-American vernacular shows that it cannot be explained as the result of dialect mixture. There remain, however, three other options to account for what is happening. (In the discussion to follow, *copula* will be used as shorthand for "main verb copula and finite auxiliary *be*.")

a. The grammatical category of the copula *to be* may be optional in AAVE.

b. The copula may have three alternate forms: *is*, *'s* and zero.

c. The copula *is* may be present regularly in the grammar, just as in other dialects, but be reduced by the contraction rules of casual speech to *'s* and then to zero.

What difference does it make which of these solutions we pick? Solution a. has some rather serious semantic implications. The finite form of the verb *to be* is more than a connecting link in English: as (2c) showed, it also carries information on tense (past versus present) and number (singular versus plural) and person (first, second, third). Information on the second and third categories is usually found in the form of the subject, but the finite verb is the main way of signaling tense. If the entire grammatical category is optional, it is possible that tense information is also missing. This would mean that sentence (2) is a statement about the present, but that (3) might apply to past or present; and that (21, 23, 24, 26, 30, 31, 32) are statements about what the person's mother is like now, but that (22, 25, 28) are not tied to the present but refer equally well to the past.

On the other hand, if we adopt solution b. or c., we assume that the underlying grammatical category, with its semantic information, is present in the speaker's mind but simply not expressed in many cases.

At this point we must begin to examine the distribution of the copula more closely. Is it true that zero can be used freely in any sentence where we would expect the copula? It turns out that this is far from the case. First, let us consider cases of the copula that do not show *is* or *are*.

The past. In the past, *was* appears regularly:

(33) I was small; I was sump'm about one years o'baby.

[M, 12, Aces, South Harlem]

(34) She was likin' me ... she was likin' George too.

[M, 18, Oscar Brothers, South Harlem]

The negative. The negative form of the present tense copula, *ain't*, appears regularly where other dialects have *isn't* or *ain't*.

(35) It ain't no cat can't get in no coop.

[M, 15, Cobras, South Harlem]

(36) My sons, they ain't but so big.

[M, 26, New York City]

We do occasionally find negative forms with a simple negative *not*, but these are relatively rare.

The first person. Whenever the subject is *I*, we regularly find the contracted form *I'm*.

(37)   I'm tired, Jeannette.

[M, 48, New York City]

(38)   I'm not no strong drinker.

[M, 15, New York City]

Pronouns ending in /t/. For the three pronouns that end in /t/, *it*, *that*, and *lot*, we find the contracted forms *i's*, *tha's*, and *what's* in the great majority of cases.

(39)   I's a real light yellow color.

[M, 15, Cobras, South Harlem]

(40)   Tha's my daily routine: women.

[M, 14, Cobras, South Harlem]

(41)   Wha's a virgin?

[M, 12, Jets, South Harlem]

Occasionally, the simple subjects *it*, *that*, *what* are found, but these are relatively rare. The predominance of *i's*, *tha's* and *wha's* will be an important factor in the ultimate explanation of what is happening here.

The nonfinite be. Without exception, we find the form *be* wherever the standard English copula would follow a modal or appear in the infinitive form.

(42)   You got to be good, Rednall!

[M, 15, Jets, South Harlem]

(43)   His wife is supposa be gettin money for this child.

[F, 48, North Carolina]

The imperative. The same situation prevails with imperatives:

(44)   Be cool, brothers!

[M, 15, Jets, South Harlem]

(45)   Don't be messin' with my old lady!

[M, 16, Jets, South Harlem]

Emphasis. We now turn to environments where the forms *is* and *are* appear regularly in AAVE. Under emphasis we find:

(46)   Allah *is* god.

[M, 16, Cobras, South Harlem]

(47) He *is* a expert.

[M, 12, T-Birds, South Harlem]

Yes-no questions. The finite forms of *be* also appear in yes-no questions.

(48) Is he dead? is he dead? Count the bullet holds in his motherfucking head.

[M, 16, Jets, South Harlem]

(49) Are you gon' give us some pussy?

[M, 13, Jets, South Harlem]

Tag questions. Tag questions are used to request confirmation from the listener; here we always find the finite forms of *be*.

(50) Is that a shock? or is it not?

[M, 13, Cobras, South Harlem]

Elliptical responses. The most interesting examples, from a syntactic point of view, are those in which we find *is* and *are* in clause-final position as the result of ellipsis, the removal of predictable material. In confirming or denying what someone else has said, we leave off all but the subject and the first member of the auxiliary:

(51) (You ain't the best sounder, Eddie!) I ain't! He is!

[M, 12, Cobras, South Harlem]

After ellipsis in comparative constructions. Within a single sentence *is* or *are* will occur in final position in a comparative clause.

(52) He is better than the girls is, now.

[M, 35, South Carolina]

(53) It always somebody tougher than you are.

[M, 25, Florida]

In (53), *is* occurs in clause-final position because we do not repeat the predicate *tough*, even though repetition would represent the meaning fairly well.

(53') *It always somebody tougher than you are tough.

In embedded clauses with wh- heads. Finally, we find a good number of complex constructions where the object of a verb is a clause headed by a *wh-* word, which has moved to the front of its clause leaving *is* or *are* at the end:

(54) That's what he is: a brother.

[M, 14, Cobras, South Harlem]

(55)   I don't care what you are.

[M, 16, Jets, South Harlem]

(56)   Do you see where that person is?

[M, 15, New York City]

2.2.4   A Solution to the Problem

We now have a long list of special environments where forms of the copula are always present in spite of the fact that, in most environments, speakers of AAVE can dispense with it. The problem for linguistic analysis is to find something in common among these environments:

(57)   a.   The past *was*.

   b.   The negative *ain't*.

   c.   The first person *I'm*.

   d.   Pronouns *i's, tha's, wha's*.

   e.   Nonfinite *to be*.

   f.   The imperative *be*.

   g.   Emphasis *He is there*.

   h.   Yes-no questions: *Is he there?*

   i.   Tag questions: ..., *is he?*

   j.   Elliptical responses: *He is!*

   k.   Comparative ellipsis: ... *than he is*.

   l.   Embedded wh- clauses: ... *what he is*.

This list of twelve undeletable environments of the copula appears to be rather miscellaneous. What can these various forms of undeletable copula have in common? At first glance, nothing. But, like many problems, this can best be attacked by a "divide and conquer" strategy. Let us consider a group of cases that strongly suggest the influence of the phonetic environment.

2.2.5   Evidence of Phonetic Conditioning

a. *Is* and *are* are deleted, but *'m* is not. It seems likely that there are phonetic processes that operate upon [z] and [r] but not upon [m].

b. *Ain't* and *be* are different from *is* and *are* in that they contain long vowels [e:] and [i:], while *is* and *are* have short, unstressed vowels, like the reduced first syllable of *about* ($=$[ə] or "shwa"). Many reduction processes of English operate to reduce and eliminate the short vowels but not the long ones.

c. *Was* and *were* differ phonetically from *is* and *are* in that they begin with a consonantal [w] instead of a vowel.

d. The forms *i's, tha's, wha's* are all connected with the fact that the contracted *'s* follows a [t], which seems to have disappeared here due to some low-level assimilation. If there is a phonetic condition that protects *'s* after /t/, and then the /t/ disappears later on, this would help explain why the *'s* is preserved.

What kind of phonetic processes might be applying here? The most likely candidate is something akin to the regular rule for the contraction of the auxiliary in English, which takes the full form *is* and converts it to *'s*. To follow through on this suggestion, we have to characterize in more detail the process of auxiliary contraction in English. (It is the same rule for the main verbs *be* and *have*; they will be included implicitly in the discussion of "auxiliary contraction" below.)

The rule of auxiliary contraction operates upon a grammatical particle that is the first member of the auxiliary, which has the form VC. The vowel V must be a completely unstressed, reduced vowel.

(58)   is   →   [əz]   →   [z]
       are   →   [ər]   →   [r]

If the auxiliary begins with a consonant, another reduction rule must remove the consonant first:

(59)   has   →   [həz]   →   [əz]   →   [z]

The single consonant is then attached to the preceding word, usually the subject of the sentence in the form of a pronoun.

(60)   He is   →   He's   =   [hiz]
       You are   →   You're =   [yʊr]
       He has   →   He's   =   [hiz]

Contraction is therefore a rule that removes shwa from an auxiliary verb where four conditions are satisfied:

(61)   a.   The auxiliary must be the first member of the verb phrase. This is the position containing the inflection that signals the information on tense: whether the sentence refers to past or present. In most dialects, contraction can't apply when this tense marker is not present (for example, it can't remove the reduced vowel of *as* in *like as not*).

       b.   The auxiliary must begin with a vowel. It can't apply to a word that begins with a full consonant, like *could*.

c.   The auxiliary must have only one consonant; contraction will not apply to words with more consonants, like *hasn't* or *won't*.

d.   The auxiliary must be a "weak word," a word whose only vowel is shwa, in a completely unstressed form.

Environments for nondeletability of the copula (59a–f) show violations of the first three conditions given above. To understand environments (g–l), we need only consider the fourth condition: that the auxiliary must be completely unstressed. Each of these environments assigns more than the minimal stress to the auxiliary. In the case of emphasis this is obvious. For yes-no questions, and tag questions, we observe that the inversion assigns at least secondary stress to the first element, the inverted auxiliary. In the last three cases the auxiliary winds up in "exposed" position, the last stressable element in the clause. In this case the normal nuclear stress rule of English assigns the primary stress to this last word.

All of the foregoing leads us to the general inference (62), which holds the key to the problem of the AAVE copula.

(62)   Where other English dialects do not permit contraction of the auxiliary, AAVE does not permit deletion.
Where other English dialects do permit contraction of the copula, AAVE permits deletion.

The following examples illustrate the parallel in the general prohibitions against contraction and the AAVE prohibitions against deletion. The * symbol is usually used to indicate intuitive reactions of unacceptability: here it refers to patterns of production that are so clear that they support predictions of what is possible or not possible.

	Other English dialects	*AAVE*
(63)	*He's as nice as he says he's.	*He's as nice as he says he.
(64)	*How beautiful you're!	*How beautiful you!
(65)	Are you going? *I'm.	Are you going? *I.
(66)	*Here I'm.	*Here I.

We might conclude from (63–66) that contraction is simply prohibited in final position, but the following show that there is more to the matter than this.

	Other English dialects	*AAVE*
(67)	*Who's it?	*Who it?
(68)	Who's IT? [in a game]	*Who IT?
(69)	*What's it?	*What it?

(70)   What's it for?   What it for? Wha's it for?

We can't say (67) with the dummy *it*, since dummy *it* is not stressable and the stress must be placed on the copula; but we can say (68) with lexical IT which accepts stress. We can't say (69), with dummy *it*, since again the copula has to take that stress; but we can say (70), when the word *for* follows to take the main nuclear stress. It seems then that a stressed syllable must follow the *is* or *are* if it is to be contracted or deleted. Yet (71–73) show that the situation is more complex:

Other English dialects	*AAVE*
(71) *He's now.	*He now.
(72) *He's unfortunately.	*He unfortunately.
(73) He's unfortunately here.	He unfortunately here.

In both (71) and (72), there are stressed forms following the copula, but we can't delete or contract. In (73), after the addition of *here*, we can contract and delete. It is evident at this point that the grammatical relations between *is* and *are* and the following elements are important to the rule. This involves the same type of phrase structure that we found to be important in interpreting sentence (2). The tree structure in (74) shows that *here* is in a close grammatical relation to *is*, so that a nuclear stress rule operating on the lower tree at left will assign the main stress to *here*. On the right, where a rule of ellipsis has removed *here*, the nuclear stress for the lower tree must stay on *is*. The sentence adverb *unfortunately* may receive primary or secondary stress, but since *is* is not in construction with *unfortunately*, the stress on this element will not act to eliminate the stress on *is*. These considerations of phrase structure apply no matter where *unfortunately* is placed. A late rule may move it into the position of (73), but this will not affect the stress pattern drastically and so does not change the possibilities of contraction and deletion.

(74)

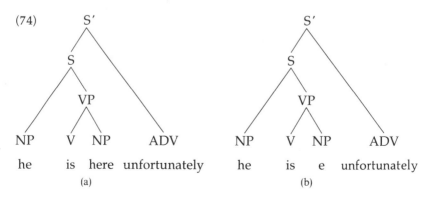

All these considerations reinforce our confidence in the general observation (62). Given these parallels between contraction and deletion, we are led to the conclusion that the absence of the copula in AAVE is due to a rule that is parallel and similar to the general auxiliary contraction rule of other dialects of English. This means that the speakers of AAVE have an unconscious knowledge that an underlying copula is present in sentences (3–32), where it is frequently absent, as well as where it is consistently present in sentences (33–56). If this is the case, it will help explain the fact that in tag questions, yes-no questions, and elliptical responses (50–53) we always get the expected form of the copula, *is* or *are*. Tag questions, for example, are formed by a regular rule that takes the auxiliary of the main verb and repeats it at the end along with the subject. The polarity is inverted, so that positive is replaced by negative, and negative by positive; thus we have the pattern:

Other English dialects	*AAVE*
(75) He's my man, is he not?	He my man, is he not?

Here the underlying form *is* will surface to give the right result, even when it is deleted in the main clause. If it were not intact in the main clause, we would find irregular tag questions with *do*. This is exactly what we do find when a verb is no longer analyzed as containing *is*, as in

(76)   He posta do it, don't he?

In this case, *is supposed to* is heard as a single fixed form *posta*, and the presence of an underlying *is* is no longer available to form the tag question *isn't he?*

2.3   Quantitative Confirmation

The qualitative arguments of section 2.2.3 are strong, and convincing to most linguists; yet, with enough ingenuity, one can always produce alternative arguments.[2] Evidence from the quantitative analysis of speech production will allow us to test the validity of the arguments given so far and to obtain even stronger confirmation. In order to test the idea that deletion is parallel to contraction, we can examine some of the independent variables that affect contraction, noting to what extent they affect deletion.

2. For example, those who did not want to believe that AAVE has an underlying copula argued that the occurrence of *is* and *are* in tag questions could be seen as parallel to *do*-support with other verbs. In other words, we do not maintain that there is an underlying *do* because of sentences like *He works hard, doesn't he?* So we need not argue that there is an underlying *is* in sentences like *He is tired, isn't he?* Sentences without verbs would produce tag questions with *is*, and sentences with verbs would produce tag questions with *do*. Equally ingenious responses can be produced to explain many of the twelve environments where *is* and *are* occur regularly.

Table 2.1
Percent of full, contracted, and deleted forms of copula by subject form for two South Harlem groups.

	Full *NP*	Pronoun	Full *NP*	Pronoun
Single interviews				
Full	56	04	67	00
Contracted	26	29	15	39
Deleted	18	67	18	61
N:	35	106	145	189
Subjects	9		15	
Group sessions				
Full	45	00	54	00
Contracted	19	23	19	42
Deleted	36	77	27	58
N:	85	30	113	75
Subjects	9		11	

One of the strongest such effects is whether the subject is a full noun phrase or a pronoun. Contraction is strongly favored when the subject is a pronoun. Table 2.1 shows the percentages of full, contracted, and deleted copula for the Cobras and the Jets in South Harlem, in two conditions: single interviews with individual members, and group sessions. The results for the two groups and the two styles are similar. In each case more full forms are shown with full noun phrase subjects and fewer with pronouns; in each case more deleted forms are shown with pronoun subjects and fewer with full noun phrase subjects. Group sessions show fewer full forms and more deletion.

But what about contraction? The expected parallel between contraction and deletion does not always appear here. For the Cobras, there is very little difference between contraction with full noun phrase and pronominal subjects. This is the result of the fact that we are treating deletion as if it had nothing to do with contraction—that it was an independent phenomenon. But the logic of the argument up until now is that deletion is a further extension of contraction: that deletion is not simply the absence of the copula, but rather the removal of a consonant that is the result of the contraction process. That is, we extend (58) to

$$(58') \quad \text{is} \quad \rightarrow \quad [\text{əz}] \quad \rightarrow \quad [\text{z}] \quad \rightarrow \quad 0$$
$$\text{are} \quad \rightarrow \quad [\text{ər}] \quad \rightarrow \quad [\text{r}] \quad \rightarrow \quad 0$$

The parallels in the permissible environments for contraction and deletion may be the result of a general resemblance between the two processes:

both involve phonological reduction. But the argument can be made much tighter, and the intricate parallels between the two sets of environments be made more understandable, if we say that deletion is *dependent* on contraction. In other words, AAVE does not drop whole words; as in most phonological processes, contraction and deletion proceed one step at a time. Contraction removes a vowel from the VC form, and then deletion removes the remaining consonant C. The set of four conditions (61) for contraction need not be repeated for deletion separately, since they follow from the simple dependence of deletion on contraction. Given this view, we then see that the true total for contraction is not the totals shown in table 2.1, but rather the total of contraction and deletion, since all deleted forms have by definition gone through contraction first. We then calculate the rate of the contraction and deletion processes by the following formulas, where F = full forms, C = contracted forms, D = deleted forms.

$$(77) \quad Contraction = \frac{C + D}{F + C + D}$$

$$(78) \quad Deletion = \frac{D}{C + D}$$

Using these definitions, we have the result shown in figure 2.1 (a–d). Here the lowest portion of each diagram shows the deleted forms, D. On top of this, we see the area representing the contracted forms, C, which were not deleted. The middle line shows the percent of forms that are first contracted and then deleted. The upper part of the diagrams shows the full forms, F, which were neither contracted nor deleted. All four diagrams show clearly the parallel between contraction and deletion processes in that both apply more frequently with pronominal subjects than with full noun subjects. Studies of older adolescent groups and adults show the same pattern.

2.3.1   The Opposing Effects of the Phonetic Environment

In many ways contraction and deletion are parallel in AAVE: in their dependence on stress reduction, on a particular phonological shape, on the preceding grammatical environment, and on the following grammatical environment.[3] But in one respect, contraction and deletion are quite

---

3. Though we will not be considering the following grammatical environment here, it has been one of the major centers of interest in the study of the historical origins of AAVE as well as the relations between contraction and deletion. Many studies have replicated the finding that both contraction and deletion have their lowest value when a noun phrase follows (*He is my brother*); next are predicate adjectives and locatives (*He is tired, He is out there*); next are progressive verbs (*He is working on it*); and finally the future with *gonna* (*He is gonna do it*).

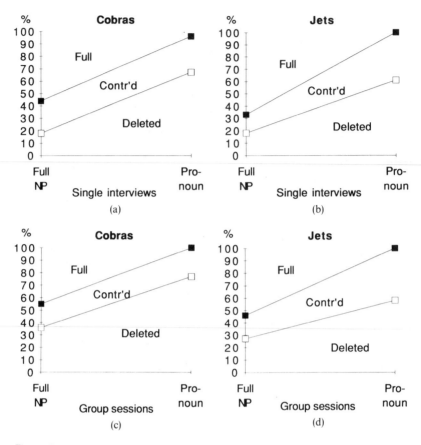

Figure 2.1
Effect of full noun phrase subject versus pronominal subject on contraction and deletion of the copula for two South Harlem groups in single interviews and group sessions. $D =$ percent contracted and then deleted; $C =$ percent contracted; $F =$ percent full forms.

different: contraction is the removal of a vowel, whereas deletion is the removal of a consonant. The following considerations lead us to believe that they will show opposing effects of the preceding phonetic environment.

The most favored syllable form in English, and in most other languages, is the open syllable CV—a single consonant followed by a single vowel. English does not favor CV-CV- as much as Italian or Japanese does, and it is rare to find long English sequences without closed syllables (CVC). Yet, when push comes to shove, the result of a reduction process will usually be a CV syllable. This sequence is easiest to pronounce, especially when speaking very fast, as in *Lemme have a piece o' pizza right away*. Next most favored is the CVC syllable type, in sequences like CVC-CVC-CVC, as in

Tom gave Matt more time. Syllables with several final consonants, CVCC and CVCCC, are on the whole disfavored. This is not because words like *first* or *hand* are hard to pronounce in isolation, but they can produce long sequences of consonants in combinations like *fist clenching* or *hand play*, with strings of four consonants in a row.[4] At the other extreme, English does not at all favor sequences of vowels, though other languages do (compare the typical Hawaiian place name *Aiea*).

Let us consider the consequences of these facts for auxiliary contraction and deletion. The result of contraction is that a single consonant is attached to the preceding words, as the spelling indicates, so that the shape of the preceding word will have the strongest effect on contraction and deletion. Some contractions will have the effect of creating CVC syllables and others will create CV syllables:

$$(79) \quad \underset{CV\ VC\ VC}{Ray\ is\ out} \xrightarrow{Contraction} \underset{CVC\ VC}{Ray's\ out} \xrightarrow{Deletion} \underset{CV\ VC}{Ray\ out}$$

$$(80) \quad \underset{CVC\ VC\ VC}{Ron\ is\ out} \xrightarrow{Contraction} \underset{CVC\ C\ VC}{Ron\ 's\ out} \xrightarrow{Deletion} \underset{CVC\ VC}{Ron\ out}$$

These examples show that the effect of contraction on syllable structure is the opposite of the effect of deletion. In (79) the subject *Ray* ends in a vowel, and contraction reduces the disfavored CV-VC form to the more favored form CVC. In (80) the subject *Ron* ends in a consonant, and contraction converts the favored CVC-VC sequence to CVCC. On the other hand, deletion in (79) changes the favored CVC-VC to the unfavored form CV-VC, while deletion in (80) resolves the cluster CVCC-VC to CVC-VC. We can infer, all other things being equal, that contraction will be favored over deletion when the subject ends in a vowel, but the reverse will be the case when the subject ends in a consonant.

Table 2.2 shows the effect of subject form on rates of contraction and deletion for the Jets and the Cobras, calculating these rates as we did in figure 2.1, and combining the data from single interviews and group interviews. Only full noun phrases are considered, since almost all pronouns, except *it*, *that* and *what*, end in a vowel. The reversal of the two effects is striking. For both the Jets and the Cobras, contraction is strongly favored when the subject ends in a vowel, and deletion is strongly favored over contraction when the subject ends in a consonant. This reversal of the phonetic conditioning of contraction and deletion further supports the proposal that the absence of the copula in AAVE is the result of a phonological deletion process that extends the effect of contraction one more

---

4. English has some words with unusually long final consonant sequences, like *sixths*, VCCCC, but most people do not pronounce all of these in natural speech. In AAVE, such combinations are almost impossible to realize.

Table 2.2
Rates of deletion and contraction by phonetic form of subject noun phrases for two South Harlem groups in single and group styles combined.

Subject ends in	Rate of contraction	N	Rate of deletion	N
Cobras				
__C	.41	46	.80	20
__V	.90	32	.41	29
Jets				
__C	.32	93	.70	30
__V	.90	32	.41	29

step, and we can be even more confident that the copula is present in the underlying structure of the grammar.

One consequence of this conclusion is that we can infer that the semantic information included in the underlying copula is preserved, since a low-level phonetic process removes phonetic information only, not semantic. This means that sentences like (3–5) and the other zero-copula sentences given above will be interpreted as statements about the present. Thus (3) *She the first one started us off* should be interpreted as referring to conditions that are true now and in general—that is, the "general present." Sentences like (5) *Michael Washington out here sellin' his rocks* will be interpreted as referring to the immediate present. None of these sentences will be heard as referring to the past, as equivalent to "She was the first one (who) started us off" or "Michael Washington was out here selling his rocks."

2.4   Experimental Approaches to the Cognitive Status of the Copula

The conclusions arrived at so far are based on inferences from the observation of speech production. We can test the conclusion that the copula is present in the underlying grammar, and is an object of cognition, by a number of experimental approaches. One such approach involves *memory tests*. It was found that many speakers of AAVE had great difficulty in repeating back certain sentence types of standard English that were outside of the AAVE grammar. These memory tests involved a betting game with real money, in which the subject won a nickel each time he repeated a sentence correctly, word for word; the members of the T-Birds, Jets, and Cobras were strongly motivated to do their best.

One of the most extreme examples involved double negatives, which are normal in AAVE. Sentences like (81a) were typically repeated back as (81b), even on the second and third try.

(81a)   He never sat at any of those desks.

(81b)   He never sat at none of those desses.

In AAVE the agreement of the negative that converts *any* to *none* is practically obligatory, and the difficulty in repeating back *any* was extreme.[5] A similar difficulty was found in repeating back sentences with the standard form of embedded questions, so that (82a) was automatically converted to (82b) by many subjects:

(82a)   I asked Alvin if Boot knew how to play basketball.

(82b)   I asked Alvin did Boot know how to play basketball.

But no sentence involving the use of the copula, no matter how complicated, posed any difficulty for repetition. The word *is* was never omitted in sentences like these:

(83)   What Alvin is, he is smart.

(84)   Boot is as good at playing basketball as he is smart in school.

In the year following the work with the T-Birds, Jets, and Cobras in South Harlem, Jane Torrey carried out a series of experiments in a second grade class in a local school. First, she recorded spontaneous speech from the thirty-odd members of the class. Next, she tested them for their knowledge of a series of standard English *-s* particles and inflections: the possessive *-s*, the plural *-s*, the third singular *-s*, and the contracted copula *'s*. Then she tested the children for their ability to make semantic distinctions based on the presence or absence of these inflections, using a method similar to the *wugs* test of Jean Berko Gleason. For the plural, children were shown pictures of one animal or two and asked to point to one or the other according to whether they were named with an *-s* or not. For the possessive, the children were shown two pictures: one of a duck in a hospital bed, with a nurse nearby; the other of a woman in a bed, with a duck dressed as a nurse standing by the bed. The subjects then heard one of two phrases —*the duck nurse* or *the duck's nurse*—and were asked to point to the right picture. For the third singular *-s*, children were given two tests. Pictures of one or two cats splashing in a puddle were to be identified by either *The cats splash* or *The cat splashes*. Pictures of a man with a stick about to hit a dog or of a dog running away from a man were to be distinguished by *The man hit the dog* or *The man hits the dog*. Knowledge of the copula was tested by similar sentences, such as *The boy hit* or *The boy's hit*, with pictures showing the boy as agent or patient of the action.

After the first series of tests Torrey exposed each child to a training program that specifically taught the meanings of the four *-s* inflections,

---

5. It was almost as extreme as the difficulty in pronouncing the *-sks* cluster in *desks*; as noted in footnote 4, this is simplified 100 percent of the time in AAVE.

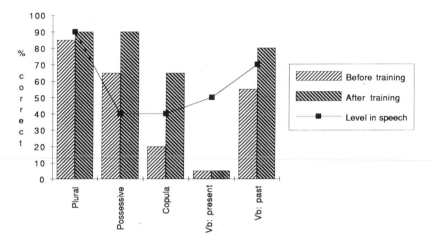

Figure 2.2
Percent correct in the use of -s inflections to obtain semantic information before and after training for second-grade children in Harlem. Points connected by the line represent the percent use of the inflection in spontaneous speech. From Torrey 1970.

and then retested the children. Figure 2.2 shows the results. The points connected by a solid line show the mean level of presence of the inflection in the spontaneous speech of the children. The bars show the percent of correct answers before and after testing. We observe that the copula was present less than 50 percent of the time. While the children had little difficulty with the plural or the possessive, they showed only 20 percent success with the copula before testing. After training, though, success with the copula increased significantly to about 65 percent correct. In contrast, there was no improvement at all in the children's ability to use the verbal third singular -s to distinguish one cat from two in *The cat splashes*. We conclude that the copula has a cognitive basis in the grammar of the children, allowing them to use it to obtain semantic information, but that the third person singular -s of the verb does not. At the same time we recognize that the knowledge of the copula among young children is not as secure as their knowledge of the plural. And, indeed, we find that some of the crucial evidence for the underlying presence of the copula is missing with preadolescents. They show no difference in the effect of a preceding consonant or vowel on contraction and deletion.

2.5   A Deep Difference: The Case of Stressed *Been*

So far, our results indicate that the differences between AAVE and other English dialects are rather superficial, the result of low-level phonetic processes that contract and delete material present in the underlying mental representation. This seems to be the case for the copula, at least for adolescents and adults, and indicates that the cognitive bases of the all English grammars are similar in this respect. Our view of the AAVE auxiliary would be misleading, though, if we left it at that. Consider sentence (85), spoken by a member of the black community in West Philadelphia:

(85)   She *been* married.

The word *been* is italicized here because it is spoken with considerable emphasis on a low pitch. Approaching this sentence with the same logic that we apply to the copula, we would infer that it is the result of the contraction and deletion of *has*, as in (85').[6]

(85')   She has been married → She 'as been married →
        She's been married → She been married.

This is indeed the conclusion that most speakers of other dialects come to when they hear this sentence. Rickford (1973) tested the semantic interpretation of this stressed *been* by a wide range of black and white subjects. He presented them with (85) and asked, did they think that the woman referred to was still married? The great majority of white subjects answered "No." Their conclusion is the result of a peculiar property of the English present perfect *has been*. This grammatical form refers to conditions continuing up to the present whenever there is an indication of duration: *She's been married for three years; she's been married for a long time.* But without any such modification, the present perfect asserts that the condition is completed and done with (though it still has an effect on the present: *She's been married and should know better than to do it again*). This use of *has been* is found in combination with any expression that refers to a state that can be turned on or off again, verb, adjective, or noun: *she's been connected, worried, happy, a member*, and so on.

So much for the white subjects. But the great majority of black subjects gave the opposite answer. In answer to the question "Is she still married?" they said "Yes." This included middle-class black people who had a good knowledge of other dialects, and were not basically vernacular speakers, as well as native speakers of AAVE. If there are no great cognitive differences between black and white speakers, how do we account for this contrast in response? Is there some underlying difference in the way that black and white speakers reason about language?

6. Here there is one more step in the chain: before contraction is applied, the initial /h/ of *has* is deleted, much like the initial /h/ of *him, her* in *Take 'im away* and *Fill 'er up.*

The answer to this question appears when we begin to notice other sentences of AAVE with stressed, low-pitch *been*. I once visited a first grade in West Philadelphia with a psychologist who was doing some experimental work there. He introduced me to a black 6-year-old boy, who then turned to him and said

(86)   I *been* know your name.

Eddie, a 15-year-old friend of my son's, was visiting our house in West Philadelphia.

(87)   WL: That's a new coat, Eddie?
       Eddie: I *been* had that for weeks.

John Baugh reports from his long-term participant-observation in the black community of Los Angeles:

(88)   They *been* called the cops, and they're still not here.

(89)   I *been* been knowing Russell.

None of these uses of *been* can be interpreted as reduced forms of the English present perfect. *They* been *called the cops* can't be interpreted as a reduced form of *They have been called the cops*; *I* been *been knowing Russell* can't be derived from *I have been been knowing Russell*. In these uses of *been* the following elements are not past participles, but transitive or intransitive verbs, usually in the past tense form. All these uses have three semantic components:

(90)   a.   A condition referred to was true in the past.

       b.   It has been true for a comparatively long time (nonrecent).

       c.   It is still true.

These three features combine to form a complex of meanings that we may call the *remote present perfect*. It is distinct from the English present perfect both formally and semantically, for the present perfect does not necessarily carry features (b) or (c). Though native speakers of AAVE are not consciously aware of these semantic features, they may focus on them in argumentative discourse. In (91), from Dayton's participant-observation in West Philadelphia, the remote feature (b) of *been* is used to disagree with the "recent" implication of *already*:

(91)   a.   They *been* left.

       b.   They left already?

       a.   They *been* left.

A similar argumentative implication is found in (92), a remark of a 15-year-old member of the Jets in the course of a card game. The implication of the question was that he was still playing; the answer strongly denied this, implying that the observer should have known that he had quit some time ago.

(92)　a.　You gonna quit?

　　　b.　I *been* quit.

It follows that the difference in response between black and white subjects in Rickford's (1973) experiment was due to the fact that the black subjects correctly perceived *been* in *she* been *married* as the AAVE remote present perfect. *If she* been *married*, she is still married. The whites, knowing nothing about this element of AAVE grammar, could only relate it to the English present perfect.

Stressed *been* is only one of many grammatical elements of AAVE that are not found in other dialects and are generally not recognized by speakers of other dialects. These include other members of the auxiliary, such as the resultative *be done* in (92) and the habitual *be* in (93), both from Dayton's observations in West Philadelphia.

(92)　If you love your enemy, they be done eat you alive in this society.

(93)　When they used to tell us that the nipples be pink on pregnant women, we be laughin'; we were laughin' 'cause it don't be like that.

Of the many aspect markers of AAVE that are never found in other dialects, habitual *be* is the only one that is generally heard and recognized in public discourse. These grammatical markers differ from those found in other dialects in profound ways. Sentences with these markers in the auxiliary do not carry the information on tense that is a part of all other English sentences. They do not invert subject and auxiliary to ask questions or to form tag questions; they do not incorporate -*n't* to form the negative. There is, for example, no AAVE question corresponding to (85), *Been she married*?

It might seem strange that white subjects know so little about these features of African-American English. After all, most of them have heard black people talk since they were children; they see many films and television shows that portray the black family with black actors. They read books in which black characters speak a dialect that is recognized as black and may actually be labeled Black English or African-American English. Yet none of this experience will enable them to recognize and interpret stressed *been* in the way that native speakers of AAVE do.

The reason for this situation is that these "deeper" or "more different" aspects of AAVE are not reproduced on the mass media. Sentences like

(86–89) and (91–93) are not heard in plays or television programs. Black actors, in their efforts to reproduce the black vernacular, unconsciously avoid the use of *been* and the other members of the AAVE auxiliary mentioned above. But they do reflect more or less faithfully the variation in the use of the copula that we have studied here. The African-American English of the media is a familiar idiom, a part of the joint world that is shared by black and white citizens of the United States. The demonstration that the absence of the copula in AAVE is an extension of familiar rules of language is consistent with the more general finding that standard and nonstandard dialects share a common cognitive base: most often, their differences are primarily adjustments in the output rules of the grammar.

Suggestions for Further Reading

Baugh, J. (1983). *Black street speech: Its history, structure and survival.* Austin: Unversity of Texas Press.
Labov, W. (1972). *Language in the inner city.* Philadelphia: University of Pennsylvania Press.
Mufwene, S., J. Baugh, G. Bailey, and W. Walter Edwards. *The structure of African-American English.*
Rickford, J. (1973). Carrying the new wave into syntax: The case of Black English *bin.* In R. Fasold and R. Shuy, eds., *Analyzing variation in language,* 162–183. Washington, DC: Georgetown University Press.

Problems

The contraction of the auxiliary that we have been discussing so far is only one of the two types of contraction that operate in the English verb phrase. The other is called "not-contraction." It is similar to auxiliary contraction in that it involves removal of a reduced vowel of (the vowel of unstressed *not*) and the attachment of the result to the preceding word.

2.1 What is the relation between these two forms of contraction? Do they compete, combine, or complement each other? Enter the possible contracted forms below for the past and present tense of the verb *to be*. For example, the first person plural in the present can be *we aren't* or *we're not*.

	PRESENT		PAST	
	Singular	*Plural*	*Singular*	*Plural*
1st person				
2nd person				
3rd person				

Are there any holes in the pattern? If so, what causes them?

2.2   Tag questions are formed by moving the first member of the auxiliary to the end of the sentence, adding contracted *not* (for positive sentences), and then adding the appropriate pronominal subject: *He's tired, isn't he?* Work out the same pattern as above, and see if there are any holes in it.

2.3   How does *not*-contraction affect the contraction and deletion of the copula in AAVE? If speakers of AAVE were to shift toward a more standard English, would they be more likely to use *not*-contraction or auxiliary contraction?

Exercise

Construct an experimental technique for measuring the degree of awareness of the grammatical structures discussed here on the part of black and white members of the speech community you are in contact with. Given a particular linguistic form, you will want to find out whether the subject can (a) recognize it as a form of English, (b) say who is likely to use this form in the speech community, (c) identify the meaning in context and/or out of context, and (d) predict the acceptability of new uses. Your experiment may test all or some of these degrees of cognitive awareness.

The framework. The experiment need not be carried out in a laboratory setting and may be more effective if you approach people outside the university. As a general setting for the experiment, you could define the task and motivate subjects by relating it to the problem of identifying native speakers of English. Immigration officials often use linguistic criteria to decide if someone was actually born in the United States: some speech forms are produced only by nonnative speakers. Such a test could be made more reliable by enlarging and refining our knowledge of the range of grammatical forms used by native speakers.

The stimuli. For test (a), you may draw on any of the examples given in this chapter, though you will want to mix them with dummy forms that are never used by native speakers. For test (b), a subset of the same items may be used. For test (c), the examples showing *been* will be more useful than those dealing with the copula; sentences parallel to (85) will be particularly useful. You may want to test the conclusion of section 2.2.4 that sentences with deleted copula cannot be heard as referring to the past. For test (d) you may want to use the nonacceptable examples of copula deletion implied in (53–56) and marked with asterisks in (63–73).

The rating scales and categories. For test (a), the scale of acceptability may have anywhere from 4 to 7 points. A 4-point scale might be labeled: "I would use it myself; some people say it; I never heard it, but some people might say it; not English at all." A 7-point scale might be simply labeled "Perfectly natural English" on one end and "No native speaker would say it" at the other. For test (b), you may want to use several different categories to elicit judgments on status: correct, colloquial, slang, nonstandard, foreign; or perhaps general English, Black English, Hispanic, Creole English; or elicit free answers. Test (d) can use the same rating scales as test (a).

The subjects. To achieve any kind of reliable result, you will probably want to have at least ten native speakers from the white community and ten from the black community. For a more refined sample, it will be helpful to categorize speakers according to their degree of familiarity with the other ethnic group; the percent of the other ethnic group in the subject's high school is a good measure. Number of close friends of the other ethnic group is another possible measure. Be sure to record the subject's age, sex, occupation, and geographic origin.

References

Bailey, B. (1968). *Jamaican creole syntax*. Cambridge: Cambridge University Press.

Bloom, L. (1970). *Language development: Form and function in emerging grammars*. Cambridge, MA: MIT Press.

Torrey, J. (1983). Black children's knowledge of standard English. *American Educational Research Journal* 20, 627–643.

Chapter 3

The Sound Structure of Mawu Words: A Case Study in the Cognitive Science of Speech

Mark Liberman

3.1 Introduction

The most intimate and habitual things in life are sometimes hard to see objectively. For instance, it seems natural and inevitable for human communication to depend on spoken words, even though this requires tens of thousands of arbitrary connections between noises and concepts. It seems natural and inevitable for human children to learn these connections over the course of a decade or so, even though this requires analyzing the behavior of adults emitting concatenations of noises referring to logically structured combinations of (often very abstract) properties of experiences. These facts are so obvious and familiar that it is not easy for us to appreciate what a strange and wonderful achievement they represent, and how far from obvious it is that this is how a system for communication among intelligent creatures should be designed.

Human vocal communication has some characteristics that are not logically necessary and are nonetheless remarkable for being so ordinary that they are hardly ever noticed.

1. Each language includes a large number of distinct words whose sound and meaning are not genetically given and therefore must be learned.

2. The number of words that are learned (estimated by Nagy and Herman (1987) to be at least forty thousand for modern American high school graduates), and the number of years available for learning them, imply that about ten words must be learned every day, on average, over a period of ten to fifteen years.

3. Most words are learned simply by observation of their use, rather than from explicit instruction, and the number of observations on which word learning is based is often small.

4. In using this large word stock, people maintain an extraordinary degree of agreement about what words were said, despite large

55

individual, geographic, and social differences in pronunciation: in an experiment reported by Doddington and Hydrick (1978), isolated words, selected at random from a set of forty thousand, each pronounced by a different and unknown speaker, were recognized by consensus of a panel of judges with an error rate of only about 2 percent.

This situation might have been different. For instance, Cheney and Seyfarth (1990) indicate that the vervet monkey's repertory of meaningful cries is genetically fixed to a substantial degree, although the number of different classes of cries identified in this case is only about ten. Some philosophers of language have argued that there is a fixed stock of basic human concepts, and so our species might have saved us all from international communications barriers—not to speak of language requirements— by expanding a system like the vervet monkey's. We might have tried to get along with a few hundred such built-in vocal symbols, using our ability to combine words into phrases whose meaning is determinable from the meaning of their parts, and our skill in pointing, making air pictures with our hands, and so on.

This is not, however, the path that human evolution has taken. Instead, each human language develops its own rather large set of essentially arbitrary vocal signs, roughly what we normally call "words." Exactly how large this set is depends on how you define its members: we do not need to count *cats* if we already have *cat*, but does *building* add to the count if *build* is already counted? What about *red herring* if we already have *red* and *herring*? The size of this set may also depend on the language (or perhaps the culture) examined. Nevertheless, if we define "word" as a piece of language whose conventional form and meaning cannot be predicted by composing smaller units contained in it, then it seems likely that normal speakers know something in the range of 10,000 to 100,000 words of their native language. The cognitive (and social!) problem of establishing such a large number of essentially arbitrary sound-meaning correspondences, and ensuring that individual children learn them in such a way as to end up able to communicate with one another across groups as well as within family groups, is a daunting one.

How do we do it?

Well, some might say that we do not. Perhaps human lexical accomplishments have been exaggerated a bit. After all, most talk is on some identifiable topic or another, restricting the likely vocabulary to a few thousand words. Within and across topics, we often use highly stereotyped word sequences; thus, the actual average uncertainty about what the next word will be is typically under a thousand and may often be under a hundred. Even so, we suffer plenty of mishearings and other communication failures.

Although these caveats have some validity, they do not change the earlier estimates of vocabulary size, learning rate, and accuracy in word transmission under good conditions. The difficulty and interest of the problem is increased by the fact that much more than words goes into the noises someone makes when talking. Speech sounds are modulated in a way that also communicates who you are, how you feel, what kind of impression you want to make, the structure of your message, and the process by which you compose it. Furthermore, what your addressee hears will be considerably changed by where you are talking (a shower stall, an office, a cathedral), by noises around you (running water, other voices, traffic, music), and perhaps by various unnatural means of transmission such as a telephone or public address system.

Somehow, listeners usually manage to hear the words that were spoken despite (or more precisely, in addition to) all these other things, both the extralexical modulations added by the speakers and the distortions imposed by the environment. This ability further emphasizes the nontrivial character of the central question: How do humans efficiently learn, remember, and use such a large number of distinct equivalence-classes of vocal noises, which we call *words*?

The answer is *phonology*—or more precisely, the linguistic sound structures that phonology studies. The rest of this paper is devoted to explaining what these sound structures are like.

The basic principle of phonology is that the notion "possible word of language X," from the point of view of pronunciation, is defined in terms of structured combinations of a small number of basic meaningless elements. Phonologists have developed a variety of theories about what these elements and structures are. The simplest idea is to suppose that the basic phonological elements are like the letters of an alphabet, each of which represents a type of vocal gesture or sound. Then phonological structures are simply strings of such letters (usually called *phonemes*), with sequence in the string representing succession in time. In fact, there is a special alphabet, known as the International Phonetic Alphabet (IPA), which aims to provide enough symbols to represent all the crucial distinctions in all the languages of the world (even though the sounds associated with an IPA symbol typically vary somewhat from language to language).

This alphabetic approach is enough to provide a basic description of the phonological system of any given language. It is possible to provide an inventory of phonemic symbols for that language so that all its words can have the distinctive aspects of their sound defined in terms of strings of those symbols; it is also possible to provide an account of the articulatory and acoustic meaning of such strings of symbols. Traditionally, the study of the distribution of phonemic symbols is the domain of the field of phonology, while the physical interpretation of those symbols is the domain of the field of phonetics.

This simple theory is enough to clarify how humans can learn, remember, and use such a large number of different words. Words are not arbitrarily distinct classes of vocal noises. Instead, a word's claims on sound are spelled out in terms of the phonological system of some particular language. This splits the problem, conceptually speaking, into two parts. Learning a given language requires figuring out what its phonological system as a whole is and how structures of phonological elements are related to vocal noises, independent of any consideration of particular words. Learning the sound of any particular word, then, requires only figuring out how to spell it phonologically. This phonological spelling is a relatively small amount of information, which might be inferred from a couple of hearings. A phonological spelling nevertheless suffices to predict the wide range of ways in which the word might be spoken by different speakers on different occasions in different contexts, because it is the phonological system as a whole that is anchored to sound. Learners' knowledge of the physical grounding of a phonological system is therefore based on every bit of experience they have ever had in talking, or listening to, the language in question, and all this experience can be brought to bear in processing any particular word.

Careful consideration of the facts of individual languages suggests that it is more insightful—scientifically more interesting—to decompose phonemic letters into smaller pieces (called *features*), organized into simple phonological structures of which syllables are the most familiar example. In this view, phonemic segments—as represented by the letters of the IPA—are actually just convenient names for pieces of these phonological structures. Hypotheses about this type of phonological organization arise naturally out of efforts to define the sound structure of words in particular languages and to model the phonetic interpretation of these structures. Such investigations indicate that the theory of phonemic letters, taken literally, is not a very good model for any particular phonological system; also, it tends to make the phonology of different languages look much more variable than it really is. When we replace a rigidly alphabetic theory of phonology with one based on structured combinations of phonological features, we get a more insightful analysis of individual languages, and we also find that the same sorts of phonological features and structures arise in the analysis of widely separated and apparently unrelated languages.

The human species has not evolved a fixed set of words. We have not even evolved a fixed set of phonemes or syllables out of which to make words. What we have evolved, it seems, is a set of basic phonological features and structures capable of specifying a wide variety of phonological systems, each of which in turn is capable of specifying the sound patterns of a set of words. This amounts to a sort of parts inventory and tool kit for designing and building the pronunciation systems of languages.

When a group of humans use this tool kit to set up a phonological system and to define the sound of a set of words in terms of it, they are ordinarily not at all aware of what they are doing, despite the considerable complexity of the problem. Doing phonology, in this practical sense, is something that just comes naturally. Each of us participates especially actively in this process during the first few years of our life; indeed, most of us are unable to achieve fully native abilities in a phonological system that we encounter later in life, no matter how carefully we study and how much we practice.

Of course, the process of creating a phonological system is never really carried out starting from nothing. Instead, an existing system is learned again by each individual, while new words are constantly added, old words die out or change their nature, and the phonological system as a whole is gradually redefined in an evolutionary process. Throughout this process of constant renewal and change, the sound system as a whole remains relatively consistent across the speech community; it retains its coherence as a system for each individual, despite the fact that speech communities throughout human history have not had official bodies such as the Académie Française to act as language police. Phonological systems remain lawful because the cognitive architecture of the human species requires them to do so.

3.2   Words in Mawu

The best way to make these basic ideas clear is to work through a concrete example in a certain amount of detail. From this perspective all human languages that have ever been studied exhibit the same basic patterns, even though their particular phonological alphabets and syllabic arrangements vary widely. As a characteristic example, we will take a look at *Mawu*, which is spoken by about 100,000 people in the Ivory Coast and Guinea. *Mawu*[1] is the name of a region, *Mawuka* is what the people who live there call themselves, and *Mawukakan* is what they call the language that they speak. Mawu is a Manding language, closely related to other languages such as Bambara and Mandinka that are spoken by millions of people in West Africa. The information and insights about Mawu in this chapter come primarily from the work of Moussa Bamba, especially Bamba (1991), and his help and advice are gratefully acknowledged. Remaining errors of fact or interpretation are the fault of the author of this chapter.

At first inspection Mawu has some unusual characteristics, such as three different kinds of nasalized vowels and a system of lexical tone with complicated rules for determining the tonal patterns of compound words

---

1. Also spelled "Mau," or "Mahou" in French orthography.

and phrases. The themes and concepts that emerge from a careful analysis of Mawu are, however, essentially the same ones that would emerge from a careful consideration of the phonology of any language. In fact, the things about Mawu phonology that are superficially most peculiar will turn out, when properly analyzed, to be strikingly similar to the comparable aspects of much more familiar languages such as French and Japanese. This abstract similarity points us toward the basic cognitive architecture underlying human speech.

It will be clearest to start with a conventional phonemic analysis, resulting in a set of phonological "letters" that can be arranged to specify the sound patterns of Mawu words. This will prepare the ground for a more insightful analysis in terms of structured combinations of phonological features.

Mawu has a simple syllable structure, compared with English, with all words aside from pronouns being made up of syllables consisting of a single consonant and a following vowel (like /ko/ "to say"), a single consonant and a following double or long vowel (like /koo/ "bone, pit, seed"), or a single consonant, one of the two *glides* symbolized in English by the letters *w* and *y* and a single following vowel (like /kwo/ "tail"). We simply need to specify what the set of consonant and vowel "letters" can be to fill out these patterns completely.

In this approach, Mawu has twenty-four consonant phonemes and twenty vowel phonemes. The nature of these "letters" of the Mawu lexical alphabet is indicated in tables 3.1 and 3.2, which are arranged in rows and columns to help indicate the nature of the corresponding mouth gestures. These tables (and also the Mawu examples that we provide) use a selection from a special set of letters called the *International Phonetic Alphabet*, or IPA, which forms a sort of universal standard for representing speech sounds. In this chapter IPA characters are used to write down Mawu examples (although a few liberties are taken with the IPA standard with respect to the notation of the second and third types of nasalized vowels).

Mawu is also a tone language, in the sense that words are distinguished according to their pitch patterns. Thus /kawa/ said with high pitch means "stone," /kawa/ said with low pitch means "cloud," and /kawa/ said with rising pitch means "shoulder." Tonal phenomena will be disregarded until the basic nontonal aspects of Mawu phonology have been presented.

The tour of Mawu phonemes begins with the seven oral vowels and the first two types of nasal vowels.

The seven oral vowels in the left-most panel of table 3.1 refer roughly to the standard American English sounds /i/ as in "beet," /e/ as in "bait," /ɛ/ as in "bet," /a/ as in "bott," /ɔ/ as in "bought," /o/ as in "boat," /u/ as in "boot." The top-to-bottom dimension in the panel represents *vowel height* or *openness*, with higher positions on the page corresponding to a higher position of the tongue and thus also to a more closed, less open

Table 3.1
Seventeen basic Mawu vowels.

Oral vowels		Nasal vowels I		Nasal vowels II	
i	u	ĩ	ũ		
e	o	ẽ	õ		
ɛ ɔ		ɛ̃ ɔ̃		ɛ̠ ɔ̠	
a		ã		a̠	

vocal tract. The left-to-right dimension in each panel of the chart very roughly divides the vowels according to front-to-back position of the tongue in the mouth, so that the tongue is raised farthest forward for /i/ and raised farthest back for /u/. Finally, the three vowels closest to the right (that is, back and high) corner of the panel—/ɔ/, /o/, /u/—are *rounded*, which is to say that they are made with rounded and protruded lips, while the other four vowels are *unrounded*.

The seven corresponding nasal vowels, in the middle panel labeled "nasal vowels I," are pronounced with just the same positions of tongue and lips, but with the *velum* (the back part of the soft palate) lowered, as it would be in American English for /ĩ/ in "mean," /ẽ/ in "main," /ɛ̃/ in "men," /ã/ in "mom," /ɔ̃/ in "dawn," /õ/ in "moan," /ũ/ in "moon."

If the nature of the nasal vowels is not clear to you, try comparing the oral vowel in (for instance) "bee" with its nasal counterpart produced by saying "bean" without actually pronouncing the final /n/. After a little practice you should be able to sense your velum going up and down while you keep your tongue and lips in the same place, to make oral and nasal versions of each vowel. If you can do that, then you are making the distinction between the Mawu words /bi/ meaning "bag" and /bĩ/ meaning "grass." Similarly /cɛ̃/ (pronounced somewhat like the name "Chen" without the final /n/) means "animal fat," while /cɛ/ (pronounced like the name "Chet" without the final /t/) means "man."

For speakers of Mawu, the seven nasal vowels are first-class phonological elements, familiar from the cradle, and not just the indirect consequence of a vowel adjacent to nasal consonants, as in English. In fact, Mawu speakers learn to distinguish two additional kinds of nasal vowels.

The nasal vowels that we have labeled type "I" are by far the most common, which is why we have given them the first roman numeral. The three vowels in the rightmost panel, labeled "nasal vowels II," are very similar in pronunciation to the type I nasal vowels. Thus, it is not always easy to tell the difference between /cɛ̃/ "animal fat," which has a nasal vowel of type I, and /cɛ̠/ "sand," which has a nasal vowel of type II.[2]

---

2. We are again disregarding tone here—the word for "animal fat" has high tone while the word for "sand" has low tone.

There are, nevertheless, several differences showing clearly that a phonological distinction exists in such pairs of words—a difference in the time course of nasality, a difference in effect on the beginning of following words, and a shift in vowel quality.

1. In very slow and careful speech, the nasal vowels of type I start out nonnasal, becoming increasingly nasal toward the end, whereas the nasal vowels of type II are fully nasal from the beginning.

2. Nasal vowels of type I cause characteristic changes in following consonants, while nasal vowels of type II (usually) do not. Thus when the word /lɑɑ/ meaning "jar" is combined with the words for "sand" and "animal fat," the initial /l/ changes to /n/ following the type I vowel but not the type II vowel: /cɛ̃ nɑɑ/ "jar of lard," but /cɛ̰ lɑɑ/ "jar of sand."

3. Especially in the case of the vowel we are writing /ɑ/, type II nasality causes a shift in vowel quality. The vowel /ɑ/, which is normally similar in sound to the vowel in standard American English "father," has as its closest type II equivalent a nasalized version of a vowel that in IPA is written [ə] and pronounced somewhat like the vowel in American English "cut." Thus, the type II nasal vowel in /sɑ̰/ meaning "snake" is something like American English "sunk" before the final consonants, while the type I nasal vowel in /sɑ̃/ meaning "rain" retains the basic /ɑ/ quality, with added nasality as might be heard in American English "psalm" before the final consonant.

In notating this second series of nasal vowels, the standard IPA notation is being abused a bit, since the IPA provides only one way to mark vowel nasality, and we have just shown that Mawukakan seems to need two. The notation used here for the second type of vowel nasality borrows the symbol (underdrawn tilde) specified by the IPA for vowels with "creaky voice," since Mawu does not use creaky voice distinctively.

Type II vowel nasality divides Mawu vowels into two groups: /ɑ/, /ɛ/ and /ɔ/, which have type II nasal versions, and /i/, /e/, /o/ and /u/, which do not. A corresponding distinction among vowels is frequently seen to play a role in the phonology of the world's languages. This distinction is especially salient in some of the other languages of West Africa, where words are ordinarily made up of vowels drawn from only one class or the other. As a result, the nature of the vocal tract gestures involved in this distinction has been carefully studied using X-rays and other methods, with the conclusion that in the vowels of the /i/ /e/ /o/ /u/ class, the root of the tongue is drawn forward, expanding the throat (or *pharynx*) cavity, while in the vowels of the /ɑ/ /ɛ/ /ɔ/ class, the root of the tongue is back, resulting in a narrower pharynx. The gesture involved in the first set of vowels is called Advanced Tongue Root, abbreviated ATR, and phonologists use this convenient abbreviation as a description for the gesture and for the corresponding class of vowels. We can say that Mawu type II nasality only occurs in non-ATR vowels.

In fact, the nasal vowel situation in Mawu is even more complex, at least superficially, than has been indicated so far. There are some words containing non-ATR vowels that share characteristics of both kinds of nasalized vowels. For example /kãã/ "love" and /mjã/ "antelope" have the shift in vowel quality characteristic of type II nasal vowels and also are fully nasalized throughout slow and careful pronunciation like type II nasal vowels; but at the same time they have the effects on following consonants typical of type I nasal vowels.

Since we have not run out of roman numerals, even though we have run out of IPA symbols, we can call vowels of this last class "type III nasalized vowels." Since they exhibit simultaneously characteristics of type I and type II, we can symbolize them in a phonemic notation by combining the diacritic mark for type I (a tilde above) with the diacritic mark for type II (a tilde below).

The existence of three distinctive types of vowel nasality is unusual—which is why the IPA does not provide for it—and might be seen as an example of the endless variability of human speech patterns. However, a consideration of the distribution of phonological features (including nasality) in Mawu syllables and words will suggest a simple reanalysis based on elements and structures that are familiar to phonologists from the analysis of many other languages. This analysis will simultaneously clarify the nature of Mawukakan and the nature of human phonological systems in general, providing a nice example of the limitations of the alphabetic metaphor, as well as a motivation for the kinds of structured combinations of features that modern phonologists postulate to explain the sound patterns of words.

First, some additional information about the phonological inventory of Mawu is needed. The set of possible consonants in Mawu is given in table 3.2.

The column labels in table 3.2 specify the *place of articulation* of the Mawu consonants. Consonants involve closing off the vocal tract, partially or completely, while in vowels the vocal tract is basically open. The closure for a Mawu consonant can occur at five different places: at the lips (a "labial" consonant such as /p/ or /b/), at the *alveolar ridge* just in back of the upper incisors (an "alveolar" consonant such as /t/ or /d/), on the hard palate a little further into the mouth (a "palatal" consonant made in roughly the same place as the consonant in English "chew"), on the soft palate still futher back in the mouth (a "velar" consonant such as /k/ or /g/), or in the larynx or "voice box" (a "glottal" consonant such as /h/

Table 3.2
Twenty-four Mawukakan consonants.

		Labial	Alveolar	Palatal	Velar	Labiovelar	Glottal
obstruents	stops voiceless	p	t	c	k	$\widehat{kp}$	
	voiced	b	d	ɟ	g	$\widehat{gb}$	
	fricatives voiceless	f	s				
	voiced	v	z				
implosives		ɓ	ɗ				
sonorants	nasals	m	n	ɲ	ŋ		
	approximants		l	j	ɰ	w	h

or the consonantal sound in English *unh-unh* meaning "no"). Mawu also has "labiovelar" consonants, in which both labial and velar closures are made at the same time, sort of like saying /k/ and /p/ or /g/ and /b/ simultaneously.

The rows in table 3.2 specify the *manner of articulation* of the Mawu consonants. Thus, a consonant whose *place of articulation* is *alveolar*—that is, whose constriction is made with the tip or blade of the tongue pressing against the alveolar ridge, just behind the top front teeth—can be of six different kinds, according to how the constriction is made, and what is happening elsewhere in the vocal tract. There are three distinct kinds of constriction in Mawu: a complete constriction (producing a *stop*); a nearly complete constriction with a turbulent flow of air through a narrow opening (producing a *fricative*), and an incomplete, relaxed constriction (producing an *approximant*). These possibilities are further distinguished by *voicing* and *nasality*. In *voiced* consonants the vocal cords (two muscular folds of tissue in the larynx) are kept together; thus, the buzzing sound typical of vowels is continued through the consonant closure, whereas in *voiceless* consonants the vocal cords are spread apart; thus, the laryngeal buzz stops during the closure and for a short time after. In *nasal* consonants, just as in nasalized vowels, the velum is lowered so that the sound is affected by the resonances of the nasal cavity.

Finally, Mawu has *implosive* consonants, in which the vocal folds are kept closed and vibrating, as in voiced consonants. The larynx is lowered during the consonant closure, so that when the closure is released, air actually flows briefly into the mouth instead of out of it. It is not clear whether to consider this special laryngeal maneuver as a different kind of voicing, or as a different kind of constriction. For convenience of tabular display, implosives are laid out in tables 3.2 and 3.3 as if they involved a different kind of constriction.

There are then sixteen logically possible combinations of the three features of constriction type, voicing, and nasality: $4 \times 2 \times 2$. Mawu makes distinctive use of only seven of these, as table 3.3 indicates.

Table 3.3
Combinations of consonant features for alveolar place.

	Velum closed (nonnasal)		Velum open (nasal)	
	Voiced	Voiceless	Voiced	Voiceless
Stop	d	t	n	
Fricative	z	s		
Implosive	ɗ			
Approximant	l			

This kind of partial cross-classification is typical of the sound systems of the world's languages. Voiceless nasal consonants do exist (for example, in Burmese), but they are quite rare. It is similarly rare for distinctive nasality to apply to fricatives and approximants. These restrictions are natural, given the physical characteristics of the articulations and sounds involved. For instance, it is difficult to maintain sufficient oral air flow for a fricative if the nasal passages are open; similarly, the basic gesture producing an implosion supposes that the vocal folds are brought together as in voiced speech, that the nasal passages are shut off, and that the oral constriction is complete.

Since these features do not interact orthogonally (that is, not all logically possible combinations in fact occur in Mawukakan phonemes), it is initially tempting to regard them as an analytic artifact, imposed because an analysis of articulatory mechanisms is most easily framed in terms of such a decomposition, but playing no real role in the cognitive structure of Mawu (or English) speech. Further investigation, though, will show that this kind of featural decomposition is essential to understanding the larger-scale sound structure of words, the variations in word pronunciation according to context, and the way that word pronunciations change over time.

In fact, a much greater degree of nonorthogonality arises in the way that basic phonological elements combine into words. These basic elements have just been described for Mawu as a set of phonemic letters in terms of which Mawu spells its words. This phonological alphabet is not actually a writing system, except insofar as a few linguists have used something like it—the Mawuka do not use their language in writing. Rather, it is a sort of theory about the cognitive structure of Mawu speech, just as similar phonological alphabets represent theories about the speech patterns of speakers of every other human spoken language. There is, however, much more to the cognitive structure of speech, among the Mawuka as among any other people, than such a phonological alphabet alone.

Mawu words are not composed of just any sequence of such phonemic segments. Among the types of sequences that do not occur are some that we may plausibly consider unpronounceable: /ptpkt/ or /mksbpi/. Some sequences that seem quite natural to English speakers are impossible in Mawu: /let/ (which would be pronounced like English "late"), /stej/ (like English "stay"), /ajl/ (like English "aisle"), and so on. On the other hand, Mawukakan has word structures that English speakers find difficult: /gbɛ/ (meaning "palm wine"), /kpako/ (meaning "coconut").

These sequence restrictions, in Mawu or in English, are based on a sort of phonological syntax, in which syllables are a typical constituent type. In discussing the internal structure of syllables, it is convenient to notate consonants with capital C and vowels with capital V. In table 3.4, capital G

Table 3.4
Mawu syllable types.

CV	/ɓa/ "goat"	/so/ "horse"	/ku/ "yam"	/je/ "squash"
CVV	/ɓaa/ "poison"	/saa/ "pistachio"	/kuu/ "bump, hill"	/joo/ "wing, feather"
CGV	/ɓja/ "loincloth"	/ɓwɛ/ "medicine"	/swa/ "monkey"	/sja/ "road"
	/fwo/ "to greet"			

is also used to mean one of the glides /w/ or /j/ (as in the beginning of English "wash" and "yes"). Leaving aside pronouns, Mawu words are made up of syllables of the three types shown in table 3.4: consonant-vowel, consonant-vowel-vowel, and consonant-glide-vowel.[3]

Mawu words can be made up of several such syllables in a row, even in the case of simple (or *monomorphemic*) words that do not contain other words or identifiable pieces of words within them. Thus, we have

CVCV	/sama/	"elephant"
CVCGV	/ɲakwa̰/	"cat"
CVVCV	/fɛɛla/	"orphan"
CGVCVV	/ʤemuu/	"citrus fruit"
CVCVV	/manɔɔ/	"kind of fish"
CVVCVV	/ɲɔɔmɛɛ/	"camel"
CVCVCV	/jabibi/	"pineapple"

Phoneme sequences that cannot be constructed by concatenating the three basic types are systematically absent from Mawu. For instance, there are no words with the form. *CVC, *CVVV, *CGVV, *CCV, *VCV (where the asterisk is used, as in syntactic examples, to mean that the form in question is not grammatically possible). This is the first reason to postulate syllablelike structures in Mawu: it enables us to give a simple account of the possible phoneme sequences in Mawu words. From what we have seen so far, Mawu words are just concatenations of the three basic syllable types. When we take a look at the distribution of the two types of vowel nasality, the evidence will become more complex; but the conclusion will stand: Mawu words are concatenations of Mawu syllables.

In the permitted CVV syllable type, the two vowels are always the same. Sequences like /toi/ or /kɛa/ are not found in Mawu. Thus, we might consider treating CVV syllables as containing long vowels—the IPA provides a symbol for this, /ː/, so that we could write the word meaning "hill" as /kuː/ instead of /kuu/. This notation certainly expresses

---

3. A small number of Mawu words borrowed from Arabic begin with a vowel, such as /ala/ "God". In most other cases, borrowed words that ought to begin with a vowel are borrowed as consonant-initial, such as /mobili/ "automobile," /burama/ "Abraham."

something true about Mawu; namely, that a syllable can have only one specification of vowel quality, even if it has two vowel segments in it. At this point the notion of a phonemic alphabet is beginning to lose its coherence, since we are either introducing a symbol that just means "repeat the previous vowel" or stating that a specification of vowel quality is shared by two adjacent symbols.

One piece is missing from the discussion so far: a demonstration that /kuu/ "hill" ends in two segments of the same type that /ku/ "yam" ends in one of. Granting that /kuu/ has the same vowel quality as /ku/ and that (allowing for speech rate, emphasis, and other sorts of timing modulation) /kuu/ is longer than /ku/, perhaps we should model vowel length as a feature, like consonant voicing, that can be present or absent in a single vowel segment. This hypothesis would simply double the number of Mawu vowel symbols by introducing a new series of long vowel phonemes, just as we introduced two (or even three) series of nasalized vowel phonemes.

Strong evidence against this length-as-a-feature analysis is provided by a Mawu language game called /ŋgoɓooɓo/. This game is similar in spirit to games familiar to English-speaking children, such as pig latin—children use it as a way to disguise their speech from those unfortunates who don't understand the rules or who are not practiced enough to decode rapidly. In /ŋgoɓooɓo/, the basic rule is to replace every vowel V with the sequence /VɓV/, where the second V is a copy of the original. Thus /ku/ "yam" becomes /kuɓu/, and /bisa/ "whip" becomes /biɓisaɓa/.

What about /kuu/ "hill"? If this word contained a single long vowel, we would expect the /ŋgoɓooɓo/ version to be /kuːɓuː/. Such a form, however, would provoke any Mawuka child to laughter. The correct outcome for /kuu/ is /kuɓuuɓu/, which is exactly what should happen if each of two separate vowels in /kuu/ is given its own /ŋgoɓooɓo/ expansion.

There is one apparent exception to the Mawu rule that the two vowels in a CVV syllable must be the same. This exception provides one more distinction between type I and type II nasalization. Remember that type I nasalization nasalizes only the end of its vowel, at least in sufficiently slow and careful speech, and spreads to the initial consonant of the following syllable in all kinds of speech, whereas type II nasalization nasalizes all of its vowel, does not spread to following consonants, and produces a change in vowel quality in /a/. Since this change in vowel quality is a useful signpost, our initial discussion of the distribution of Mawu vowel nasality will focus on /a/.

Type II nasalization acts like any other vowel feature with respect to VV sequences: If one of the adjacent vowel segments has type II nasalization, then both must. Thus, there are words such as /daa/ "curse," /saa/ "funeral," /faa/ "power," in which two adjacent identical vowels also share type II nasalization. There are no words containing sequences such as /aa/ or /aa̰/, in which two adjacent vowels differ in type II nasalization.

The distribution of type I nasalization in CVV syllables is, however, completely different. There are many CVV words in which the first vowel is not nasalized at all, while the second vowel has type I nasalization: thus /caã/ "peanut," /ɓaã/ "dike," /kaã/ "to sew." There are no words containing VV sequences such as /ãa/ or /ãã/.

Type I nasalization, unlike all other vowel features, is thus limited to the very end of such syllables. It cannot apply to the first of a pair of non-ATR vowels, unlike all other vowel features, which must be shared by both vowels in such a case. Even in a CV syllable, it only affects the end of the vowel, at least if speech is slow enough to permit such a contour of nasality to be distinguished. Furthermore, it readily spreads to influence the initial consonant of a following syllable in a systematic pattern according to which voiceless consonants become voiced; voiced stops and fricatives become prenasalized (that is, they acquire a short nasal segment at their beginning); and glides, liquids, and implosives all become the corresponding nasal consonants. Nasal consonants are not affected. Examples of these outcomes are given in table 3.5 for the labial and alveolar consonants. These examples have been constructed using the word /jã/, meaning "here"; in combination with a following noun X, it means something like "X of this place," or "local X."

The pattern exemplified in table 3.5 has certain well-defined structural limits. For instance, it does not apply between the end of one syntactic clause and the beginning of the next, or even between a verb and a following adverbial. These limits provide some interesting clues of a

Table 3.5
Mawu nasal assimilation.

Consonant	Result	Example
p	mb	/jã/ + /pinɛ/ ⇒ [jãmbinɛ] "local wheel"
b	mb	/jã/ + /ba/ ⇒ [jãmba] "local river"
f	mv	/jã/ + /fyɛ/ ⇒ [jãmvyɛ] "local plantation"
v	mv	/jã/ + vũ/ ⇒ [jãmvũ] "local basket"
ɓ	m	/jã/ + /ɓa/ ⇒ [jãma] "local goat"
t	nd	/jã/ + /tuu/ ⇒ [jãnduu] "local oil"
d	nd	/jã/ + /di/ ⇒ [jãndi] "local honey"
s	nz	/jã/ + /so/ ⇒ [jãnzo] "local horse"
z	nz	/jã/ + /zoolo/ ⇒ [jãnzoolo] "local zoolo-worm"
ɗ	n	/jã/ + /ɗyemuu/ ⇒ [jãnyemuu] "local citrus fruit"
l	n	/jã/ + /lɔɔ/ ⇒ [jãnɔɔ] "local firewood"

purely phonological character to the constituent structure of Mawu sentences. However, within constituents of the appropriate type—including words, compound words, and combinations of nouns with adjectives, verbs and auxiliary verbs, and so forth—this pattern of influence of the type I nasal feature on a following initial consonant is entirely automatic and exceptionless. It does not matter what the words are. If a type I nasal is followed by an initial consonant that is not already a nasal, that consonant will change according to the pattern in table 3.5.

The effect shown in table 3.5 clearly involves the spread of nasality from type I nasals to following consonants. Such effects are called *assimilation* by phonologists. Assimilation effects clearly involve the influence of an articulatory gesture on its neighbor—here the velum is staying down a little longer. This effect cannot, though, be treated purely as a matter of articulatory laziness. For one thing, this assimilatory effect does not occur with type II nasal vowels, which have a lowered velum, just as type I vowels do. For another thing, the affected consonant articulations are changing in other ways besides a lowered velum. Approximants are becoming regular nasal consonants with full oral closure, voiceless consonants are becoming voiced as well as prenasalized, and so forth. Mawu nasal assimilation is thus being mediated by the phonological system, both in the definition of when it happens and in the results when it does happen.

The assimilation effect shown in table 3.5 gives us a reliable test for the presence of type I nasality in a syllable-final vowel, just as the shift in quality of a type II nasal /ɑ/ (roughly from the vowel of "non" to the vowel of "nun") gives us a reliable indication of the presence of type II nasality in any vowel. There is a third test that tells us whether a vowel has any sort of nasality at all. Table 3.6 shows that in the language game ŋgoɓooɓo, a nasal vowel of whatever type is doubled according to the pattern VmV rather than VɓV.

Table 3.6
ŋgoɓooɓo with nasal vowels.

Word	Gloss	ŋgoɓooɓo
sã	rain	sama
sạ	snake	sama
g͡bã	celibate	g͡bama
kɔ̣ɔ	hunger	kɔmɔɔmɔ
dạ̃ạ̃	clock	damaama
kaã	to sew	kaɓaama

The shift to /m/ from /ɓ/ is the expected consequence of nasalization caused by a type I nasal vowel, as shown earlier in table 3.5. In ŋgoɓooɓo, the nasal aspect of any sort of nasalized vowel has this same effect, thus underlining the point that we are really dealing with the same nasal feature in different disguises. Furthermore, all vowels in ŋgoɓooɓo wind up being oral. Their nasality, if they had any, is transferred to the /ɓ/, turning it into /m/. The result is to "uncover" the basic identity of the type II and III nasal vowels with the type I nasal vowels and with nonnasalized vowels; they all become one set of seven vowels; phonemic nasality and any consequent quality changes are removed. This underlines the point that we are really dealing with the same nonnasal vowel features, with the basic seven vowels of Mawu transformed into twenty superficial vowel phonemes by various sorts of interaction with nasality.

Table 3.7 summarizes what we know about the permitted interactions of the various effects of nasality in Mawu CVV syllables whose vowel is /ɑ/. The first five columns represent questions that we can ask about a form. Columns 1 and 2 ask "does the first (or second) vowel shift in quality to schwa?" as type II nasal /ɑ/ does. Columns 3 and 4 ask "does the first (or second) vowel replicate with mV in ŋgoɓooɓo?" as all nasal vowels do. Column 5 asks "does the first consonant of a following word undergo nasal assimilation?" as consonants do following type I nasal vowels. Column 6 presents the phoneme sequence that corresponds to the answer to these questions.

The four rows in table 3.7 are the only possible configurations of answers to these questions, and also the only four nasal vowel sequences, that Mawu allows. One simple way to summarize what table 3.7 tells us is that CVV syllables, like CV syllables, permit exactly four types of vowels: nonnasal, nasal type I, nasal type II, and nasal type III. If there really were four basic types of vowel letters freely co-occurring, we would expect CVV syllables to have $4 \times 4 = 16$ possibilities of nasality type, not just four.

Table 3.7
Possible distributions of nasality in Mawu ɑɑ sequences.

1 V1 ə	2 V2 ə	3 V1 ŋg m	4 V2 ŋg m	5 C assimilation	6 phoneme sequence
no	no	no	no	no	ɑɑ
no	no	no	yes	yes	ɑ̃
yes	yes	yes	yes	no	ɑ̠ɑ̠
yes	yes	yes	yes	yes	ɑ̠ɑ̠̃

Table 3.8
Impossible distributions of nasality in Mawu ɑɑ sequences.

1 V1 ə	2 V2 ə	3 V1 ŋg m	4 V2 ŋg m	5 C assimilation	6 phoneme sequence
no	no	yes	no	no	ãɑ
no	yes	no	yes	no	ɑɑ̰
yes	no	yes	no	no	ɑ̰ɑ
yes	no	yes	yes	yes	ɑ̰ã
no	yes	yes	yes	no	ãɑ̰
no	yes	yes	yes	yes	ãɑ̰̃

Table 3.8 gives examples of configurations of answers that seem plausible in the abstract, and are predicted by free combination of vowel phonemes, but are not in fact possible in Mawu for the vowel /ɑ/.

The situation for the other six vowels is similar. The vowels /ɔ/ and /ɛ/ (with roughly the sound of the vowels in American English "awe" and "Ed") are just like /ɑ/, except that the clear vowel quality shift caused by type II nasalization in /ɑ/ does not occur. We can thus disregard the first two columns, and ask about the pattern of answers in the third through fifth columns. Here, as in the case of /ɑ/, only four of the eight logically possible combinations can be found, and the four possibilities are exactly as they are for /ɑ/.

The vowels /i/, /e/, /u/, /o/ have a still simpler pattern. For these vowels there are only two rows in a table giving the possible constellation of answers to these questions for two-vowel sequences. These two rows represent an oral pattern, where there is no vowel nasality of any sort at all in the syllable and the answer to all questions is "no" and a nasal pattern. The nasal pattern (for these four vowels) always produces nasal assimilation in following consonants, and it always produces ŋgoɓooɓo nasality in the second vowel of a two-vowel sequence. As for the ŋgoɓooɓo treatment of the first vowel in two-vowel sequences whose second element is nasal, it is always oral for /e/ and /o/, and always nasal for /i/ and /u/. Thus, in none of the four vowels is there any option for the treatment of the first of a VV sequence in case the second is nasal, and so there is only one kind of nasalized-vowel syllable, whether its shape is CV or CVV.

Many readers will by now have recognized that the apparent complexity of the Mawu system of vowel nasality is just a consequence of our misapplication of the alphabetic metaphor. Aiming to represent Mawu words as sequences of letters, each representing a distinctive class of speech sounds, we ended up with a system of twenty vowel phonemes interacting with one another and with adjacent consonants in a complex way.

There is a much simpler way to look at things. Type I nasal vowels, as noted before, are mainly a phenomenon of the syllable margin: They usually occur only in the second of a VV pair, and they affect the initial consonants of following syllables; in slow pronunciations only the end of a type I nasal vowel is nasalized.

Suppose we represent type I nasality as an optional element at the end of the syllable, symbolized X. Now Mawu syllable types become CV, CVX, CVV, CVVX, CGV, and CGVX. The type I nasal vowel phonemes vanish from the analysis—they are just the phonetic interpretation of VX sequences, X causing preceding vowels to assimilate in nasality just as it causes such assimilation in following consonants. The three type II nasal vowels remain—they are intrinsically nasalized vowels. The type III nasal vowel phonemes also vanish from the analysis—they are just concatenations of the type II nasal vowels with the element X. Mawu is left with a system of seven oral and three (intrinsically) nasal vowels, a state of affairs that is quite similar to the vowel inventories of many other and more well-known languages, such as French.

The complex distribution of the various types of Mawu vowel nasality, laid out in tables 3.7 and 3.8 and the subsequent discussion, now follows from two simple principles: VV sequences must be repetitions of the same vowel (nasal or otherwise), and X is an optional syllable-final element, occurring freely after all possible syllables. There are now guaranteed to be a maximum of four types of syllable with respect to vowel nasality for the non-ATR vowels, whether the syllable shape is CV or CVV or CGV:

1. no nasality at all;
2. nasality due to element X following the syllable;
3. intrinsic nasality of the vowel(s) in the syllable;
4. both intrinsic vowel nasality and element X following the syllable.

In the case of the ATR vowels, intrinsic vowel nasality cannot occur, since the Mawu inventory of vowels includes nasalized versions only of the non-ATR cases /ɑ/, /ɔ/, /ɛ/, and not the ATR cases /i/, /e/, /u/, /o/. As a result, the only choice for the ATR vowels is whether or not element X is present at the end of the syllable or not. Thus, there is just one type of nasalized-vowel possibility for syllables containing these four vowels, whether the syllable contains a single vowel or a VV sequence, and this nasality is always of the type that spreads to following consonants. In the case of the high vowels /i/ and /u/, there is one extra wrinkle: the nasality produced by element X at the end spreads to the first vowel of a VV sequence, so that the ŋgoɓooɓo output of the first vowel as well as the second has /m/ rather than /ɓ/ in these cases.

What is this element X? Well, it is certainly nasal in character; however, it is not a vowel. If it were, it should add an extra V6V sequence in ŋgo6oo6o, which it does not, and it would also violate the general Mawu constraint against CVVV syllables. Neither is it a consonant, in the normal sense—there is no associated constriction in the vocal tract, just the lowering of the velum to produce nasality. Thus X seems to be a pure floating nasal feature, free of any other content. In what follows, we will therefore write it as a floating IPA nasal diacritic / ~/.

This whole situation is a familiar story to those who have looked at the sound systems of even a small sample of the world's languages. It is normal for syllable structure to play a strong role in the permitted distribution of phonological features. ATR and nasality are common, almost ubiquitous as distinctive features in the phonological systems of the world. Syllable types CV and CVV are among the most common and natural of phonological structures. CVN (where N is a nasal consonant of some sort) is almost as simple and natural a syllable structure as CV is, and it is quite common for languages to allow only such a nasal as a syllable-final element. It is normal for such syllable-final nasals to produce assimilatory effects in the preceding vowel and to assimilate in place of articulation to a following consonant. When the syllable-final nasal does not assimilate in place to a following consonant, its closure often becomes very weak (as in Japanese) or vanishes, leaving bare nasality behind (as in French and often in Mandarin Chinese).

The basic phonological building blocks of the Mawu nasal vowel situation are, then, widespread and natural ones. Mawu assembles these routine building blocks in a slightly unusual way, permitting intrinsically nasalized vowels to co-occur freely with syllable-final nasal elements, never treating the syllable-final nasal elements as an independent consonantal constriction. As a result, its phonological system seems to have a peculiar, unheard-of characteristic—three distinct kinds of nasalized vowels—requiring us to add to the already-unwieldy IPA standard and to recognize yet another odd quirk of human linguistic culture. However, this apparent peculiarity is only the result of superficial misanalysis, and a more careful examination yields an empirically more accurate description of Mawu, which also reaffirms the abstract unity of human phonological systems.

One characteristic of this analysis deserves special note. In isolation, or in final position in an utterance, there is apparently no articulatory or acoustic difference at all between what we originally called type II and type III nasal vowels, that is, between an intrinsically nasal vowel, and an intrinsically nasal vowel followed by a floating nasal element. The intrinsically nasal vowel already causes the velum to be fully lowered, and there is no extra duration or other sign of the floating nasal element, whose existence is purely potential in this case. This potential is actualized only when another word follows whose initial consonant is not already nasal, since the floating nasal will spread, whereas the "bound" nasal feature instrinsic to the nasalized vowel will not. The spreading nasal feature is easy enough to hear, changing for instance /l/ to /n/. Thus /swą/ "odor" and /swą~/ "dish of pounded yam" are both identically [swą] in isolation, or if followed by a word beginning with a nasal consonant; but they will be clearly distinguished if followed by an element of another type, such as the plural element /lu/: [swąlu] vs. [swąnu].

In such cases phonological representation of Mawu words may contain an element that cannot be heard or spoken in even the most careful isolated citation-form pronunciation, but which comes out in a clear and systematic way through its effect on a following word, if one is present. We will soon see that a similar state of affairs applies in an even more thoroughgoing way in the case of Mawu tone. Such cases underline the abstract coherence of the phonological system, which finds little difficulty in establishing and preserving such distinctions because they are simple expressions of its basic combinatoric nature.

Mawu makes one additional use of bare nasality that is worthy of comment. There is one word—namely, the first person singular pronoun "I"— that consists solely of a bare nasal feature. Mawu pronouns in general conspicuously flout the normal syllable structure restrictions of the language, which require syllables (and thus words) to start with a consonant.

~	"I"	H
i	"you"	H
ɑ	"he, she, it"	L
ã	"we"	H(L)
ɑ	"you-all"	H
i	"they"	L

The last column gives the tone—Mawu is a tone language, remember? We will learn what the tonal categories mean shortly. Except for "I," the pronouns are all single vowels. The "I" pronoun behaves as if it were a floating nasal feature: it produces assimilatory changes in following consonants similar to those we presented earlier.

This allows us to explain where the language-game name ŋgoɓooɓo comes from. Sharp-eyed readers may have noticed that the first syllable of this word is an exception to the generalizations about Mawu syllable structure that we have been claiming. In fact, this word comes from the phrase / ~ko o/, in which / ~/ means "I," /ko/ is a verb meaning "say," and /o/ is a mark of emphasis, so that the whole phrase means something like "I say!" With nasal assimilation this becomes /ŋgoo/, which in turn is subjected to the normal rule of the language game to produce /ŋgoɓooɓo/.

Many languages, including some that are quite closely related to Mawu, have an independent series of prenasalized stops. In Mawu, however, these segments are always derived from the sequence of a floating nasal feature with a voiced stop or fricative, and so there is no reason to set them up as an independent choice to be made in specifying the sound pattern of words.

Although phonological features are not usually seen in such a transparently unbound state as Mawu floating nasality, many aspects of language sound structures argue in favor of representing words as structured combinations of features rather than simply as strings of phonemic symbols. We have already seen examples of three of these motivations:

1. *Phonological inventories.* In specifying the distinctive sound elements of a language, it is natural to use featural concepts such as "place of articulation," " voicing," "nasality" and so on.

2. *Combinatory constraints.* In specifying the combinations and sequences of distinctive sound elements that can be used to define the sound of words, it is natural to use concepts such as "consonant," "vowel," "syllable" and so forth, which provide a kind of structural framework on which distinctive features can be arranged.

3. *Contextual variation.* In specifying how word pronunciation changes depending on adjacent words, it is natural to refer to effects such as the assimilation of features in a structural setting.

Treating Mawu nasality in terms of the distribution of a nasal feature in syllabic structures produces a description that is simple and quasi-universal in character, rather than complex and highly particular to Mawu. Such successful analyses show that language sound patterns instantiate simple, effective, but rather abstract cognitive structures that recur across languages.

There is a fourth kind of motivation for thinking of a phonological representation as a structured combination of features instead of as a sequence of phonemic letters. In some cases different phonological features seem to operate on completely different scales of time and space. Phonologists call these different strands of featural activity *tiers*, and Mawu tone provides a good example. Mawu words can be distinguished by their pitch patterns, and these distinctive pitch patterns are naturally modeled as simple sequences of distinctive high (H) and low (L) tones rather than as arbitrary melodies. This aspect of Mawu phonology has a curious characteristic: All words, regardless of their length, exhibit one of exactly four possible tone patterns.

Table 3.9 shows a sample of monosyllabic Mawu words that differ minimally in tone. In these cases the way that the speaker modulates the pitch of his or her voice makes the difference between words. The CV

Table 3.9
Mawu tone patterns.

L	LH(L)	H	H(L)
si		si	si
"life"		"seed"	"fly"
	so	so	
	"horse"	"village"	
g͡ba			g͡ba
"kitchen"			"hut"
saa	saa	saa	saa
"sheep"	"salary"	"squash seed"	"charm"

syllable /so/ said with pitch rising from low to high means "horse," while /so/ said with pitch starting high and remaining high means "village." Table 3.9 shows that monosyllabic Mawu nouns, even if only a single vowel is present, can have four distinctive pitch patterns: low tone, which is written L; rising tone, which is written LH(L); and two kinds of high tone, which we write as H and H(L).

In isolation, patterns H and H(L) sound exactly alike; thus, /si/ "seed" and /si/ "fly" are pronounced identically if said in isolation. The difference comes out only in combination forms. For instance, the Mawuka indicate plurality with an element /lu/ that occurs following the noun phrase to be pluralized. The plural element /lu/ has no distinctive tone of its own—its tone is always predictable from context. When added directly to a noun with the H tone pattern, /lu/ also has a high tone, so that /si/ H "seed" + /lu/ is /silu/ HH "seeds," with a high tone on both syllables. When added to a noun with the H(L) tone pattern, /lu/ has a low tone, so that /si/ H(L) "fly" + /lu/ is /silu/ HL "flies," said with a falling tone pattern.

The parenthesized low tone in the H(L) pattern is similar in character to the floating nasal element when it follows an intrinsically nasalized vowel, such as in the word /swɑ~/ "starch dish." This floating nasal element makes no difference pronounced in isolation, since the preceding vowel is already nasal, but emerges when a following nonnasal consonant is available to be nasalized. Similarly, the floating L tone is not pronounced in isolation; it takes effect only when a following syllable gives it space to dock.

The final floating low tone in words like /si/ H(L) "fly" differs from the final floating nasal in words like /ka~/ "neck," where the preceding vowel is not intrinsically nasal, and therefore is partly nasalized by the floating nasal feature. Logically, a final floating low tone should be able to affect the pitch pattern of the preceding vowel in /si/ H(L), producing a falling tone. This, however, does not happen. A similar state of affairs applies in the case of rising-tone words such as /so/ LH(L) "horse." Such words start low and end high; but, following a rising-tone word, a determiner element such as /lu/ will get a low tone.

For the purposes of the present discussion, the main point is that every Mawu word has one of the four tone patterns L, LH(L), H, H(L). This is true for the monosyllabic words shown in table 3.9, and it is equally true for longer words, including borrowed words.

L	/namaa/ "paralytic"	/safɛɛni ~/ "donkey"
LH(L)	/sukuu/ "kind of dance"	/falati/ "provocation"
H	/namaa/ "trouble"	/ɲamakuu~/ "ginger"
H(L)	/ɲɔɔmɛɛ/ "camel"	/bɔlɔsi/ "brush"

The patterns L, H, and H(L) assign a uniform phonological tone to the whole word, either low or high. The pattern LH(L) requires a transition from low tone to high tone somewhere in the word. If tone were freely contrastive on vowels or syllables in Mawu, we might expect to see words differing only where this rise takes place. Instead, the location of the rise is predictable from the rest of the phonological spelling of the word. The final high tone is associated with the last vowel of the word, and the initial low tone is associated with the first vowel of the word. If the word has only one or two vowels, there is nothing more to say. If there are three or more vowels, then the initial low tone spreads as long as it encounters only vowels or approximant consonant. The first sufficiently strong consonant will form the boundary between the low tone region and the high tone region. For example, the three vowels of /salaba/ LH "lamp wick" will have the tone pattern LLH, while the three vowels of /ja~galo/ LH "sickness" will have the tone pattern LHH.

The only tonal choice that can thus be made for a Mawu word is to pick one of the four tonal patterns. The four options are the same whether the word has one vowel in it or six vowels. This is a clear example of the way in which phonological features sometimes operate on distinct strands, or *tiers*. In Mawu the phonological spelling of a word on the tonal tier is decoupled from its spelling in terms of consonants and vowels or even syllables. If we had to describe Mawu tone in terms of high- and low-pitched varieties of vowel phonemes, we would have to use schematic descriptions of sequences of these classes of vowels to describe the set of possible tonal categories. It is much simpler just to talk about whole words having tone patterns like L or H or LH(L).

Such independence of the tonal tier is commonly found, but in other tone languages the tonal choices available in constructing a word may be more closely linked to the rest of its phonological spelling. In Yoruba each vowel may be given one of the three phonologically distinct tone levels (low, mid, or high); and in Mandarin Chinese each syllable may have one of four tone patterns that may be described as high, rising, low, or falling.

In the case of Mawu, there is good evidence that the limitation of words to four basic tonal patterns is part of what every speaker understands implicitly about the language. For instance, the limitation is maintained in a systematic way for compound words, even newly minted ones. Mawu has a productive system for making new words out of old ones—nouns, verbs, adjectives, and adverbs can all be made this way. One aspect of this derivational system is the combination of two words into a compound word, just as with English compounds such as "phonebook," "horsehair," and "oxcart."

When a Mawu compound is made in this way, its tone pattern is predictable on the basis of the tone patterns of its constituent parts. Not only is the output predictable, but the predicted output in each case is also one of the four basic tonal patterns. Table 3.10 shows the outcome for each of the sixteen possible inputs.

Thus, /jɛɛ/ H "fish" combines with /ku~/ L "head" to make /jɛɛku~/ H "fish head"; /ku~/ L "head" combines with /sye/ H(L) "hair" to make LH(L) "head hair," /caa~/ L "peanut" combines with /fyɛ/ H "farm" to make /caa~fyɛ/ L "peanut farm"; /la/ H "mouth, door" combines with /kuu/ L "hill, bump" to make /lakuu/ H "chin."

Table 3.10
Tone of Mawu compound words.

Tone of word 1	Tone of word 2	Tone of resulting compound
L	L	L
L	LH(L)	LH(L)
L	H	L
L	H(L)	LH(L)
LH(L)	L	L
LH(L)	LH(L)	LH(L)
LH(L)	H	L
LH(L)	H(L)	LH(L)
H	L	H
H	LH(L)	H(L)
H	H	H
H	H(L)	H(L)
H(L)	L	H
H(L)	LH(L)	H(L)
H(L)	H	H
H(L)	H(L)	H(L)

As these examples suggest, such compounds can sometimes be somewhat idiosyncratic in the way that their meaning is related to the meanings of their parts, but they can also be formed in quite a regular way. For instance, /faa/ L "skin, rind" can be combined with the word for any animal, fruit, or vegetable to make a compound word to refer to its skin or rind, and all such compounds will follow the tonal relationships laid out in table 3.10.

Of course, it is also possible to make various sorts of phrases out of the same words—somewhat like the difference between English "banana peel" and "peel of a banana"—and the tone pattern of such phrasal combinations will not necessarily remain among the lexically possible patterns. Thus /gɔɔ/ H "banana" combines with /faa/ L "skin' by the principles of table 3.10 to make /gɔɔfaa/ H "banana peel," but the combination /gɔɔfaa/ H(L) "skin of a banana" is also possible.

The principles in table 3.10 can apply recursively to create compound words of three or more elements, such as /kawacelwa/ H "quarry," made from /kawa/ H "rock," /ce/ L "to break by striking," /lwa/ H "place." Such examples also stay within the lexical pattern of four possible tone patterns, which is a durable characteristic of the notion "possible word of Mawu."

The situation as we have described it seems complex enough. Imagine how difficult it would be to encompass it at all in a purely alphabetic theory, in which tonal categories might be expressed as varieties of vowels, whose co-occurrences at the level of simple and compound words would have to be restricted so as to be consistent with the patterns so far described. By treating tonal phenomena as a separate strand or tier of activity, at least the basic tonal facts of Mawu can be laid out in a straightforward fashion.

As in the case of the three types of nasal vowels, however, the reader ought again to be restless and suspicious. What could be the real meaning of these rather odd constraints? Why limit tone patterns to four, and why limit them to this particular, somewhat odd, set of four patterns, two of which have floating tones that are hidden except when a toneless particle follows? Having decided on such a limitation, why maintain it in compound words through the particular pattern of combination rules expressed in table 3.10?

As with the matter of three types of nasal vowels, we might simply shrug and mention the boundless variability of the human imagination. In fact, the description given here has only begun to scratch the surface of the complex tonal phonology of Mawu. As in the nasal vowel case, though, a more careful consideration of a wider variety of facts suggests a simple and rational account, although a slightly more abstract one, according to which Mawu looks very much like many other languages. Such an account has been proposed in Bamba (1991). We can see the essence of his proposal—the presentation here is superficially a bit different—by considering an analogy to the facts of Japanese.

The Tokyo dialect of Japanese is usually described (Haraguchi 1977; Poser 1984; Pierrehumbert and Beckman 1988) as having lexically distinctive accent. Any syllable in a word may be accented, or none may be. Thus, *hashi* with initial-syllable accent means "chopsticks," *hashi* with final-syllable accent means "bridge," and *hashi* with no accent at all means "edge." All words typically begin on a low pitch, rising immediately if the first syllable is long,[4] or just after the first syllable if it is short. An accent is realized as a fall in pitch just after the accented syllable, while an accentless word stays high to the end. It is therefore said that the final-syllable accent and the accentless case are usually pronounced in the same way; however, when a particle such as the subject marker *-ga* follows, a final-accented word expresses its latent pitch fall with a low tone on the following particle, while the particle remains high following an accentless word.

In the Osaka dialect an additional degree of tonal differentiation is possible. Whether the word is accented or accentless, it may begin with a low tone or a high tone. Thus, in Osaka Japanese, there are four types of words from the point of view of tone and accent:

1. low beginning, accentless;
2. low beginning, accented;
3. high beginning, accentless;
4. high beginning, accented.

These are essentially the same as the four tonal types of Mawu. The Mawu tone patterns H(L) and LH(L) are like final-accented words in Tokyo Japanese, with the final floating L tone only emerging if a particle is added so as to give it a place to dock. The Mawu tone patterns L and LH(L) are like the low-beginning words of Osaka Japanese, accentless and accented respectively, while the tone patterns H and H(L) are like the corresponding high-beginning words.

The similarity is disguised by a few differences. In Osaka Japanese an accent can be on any vowel, except that high-beginning words cannot be final-accented, and low-beginning words cannot be initial-accented. In Mawu, on the other hand, an accent, if present, can only be on the final vowel, regardless of whether the word begins high or low; but high and low beginnings can freely combine with presence or absence of accent even in monosyllables. Thus, Osaka Japanese cannot exhibit the full range of four categories on monosyllabic words, as Mawu does; on the other

---

4. Long syllables in Japanese contain two vowels, or a vowel and a syllable-final consonant.

hand, Mawu cannot exhibit the range of options for accent placement in polysyllabic words that Japanese does.

In Osaka Japanese, because we can place an accent almost anywhere in polysyllabic words, we tend to think of the facts primarily in terms of variable stress or accent, although they clearly have a tonal dimension as well. In Mawu, the four tonal patterns remain available in words with only one vowel, and the options for accentuation are only final-syllable accent or absence of accent, without any variation in accent location. We therefore tend to think of the facts primarily in terms of tone, although they have an accentual dimension that comes out more clearly as a wider range of phenomena are examined.

As a further demonstration of the fundamental similarity, consider the treatment of compound nouns in Osaka Japanese. Such compounds remain within the basic scheme of the language; they may begin high or low, and they may be accented or accentless. Whether or not the compound is accented depends on the second member, whereas whether or not the compound has a high beginning or a low beginning depends on the first member.

The basic relationship is given in table 3.11. We can ignore whether or not the first word is accented, and likewise whether or not the second word starts low or high, because these questions will have no impact on the starting tone or the accentuation of the compound. Each cell in the table shows the outcome for the whole compound, as a function of whether the first word starts low or high, and whether the second word is accented or accentless.

Table 3.11, representing the compounding facts for Osaka Japanese, is exactly a schematic form of table 3.10, which presented the compounding facts for Mawu! The abstract ingredients in both cases are the same—the formation of compound words in a phonological system whose words can be high or low at their beginning and may also be either accented or not. In both cases the basic outcome is the same: Compound words remain within the system, exhibiting the same range of tonal/accentual behaviors as simple words do, with the initial-tone specification of the compound taken from its initial word and the accentuation of the compound determined by the final word. In the two languages both simple and compound

Table 3.11
Compound nouns in Osaka Japanese.

	Word 2 is accented	Word 2 is accentless
Word 1 begins L	Result begins L, is accented	Result begins L, is accentless
Word 1 begins H	Result begins H, is accented	Result begins H, is accentless

words remain limited to the four basic patterns because the elements of the patterns are defined phonologically at the level of the word and not at the level of the individual vowel or even syllable.

It is clear that a single theory of tone and accent should be able to encompass both the Mawu and the Japanese systems, since the facts, in a slightly abstracted form, are essentially the same in both cases. A careful consideration of the distributional peculiarities in each language leads us to an analysis that makes otherwise odd and complex phenomena seem sensible and simple. Curiously, the analysis is nearly the same for (this aspect of) two languages spoken at opposite ends of the world by peoples who have surely been separated for a long time. This similarity cannot be due to cultural influence or to inheritance of a shared feature from a common parent language. Instead, it can only mean that both peoples happen to have picked up the same pieces from the phonological tool kit that is the common property of humanity.

3.3   Conclusion

This discussion has omitted many complex and interesting aspects of the Mawu phonological system; for instance, a striking range of tonal phenomena arise when words are combined into phrases. Also omitted have been many fascinating phenomena from other languages of the world: clicks, voice quality variation, vowel harmony, introduction and deletion of features and segments to achieve proper syllable structure, and so on.

The point, however, has not been to present a complete description of any one language, nor has it been to list schematically the components of the universal phonological parts inventory and tool kit. Instead, a detailed analysis of two apparently peculiar facts of Mawu word-level phonology—the three classes of nasal vowels and the restriction to four word-level tonal patterns—has aimed to show that these apparent oddities arise naturally out of the interaction of simple elements and structures that are also part of the phonological systems of much more familiar languages. This demonstration exemplifies concretely what phonological analysis is like and why it tells us something important about the cognitive structures that underlie human speech.

Suggestions for Further Reading

The efforts of phonologists and phoneticians to define the notion *possible word of such-and-such a language*, carried out in careful detail across many languages, has led to a general picture of the phonological parts bin and tool box out of which the world's languages form their phonological systems. Although these systems exhibit a fascinating and perhaps even endless variety of superficial differences, just as biological forms of other other sorts do, careful analysis always shows us deeper similarities, reflecting the fact that these systems are all built out of the same sort of stuff by the same sorts of processes. An excellent introduction to modern phonology, presented in breadth and also in considerable depth, can be found in Kenstowicz 1993.

Theories of phonology have improved a great deal over the past thirty years, with the result that a trained phonologist begins to work on a new language with a set of analytic tools producing insightful analyses of many of its phonological phenomena. This process of improvement continues, as new ways of thinking shed light on old problems and as new analyses strengthen or undermine existing theories. For examples of how a fresh perspective can improve on familiar analyses while offering a convincing account of new phenomena, see Prince and Smolensky, 1995 or McCarthy and Prince, 1995.

Problems

3.1 *An alien language.* Imagine an intelligent race of creatures in another galaxy whose system of communication includes nothing at all analogous to a human phonological system. In particular, they have no culturally specific combinatory system of meaningless elements out of which basic meaningful ones are made. If their communications system has an inventory of basic meaningful elements, it can be genetically given, or culturally variable, as you please, as long as it is not built on top of anything like a phonology.

Describe how this alien communications system works. Try to be specific and to avoid concepts like direct transfer of thoughts, unless you have a concrete and physically plausible idea about how this might occur.

Why might a species evolve in the direction of your system? What would be the advantages and disadvantages compared with the human system of spoken language?

3.2 *How many possible words are there in Mawu?* Keeping in mind the number of consonants and vowels, the set of possible syllable structures, the distribution of final nasal elements, and the tonal system, how many monosyllabic words could there be in Mawu? How many two-syllable words? How many words of three syllables? (Assume that seventeen initial consonant-glide sequences are possible and that there are no other constraints on feature co-occurrences beyond those mentioned in this chapter.)

3.3 *Comparison of Mawu and Bambara nasality.* The table below compares certain Mawu words with their cognates in Bambara, a related Manding language. The Bambara words are given in their standard spelling, in which a syllable-final nasal indicates a preceding nasalized vowel.

Bambara	Mawu	gloss
so	so	"horse"
ba	ba	"river"
fin	fĩ~	"black"
basa	basa	"lizard"
faga	faa	"to kill"
fara	faa	"skin, rind"
kolo	koo	"bone"
kelen	kee~	"one"
sula	swa	"monkey"

Bambara	Mawu	gloss
todi	twe	"toad"
fila	fja	"two"
kɔŋɔ	kɔ̰ɔ̰	"hunger"
kuna	kwa̰	"bitter"
suma	swa̰	"slow"
sunan	swa̰˜	"millet"
wari	wɛɛ	"money"
sali	sɛɛ	"to pray"

Based on the information in this table, predict the Mawu equivalents of the Bambara words /furu/ "stomach," /togo/ "hut," /fali/ "donkey," /mina/ "to catch," /falin/ "to germinate," /kɔnɔn/ "pearl."

Now can you predict the Bambara equivalents of the Mawu words /muu/ "flour," /wuu/ "dog," /saa/ "sheep," /saa/ "to pay"?

Do you think it is harder for Bambara speakers to understand Mawu or for Mawu speakers to undertand Bambara?

References

Bailleul, C. (1981). *Petit dictionaire bambara-francias francias-bambara.* Avebury, England.

Bamba, M. (1991). *De l'interaction entre tons et accent.* Ph.D. thesis, Université du Québec à Montréal.

Cheney, D. L., and R. M. Seyfarth (1990). *How monkeys see the world: Inside the mind of another species.* Chicago: University of Chicago Press.

Doddington, G. R., and B. M. Hydrick (1978). High performance speaker-independent word recognition. *J. Acoust. Soc. Am.,* 64S1:S182.

Haraguchi, S. (1977). *The tone pattern of Japanese.* Tokyo: Kaitakusha.

Kenstowicz, M. (1993). *Phonology in generative grammar.* Oxford: Blackwell.

McCarthy, J. J., and A. S. Prince (1995). *Prosodic morphology.* Cambridge, MA: MIT Press.

Nagy, W. E., and P. A. Herman (1987). Breadth and depth of vocabulary acquisition: Implications for acquisition and instruction. In M. G. McKeown and M. E. Curtis, eds., *The nature of vocabulary acquisition.* Hillsdale, N.J.: Erlbaum. 19–35.

Pierrehumbert, J. B., and M. E. Beckman (1988). *Japanese tone structure.* Cambridge, MA: MIT Press.

Poser, W. J. (1984). *The phonetics and phonology of tone and intonation in Japanese.* Ph.D. thesis, Massachusetts Institute of Technology.

Prince, A., and P. Smolensky (1995). *Optimality theory: Constraint interaction in generative grammar.* Cambridge, MA: MIT Press.

Chapter 4
Exploring Developmental Changes in Cross-Language Speech Perception
Janet F. Werker

One of the most remarkable attributes of being human is the ability to acquire language, and considerable research in cognitive science has been directed toward understanding the processes and capabilities that make this feat possible. In order to acquire a spoken language, the listener must be able to parse the continuous stream of speech into sentences, clauses, words, syllables, and phonemes and to represent the information at each level. A phoneme is a subsyllabic unit, and the difference in a single phoneme can convey different meanings (for example, *big* versus *dig* or *bat* versus *bet*).

There are differences between languages in the phoneme inventory. For instance, the distinction between /r/ and /l/ is important in English: the word "rate" means something quite different than the word "late"; however, this difference is not phonemic—it does not signal a difference in meaning—in Japanese. Similarly, the difference between a dental /t/ and retroflex /T/ is not phonemic in English, although it can signal a difference in meaning in Hindi. Thus, for an English-learning child, the word *table* refers to a single class of items irrespective of whether the /t/ is produced with the tongue behind the front teeth (dental), on the ridge behind the teeth (alveolar), or with the underside of the tongue tip against the roof of the mouth (retroflex). For a Hindi-learning child, though, the dental and retroflex /t'/ are both phonemes and thus can signal different words. Clearly, then, English or Hindi children—like all children in the world—require some working knowledge of the phonology (the sound structure) of their native language in order to map sound on to meaning.

The focus of this chapter is to describe the quest by psychologists and linguists to understand the mechanisms and processes by which children acquire sensitivity to the sound structure, particularly the phoneme inventory, of their native language. The chapter will begin with a brief review of the remarkable speech perception abilities of young infants. This will be followed by a description of the research showing how these initial capacities are shaped and influenced by exposure to different languages. Finally, some of the issues raised in attempting to explain these findings will be discussed. In reading this chapter, you will find that by the end of the first year of life, long before many infants have even acquired their first word, speech perception capacities have been modified to match the properties of the sound structure of the native language.

4.1   Speech Perception Sensitivities in Very Young Infants

In 1971 Eimas et al. published an influential paper in *Science* showing that infants 1–4 months of age are able to discriminate computer-synthesized examples of the syllables /ba/ and /pa/, which differ in only the initial phoneme. Eimas and colleagues also tested infants on their ability to discriminate various instances of the syllable /ba/ that differed by exactly the same amount as the /ba/ versus /pa/ stimuli. This clarified whether infants are exquisitely sensitive to any small acoustic differences or whether they are most sensitive to those differences that have been used by languages of the world to distinguish meaning. The infants were unable to discriminate these equal-sized acoustic differences from within the /ba/ category. Subsequent studies by the original authors and several other researchers confirmed this basic finding. Infants are able to discriminate nearly every phonemic contrast on which they have been tested, but they typically fail to discriminate equal-sized acoustic differences that specify two variations of the same phoneme.

This ability to discriminate phonemic contrasts extends to syllables the infant has never before heard. For example, young Kikuyu-learning infants can discriminate phonemic contrasts that are used in English but not in Kikuyu (Streeter 1975), and young Japanese-learning infants can discriminate contrasts that are used in English but not in Japanese (Tsushima et al. 1994). Young English-learning infants can discriminate consonant contrasts that are used in Czech (Trehub 1976), Hindi (Werker et al. 1981), Nthlakampx (Werker and Tees 1984a), Spanish (Aslin et al. 1981), and Zulu (Best, McRoberts, and Sithole 1988), to name but a few. They also seem to discriminate nonnative vowel contrasts (Trehub 1973; Polka and Werker 1994). These results suggest that rather than having to learn about important differences in speech, infants are equipped—undoubtedly through evolution—with sensitivities that make them "universal listeners," ready to learn any of the world's languages.[1]

In contrast to these language-general sensitivities shown by young infants, under many circumstances adults have difficulty discriminating

1. See Werker and Tees (1992) for a discussion of how evolution propels epigenetic processes.

syllables differing by only a single phoneme if that particular phonemic contrast is not used in their native language. Without training, Japanese adults have difficulty discriminating the difference between /ra/ and /la/ (Strange and Jenkins 1978), English adults have difficulty discriminating certain Hindi (Werker et al. 1981), Nthlakampx (Werker and Tees 1984a), and Czech (Trehub 1976) contrasts, and may even need short familiarization periods to discriminate acoustically quite salient nonnative distinctions (Pisoni et al. 1982; Werker and Logan 1985).

4.2   Early Effects of the Language Environment

If infants are "universal listeners" but adults sometimes have difficulty discriminating nonnative phonemic contrasts, then there must be a decline across age in cross-language speech perception performance. This contradicts the typical expectation that there will be age-related increases in ability and age-related improvements in performance. To see if the pattern of broad-based abilities in infancy and subsequent decline is accurate, a series of studies tested infants and adults on the same nonnative contrasts in the same procedure.

In an initial study Werker et al. (1981) compared English-learning infants aged 6–8 months with both English-speaking adults and Hindi-speaking adults on their ability to discriminate the English (and Hindi) /ba/-/da/ phoneme distinction plus two (non-English) Hindi contrasts selected to vary on their potential difficulty. The Hindi retroflex versus dental contrast, /Ta/-/ta/, involves two consonants that vary on the precise location of the tongue. The Hindi breathy voiced and voiceless unaspirated contrast, /t^ha/-/d^ha/ involves a difference in the timing and shape of the opening of the vocal cords upon release of the consonant. Significantly, neither of these Hindi phoneme contrasts is used to distinguish meaning in English.

All stimuli were produced by a native Hindi speaker who was also a trained linguist. Several exemplars of each phoneme were recorded, and eight from each category were selected. The final stimuli that were selected were uniformly rated as excellent exemplars by native speakers. Also, care was taken to ensure that the exemplars specifying each contrast (such as the /t^ha/'s and the /d^ha/'s) were overlapping in intensity, duration, fundamental frequency, and intonation contour so that listeners could not use these nonphonetic acoustic cues to distinguish the contrasts.

A method of testing was adopted that can be implemented in very similar forms with infants (5 1/2 months or older), children, and adults to ensure that subjects of different ages are tested in an equally sensitive procedure. The procedure used with infants is called the Conditioned Head

Turn, and the adult procedure is a close variate. Basically, this is a category change task in which the subject has to monitor a continuous background of syllables from one phonetic category (for example, /ba/), and signal when the stimuli change to a contrasting phonetic category (for example, /da/). Infants are conditioned to turn their head toward the speaker when a change is presented. Correct head turns are reinforced with interesting, lighted toys (such as drumming bears) and verbal praise from the experimenter. Adults and children signal detection of this change by pressing a button. Their correct responses are reinforced with a flashing light. Incorrect responses are not reinforced. A picture of an infant performing in the Conditioned Head Turn procedure is shown in figure 4.1.

The results from this early study comparing Hindi-speaking adults, English-speaking adults, and English-learning infants were consistent with the prediction of language-universal infant sensitivities and subsequent decline. Virtually all subjects in all groups could discriminate the /ba/-/da/ contrast—a distinction that is common across the world's languages and used in both English and Hindi. The six–eight-month-old English-learning infants and the Hindi-speaking adults could easily discriminate both Hindi

Figure 4.1
Madeleine performing in the Conditioned Head Turn Procedure. In this case, she has just successfully turned her head upon detecting a change in the speech sound stimulus. Her correct head turn is being reinforced with the lighting and activation of the toy animal, and with praise from the experimenter. (Photo courtesy Steve Heine)

contrasts. The English-speaking adults, however, had trouble discriminating the Hindi contrasts, showing particular trouble with the more difficult retroflex/dental place-of-articulation distinction (Werker et al. 1981). These results are summarized in figure 4.2.

To ascertain the age at which language experience first influences phonetic perception, Werker and Tees began a series of experiments testing children of different ages. First, ages were selected to test Lenneberg's hypothesis of a critical period for language acquisition (Lenneberg 1967). Lenneberg argued for a critical period for acquiring spoken language ending around the onset of puberty on the basis of data from children acquiring a second language and from reacquisition of spoken language after brain injury at different ages. His writings were so influential that it was reasoned that a similar critical period might apply to language perception. To test for this critical period, children of 12 and 8 years were tested, with the expectation that the 8-year-olds but not the 12-year-olds would be able to discriminate nonnative contrasts. English-speaking children of both ages, however, performed like English-speaking adults and were unable to discriminate the Hindi non-English phonemes. The study was extended to 4-year-old children, who actually performed most poorly of

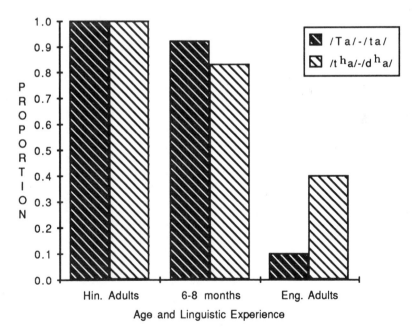

Figure 4.2
Proportion of subjects reaching criterion as a function of age and language contrast. Adapted from Werker et al. 1981.

all on the nonnative contrasts. Importantly, their poor performance was not due to task difficulties as they performed well on an English /ba/-/da/ distinction, and as 4-year-old Hindi-speaking children performed well on the Hindi contrasts (Werker and Tees 1983). These findings revealed that experience must begin to influence speech perception long before age 4, certainly well before the critical period suggested by Lenneberg.

In 1984 Werker and Tees continued a series of experiments designed to test even younger children to establish the age at which the decline is first evident. English-learning infants of 6–8, 8–10, and 10–12 months of age were tested on their ability to discriminate the Hindi (/Ta/-/ta/) contrast and the Nthlakampx /k'i/-/q'i/ contrast. Almost all the infants aged 6–8 months could discriminate both non-English contrasts, but the pattern was entirely different for older infants. As shown in the top part of figure 4.3, very few of the infants aged 10–12 months could discriminate either the Hindi or the Nthlakampx contrast (Werker and Tees 1984a). The infants aged 8–10 months showed an intermediate pattern of performance—with about half discriminating and half not discriminating the nonnative contrasts. As shown in the lower part of figure 4.3, the same basic pattern was revealed in a longitudinal study in which a small group of infants (six) were retested at two-month intervals (Werker and Tees 1984a) from ages 7 through 11 months. Finally, to ensure that the effect was due to experience with the language, a small number of Hindi and Nthlakampx-learning infants aged 11–12 months were tested and were found to be able to discriminate their native contrasts.[2]

This pattern of change between 6 and 12 months of age has been reported for a different retroflex/dental distinction (/Da/-/da/) (Werker and Lalonde 1988) and for three Zulu contrasts: a bilabial plosive/ implosive distinction, a lateral fricative voiced/voiceless contrast, and a velar voiceless/ejective stop distinction (Best 1994). The change for the Nthlakampx contrast has also been replicated by Best et al. (in press). In a comparable series of experiments Tsushima et al. (1994) showed an analogous pattern for Japanese-learning infants. The Japanese infants of 6–8, but not 10–12 months of age can discriminate the English (non-Japanese) /ra/-/la/ distinction. Finally, although there is some evidence that language specific influences might begin to influence vowel perception at an

---

2. Before being tested on the non-English contrasts, the infants were required first to show that they could perform in the Head Turn procedure on the English /ba/-/da/ distinction. All infants were then given twenty-five trials on which to reach discrimination criterion on a non-English contrast. Before concluding that any infant who failed to reach criterion in that number of trials could really *not* discriminate a nonnative contrast and had not just lost interest in the procedure, all such infants were subsequently retested on the English /ba/-/da/ distinction. The data were only retained as meaningful from infants who passed the /ba/-/da/ test both before and after failing the nonnative contrast.

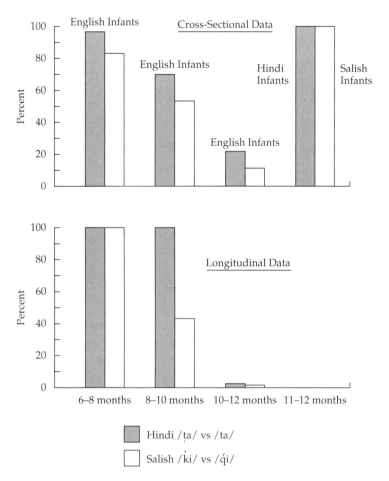

Figure 4.3
Proportion of infant subjects from three age groups and various language backgrounds reaching criterion on the Hindi and Salish contrasts. From Werker and Tees 1984a, 61.

earlier age—by 6 months—than they do consonant perception (Kuhl et al. 1992; Polka and Werker 1994), there is evidence of further change between 6 and 12 months of age, by which time infants' performance on nonnative vowel contrasts declines to the level of their performance on nonnative consonant contrasts (Polka and Werker 1994).

What can we conclude from these findings? First, infants stop being "universal listeners" for phoneme distinctions by the end of the first year of life. Second, it appears that the role of experience is to "maintain" those perceptual sensitivities that are already evident in the young infant. Without such exposure, initial abilities will be lost. The classic example of loss of perceptual ability following lack of exposure is the demonstration by

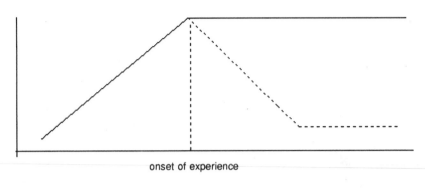

onset of experience

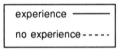

experience ———
no experience - - - - -

Figure 4.4
A representation of the Maintenance/loss model of experiential influences on perceptual development. Adapted from Gottlieb 1981.

Hubel and Wiesel that some cells in the visual cortex are designed to respond quite selectively to certain kinds of input. On the basis of early data, it was believed that if deprived of the appropriate input (such as vertical lines) for a sufficiently long time during a critical or sensitive period of development (for example, Wiesel and Hubel 1965), these cells atrophy. Irrespective of what happens later in life, these cells can no longer fire to the kind of information they were designed to detect (see Tees 1986 for a critique). Extrapolating to the field of speech perception, it was similarly believed that lack of exposure for a criterial amount of time should lead to permanent loss of the ability to discriminate nonnative phonemic contrasts.

Maintenance/loss is only one of the many possible roles experience might play in perceptual development (see Gottlieb 1981 for other possible roles). The Maintenance/loss model is shown in figure 4.4. The central assumption of this model when applied to speech perception is that the neonate is equipped with sensitivity to all possible phonemes of all languages. The role of experience is to maintain sensitivity to only those phonemes that the infants hears. Sensitivity to nonexperienced (nonnative) contrasts declines and/or disappears.

4.3   Problems for the Maintenance View

The data reviewed above are most consistent with a Maintenance role of experience, but there are fundamental problems with this view. First, the

Maintenance/loss model suggests that declines in sensitivity should follow lack of exposure and should be permanent and absolute. Although adults perform more poorly than infants on nonnative phoneme contrasts, there are conditions under which continuing adult sensitivity can be demonstrated. In one of the more intriguing demonstrations, it was shown that if the critical acoustic information in the speech contrast is presented alone so that the syllables no longer sound like speech, adults can discriminate nonnative contrasts. To illustrate, Werker and Tees (1984b) presented adult English speakers with either the ejective portion alone from the Nthlakampx /k'i/-/q'i/ contrast (telling listeners that it was water dropping into a bucket and that they should signal when the bucket was switched) or a truncated portion of the Hindi retroflex/dental (/Ta/-/ta/) contrast. In each case adult English speakers discriminated the shortened pairs with ease, but they still failed to distinguish the full syllables even when tested on them immediately after being presented with the shortened portions. Furthermore, adults can be "taught" to discriminate the full syllables if given enough training trials, or if tested in sensitive procedures with low memory demands (Pisoni et al. 1982; Werker and Logan 1985). Thus, it appears that the age-related decline in performance is evident only for stimuli that sound speechlike, and only in testing contexts that have processing demands similar to the memory and uncertainty demands required in everyday language processing. The age-related decline is not permanent and absolute, as would be predicted by a Maintenance/loss view.

A second problem for the Maintenance view is that neither the ages nor the form of the findings maps on to that predicted. According to a Maintenance model, one would predict that total duration of "misuse" would best predict poor performance—or, at least, that performance would decline to some "floor" level at which it would remain. It would be incompatible with a Maintenance model to expect a decline and then a recovery. Recall, however, that Werker and Tees (1983) found that English 4-year-old children perform more poorly than older children and adults do. Specifically, performance on the Hindi retroflex/dental (/Ta/-/ta/) contrast was found to be poor from age 10–12 months through adulthood; however, the pattern of findings for a perceptually easier Hindi voicing contrast was quite different. English-learning infants aged 6–8 months showed high levels of discrimination. Children of 10–12 months and 4 years of age showed poor discrimination. Of critical importance, adults and children 8 and 12 years of age showed better discrimination than the younger children did. A similar pattern has been reported more recently by Best (1994) for a different consonant contrast. Finally, Polka and Werker (1994) reported that adult English speakers can discriminate the German front/back vowel contrasts, whereas infants aged 10–12 months cannot. These findings present a serious challenge to the Maintenance model.

The Maintenance model's requirement of permanent change early in life might also predict that declines in perceptual sensitivity will be reflected in production difficulties. This prediction is, however, incompatible with the known fact that children far older than 10–12 months of age can move to a new country and acquire a new language with no trace of an accent (see the chapter by Gleitman and Newport in this volume). Indeed, the best estimates are that children up to at least 6 years of age, and possibly later, remain accent-free when acquiring a new language. An adequate model of age-related changes in speech perception has to be able to account for these data.

Another problem for the Maintenance view is that some nonnative contrasts are easy for adults to discriminate, even with no training at all. In a classic example Best, McRoberts, and Sithole (1988) tested infants and adults on their ability to discriminate a nonnative contrast that not only is absent from the native language but also comprises phones that are completely unlike any occurring in the native language. Best and colleagues selected an apical/lateral click contrast from the Zulu language because clicks are not used at all in the English language; thus, it can be safely assumed that English speakers have not been exposed to these phones— at least not in a linguistic context.[3]

Testing was conducted with English-learning infants 6–8, 8–10, 10–12, and 12–14 months of age, as well as with Zulu- and English-speaking adults. As expected, Zulu adults easily discriminated the click contrast. According to a Maintenance/loss explanation, older infants and adults should be unable to discriminate a phonetic contrast comprised of phones not heard in the input. Contrary to this prediction, Best and colleagues found that English subjects of all ages could easily discriminate the apical/lateral click contrast. Infants of 10–12 and even 12–14 months of age performed as well as both Zulu adults and infants aged 6–8 months. Similarly, English adults discriminated this contrast with ease.

On the basis of these results, Best and colleagues proposed that it is not just experience or lack thereof that leads to a change in speech perception performance; instead, the experience needs to map on to the phonology of the language of input. Phones that are similar to those used in the native language will be susceptible to reorganization, but phones that are completely unlike the phonetic repertoire of the language of input will not be assimilated to native-language phones and will remain discriminable. These nonassimilable phones will be treated as any other nonspeech signal, and

---

3. Subjects may have been exposed to these sounds in a nonlinguistic context. The apical click sounds something like the 'tsk tsk' nonspeech sound we make, and the lateral click is something like the click one makes to urge a horse to run faster. Even so, it can be safely assumed that these sounds would be extremely rare in the input.

will be discriminable on the basis of any available acoustic information. (See Best 1994 for a fuller description of the proposed model and for a review of more recent research.)

A recent series of experiments by Pegg and Werker (1994) provides a new kind of challenge to the Maintenance/loss view. In this research subjects were tested on their ability to discriminate phones that infants "hear" in their native language but that do not have functional phonemic significance (are not used to distinguish meaning). The phones investigated were two allophone variates. Briefly, allophones are variations on phonemes that occur within a language but do not function to contrast meaning. Some allophonic variation is random (speakers might vary in how far they push their tongue between their front teeth when pronouncing [th]), whereas other allophonic variation is systematic and predictable. Either way, if the variation exists in the input, listeners have had "experience" hearing it. Thus, if simple exposure to phonetic variation is adequate to maintain discriminability, then listeners should be able to discriminate the phonetic variation that occurs in allophones (see MacKain 1982 for an early discussion of this issue).

To test this hypothesis, Pegg and Werker (1994) compared adult English speakers with English-learning infants of 6–8 and 10–12 months of age on their ability to discriminate a systematic allophone distinction that occurs in English. The phonetic distinction selected involves allophonic variations in the English phonemes /d/ and /t/. In English, the /t/ produced in initial position in a word is classified as voiceless, aspirated (phonetically transcribed [tʰ]). The /d/ in initial position is voiced, unaspirated, and is transcribed phonetically as [d]. The /t/ following /s/ in "st" words has characteristics of both initial position /t/ and initial position /d/; nevertheless, when the [s] is removed from (s)t words (hereafter referred to as (s)/t/),[4] English speakers perceive it as a /d/, and, indeed, consistently rate it as a "good" token of /d/.

To examine the effect of experience on perception of an allophone distinction, Pegg and Werker tested infants of 6–8 and 10–12 months of age, as well as English-speaking adults, on their ability to discriminate multiple exemplars of (s)/ta/ from multiple exemplars of /da/ using the Conditioned Head Turn procedure. The results revealed that the majority (but not all) of English adults discriminate this allophone difference, as do the majority of infants aged 6–8 months; however, almost none of the infants aged 10–12 months who were tested were able to discriminate this comparison. (For a fuller description, see Pegg 1995.)

---

4. It is still transcribed phonemically as a /t/ because it patterns phonologically as a /t/. For example, voiceless stop consonants such as /t/ can occur before /r/ in words such as *tree* or *street*, but we cannot have voiced consonants such as /d/ occur before /r/ in words.

These results are quite interesting. First, the results from the adults show that adult listeners can perceive a systematic allophonic distinction, even when both allophones are categorized as variations in /da/. Second, the results from the 6–8-month-old infants broaden the meaning of "language-universal" phonetic sensitivity in young infants. Here many young infants discriminate a phonetic distinction that is systematic and natural, but that is not used (with this precise form of phonetic variation) as a phonemic contrast in any of the world's languages. Finally, the results from the 10–12-month-old infants are most clear. Infants this age are unable to discriminate the allophone variates, even though they hear them in their everyday language and even though the majority of adult speakers of the language can discriminate them. This finding confirms that simply "hearing" phonetic forms in the input language is not necessarily sufficient to maintain discriminability at 10–12 months.

Taken together, these studies suggest that the Maintenance hypothesis is inadequate to account for the results to date. Indeed, instead of a pattern such as that shown in figure 4.4, the effects of experience on perceptual performance seem to show high levels of ability in the young infant, a dip from 10 months to at least 4 years of age, and recovery of function some time after. (See figure 4.5.) Thus, an alternative explanation is required.

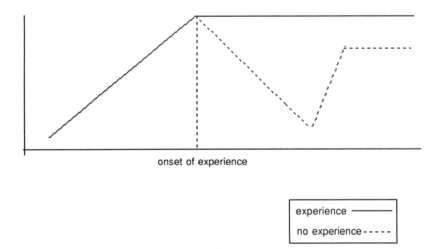

onset of experience

experience ———
no experience - - - - -

Figure 4.5
A representation of the data from studies of cross-language phoneme discrimination with subjects of different ages showing a decline in performance toward the end of the first year of life followed by an improvement in discrimination performance between early childhood and adulthood.

4.4   A New Approach: Functional Reorganization

If the change in phoneme discrimination does not involve an absolute "loss" of sensitivity as a function of experience, what might it involve? One possibility that has been suggested is that the change in nonnative phoneme discrimination involves some kind of functional reorganization (Werker and Pegg 1992). The central assumption of this Functional Reorganization Hypothesis is that children's changing sensitivities reflect not absolute, hardware changes in the auditory system, but rather the needs of the developing linguistic system. According to this explanation, the "universal" sensitivities seen in the newborn infant may continue to be present across the life span, and thus may show up in adults under certain kinds of testing conditions. The changes seen in perceptual performance across the first year of life do not reflect changes in the hard-wiring of the brain; instead, they reflect the operation of postperceptual processes that allow the infant to attend to only phonetic information that distinguishes meaning.

The Functional Reorganization Hypothesis can account nicely for much of the data. It appears that very young infants respond to any detectable phonetic variation in the speech signal—a response bias that prepares the child to acquire any of the world's language. Young infants are therefore listening functionally to as many aspects of the phonology as they can pick up. Adults, on the other hand, have a bias for phonemic information and most readily and reliably discriminate phones that distinguish meaning; however, adults are also able to listen strategically for nonphonemic variation if required by particular task conditions. It is infants 10–12 months of age, and possibly even children up to at least 4 years who seem constrained to listen only to that information that might be used to distinguish meaning. Why might the older infant and young child be so constrained?

Starting at around 1 year of age, infants are poised to begin to learn words, a task they will devote considerable energy to over the next several years. A language-specific bias to attend to only those differences that are used to contrast meaning in the native language will help the child map sound on to meaning. Sensitivity to too much variation could result in errors, making the child map different meanings on to different productions of a single phoneme. Attention to just that variation that is phonemic in the native language would protect the child from this kind of error and would make the word-learning process that much more efficient.

This explanation can account for the findings reported by Best and colleagues (1988) that sounds completely unlike those used in the native language (Zulu clicks) are not subject to reorganization (and stay discriminable) since they are not perceived as part of the linguistic system. As noted by Best (1994), they remain discriminable as nonspeech sounds. It can also account for the recent research by Pegg and Werker showing that infants of 10–12 months stop discriminating two allophonic variates that occur in the native language but are not used to distinguish meaning. The Functional Reorganization Hypothesis requires that infants of this age treat such stimuli as the same.

Because the Functional Reorganization Hypothesis does not involve a change in the neural hardware that supports "universal" discrimination in the young infant, the underlying sensitivity to nonnative distinctions is not lost. Adults, whose vocabularies are well established and relatively stable, have the cognitive "distance" and strategic skills to listen for whatever information is required in a particular task. Thus, if the task requires listening to nonnative phonetic distinctions, the adults will—with varying amounts of practice or training—be able to demonstrate such an ability. Similarly, young children moving to a new linguistic environment would have the auditory sensitivity to listen to the relevant phonetic detail to acquire words in their new language. This could account for the finding that young children can move into a new language environment and acquire a second language accent-free.

4.5   Residual Problems for the Functional Recorganization Hypothesis

There are two residual problems for the Functional Reorganization Hypothesis. First, there does seem to be a critical period for language acquisition, including acquisition of accent. The Functional Reorganization Hypothesis would imply that there is continuing flexibility throughout life for acquisition of the phonological structure of a new language. And, indeed, there does seem to be flexibility throughout life for discriminating nonnative phonetic contrasts; but, as noted above, although young children can acquire a second language accent-free, older children and adults cannot. The fact that adults and older children who learn a second language still have an accent (even though they can learn to discriminate the phonetic elements) could be an instance of perceptual flexibility being greater than productive flexibility. There could be a "critical period" for acquisition of the ability to "speak" a new language without an accent, but the ability to perceive the phonological detail in new languages could remain open (see Flege 1992). It is important to note, however, that although adults can improve their performance on nonnative phonetic contrasts, they seldom reach "native" levels of performance (Polka 1992). This remaining difference in perceptual sensitivity may be akin to the "accent" shown by adult second-language learners.

A second problem for the Functional Reorganization Hypothesis is that there appears to be a mismatch between the kinds of perceptual sensitivities shown by infants and those shown by young children. For years there have been reports that children aged 2 to 5 have difficulty discriminating syllables and/or words that differ in only a single phoneme (for a review see Barton 1976). At first blush, it would seem that these results are incompatible with the Functional Reorganization Hypothesis, since it would predict that children should be listening for just that kind of information. Similarly, if children are listening to native language phonemic information, they should be able to use it when learning new words. There is as yet no evidence, though, that infants aged 12–18 months can use fine phonetic detail when learning new words. Indeed, children of this age treat phonetically similar nonsense words as identical and seem unable to pair them with distinct objects (e.g., they treat "dog" and "bog" as variations in the word *dog*). (See Werker and Pegg 1992; Werker and Stager 1995.)

How can the Functional Reorganization Hypothesis be correct if children are not using language-specific phonemic information in word-learning tasks? The answer to this question is not known, but some speculation is provided below. In addition to the influences on consonant and vowel perception, the ambient language exerts profound influences on other aspects of speech processing during the first year of life, with language-specific tuning first evident for the more global properties of the native language (Jusczyk et al. 1992; Mehler et al. 1988). Also, by 10 months of age infants display a variety of cognitive advances that could be important for the way they pick up and use linguistic information. By this age infants are able to detect, remember, and compare separate sources of information. Perhaps most relevant, they are able for the first time to form perceptual categories on the basis of arbitrary correlations of features (Younger and Cohen 1983). One possibility is that these emerging cognitive skills allow the infant to detect the correspondence between certain kinds of speech sounds and regular, systematic use by adults. Indeed, there is evidence that by 10 months of age the infant may for the first time have the cognitive skills in place to selectively attend to just that information in consonants and vowels that is criterial in defining native-language phonemic categories (Lalonde and Werker, in press). Finally, just as prosodic structure might help a child find larger linguistic units such as clauses and phrases (Gleitman et al. 1988), prior tuning to the more global properties of the native language may provide a familiar prosodic context that helps the child find criterial phonetic detail (Christophe, Dupoux, and Mehler 1993; Jusczyk, in press). See also Morgan and Saffran (in press).

Selective perception of native-language phonemic distinctions may not automatically propel the child into using all the details in their perceptual representations in word-learning tasks. Indeed, just as children over-generalize in applying the meaning of words in the early stages of language acquisition (Clark 1983), they may overgeneralize in applying the sounds of words in the early stages of language acquisition. The language-specific phonemic perceptual categories established during the latter part of infancy may provide the child with the arsenal of capabilities required to map sound on to meaning, but children may only sample from that arsenal as required to distinguish one word from another in their lexicon. Thus, if they have a vocabulary of only fifty words, very little information might be required to distinguish those words from one another. This is consistent with some of the findings in child phonology, which suggest that, in the early stages of word learning, children represent the phonological structure of words at their most global level (Ferguson and Farwell 1975). As children acquire more words, there is pressure to "fill in" more information. At this time the child may use more of the capacity provided by the language-specific tuning that occurred during the first year of life. Support for this possibility is provided by Barton's work (1976) showing that if children know words very, very well, even 2-year-old children show evidence of easily distinguishing words that differ in only a single, minimal phoneme distinction (for example, "pear" vs. "bear").

According to this line of reasoning, the Functional Reorganization Hypothesis may be maintained in an altered form. Experience and cognitive development allow children to attend selectively to only the phonetic detail that is important for defining the phonemic categories of their native language. Children, however, need use only parts of that available information in word-learning situations, representing no more detail than is required to distinguish items in their lexicon. Finally, once children have a working knowledge of the phonology of the native language, tests of word discrimination are no longer simple perceptual tasks. They are now tasks that require children to use the detail available in their representations of those words. If children represent words only globally, then tests of word discrimination will reveal gaps in detail, unless, as is the case in the Barton study above, there has been sufficient pressure to "fill in" the entire phonetic representation.

4.6   Summary

Research in cross-language speech perception has revealed a number of findings that provide insight into the relations between initial perceptual biases and subsequent language acquisition. To summarize briefly, young infants show a sensitivity to many "universal" properties of human languages, including an ability to discriminate both native and nonnative phonetic contrasts. During the first year of life infants' performance on speech perception tasks changes to reflect enhanced sensitivity to the properties of the native language. Language-specific discrimination of many aspects of the native language—most clearly consonant contrasts— is first seen at around 9–10 months of age. This change in sensitivity to phonetic contrasts occurs not simply from lack or presence of exposure, but from exposure to phonetic contrasts that are used to contrast meaning in the native language. Furthermore, this age-related change in performance on nonnative phonetic contrasts is not absolute. When tested under more sensitive, or nonlinguistic, testing conditions, older subjects are still able to discriminate nonnative distinctions. Indeed, adults seem to be able to strategically listen for whatever detail in speech sounds is required for successful performance in a task. Children, though, at least up to age 4, are less able to engage in such strategic activity and seem constrained to listen to only native language phonemic differences.

When the original finding of age-related declines in performance on nonnative speech perception tasks was reported, it was viewed as an instance of a Maintenance/loss phenomenon in perceptual development. With the emergence of new data, as summarized above, the Maintenance explanation became less viable. A Functional Reorganization Hypothesis was proposed in which the age-related changes are understood in terms of the functional linguistic tasks the child faces at different stages in development. This hypothesis is helpful in understanding the data collected to date.

The residual problems with the Functional Reorganization Hypothesis point to fascinating new areas of research that will potentially link findings in speech perception and phonological acquisition to the kinds of patterns that have previously been described in the acquisition of both syntax (maturational constraints, bootstrapping) and semantics (overgeneralizations). The unanswered questions also point to areas of possible synthesis between language acquisition, perceptual development, and emerging cognitive capabilities. In conclusion, it appears that in order to fully understand age-related changes in speech perception we have to consider not just the capabilities given by nature and the role the input plays in shaping those capabilities, but also the particular challenges the child faces at each juncture in language acquisition and the potential contribution of developing cognitive skills.

Suggestions for Further Reading

Ferguson, C. A., L. Menn, and C. Stoel-Gammon, eds. (1992). *Phonological development: Models, research, and implications.* Parkton, MD: York Press.
Gottlieb, G. (1981). Roles of early experience in species-specific perceptual development. In

R. N. Aslin, J. R. Alberts, and M. R. Petersen, eds., *Development of Perception*. Vol. 1. New York: Academic Press.

Jusczyk, P. (1993). From general to language-specific capacities: The WRAPSA Model of how speech perception develops. *Journal of Phonetics* 21, 3–28.

Kuhl, P. K. (1993). Innate predispositions and the effects of experience in speech perception: The perceptual magnet theory. In B. de Boysson-Bardies, S. de Schonen, P. Jusczyk, P. McNeilage, and J. Morton, eds., *Developmental neurocognition: Speech and face processing in the first year of life*, 275–288. Dordrecht, Netherlands: Kluwer.

Liberman, A. M., F. S. Cooper, D. P. Shankweiler, and M. Studdert-Kennedy (1967). Perception of the speech code. *Psychological Review* 74, 431–461.

MacKain, K. S. (1982). Assessing the role of experience on infants' speech discrimination. *Journal of Child Language* 9, 527–542.

Miller, J. L., and P. D. Eimas (in press). *Handbook of perception and cognition*. Vol. 11, *Speech, language, and communication*. Orlando, FL: Academic Press.

Morgan, J., and Demuth, K. (in press). *Signal to syntax*. Hillsdale, NJ: Erlbaum.

Strange, W. (Ed.) (in press). *Speech perception and linguistic experience: Theoretical and methodological issues in cross-language speech research*. Timonium, MD: York Press.

Problems

4.1 Briefly describe the effects of experience on perception of nonnative consonant contrasts.

4.2 Summarize the data that pose a problem for a simple Maintenance/loss explanation of age-related changes in speech perception.

4.3 Point out similarities and differences in the data on acquisition of foreign language production in comparison to foreign language perception.

Questions for Further Thought

4.1 Critically discuss different theoretical frameworks that might be considered for explaining age-related changes in cross-language speech perception.

4.2 What are some of the limitations in the conclusions that can be drawn from data presented in this chapter, and what kinds of experiments might you design to address those limitations?

4.3 How do developmental changes in speech perception parallel other common patterns in language acquisition?

References

Aslin, R. N., D. B. Pisoni, B. L. Hennessy, and A. J. Perey (1981). Discrimination of voice onset time by human infants: New findings and implications for the effect of early experience. *Child Development* 52, 1135–1145.

Barton, D. (1976). The role of perception in the acquisition of phonology. Stanford University Ph.D. dissertation reproduced by the Indiana University Linguistics Club, Bloomington.

Best, C. T. (1994). The emergence of language-specific phonemic influences in infant speech perception. In J. Goodman and H. Nusbaum, eds., *The transition from speech sounds to spoken words: The development of speech perception*. Cambridge, MA: MIT Press.

Best, C. T., R. La Fleur, and G. W. McRoberts (in press). Divergent developmental patterns for infants' perception of two non-native contrasts. *Infant Behavior and Development*.

Best, C. T., G. W. McRoberts, and N. N. Sithole (1988). The phonological basis of perceptual loss for non-native contrasts: Maintenance of discrimination among Zulu clocks by English-speaking adults and infants. *Journal of Experimental Psychology: Human Perception and Performance* 14, 345–360.

Christophe, A., E. Dupoux, and J. Mehler (1993). How do infants extract words from the speech stream? A discussion of the bootstrapping problem for lexical acquisition. In E. V. Clark, ed., *Proceedings of the 24th Annual Child Language Research Forum*, Stanford, CA.

Clark, E. (1983). Meanings and concepts. In J. Flavell and E. Markman, eds., *Handbook of child psychology*. Vol. 3. New York: Wiley.

Eimas, P. D., E. R. Siqueland, P. Jusczyk, and J. Vigorito (1971). Speech perception in infants. *Science* 171, 303–306.

Ferguson, C. A., and C. B. Farwell (1979). Words and sounds in early language acquisition. *Language* 51, 419–439.

Flege, J. E. (1992). Effects of age of learning on second language (L2) production. In C. A. Ferguson, L. Menn, and C. Stoel-Gammon, eds., *Phonological development: Models, research, and implications*. Parkton, MD: York Press.

Gleitman, L., H. Gleitman, B. Landau, and E. Wanner (1988). Where the learning begins: Initial representations for language learning. In F. Newmeyer, ed., *The Cambridge linguistics survey*. Cambridge: Cambridge University Press.

Gottlieb, G. (1981). Roles of early experience in species-specific perceptual development. In R. N. Aslin, J. R. Alberts, and M. R. Petersen, eds., *Development of perception*. Vol. 1. New York: Academic Press.

Jusczyk, P. W. (in press). Language acquisition: Speech sounds and the beginnings of phonology. In J. L. Miller and P. D. Eimas, eds., *Handbook of perception and cognition*. Vol. 11, *Speech, language, and communication*. Orlando, FL: Academic Press.

Jusczyk, P. W., D. G. Kemler Nelson, K. Hirsh-Pasek, L. Kennedy, A. Woodward, and J. Piwoz (1992). Perception of acoustic correlates of major phrasal units by young infants. *Cognitive Psychology* 24, 252–293.

Kuhl, P. K., K. A. Williams, F. Lacerda, K. N. Stevens, and B. Lindblom (1992). Linguistic experience alters phonetic perception in infants by 6 months of age. *Science* 255, 606–608.

Lalonde, C. E., and J. F. Werker (in press). Cognitive influences on cross-language speech perception in infancy. *Infant Behavior and Development*.

Lenneberg, E. H. (1967). *Biological foundations of language*. New York: Wiley.

Mehler, J., P. W., Jusczyk, G. Lambertz, N. Halstead, J. Bertoncini, and C. Amiel-Tison (1988). A precursor of language acquisition in young infants. *Cognition* 29, 143–178.

Morgan, J. L., and J. R. Saffran (in press). Emerging integration of segmental and suprasegmental information in prelingual speech segmentation. *Child Development*.

Pegg, J. E. (1995). Infant and adult perception of an English phonetic distinction. Ph.D. dissertation. The University of British Columbia.

Pegg, J. E., and J. F. Werker (1994). Age related changes in perception of an allophone distinction in infancy. Presented at the International Conference on Infant Studies, Paris, June 3–5.

Pisoni, D. B., R. N. Aslin, A. J. Perey, and B. L. Hennessy (1982). Some effects of laboratory training on identification and discrimination of voicing contrasts in stop consonants. *Journal of Experimental Psychology: Human Perception and Performance* 8, 298–314.

Polka, L. (1992). Characterizing the influence of native experience on adult speech perception. *Perception and Psychophysics* 52, 37–52.

Polka, L., and J. F. Werker (1994). Developmental changes in perception of non-native vowel contrasts. *Journal of Experimental Psychology: Human Perception and Performance* 20, 421–435.

Stager, C. L., and J. F. Werker (1995). Phonetic similarity influences learning word-object associations in 14-month-old infants. American Psychological Society Meeting, New York, NY. June 29–July 2.

Strange, W., and J. Jenkins (1978). Role of linguistic experience in the perception of speech. In R. D. Walk and H. L. Pick, eds., Perception and experience. New York: Plenum Press.

Streeter, L. A. (1976). Language perception of 2-month-old infants shows effects of both innate mechanisms and experience. Nature 259, 39–41.

Tees, R. C. (1986). Experience and visual development: Behavioral evidence. In W. T. Greenough and J. M. Juraska, eds., Developmental neuropsychobiology. New York: Academic Press.

Trehub, S. E. (1973). Infants' sensitivity to vowel and tonal contrasts. Developmental Psychology 9, 91–96.

Trehub, S. E. (1976). The discrimination of foreign speech contrasts by infants and adults. Child Development 47, 466–472.

Tsushima, T., O. Takizawa, M. Sasaki, S. Shiraki, K. Nishi, M. Kohno, P. Menyuk, and C. Best (1994). Discrimination of English /r-l/ and /w-y/ by Japanese infants 6–12 months: Language-specific developmental changes in speech perception abilities. Paper presented at the International Conference on Spoken Language. Yokohama, Japan.

Werker, J. F., J. H. V. Gilbert, K. Humphrey, and R. C. Tees (1981). Developmental aspects of cross-language speech perception. Child Development 52, 349–353.

Werker, J. F., and C. E. Lalonde (1988). Cross-language speech perception: Initial capabilities and developmental change. Developmental Psychology 24, 672–683.

Werker, J. F., and J. S. Logan (1985). Cross-language evidence for three factors in speech perception. Perception & Psychophysics 37, 35–44.

Werker, J. F., and J. F. Pegg (1992). Infant speech perception and phonological acquisition. In C. Ferguson, L. Menn, and C. Stoel-Gammon, eds., Phonological Development: Models, Research, and Implications, 285–312. Parkton, MD: York Press.

Werker, J. F., and R. C. Tees (1983). Developmental change across childhood in the perception of non-native speech sounds. Canadian Journal of Psychology 37, 278–286.

Werker, J. F., and R. C. Tees (1984a). Cross-language speech perception: Evidence for perceptual reorganization during the first year of life. Infant Behavior and Development 7, 49–63.

Werker, J. F., and R. C. Tees (1984b). Phonemic and phonetic factors in adult cross-language speech perception. Journal of the Acoustical Society of America 75, 1866–1878.

Werker, J. F., and R. C. Tees (1992). The organization and reorganization of human speech perception. In M. Cowàn, ed., Annual Review of Neuroscience 15, 377–402.

Wiesel, T. N., and D. H. Hubel (1965). Journal of Neurophysiology 28, 1060–1072.

Younger, B. A., and L. B. Cohen (1983). Infant perception of correlations among attributes. Child Development 54, 858–867.

Chapter 5
Why the Child Holded the Baby Rabbits:
A Case Study in Language Acquisition

Steven Pinker

5.1 Introduction: The Creativity of Language Users

Human language is one of the wonders of the natural world. Unlike other species' calls and cries, which convey a fixed set of messages—such as warnings of danger or claims to territory—the noises that come out of our mouths can convey an unlimited number of different, precise, structured, brand-new propositions. I can put together sentences that can tell you anything from how to build a small thermonuclear device in your basement, to the mating habits of the octopus, to the latest twists in your favorite soap opera plot. You would never have heard these sentences before, but you would recognize them as English and understand their meanings. The number of sentences that a human can produce and understand is astonishing—a hundred million trillion different sentences twenty words or less, according to one estimate. Indeed, a person is capable, in principle, of producing an *infinite* number of sentences (putting aside the fact all humans are mortal). By the same logic that allows us to say that there are an infinite number of numbers (if you ever think you have listed them all, I can create a new one by adding 1 to the largest), there are an infinite number of sentences: if you ever think you have listed them all, I can create a new one by adding *He wrote that . . .* to the longest.

A human head is not big enough to store an infinite number of sentences, or even a hundred million trillion sentences. So what we know when we know a language is a program, or recipe, or set of rules, that can string words together in an unlimited number of systematic combinations. This set of rules is sometimes called a *mental grammar* (which is not to be confused with the prescriptive, or school, grammars that dictate how one "ought" to write and talk in standard English, a different matter entirely). A mental grammar contains rules that define sentences by concatenating

Preparation of the chapter was supported by NIH grant HD 18381, NSF Grant BNS 91-09766, and the McDonnell-Pew Center for Cognitive Neuroscience at MIT.

pieces of sentences, and define those pieces in terms of smaller pieces, and so on. For example, a sentence consists of a subject and a predicate, and a predicate consists of a verb and an object and possibly another whole sentence embedded inside—a trick called "recursion" that can create arbitrarily long sentences with sentences inside them, such as *I think that he thinks that she thinks that....* The nature of mental grammars is discussed in chapter 10; how they are put to use is discussed in chapter 8. In this chapter we will explore a crucial aspect of mental grammars: how children develop them.

The way that babies develop language is as wondrous a phenomenon as the way that adults use language. Indeed, the linguist Noam Chomsky revolutionized the study of language in the late 1950s by pointing out that language acquisition is the key to understanding the nature of language.

Obviously, children are not born with the mental rules for any particular language—a baby will acquire English or Japanese or Cherokee or Swahili, depending on where it is brought up; but, just as obviously, babies are not taught the rules of those languages. Parents just talk to their children; they do not give them grammar lessons. Somehow, the children must distill the rules out of their parents' sentences. And this is a difficult problem for any computational system to solve. By the time they are in their threes, normal children speak their language fluently. They have heard only a finite number of sentences from their parents—however many they can listen to in those three years—but have developed the ability to produce and understand an infinite number of new sentences. They cannot just memorize their parents' sentences; they have to take leaps, and make guesses about what other kinds of word combinations are possible in the language. Logically speaking, there are an infinite number of legitimate ways of making such leaps. A child *could* conclude that English consists of all the sentences heard so far, plus their right-to-left mirror images (perhaps to convey the opposite of the sentence's original meanings), or of all the sentences heard so far, plus the same sentences with their auxiliaries omitted (*He taken a ride*), or of all those sentences, plus the same ones with the word *what* stuck in front of them (to turn them into questions), and so on. All those leaps but one—the correct mental grammar for English—are wrong, but they are all consistent with the parents' speech. How do children make just the right leap?

Chomsky pointed out that the only way for children to solve this problem is to be innately equipped with mental machinery that forces them to analyze sentences only in certain ways, and thus to pull out only certain kinds of rules and principles—the ones that in fact underlie humanly possible languages. He called this machinery *universal grammar.* Among the psychologists and linguists who study language, there is a controversy over whether universal grammar is an independent "mental organ," or a special case of more general principles of mental life (used in other domains such as problem solving and social interactions); but it is a logical necessity that children's mental learning mechanisms be constrained in *some* way, for otherwise they could not generalize correctly beyond their parents' sentences to the rest of the language.

5.2   Overregularization: A Case Study of Grammatical Creativity

In this chapter we will try to understand the process of language acquisition by focusing on a very clear example where we can catch children in the act of generalizing beyond what they hear from their parents. By their late twos, all normal children produce sentences like the following:

My teacher holded the baby rabbits and we patted them.
Hey, Horton heared a Who.
I finded Renée.
I love cut-upped egg.
Once upon a time a alligator was eating a dinosaur and the dinosaur was eating the alligator and the dinosaur was eaten by the alligator and the alligator goed kerplunk.

Obviously, no adult who speaks standard English goes around saying *heared*, *finded*, or *goed*, so children could not have memorized these verbs from their parents. They must have abstracted a rule—something like "to form the past tense, add the *-ed* sound to the end of the verb"—and are trying it out on "irregular" verbs that don't ordinarily submit to the rule, like *to go*. (They also try it out on verbs that they have created themselves, like to *cut-up*, a misanalysis of the verb-plus-particle combination *cut + up*.) Indeed, experimental psychologists have shown, in a different way, that preschool children are quite willing to apply the past tense rule to new verbs to create brand-new past tense forms. In 1958 Jean Berko (now Berko-Gleason) ran a simple but ingenious experiment. Showing children a picture of a man swinging a club, she said, "Here is a man who knows how to *rick*. He did the same thing yesterday. He...." Most of the preschool children eagerly filled in the blank with the correct new form *ricked*. Similarly, when asked to complete a sentence about more than one *wug* (a little cartoon bird), they created *wugs*; and in honor of that bird the experimental paradigm is now called the *wug*-test.

5.2.1   The Course of Rule Development

Children's willingness to apply the English past tense rule to inappropriate and novel verbs offers us a window on their acquisition of productive grammatical rules. We can even see the acquisition of the rule happen before our eyes, as we follow children's early language development. Children produce isolated words around the age of one and combine them into two-word microsentences like *See baby* and *More milk* around age one and a half. By their twos, children are producing longer and more complex sentences, and they are beginning to supply the obligatory functional morphemes like *-ing*, *-ed*, and *-s*, and auxiliaries. Somewhere between the ages of late one and late two, the first "overregularization error" (as forms like *goed* and *holded* are called) appears—a clear sign that the child has acquired something like the past tense rule.

Interestingly, children do not avoid past tense forms before using the rule. Indeed, for months on end they can use irregular past tense forms correctly, like *held*, *went*, and *heard*, together with a smattering of regular forms, like *played* and *used*. Presumably, they simply memorized those forms from their parents' speech and were using them just like any other words (with the "pastness" just a part of the words' meanings). At some point they "notice" (not consciously, of course) that many words come in two, ever-so-slightly different versions: *walk* and *walked*, *use* and *used*, *play* and *played*, *push* and *pushed*, and so on. Of course, the child could, logically speaking, simply chalk these up to variations in pronunciation or speaking style. But if universal grammar says something like "There exist rules for adding affixes onto words to signal tense, number, person, gender, and so on—Watch out for them!" the child would therefore be impelled to look for some systematic rule underlying the variation. By subtracting *walk* from *walked*, *push* from *pushed*, and so on, the child can pull out the *-ed*; by checking for what correlates with the use of the *-ed* versions, the child can notice that Mom and Dad always use it when they are describing events that are over and done with, and therefore that adding *-ed* signifies "past tense." (The child must also be forced to assume that the rule is *obligatory* —you can't say *I eat breakfast earlier this morning*, even though the meaning is completely clear.) Having acquired the rule, children can feed any verb into it, regular or irregular; thus, they start saying *goed* and *holded* in circumstances where earlier they might have said *went* and *held*.

Child psychologists call the whole sequence "U-shaped development" because if you plot the child's performance over time—specifically, the number of past tense forms of irregular verbs that are correct past tense forms, as opposed to overgeneralizations—the curve starts at 100 percent and then dips down (in one sense, the child is getting *worse* while growing older) before rising back to 100 percent by adulthood. U-shaped development is always an interesting phenomenon because it reflects some qualitative change in the child's development, not just better and better approximations of adult performance.

5.2.2.   Explaining Rule Development Is Not So Easy

The story I just told is an oversimplification in many little ways that we can ignore for the time being (for example, the past tense suffix is actually pronounced in three different ways in *walked, jogged,* and *patted,* and the child must cope with this), and in one big way that we cannot ignore. Here is the problem. I have told you that children start to say *holded* because they have acquired the "add -*ed*" rule. But adults have the "add -*ed*" rule, too, but they *don't* say *holded.* If they did, we would not call the child's form an "error" to begin with, and I could never have used these forms as an example of children's creative use of grammatical rules, the whole point of the example! Something very important is missing from the story: the difference between children and adults, and how children eventually eliminate that difference as they grow up.

A first guess might be that language development is driven by communication: children improve their language in directions that allow them to communicate their wishes more effectively. Wrong! There is nothing unclear about the meaning of *holded.* In fact, as long as children are willing to make overregularization errors, their language is *more* communicative than adults'. There are about twenty-five irregular verbs in adult English that don't change their forms in the past tense, like *cut, set,* and *put*; thus they are ambiguous between past and nonpast. *On Wednesday I cut the grass* could mean last Wednesday, next Wednesday, or every Wednesday. The childlike form *On Wednesday I cutted the grass* could mean only a preceding Wednesday. A language is obviously a very powerful form of communication, but children must not be acquiring all of its details *because* they help in communication; they learn adult English because they can't help it, and just use it, whatever its strengths and weaknesses.

A second guess is that adults don't say *holded* and *goed* because they have never heard other adults say them. Wrong again. This hypothesis predicts that adults could not pass a *wug*-test, which is absurd. New verbs enter the language all the time, like *to diss, to mosh, to snarf, to frob, to wild, to mung, to flame,* and so on. Surely adults who learn *diss* in the present tense do not have to wait to hear someone else say *dissed* before they can say it; the forms *dissed* and *dissing* are created automatically. So, we cannot explain why adults avoid *holded* by saying that they've never heard anyone else say *holded.* Adults have never heard anyone else say *dissed,* either, but they don't avoid *dissed.*

The problem with overregularizations is not that they have never been heard before; it's that the irregular counterpart *has* been heard. There must be a piece of adult psychology that causes the experience of hearing an irregular form like *held* to block the subsequent application of the regular "add -*ed*" rule to that item. Some linguists have called this mechanism the

Blocking principle. This means that an idiosyncratic form listed in the mental dictionary as corresponding to a particular grammatical modification of a word (past tense, in this case) blocks the application of a general rule that would effect the same grammatical modification. Thus, *held*, listed as an idiosyncratic past tense form of *hold*, blocks application of the regular past tense rule, preempting *holded*; *geese*, listed as a plural of *goose*, blocks *gooses*; *better*, listed as a comparative of the adjective *good*, blocks *gooder*.

So, maybe children lack the Blocking principle and have to learn it. This explanation is no help, though, until we figure out how they *could* learn it, and that raises a very big problem related to the logic of learning. To learn the Blocking principle, children have to know that forms like *holded* are ungrammatical. Now, they can't conclude that *holded* is ungrammatical simply because they have not heard adults use *holded*; they have not heard adults use *ricked* either, and they are happy to say *ricked* (and must continue to make such leaps as adults in order to be able to produce *flamed, dissed, moshed*, and so on. The only way of knowing that *holded* is ungrammatical is to use it and be corrected, or to get some other negative feedback signal from adults like disapproval, a puzzled look, or a non sequitur response. But it does not appear that parents provide such systematic feedback (which is sometimes called *negative evidence*). After all, if they did, they would be correcting or disapproving their young children almost all the time, since most of toddlers' sentences are ungrammatical in some way or another. No, parents care much more about truth and good behavior than grammaticality, as we can see in the following typical dialogues:

Child: Mamma isn't boy, he a girl.
Mother: That's right.

Child: And Walt Disney comes on Tuesday.
Mother: No, he does not.

The psychologists Roger Brown and Camille Hanlon (1970) verified this impression quantitatively. They examined transcripts of the natural conversations of three children they were studying, with the pseudonyms Adam, Eve, and Sarah (the first three names in the Bible), and divided their sentences into grammatical and ungrammatical lists. For each sentence they checked whether the parent expressed approval (such as "Yes, that's good") or disapproval. The proportion was the same for grammatical sentences and ungrammatical ones, so the child can get no information about grammar from such responses. They also checked whether children might learn about the state of their grammar by noticing whether they are being understood. They looked at children's well-formed and badly formed questions, and whether parents seemed to answer them appropriately, as if they understood them, or with non sequiturs. Again, there was no correlation; *What you can do?*, like *holded*, may not be English, but it is perfectly understandable. We can conclude that children do not seem to have access to information about which of their words or sentences are ungrammatical.

To be fair, there has been some controversy about this point, and a few psychologists have tried to show that there are very subtle and probabilistic patterns in some parents' reactions to their children that might give the children information about which of their utterances are ungrammatical. But the psychologist Gary Marcus (1993) has shown that even these patterns are so unreliable as to be useless (children would have to repeat each error verbatim hundreds of times to get reliable feedback information, because most of the time parents react the same way to grammatical sentences as to ungrammatical ones). The physician-psychologist Karin Stromswold (1995) has an even more dramatic demonstration that parental feedback cannot be very important. She studied a child who, for unknown neurological reasons, was congenitally unable to talk. He was an avid listener, though, and when tested was able to understand complicated sentences perfectly and to judge accurately whether a sentence was grammatical or ungrammatical (including correct dismissals of many overregularized test items like *holded*). The boy's abilities show that children certainly do not *need* negative evidence to learn grammatical rules properly, even in the unlikely event that their parents provided it.

5.3   A Simple Explanation of Overregularization—That Works

Logically speaking, given the knowledge that forms like *holded* are not English, children could learn the Blocking principle. Since this is unlikely— children have no direct evidence that *holded* is not English—we can turn to an alternative: Given the Blocking principle, children could learn that forms such as *holded* are not English; they would just have to hear their parents say *held*. Perhaps Blocking is part of Chomsky's innate universal grammar and is a cause, rather than an effect, of the child's language learning.

But we need one more assumption to get this theory to work. If children had a Blocking mechanism, they should never say *holded* to begin with—having heard their parents say *held* even once, they should block the rule from applying to it! The extra needed assumption comes from an uncontroversial principle of the psychology of memory, known for over a hundred years. People do not remember an arbitrary pairing (like a name with a face, or a treaty with a date) perfectly on a single exposure. It often takes repeated encounters, with the probability of successful retrieval increasing with each encounter (presumably reflecting an increase in the "strength" or clarity of the trace of the pairing as it is stored in memory). Now children, by definition, have not lived as long as adults. So children have experienced everything in life fewer times than an adult has, including hearing the past tense forms of irregular verbs. If children have heard *held* less often, their memory trace for it will be weaker, and retrieval less reliable. Some of the time, when they are trying to express the concept of holding in the past, *held* will not pop into mind (or at least, not quickly enough to get it out in that sentence). If they are at an age at which they have already acquired the regular past tense rule, they will apply it to *hold*, creating *holded*, so as to satisfy the constraint that tense must be marked in all sentences. Prior to that age, when they failed to retrieve *held*, they had no choice but to say *hold*.

This account, which combines a simple idea from linguistics (Blocking as part of the child's innate universal grammar) and a simple idea from psychology (memory retrieval is fallible, with a probability that increases with increasing number of exposures to the pair), has a number of advantages. For one thing, it removes the paradox about why children get worse, and how they get better in the absence of parental feedback. The irregular forms that the child uses early on do not go anywhere once the child has acquired the regular rule, nor are those forms ever incapable of blocking overregularization: they just have to be retrieved from memory to be able to do the blocking, and they are retrieved probabilistically. The cure for overregularization is living longer, hearing the irregulars more often, and consolidating them in memory, improving retrievability.

Indeed, according to this account, we do not even need to posit any qualitative difference between the mind of the child and the mind of the adult, and so the account has parsimony on its side. In fact, it is deducible from the very logic of irregularity, supplemented only by the simple assumption that memory is fallible. What is the past tense form of the verb *to shend*, meaning "to shame"? If you answered *shended*, then you have overregularized; the correct form is *shent*. Of course, this "error" is not surprising. Irregular forms are not predictable (that is what "irregular" means), so the only way you could have produced *shent* was if you had previously heard it and remembered it. But you have heard it zero times, so you can't have remembered it. Now, if in two years you were asked the question again and overregularized it once more, it would still not be surprising, because you would have heard it only once. Many verbs for a given child will be like *shent* for you: never heard; heard but not attended to; heard and attended to, but not enough times to be able to recall it on demand reliably. The *holded* phenomenon has been demystified from beginning to end.

5.4   Evidence for the Blocking-Plus-Retrieval-Failure Theory

Even the most beautiful theory can be killed by an ugly fact, so we have to examine the facts before we can be content that we have understood this example of language acquisition in action. Gary Marcus and I have assembled ten facts that we think support the overall story fairly nicely (Marcus et al. 1992).

First, we looked at the actual *rate* of making the errors. The theory predicts that the child's linguistic system is at all times designed to suppress regularization of verbs remembered to be irregular. This suppression cannot be perfect because the child's memory is not perfect, but it is as good as the child's memory retrieval process. If we assume that children's memory for words, though imperfect, is good (the child is, after all, successfully using thousands of words, and acquiring them at a rate of approximately one every two waking hours), then overregularization should be the exception, not the rule, representing the occasional breakdown of a system that is built to suppress the error.

Marcus and I examined computer-based transcripts of the spontaneous speech of twenty-five individual children, together with transcripts of another fifty-eight children speaking with one another in various-sized groups. We looked at their rates of overregularization, calculated as the number of errors (such as *holded* and *helded*) divided by the number of opportunities for the child to make an error, which we conservatively estimated by adding the number of errors to the number of correct past tense forms like *held*. The mean rate across children was only 4.2 percent; the median only 2.5 percent! That is, more than 95 percent of the time when a child uttered the past tense form of an irregular verb, it was the correct form like *held*, not an error like *holded*.

Moreover, once children began to overregularize at all, they kept doing it at this low rate pretty steadily throughout the preschool years (2 to 5). That is, the 2.5 percent rate is not a misleading statistic resulting from averaging together, say, thirty-nine months in which the child was 100 percent correct and one month in which the child had completely reorganized his or her grammar and was 100 percent incorrect. The top curve in figure 5.1 shows the percent correct (excluding ambiguous tenseless forms like *hold*) for the boy called Adam. You can see the transition from correct performance to occasional errors (the left arm of the very roughly "U-shaped" development); but once the errors are made, they are made at roughly the same rate for years. This is just what we would expect if the errors were sporadic malfunctions, not a product of a qualitatively different kind of system.

The low rate is also not an artifact of averaging together a few verbs that are always overregularized (which would be a mystery on our simple

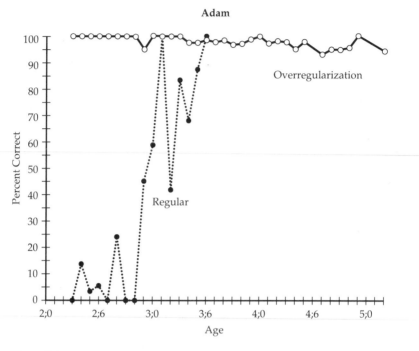

Figure 5.1
"Overregularization" curve: Percentage of Adam's irregular past tense forms (e.g., *held* or *holded*) that are correct (e.g., *held*). Equivalent to 100 percent − overregularization rate.

"Regular" curve: Proportion of Adam's regular verbs in obligatory past tense contexts (e.g., *He walk* or *He walked*) that were correctly marked for tense (e.g., *He walked*).

theory) with many verbs that are never overregularized. We found that no verb was immune to overregularization, not even the verbs that a child had used correctly before beginning to overregularize: a child might use *felt* when young, then both *felt* and *feeled* when slightly older. Nor did we find verbs that one can conclude are *always* overregularized. There were a few, to be sure, but they were always verbs represented by tiny, possibly misleading samples. A child might have said *holded* once and *held* zero times, for an error rate of 100 percent; but, if the tape recorder had happened to catch him on a different day, it could have been *held* once and *holded* zero times, for an error rate of 0 percent. Whenever a child used a verb in the past tense often enough for us to get a reliable sample, avoiding this problem, we virtually always found that the error percentage was in the single digits. Once again, it looks as though overregularization is fairly haphazard from one moment to another. In fact, children can use the correct and overregularized version of the same verb in quick succession, like this: "Daddy comed and said 'hey, what are you doing laying down?' And then a doctor came ..."

Second, there is some predictability as to which verbs are overregularized more often, and it fits nicely with the theory that memory retrieval failure is a prime culprit. We counted how often the children's parents used each irregular verb in the past tense (fortunately, the parents' speech, not just the children's, was included in the transcripts). The prediction is: if a parent uses *brought* and *told* more often than, say, *froze* and *wound*, the child should have a stronger memory trace for *brought* and *told* than for *froze* and *wound*, and hence should say *bringed* and *telled* less often than *freezed* and *winded*. Actually, we compared ninety irregular verbs, not just four, and found that, as predicted, every single child made more errors on the verbs that the parents used less often in the past tense: the correlations between overregularization rates and frequency in parental speech averaged $-.33$.

A third kind of evidence comes from examining what happens to the *regular* verbs at the point at which the child first makes an error with the irregulars. The lower curve in figure 5.1 plots the percentage of time Adam correctly marked regular verbs for past tense (that is, with *-ed*) in contexts that required past tense marking: that is, how often he said *Yesterday he walked* as opposed to *Yesterday he walk*. As you can see, before beginning to overregularize, Adam left regular verbs unmarked most of the times in which they should have been marked. After he began overregularizing, he started to mark them more often than not. Indeed, the curve for correct marking of regular verbs ascends steeply at just the point at which Adam first overregularized. If we assume that this is the age at which he acquired a well-functioning "add *-ed*" rule, the data can be explained nicely. In the first phase Adam was stuck with the past tense forms that he had memorized, both regular and irregular. If he lacked the past tense form for a verb, or if he had a past tense form in memory but could not recall it instantly, then that was just too bad for the syntax of the sentence; he had no choice but to use the bare verb stem. But in the second phase he had the *-ed* rule available to fill any memory vacuum. This allowed him to mark regular verbs correctly *and* to mark irregular verbs incorrectly, as overregularizations—as if marking an irregular incorrectly is better than not marking it at all. The graph, in a sense, catches Adam in the act of growing a rule.

A fourth kind of evidence confirms that children are not radically reorganizing their grammars when they begin to overregularize (which would by mysterious) but are simply adding to it. Remember that at the ages in which children overregularize, they do so only around 4 percent of the time. Where do those four percentage points' worth of errors come from? Are they produced in the kinds of sentences for which Adam, before he acquired the rule, would have produced a correct irregular form like *held*?

Or are they produced in the kinds of sentences for which he would have produced a bare stem like *hold*? That is, are the errors driving out correct forms like *held* (a mysterious step backward on the road to adult language), or are they merely driving out a different kind of error, *hold*? We cannot know with certainty, but here is a statistic suggesting that these new errors are taking the place of old errors. In phase 1, Adam used correct forms like *He held it* 74 percent of the time, and made errors like *He hold it* 26 percent of the time. In phase 2 he used *He held it* 89 percent of the time, *He hold it* 9 percent of the time, and *He holded it* 2 percent of the time. It looks as if the overregularizations are occurring at the expense of the forms that used to be bare-stem errors, not at the expense of correct forms; the correct forms just get likelier and likelier as the child gets older. We thus see no real regression or reorganization or backsliding, just a sophisticated kind of error (since it represents an effort to mark tense) replacing a simpler kind (no marking at all).

Fifth, we looked at the results of a certain kind of experiment, in which children are asked to act like little linguists and tell the experimenter whether certain words are grammatical or ungrammatical. Of course, children do not know what the word *grammatical* means, so clever games have to be invented to tap their intuitions of grammaticality indirectly. Typically, the experimenter has a puppet say various things, and the child is asked to judge whether the puppet "said something silly."

Now, one has to be careful in interpreting any experiment in psychology in which the subject gives the equivalent of a "yes" or "no" answer in trying to detect the presence of some condition (perception researchers call these "signal detection" problems). In most cases the subject will have some degree of confidence in whether the condition is present (say, whether a light came on, or whether a sentence is grammatical), and then will have to decide whether that confidence level is high enough to warrant saying "yes" or "no" (or, for the child, "not silly" or "silly"). That decision will be influenced not only by the subject's actual degree of certainty but also by the subject's willingness to say "yes" or "no" more than a certain proportion of the time when there is any doubt at all. This will depend on the subject's feelings of the costs and benefits of saying "yes" when the condition is absent (a false alarm) versus saying "no" when the condition is present (a miss). In these experiments in particular, each child will have a different willingness to say "silly!" depending on his sense of politeness, fun, and many other factors that we cannot precisely measure. The point of this methodological digression is that it is not easy to interpret the percent-correct measure from any psychology experiment in which the subject gives a yes-or-no answer. It is generally sounder to *compare* the subject's "yes" rate when the condition is actually present with the "yes" rate when the condition is absent.

In these experiments (conducted by the psychologist Stan Kuczaj, 1978), the children, who ranged in age from 3 to 9, failed to say "silly" to many overregularizations—as many as 89 percent for some children. Does this mean that their mental grammars actually accept overregularizations? Not necessarily—they could just be shy about calling the experimenter's puppet "silly." A better way to look at the data is to compare how often they said "silly" when the puppet used an overregularization and when the puppet used a correct past tense form. In virtually every test the children were statistically *more* likely to call the overregularized form "silly"; this suggests that their grammars really did deem those forms worse, despite their occasional errors.

A sixth and related kind of evidence is anecdotal. Some psycholinguists have tried using their own children's overregularizations when talking to the children, just for fun. The children were not amused:

Parent: Where's Mommy?
Child: Mommy goed to the store.
Parent: Mommy goed to the store?
Child: NO! (*annoyed*) Daddy, I say it that way, not you.

Child (a different one):   You readed some of it too ... she readed all the rest.
Parent: She read the whole thing to you, huh?
Child: Nu-uh, you read some.
Parent: Oh, that's right, yeah. I readed the beginning of it.
Child: Readed? (*annoyed surprise*) Read! (*pronounced "red"*)
Parent: Oh, yeah, read.
Child: Will you stop that, Papa?

Again, it looks as though the children, at some level in their minds, compute that overregularizations are ungrammatical even if they sometimes use them themselves.

A seventh bit of evidence also comes from adult overregularizations— but this time accidental ones. If you listen long enough, you will hear *adults* saying things like *drived* and *blowed* as slips of the tongue. (Occasionally I hear my students chuckling softly in lectures, and one will later point out to me that I have done it myself.) Not very often, of course— perhaps a few thousandths of a percent of the time—but the fact that adults make them at all suggests that the errors themselves do not have to be the product of a different kind of mental grammar. Indeed, the psychologist Michael Ullman (Ullman et al. 1993) has found that as adults get older and their memory gets less and less reliable, they begin to make overregularizations more often, at least in experiments. (So perhaps the full developmental curve is tilde-shaped, not U-shaped.)

An eighth kind of evidence involves a gray area where adults, like children, use both overregularized and correct forms of a verb, but even the adults are not sure which is "correct." Most Americans are unsure about the best past tense form of certain irregular verbs. For example, is it *dreamed* or *dreamt? Dived* or *dove? Leapt* or *leaped? Slitted* or *slit? Slayed* or *slew? Strided* or *strode?* These indecisive verbs are lower in frequency of use (at least in the written language) than verbs for which there is no doubt among speakers (such as *went, came, told,* and the like; Marcus et al. 1992; Ullman 1993). And in a study asking people to give ratings to the regular and irregular forms of several hundred verbs (Ullman 1993), we found that the more often the irregular version of one of these verbs is found in the written language, compared with the regular version, the better the irregular form sounded to the people.

The explanation is as follows. Say you have heard *strode,* an uncommon verb, only a few times in your life—more often than *shent,* of course, but far far less often than *held.* You would have a weak, fuzzy memory trace for *strode.* You would recognize it when you heard it, but when you tried to say it, you'd have a little voice in your mind's ear shouting "*strode!*" but not so strong as to block the regular rule from applying to *stride;* you might thus go ahead and say *strided.* For verbs uncommon enough for many people to be in doubt about the irregular, but still lively enough for the irregular form to be recognizable, this can sometimes lead to a chaotic situation in the language community as a whole. Some people use *strided,* others use *strode,* and still others—hearing various parents and neighbors using one or another without rhyme or reason—simply memorize them both and use them interchangeably in their own speech.

But for even rarer verbs, adults' systematic "overregularizations" could create a vicious circle: the adults would use the irregular form less and less; thus their neighbors and children would themselves hear the irregular form used less and less, causing their memory traces for the irregular to be weak, causing *them* to use the irregular form less (overregularize it more), causing *their* neighbors and children to hear it less, and so on. An irregular form that falls below a certain level of usage could simply disappear from the language after a few generations. This is precisely what has happened in the history of English. Old English (the version of English spoken before the twelfth century) had many more irregular verbs than modern English does, such as *chide-chid, abide-abode, cleave-clove,* and *geld-gelt* (look it up). As time passes, some verbs wane in popularity, and one can imagine a time when, say, the verb *to geld* had slipped so far that a majority of adults could have lived their lives seldom having heard its past tense form *gelt.* When pressed, they would have used *gelded;* the verb had become regular for them—and for all subsequent generations.

The linguist Joan Bybee has tested this scenario using "diachronic" evidence (lingo for historical change, as opposed to the "synchronic" evidence about the state of the language at any one time), and this gives us a ninth piece of evidence. Bybee examined thirty-three surviving verbs that were irregular in Old English. Fifteen have come through in Modern English as irregular verbs; eighteen have become regular (such as *chide*). The surviving irregulars have a mean frequency in modern written English of 515 uses per million words of text (137/million for past tense forms alone); the regularized verbs have a mean frequency of 21/million (5/million in the past tense). That is, the English language over the centuries behaves just as children and adults do today: it regularizes the rarer irregular verbs. Presumably, this is because children today, adults today, children of yesteryear, and adults of yesteryear all have the same psychology of language.

The tenth kind of evidence comes form the statistics of twentieth-century English vocabulary. If the survival of an irregular form against the pressures of children's (and adults') regularizing them depends on high frequency, then we should find that clear irregular verbs tend to be the commonly used ones in the language. Regular verbs, on the other hand, can be formed by a rule whenever a past tense form is needed, and hence a regular verb can have a past tense form regardless of its frequency; it can be common or rare. (Note that it is not a logical necessity that every word have a predictable inflected form. Often a language will simply lack a rule for some category, as English does for inhabitants of a city. While everyone knows that residents of London are *Londoners*, residents of Boston are *Bostonians*, not *Bostoners*, and non-natives generally shrug when asked for the names of residents of St. Louis, Falmouth, Tel Aviv, and so on. Verbs are different: no matter how obscure, everyone can guess a past tense form for any verb.)

Computational linguists at Brown University have assembled the frequency statistics for one million words of English text, including newspapers, popular books, textbooks, and many other sources. The texts contained 4,291 different verbs. Here are the top ten in frequency:

1. be   39,175/million
2. have   12,458
3. do   4,367
4. say   2,765
5. make   2,312
6. go   1,844
7. take   1,575
8. come   1,561
9. see   1,513
10. get   1,486

Note that all ten are irregular! (Just as striking is the fact that the third person singular present inflection, whose regular form is -s as in *He walks*, has only four irregular exceptions: *is, has, does, says*. They constitute the four most frequent verbs in English.) There are a thousand verbs tied for *least* frequent in the Brown sample, all having a frequency of one occurrence per million. Here are the first few:

3791.	abate	1/million
3791.	abbreviate	1
3791.	abhor	1
3791.	ablate	1
3791.	abridge	1
3791.	abrogate	1
3791.	acclimatize	1
3791.	acculturate	1
3791.	admix	1
3791.	adsorb	1

As you can see, these are all regular. More precisely, 982 of the bottom 1,000 are regular, and one is a genuine irregular—the slightly quaint-sounding *smite-smote*. Another sixteen irregulars snuck in (a nice colloquial irregular!) in disguise: two-piece words that consist of an irregular *root* (the smallest unanalyzable piece of a word) plus a prefix: *bethink, forswear, inbreed, mis-read, outdraw, outfight, overbear, overdrive, overlie, overwrite, presell, regrind, spellbind, unbend, unbind, unwind.* Incidentally, some of these prefix-plus-root combinations show some interesting properties of the human language system. The regular form sounds completely awful (*bethinked, forsweared, inbreeded, mis-readed*, and so on), despite the low frequency of the whole irregular form. The fact that the *roots* are high in frequency (*think-thought, swear-swore*, and so on) seems to be enough to block the regular rule. This shows that people mentally analyze words into a prefix plus a root, when they can; it is the root that does the blocking (so a familiar root inside an unfamiliar word, as in *bethink*, blocks regular *bethinked*). But for many of these verbs, the irregular form also sounds strange, like *bethought, forswore, overdrove, spellbound*, presumably because of the unfamiliarity of the entire two-piece word. Because we snip words into their parts when figuring out how to inflect them, these verbs have no perfectly natural sounding past tense forms: the regular is blocked by the fairly frequent irregular root, but the irregular is weakened by the unfamiliarity of the word as a whole.

5.5   Past Tense Overregularization and Connectionist Modeling

I have been writing as if children's creative errors with -ed can be accounted for only by assuming that there is an "add -ed" rule in the child's head. But there are alternatives. Perhaps children use some kind of *analogy* from words they already know. They might say *holded* because *hold* sounds like *fold, mould,* and *scold,* and the past tenses of those verbs are regular *folded, moulded,* and *scolded.* Of course, some verbs, like *sing* and *ring,* do not rhyme exactly with any common regular verbs, but children still might be using bits and pieces of partially similar verbs they have heard, like *sipped, banged, rimmed,* and *rigged,* to assemble the analogous *singed* and *ringed.*

Until recently, no one knew how exactly this kind of complex analogizing would work, so it was not clear what to make of this alternative. But the school of computer modeling called *parallel distributed processing* (PDP), *connectionism,* or *artificial neural networks* (see the chapter by James Anderson in volume 4) introduced a new set of possible mental mechanisms to the field of psychology. One of them, called a *pattern associator,* is designed both to memorize specific pairs of items in a training set *and* to generalize them to new forms using complex partial analogies. In such networks an input is usually represented as a pattern of activation in a large collection of "units," each corresponding to a feature of the input item (a "distributed representation"). An output is represented as a pattern of activation on a second collection of units. Each input unit is connected to each output unit by a link whose weight is modifiable by training; sometimes one or more layers of "hidden" units stand between the input and the output layers. Some theorists treat the units as very simple models of neurons and treat the networks as models of the brain's massively parallel circuitry.

David Rumelhart and James McClelland (1986) devised a pattern associator model of the acquisition of past tense forms that acquired hundreds of regular and irregular verbs, and it generalized properly to dozens of new verbs that it had not been trained on. More strikingly, the model appeared to go through a U-shaped developmental sequence, first producing irregular verb forms correctly and later overregularizing them. But the model had no explicit representation of words and rules, nor any distinction between regular and irregular systems. It was just a single pattern associator network consisting of an array of input units, an array of output units, and a matrix of modifiable weighted links between every input and every output. The verb stem was represented by turning on a subset of input nodes, each corresponding to a sound pattern in the stem. For example, one unit might represent "vowel between two consonants"; another might represent "stop consonant at the end of the word"; a third might represent "high vowel between a sibilant consonant and a non-sibilant consonant." To represent the verb stem *pass,* the first and second units (and dozens of others) would be turned on; the third (and dozens of others) would be left off. This sent a signal across each of the links to the output nodes, which represent the sounds of the past tense form. Each output node would sum its incoming signals and turn on if the sum exceeded a threshold; the output form would be the word most compatible with the set of active output nodes. During the learning phase the past tense form computed by the network is juxtaposed with the correct version provided by a "teacher," and the strengths of the links and thresholds are adjusted so as to reduce the difference. By recording and superimposing associations between stem sounds and past sounds, the model improves its performance and can generalize to new forms to the extent that their sounds overlap with old ones. This process is qualitatively the same for regular and irregular verbs: *stopped* is produced because input *op* units were linked to output *opped* units by previous verbs; *clung* is produced because *ing* was linked to *ung*.

Here is how Rumelhart and McClelland got their model to make overregularization errors after a period of correct performance, as we see in children. They reasoned that if children acquire verbs in order of decreasing frequency, they will develop a vocabulary with an increasing proportion of regular verbs as they begin to run out of the high-frequency irregulars and encounter more and more regular verbs. In particular, they noted that children seem to undergo an explosion in vocabulary development early in life, which could result in a sudden influx of a large number of regular verbs. They imagined an extreme case: The child first learns the dozen or so commonest verbs (which are almost all irregular), followed by an explosive acquisition of the next four hundred or so verbs, of which about 80 percent are regular. The network, bombarded by verbs showing the regular pattern, would strengthen many links between stem units and the units defining the sounds of the *-ed* ending. These newly modified links overwhelmed the existing links between features of irregular stems and the features of their idiosyncratic pasts, resulting in overregularization.

5.5.1   Testing Rules Versus Analogies

Is there any way to tell whether children's overregularization errors are due to overapplication of a mental rule or the effect of automatically analogizing from the patterns found in regular verbs? Marcus, Ullman, and I thought up several empirical tests.

First, we looked at the key assumption that during the child's development, overregularization was triggered by a sudden influx of regular verbs. What would this mean, concretely? It could mean that parents were suddenly using many more regular verbs in the past tense when talking to their children. We checked this assumption by counting the number of sentences with regular verbs and with irregular verbs used by the parents of Adam, Eve, and Sarah as the children grew. We found that the proportion remained constant from 2 years of age to 5 years of age, about 30 percent regular. Thus a key assumption of the model turns out not to be true. This might seem odd, given that early conversations would presumably favor common irregular verbs like *make* and *do*, and later ones would make their way down to less common regular ones like *abhor* and *abrogate*, to take an extreme example. But *make, do, hold,* and so on are indispensable general-purpose verbs that people of all ages need to use; *abhor, abrogate,* and the like complete with *each other* for air time in conversation, leaving the proportion of regular verb forms more or less constant.

Even when we looked at the number of different kinds of verbs in the child's vocabulary (the "types"), as opposed to how often each verb is used (the "tokens"), we found no synchrony between the acquisition of regular verbs and the beginning of overregularization. There is an increase in the rate of vocabulary growth, to be sure, and that increase, as one would expect, results in an influx of regular verbs because most of the irregulars were learned at the beginning of development. But the spurt occurs when they are in their mid-to-late 1s, about a year earlier than the first overregularization error, which tends to occur in the mid-to-late 2s. During the ages in which children overregularize, the regulars are pouring in at a lower rate than when the children are using the irregulars correctly, exactly the opposite to what would have to happen to get a pattern-associator network to overregularize.

Second, we looked at the similarity between the overregularization errors and existing regular verbs. If *holded* is an analogy from similar verbs like *folded*, then the greater the number of similar regular verbs there are, and the more frequent each one is, the more likely the error should be, compared with other verbs. *Holded* might be a more common error than *drinked*, for example, because *holded* is attracted to frequent *folded* and to a lesser extent *scolded* and *moulded*, whereas *drinked* is attracted to relatively low-frequency *blinked* and nothing else. But when we did the calculations (correlating overregularization rates of the different verbs against the sums of the frequencies of the regular verbs that rhymed with them), we found no consistent correlation.

Third, we looked to see whether children's overregularizations simply followed similarity of sound, or whether they were made within the context of an entire system of mental grammar. The main idea was that if children go just by sound, they should overregularize a given verb sound at the same rate regardless of the grammatical status of the verb. But there are two cases where a given verb sound can behave in very different ways in terms of how children form their past tenses.

One of them, studied by Stromswold (1990), involves auxiliaries. As indicated in chapters 2 and 10, auxiliaries are a special kind of verb: They belong to the closed functional categories, as opposed to the open lexical categories, and are completely sequestered from the kinds of grammatical rules that apply to verbs in general. (For example, you can't say *to must, musted, musting, have musted*, and so on). Conveniently, some of the auxiliaries in English also come in ordinary, nonauxiliary versions. *Do* can be an auxiliary, as in *I didn't eat* and *Did he eat*, but it can also be an ordinary verb meaning "act," as in *Do something!* and *We did it.* *Have* can be an auxiliary, as in *They have gone*, but it can also be an ordinary verb meaning "possess," as in *We have a Volvo.* And *be* can be an auxiliary, as in *He is running* or *It is being washed*, but it can also be an ordinary verb meaning "in the state of," as is *She is sick* and *He is a fool.* Interestingly, these verbs come in the same irregular forms whether they are being used as auxiliaries or as ordinary verbs: *does* and *did, has* and *had, am, is, are, was, were, been*. Moreover, the semantic relations are the same in all cases: the relation between *have a book* and *had a book* is the same as the relation between *have eaten* and *had eaten; I am tired* is to *I was tired* as *I am resting* is to *I was resting.* Clearly, there are too many of these parallelisms to be coincidental, and a parsimonious assumption is that the irregular forms of the main verb and of the auxiliary versions are stored in the same mechanism. But their susceptibility to overregularization is qualitatively different: In a sample of forty thousand child sentences containing these verbs, Stromswold found that the ordinary verb versions are overregularized at rates comparable to those I have been talking about (around 5 percent), whereas the auxiliary versions of the same verbs were *never* overregularized —0 errors. That is, children said *Look what he doed* but never *What doed he make;* they said *We haved a house* but never *We haved gone;* they said *He be'd sleepy* but never *He be'd sleeping.* This shows that they cannot just be analogizing on the basis of sound; if so, they would overregularize each of these sounds equally often, whether used as auxiliaries or as ordinary verbs.

Here is another interesting case where children care about a verb's grammar, not just its sound, in deciding how to put it in the past tense. An interesting quirk of grammar is that verbs intuitively perceived as derived from nouns or adjectives are always regular, even if they are similar or identical to an irregular verb. Thus one says *grandstanded*, not *grandstood; flied out* in baseball (hit *a fly*), not *flew out; high-sticked* in hockey, not *high-stuck.* The explanation is that an irregular memorized form is a linkage between two word roots, the atomic sound-meaning pairings stored in the mental lexicon; it is not a link between two words or sound patterns directly. *High-stuck* sounds silly because the verb is tacitly perceived as being based on the noun root (*hockey*) *stick*, and noun roots cannot be listed in the lexicon as having any past tense form (the past tense of a noun makes no sense semantically), let alone an irregular one. Because its root is not the verb *stick*, there is no route by which *stuck* can be made available; to obtain a past tense form, the speaker must apply the regular rule, which serves as the default.

Now the question is, Are children sensitive to this subtle grammatical distinction? We found that they were (Kim, Marcus, Pinker, Hollander, and Coppola, 1994). We did a *wug*-test with a twist: half of the new verbs were homophonous with irregulars but were obviously based on nouns, like *to fly* in the sense of "to cover a piece of paper with flies" or *to ring* in the sense of "to put a ring on something." The 4-year-old children we tested regularized the verbs much more often when they were based on nouns (just like the adults who first said *grandstanded* and *flied out*) than when they were just plain irregular verbs, like "flying down the road" or "ringing a bell." Once again, children are not just overregularizing according to similarity of sound; they apply the regular suffix most often when the grammar of English demands it.

But we did find one correlation that *was* predicted by the connectionist pattern associator model. Though irregular verbs do not seem to be analogized to regulars, they might be analogized to *other irregulars*. We already know that irregular verbs fall into families of similar verbs: *ring-rang, drink-drank, sink-sank, shrink-shrank,* and so on; *grow-grew, know-knew, throw-threw, fly-flew,* and so on; *feed-fed, breed-bred, creep-crept,* and so on. Perhaps the irregulars come in these clusters because each member of the cluster serves as an analogy that helps in the memorization of all the others; it is easy to memorize *sink-sank* because it rhymes with *drink-drank.* (This is exactly what happens in connectionist pattern-associators because *sink* is represented by turning on many of the same units that are used by *drink*; thus, *sink* can exploit the connections to the irregular units for *ank* that have already been learned for *drank*). We found some good evidence for this effect when we looked at children's overregularization errors: The greater the number of rhyming irregular family members a verb had and the more common those rhyming members were in parents' speech, the less often the children overregularized them.

The analogizing of an irregular pattern, in fact, helps people not only to memorize verbs but also, once in a while, to apply it creatively to create new irregular forms. Children occasionally (about two-tenths of 1 percent of the opportunities) overapply irregular patterns, as in *wipe-wope* (compare *write-wrote*), *bring-brang* (compare *sing-sang*), and *write-writ* (compare *bite-bit*). And even adults are occasionally tempted, sometimes as a form of slang or humor (*squeeze-squoze,* or e.g., on the T-shirt that used to be sold by a famous Boston restaurant: "I got scrod at Legal Seafood"). A few of these kinds of innovations can make inroads into the language—like the form *snuck* I used earlier, a fairly recent creation (late nineteenth century) based on *stick-stuck*.

Does the demonstration of analogizing among irregular verbs contradict all those earlier findings showing that children were not engaging in connectionist-style analogizing? Not at all. Connectionist pattern associators may not be accurate models of the regular rule, but they may be accurate models of the memory system in which the irregulars are stored. Just as we noted early on that frequently heard words are easier to memorize, it seems that words that fall into mutually similar families are easier to memorize—and pattern associators display both those properties. Indeed, this might resolve an ongoing debate in cognitive science over whether rule systems or connectionist networks are better models of language processes. Both approaches might be right, but for different parts of the mind: rules for the combinatorial system underlying grammar, networks for the memory underlying word roots.

5.6   Conclusions

Why obsess over babytalk like *We holded the rabbits*? Because it is a simple enough example to study in great scientific detail but representative of important general problems in understanding language and language acquisition. In particular, it has led us to make the following observations.

1. A language contains rules that can generate an infinite number of brand-new word-forms and sentences.

2. When learning a language, children have to generalize from a finite sample of parental speech to the infinite set of sentences that define the language as a whole. Since there are an infinite number of ways to do this but only one is correct, children must be innately guided to the correct solution by having some kinds of principles governing the design of human language built in.

3. We can catch children in the act of generalizing when they use one of the general rules of English to create a form that they could not have heard from their parents. Children must be generalizing such a rule when they apply it to irregular verbs, as in *holded*, or to novel verbs in experiments, as in *ricked*.

4. Children command not just rules but memorized words, like *held*; they use the memorized irregular forms both prior to, and simultaneously with, the overgeneralized, rule-created forms.

5. Children's simultaneous use of correct and incorrect forms poses the puzzle of how they unlearn the incorrect forms, given that the incorrect forms are expressive and useful, and are not reliably corrected by parents.

6. The puzzle can be solved if children command one of the basic design features of language: the "Blocking" principle, whereby a rule is prevented from applying if there is a grammatically equivalent

irregular form in the memorized mental dictionary. As long as they can remember an irregular, they can stop producing the overregularized version.

7. The course of language development in this area can be explained straightforwardly, as an interaction between the innate organization of language (rules, words, and the Blocking principle that relates them) and the child's experience with parental speech. Early on, children just memorize words (*held*), though not perfectly. Later they formulate the regular past tense rule "add -*ed*" from memorized regular pairs like *walk-walked*. Now equipped with the rule, whenever they fail to retrieve an irregular past form from memory, they can apply the rule, resulting in an overregularization error. As they hear the irregular more and more often, they remember it better and better, block the rule more and more reliably, and make the errors less and less often.

8. There is considerable evidence for this hypothesis, in the form of demonstrations that children's language is organized much like adults', just with noisier retrieval of irregulars. The errors are uncommon, occur sporadically over all ages and verbs, and occur more often for less frequent irregular verbs. Children judge correct irregulars as better-sounding than their own errors. Adults, when they are put in the same circumstances that children invariably are in— insufficient experience hearing irregular forms—do what children do, namely, apply the regular rule to those forms. This is true both now and over the entire history of the language, and the regularizing tendencies of children and adults over the centuries have shaped the frequency structure of the language as we find it today.

9. Analogy plays a clear role in language. Children, and adults, occasionally analogize the pattern in one irregular verb to a new irregular verb (*write-wrote* → *bite-bote*). They also find it easier to memorize irregular verbs when they are similar to other irregular verbs. This analogizing is a hallmark of connectionist or parallel distributed processing pattern associators; it suggests that human memory might be like a pattern associator. The regular suffix, in contrast, does not seem to be applied by analogy: Children do not apply it more readily at the ages at which they have recently learned a bunch of regular verbs, and they do not apply it more readily to the verbs that are more similar to existing regular verbs. Moreover, generalizations of the regular pattern can bypass the word-sound system altogether and are applied (by children and adults) to irregular-sounding verbs that lack verb roots (that is, verbs derived from nouns). This shows that the regular suffix applies to the category of "verbs" across the board, not just verbs with familiar sounds.

Suggestions for Further Reading

A general introduction to language can be found in my book *The Language Instinct*, 1994. Chapters 2 and 9 are about language acquisition in general, and chapter 5 is about words and word structure, including regular and irregular inflection. The logical problem of language acquisition is discussed in detail by Wexler and Culicover 1980 and by Pinker 1979, 1984, 1987, 1989.

The latest facts and previous literature on overregularization in children are summarized in a *Monograph of the Society for Research in Child Development* by Gary Marcus et al. 1992. Marchman and Bates 1993 present an alternative account of the developmental data, which elicited a reply in one of the chapters of Marcus et al. 1992. Stemberger 1993 has found an interesting additional contributor to children's errors: children overregularize more if the vowel of the stem is more psychologically "natural" than the vowel of the past tense form.

The data on children's spontaneous speech errors come from an analysis of portions of the Child Language Data Exchange System, a computer archive of transcripts of children's conversations and related language materials. It is described in MacWhinney and Snow 1985, 1990, and in MacWhinney 1995. Roger Brown's study of the language of three children is reported in Brown 1973.

The general theory that the English past tense captures the two main psychological systems underlying language—rules of grammar and a memorized lexicon—is laid out in Pinker 1991, in Pinker and Prince 1994, and in Marcus et al. 1995, together with a review of the supporting evidence. Some of that evidence is reported in individual journal articles: On *flied out* and the process of regularizing irregular-sounding verbs derived from nouns, see Kim et al. 1991 and Kim et al. 1994. On analogies from regular and irregular verbs, see Prasada and Pinker 1993. For an interesting comparison of English-speaking children with German-speaking children, see Clahsen et al. 1993, and Clahsen, Marcus, and Bartke 1993. Marcus (in press) looks at children's overregularization of nouns. Stromswold 1990 compared overregularization of auxiliary and nonauxiliary verbs. Marcus (1993) examined parental "negative evidence" in language acquisition, a question first examined by Brown and Hanlon 1970.

The connectionist approach to cognition is explained in a recent textbook by Quinlan (1992). It was originally explained and defended in detail, with many case studies, in the two-volume set *Parallel Distributed Processing*, edited by David Rumelhart and James McClelland (1986). Rumelhart and McClelland's model of the acquisition of the past tense is described in one of the chapters in volume 2 of that set. The PDP volumes inspired a vigorous debate among cognitive psychologists, beginning with the three critical essays in a special issue of the journal *Cognition* in 1988 (volume 28) that was reprinted as a book by Pinker and Mehler 1988. The paper by Fodor and Pylyshyn 1988 reprinted in that volume is considered the principal general critique of the connectionist approach, and it led to replies by Chater and Oaksford 1990 and others (see the Quinlan book). The paper by Pinker and Prince (1988) examined Rumelhart and McClelland's past tense model as a concrete illustration of the strengths and weaknesses of connectionism, and it led to alternative connectionist past tense models defended by MacWhinney and Leinbach 1993, Plunkett and Marchman 1991, 1993, Hare and Elman 1993, and Daugherty and Seidenberg 1992.

Problems

Here is a list of the verb stems that have irregular past tense forms in modern standard American and British English:

alight, arise, awake, be, bear, beat, become, befall, beget, begin, behold, bend, beset, beshit, bespeak, bid, bind, bite, bleed, blow, break, breed, bring, build, burn, burst, buy, cast, catch, choose, cling, come, cost, creep, cut, deal, dig, dive, do, draw, dream, drink, drive, dwell, eat, fall, feed, feel, fight, find, fit, flee, fling, fly, forbear, forbid, foretell, forget, forgive, forgo, forsake, forswear, freeze, get, give, go, grind, grow, hang, have, hear, heave, hide, hit, hold, hurt, keep, kneel, knit, know, lead, leap, learn, leave, lend, let, lie, light, lose, make, mean, meet, mislead, mistake, partake, plead, prove, put, quit, read, rend, rid, ride, ring, rise, run, say, see, seek, sell, send, set, sew, shake, shear, shed, shine, shit, shoot, show, shrink, shut, sing, sink, sit, slay, sleep, slide, sling, slink, slit, smell, smite, sneak, sow, speak, speed, spell, spend, spill, spin, spit, split, spoil, spread, spring, stand, steal, stick, sting, stink, strew, stride, strike, string, strive, swear, sweep, swell, swim, swing, take, teach, tear, tell, think, thrive, throw, thrust, tread, undergo, understand, upset, wake, wear, weave, wed, weep, wet, win, wind, withdraw, withstand, wring, write

5.1 (a) Pull out a family of verbs (with five to twenty different verbs) such that the verb stems are all similar to one another and the past tense forms are all similar to one another. (b) Formulate a rule that would precisely convert the stems to the past tense forms for as many verbs as possible in the family (that is, a set of instructions of the form "if a verb has the following sequence of vowels and consonants, then convert such-and-such a vowel to such-and-such a vowel, and such-and-such a consonant to such-and-such a consonant"). There will be positive exceptions of your rule—verbs that fit the "if" part but whose past tense is different from what you get when you apply the "then" part. (c) Give an example of a verb that is a positive exception to your rule, and show how it is one. There will also be negative exceptions: verbs that don't fit the "if" part of your rule, but which have a past tense form that is similar to the one that would have been created by the "then" part. (e) Give an example of a verb that is a negative exception to your rule, and show how it is one. (f) Given what you now know about this family of verbs, what can you say about how a child might learn their past tense forms?

5.2 (a) List all the verbs for which you would use a *regular* past tense form (for example, most people would say *heaved* as the past tense for *heave*, but it is listed here because the form *hove* exists in English as well). List their irregular forms as well (use a dictionary if you have to). (b) Now list an equal number of verbs for which you would *never* use the regular form (for example, no adult would say *telled*). (c) Are there any systematic differences between the (a) verbs and the (b) verbs? (d) Could those differences explain why a child might overregularize any of the verbs in your (a) list?

5.3 In English, one can turn a noun into a verb in several ways: *I pocketed the money* (put it into a pocket); *She peeled the carrot* (took the peel off); *He elbowed his way in* (used his elbow as an instrument); *I'm all gamed out* (I've had enough games); *She chickened out* (acted like a chicken). (a) Find three verbs in the list of irregular verbs that are homophonous (have the same sound) as a noun. (b) Find, or make up, a verb based on that noun. (c) Make up a sentence in which the verb is used in the past tense. (d) Is the past tense form the same as, or different from, that of the original irregular verb you chose? (e) If there is a difference, explain it.

References

Berko, J. (1958). The child's learning of English morphology. *Word* 14, 150–177.

Brown, R. (1973). *A first language: The early stages.* Cambridge, MA: Harvard University Press.

Brown, R., and C. Hanlon (1970). Derivational complexity and order of acquisition in child speech. In J. R. Hayes, ed., *Cognition and the development of language.* New York: Wiley.

Chater, N., and M. Oaksford (1990). Autonomy, implementation and cognitive architecture: A reply to Fodor and Pylyshyn. *Cognition* 34, 93–108.

Clahsen, H., M. Rothweiler, A. Woest, and G. F. Marcus (1993). Regular and irregular inflection in the acquisition of German noun plurals. *Cognition* 45, 225–255.

Clahsen, H., G. Marcus, and S. Bartke (1993). Compounding and inflection in German child language. *Essex Research Reports in Linguistics* 1, Colchester, England.

Daugherty, K., and M. Seidenberg (1992). Rules or connections? The past tense revisited. *Proceedings of the Fourteenth Annual Conference of the Cognitive Science Society, 259–264*. Hillsdale, NJ: Erlbaum.

Fodor, J. A., and Z. Pylyshyn (1988). Connectionism and cognitive architecture. A critical analysis. *Cognition* 28, 3–71.

Hare, M., and J. Elman (1993). A connectionist account of English inflectional morphology: Evidence from language change. In *Proceedings of the Fourteenth Annual Conference of the Cognitive Science Society, 265–270*. Hillsdale, NJ: Erlbaum.

Kim, J. J., S. Pinker, A. S. Prince, and S. Prasada (1991). Why no mere mortal has ever flown out to center field. *Cognitive Science* 15, 173–218.

Kim, J. J., G. Marcus, S. Pinker, M. Hollander, and M. Coppola (1994). Sensitivity of children's inflection to morphological structure. *Journal of Child Language* 21, 173–209.

Kuczaj, S. A. (1978). Children's judgments of grammatical and ungrammatical past-tense forms. *Child Development* 49, 319–326.

MacWhinney, B. (1995). *The CHILDES Project: Computational tools for analyzing talk* (2nd ed.). Hillsdale, NJ: Erlbaum.

MacWhinney, B., and J. Leinbach (1991). Implementations are not conceptualizations: Revising the verb learning model. *Cognition* 40, 121–157.

MacWhinney, B., and C. E. Snow (1985). The Child Language Data Exchange System. *Journal of Child Language* 12, 271–296.

MacWhinney, B., and C. E. Snow (1990). The Child Language Data Exchange System: An update. *Journal of Child Language* 17, 457–472.

Marchman, V., and E. Bates (1993). Continuity in lexical and morphological development: A test of the critical mass hypothesis. *Journal of Child Language* 21, 339–366.

Marcus, G. F. (1993). Negative evidence in language acquisition. *Cognition* 46, 53–85.

Marcus, G. F. (in press). Children's overregularization of English plurals: A quantitative analysis.

Marcus, G. F., U. Brinkmann, H. Clahsen, R. Wiese, and S. Pinker (1995). German inflection: The exception that proves the rule. Submitted to *Cognitive Psychology*.

Marcus, G., S. Pinker, M. Ullman, M. Hollander, T. J. Rosen, and F. Xu (1992). Overregularization in language acquisition. *Monographs of the Society for Research in Child Development* 57 (4, Serial No. 228).

Pinker, S. (1979). Formal models of language learning. *Cognition* 1, 217–283.

Pinker, S. (1984). *Language learnability and language development*. Cambridge, MA: Harvard University Press.

Pinker, S. (1987). The bootstrapping problem in language acquisition. In B. MacWhinney, ed., *Mechanisms of language acquisition*. Hillsdale, NJ: Erlbaum.

Pinker, S. (1989). *Learnability and cognition: The acquisition of argument structure*. Cambridge, MA: MIT Press.

Pinker, S. (1991). Rules of language. *Science* 253, 530–535. Reprinted in P. Bloom, ed., *Language acquisition: Core readings*. Cambridge, MA: MIT Press.

Pinker, S. (1994a). *The language instinct*. New York: Morrow. London: Penguin.

Pinker, S., and J. Mehler, eds. (1988). *Connections and symbols*. Cambridge, MA: MIT Press.

Pinker, S., and A. Prince (1988). On language and connectionism: Analysis of a parallel distributed processing model of language acquisition. *Cognition* 28, 73–193.

Pinker, S., and A. Prince (1994). Regular and irregular morphology and the psychological status of rules of grammar. In S. D. Lima, R. L. Corrigan, and G. K. Iverson (eds.), *The reality of linguistic rules*. Philadelphia: Benjamin.

Plunkett, K., and V. Marchman (1991). U-shaped learning and frequency effects in a multi-layered perceptron: Implications for child language acquisition. *Cognition* 38, 43–102.

Plunkett, K., and V. Marchman (1993). From rote learning to system building. *Cognition* 48, 21–69.

Prasada, S., and S. Pinker (1993). Generalizations of regular and irregular morphological patterns. *Language and Cognitive Processes* 8, 1–56.

Quinlan, P. (1992). *An introduction to connectionist modeling*. Hillsdale, NJ: Erlbaum.

Rumelhart, D., and J. McClelland (1986). On learning the past tenses of English verbs. Implicit rules or parallel distributed processing? In J. McClelland, D. Rumelhart, and the PDP Research Group, *Parallel distributed processing: Explorations in the microstructure of cognition*. Cambridge, MA: MIT Press.

Rumelhart, D., J. McClelland, and the PDP Research Group (1986). *Parallel distributed processing: Explorations in the microstructure of cognition*. Cambridge, MA: MIT Press.

Stemberger, J. (1993). Vowel dominance in overregularizations. *Journal of Child Language* 20, 503–521.

Stromswold, K. J. (1990). Learnability and the acquisition of auxiliaries. Doctoral dissertation, Department of Brain and Cognitive Sciences, MIT.

Stromswold, K. J. (1995). What a mute child tells us about language. Unpublished manuscript, Rutgers University.

Ullman, M. (1993). The computation and neural localization of inflectional morphology. Doctoral dissertation, Department of Brain and Cognitive Sciences, MIT.

Ullman, M., S. Corkin, S. Pinker, M. Coppola, J. Locascio, and J. H. Growdon (1993). Neural modularity in language: Evidence from Alzheimer's and Parkinson's disease. (abstract) Paper presented at the 23rd Annual Meeting of the Society for Neuroscience, Washington DC.

Wexler, K., and P. Culicover (1980). *Formal principles of language acquisition*. Cambridge, MA: MIT Press.

Chapter 6
Language Acquisition
Steven Pinker

6.1 Introduction

Language acquisition is one of the central topics in cognitive science. Every theory of cognition has tried to explain it; probably no other topic has aroused such controversy. Possessing a language is the quintessentially human trait: all normal humans speak, no nonhuman animal does. Language is the main vehicle by which we know about other people's thoughts, and the two must be intimately related. Every time we speak we are revealing something about language, so the facts of language structure are easy to come by; these data hint at a system of extraordinary complexity. Nonetheless, learning a first language is something every child does successfully in a matter of a few years and without the need for formal lessons. With language so close to the core of what it means to be human, it is not surprising that children's acquisition of language has received so much attention. Anyone with strong views about the human mind would like to show that children's first few steps are steps in the right direction.

Language acquisition is not only inherently interesting; studying it is one way to look for concrete answers to questions that permeate cognitive science:

6.1.1 Modularity

Do children learn language using a "mental organ," some of whose principles of organization are not shared with other cognitive systems such as perception, motor control, and reasoning (Chomsky 1975, 1991; Fodor 1983)? Or is language acquisition just another problem to be solved by general intelligence, in this case the problem of how to communicate with other humans over the auditory channel (Putnam 1971; Bates 1989)?

Preparation of the chapter was supported by NIH grant HD 18381 and NSF grant BNS 91-09766, and by the McDonnell-Pew Center for Cognitive Neuroscience at MIT.

6.1.2   Human Uniqueness

A related question is whether language is unique to humans. At first glance the answer seems obvious. Other animals communicate with a fixed repertoire of signals, or with analogue variation like the mercury in a thermometer. But none appears to have the combinatorial rule system of human language, in which symbols are permuted into an unlimited set of combinations, each with a determinate meaning. On the other hand, many other claims about human uniqueness, such as that humans were the only animals to use tools or to fabricate them, have turned out to be false. Some researchers have thought that apes have the capacity for language but never profited from a humanlike cultural milieu in which language was taught, and they have thus tried to teach apes languagelike systems. Whether they have succeeded, and whether human children are really "taught" language themselves, are questions we will soon come to.

6.1.3   Language and Thought

Is language simply grafted on top of cognition as a way of sticking communicable labels onto thoughts (Fodor 1975; Piaget 1926)? Or does learning a language somehow mean learning to think in that language? A famous hypothesis, outlined by Benjamin Whorf (1956), asserts that the categories and relations we use to understand the world come from our particular language, so that speakers of different languages conceptualize the world in different ways. Language acquisition, then, would be learning to think, not just learning to talk.

This is an intriguing hypothesis, but virtually all modern cognitive scientists believe that it is false (see Pinker 1994a). Babies can think before they can talk (chapter 1 and chapter 8 of volume 2.) Cognitive psychology has shown that people think not just in words but in images (see chapter 7 of volume 2) and abstract logical propositions (see chapter 12). And linguistics has shown that human languages are too ambiguous and schematic to use as a medium of internal computation; when people think about "spring," surely they are not confused as to whether they are thinking about a season or something that goes "boing"—and if one word can correspond to two thoughts, thoughts cannot be words.

But language acquisition has a unique contribution to make to this issue. As we shall see, it is virtually impossible to show how children could learn a language unless one assumes that they have a considerable amount of nonlinguistic cognitive machinery in place before they start.

6.1.4   Learning and Innateness

All humans talk but no house pets or house plants do, no matter how pampered, so heredity must be involved in language. But a child growing up in Japan speaks Japanese, whereas the same child brought up in California would speak English, so the environment is also crucial. Thus, there is no question about whether heredity or environment is involved in language or even whether one or the other is "more important." Instead, language acquisition might be our best hope of finding out *how* heredity and environment interact. We know that adult language is intricately complex, and we know that children become adults; therefore, something in the child's mind must be capable of attaining that complexity. Any theory that posits too little innate structure, so that its hypothetical child ends up speaking something less than a real language, must be false. The same is true for any theory that posits too much innate structure, so that the hypothetical child can acquire English but not, say, Bantu or Vietnamese.

And not only do we know about the *output* of language acquisition, we know a fair amount about the *input* to it, namely, parents' speech to their children. So even if language acquisition, like all cognitive processes, is essentially a "black box," we know enough about its input and output to be able to make precise guesses about its contents.

The scientific study of language acquisition began around the same time as the birth of cognitive science, in the late 1950s. We can see now why that is not a coincidence. The historical catalyst was Noam Chomsky's review of Skinner's *Verbal Behavior* (Chomsky 1959). At that time Anglo-American natural science, social science, and philosophy had come to a virtual consensus about the answers to the questions listed above. The mind consisted of sensorimotor abilities plus a few simple laws of learning governing gradual changes in an organism's behavioral repertoire. Language, therefore, must be learned, it cannot be a module, and thinking must be a form of verbal behavior, since verbal behavior is the prime manifestation of "thought" that can be observed externally. Chomsky argued that language acquisition falsified these beliefs in a single stroke: Children learn languages that are governed by highly subtle and abstract principles, and they do so without explicit instruction or any other environmental clues to the nature of such principles. Hence, language acquisition depends on an innate, species-specific module that is distinct from general intelligence. Much of the debate in language acquisition has attempted to test this once-revolutionary, and still controversial, collection of ideas. The implications extend to the rest of human cognition.

6.2   The Biology of Language Acquisition

Human language is made possible by special adaptations of the human mind and body that occurred in the course of human evolution and which are put to use by children in acquiring their mother tongue.

6.2.1   Evolution of Language

Most obviously, the shape of the human vocal tract seems to have been modified in evolution for the demands of speech. Our larynxes are low in our throats, and our vocal tracts have a sharp right-angle bend that creates two independently modifiable resonant cavities (the mouth and the pharynx or throat) which define a large two-dimensional range of vowel sounds (see the chapter by Liberman in this volume). But it comes at a sacrifice of efficiency for breathing, swallowing, and chewing (Lieberman 1984). Before the invention of the Heimlich maneuver, choking on food was a common cause of accidental death in humans, causing six thousand deaths a year in the United States. The evolutionary selective advantages for language must have been very large to outweigh such a disadvantage.

It is tempting to think that if language evolved by gradual Darwinian natural selection, we must be able to find some precursor of it in our closest relatives, the chimpanzees. In several famous and controversial demonstrations, chimpanzees have been taught some hand-signs based on American Sign Language, to manipulate colored switches or tokens, or to understand some spoken commands (Gardner and Gardner 1969; Premack and Premack 1983; Savage-Rumbaugh 1991). Whether one wants to call these abilities "language" is not really a scientific question but a matter of definition: how far we are willing to stretch the meaning of the word *language*.

The *scientific* question is whether the chimps' abilities are *homologous* to human language—that is, whether the two systems show the same basic organization owing to descent from a single system in their common ancestor. For example, biologists do not debate whether the winglike structures of gliding rodents may be called "genuine wings" or something else (a boring question of definitions). It is clear that these structures are not homologous to the wings of bats, because they have a fundamentally different anatomical plan, reflecting a different evolutionary history. Bats' wings are modifications of the hands of the common mammalian ancestor; flying squirrels' wings are modifications of its rib cage. The two structures are merely *analogous*: similar in function.

Though artificial chimp signaling systems have some analogies to human language (for example, use in communication, combinations of more basic signals), it seems unlikely that they are homologous. Chimpanzees require massive regimented teaching sequences contrived by humans to acquire quite rudimentary abilities, mostly limited to a small number of signs, strung together in repetitive, quasi-random sequences, used with the intent of requesting food or tickling (Terrace, Petitto, Sanders, and Bever 1979; Seidenberg and Petitto 1979, 1987; Seidenberg 1986; Wallman 1992; Pinker 1994a). This contrasts sharply with human children, who pick up thousands of words spontaneously, combine them in structured sequences where every word has a determinate role, respect the word order of the adult language, and use sentences for a variety of purposes such as commenting on interesting events.

This lack of homology does not, by the way, cast doubt on a gradualistic Darwinian account of language evolution. Humans did not evolve directly from chimpanzees. Both derived from a common ancestor, probably around six or seven million years ago. This leaves about 300,000 generations in which language could have evolved gradually in the lineage leading to humans, after it split off from the lineage leading to chimpanzees. Presumably, language evolved in the human lineage for two reasons: Our ancestors developed technology and knowledge of the local environment in their lifetimes, and they were involved in extensive reciprocal cooperation. This allowed them to benefit by sharing hard-won knowledge with their kin and exchanging it with their neighbors (Pinker and Bloom 1990).

6.2.2   Dissociations between Language and General Intelligence

Humans evolved brain circuitry, mostly in the left hemisphere surrounding the sylvian fissure, that appears to be designed for language, though how exactly its internal wiring gives rise to rules of language is unknown (see the chapter by Zurif in this volume). The brain mechanisms underlying language are not just those allowing us to be smart in general. Strokes often leave adults with catastrophic losses in language (see the chapter by Zurif; also Pinker 1994a), though not necessarily impaired in other aspects of intelligence, such as those measured on the nonverbal parts of IQ tests. Similarly, there is an inherited set of syndromes called Specific Language Impairment (Gopnik and Crago 1993; Tallal, Ross, and Curtiss 1989), which is marked by delayed onset of language, difficulties in articulation in childhood, and lasting difficulties in understanding, producing, and judging grammatical sentences. By definition, specifically language impaired people show such deficits despite the absence of cognitive problems like retardation, sensory problems like hearing loss, and social problems like autism.

More interestingly, there are syndromes showing the opposite dissociation, where excellent language abilities coexist with severe retardation. These cases show that language development does not depend on fully functioning general intelligence. One example comes from children with Spina Bifida, a malformation of the vertebrae that leaves the spinal cord unprotected, often resulting in hydrocephalus, an increase in pressure in the cerebrospinal fluid filling the ventricles (large cavities) of the brain, distending the brain from within. Hydrocephalic children occasionally end up significantly retarded but can carry on long, articulate, and fully grammatical conversations, in which they earnestly recount vivid events that are, in fact, products of their imaginations (Cromer 1992; Curtiss 1989;

Pinker 1994a). Another example is Williams Syndrome, an inherited condition involving physical abnormalities, significant retardation (the average IQ is about 50), incompetence at simple everyday tasks (tying shoelaces, finding one's way, adding two numbers, and retrieving items from a cupboard), social warmth and gregariousness, and fluent, articulate language abilities (Bellugi et al. 1990).

6.2.3   Maturation of the Language System

As the chapter by Gleitman and Newport suggests, the maturation of language circuits during a child's early years may be a driving force underlying the course of language acquisition (Pinker 1994a, chapter 9; Bates, Thal, and Janowsky 1992; Locke 1992; Huttenlocher 1990). Before birth, virtually all the neurons (nerve cells) are formed, and they migrate into their proper locations in the brain. But head size, brain weight, and thickness of the cerebral cortex (gray matter)—where the synapses (junctions) subserving mental computation take place—continue to increase rapidly in the year after birth. Long-distance connections (white matter) are not complete until 9 months, and they continue to grow their speed-inducing myelin insulation throughout childhood. Synapses continue to develop, peaking in number between 9 months and 2 years (depending on the brain region), at which point the child has 50 percent more synapses than the adult. Metabolic activity in the brain reaches adult levels by 9 to 10 months and soon exceeds it, peaking around the age of 4. In addition, huge numbers of neurons die in utero, and the dying continues during the first two years before leveling off at age 7. Synapses wither from the age of 2 through the rest of childhood and into adolescence, when the brain's metabolic rate falls back to adult levels. Perhaps linguistic milestones like babbling, first words, and grammar require minimum levels of brain size, long-distance connections, or extra synapses, particularly in the language centers of the brain.

Similarly, one can conjecture that these changes are responsible for the decline in the ability to learn a language over the lifespan. The language learning circuitry of the brain is more plastic in childhood; children learn or recover language when the left hemisphere of the brain is damaged or even surgically removed (though not quite at normal levels), but comparable damage in an adult usually leads to permanent aphasia (Curtiss 1989; Lenneberg 1967). Most adults never master a foreign language, especially the phonology, giving rise to what we call a "foreign accent." Their development often fossilizes into permanent error patterns that no teaching or correction can undo. There are great individual differences, which depend on effort, attitudes, amount of exposure, quality of teaching, and plain talent.

Many explanations have been advanced for children's superiority: they can exploit the special ways that their mothers talk to them, they make errors unself-consciously, they are more motivated to communicate, they like to conform, they are not xenophobic or set in their ways, and they have no first language to interfere. But some of these accounts are unlikely, given what we will learn about how language acquisition works later in this chapter. For example, children can learn a language without the special indulgent speech from their mothers; they make few errors, and they get no feedback for the errors they do make. And it can't be an across-the-board decline in learning. There is no evidence, for example, that learning words (as opposed to phonology or grammar) declines in adulthood.

The chapter by Gleitman and Newport shows how sheer age seems to play an important role. Successful acquisition of language typically happens by 4 (as we shall see in the next section), is guaranteed for children up to the age of 6, is steadily compromised from then until shortly after puberty, and is rare thereafter. Maturational changes in the brain, such as the decline in metabolic rate and number of neurons during the early school age years, and the bottoming out of the number of synapses and metabolic rate around puberty, are plausible causes. Thus, there may be a neurologically determined "critical period" for successful language acquisition, analogous to the critical periods documented in visual development in mammals and in the acquisition of songs by some species of birds.

6.3   The Course of Language Acquisition

Although scholars have kept diaries of their children's speech for over a century (Charles Darwin was one of the first), it was only after portable tape-recorders became available in the late 1950s that children's spontaneous speech began to be analyzed systematically within developmental psychology. These naturalistic studies of children's spontaneous speech have become even more accessible now that they can be put into computer files and can be disseminated and analyzed automatically (MacWhinney and Snow 1985, 1990; MacWhinney 1991). They are complemented by experimental methods. In *production* tasks, children utter sentences to describe pictures or scenes, in response to questions, or to imitate target sentences. In *comprehension* tasks, they listen to sentences and then point to pictures or act out events with toys. In *judgment* tasks, they indicate whether or which sentences provided by an experimenter sound "silly" to them.

As the chapter by Werker in this volume shows, language acquisition begins very early in the human lifespan, and begins, logically enough, with the acquisition of a language's sound patterns. The main linguistic accomplishments during the first year of life are control of the speech musculature and sensitivity to the phonetic distinctions used in the parents' language. Interestingly, babies achieve these feats before they produce or understand words, so their learning cannot depend on correlating sound with meaning. That is, they cannot be listening for the difference in sound between a word they think means *bit* and a word they think means *beet*, because they have learned neither word. They must be sorting the sounds directly, somehow tuning their speech analysis module to deliver the phonemes used in their language (Kuhl et al. 1992). The module can then serve as the front end of the system that learns words and grammar.

Shortly before their first birthday, babies begin to understand words, and around that birthday, they start to produce them (see Clark 1993; Ingram 1989). Words are usually produced in isolation; this one-word stage can last from two months to a year. Children's first words are similar all over the planet. About half the words are for objects: food (*juice, cookie*), body parts (*eye, nose*), clothing (*diaper, sock*), vehicles (*car, boat*), toys (*doll, block*), household items (*bottle, light*), animals (*dog, kitty*), and people (*dada, baby*). There are words for actions, motions, routines (*up, off, open, peekaboo, eat,* and *go*), and modifiers (*hot, allgone, more, dirty,* and *cold*). Finally, there are routines used in social interaction, like *yes, no, want, bye-bye,* and *hi*— few of which, like *look at that* and *what is that*, are words in the sense of memorized chunks, though they are not single words for the adult. Children differ in how much they name objects or engage in social interaction using memorized routines, though all children do both.

Around 18 months of age, language changes in two ways. Vocabulary growth increases; the child begins to learn words at a rate of one every two waking hours and will keep learning at that rate or faster through adolescence (Clark 1993; Pinker 1994). And primitive syntax begins, with two-word strings like the following:

All dry.	All messy.	All wet.
I sit.	I shut.	No bed.
No pee.	See baby.	See pretty.
More cereal.	More hot.	Hi Calico.
Other pocket.	Boot off.	Siren by.
Mail come.	Airplane allgone.	Bybebye car.
Our car.	Papa away.	Dry pants.

Children's two-word combinations are highly similar across cultures. Everywhere children announce when objects appear, disappear, and move about, point out their properties and owners, comment on people doing things and seeing things, reject and request objects and activities, and ask about who, what, and where. These sequences already reflect the language being acquired: in 95 percent of them, the words are properly ordered (Braine 1976; Brown 1973; Pinker 1984; Ingram 1989).

Even before they put words together, babies can comprehend a sentence using its syntax. For example, in one experiment, babies who spoke only in single words were seated in front of two television screens, each of which featured a pair of adults dressed up as Cookie Monster and Big Bird from *Sesame Street*. One screen showed Cookie Monster tickling Big Bird; the other showed Big Bird tickling Cookie Monster. A voice-over said, "Oh look!!! Big Bird is tickling Cookie Monster!! Find Big Bird tickling Cookie Monster!!" (Or vice versa.) The children must have understood the meaning of the ordering of subject, verb, and object, because they looked more at the screen that depicted the sentence in the voice-over (Hirsh-Pasek and Golinkoff 1991).

Children's output seems to meet up with a bottleneck at the output end (Brown 1973; Bloom 1970; Pinker 1984). Their two- and three-word utterances look like samples drawn from longer potential sentences expressing a complete and more complicated idea. Roger Brown, one of the founders of the modern study of language development, noted that although the three children he studied intensively never produced a sentence as complicated as *Mother gave John lunch in the kitchen*, they did produce strings containing all of its components, and in the correct order (Brown 1973, p. 205):

Agent (*Mother*	Action *gave*	Recipient *John*	Object *lunch*	Location *in the kitchen.*)
Mommy	fix.			
Mommy			pumpkin.	
Baby				table.
Give		doggie.		
	Put		light.	
	Put			floor.
I	ride		horsie.	
Tractor	go			floor.
	Give	doggie	paper.	
	Put		truck	window.
Adam	put		it	box.

Between the late 2s and mid-3s, children's language blooms into fluent grammatical conversation so rapidly that it overwhelms the researchers who study it; no one has worked out the exact sequence. Sentence length increases steadily and, because grammar is a combinatorial system, the number of syntactic types increases exponentially, doubling every month, reaching the thousands before the third birthday (Ingram 1989, p. 235; Brown 1973; Limber 1973; Pinker 1984). For example, here are snapshots of the development of one of Brown's longitudinal subjects, Adam, in the year following his first word combinations at the age of 2 years and 3 months (Pinker 1994a):

2;3: Play checkers. Big drum. I got horn.

2;4: See marching bear go? Screw part machine.

2;5: Now put boots on. Where wrench go? What that paper clip doing?

2;6: Write a piece a paper. What that egg doing? No, I don't want to sit seat.

2;7: Where piece a paper go? Dropped a rubber band. Rintintin don't fly, Mommy.

2;8: Let me get down with the boots on. How tiger be so healthy and fly like kite? Joshua throw like a penguin.

2;9: Where Mommy keep her pocket book? Show you something funny.

2;10: Look at that train Ursula brought. You don't have paper. Do you want little bit, Cromer?

2;11: Do want some pie on your face? Why you mixing baby chocolate? I said why not you coming in? We going turn light on so you can't see.

3;0: I going come in fourteen minutes. I going wear that to wedding. Those are not strong mens. You dress me up like a baby elephant.

3;1: I like to play with something else. You know how to put it back together. I gon' make it like a rocket to blast off with. You want to give me some carrots and some beans? Press the button and catch it, sir. Why you put the pacifier in his mouth?

3;2: So it can't be cleaned? I broke my racing car. Do you know the light wents off? When it's got a flat tire it's need a go to the station. I'm going to mail this so the letter can't come off. I want to have some espresso. Can I put my head in the mailbox so the mailman can know where I are and put me in the mailbox? Can I keep the screwdriver just like a carpenter keep the screwdriver?

Normal children can differ by a year or more in their rate of language development, though the stages they pass through are generally the same regardless of how stretched out or compressed. Adam's language development, for example, was relatively leisurely; many children speak in complex sentences before they turn 2.

During the grammar explosion, children's sentences are getting not only longer but more complex, with fuller trees, because the children can embed one constituent inside another. Whereas before they might have said *Give doggie paper* (a three-branch verb phrase) and *Big doggie* (a two-branch noun phrase), they now say *Give big doggie paper*, with the two-branch NP embedded inside the three-branch VP. The earlier sentences resembled telegrams, missing unstressed function words like *of, the, on*, and *does*, as well as inflections like *-ed, -ing*, and *-s*. By the 3s, children are using these function words more often than they are omitting them, many in more than 90 percent of the sentences that require them. A full range of sentence types flower—questions with words like *who, what*, and *where*, relative clauses, comparatives, negations, complements conjunctions, and passives. These constructions appear to display most, perhaps even all, of the grammatical machinery needed to account for adult grammar.

Though many of the young 3-year-old's sentences are ungrammatical for one reason or another, it is because there are many things that can go wrong in any single sentence. When researchers focus on a single grammatical rule, counting how often a child obeys it and how often the child flouts it, the results are very impressive. For just about every rule that has been looked at, 3-year olds obey it a majority of the time (Stromswold 1990; Pinker 1984, 1989; Crain 1992; Marcus et al. 1992). As we have seen, children rarely scramble word orders and, by the age of 3, come to supply most inflections and function words in sentences that require them. Though our ears perk up when we hear errors like *mens, wents, Can you broke those?, What he can ride in?, That's a furniture, Button me the rest*, and *Going to see kitten*, the errors occur in anywhere from 0.1 percent to 8 percent of the the opportunities for making them; more than 90 percent of the time, the child is on target. Chapter 3 of this volume follows one of those errors in detail.

Children do not seem to favor any particular kind of language (indeed, it would be puzzling how any kind of language could survive if children did not easily learn it!). They swiftly acquire free word order, SOV and VSO orders, rich systems of case and agreement, strings of agglutinated suffixes, ergative case marking, and whatever else their language throws at them, with no lag relative to their English-speaking counterparts. Even grammatical gender, which many adults learning a second language find mystifying, presents no problem: children acquiring languages like French, German, and Hebrew acquire gender marking quickly, make few errors, and never use the association with maleness and femaleness as a false criterion (Levy 1983). It is safe to say that except for constructions that are rare, predominantly used in written language, or mentally taxing even to an adult (like *The horse that the elephant tickled kissed the pig*), all parts of all languages are acquired before the child turns 4 (Slobin 1985a/1992).

6.4 Explaining Language Acquisition

How do we explain the course of language acquisition in children—most importantly, their inevitable and early mastery? Several kinds of mechanisms are at work. As we saw in section 6.2.3, the brain changes after birth, and these maturational changes may govern the onset, rate, and adult decline of language acquisition capacity. General changes in the child's information processing abilities (attention, memory, short-term buffers for acoustic input and articulatory output) could leave their mark as well. In chapter 5 of this volume, I show how a memory retrieval limitation—children are less reliable at recalling that *broke* is the past tense of *break*—can account for a conspicuous and universal error pattern, overregularizations like *breaked* (see also Marcus et al. 1992).

Many other small effects have been documented where changes in information processing abilities affect language development. For example, children selectively pick up information at the ends of words (Slobin 1973) and at the beginnings and ends of sentences (Newport, Gleitman, and Gleitman 1977), presumably because these are the parts of strings that are best retained in short-term memory. Similarly, the progressively widening bottleneck for early word combinations presumably reflects a general increase in motor planning capacity. Conceptual development (see chapter 4 in volume 3), too, might affect language development: if a child has not yet mastered a difficult semantic distinction, such as the complex temporal relations involved in *John will have gone*, he or she may be unable to master the syntax of the construction dedicated to expressing it.

The complexity of a grammatical form has a demonstrable role in development: Simpler rules and forms appear in speech before more complex ones, all other things being equal. For example, the plural marker -s in English (for example, *cats*), which requires knowing only whether the number of referents is singular or plural, is used consistently before the present tense marker -s (*he walks*), which requires knowing whether the subject is singular or plural *and* whether it is a first, second, or third person *and* whether the event is in the present tense (Brown 1973). Similarly, complex forms are sometimes first used in simpler approximations. Russian contains one case marker for masculine nominative (that is, a suffix on a masculine noun indicating that it is the subject of the sentence), one for feminine nominative, one for masculine accusative (used to indicate that a noun is a direct object), and one for feminine accusative. Children often use each marker with the correct case, never using a nominative marker for accusative nouns or vice versa, but they do not properly use the masculine and feminine variants with masculine and feminine nouns (Slobin 1985b).

These global trends, though, do not explain the main event: how children succeed. Language acquisition is so complex that one needs a precise framework for understanding what it involves—indeed, what learning in general involves.

6.4.1 Learnability Theory

What is language acquisition, in principle? A branch of theoretical computer science called *Learnability Theory* attempts to answer this question (Gold 1967; Osherson, Stob, and Weinstein 1985; Pinker 1979). Learnability theory has defined learning as a scenario involving four parts (the theory embraces all forms of learning, but I will use language as the example):

1. *A class of languages.* One of them is the "target" language, to be attained by the learner, but the learner does not, of course, know which it is. In the case of children, the class of languages would consist of the existing and possible human languages; the target language is the one spoken in their community.

2. *An environment.* This is the information in the world that the learner has to go on in trying to acquire the language. In the case of children, it might include the sentences that parents utter, the context in which they utter them, feedback to the child (verbal or nonverbal) in response to the child's own speech, and so on. Parental utterances can be a random sample of the language, or they might have some special properties: They might be ordered in certain ways, sentences might be repeated or only uttered once, and so on.

3. *A learning strategy.* The learner, using information in the environment, tries out "hypotheses" about the target language. The learning strategy is the algorithm that creates the hypotheses and determines whether they are consistent with the input information from the environment. For children, it is the "grammar-forming" mechanism in their brains, their "language acquisition device."

4. *A success criterion.* If we want to say that "learning" occurs, presumably it is because the learners' hypotheses are not random, but that by some time the hypotheses are related in some systematic way to the target language. Learners may arrive at a hypothesis identical to the target language after some fixed period of time; they may arrive at an approximation to it; they may waver among a set of hypotheses, one of which is correct.

Theorems in learnability theory show how assumptions about any of the three components impose logical constraints on the fourth. It is not hard to show why learning a language, on logical grounds alone, is so hard. As in all "induction problems" (uncertain generalizations from instances), there are an infinite number of hypotheses consistent with any

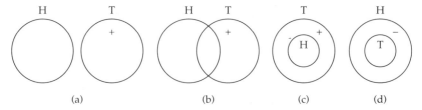

Figure 6.1
Four situations that a child could be in while learning a language. Each circle represents the set of sentences constituting a language. "H" stands for "hypothesized language"; "T" stands for "target language." "$+$" indicates a grammatical sentence in the language; "$-$" indicates an ungrammatical sentence.

finite sample of environmental information. Learnability theory shows which induction problems are solvable and which are not.

A key factor is the role of *negative evidence,* or information about which strings of words are not sentences in the language to be acquired. Human children might get such information by being corrected every time they speak ungrammatically. If they are not—and as we shall see, they probably are not—the acquisition problem is all the harder. Consider figure 6.1, where languages are depicted as circles corresponding to sets of word strings, and where all the logical possibilities for how the child's language could differ from the adult language are depicted. There are four possibilities: (a) The child's hypothesis language (H) is disjoint from the language to be acquired (the "target language," T). That would correspond to the state of a child who is learning English and cannot say a single well-formed English sentence; for example, the child might be able to say only things like *we breaked it,* and *we goed,* never *we broke it* or *we went.* (b) The child's hypothesis and the target language intersect. Here the child would be able to utter some English sentences, like *he went.* However, he or she would use strings of words that are not English, such as *we breaked it;* and some sentences of English, such as *we broke it,* would still be outside their abilities. (c) The child's hypothesis language is a subset of the target language. This would mean that the child would have mastered some of English, but not all of it, but that everything the child had mastered would be part of English. The child might not be able to say *we broke it* but would be able to say some grammatical sentences, such as *we went;* no errors such as *she breaked it* or *we goed* would occur. The final logical possibility is (d), where the child's hypothesis language is a superset of the target language. That would occur, for example, if the child could say *we broke it, we went, we breaked it,* and *we goed.*

In cases (a–c) the child can learn that the hypothesis is incorrect by hearing "positive evidence" (indicated by the "$+$" symbol); parental sentences that are in the target language but not in the child's hypothesized one, such as *we broke it*. This is impossible in case (d); negative evidence (such as corrections of the child's ungrammatical sentences by his or her parents) would be needed. In other words, without negative evidence, if a child guesses too large a language, the world can never tell him that he is wrong.

This has several consequences. For one thing, the most general learning algorithm one might conceive of—one that is capable of hypothesizing any grammar, or any computer program capable of generating a language—is useless. Without negative evidence (and even in many cases with it), there is no general-purpose, all-powerful learning machine; a machine must in some sense "know" something about the constraints in the domain in which it is learning.

More concretely, if children don't receive negative evidence (see section 6.6.2) we have a lot of explaining to do, because overly large hypotheses are very easy for the child to make. For example, children actually do go through stages in which they use two or more past tense forms for a given verb, such as *broke* and *breaked*—this case is discussed in detail in chapter 5 of this volume. They derive transitive verbs from intransitives too freely: where an adult might say *The girl giggled* but not *Don't giggle me!* children can say both (Bowerman 1982b; Pinker 1989). In each case they are in situation (d) in figure 6.1, and, unless their parents slip them some signal in every case that lets them know they are not speaking properly, it is puzzling that they eventually stop. That is, we would need to explain how they grow into adults who are more restrictive in their speech. Another way of putting it is that it is puzzling that the English language doesn't allow *don't giggle me* and *she eated*, given that children are tempted to grow up talking that way. If the world is not telling children to stop, something in their brains is, and we have to find out who or what is causing the change.

Let's now examine language acquisition in the human species by breaking it down into the four elements that give a precise definition to learning: the target of learning, the input, the degree of success, and the learning strategy.

6.5 What Is Learned

To understand how X is learned, you first have to understand what X is. Linguistic theory is thus an essential part of the study of language acquisition (see chapter 10 in this volume). Linguistic research tries to do three things. First, it must characterize the facts of English and all the other languages whose acquisition we are interested in explaining. Second, since children are not predisposed to learn English or any other language, linguistics has to examine the structure of other languages. In particular, linguists characterize which aspects of grammar are universal, prevalent, rare, and nonexistent across languages. Contrary to early suspicions, languages do not vary arbitrarily and without limit; there is by now a large catalog of *language universals*, properties shared exactly, or in a small number of variations, by all languages (see Comrie 1981; Greenberg 1978; Shopen 1985). This obviously bears on what children's language acquisition mechanisms find easy or hard to learn.

And one must go beyond a mere list of universals. Many universal properties of language are not specific to language but are simply reflections of universals of human experience. All languages have words for "water" and "foot" because all people need to refer to water and feet; no language has a word a million syllables long because no person would have time to say it. But others might be specific to the innate design of language itself. For example, if a language has both derivational suffixes (which create new words from old ones, like *-ism*) and inflectional suffixes (which modify a word to fit its role in the sentence, like plural *-s*), then the derivational suffixes are always closer to the word stem than the inflectional ones are. For example, in English one can say *Darwinisms* (derivational *-ism* closer to the stem than inflection *-s* is) but not *Darwinsism*. It is hard to think of a reason how this law would fit into any universal law of thought or memory: why would the concept of two ideologies based on one Darwin be thinkable, but the concept of one ideology based on two Darwins (say, Charles and Erasmus) not be thinkable (unless one reasons in a circle and declares that the mind must find *-ism* to be more cognitively basic than the plural, because that's the order we see in language)? Universals like this, that are specifically linguistic, should be captured in a theory of *universal grammar* (UG) (Chomsky 1965, 1981, 1991). UG specifies the allowable mental representations and operations that all languages are confined to use. The theory of universal grammar is closely tied to the theory of the mental mechanisms that children use in acquiring language; their hypotheses about language must be couched in structures sanctioned by UG.

To see how linguistic research cannot be ignored in understanding language acquisition, consider the sentences below. In each of the examples a learner who heard the (a) and (b) sentences could quite sensibly extract a general rule that, when applied to the (c) sentence, yields version (d). Yet the result is an odd sentence that no one would say:

1. a. John saw Mary with her best friend's husband.
   b. Who did John see Mary with?

   c. John saw Mary and her best friend's husband.
   d. *Who did John see Mary and?

2. a. Irv drove the car into the garage.
   b. Irv drove the car.

   c. Irv put the car into the garage.
   d. *Irv put the car.

3. a. I expect the fur to fly
   b. I expect the fur will fly.

   c. The fur is expected to fly.
   d. *The fur is expected will fly.

4. a. The baby seems to be asleep.
   b. The baby seems asleep.

   c. The baby seems to be sleeping.
   d. *The baby seems sleeping.

5. a. John liked the pictures of Bill that Mary took.
   b. John liked Mary's pictures of Bill.

   c. John liked the pictures of himself that Mary took.
   d. *John liked Mary's pictures of himself.

The solution to the problem must be that children's learning mechanisms ultimately do not allow them to make what would otherwise be a tempting generalization. For example, in (1), constraints that prevent extraction of a single phrase out of a coordinate structure (phrases joined by a word like *and* or *or*) would block what otherwise would be a natural generalization from other examples of extraction, such as 1(a–b). The other examples present other puzzles that the theory of universal grammar, as part of a theory of language acquisition, must solve. Because of the subtlety of these examples—and the abstractness of the principles of universal grammar that must be posited to explain them—Chomsky has claimed that the overall structure of language must be innate, based on his paper-and-pencil examination of the facts of language alone.

6.6 Input

To understand how children learn language, we have to know what aspects of language (from their parents or peers) they have access to.

6.6.1 Positive Evidence

Children clearly need some kind of linguistic input to acquire a language. There have been occasional cases in history where abandoned children have somehow survived in forests, such as Victor, the wild boy of Aveyron (subject of a film by François Truffaut). Occasionally, modern children have grown up wild because depraved parents have raised them silently in dark rooms and attics; the chapter by Gleitman and Newport in this volume discusses some of those cases. The outcome is always the same: the children, when found, are mute. Whatever innate grammatical abilities there are, they are too schematic to generate concrete speech, words, and grammatical constructions on their own.

Children do not, on the other hand, need to hear a full-fledged language to end up with one. As long as they are in a community with other children and have some source for individual words, they will invent one on their own, often in a single generation. Children who grew up in plantations and slave colonies were often exposed to a crude pidgin that served as the lingua franca in these babels of laborers. But they grew up to speak genuinely new languages, expressive "creoles" with their own complex grammars (Bickerton 1984; see also the chapter by Gleitman and Newport). The sign languages of the deaf arose in similar ways. Indeed, they arise spontaneously and quickly wherever there is a community of deaf children (Senghas 1994; Kegl 1994).

Children most definitely *do* need to hear an existing language to learn *that* language, of course. Children with Japanese genes do not find Japanese any easier than English, or vice versa; they learn whichever language they are exposed to. The term "positive evidence" refers to the information available to the child about which strings of words are grammatical sentences in the target language.

By "grammatical," incidentally, linguists and psycholinguists mean only those sentences that sound natural in colloquial speech, not necessarily those that would be deemed "proper English" in formal written prose. Thus split infinitives, dangling participles, slang, and so on are "grammatical" in this sense (and indeed, are as logical, systematic, expressive, and precise as "correct" written English, often more so; see chapter 2 and Pinker 1994a). Similarly, elliptical utterances (such as when the question *Where are you going?* is answered with *To the store*) count as grammatical. Ellipsis is not just random snipping from sentences, but is governed by rules that are part of the grammar of one's language or dialect. For example, the grammar of casual British English allows you to answer the question *Will he go?* by saying *He might do*, whereas the grammar of American English does not allow it.

Given this scientific definition of "grammatical," do we find that parents' speech counts as "positive evidence"? That is, when a parent uses a sentence, can the child assume that it is part of the language to be learned, or do parents use so many ungrammatical sentences—random fragments, slips of the tongue, hesitations, and false starts—that the child would have to take much of it with a grain of salt? Fortunately for the child, the vast majority of the speech they hear during the language-learning years is fluent, complete, and grammatically well formed: 99.93 percent, according to one estimate (Newport, Gleitman, and Gleitman 1977). Indeed, this is true of conversation among adults in general (Labov 1969).

Thus, language acquisition is ordinarily driven by a grammatical sample of the target language. Note that this is true even for forms of English that people unthinkingly call "ungrammatical," "fractured," or "bad English," such as rural American English (*them books; he don't; we ain't; they drug him away*) and urban black English (*She walking; He be working*; see chapter 2 of this volume). These are not corrupted versions of standard English; to a linguist they look just like different dialects, as rule-governed as the southern England dialect of English that, for historical reasons, became the standard several centuries ago. Scientifically speaking, the grammar of working-class speech—indeed, every human language system that has been studied—is intricately complex, though different languages are complex in different ways.

6.6.2   Negative Evidence

Negative evidence refers to information about which strings of words are not grammatical sentences in the language, such as corrections or other forms of feedback from a parent that tell the child that one of his or her utterances is ungrammatical. As mentioned in section 6.4.1, it is very important for us to know whether children get and need negative evidence, because in the absence of negative evidence, children who hypothesize a rule that generates a superset of the language will have no way of knowing that they are wrong (Gold 1967; Pinker 1979, 1989). If children do not get, or do not use, negative evidence, they must have some mechanism that either avoids generating too large a language—the child would be conservative—or that can recover from such overgeneration.

Roger Brown and Camille Hanlon (1970) attempted to test B. F. Skinner's behaviorist claim that language learning depends on parents' reinforcement of children's grammatical behaviors. Using transcripts of naturalistic parent-child dialogue, they divided children's sentences into ones that were grammatically well formed and ones that contained grammatical errors. They then divided adults' responses to those sentences into ones that expressed some kind of approval (such as, *"yes, that's good"*) and those that expressed some kind of disapproval. They looked for a correlation, but failed to find one; parents did not differentially express approval or disapproval to their children contingent on whether the child's prior utterance was well formed or not (approval depends, instead, on whether the child's utterance is *true*). Brown and Hanlon also looked at children's well-formed and badly formed question and whether parents seemed to answer them appropriately, as if they understood them, or with non sequiturs. They found that parents do not understand their children's well-formed questions any better than their badly formed ones.

Other studies (such as Hirsh-Pasek, Treiman, and Schneiderman 1984; Demetras, Post, and Snow 1986; Penner 1987; Bohannon and Stanowicz 1988) have replicated that result, but with a twist. Some have found small statistical contingencies between the grammaticality of some kinds of sentences from some children and the kind of follow-up given by their parents; for example, whether the parent repeats the sentence verbatim, asks a follow-up question, or changes the topic. But Marcus (1993) has found that these patterns fall far short of negative evidence (reliable information about the grammatical status of any word string). Different parents react in opposite ways to their children's ungrammatical sentences, and many forms of ungrammaticality are not reacted to at all—leaving a given child unable to know what to make of any parental reaction. Even when a parent does react differentially, a child would have to repeat a particular error verbatim hundreds of times to eliminate the error, because the parent's reaction is only statistical; the feedback signals given to ungrammatical sentences are also given nearly as often to *grammatical* sentences.

Stromswold (1994) has an even more dramatic demonstration that parental feedback cannot be crucial. She studied a child who, for unknown neurological reasons, was congenitally unable to talk. He was a good listener, though; and, when tested, he was able to understand complicated sentences perfectly and to judge accurately whether a sentence was grammatical or ungrammatical. The boy's abilities show that children certainly do not *need* negative evidence to learn grammatical rules properly, even in the unlikely event that their parents provided it.

These results, though of profound importance, should not be too surprising. Every speaker of English judges sentences such as *I dribbled the floor with paint* and *Ten pounds was weighed by the boy* and *Who do you believe the claim that John saw?* and *John asked Mary to look at himself* to be ungrammatical. But it is unlikely that every such speaker has at some point uttered these sentences and benefited from negative evidence. The child must have mental mechanisms that rule out vast numbers of "reasonable" strings of words without any outside intervention.

6.6.3   Motherese

Parents and caretakers in most parts of the world modify their speech when talking to young children, an example of how people in general use several "registers" in different social settings. Speech to children is slower, shorter, in some ways (but not all) simpler, higher-pitched, more exaggerated in intonation, more fluent and grammatically well formed, and more directed in content to the present situation, compared with speech among adults (Snow and Ferguson 1977). Many parents also expand their children's utterances into full sentences or offer sequences of paraphrases of a given sentence.

One should not, though, consider this speech register, sometimes called Motherese, to be a set of "language lessons." Though mothers' speech may seem simple at first glance, in many ways it is not. For example, speech to children is full of questions—sometimes a majority of the sentences. If you think that questions are simple, just try to write a set of rules that accounts for the following sentences and nonsentences:

6. He can go somewhere.
    Where can he go?
    *Where can he go somewhere?
    *Where he can go?
    *Where did he can go?

7. He went somewhere.
    Where did he go?
    He went WHERE?
    *Where went he?
    *Where did he went?
    *Where he went?
    *He did go WHERE?

8. He went home.
    Why did he go home?
    How come he went home?
    *Why he went home?
    *How come did he go home?

Linguists struggle over these facts (see chapters 10 and 12 of this volume), some of the most puzzling in the English language. But these are the constructions that infants are bombarded with and that they master in their preschool years.

Chapter 1 gives another reason for doubting that Motherese is a set of language lessons. Children whose mothers use Motherese more consistently don't pass through the milestones of language development any faster (Newport, Gleitman, and Gleitman 1977). Furthermore, there are some communities with radically different ideas about children's proper place in society. In some societies, for example, people tacitly assume that children are not worth speaking to and do not have anything to say that is worth listening to. Such children learn to speak by overhearing streams of adult-to-adult speech (Heath 1983). In some communities in New Guinea, mothers consciously try to teach their children language, but not in the style familiar to us, of talking to them indulgently. Rather, they wait until a third party is present and coach the child as to the proper, adultlike sentences that they should use (see Schieffelin and Eisenberg 1981). Nonetheless, those children, like all children, grow up to be fluent language speakers. It surely must help children when their parents speak slowly, clearly, and succinctly to them, but their success at learning can't be explained by any special grammar-unveiling properties of parental babytalk.

6.6.4   Prosody

Parental speech is not a string of printed words on a ticker-tape, nor is it in a monotone like that of science-fiction robots. Normal human speech has a pattern of melody, timing, and stress called prosody. And Motherese directed to young infants has a characteristic, exaggerated prosody of its own: a rise and fall contour for approving, a set of sharp staccato bursts for prohibiting, a rise pattern for directing attention, and smooth, low legato murmurs for comforting. Fernald (1992) has shown that these patterns are very widespread across language communities and may be universal. The melodies seem to attract the child's attention—marking the sounds as speech as opposed to stomach growlings or other noises—and might distinguish statements, questions, and imperatives, delineate major sentence boundaries, and highlight new words. When given a choice, babies prefer to listen to speech with these properties than to speech intended for adults (Fernald 1984, 1992; Hirsh-Pasek et al. 1987).

In all speech a number of prosodic properties of the speech wave, such as lengthening, intonation, and pausing, are influenced by the syntactic structure of the sentence (Cooper and Paccia-Cooper 1980). Just listen to how you would say the word *like* in the sentence *The boy I like slept* compared with *The boy I saw likes sleds*. In the first sentence the word *like* is at the boundary of a relative clause and is drawn out, exaggerated in intonation, and followed by a pause; in the second, it is in the middle of a verb phrase and is pronounced more quickly, uniformly in intonation, and is run together with the following word. Some psychologists (such as Gleitman and Wanner 1984; Gleitman 1990) have suggested that children use this information in the reverse direction, reading the syntactic structure of a sentence directly off its melody and timing. We will examine the hypothesis in section 6.8.2.

6.6.5   Context

Children do not hear sentences in isolation, but in a context. No child has learned language from the radio; indeed, children rarely, if ever, learn language from television. Ervin-Tripp (1973) studied hearing children of deaf parents whose only access to English was from radio or television broadcasts. The children did not learn any speech from that input. One reason is that without already knowing the language, it would be difficult for a child to figure out what the characters in the unresponsive televised worlds are talking about. In interacting with live human speakers, who tend to talk about the here and now in the presence of children, the child can be more of a mind reader, guessing what the speaker might have meant (Macnamara 1972, 1982; Schlesinger 1971). That is, before children have learned syntax, they know the meaning of many words, and they might be able to make good guesses as to what their parents are saying based on their knowledge of how the referents of these words typically act (for example, people tend to eat apples, but not vice versa). In fact, parental speech to young children is so redundant with its context that a person with no knowledge of the order in which parents' words are spoken, only the words themselves, can infer from transcripts, with high accuracy, what was being said (Slobin 1977).

Many models of language acquisition assume that the input to the child consists of a sentence and a representation of the meaning of that sentence, inferred from context and from the child's knowledge of the meanings of the words (for example, Anderson 1977; Berwick 1985; Pinker 1982, 1984; Wexler and Culicover 1980). Of course, this cannot literally be true—children do not hear every word of every sentence and surely do not, to begin with, perceive the entire meaning of a sentence from context. Blind children, whose access to the nonlinguistic world is obviously severely limited, learn language without many problems (Landau and Gleitman 1985). And when children do succeed in guessing a parent's meaning, it cannot be by simple temporal contiguity. For example, Gleitman (1990) points out that when a mother arriving home from work opens the door, she is likely to say, "What did you do today?," not "I'm opening the door." Similarly, she is likely to say "Eat your peas" when her child is, say, looking at the dog, and certainly not when the child is already eating peas.

Still, the assumption of context-derived semantic input is a reasonable idealization, if one considers the abilities of the whole child. The child must keep an updated mental model of the current situation, created by mental faculties for perceiving objects and events and the states of mind and communicative intentions of other humans. The child can use this knowledge, plus the meanings of any familiar words in the sentence, to infer what the parent probably meant. In section 6.8.3 we will discuss how children might fill the important gaps in what they can infer from context.

6.7   What and When Children Learn

People do not reproduce their parents' language exactly. If they did, we would all still be speaking like Chaucer. But in any generation, in most times, the differences between parents' language and the one their children ultimately acquire is small. And remember that, judging by their spontaneous speech, we can conclude that most children have mastered their mother tongue (allowing for performance errors due to complexity or rarity of a construction) sometime in their 3s. It seems that the success criterion for human language is something close to full mastery and in a short period of time.

To show that young children really have grasped the design plan of language, rather than merely approximating it with outwardly convincing routines or rules of thumb that would have to be supplanted later in life, we cannot rely just on what they say; we have to use clever experimental techniques. Let's look at two examples that illustrate how even very young children seem to obey the innate complex design of universal grammar.

Earlier, I mentioned that in all languages, if there are derivational affixes that build new words out of old ones, like $-ism$, $-er$, and $-able$, and inflectional affixes that modify a word according to its role in the sentence, like $-s$, $-ed$, and ing, then the derivational affix appears inside the inflectional one: $Darwinisms$ is possible, $Darwinsism$ is not. This and many other grammatical quirks were nicely explained in a theory of word structure proposed by Paul Kiparsky (1982).

Kiparsky showed that words are built in layers or "levels." To build a word, you can start with a root like $Darwin$. Then you can apply rules of a certain kind to it, called level 1 rules, to yield a more complex word. For example, there is a rule adding the suffix $-ian$, turning the word into $Darwinian$. Level 1 rules, according to the theory, can affect the sound of the stem; in this case the syllable carrying the stress shifts from Dar to win. Level 2 rules apply to a word after any level 1 rules have been applied. An example of a level 2 rule is the one that adds the suffix $-ism$, yielding, for example, $Darwinism$. Level 2 rules generally do not affect the pronunciation of the words they apply to; they just add material onto the word, leaving the pronunciation intact. (The stress in $Darwinism$ is the same as it was in $Darwin$.) Finally, level 3 rules apply to a word after any level 2 rules have been applied. The regular rules of inflectional morphology are examples of level 3 rules. An example is the rule that adds an $-s$ to the end of a noun to form its plural—for example, $Darwinians$ or $Darwinisms$.

Crucially, the rules cannot apply out of order. The input to a level 1 rule must be a word root. The input to a level 2 rule must be either a root or the output of level 1 rules. The input to a level 3 rule must be a root, the output of level 1 rules, or the output of level 2 rules. That constraint yields predictions about what kinds of words are possible and what kinds are impossible. For example, the ordering makes it possible to derive $Darwinianism$ and $Darwinianisms$, but not $Darwinsian$, $Darwinsism$, and $Darwinismian$.

Now, irregular inflection, such as the pairing of *mouse* with *mice*, belongs to level 1, whereas regular inflectional rules, such as the one that relates *rat* to *rats*, belongs to level 3. Compounding, the rule that would produce *Darwin-lover* and *mousetrap*, is a level 2 rule, in between. This correctly predicts that an irregular plural can easily appear inside a compound, but a regular plural cannot. Compare the following:

mice-infested; *rats-infested
men-bashing; *guys-bashing
teethmarks; *clawsmarks
feet-warmer; *hands-warmer
purple people-eater; *purple babies-eater

Mice-infested is a possible word, because the process connecting *mouse* with *mice* comes before the rule combining either noun with *infested*. However, *rats-infested*, even though it is cognitively quite similar to *mice-infested*, sounds strange; we can say only *rat-infested* (even though by definition one rat does not make an infestation).

Peter Gordon (1986) had children between the ages of 3 and 5 participate in an elicited-production experiment in which he would say, "Here is a puppet who likes to eat _____. What would you call him?" He first provided a response for several singular mass nouns, like *mud*, beforehand, so that the children were aware of the existence of the "x-eater" compound form. In the crucial examples, involving count nouns and their plurals, children behaved just like adults: a puppet who likes to eat a mouse was called a *mouse-eater*, a puppet who likes to eat a rat was called a *rat-eater*, a puppet who likes to eat mice was called either a *mouse-eater* or a *mice-eater*—but—a puppet who likes to eat rats was called a *rat-eater*, never a *rats-eater*. Interestingly, children treated their own overregularizations, such as *mouses*, exactly as they treated legitimate regular plurals: they would never call the puppet a *mouses-eater*, even if they used *mouses* in their own speech.

Even more interestingly, Gordon examined how children could have acquired the constraint. Perhaps, he reasoned, they had learned the fact that compounds can contain either singulars or irregular plurals, never regular plurals, by keeping track of all the kinds of compounds that do and do not occur in their parents' speech. But it turns out that they would have no way of learning that fact. Although there is no grammatical reason why compounds would not contain irregular plurals, the speech that most children hear does not contain any. Compounds like *toothbrush* abound; compounds containing irregular plurals like *teethmarks*, *people-eater*, and *men-bashing*, though grammatically possible, are statistically rare, according to the standardized frequency data that Gordon examined, and he found none that was likely to appear in the speech children hear. Therefore children were willing to say *mice-eater* and unwilling to say *rats-eater* with no good evidence from the input that that is the pattern required in English. Gordon suggests that this shows that the constraints on level ordering may be innate.

Let's now go from words to sentences. Sentences are ordered strings of words. No child could fail to notice word order in learning and understanding language. But most regularities of language govern hierarchically organized structures—words grouped into phrases, phrases grouped into clauses, clauses grouped into sentences (see chapters 10, 12, and 1 of this volume). If the structures of linguistic theory correspond to the hypotheses that children formulate when they analyze parental speech and form rules, children should create rules defined over hierarchical structures, not simple properties of linear order such as which word comes before which other word or how close two words are in a sentence. The chapter by Gleitman and Newport discusses one nice demonstration of how adults (who are, after all, just grown-up children) respect constituent structure, not simple word order, when forming questions. Here is an example making a similar point that has been tried out with children.

Languages often have embedded clauses missing a subject, such as *John told Mary to leave*, where the embedded "downstairs" clause *to leave* has no subject. The phenomenon of *control* governs how the missing subject is interpreted. In this sentence it is Mary who is understood as having the embedded subject's role, that is, the person doing the leaving. We say that the phrase *Mary* "controls" the missing subject position of the lower clause. For most verbs, there is a simple principle defining control. If the upstairs verb has no object, then the subject of the upstairs verb controls the missing subject of the downstairs verb. For example, in *John tried to leave, John* is interpreted as the subject of both *try* and *leave*. If the upstairs verb has a subject and an object, then it is the object that controls the missing subject of the downstairs verb, as we saw in *John told Mary to leave*.

In 1969 Carol Chomsky published a set of classic experiments in developmental psycholinguistics. She showed that children apply this principle quite extensively, even to the handful of verbs that are exceptions to it. In act-out comprehension experiments on children between the ages of 5 and 10, she showed that even relatively old children were prone to this kind of mistake. When told "Mickey promised Donald to jump; make him jump," the children made Donald, the object of the first verb, do the jumping, in accord with the general principle. The "right answer" in this case would have been Mickey, because *promise* is an exception to the principle, calling for an unusual kind of control where the subject of the upstairs verb, not the object of the upstairs verb, should act as controller.

But what, exactly, is the principle that children are overapplying? One possibility can be called the Minimal Distance Principle: the controller of the downstairs verb is the noun phrase nearest to it in the linear string of words in the sentence. If children analyze sentences in terms of linear order, this should be a natural generalization; however, it is not right for the adult language. Consider the passive sentence *Mary was told by John to leave*. The phrase *John* is closest to the subject position for *leave*, but adult English speakers understand the sentence as meaning that Mary is the one leaving. The Minimal Distance Principle gives the wrong answer here. Instead, for the adult language, we need a principle sensitive to grammatical structure, such as the "c-control" structural relation discussed in this volume's chapter 10. Let's consider a simplified version, which we can call the Structural Principle. It might say that the controller of a missing subject is the grammatical object of the upstairs verb if it has one; otherwise, it is the grammatical subject of the upstairs verb (both of them c-command the missing subject). The object of a preposition in the higher clause, however, is never allowed to be a controller, basically because it is embedded "too deeply" in the sentence's tree structure to c-command the missing subject. That's why *Mary was told by John to leave* has *Mary* as the controller. (It is also why, incidentally, the sentence *Mary was promised by John to leave* is unintelligible—it would require a prepositional phrase to be the controller, which is ruled out by the Structural Principle.)

It would certainly be understandable if children were to follow the Minimal Distance Principle. Not only is it easily stated in terms of surface properties that children can easily perceive, but the kinds of sentences that would disconfirm it, like *Mary was told by John to leave*, are nonexistent or rare in parents' speech. Michael Maratsos (1974) did the crucial experiment. He gave children such sentences and asked them who was leaving. Of course, on either account children would have to be able to understand the passive construction to interpret these sentences, and Maratsos gave them a separate test of comprehension of simple passive sentences to select the children who could do so. And indeed, he found that those children interpreted passive sentences with missing embedded subjects just as adults would. That is, in accord with the Structural Principle and in violation of the Minimal Distance Principle, they interpreted *Mary was told by John to leave* as having the subject, Mary, do the leaving, that is, as the controller. The experiment shows how young children have grasped the abstract structural relations in sentences and have acquired a grammar of the same design as that spoken by their parents.

6.8   The Child's Language-Learning Algorithm

Here is the most basic problem in understanding how children learn a language: The input to language acquisition consists of sounds and situations; the output is a grammar specifying, for that language, the order and arrangement of abstract entities like nouns, verbs, subjects, phrase structures, control, and c-command (see chapters 10 and 12 of this volume, also the demonstrations in this chapter and in chapter 1). Somehow, the child must discover these entities to learn the language. We know that even preschool children have an extensive unconscious grasp of grammatical structure, thanks to the experiments discussed in section 6.7, but how has the child managed to go from sounds and situations to syntactic structure?

Innate knowledge of grammar itself is not sufficient. It does no good for the child to have written down in his brain "There exist nouns"; children need some way of *finding* them in parents' speech so that they can determine, among other things, whether the nouns come before the verb, as in English, or after, as in Irish. Once children find nouns and verbs, any innate knowledge would immediately be helpful, because they could then deduce all kinds of implications about how to use them. But finding them is the crucial first step, and it is not an easy one.

In English, nouns can be identified as those things that come after articles, get suffixed with -s in the plural, and so on. But the infant obviously doesn't know that yet. Nouns do not occur in any constant position in a sentence across the languages of the world, and they are not said with any particular tone of voice. Nor do nouns have a constant meaning— they often refer to physical things, like dogs, but don't have to, as in *The days of our lives* and *The warmth of the sun*. The same is true for other linguistic entities, such as verbs, subjects, objects, auxiliaries, and tense. Since the child must somehow "lift himself up by his bootstraps" to get started in formulating a grammar for the language, this is called the "bootstrapping problem" (see Pinker 1984, 1987, 1989, 1994; Morgan 1986; Gleitman 1990; and the contributors to Morgan and Demuth 1995). Several solutions can be envisioned.

6.8.1   Extracting Simple Correlations

One possibility is that the child sets up a massive correlation matrix and tallies which words appear in which positions, which words appear next to which other words, which words get which prefixes and suffixes in which circumstances, and so on. Syntactic categories would arise implicitly as the child discovers that certain sets of properties are mutually intercorrelated in large sets of words. For example, many words tend to occur between a subject and an object, are inflected with -s when the subject is singular and in the third person and the tense is present, and often appear after the word *to*. This set of words would be grouped together as the equivalent of the "verb" category (Maratsos and Chalkley 1981).

There are two problems with this proposal. The main one is that the features that the prelinguistic child is supposed to be cross-referencing are not audibly marked in parental speech. Rather, they are perceptible only to a child who has already analyzed the grammar of the language—just what the proposal is trying to explain in the first place! How are prelinguistic children supposed to find the "subject" of the sentence in order to correlate it with the ending on the words they are focusing on? A subject is not the same thing as the first word or two of the sentence (as in *The big bad wolf huffed and puffed*) or even the first phrase (*What did the big bad wolf do?*). We have a dilemma. If the features defining the rows and columns of the correlation matrix are things that are perceptible to the child, like "first word in a sentence," then grammatical categories will never emerge, since they have no consistent correlation with these features. But if the features are the things that do define grammatical categories, like agreement and phrase structure position, the proposal assumes just what it sets out to explain, namely, that the child has analyzed the input into its correct grammatical structures. Somehow, the child must break into this circle. It is a general danger that pops up in cognitive psychology whenever anyone proposes a model that depends on correlations among features; there is always a temptation to glibly endow the features with the complex, abstract representations whose acquisition one is trying to explain.

The second problem is that, without prior constraints on the design of the feature-correlator, there are an astronomical number of possible intercorrelations among linguistic properties for the child to test. To take just two, the child would have to determine whether a sentence containing the word *cat* in third position must have a plural word at the end, and whether sentences ending in words ending in *d* are invariably preceded by words referring to plural entities. Most of these correlations never occur in any natural language. It would be a mystery, then, why children are built with complex machinery designed to test for them—though another way of putting it is that it would be a mystery why there are no languages exhibiting certain kinds of correlation, given that children are capable of finding them.

6.8.2   Using Prosody

A second way in which the child could begin syntax learning would be to attend to the prosody of sentences and to posit phrase boundaries at points in the acoustic stream marked by lengthening, pausing, and drops in fundamental frequency. The proposal seems attractive because prosodic properties are perceptible in advance of knowing any syntax, so at first glance, prosody seems like a straightforward way for a child to break into the language system.

But on closer examination, the proposal does not seem to work (Pinker 1987, 1994b; Fernald and McRoberts, in press; Steedman, in press). Just as gold glitters, but all that glitters is not gold, syntactic structure affects aspects of prosody, but aspects of prosody are affected by many things besides syntax. The effects of emotional state of the speaker, intent of the speaker, word frequency, contrastive stress, and syllabic structure of individual words are all mixed together, and there is no way for a child to disentangle them from the sound wave alone. For example, in the sentence *The baby ate the slug*, the main pause coincides with the major syntactic boundary between the subject and the predicate. But a child cannot work backwards and assume that the main pause in an input sentence marks the boundary between the subject and the predicate. In the similar sentence *He ate the slug*, the main pause is at the more embedded boundary between the verb and its object.

Worse, the mapping between syntax and prosody, even when it is consistent, is consistent in different ways in different languages. A young child cannot, therefore, use any such consistency, at least not at the very beginning of language acquisition, to decipher the syntax of the sentence; it itself is one of the things that has to be learned.

6.8.3   Using Context and Semantics

A third possibility (see Pinker 1984, 1989; Macnamara 1982; Grimshaw 1981; Wexler and Culicover 1980; P. Bloom, 1994) exploits the fact that there is a one-way contingency between semantics and syntax in the basic sentences of most of the world's languages. Though not all nouns are physical objects, all physical objects are named by nouns. Similarly, if a verb has an argument playing the semantic role of "agent," then that argument will be expressed as the subject of basic sentences in language after language. (Again, this does not work in reverse: the subject is not necessarily an agent. In *John liked Mary* the subject is an "experiencer"; in *John pleased Mary* it is an object of experience; in *John received a package* it is a goal or recipient; in *John underwent an operation* it is an affected entity.) Similarly, entities directly affected by an action are expressed as objects (but not all objects are entities affected by an action); actions themselves are expressed as verbs (though not all verbs express actions). Even phrase structure configurations have semantic correlates; arguments of verbs reliably appear as "sisters" to them inside the verb phrase in phrase structure trees (see the chapter by Lasnik in this volume).

If children assume that semantic and syntactic categories are related in restricted ways in the early input, they could use semantic properties of words and phrases (inferred from context; see section 6.5) as evidence that they belong to certain syntactic categories. For example, a child can infer that a word designating a person, place, or thing is a noun, that a word designating an action is a verb, that a word expressing the agent argument of an action predicate is the subject of its sentence, and so on. For example, upon hearing the sentence *The cat chased the rat*, the child can deduce that in English the subject comes before the verb, that the object comes after the verb, and so on. This would give the child the basis for creating the phrase structure trees that allow him or her to analyze the rules of the language.

Of course, a child cannot literally create a grammar that contains rules like "Agent words come before action words." This would leave the child no way of knowing how to order the words in sentences such as *Apples appeal to Mary* or *John received a package*. But once an initial set of rules is learned, items that are more abstract or that do not follow the usual patterns relating syntax and semantics could be learned through their distribution in already learned structures. That is, the child could now infer that *Apples* is the subject of *appeal*, and that *John* is the subject of *receive*, because they are in subject position, a fact the child now knows thanks to the earlier *cat-chased-rat* sentences. Similarly, the child could infer that *appeal* is a verb to begin with because it is in the "verb" position.

6.9   Acquisition in Action

What do all these arguments mean for what goes on in a child's mind moment by moment as he or she is acquiring rules from parental speech? Let's look at the process as concretely as possible.

6.9.1   Bootstrapping the First Rules

First imagine a hypothetical child trying to extract patterns from the following sentences, without any innate guidance as to how human grammar works.

> Myron eats lamb.
> Myron eats fish.
> Myron likes fish.

At first glance, one might think that the child could analyze the input as follows. Sentences consist of three words: the first must be *Myron*, the second either *eats* or *likes*, the third *lamb* or *fish*. With these micro-rules, the child can already generalize beyond the input, to the brand new sentence *Myron likes chicken*.

But let's say the next two sentences are

> Myron eats loudly.
> Myron might fish.

The word *might* gets added to the list of words that can appear in second position, and the word *loudly* is added to the list that can appear in third position. But look at the generalizations this would allow.

>Myron might loudly.
>Myron likes loudly.
>Myron might lamb.

This is not working. The child must couch rules in grammatical categories like noun, verb, and auxiliary, not in actual words. That way, *fish* as a noun and *fish* as a verb can be kept separate, and the child would not adulterate the noun rule with instances of verbs and vice versa. If children are willing to guess that words for objects are nouns, words for actions are verbs, and so on, they would have a leg up on the rule-learning problem.

But words are not enough; they must be ordered. Imagine the child trying to figure out what kind of word can occur before the verb *bother*. It cannot be done:

>That dog bothers me. [*dog*, a noun]
>What she wears bothers me. [*wears*, a verb]
>Music that is too loud bothers me. [*loud*, an adjective]
>Cheering too loudly bothers me. [*loudly*, an adverb]
>The guy she hangs out with bothers me. [*with*, a preposition]

The problem is obvious. There *is* a certain something that must come before the verb *bother*, but that something is not a kind of word; it is a kind of *phrase*, a noun phrase. A noun phrase always contains a head noun; but that noun can be followed by many other phrases, so it is pointless to try to learn a language by analyzing sentences word by word. The child must look for phrases—and the experiments on grammatical control discussed in section 6.7 show that they do.

What does it mean to look for phrases? A phrase is a group of words. Most of the logically possible groups of words in a sentence are useless for constructing new sentences, such as *wears bothers* and *cheering too*, but the child, unable to rely on parental feedback, has no way of knowing this. So once again, children cannot attack the language learning task like some logician free of preconceptions; they need prior constraints. We have already seen where such constraints could come from. First, the child could assume that parents' speech respects the basic design of human phrase structure: phrases contain heads (for example, a noun phrase is built around a head noun); arguments are grouped with heads in small phrases, sometimes called X-bars (see the chapter by Lasnik in this volume); X-bars are grouped with their modifiers inside large phrases (Noun Phrase, Verb Phrase, and so on); phrases can have subjects. Second, since the meanings of parents' sentences are guessable in context, the child could use the meanings to help set up the right phrase structure. Imagine that a parent says *The big dog ate ice cream*. A child who already knows the words *big*, *dog*, *ate*, and *ice cream* can guess their categories and grow the first branches of a tree:

In turn, nouns and verbs must belong to noun phrases and verb phrases, so the child can posit one for each of these words. And if there is a big dog around, the child can guess that *the* and *big* modify *dog* and connect them properly inside the noun phrase:

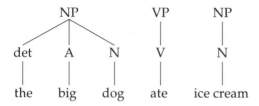

If the child knows that the dog just ate ice cream, he or she can also guess that *ice cream* and *dog* are arguments of the verb *eat*. *Dog* is a special kind of argument because it is the causal agent of the action and the topic of the sentence; hence, it is likely to be the subject of the sentence and therefore attaches to the "S." A tree for the sentence has been completed:

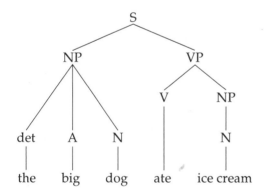

The rules and dictionary entries can be peeled off the tree:

S → NP VP
VP → det A N
VP → V NP
dog: N
ice cream: N
ate: V; eater = subject, thing eaten = object

the: det
big: A

This hypothetical example shows how a child, if suitably equipped, could learn three rules and five words from a single sentence in context.

The use of part-of-speech categories, phrase structure, and meaning guessed from context are powerful tools that can help the child in the daunting task of learning grammar quickly and without systematic parental feedback (Pinker 1984). In particular, there are many benefits to using a small number of categories like N and V to organize incoming speech. By calling both the subject and object phrases NP, rather than, say, Phrase #1 and Phrase #2, the child automatically can apply knowledge about nouns in subject position to nouns in object position, and vice versa. For example, our model child can already generalize, using the *dog* as an object, without having heard an adult do so, and the child tacitly knows that adjectives precede nouns not just in subjects but in objects, again without direct evidence. The child knows that if more than one *dog* is *dogs* in subject position, more than one *dog* is *dogs* in object position.

More generally, English allows at least eight possible phrase-mates of a head noun inside a noun phrase, such as *John's* dog; dogs *in the park*; *big* dogs; dogs *that I like*; and so on. In turn, there are about eight places in a sentence where the whole noun phrase can go, such as *Dog* bites man; Man bites *dog*; A *dog's* life; Give the boy *a dog*; Talk to *the dog*; and so on. There are three ways to inflect a noun: *dog, dogs, dog's*. And a typical child by the time of high school has learned something like twenty thousand different nouns (Miller 1991; Pinker 1994a). If children had to learn all the combinations separately, they would need to listen to about 123 million different sentences. At a rate of a sentence every ten seconds, ten hours a day, it would take over a century. But by unconsciously labeling all nouns as "N" and all noun phrases as "NP," the child has only to hear about twenty-five different kinds of noun phrase and can learn the nouns one by one; the millions of possible combinations fall out automatically.

Indeed, if children are constrained to look for only a small number of phrase types, they automatically gain the ability to produce an infinite number of sentences, one of the hallmarks of human language. Take the phrase *the tree in the park*. If the child mentally labels *the park* as an NP, and also labels *the tree in the park* as an NP, the resulting rules generate an NP inside a PP inside an NP—a loop that can be iterated indefinitely, as in *the tree near the ledge by the lake in the park in the city in the east of the state.* . . . In contrast, a child who was free to label *in the park* as one kind of phrase, and *the tree in the park* as another, would be deprived of the insight that the phrase contains an example of itself. The child would be limited to reproducing that phrase structure alone.

With a rudimentary but roughly accurate analysis of sentence structure set up, a learner can acquire other parts of language systematically. Abstract words, such as nouns that do not refer to objects and people, can be learned by paying attention to where they sit inside a sentence. Since *situation* in *The situation justifies drastic measures* occurs inside a phrase in NP position, it must be a noun. If the language allows phrases to be scrambled around the sentence (as do Latin and the Australian aboriginal language Warlpiri), the child can discover this feature upon coming across a word that cannot be connected to a tree in the expected place without crossing branches (in section 6.9.3, we will see that children do seem to proceed in this order). The child's mind can also know what to focus on in decoding whatever case and agreement inflections the language might contain: A noun's inflection can be checked to see if it appears whenever the noun appears in subject position, in object position, and so on; a verb's inflection can be checked for tense, aspect, and the number, person, and gender of its subject and object. The child need not bother checking whether the third word in the sentence referred to a reddish or a bluish object, whether the last word was long or short, whether the sentence was being uttered indoors or outdoors, and billions of other fruitless possibilities that a purely correlational learner would have to check.

6.9.2   The Organization of Grammar as a Guide to Acquisition

A grammar is not a bag of rules; there are principles that link the various parts together into a functioning whole. The child can use such principles of universal grammar to allow one bit of knowledge about language to affect another. This helps solve the problem of how the child can avoid generalizing to too large a language, which in the absence of negative evidence would be incorrigible. In cases where children do overgeneralize, these principles can help the child recover: if there is a principle that says that A and B cannot coexist in a language, a child acquiring B can use it to catapult A out of the grammar.

Blocking and Inflectional Overregularization

Chapter 5 of this volume presents a good example. The *Blocking principle* in morphology dictates that an irregular form listed in the mental dictionary as corresponding to a particular inflectional category (say, past tense) blocks the application of the corresponding general rule. For example, adults know the irregular form *broke*, and that prevents them from applying the regular "add -ed" rule to *break* and saying *breaked*. But because children have not heard *broke* enough times to remember it reliably on demand, they sometimes fail to block the rule and thus occasionally say *breaked*. As they hear *broke* enough times to recall it reliably, Blocking would suppress the regular rule, and they would gradually recover from these overgeneralization errors (Marcus et al. 1992).

Interactions between Word Meaning and Syntax

Here is another example in which a general principle rules out a form in the adult grammar, but in the child's grammar the crucial information allowing the principle to apply is missing. As the child's knowledge increases, the relevance of the principle to the errant form manifests itself, and the form can be ruled out so as to make the grammar as a whole consistent with the principle.

Every verb has an "argument structure": a specification of what kinds of phrases it can appear with (Pinker 1989). A familiar example is the distinction between a transitive verb like *devour*, which requires a direct object (you can say *He devoured the steak* but not just *He devoured*) and an intransitive verb like *dine*, which does not (you can say *He dined* but not *He dined the steak*). Children sometimes make errors with the argument structures of verbs that refer to the act of moving something to a specified location (Bowerman 1982b; Gropen et al. 1991a):

> I didn't fill water up to drink it; I filled it up for the flowers to drink it.
> Can I fill some salt into the bear? [a bear-shaped salt shaker]
> I'm going to cover a screen over me.
> Feel your hand to that.
> Terri said if this [a rhinestone on a shirt] were a diamond then people would be trying to rob the shirt.

A general principle of argument structure is that the argument that is affected in some way (the particular way is specified by the verb) gets mapped onto the syntactic object. This is an example of a "linking rule," which links semantics with syntax (and which is an example of the contingency a young child would have employed to use semantic information to bootstrap into the syntax). For example, for adults, the "container" argument (where the water goes) is the direct object of fill—*fill the glass with water*, not *fill water into the glass*—because the mental definition of the verb *fill* says that the glass becomes full, but says nothing about how that happens (one can fill a glass by pouring water into it, by dripping water into it, by dipping it into a pond, and so on). In contrast, with a verb like *pour*, it is the "content" argument (the water) that is the object—*pour water into the glass*, not *pour the glass with water*—because the mental definition of the verb *pour* says that the water must move in a certain manner (downward, in a continuous stream) but does not specify what happens to the container (the water might fill the glass, merely wet it, end up beside it, and so on). In both cases the entity specified as "affected" ends up as the object, but for *fill*, it is the object whose *state* is affected (going from not full to full), whereas for *pour*, it is the object whose *location* is affected (going from one place to a lower one).

Now, let's say children mistakenly think that *fill* refers to a manner of motion (presumably, some kind of tipping or pouring) instead of to an end state of fullness. (Children commonly use end-state verbs as manner verbs: for example, they think that *mix* just means *stir*, regardless of whether the stirred ingredients end up mixed together; Gentner 1978). If so, the linking rule for direct objects would cause them to make the error we observe: *fill x into y*. How could they recover? When children observe the verb *fill* in enough contexts to realize that it actually encodes the end state of fullness, not a manner of pouring or any other particular manner (for example, eventually they may hear someone talking about *filling* a glass by leaving it on a window sill during a storm), they can change their mental dictionary entry for *fill*. As a result, they would withdraw it from eligibility to take the argument structure with the contents as direct object, on the grounds that it violates the constraint that "direct object = specifically affected entity." The principle could have existed all along but only been deemed relevant to the verb *fill* when more information about its definition had been accumulated (Gropen et al. 1991a, 1991b; Pinker 1989).

There is evidence that the process works in just that way. Gropen et al. (1991a) asked preschool children to select which picture corresponded to the sentence *She filled the glass with water*. Most children indiscriminately chose any picture showing water pouring; they did not care whether the glass ended up full. This shows that they do misconstrue the meaning of *fill*. In a separate task, the children were asked to describe in their own words what was happening in a picture showing a glass being filled. Many of these children used incorrect sentences like *He's filling water into the glass*. Older children tended to make fewer errors of both verb meaning and verb syntax, and children who got the verb meaning right were less likely to make syntax errors and vice versa. In an even more direct demonstration, Gropen et al. (1991b) taught children new verbs like *to pilk*, referring to actions like moving a sponge over to a cloth. For some children the motion had a distinctive zigzag manner, but the cloth remained unchanged. For others the motion was nondescript, but the cloth changed color in a litmuslike reaction when the sponge ended up on it. Though none of the children heard the verb used in a sentence, when asked to describe the event, the first group said that the experimenter was *pilking the sponge*, whereas the second group said that he was *pilking the cloth*. This is just the kind of inference that would cause a child who finally figured out what *fill* means to stop using it with the wrong direct object.

Interestingly, the connections between verbs' syntax and semantics go both ways. Gleitman (1990) points out that there are some aspects of a verb's meaning that are difficult, if not impossible, for a child to learn by observing only the situations in which the verb is used. For example, verb pairs like *push* and *move*, *give* and *receive*, *win* and *beat*, *buy* and *sell*, *chase* and *flee*, and *drop* and *fall* often can be used to describe the same event; only the perspective assumed by the verb differs. Also, mental verbs like *see*, *know*, and *want* are difficult to infer merely by observing their contexts. Gleitman suggests that the crucial missing information comes from the syntax of the sentence. For example, *fall* is intransitive (*it fell*, not *John fell the ball*); *drop* can be transitive (*He dropped the ball*). This reflects the fact that the meaning of *fall* involves the mere act of plummeting, independent of who, if anyone, caused it, whereas the extra argument of *drop* refers to an agent who is causing the descent. A child could figure out the meaning difference between the two by paying attention to the transitive and intransitive syntax—an example of using syntax to learn semantics, rather than vice versa. (Of course, it can work only if the child has acquired some syntax to begin with.) Similarly, a verb that appears with a clause as its complement (as in *I think that ...*) must refer to a state involving a proposition, and not, say, of motion (there is no verb like *He jumped that he was in the room*). Therefore, a child hearing a verb appearing with a clausal complement can infer that it might be a mental verb.

Naigles (1990) conducted an experiment suggesting that children indeed can learn some of a verb's meaning from the syntax of a sentence it is used in. Children 24 months old first saw a video of a rabbit pushing a duck up and down, while both made large circles with one arm. One group of children heard a voice saying "The rabbit is gorping the duck"; another heard "The rabbit and the duck are gorping." Then both groups saw a pair of screens: one showed the rabbit pushing the duck up and down, neither making arm circles; the other showed the two characters making arm circles, neither pushing down the other. In response to the command "Where's gorping now? Find gorping!" the children who heard the transitive sentence looked at the screen showing the up-and-down action, and the children who heard the intransitive sentence looked at the screen showing the making-circles action. (For a general discussion of how children could use verb syntax to learn verb semantics and vice versa, see Pinker 1994b.)

6.9.3   Parameter-Setting and the Subset Principle

A striking discovery of modern generative grammar is that natural languages seem to be built on the same basic plan. Many differences among languages represent not separate designs but different settings of a few "parameters" that allow languages to vary, or different choices of rule types from a fairly small inventory of possibilities. The notion of a "parameter" is borrowed from mathematics. For example, all of the equations of the form $y = 3x + b$, when graphed, correspond to a family of parallel lines with a slope of 3; the parameter b takes on a different value for each line, and corresponds to how high or low it is on the graph. Similarly, languages may have parameters (see the chapter by Lasnik in this volume).

For example, all languages in some sense have subjects, but there is a parameter corresponding to whether a language allows the speaker to omit the subject in a tensed sentence with an inflected verb. This "null subject" parameter (sometimes called PRO-drop) is set to "off" in English and to "on" in Spanish and Italian (Chomsky 1981). In English one can't say *Goes to the store*, but in Spanish, one can say the equivalent. The reason that this difference is said to be a "parameter," rather than an isolated fact, is that it predicts a variety of more subtle linguistic facts. For example, in null subject languages, one can also use sentences like *Who do you think that left?* and *Ate John the apple*, which are ungrammatical in English. This is because the rules of a grammar interact tightly; if one thing changes, it will have a series of cascading effects throughout the grammar. For example, *Who do you think that left?* is ungrammatical in English because the surface subject of the verb *left* is an inaudible "trace" left behind when the underlying subject, *who*, was moved to the front of the sentence. For reasons we need not cover here, a trace cannot appear after a word like *that*, so its presence taints the sentence. Recall that in Spanish, one can delete subjects. Therefore, one can delete the trace subject of *left*, just like any other subject (yes, one can "delete" a mental symbol even though it would have made no sound to begin with). Since the trace is no longer there, the principle that disallows a trace in that position is no longer violated, and the sentence sounds fine in Spanish.

On this view the child would set parameters on the basis of a few examples from the parental input, and the full complexity of a language will ensue when those parameterized rules interact with one another and with universal principles. The parameter-setting view can help explain the universality and rapidity of the acquisition of language, despite the arcane complexity of what is and is not grammatical (for example, the ungrammaticality of *Who do you think that left?*). When children learn one fact about a language, they can deduce that other facts are also true of it without having to learn them one by one.

This raises the question of how the child sets the parameters. One suggestion is that parameter settings are ordered and that children assume a particular setting as the default case, moving to other settings as the input evidence forces them to (Chomsky 1981). But how would the parameter settings be ordered? One very general rationale comes from the fact that children have no systematic access to negative evidence. Thus, for every case in which parameter setting A generates a subset of the sentences generated by setting B (as in diagrams (c) and (d) of figure 6.1), the child must first hypothesize A, then abandon it for B only if a sentence generated by B but not by A was encountered in the input (Pinker 1984; Berwick, 1985; Osherson, Stob, and Weinstein 1985). The child would then have no need for negative evidence; he or she would never guess too large a language to begin with. (For settings that generate languages that intersect or are disjoint, as in diagrams (a) and (b) of figure 6.1, either setting can be discarded if incorrect, because the child will eventually encounter a sentence that one grammar generates but the other does not.)

Much interesting research in language acquisition hinges on whether children's first guess from among a set of nested possible languages really is the smallest subset. For example, some languages, like English, mandate strict word orders; others, such as Russian and Japanese, list a small set of admissible orders; still others, such as the Australian aborigine language Warlpiri, allow almost total scrambling of word order within a clause. Word order freedom thus seems to be a parameter of variation, and the setting generating the smallest language would obviously be the one dictating fixed word order. If children follow the Subset Principle, they should assume, by default, that languages have a fixed constituent order. They would back off from that prediction if and only if they heard alternative word orders, which indicate that the language does permit constituent order freedom. The alternative is that the child could assume that the default case was constituent order freedom.

If fixed order is indeed the default, children should make few or no word order errors for a fixed-order language like English, and might be conservative in learning freer-word-order languages, sticking with a subset of the sanctioned orders (whether they in fact are conservative would depend on how much evidence of multiple orders they need before leaping to the conclusion that multiple orders are permissible, and on how frequent in parental speech the various orders are). If, on the other hand, free order is the default, children acquiring fixed-word-order languages might go through a stage of overgenerating (saying *give doggie paper*; *give paper doggie*; *paper doggie give*; *doggie paper give*; and so on), while children acquiring free-word-order languages would immediately be able to use all the orders. In fact, as I have mentioned, children learning English never leap to the conclusion that it is a free-word-order language and speak in multiple, often ungrammatical orders (Brown 1973; Braine 1976; Pinker 1984; Bloom, Lightbown, and Hood 1975). Logically speaking, though, that would be consistent with what they hear if they were willing to entertain the possibility that their parents were just conservative speakers of Korean, Russian, or Swedish, where several orders are possible. But children learning Korean, Russian, and Swedish *do* sometimes (though not always) err on the side of caution, using only one of the orders allowed in the language pending further evidence (Brown 1973). It looks as if fixed order is the default, just as the Subset Principle would predict.

Wexler and Manzini (1987) present a particularly nice example concerning the difference between "anaphors" like *herself* and "pronouns" like *her*. An anaphor has to have its antecedent lie a small distance away (measured in terms of phrase size, of course, not number of words); the antecedent is said to be inside the anaphor's "governing category." That is why the sentence *John liked himself* is fine, but *John thought that Mary liked himself* is ungrammatical: *himself* needs an antecedent (like *John*) within the same clause as itself, which it has in the first example but not in the second. Different languages permit different-size governing categories for the equivalents of anaphors like *himself*; in some languages, the translations of both sentences are grammatical. The Subset Principle predicts that children should start off assuming that their language requires the tiniest possible governing category for anaphors, and then expand the possibilities outward as they hear the telltale sentences. Interestingly, for pronouns like *her*, the ordering is predicted to be the opposite. Pronouns *may not* have an antecedent within their governing categories: *John liked him* (meaning *John liked himself*) is ungrammatical, because the antecedent of *him* is too close, but *John thought that Mary liked him* is fine. Sets of languages with bigger and bigger governing categories for pronouns allow fewer and fewer grammatical possibilities, because they define larger ranges in which a pronoun prohibits its antecedent from appearing—an effect of category size on language size that is in the opposite direction to the one that applies to anaphors. Wexler and Manzini thus predict that for pronouns, children should start off assuming that their language requires the *largest* possible governing category, and then shrink the possibilities *inward* as they hear the telltale sentences. They review experiments and spontaneous speech studies that provide some support for this subtle pattern of predictions.

6.10   Conclusion

The topic of language acquisition implicates the most profound questions about our understanding of the human mind, and its subject matter, the speech of children, is endlessly fascinating. The attempt to understand it scientifically, though, is guaranteed to bring on a certain degree of frustration. Languages are complex combinations of elegant principles and historical accidents. We cannot design new ones with independent properties; we are stuck with the confounded ones entrenched in communities. Children, too, were not designed for the benefit of psychologists: their cognitive, social, perceptual, and motor skills are all developing at the same time that their linguistic systems are maturing and their knowledge of a particular language is increasing; none of their behavior reflects one of these components acting in isolation.

Given these problems, it may be surprising that we have learned anything about language acquisition at all, but we have. When we have, I believe, it is only because a diverse set of conceptual and methodological tools has been used to trap the elusive answers to our questions: neurobiology, ethology, linguistic theory, naturalistic and experimental child psychology, cognitive psychology, philosophy of induction, and theoretical and applied computer science. Language acquisition, then, is one of the best examples of the indispensability of the multidisciplinary approach called cognitive science.

Suggestions for Further Reading

A general introduction to language can be found in Pinker 1994a, from which several portions of this chapter were adapted. Besides a chapter on language acquisition, there are chapters on syntactic structure, word structure, universals and change, prescriptive grammar, neurology and genetics, and other topics.

The logical problem of language acquisition is discussed in detail by Wexler and Culicover 1980, by Pinker 1979, 1984, 1987, 1989, by Osherson, Stob, and Weinstein 1985, by Berwick 1985, and by Morgan 1986. Pinker 1979 is a nontechnical introduction. The study of learnability within theoretical computer science has recently taken interesting new turns, reviewed in Kearns and Vazirani 1994, though with little discussion of the special case we are interested in—language acquisition. Brent 1995 contains state-of-the-art computer models of language acquisition, though not all are intended as models of the child.

The most comprehensive recent textbook on language development is Ingram 1994. Among other recent textbooks, Gleason 1993 has a focus on children's and mothers' behavior, whereas Atkinson 1992, Goodluck 1991, and Crain and Lillo-Martin (in press) have more of a focus on linguistic theory. P. Bloom 1993 is an excellent collection of reprinted articles, organized around the acquisition of words and grammar. Hoekstra and Schwartz 1994 is a collection of recent papers more closely tied to theories of generative grammar. Fletcher and MacWhinney 1995 has many useful survey chapters; see also the surveys by Paul Bloom in Gernsbacher 1994 and by Michael Maratsos in Mussen 1983 (4th edition; 5th edition in preparation at the time of this writing).

Earlier collections of important articles include Krasnegor et al. 1991, MacWhinney 1987, Roeper and Williams 1987, Wanner and Gleitman 1982, Baker and McCarthy 1981, Fletcher and Garman 1979, Ferguson and Slobin 1973, Hayes 1970, Brown and Bellugi 1964, and Lenneberg 1964. Slobin 1985a/1993 is a large collection of major reviews on the acquisition of particular languages.

The most ambitious attempts to synthesize large amounts of data on language development into a cohesive framework are Brown 1973, Pinker 1984, and Slobin 1985b. Clark 1993 reviews the acquisition of words. Locke 1993 covers the earliest stages of acquisition, with a focus on speech input and output. Morgan and Demuth (in press) contains papers on children's perception of input speech and its interaction with their language development.

Problems

6.1 "Negative evidence" is reliable information available to a language learner about which strings of words are ungrammatical in the language to be acquired. Which of the following would, and would not, count as negative evidence? Justify your answers.

a. Mother expresses disapproval every time Junior speaks ungrammatically.

b. Father often rewards Junior when he speaks grammatically and often punishes him when he speaks ungrammatically.

c. Mother wrinkles her nose every time Junior speaks ungrammatically and never wrinkles her nose any other time.

d. Father repeats all of Junior's grammatical sentences verbatim and converts all his ungrammatical sentences into grammatical ones.

e. Mother blathers incessantly, uttering all the grammatical sentences of English in order of length—all the two-word sentences, then all the three-word sentences, and so on.

f. Father corrects Junior whenever he produces an overregularization like *breaked*, but never corrects him when he produces a correct past tense form like *broke*.

g. Whenever Junior speaks ungrammatically, Mother responds by correcting the sentence to the grammatical version. When he speaks grammatically, Mother responds with a follow-up that merely recasts the sentence in different words.

h. Whenever Junior speaks ungrammatically, Father changes the subject.

i. Mother never repeats Junior's ungrammatical sentences verbatim, but sometimes repeats his grammatical sentences verbatim.

j. Father blathers incessantly, producing all possible strings of English words, furrowing his brows after every ungrammatical string and pursing his lips after every grammatical sentence.

6.2   Consider three languages. Language A is English, in which a sentence must contain a grammatical subject: *He ate the apple* is good; *Ate the apple* is ungrammatical. In Language B the subject is optional, but the verb always has a suffix that agrees with the subject (whether it is present or absent) in person, number, and gender. Thus *He ate-3MS the apple* is good (assume that "*3MS*" is a suffix, like *-o* or *-ik*, that is used only when the subject is third person masculine singular), as is *Ate-3MS the apple*. (Those of you who speak Spanish or Italian will see that this hypothetical language is similar to them.) Language C has no inflection on the verb but allows the subject to be omitted: *He ate the apple* and *Ate the apple* are both good.

Assume that a child has no access to negative evidence, but knows that the language to be learned is one of the three above. Does the child have to entertain these hypotheses in any fixed order? If so, what is it? What learning strategy would guarantee that the child would arrive at the correct language? Show why.

6.3   Imagine a verb *pilk* that means "to have both of one's elbows grabbed by someone else," so *John pilked Bill* meant that Bill grabbed John's elbows.

a. Why is this verb unlikely to occur in English?

b. If children use semantic context and semantics-syntax linking rules to bootstrap their way into a language, what would a languageless child infer about English upon hearing "This is pilking" and seeing Bill grab John's elbows?

c. If children use semantic context and semantics-syntax linking rules to bootstrap their way into a language, what would a languageless child infer about English upon hearing "John pilked Bill" and seeing Bill grab John's elbows?

d. If children use semantic context and semantics-syntax linking rules to bootstrap their way into a language, what would a child have to experience in order to learn English syntax *and* the correct use of the word *pilk*?

References

Anderson, J. (1977). Induction of augmented transition networks. *Cognitive Science* 1, 125–157.

Atkinson, M. (1992). *Children's syntax: An introduction to principles and parameters theory.* Cambridge, MA: Blackwell.

Baker, C. L., and J. McCarthy, eds. (1981). The logical problem of language acquisition. Cambridge, MA: MIT Press.

Bates, E. (1989). Functionalism and the competition model. In B. MacWhinney and E. Bates, eds., *The crosslinguistic study of sentence processing.* New York: Cambridge University Press.

Bates, E., D. Thal, and J. S. Janowsky (1992). Early language development and its neural correlates. In I. Rapin and S. Segalowitz, eds., *Handbook of neuropsychology.* Vol. 6, *Child Neurology.* Amsterdam: Elsevier.

Bellugi, U., A. Bihrle, T. Jernigan, D. Trauner, and S. Doherty (1990). Neuropsychological, neurological, and neuroanatomical profile of Williams Syndrome. *American Journal of Medical Genetics Supplement* 6, 115–125.

Berwick, R. C. (1985). *The acquisition of syntactic knowledge.* Cambridge, MA: MIT Press.

Bickerton, D. (1984). The language bioprogram hypothesis. *Behavioral and Brain Sciences* 7, 173–221.

Bloom, L. (1970). *Language development: Form and function in emerging grammars.* Cambridge, MA: MIT Press.

Bloom, L., P. Lightbown, and M. Hood (1975). Structure and variation in child language. *Monographs of the Society for Research in Child Development* 40.

Bloom, P., ed. (1993). Language acquisition: Core readings. Cambridge, MA: MIT Press.

Bloom, P. (1994). Possible names: The role of syntax-semantics mappings in the acquisition of nominals. In L. Gleitman and B. Landau, eds., *The acquisition of the lexicon.* Cambridge, MA: MIT Press.

Bohannon, J. N., and L. Stanowicz (1988). The issue of negative evidence: Adult responses to children's language errors. *Developmental Psychology* 24, 684–689.

Bowerman, M. (1982a). Evaluating competing linguistic models with language acquisition data: Implications of developmental errors with causative verbs. *Quaderni di Semantica* 3, 5–66.

Bowerman, M. (1982b). Reorganizational processes in lexical and syntactic development. In E. Wanner and L. Gleitman, eds., *Language acquisition: The state of the art.* New York: Cambridge University Press.

Braine, M. D. S. (1976). Children's first word combinations. *Monographs of the Society for Research in Child Development* 41.

Brent, M., ed. (1995). Special issue of *Cognition* on computational models of language acquisition.

Brown, R. (1973). *A first language: The early stages.* Cambridge, MA: Harvard University Press.

Brown, R., and U. Belluqi, eds. (1964). Special issue of *Harvard Educational Review.*

Brown, R., and C. Hanlon (1970). Derivational complexity and order of acquisition in child speech. In J. R. Hayes, ed., *Cognition and the development of language.* New York: Wiley.

Chomsky, C. (1969). *Acquisition of syntax in children from 5–10.* Cambridge, MA: MIT Press.

Chomsky, N. (1959). A review of B. F. Skinner's *Verbal behavior. Language* 35, 26–58.

Chomsky, N. (1975). *Reflections on language.* New York: Random House.

Chomsky, N. (1981). *Lectures on government and binding.* Dordrecht, Netherlands: Foris.

Chomsky, N. (1991). Linguistics and cognitive science: Problems and mysteries. In A. Kasher, ed., *The Chomskyan turn.* Cambridge, MA: Blackwell.

Clark, E. V. (1993). *The lexicon in acquisition.* New York: Cambridge University Press.

Comrie, B. (1981). *Language universals and linguistic typology.* Chicago: University of Chicago Press.

Cooper, W. E., and J. Paccia-Cooper (1980). *Syntax and speech*. Cambridge, MA: Harvard University Press.

Crain, S. (1992). Language acquisition in the absence of experience. *Behavioral and Brain Sciences* 14, 597–650.

Crain, S., and D. Lillo-Martin (in press). *Language acquisition*. Cambridge, MA: Blackwell.

Cromer, R. F. (1992). *Language and thought in normal and handicapped children*. Cambridge, MA: Blackwell.

Curtiss, S. (1989). The independence and task-specificity of language. In A. Bornstein and J. Bruner, eds., *Interaction in human development*. Hillsdale, NJ: Erlbaum.

Demetras, M. J., K. N. Post, and C. E. Snow (1986). Feedback to first language learners: The role of repetitions and clarification questions. *Journal of Child Language* 13, 275–292.

Ervin-Tripp, S. (1973). Some strategies for the first two years. In T. E. Moore, ed., *Cognitive development and the acquisition of language*. New York: Academic Press.

Ferguson, C., and D. I. Slobin, eds. (1973). *Studies of child language development*. New York: Holt, Rinehart and Winston.

Fernald, A. (1984). The perceptual and affective salience of mothers' speech to infants. In L. Feagans, C. Garvey, and R. Golinkoff, eds., *The origins and growth of communication*. Norwood, NJ: Ablex.

Fernald, A. (1992). Human maternal vocalizations to infants as biologically relevant signals: An evolutionary perspective. In J. H. Barkow, L. Cosmides, and J. Tooby, eds., *The adapted mind: Evolutionary psychology and the generation of culture*. New York: Oxford University Press.

Fernald, A., and G. McRoberts (in press). Prosodic bootstrapping: A critical analysis of the argument and the evidence. In J. L. Morgan and K. Demuth, eds., *Signal to syntax*. Hillsdale, NJ: Erlbaum.

Fletcher, P., and M. Garman, eds. (1979). *Language acquisition*. New York: Cambridge University Press.

Fletcher, P., and B. MacWhinney, eds. (1995). *The handbook of child language*. Cambridge, MA: Blackwell.

Fodor, J. A. (1975). *The language of thought*. Cambridge, MA: Harvard University Press.

Fodor, J. A. (1983). *The modularity of mind*. Cambridge, MA: Bradford Books/MIT Press.

Gardner, R. A., and B. T. Gardner (1969). Teaching sign language to a chimpanzee. *Science* 165, 664–672.

Gentner, D. (1978). On relational meaning: The acquisition of verb meaning. *Child Development* 49, 988–998.

Gernsbacher, M. A., ed. (1994). *Handbook of psycholinguistics*. San Diego: Academic Press.

Gleason, J. Berko, ed. (1993). *The development of language*. 3rd ed. New York: Macmillan.

Gleitman, L. R. (1990). The structural sources of verb meaning. *Language Acquisition* 1, 3–55.

Gleitman, L. R., and E. Wanner (1984). Richly specified input to language learning. In O. Selfridge, E. L. Rissland, and M. Arbib, eds., *Adaptive control of ill-defined systems*. New York: Plenum.

Gold, E. (1967). Language identification in the limit. *Information and Control* 10, 447–474.

Goodluck, H. (1991). *Language acquisition: a linguistic introduction*. Cambridge, MA: Blackwell.

Gopnik, M., and M. Crago (1991). Familiar aggregation of a genetic language disorder. *Cognition* 39, 1–50.

Greenberg, J., ed. (1978). *Universals of human language*. Vol. 4, *Syntax*. Stanford, CA: Stanford University Press.

Grimshaw, J. (1981). Form, function, and the language acquisition device. In C. L. Baker and J. McCarthy, eds., *The logical problem of language acquisition*. Cambridge, MA: MIT Press.

Gropen, J., S. Pinker, M. Hollander, and R. Goldberg (1991a). Syntax and semantics in the acquisition of locative verbs. *Journal of Child Language* 18, 115–151.

Gropen, J., S. Pinker, M. Hollander, and R. Goldberg (1991b). Affectedness and direct objects: The role of lexical semantics in the acquisition of verb argument structure. *Cognition* 41, 153–195.

Hayes, J. R., ed. (1970). *Cognition and the development of language.* New York: Wiley.

Heath, S. B. (1983). *Ways with words: Language, life, and work in communities and classrooms.* New York: Cambridge University Press.

Hirsh-Pasek, K., D. G. N. Nelson, P. W. Jusczyk, K. W. Cassidy, B. Druss, and L. Kennedy, (1987). Clauses are perceptual units for young infants. *Cognition* 26, 269–286.

Hirsh-Pasek, K., R. Treiman, and M. Schneiderman (1984). Brown and Hanlon revisited: Mothers' sensitivity to ungrammatical forms. *Journal of Child Language* 11, 81–88.

Hirsh-Pasek, K., and R. M. Golinkoff (1991). Language comprehension: A new look at some old themes. In N. Krasnegor, D. M. Rumbaugh, R. L. Schiefelbusch, and M. Studdert-Kennedy, eds., *Biological and behavioral determinants of language development.* Hillsdale, NJ: Erlbaum.

Hoekstra, T., and B. Schwartz, eds. (1994). *Language acquisition studies in generative grammar.* Philadelphia: John Benjamins.

Huttenlocher, P. R. (1990). Morphometric study of human cerebral cortex development. *Neuropsychologia* 28, 517–527.

Ingram, D. (1994). *First language acquisition: Method, description, and explanation,* 2nd ed. New York: Cambridge University Press.

Kearns, M. J., and U. V. Vazirani (1994). *An introduction to computational learning theory.* Cambridge, MA: MIT Press.

Kegl, J. (1994). The Nicaraguan sign language project: An overview. *Signpost* 7, 32–39.

Kiparsky, P. (1982). Lexical phonology and morphology. In I. S. Yang, ed., *Linguistics in the morning calm.* Seoul: Hansin.

Krasnegor, N. A., D. M. Rumbaugh, R. L. Schiefelbusch, and M. Studdert-Kennedy, eds., (1991) *Biological and behavioral determinants of language development.* Hillsdale, NJ: Erlbaum.

Kuhl, P., K. A. Williams, F. Lacerda, K. N. Stevens, and B. Lindblom (1992). Linguistic experience alters phonetic perception in infants by six months of age. *Science* 255, 606–608.

Labov, W. (1969). The logic of nonstandard English. *Georgetown Monographs on Language and Linguistics* 22, 1–31.

Landau, B., and L. R. Gleitman (1985). *Language and experience.* Cambridge, MA: Harvard University Press.

Lenneberg, E. H. (1967). *Biological foundations of language.* New York: Wiley.

Lenneberg, E. H., ed. (1984). *New directions in the study of language.* Cambridge, MA: MIT Press.

Levy, Y. (1983). It's frogs all the way down. *Cognition* 15, 75–93.

Lieberman, P. (1984). *The biology and evolution of language.* Cambridge, MA: Harvard University Press.

Limber, J. (1973). The genesis of complex sentences. In T. E. Moore, ed. *Cognitive development and the acquisition of language.* New York: Academic Press.

Locke, J. L. (1992). Structure and stimulation in the ontogeny of spoken language. *Developmental Psychobiology* 28, 430–440.

Locke, J. L. (1993). *The child's path to spoken language.* Cambridge, MA: Harvard University Press.

Macnamara, J. (1972). Cognitive basis of language learning in infants. *Psychological Review* 79, 1–13.

Macnamara, J. (1982). *Names for things: A study of child language*. Cambridge, MA: MIT Press.

MacWhinney, B. (1991). *The CHILDES project: Computational tools for analyzing talk*. 2nd ed. Hillsdale, NJ: Erlbaum.

MacWhinney, B., ed. (1987). *Mechanisms of language acquisition*. Hillsdale, NJ: Erlbaum.

MacWhinney, B., and C. Snow (1985). The child language data exchange system. *Journal of Child Language* 12, 271−296.

MacWhinney, B., and C. Snow (1990). The child language data exchange system: An update. *Journal of Child Language* 17, 457−472.

Maratsos, M. P. (1974). How preschool children understand missing complement subjects. *Child Development* 45, 700−706.

Maratsos, M. P., and M. Chalkley (1981). The internal language of children's syntax: The ontogenesis and representation of syntactic categories. In K. Nelson, ed., *Children's Language*. Vol. 2. New York: Gardner Press.

Marcus, G. F. (1993). Negative evidence in language acquisition. *Cognition, 46*, 53−85.

Marcus, G. F., S. Pinker, M. Ullman, M. Hollander, T. J. Rosen, and F. Xu (1992). Overregularization in language acquisition. *Monographs of the Society for Research in Child Development 57*.

Miller, G. A. (1991). *The science of words*. New York: W. H. Freeman.

Morgan, J. L. (1986). *From simple input to complex grammar*. Cambridge, MA: MIT Press.

Morgan, J. L., and K. Demuth, eds. (in press). *Signal to syntax*. Hillsdale, NJ: Erlbaum.

Mussen, P., ed. (1983). *Carmichael's manual of child psychology*. 4th ed. New York: Wiley.

Naigles, L. (1990). Children use syntax to learn verb meanings. *Journal of Child Language* 17, 357−374.

Newport, E., H. Gleitman, and E. Gleitman (1977). Mother, I'd rather do it myself: Some effects and non-effects of maternal speech style. In C. E. Snow and C. A. Ferguson, eds., *Talking to children: Language input and acquisition*. Cambridge: Cambridge University Press.

Osherson, D. N., M. Stob, and S. Weinstein (1985). *Systems that learn*. Cambridge, MA: MIT Press.

Penner, S. (1987). Parental responses to grammatical and ungrammatical child utterances. *Child Development* 58: 376−384.

Piaget, J. (1926). *The language and thought of the child*. New York: Routledge & Kegan Paul.

Pinker, S. (1979). Formal models of language learning. *Cognition* 7, 217−283.

Pinker, S. (1984). *Language learnability and language development*. Cambridge, MA: Harvard University Press.

Pinker, S. (1987). The bootstrapping problem in language acquisition. In B. MacWhinney, ed., *Mechanisms of language acquisition*. Hillsdale, NJ: Erlbaum.

Pinker, S. (1989). *Learnability and cognition: The acquisition of argument structure*. Cambridge, MA: MIT Press.

Pinker, S. (1994a). *The language instinct*. New York: Morrow.

Pinker, S. (1994b). How could a child use verb syntax to learn verb semantics? *Lingua 92*, 377−410. Reprinted in L. Gleitman and B. Landau, eds., *The acquisition of the lexicon*. Cambridge, MA: MIT Press.

Pinker, S., and P. Bloom (1990). Natural language and natural selection. *Behavioral and Brain Sciences 13*, 707−784.

Premack, D., and A. J. Premack (1983). *The mind of an ape*. New York: Norton.

Putnam, H. (1971). The "innateness hypothesis" and explanatory models in linguistics. In J. Searle, ed., *The philosophy of language*. New York: Oxford University Press.

Roeper, T., and E. Williams, eds. (1987). *Parameter-setting and language acquisition*. Dordrecht, Netherlands: Reidel.

Savage-Rumbaugh, E. S. (1991). Language learning in the bonobo: How and why they learn. In N. A. Krasnegor, D. M. Rumbaugh, R. L. Schiefelbusch, and M. Studdert-Kennedy, eds., *Biological and behavioral determinants of language development*. Hillsdale, NJ: Erlbaum.

Schieffelin, B., and A. R. Eisenberg (1981). Cultural variation in children's conversations. In R. L. Schiefelbusch and D. D. Bricker, eds., *Early language: Acquisition and intervention*. Baltimore: University Park Press.

Schlesinger, I. M. (1971). Production of utterances and language acquisition. In D. I. Slobin, ed., *The ontogenesis of grammar*. New York: Academic Press.

Seidenberg, M. S. (1986). Evidence from great apes concerning the biological bases of language. In W. Demopoulos and A. Marras, eds., *Language learning and concept acquisition*. Norwood, NJ: Ablex.

Seidenberg, M. S., and L. A. Petitto (1979). Signing behavior in apes: A critical review. *Cognition 7*, 177–215.

Seidenberg, M. S., and L. A. Petitto (1987). Communication, symbolic communication, and language: Comment on Savage-Rumbaugh, McDonald, Sevcik, Hopkins, and Rupert (1986), *Journal of Experimental Psychology: General 116*, 279–287.

Senghas, A. (1994). Nicaragua's lessons for language acquisition. *Signpost, 7*, 32–39.

Shopen, T., ed. (1985). *Language typology and syntactic description*. Vol. 2, *Complex constructions*. New York: Cambridge University Press.

Slobin, D. (1973). Cognitive prerequisites for the development of grammar. In C. Ferguson and D. I. Slobin, eds., *Studies in child language development*. New York: Holt, Rinehart and Winston.

Slobin, D. I. (1977). Language change in childhood and in history. In J. Macnamara, ed., *Language learning and thought*. New York: Academic Press.

Slobin, D. I., ed. (1985a/1992). *The crosslinguistic study of language acquisition*. Vols. 1 and 2, 1985; Vol. 3, 1992. Hillsdale, NJ: Erlbaum.

Slobin, D. I. (1985b). Crosslinguistic evidence for the language-making capacity. In D. I. Slobin, ed., *The crosslinguistic study of language acquisition*. Vol. 2, *Theoretical issues*. Hillsdale, NJ: Erlbaum.

Snow, C. E., and C. A. Ferguson (1977). *Talking to children: Language input and acquisition*. Cambridge: Cambridge University Press.

Steedman, M. (in press). Phrasal intonation and the acquisition of syntax. In J. Morgan and K. Demuth, eds., *Signal to syntax*. Hillsdale, NJ: Erlbaum.

Stromswold, K. (1994). What a mute child tells us about language. Unpublished manuscript, Rutgers University.

Tallal, P., R. Ross, and S. Curtiss (1989). Familial aggregation in specific language impairment. *Journal of Speech and Hearing Disorders, 54*, 167–171.

Terrace, H., L. A. Petitto, R. J. Sanders, and T. G. Bever (1979). Can an ape create a sentence? *Science 206*, 891–902.

Wallman, J. (1992). *Aping language*. New York: Cambridge University Press.

Wanner, E., and L. Gleitman, eds. (1982). *Language acquisition: The state of the art*. New York: Cambridge University Press.

Wexler, K., and P. Culicover (1980). *Formal principles of language acquisition*. Cambridge, MA: MIT Press.

Wexler, K., and R. Manzini (1987). Parameters and learnability in binding theory. In T. Roeper and E. Williams, eds., *Parameters and linguistic theory*. Dordrecht, Netherlands: Reidel.

Whorf, B. (1956). *Language, thought, and reality*. Cambridge, MA: MIT Press.

Chapter 7

Speaking and Misspeaking

Gary S. Dell

Several years ago, U.S. President Gerald Ford toasted Egyptian President Anwar Sadat and "the great people of Israel—Egypt, excuse me." Later this incident was reported to me by a friend like this: "I heard Freud made a Fordian slip... [laughs] wait..." Whether we like it or not, slips of the tongue are a fact of life. For normal speakers of English, one or two errors occur on average about every thousand words (Garnham et al. 1981; Hotopf 1983) and, as far as we can tell, all speakers of all languages make them. Analogous errors occur in sign languages and in writing and typing—basically in all media in which language is produced.

Besides providing a source of amusement, embarrassment, and armchair psychoanalysis, speech errors are an excellent source of data for understanding the nature of language and how it is produced. It is useful to think of slips as data for language in the same way that collisions of atoms and subatomic particles provide data for physics. Consider the slip of saying "darn bore" for "barn door." It is as if the words *barn* and *door* "collided" and broke apart into pieces that then recombined to make new words. By studying word collisions such as these, we can determine the nature of the pieces of language and the laws that govern their combinations. In the case of "darn bore" for "barn door" we might characterize the slip as the *exchange* of /b/ and /d/, thus providing evidence that things such as /d/ and /b/, *phonemes*, are building blocks of speech. We might furthermore hypothesize from the fact that the /d/ from *door* moved to a word-initial position to make *darn* and that the /b/ from *barn* moved to a word-initial position to make *bore* that the phonemes are coded for position. In general, by looking at many such errors, one can formulate and test hypotheses about language production. In this chapter we will examine both how researchers use speech errors as data in cognitive science and some of their conclusions.

7.1 Studying Slips of the Tongue

How do you get a sizable number of slips to study? The easiest thing to do is to collect them from natural speech. Often, researchers attempt to write down all of the slips that they hear. This is what Meringer and Mayer (1895), the first to systematically study speech errors, did. It was soon recognized, though, that trying to listen for and write down all slips conflicts with normal living and, hence, creates a sample biased toward errors that are most noticeable—often the bizarre or funny slips, such as the two "Fordian" slips presented above. Consequently, many collectors listen for slips only during short periods of time when they are able to attend to error monitoring. Even though this method can miss and miscode errors (Ferber 1993), trained collectors who work only at specific times have gathered large and valuable collections. The most accurate way to build a collection, however, is to tape-record speech samples and then to study the recording carefully for errors. This time-consuming work, however, rarely gets enough errors for quantitative tests of hypotheses. For example, Garnham et al. (1981) went through a sample of around 200,000 words and came up with fewer than 200 slips.

Because of the limitations associated with collections of natural slips, some investigators try to bring the phenomenon into the laboratory by creating slips in controlled experiments. For example, Baars, Motley, and MacKay (1975) presented subjects with written word pairs, at a rate of about one pair per second. After some pairs a tone sounded, directing the subject to say the most recent pair as quickly as possible. By cleverly setting up the word pair sequence, these researchers were able to induce phoneme exchanges in about 10 percent of the trials. In fact, their experiment made a significant discovery, namely, that exchanges such as "beal dack" for "deal back," in which the spoken output consists of nonwords, are about three times less likely than exchanges that create words, such as "bean dad" for "dean bad." This conclusion was possible because their experiment controlled for other possible factors by comparing the slip rate to pairs such as "deal back," whose initial consonants exchange to produce nonwords, with an equal number of similar pairs such as "dean bad," which exchange to produce words. This ability to test specific hypotheses, while controlling for extraneous factors, is an advantage of the experimental approach over natural error collection. Furthermore, experiments allow for accurate recordings. Of course, one must acknowledge the disadvantages as well: By creating artificial slips, the experimenter may be altering the processes of speech production to such an extent that the artificial slips are not indicative of natural production. In general, one hopes that conclusions from experimental and natural data agree because each method compensates for shortcomings in the other. To a large extent, such agreement is the case (Stemberger 1992).

7.2   The Freudian Approach

Most people associate the study of speech errors with Freud and with the claim that slips result from a conflict between what one plans to say and some unconscious intention. Often, the slip will reveal the repressed intention, according to this view; for example, Freud (1901/1958) interpreted an error from a patient who replaced the German word *schwer* ("heavy") with *Schwest* (first syllable of "sister") as evidence for the speaker's unconscious concern about his sister. Notice that the tendency for phonological exchanges to create words over nonwords discovered in the 1975 Baars experiment can be seen as support for the claim that slips reveal thoughts other than intended ones. It is, however, a big jump to conclude next that the revealed unintended thoughts were *repressed* and that the slip actually has the *function* of giving that thought expression. In fact, the orthodox Freudian view of speech errors has at least three problems. First, the approach is characterized by interpretation of slips *after the fact*. So, if a host introduces a guest like this: "It is my great pleasure to prevent...I mean, present ...," one could speculate that this introduction is not being made with the greatest of pleasure, at least unconsciously. But how are we to verify that this is the case? The way to validate a scientific statement is to derive and test predictions from it. Although one could imagine trying to predict future slips that this host might make from some hypothesized unconscious attitude toward the guest, in practice such predictions would be nearly impossible to derive. Consequently, empirical tests of Freudian after-the-fact interpretations of slips are lacking. (For a review of such attempts see Baars 1992). The second problem is that, when one looks informally for psychodynamic influences in slips that are collected from unbiased sources such as tape recordings, one is hard-pressed to find them, (Ellis 1980). So, Freudian interpretations may be hard to come up with for most real slips, even when one tries after the fact.[1] Finally, even if we grant that slips are psychodynamically caused, we are going to have to acknowledge that this perspective offers little insight into the complexity of the data. As we will show, speech errors come in all shapes and sizes, but we can make sense of this complexity only by adopting an alternative perspective, one that focuses on the structure of language and its use.

---

1. Of course, one can always counter this objection by saying that interpreting an error requires more knowledge than is typically available. If so, though, we are back to the difficulty of the testability of the theory.

7.3   A Cognitive Science Approach

The alternative to the Freudian view that this chapter develops is that the characteristics of slips are the result of the information-processing requirements of producing language. We will thus try to explain why someone says "prevent" instead of "present," not by discovering their repressed wishes but by explicating the *task* of utterance generation.

It may seem odd to refer to everyday talking as a task, because our impression is that it does not require a great deal of mental computation. This impression is wrong. First of all, an utterance is a very complex thing. As other chapters in this volume show, utterances can be described in several different ways. More precisely, each sentence is associated with distinct representations for each type of linguistic knowledge. These types of knowledge, or *levels*, include *semantics*, which represents the meaning of the utterance; *syntax*, which specifies the words and their arrangement; and *phonology*, which deals with the sounds of the words. Each level's representation focuses on different facts about the utterance; for example, the syntactic representation of "pass the salt" would, among other things, indicate that "pass" is the main verb, and that "the salt" is a noun phrase and direct object of "pass." The phonological representation would specify the sounds that make up each syllable, for example, that *the* is pronounced as "thuh" rather than "thee" in this context. To construct a sentence such as "pass the salt," one must mentally represent its meaning, choose words and determine their arrangement, and specify the sounds of the words; that is, one must build semantic, syntactic, and phonological representations of the utterance. Moreover, at each level there are rules to be followed; for instance, the direct object "the salt" must follow, not precede, the verb. Or, the word *the* must be pronounced "thuh" if it is before a word beginning with a consonant. In short, utterances are associated with rules and representations at more than one linguistic level, and the language production system must deal with this complexity.

The fact that utterances are constructed at different levels is closely related to another property of language, its *creativity*. A great many of the sentences that we utter are being spoken for the first time. Our ability to combine words in new ways can be thought of as syntactic creativity. Other levels of representation are also associated with creativity of a sort. We have the ability to produce and recognize novel words made up of existing morphemes, as in the sentence "My musical tastes are pre-Bachian." The term "pre-Bachian" illustrates *morphological* creativity, morphology being a linguistic level concerned with word building that is sometimes distinguished from syntax and phonology. There is even a form of phonological creativity associated with the fact that we see some novel combinations of speech sounds as potential words (for example, *snurk*), while others (like *nsukf*) could never be considered words because they are not pronounceable. In sum, language allows for creativity in the way that words—and to a lesser extent, morphemes and sounds—are combined. The language production system must reflect this fact.

A final aspect of language production is that the relevant decisions have to be made fast. A speaker produces more than three words per second, each word having been chosen from a vocabulary of more than forty thousand words. What is more, most of these words consist of several speech sounds, each of which must be produced in correct sequence. These temporal constraints contribute greatly to the task of production.

Thus, we see that our impression of the effortlessness of talking is misleading. Generating an utterance requires the rapid building of novel combinations of linguistic units, a process that must go on at several linguistic levels and, hence, must be sensitive to a variety of rules—rules about word order, word building, and word pronunciation. Given all these complications, one should not be surprised that errors occur. However, the hypothesis that cognitive science offers about speech errors is more specific than just saying that slips occur because talking is hard. I will show, rather, that the characteristics of slips are derivable from what is known about language and language production. In particular I offer the hypothesis that slips occur and have the properties that they do because of the need for creativity at each linguistic level. To defend this idea, we first need to look more closely at the data.

7.4   Kinds of Slips

One of the most noticeable things about speech errors is that different-sized linguistic units can slip. The *Egypt-Israel* example involves the substitution of one word for another, while the *barn door—darn bore* slip was characterized as the exchange of phonemes. Linguistic theory proposes the existence of a variety of linguistic units smaller than a sentence: clause, phrase, word, morpheme, syllable, syllable part (such as the VC part of a CVC syllable), consonant cluster, phoneme, phonological feature. For each of these unit sizes, there seem to be slips.[2] The examples (1)–(6) below illustrate some of the types. In all cases the target utterance is "I wanted to read the letter to my grandmother."[3]

---

2. Of course, there is variation depending on the language being spoken; for example, if a language has no consonant clusters, then there can be no consonant cluster slips. The data presented in this chapter come from English, but the conclusions that we offer are hypothesized to be true for other languages. In general, though, there is a need for the study of slips in languages other than English and German.

3. Unlike the other examples given, these were not actually occurring slips.

(1)   phrase (exchange)—"I wanted to read *my grandmother* to *the letter."*

(2)   word (noncontextual substitution)—"I wanted to read the *envelope* to my grandmother."

(3)   inflectional morpheme (shift)—"I want to read*ed* the letter to my grandmother."

(4)   stem morpheme (exchange)—"I *read*ed to *want* the letter to my grandmother."

(5)   consonant cluster (anticipation)—"I wanted to read the *gr*etter to my grandmother."

(6)   phonological feature (anticipation or perseveration)—"I wanted to read the letter to my *b*randmother."

Notice that each slip is categorized with regard to both the size of the slipping unit and the nature of the disturbance. We have already seen examples of exchanges before, such as "Freud made a Fordian slip," where two parts of the speech stream exchange places, leaving something between them undisturbed. In the phrasal exchange (1), the noun phrases exchange, leaving the "to" in place. Error (4) involves the exchange of the stem morphemes "want" and "read," leaving in place the "ed" and "to." *Anticipations* and *perseverations* are closely related to exchanges. In (5), the consonant cluster /gr/ is anticipated; that is, it comes out earlier than it should and replaces some other material—the sound /l/ in this case. Notice that had the slip been "...*gr*etter to my *l*andmother," we would call it an exchange. A perseveration is the reverse of an anticipation, for example, "a letter to my *l*andmother." Sometimes, we cannot tell whether a substitution is an anticipation or perseveration. In (6) the sound /g/ is replaced with /b/. Where did the /b/ come from? One possibility is that this is a phonological feature error. If the sound /g/, which contains the *velar* feature (for a back place of articulation), acquires the *bilabial* feature (front place of articulation) of the sound /m/, the resulting sound is a /b/. However, there are two /m/'s that could have supplied the bilabial feature, one in "my" and one in "grandmother." Hence, we cannot say whether this feature was anticipated or perseverated or, for that matter, whether both /m/'s together caused the error to occur. *Shift* errors, like exchanges, anticipations, and perseverations, involve the movement of some linguistic unit, such as the past tense morpheme *ed* in error (3). The difference is that, in a shift, the moving unit does not replace anything; it just jumps from its correct spot to an earlier or later location. Error (2) is an example of a *noncontextual* slip. These occur when a linguistic unit from outside of the intended utterance is spoken. In the noncontextual word substitution (2), "envelope" replaces "letter," likely because of its similarity in meaning.

There are four points I would like to make about these error types. First, it should be clear that speech can go wrong in many different ways. This by itself shows something of the complexity of language production. Second, slips are not just a random scrambling of sounds; rather, there are strong constraints on how things go awry. For example, when a unit participates in an exchange, it likely exchanges with another of more or less the same size and kind (such as the two noun phrases in (1)). Similarly, when the *ed* shifted positions in (3), it moved to the end of another word, as is fitting for a suffix. The third point is that interference can come both from within the utterance as in examples (1) and (3–6) and from outside the utterance as in example (2). It appears that, when we are attempting to produce a particular word or sound, other linguistic material has the potential to be spoken: material from upcoming words, from previously spoken words, and from items that are not intended anywhere in the utterance. Another way to say this is that when we should be *activating* a particular unit, other units are partially activated as well.

Finally, it should be pointed out that it is not easy to categorize slips. For instance, we could not tell if error (6) was an anticipation or a perseveration. In fact, error categorization is always a theory-laden decision. For example, a theory that explains error (6) as the movement of a particular token of a linguistic unit from one place to another would require that the error be called either a perseveration or an anticipation, but not both. An alternate theory might allow that the error is both at once, for instance, because the theory thinks of anticipatory and perseveratory influences as sources of excitation that can sum together. Consider another example of ambiguity, the "Freud made a Fordian slip" case. Normally, this would be called an exchange of stem morphemes, *Freud* and *Ford*. But it also could be categorized as the exchange of the /roy/ and /or/ sound sequences. Here is where theory comes in. It so happens that the /roy/ and /or/ parts of *Freud* and *Ford*, respectively, are not considered to be single linguistic units in theories of phonological structure. It is simpler, therefore, to hypothesize that whole morphemes exchanged, rather than to say that it so happened that the particular phoneme sequences /roy/ and /or/ exchanged. In fact, some additional support for saying that the slip is really an exchange of meaningful units, rather than particular sounds, comes from the fact that the two morphemes are both proper names. In general, though, one cannot be sure about what unit or units are slipping. Particular categorization decisions are always going to be theory-laden. This fact, in turn, means that one must be careful when interpreting error patterns as support for theory, notably when the theory was assumed beforehand in the categorization.

Despite the ambiguities in categorization, there appear to be some solid facts regarding the size of the linguistic units that slip. Figure 7.1 (adapted

FREQUENCIES OF UNITS IN ERRORS

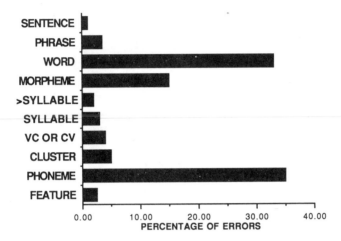

Figure 7.1
Rough estimate of the frequencies of linguistic units in exchange errors. Figure is from Bock 1991.

from Bock 1991) shows the relative rates at which the units participate in exchanges (based on error rates from English natural collections, cited by Stemberger 1982; Garrett 1975; and Shattuck-Hufnagel 1983). I have chosen to focus on exchanges here because these errors are more easily noticed and are, consequently, less likely to be missed by collectors. Although all the various-sized linguistic units do participate in exchanges, some units are much more vulnerable than others. There are two large bumps in the graph, and one medium-sized bump. The large bumps are at the level of the word and the level of the single phoneme. The medium bump is at the level of the morpheme. Why these units? Researchers suggest that the most slippable units are the most basic units in language production, and that each of these—the word, the morpheme, and the phoneme—is the building block for a particular linguistic level. The word is the basic unit for the syntactic level, and the phoneme is the basic unit of the phonological level. The fact that there is a medium-sized bump at the morpheme suggests that we may also wish to consider the possibility of a separate morphological level. In sum, the distribution of the frequency of slip sizes corresponds roughly with the levels of language that linguists have derived for independent reasons.

Why is each linguistic level associated with slips that are predominantly of a particular size? I believe that one must take the "building block" analogy very seriously. The claim is that, when one produces a sentence, one first *builds* a syntactic structure whose elementary units are words. Then one *builds* any morphologically complex words out of existing morphemes. Finally, one *builds* the sound structure of individual words out of phonemes. Now, the alternative to building a representation is to have it prefabricated, stored, and called into action when it is needed. Let us call this alternative to building a representation, *retrieving* a representation. So, the claim is that, to the extent that a representation is built rather than retrieved, you can get slips, predominantly those involving the building blocks of that representation. Slips arise where there is some creativity in the production process—where the system actually builds rather than retrieves. This seems intuitively correct because slips are, themselves, creative combinations of units. When one says "I have to fill up my gas with car," one has produced a novel combination of words. Or in the error "In concludement ..." (for *conclusion*), the speaker has built a new "word" out of old morphemes. Finally, when one says "thollow hud" (for *hollow thud*), one has creatively arranged phonemes to make new pronounceable strings. Let us consider the relation between slips and linguistic creativity in more detail by considering, first, word errors and their relation to syntactic processes, and then errors involving individual speech sounds and phonological processes.

7.5   Word Errors and the Building of Sentences

One of the most striking facts about word slips, such as exchanges, anticipations, perseverations, and noncontextual substitutions, is that they obey a *syntactic category rule*. When one word erroneously replaces another, most of the time the target and substituting word are of the same syntactic category.[4] Nouns slip with nouns, verbs with verbs, and so on. Consider the examples that we've seen thus far. *Egypt*, a proper noun, was replaced by *Israel*, another proper noun; *gas* and *car*, both nouns, exchanged places. Other examples include the exchange of verbs in "Once I *stop*, I can't *start*," or prepositions in "Every time I put one of these buttons *off*, another one comes *on*." One way to account for these facts is to assume that these errors occur during the construction of a syntactic representation of the utterance. More specifically, it has been suggested that the processing goes like this: Based on the intended meaning of the utterance (the semantic representation), words are retrieved from the mental lexicon, the store of words that we already know. For example, if one wished to state the universal proposition that DOGS CHASE CATS, the nouns *dog* and *cat*

4. For word substitutions, the effect is very strong, 95 percent of the time (Fay and Cutler 1977). For exchanges, the effect is also very strong, provided that the exchanged words are far apart (Garrett 1975).

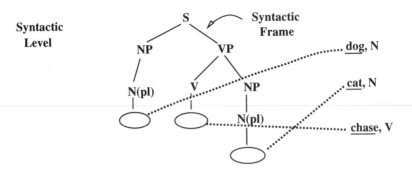

Figure 7.2
A syntactic frame for "dogs chase cats."

and the verb *chase* might be retrieved. Furthermore, a syntactic *frame* is constructed that indicates the potential structure of the sentence. This frame, an example of which is shown in figure 7.2, can be thought of as a tree that indicates the grammatical relations among the words in the sentence. The frame by itself, however, does not initially contain any words; it has empty *slots* for the words to go into, slots that are assumed to be labeled for syntactic category. In our example the frame might specify that there is to be a noun phrase, consisting of a plural noun that is the subject of the sentence followed by a main verb in the present tense and another plural noun that is the direct object. Now, to actually complete the representation, the words retrieved from the lexicon have to be inserted into the frame slots. How is it known which words go in which slots? The labels on the slots are assumed to guide insertion. *Chase*, being a verb, will go only in the verb slot, and *dog* and *cat* will go only in noun slots. But what determines which noun goes where? Presumably, the semantic representation distinguishes between the chaser, or *agent*, and the chased, or *patient*; and there is a rule for this frame that the agent goes in the first, or subject, noun phrase. If there is some difficulty in making use of the semantic representation, then one might expect errors of insertion, such as the exchange "Cats chase dogs." But, even though the insertion went wrong in this example, it was nonetheless correct in that nouns went into noun slots.

Word errors that obey the syntactic category rule, particularly exchanges, provide good evidence for the idea that sentences are built by placing (and sometimes misplacing) word units in labeled slots in syntactic frames. This suggests that the errors ultimately arise because of the need for the syntactic level to be creative. A system that knows the nouns *cat* and *dog*, the verb *chase*, and the structural frame shown in figure 7.2 not only is capable of building "Dogs chase cats" but can also make "Cats chase dogs." This is possible because the system separates syntactic patterns (the frame) from the words, with the result that the system implies the existence of sentences other than those that may have already been produced. So, because the system must be capable of producing "Cats chase dogs" when it wants to, it may also produce "Cats chase dogs" when it does not want to.

The proposal that word slips result from the system's creativity is consistent with other facts. For instance, sometimes one's utterances are not novel. How many times have you said "What time is it?" or "Excuse me, please"? It has been suggested that producing nonnovel utterances may involve retrieval of a prefabricated representation, rather than the building of a representation by actively inserting words into frame slots (for example, MacKay 1982). If this is so, one would expect fewer slips in nonnovel utterances. Experiments that have examined the effects of practicing particular utterances have shown that this expectation is true (Schwartz et al. 1994). Another example of the influence of the system's creativity concerns syntactic flexibility. Often, the same semantic representation can be associated with more than one syntactic representation. Consider the fact that "Dogs chase cats" means roughly the same thing as "Cats are chased by dogs." Hence, when one wishes to make a statement about dogs as chasers and cats as chasees, one must choose between a frame for the active voice or the passive voice. It has been suggested by Ferriera (1994) that this flexibility could contribute to error. Suppose that the active voice frame is eventually chosen but that the passive frame was a strong contender, losing out only at the end. It may then happen that the rule for assigning *dog* and *cat* to noun positions appropriate for the passive—namely, assign the patient to the subject position—may be erroneously called upon. The result of the passive assignment rule and the active frame is the error "Cats chase dogs." An actual error that suggests the influence of syntactic flexibility is "I'm mailing a *mother* to my *letter*." This could have resulted from a mix of the frame for "I'm mailing a letter to my mother" and the assignment of nouns suitable for "I'm mailing my mother a letter."

7.6   Semantic and Phonological Relations in Word Errors

Thus far, we have said that word errors obey a syntactic category rule: A word is erroneously replaced with another of the same category. In fact, this rule is the main reason that word errors are said to be associated with the construction of a syntactic representation. This raises the question: Do the other properties of words—their semantic and phonological properties, for instance—also play a role in word errors? The answer is that they do play a role, but a different and arguably less central role. Consider semantic relations. It is common for one kind of word error, noncontextual word substitutions, to involve a semantically similar error word replacing the target word. For example, *knee* might replace *elbow*, or *black* might replace *white*. *Israel* for *Eygpt* is another clear example. For other kinds of word errors, such as exchanges, anticipations, and perseverations, semantic similarity between the interacting words is less evident; for instance, "I'm writing a *mother* to my *letter*." In addition to semantic similarity between the error and target words, one can see more complex relations due to meaning. When a speaker says "Lizst's second Hungarian *restaurant*," where "Hungarian *rhapsody*" was intended, the replacing and replaced words are themselves not semantically related. It seems, however that both words are associated to *Hungarian*, suggesting that the intention to say *Hungarian* brought along the associated *restaurant*.

What about phonological relations in word errors? Is there any tendency for words related in sound to replace one another in slips? If you have been trying to analyze the word slips presented thus far, you may already have an opinion on this matter. In *restaurant* for *rhapsody*, both words begin with /r/ and are three syllables long with first-syllable stress. Another example that we gave involved an exchange of *start* and *stop*, both beginning with /st/. It certainly looks as if the interacting words in word slips sometimes are phonologically related. In fact, there are many slips in which the only similarity between the words is phonological, aside from the words' similarity in syntactic category, for instance, *prevent* for *present* (the verb preSENT). But we must be careful when drawing conclusions about the effect of phonological relations or, for that matter, about any kind of similarity between error and target words. This is because, thus far, we have been doing the same thing that Freud did—we have been interpreting slips after the fact. When we see a slip of *prevent* for *present*, we say, "I bet this one occurred because of the phonological similarity." The problem is that the similarity may have arisen by chance. How, then, can you tell whether phonological similarity matters? Well, for a single error, you cannot. But it can be shown that there is a tendency for error and target words to be phonologically similar by assessing the degree to which a representative sample of word errors exhibits the similarity and by comparing that degree with what would be expected if words randomly replaced one another. There are a number of predictions that can be tested. For example, do the target and error words share their initial sounds more often than chance, or their main vowels, or their stress patterns? In general, tests of these and related predictions show that phonological relations are quite strong in word substitution errors and seem to be present in other word errors such as exchanges (Dell and Reich 1981; Harley 1984). For example, substituted words in English share the initial sound with their corresponding target words around 35 percent of the time. By chance, you would expect this to happen only around 5 percent of the time.

When we speak of the semantic, syntactic, and phonological similarity between slipping words, we are dealing with information that is associated with different linguistic levels. How is it that all these different levels are involved in word errors? We have said that the word substitution errors may *happen* at the syntactic level, and our main reason for this was that the interacting words in substitutions, exchanges, and other word errors are constrained to be in the same syntactic category. The effect is so strong that we called it the *syntactic category rule*. There is no such "rule" with regard to semantic or phonological similarity; rather, semantic and phonological effects are best described as tendencies or influences. Hence, we can say that when one word replaces another, they are *required* to be of the same major syntactic category and will *tend* to show other aspects of similarity.

We have suggested that the similarity of syntactic category arises because word errors occur when the wrong words are inserted into syntactically labeled slots in syntactic frames. How, then, do semantic and phonological similarity work? It is reasonable to suppose that semantically and phonologically similar words become activated in the process of retrieving a target word; thus, these have some chance of erroneously replacing the target. The case of semantic similarity is more straightforward and so we consider it first. The semantic representation contains *concepts*, such as the concepts of GIRL, DOG, BIG, and so on. These are associated with one another so that when one processes a particular concept, related concepts become activated. Often, the concepts are described as existing in a *semantic network*, with related concepts connecting to one another, and with each concept connecting to the word(s) that encode(s) it (see, for example, Roelofs 1992). Retrieval processes involve the *spreading of activation*. Concepts in the semantic representation are activated and this activation spreads to associated words and concepts, with the result that, normally, the correct words are strongly activated. It is these strongly activated words that are given the opportunity to be inserted into slots in the syntactic representation. Because semantically related concepts are connected to one another, however, words that are semantically related to target words become active as well, thus increasing the chance that they will be erroneously inserted into slots. For example, when *girl* is a target, *boy*, *woman*, and other words will have some activation. This will be particularly true if any of these words was previously spoken or was about to be spoken. So, *boy* might have a small chance of replacing *girl* as a noncontextual substitution error ("The boy...er...girl is on the swing"), but a greater chance of replacing *boy* an anticipation ("The boy...er...girl is next to the boy").

It makes sense that speakers err by sometimes replacing a target word with a semantically related word because they are supposed to choose words based on meaning. How is it, then, that word slips can also involve phonological relations? We certainly do not deliberately choose words because of their sounds, unless we are punning or making poetry. My view is that phonological effects on word slips reflect the spreading of activation from a target word to the target word's phonemes, and from there to other nontarget words that share those sounds. Let me be more concrete by using figure 7.3. Consider how the verb *prevent* might replace the verb *present*. First, the concept of *present* is activated and activation spreads to the word unit for *present*. This word unit stands for the word-*as-a-whole*, and it is what we assume is inserted into slots in the syntactic representation. However, when the word unit for *present* is activated, the activation continues to spread to its associated sounds. Notice how the semantic network has grown. It no longer has just concepts and words but also contains units for individual speech sounds. Instead of calling it a semantic network, then, it might be best to call it a *lexical network* to reflect the fact that it contains all the relevant information about words: their associated concepts, their syntactic properties, and their sounds. Now, to return to the example, as the sounds of *present* become activated, their activation continues to spread, and some of it can spread "upwards" to words that possess these sounds, such as *prevent*. Because *prevent* is also a verb, it may end up going in the verb slot that *present* was supposed to go in, thus creating the slip.

One explanation for why there are phonological influences in word errors is, therefore, that the retrieval of target words also activates phonologically related words through activation spreading down to sounds and back up to words. But why would we want to propose that activation moves from sounds to words during language production? Isn't the whole idea to go from meaning to words to sounds? Yes, it is. But we must remember that our lexical knowledge is not just used for talking. It is also used for listening. It may be the case that the lexical network allows activation to spread in both directions because it is used for both production and comprehension.

The proposal that phonological influences on word errors are caused by activation spreading down to sounds and back up to words is controversial. Many researchers claim that, when processes are at the syntactic level, information associated with later levels, such as phonological information, should not be active. This claim, known as the *modularity hypothesis*,

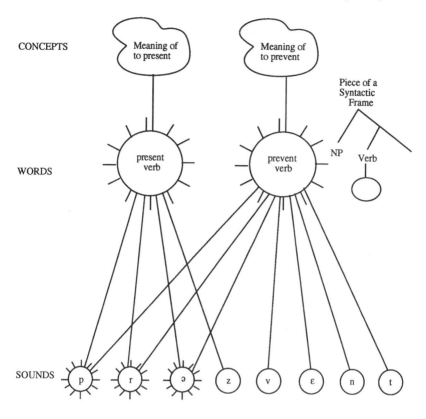

CONCEPTS

WORDS

SOUNDS

LEXICAL NETWORK

Figure 7.3
A piece of the lexical network showing how "present" might slip to "prevent" from the spreading of activation.

derives from the fact that the rules at each linguistic level are, for the most part, stated only in terms of information that is properly part of that level. For instance, it is generally true that syntactic rules do not refer to phonological information. You never see syntactic rules like this: If an adjective begins with a vowel, then it follows the noun it modifies; otherwise, it precedes the noun. If syntactic rules do not refer to phonological information, then the language production system does not need to activate the sounds of words when it is building the syntactic representation of the utterance. So, according to the modularity hypothesis, when words are being retrieved for slots in the syntactic representation, one might expect semantically related competing words to be active—because words should be retrieved based on meaning—but not phonologically related words. But how does the modularity hypothesis explain the fact that word substitution errors often do exhibit phonological relations? It is assumed that errors such as *prevent* for *present* occur at some later stage in production, after words are retrieved based on meaning and inserted into slots in the syntactic representation. In fact, phonologically related word substitution errors are often categorized as a different kind of error, called *malapropisms*. If malapropisms occur at a postsyntactic linguistic level, the influence of sound similarity on them is not so unexpected.

Which is correct, then, the modularity hypothesis or the spreading activation view? Both ideas have an account of the semantic and phonological influences on word errors. The modularity hypothesis, however, predicts that the semantic and phonological influences should be separate. An error will be caused either semantically or phonologically, but not by both relations at once. Of course, it may happen that a particular error will look as though both influences are at work, but this would be a fortuitous occurrence. In contrast, the spreading activation view predicts that semantic and phonological influences can *combine* to increase the chance of the slip. For example, consider the slip of *stop* for *start*, which is called a *mixed error*. According to the spreading activation view, when one is retrieving the word unit for *start*, some activation spreads to *stop* directly because it is related in meaning to *start*; and some activation also gets to it via the shared phonemes /st/. The two sources of activation converge on *stop*, greatly increasing its chances of being selected. According to the modularity hypothesis, the mixed error would be either a semantic slip that happened by chance to be phonologically similar, or a malapropism that happened to be semantically similar. Clearly, the two hypotheses make different predictions about the likelihood of these mixed errors. It turns out that errors that look to be both semantic and phonological are unexpectedly common in speech error collections. Specifically, if one identifies a set of word substitutions that have strong semantic relations, one finds that the phonological similarity between the error and target in this set is greater than what would be expected by chance (del Viso et al. 1991; Dell and Reich 1981; Harley 1984). This supports the spreading activation view over the modularity view.[5]

In summary, one can profitably view word slips as reflecting the syntactic creativity of language and a process of lexical retrieval that is sensitive to meaning and sound. The syntactic class rule suggests that the errors occur during the construction of a syntactic representation. Retrieving

---

5. The modularity view can still be maintained with additional assumptions (see Levelt et al. 1991).

words for this representation, however, allows for both semantic and phonological information to play a role in word errors.

7.7 Phonological Errors

Thus far, we've been talking mostly about errors in which whole words or morphemes slip. As figure 7.1 shows, it is quite common for meaningless parts of words to slip as well. These slips, called *phonological* or *sound errors*, are assumed to arise during the construction of the phonological representation.

Just as with the word errors, sound errors may reflect creative processes in speaking. That is, when one says "thollow hud" for "hollow thud," one is creating two new "words." Now, it may seem odd to associate phonological errors with creativity because one does not seem to create words out of phonemes in the same way that one creates sentences out of words. We do not have all possible sentences stored in our heads; hence, we must build rather than retrieve them. In contrast, the sound sequences that make up words are, for the most part, stored in memory. One would think that constructing a phonological representation of a word is more an act of retrieval than an act of building. However, I claim that phonological errors tell us that there is a sense in which we actually build words out of sounds—they are not just prefabricated entities.

Let us look at some of the properties of phonological errors. Here are some examples taken from Fromkin (1973):

(7) "a reading list" spoken as "a leading list" (phoneme anticipation)

(8) "an early period" spoken as "a pearly period" (anticipatory addition
     of a phoneme)

(9) "black boxes" spoken as "back bloxes" (phoneme shift)

(10) "beef noodle" spoken as "beef needle" (phoneme perseveration)

(11) "heap of junk" spoken as "hunk of jeep" (rhyme exchange)

(12) "squeaky floor" spoken as "fleaky squoor" (consonant cluster
      exchange)

The first thing to notice about these slips is that they involve a slip of a single phoneme or, less likely, a group of phonemes. When the slip is more than a single phoneme, it is usually either a consonant cluster, such as /skw/ or /fl/ as in example (12); or it is a part of the syllable known as the *rhyme*, the part that remains when its initial consonants are removed ("unk" and "eep" from example (11)). The fact that multiphoneme sound errors often correspond to clusters and rhymes is quite interesting, because phonologists have proposed the existence of these groupings of phonemes for independent reasons. For example, rules about which syllables are stressed refer to the rhyme part of the syllable. From the phonologist's perspective, words are composed of a hierarchical grouping of sounds, in the same way that sentences are a hierarchical grouping of words.

A second important aspect of sound errors is that there are strong constraints about what sounds can replace what sounds. Specifically, consonants replace consonants, and vowels replace vowels (see MacKay 1970); in fact, this property of sound errors is so strong that it can be characterized as a rule. The likelihood of an error such as "ant" being spoken as "ano" (replacing the consonant /t/ with the vowel /ow/) seems to be close to zero. This *consonant-vowel rule* is very much analogous to the syntactic category rule that we applied to word errors. Phonemes of the same type (vowels, consonants) replace one another in the same way that words of the same type (nouns, verbs, and so on) replace one another.

A third property of sound errors is that the slips are just about always well formed or pronounceable. They obey the *phonological rules* of the language (Fromkin 1971; Wells 1951). Even though some of the slips above were nonwords, such as "fleaky" and "bloxes," these are potential words because they exhibit the basic patterns of English words. Strings of sounds not exhibiting these patterns, like "lfeak" or "ngofg," simply do not show up in speech error collections. This finding, moreover, is not entirely due to error collectors' inabilities to hear ill-formed strings, because slips that are recorded in laboratory experiments also seem to have a strong tendency to be well formed. Another kind of rule that sound errors obey is illustrated by example (8). When the /p/ from *period* added itself on to *early*, the intended word *an* became *a*. The error was thus not only well formed in the sense that "pearly" is a pronounceable string of English, but also in that the error adhered to the rule that the form of *a/an* depends on whether the following word begins with a vowel or a consonant.

In general, sound errors are quite well behaved. They respect the hierarchical structure of the syllable, the vowel and consonant categories, and the rules that specify how sounds are put together. Because slips respect these properties, they create either actual words, such as "leading list," or, more interestingly, potential words—strings of sounds that adhere to the sound patterns of the language being spoken. This brings us to the link between slips and creativity. Just as the syntactic system must be creative to make novel sentences, the phonological system should have the potential to recognize and to produce novel words. No speaker of a language has a completely fixed vocabulary because, nearly every day, one is exposed to new words. Perhaps, for example, you experienced the words *malapropism* and *velar* for the first time when reading this chapter. And even if you do not remember what they mean, you would be perfectly capable of pronouncing them. This ability to deal with novel words suggests that phonological representations are not always retrieved ready-made from the set of words that we know. Instead, we can create new phonological representations when we need to. I suggest that we also create new phonological representations when we don't want to. These are what sound errors are.

Because of the need for the phonological system to be creative, researchers have proposed that the phonological representation is constructed in much the same way as the syntactic representation—linguistic units are inserted into slots in a structural frame. In the case of the phonological representation, the frame looks something like that in figure 7.4. The frame corresponds roughly to a word, specifying the number of syllables in the word and subsyllabic structure. At the bottom are slots that are labeled for consonant or vowel. So, whereas the syntactic frame slots hold words and are labeled for syntactic category, the phonological frame slots contain individual phonemes and are labeled for type of phoneme.

Let's consider how the phonological representation of the word *read* (/rid/) is built. We will assume the same kind of spreading activational processes that we proposed for the building of syntactic representations. First, a frame is assembled specifying that the word has one syllable and that this syllable has slots for three phonemes, labeled consonant, vowel, and consonant. At the same time the phonemes of the word are being retrieved by the spreading of activation in the lexical network. Activation spreads down from the verb *read* to its phonemes. These activated phonemes are then inserted into the slots. The vowel /i/ goes in the vowel slot and the consonants /r/ and /d/ go in consonant slots. How do the

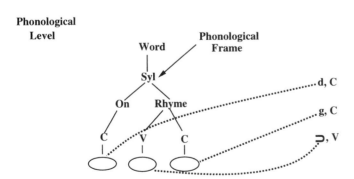

Figure 7.4
A phonological frame for the word "dog."

consonants know which slot to go to? That is, what makes "read" as opposed to "dear" happen? There are two possibilities. One is that the order of the consonants is specified by how activated they are; so, /r/ is more activated than /d/, and this causes /r/ to go in the first available consonant slot. The other possibility is that the activated phonemes and the slots are labeled as to whether they are syllable-initial or syllable-final. Hence the retrieved /r/ is a special syllable-initial /r/, and the /d/ is a syllable-final one. At present, some researchers believe that the consonants are labeled for position (for example, MacKay 1987), while others hold that position is represented just by the order in which they are activated (Meyer 1991). In either case, though, there is some mechanism that keeps initial and final consonants out of one another's slots. Whatever this mechanism is, though, it is a very powerful one because we do not see speech errors in which the initial and final consonants of a word are exchanged. "Read" never slips to "dear."

Words such as read do often participate in slips where intruding sounds come from nearby words such as "leading list" for "reading list." How does this happen? In general, a slip occurs when the wrong phoneme goes in a slot, or when a slot fails to get a phoneme, or when a slot is incorrectly added to a frame. In the "leading list" case the problem is one of the wrong phoneme in a slot. When the phonological representation for reading is being built, the syntactic level has probably already built the noun phrase reading list; that is, in the syntactic representation, the word units for reading and list have already been inserted into syntactic slots. Consequently, when one is trying to specify the phonemes of reading, the word list has already been selected. This means that the word unit for list may possess some activation, which could spread down to its phonemes. Thus there is some chance that /l/ will be activated enough to replace a consonant in reading, creating the slip "leading." The fact that /l/, the initial consonant of list, replaces the initial consonant /r/ can be taken as evidence that the slots may be labeled for syllable or word position. Other factors that could be at work in this slip are the similarity in sound between /r/ and /l/ and the fact that leading is a real word (see Stemberger 1992, for a review of factors involved in sound errors).

One of the most important properties of sound errors is that they occur only rarely on short, common words known as function words. Function words are articles, prepositions, pronouns, auxiliary verbs, and conjunctions. Instead, sound errors occur predominantly on nouns, verbs, and adjectives, or content words. For example, phoneme exchanges between an adjective and a noun, such as "heft hemisphere" for "left hemisphere" are common; but an exchange involving an article and a noun, such as "kuh that" for "the cat," would happen only rarely. In fact, I have not come across a single sound error involving the word *the*, even though *the* occurs once every fifteen words in English, on average.

Why are sound errors largely confined to content words? One very interesting hypothesis is that function words are treated differently from content words during the construction of the phonological representation. Function words belong to syntactic categories that are *closed*; that is, the set of articles, prepositions, pronouns, and so on that you know is fixed and does not change. The content word categories, however, are *open*. We are constantly learning new nouns, verbs, and adjectives. Hence, we really need creativity in the phonological representation for only the content words. Once we have acquired our native language, we have no need to create new function words. The lack of sound errors in function words can thus be taken as evidence for the proposal that slips happen most often where the system must allow for the production of new combinations. Perhaps the process of actively inserting phonemes into slots in phonological frames does not take place for function words (see Garrett 1975). Alternately, function words' sounds tend not to slip because these words are quite common and hence benefit from frequent practice (see MacKay 1987).

7.8 Word and Sound Errors and Linguistic Creativity

To conclude the discussion of error data, let us compare the creativity of the phonological and syntactic systems. Clearly, the speaker's ability to combine words to make new sentences is called upon much more often than the ability to combine sounds to make new words. Most of the sentences we utter are new, whereas nearly every one of the words that we produce is familiar. Given this, it seems incongruous that figure 7.1 shows phoneme exchanges as occurring about as often as word exchanges. In fact, it may be that phoneme errors are even *more* likely than word errors because phoneme slips are harder for error collectors to catch. Why, then, are phoneme errors as common as (or more common than) word errors, given our view that the errors occur most where there is the greatest need for creativity? The answer may lie in the fact that speakers must produce more phonemes than words. The last sentence ("The answer may lie ...") takes around five seconds to say and contains fifteen words and around fifty-six phonemes. The greater rate at which decisions must be made at the phonological level (around eleven phonemes per second), in comparison with the syntactic level (around three words per second), may thus account for the unexpectedly high rate of sound errors. Some support for this claim comes from experiments that I have been doing in which speakers produce tongue twisters at different speech rates. Speech rate has a large effect on the chance of making a sound error. When one speaks at a rate of around fifteen phonemes per second, sound errors are quite common, about one slip every ten words; however, when the speech rate is extremely slow, four phonemes per second, there are virtually no slips. Perhaps, then, the degree to which the phonological level is error-prone may reflect both its capacity for creativity (which is less than that of the syntactic level) and the speed with which its basic units must be selected (which is more than that of the syntactic level).

In summary, we have seen that slips can occur at different linguistic levels and that they seem to reflect the fact that language allows for the creative combination of linguistic units at these levels. Furthermore, we have suggested that at the syntactic and phonological levels, a hierarchical frame is constructed; the slots in that frame are filled with the appropriate linguistic units—words at the syntactic level and phonemes at the phonological level. By using frames in this way, the system is capable of producing novel but rule-governed combinations of units. Finally, it was hypothesized that linguistic units are retrieved by spreading activation through a network of units standing for concepts, words, and sounds. Slips are simply the natural consequences of all of these processes. When the system attempts to retrieve some particular linguistic unit, others become activated as well and, hence, it will sometimes happen that the wrong units are inserted into the slots. Luckily for us, this doesn't happen too often.

7.9   Conclusions—Slips and Cognitive Science

We began this chapter by promising to take a cognitive science approach to speech errors rather than a Freudian one. We sought explanation for the properties of slips by looking at the nature of language and how it is produced, rather than by looking at repressed memories. There is another important aspect of modern research on speech errors that is consistent with cognitive science. This is the use of computational models. By translating one's theory into a computer program, one can see whether the theory in fact behaves the way one expects it to. This translation has been particularly important for accounting for speech error data because there are so many factors at work in producing errors. For example, when one is selecting a particular target word for a slot in the syntactic representation, one must consider the semantic, syntactic, and phonological properties of all the surrounding words in the utterance, plus the relation of the target word to other similar words that might not be in the utterance. To explore the consequences of these factors, many researchers have found it worthwhile to build computational models. In essence, they make models that can "talk" and examine the "slips" that the models make. To the extent that a model slips in the same way that people do, the theory that inspired the model gains support. It turns out that the particular approach to language production presented here—an approach based on spreading activation—has often been translated into computational terms. As it is beyond the scope of this chapter to present the characteristics of particular models, the interested reader should consult the following references: Berg 1988; Dell 1986, 1988; Harley 1993; Houghton 1990; MacKay 1987; Martin et al. 1994; Roelofs 1992; Schade and Berg 1992; and Stemberger 1985.

In conclusion, the study of speech errors is a good example of the interdisciplinary nature of cognitive science. Linguistics provides theories about the nature of language—its levels, units, and rules. Psychology provides hypothesized processing mechanisms, such as memory retrieval being carried out by spreading activation. And, finally, the consequences of wedding linguistic theory and psychological processing mechanisms can be made concrete by employing computational models.

Suggestions for Further Reading

Freud 1901/58 is the principal statement of the hypothesis that slips are related to repressed intentions. Fromkin 1971, Garrett 1975, and MacKay 1970 outline approaches based on linguistic and psycholinguistic theory. Garrett and Fromkin, in particular, show how errors are associated with different linguistic levels. Shattuck-Hufnagel 1979 shows how the variety of phonological errors can be accounted for by assuming breakdowns in the way that phonemes are inserted into slots in phonological frames. Dell 1986, Stemberger 1985, and MacKay 1987 present broad spreading activation theories of production that deal with speech errors. Levelt 1989 is a general text on language production and shows how speech error data fit with other psycholinguistic and linguistic data. Dell, Juliano, and Govindjee 1993 is an example of a recent neural network model of speech errors. Bock and Levelt 1994 provide a review of modern theories of syntactic encoding in production.

Problems

7.1 Categorize these errors with respect to the size of the slipping unit and the nature of the disruption.

    a. petty cash → ketty pash
    b. cup of coffee → cuff of coffee
    c. Class will be about discussing the test → ... discussing the class
    d. pass the pepper → pass the salt
    e. spill beer → speer bill
    f. Eerie stamp → steerie stamp
    g. The squeaky wheel gets the grease → The skreeky gwease gets the wheel

7.2 Here is a type of error that we didn't discuss, called a blend. Instead of saying a "tennis athlete" or "tennis player," a person says "tennis athler." Explain how this might happen, according to the theory of production presented in the chapter.

7.3   The "tip-of-the-tongue" phenomenon is reasonably common. Here's an example: "That guy is amazing. He's so ... I can't think of the word. It's long and begins with o or b or something, it's not 'bodacious' ... obnoxious!... that's the word I wanted."

Using the theory of production outlined in the chapter, identify the point in the production process where the tip-of-the-tongue state is occurring.

7.4   Phonological slips happen only rarely in function words. The chapter gave two possible reasons—function words are members of closed categories, and function words are highly frequent. Try to think of other reasons why function words are relatively immune to their sounds slipping.

Question for Further Thought

7.1   Collect speech errors for around two hours sometime when you are hearing spontaneous speech (as in class or at a party). Note any problems you had in detecting and accurately recording slips.

References

Baars, B. J. (1992). *Experimental slips and human error: Exploring the architecture of volition.* New York: Plenum Press.

Baars, B. J., M. Motley, and D. MacKay (1975). Output editing for lexical status in artificially elicited slips of the tongue. *Journal of Verbal Learning and Verbal Behavior* 14, 382–391.

Berg, T. (1988). *Die Abbildung des Sprachproduktionprozess in einem Aktivationsflussmodell.* Tuebingen: Max Niemeyer.

Bock, K. (1991). A sketchbook of production problems. *Journal of Psycholinguistic Research* 20, 141–160.

Bock, K., and W. J. M. Levelt (1994). Language production: Grammatical encoding. In M. A. Gernsbacher, ed., *Handbook of psycholinguistics.* Orlando, FL: Academic Press.

del Viso, S., J. M. Igoa, and J. E. García-Alba (1991). On the autonomy of phonological encoding: Evidence from slips of the tongue in Spanish. *Journal of Psycholinguistic Research* 20, 161–185.

Dell, G. S. (1986). A spreading activation theory of retrieval in language production. *Psychological Review* 93, 283–321.

Dell, G. S. (1988). The retrieval of phonological forms in production: Tests of predictions from a connectionist model. *Journal of Memory and Language* 27, 124–142. Reprinted (1989) in W. Marslen-Wilson, ed., *Lexical representation and process*, 136–165. Cambridge, MA: MIT Press.

Dell, G. S., and P. A. Reich (1981). Stages in sentence production: An analysis of speech error data. *Journal of Verbal Learning and Verbal Behavior* 20, 611–629.

Dell, G. S., C. Juliano, and A. Govindjee (1993). Structure and content in language production: A theory of frame constraints in phonological speech errors. *Cognitive Science* 17, 149–196.

Ellis, A. W. (1980). On the Freudian theory of speech errors. In V. A. Fromkin, ed., *Errors in linguistic performance. Slips of the tongue, ear, pen, and hand.* London: Academic Press.

Fay, D., and A. Cutler (1977). Malapropisms and the structure of the mental lexicon. *Linguistic Inquiry* 8, 505–520.

Ferber, R. (1993). *Wie valide sind versprechersammlungen?* Bern: Peter Lang.

Ferreira, V. (1994). Syntactic flexibility in language production. Paper presented at Midwestern Psychological Association, Chicago.

Freud, S. (1958). *Psychopathology of everyday life*. Translated by A. A. Brill. New York: New American Library (original work published 1901).

Fromkin, V. A. (1971). The non-anomalous nature of anomalous utterances. *Language* 47, 27–52.

Fromkin, V. A. (1973). Introduction. In V. A. Fromkin, ed., *Speech errors as linguistic evidence*, 11–45. The Hague: Mouton.

Garnham, A., R. C. Shillcock, G. D. A. Brown, A. I. D. Mill, and A. Cutler (1981). Slips of the tongue in the London-Lund corpus of spontaneous conversation. *Linguistics* 19, 805–817.

Garrett, M. F. (1975). The analysis of sentence production. In G. H. Bower, ed., *The psychology of learning and motivation*, 133–175. San Diego: Academic Press.

Harley, T. A. (1984). A critique of top-down independent levels models of speech production: Evidence from non-plan-internal speech errors. *Cognitive Science* 8, 191–219.

Harley, T. A. (1993). Phonological activation of semantic competitors during lexical access in speech production. *Language and Cognitive Processes* 8, 291–307.

Hotopf, W. H. N. (1983). Lexical slips of the pen and tongue. In B. Butterworth, ed., *Language production*. Vol. 2. San Diego: Academic Press.

Houghton, G. (1990). The problem of serial order: A neural network model of sequence learning and recall. In R. Dale, C. Mellish, and M. Zock, eds., *Current research in natural language generation*, 287–319. London: Academic Press.

Levelt, W. J. M. (1989). *Speaking: From intention to articulation*. Cambridge, MA: MIT Press.

Levelt, W. J. M., H. Schriefers, D. Vorberg, A. S. Meyer, T. Pechmann, and J. Havinga (1991). The time course of lexical access in speech production: A study of picture naming. *Psychological Review* 98, 122–142.

MacKay, D. G. (1970). Spoonerisms: The structure of errors in the serial order of speech. *Neuropsychologia* 8, 323–350.

MacKay, D. G. (1982). The problems of flexibility, fluency, and speed-accuracy trade-off in skilled behaviors. *Psychological Review* 89, 483–506.

MacKay, D. G. (1987). *The organization of perception and action: A theory for language and other cognitive skills*. New York: Springer-Verlag.

Martin, N., E. M. Saffran, and G. S. Dell (submitted). Recovery in deep dysphasia: Evidence for a relation between auditory-verbal-STM capacity and lexical errors in repetition.

Martin, N., G. S. Dell, E. Saffran, and M. F. Schwartz (1994). Origins of paraphasias in deep dysphasia: Testing the consequence of a decay impairment to an interactive spreading activation model of lexical retrieval. *Brain and Language* 47, 609–660.

Meringer, R., and K. Meyer (1895). *Versprechen und Verlesen*. Stuttgart: Goschensche.

Meyer, A. S. (1991). The time course of phonological encoding in language production: Phonological encoding inside a syllable. *Journal of Memory and Language* 30, 69–89.

Roelofs, A. (1992). A spreading-activation theory of lemma retrieval in speaking. *Cognition* 42, 107–142.

Schade, U., and T. Berg (1992). The role of inhibition in a spreading activation model of language production. II. The simulational perspective. *Journal of Psycholinguistic Research* 6, 435–462.

Schwartz, M. F., E. M. Saffran, D. E. Bloch, and G. S. Dell (1994). Disordered speech production in aphasic and normal speakers. *Brain and Language* 47, 52–58.

Shattuck-Hufnagel, S. (1979). Speech errors as evidence for a serial-order mechanism in sentence production. In W. E. Cooper and E. C. T. Walker, eds., *Sentence processing: Psycholinguistic studies presented to Merrill Garrett*, 295–342. Hillsdale, NJ: Erlbaum.

Shattuck-Hufnagel, S. (1983). Sublexical units and suprasegmental structure in speech production planning. In P. F. MacNeilage, ed., *The production of speech*, 109–136. New York: Springer-Verlag.

Stemberger, J. P. (1982). *The lexicon in a model of language production.* Unpublished doctoral dissertation, University of California, San Diego.

Stemberger, J. P. (1985). An interactive activation model of language production. In A. W. Ellis, ed., *Progress in the psychology of language.* Vol. 1, 143–186. Hillsdale, NJ: Erlbaum.

Stemberger, J. P. (1992). The reliability and replicability of speech error data. In B. Baars, ed., *Experimental slips and human error: Exploring the architecture of volition.* New York: Plenum Press.

Wells, R. (1951). Predicting slips of the tongue. *Yale Scientific Magazine,* 3, 9–30.

Chapter 8

Comprehending Sentence Structure

Janet Dean Fodor

8.1 From Word String to Sentence Meaning

8.1.1 Deducing Structure

When we hear or read a sentence, we are aware more or less instantaneously of what it means. Our minds compute the meaning somehow, on the basis of the words that comprise the sentence. But the words alone are not enough. The sentence meanings we establish are so precise that they could not be arrived at by just combining word meanings haphazardly. A haphazard word combiner could misunderstand (1) as meaning that all bears love; it could interpret (2) as meaning that pigs fly and rabbits can't.

(1)   Love bears all.

(2)   Pigs and rabbits can't fly.

But people (except when something is badly wrong) do not comprehend sentences in so vague a way. We combine word meanings according to a precise recipe that is provided by the syntax of the language. A sentence is more than a string of words. It is a highly structured object in which the words are organized into phrases and clauses in accord with general principles of syntactic patterning. For instance, the string of words in (2) does not have the structure shown by the brackets in (3a). Its structure is (3b), and this is why it means what it does.

(3)   a.   [Pigs [and rabbits can't] fly].

     b.   [Pigs and rabbits] [can't fly].

What is interesting is that this syntactic structure that drives sentence comprehension is not manifest in the stimulus. It is there but not overtly displayed. It is not reliably marked in the phonetic form of a spoken sentence or in the orthographic form of a written one. The prosody of the sentence (the melody and timing with which it is spoken; see chapter 9) does usually reflect some aspects of the syntactic structure, but not all; in written language, structural information is missing entirely except as indicated by an occasional comma. Thus, if perceivers are to use syntactic structure in comprehending sentences, it seems that they must first deduce the syntactic structure.

In order to do so, they must be applying their knowledge of the structural principles of the language. Different natural languages (English, Spanish, Japanese, and so forth) exhibit slightly (not entirely) different sentence patterns, which shape their sentences and dictate how word meanings are to be integrated. Linguists study languages in order to discover what these patterns are. But the speakers and perceivers of a language evidently have this information in their heads. We can't introspect about it, we have no conscious access to it (which is why linguists have to infer it laboriously by observing sentences just as entomologists observe insects); but we acquire this knowledge as infants learning the language, and we draw on it, unconsciously and automatically, to calculate sentence structure every time we speak or understand.

For example, people who know English know that the subject of sentence (1) is the abstract noun *love* and that its verb is *bears*, even though *love* can be a verb in other contexts and *bears* can be a noun. The fact that *love* is the subject here and not the verb follows from the facts of English grammar. In English (though not in Welsh or Maori) a sentence cannot begin with a verb unless it is an auxiliary verb (like *may* in *May Charlotte leave early?*) or an imperative verb (as in *Watch your back!*) or in a special "topicalized" construction such as *Leave you I must but forget you I never will*. Sentence (1) does not fit any of these patterns. The beginning of it may look like an imperative (*Love bears, don't fear them!*) but at least in modern English the *all* at the end of (1) scotches this possibility. Therefore the first word of (1) is not a verb. It is not an adjective or a preposition or anything else, so it must be a noun. This fact then entails that the next word, *bears*, functions as a verb here, not as a noun. This is because in English (unlike Korean) the subject cannot be followed directly by the object (or other noun phrase); the verb must come between them. (There can be two nouns in a row in English if they form a compound noun, like *honey bees*; but *love bears* does not work as a compound noun in (1).)

Perceivers thus PROJECT structure onto a string of words, deducing it from their mentally stored grammar of the language. This is an extraordinary feat that underlies even the most ordinary uses of language. Psycholinguists are interested in finding out HOW people put their unconscious grammatical knowledge to work. What exactly are these mental deductions, which so rapidly and reliably deliver sentence meanings to our conscious minds? They are not directly observable, so we need to be resourceful in finding methods for investigating them. One strategy that can be helpful is to look at extreme cases, where a great many properties of the sentence have to be projected from very little perceptible evidence. These would be sentences where the ratio of "invisible" structure to overt words is very high. An example is (4).

(4)   The rat the cat the dog worried chased ate the malt.

This is what is called a doubly center-embedded relative clause construction; it has one relative clause in the middle of another relative clause in the middle of a main clause. It was noticed some years ago by Yngve (1960) that sentences like this, though well formed in accord with the syntactic rules of English, are extremely difficult to structure and understand. Parts of (4) are easy enough to parse. The phrase *the cat the dog worried* is clear, and if we call this cat *Socks*, the sentence would be *The rat Socks chased ate the malt*, which is also comprehensible. But apparently there is just too much structure in (4) as a whole for our mental comprehension routines to cope with. Miller and Chomsky (1963) and, more recently, Frazier (1985) have observed that doubly center-embedded relative clause constructions have a very dense syntactic structure. A tree diagram of the structure of (4) is shown in (5), and you can see that it has many nonterminal (higher) nodes relative to its terminal (word-level) nodes. This is especially true at the beginning of the sentence, where the first six words require three clause structures to be built. Compare this with the structure shown in (6) for a sentence which has the same number of words but has fewer nodes more evenly distributed, and which is perfectly easy to understand.[1]

1. In this chapter, traditional tree diagrams (or structural bracketings) and category labels will be used to represent sentence structures. S = sentence or clause; NP = noun phrase; VP = verb phrase; Det = determiner (article). Readers should note that newer conventions (e.g., clauses as CP or IP) are in use in many recent works in linguistics.

(5)

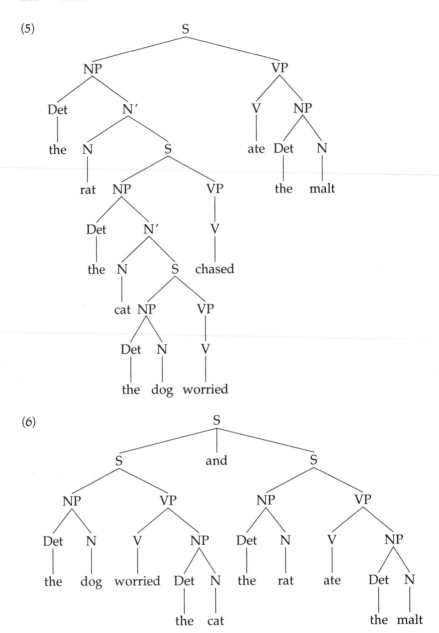

(6)

The difficulty of (4) (and other sentences with multiple center-embeddings) shows that our mental sentence comprehension routines, though remarkably efficient most of the time, do have their limits.

8.1.2 Empty Categories

Another way in which a sentence can have a high load of structure to be projected by the perceiver is if some of its constituents do not overtly appear in the word string. These non-overt constituents are what linguists call *empty categories*. They are *categories* in the syntactician's sense; that is, they are noun phrases or verbs or relative pronouns, and so forth. They are *empty* in the sense of lacking any phonological (or orthographic) realization. Thus, an empty category is a piece of the sentence structure, but it is not pronounced (or written) by the sentence producer, so it is not audible (or visible) to the sentence perceiver. The perceiver must deduce both its existence and its properties. An example is the "missing" verb *flew* in the second clause of sentence (7).

(7)   John flew to Paris, and Mary to Chicago.

Mary is a noun phrase (NP) and *to Chicago* is a prepositional phrase (PP). A clause cannot normally consist of just an NP followed by a PP; it must have a verb. It seems reasonable to suppose, then, that the structure of (7) is (8), where there is a verb in both clauses in accord with general structural principles, but where the second verb is phonologically empty.

(8)

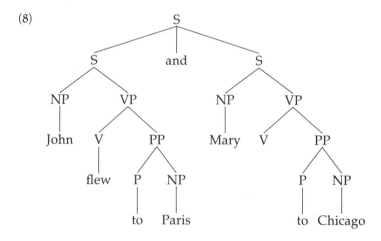

The empty verb has a quite specific meaning. The second clause of (7) clearly means that Mary FLEW to Chicago, not that she drove to Chicago, or that she wrote to Chicago, and so forth. On the other hand, if the first clause of (7) had been *John drove to Paris*, then the second clause would have meant that Mary DROVE to Chicago, not that she flew there. It is always the verb in the first clause that identifies the empty verb in the second clause. Thus, the grammar of English does not allow just any verb in any context to be empty; there are strict principles governing where empty categories (henceforth ECs) can appear in sentences and how they can be interpreted. If there were not, it would be impossible for perceivers to reconstruct ECs as they compute the sentence structure.

Sentence (4) above also contains some ECs, though they are not shown in (5). (If they were, the contrast in complexity between (5) and (6) would be even clearer.) A relative clause in English, as in many languages, has a "gap" in it where a noun phrase would normally appear. Consider example (9), which is the simplified version of (4) with just one relative clause.

(9)   The rat Socks chased ate the malt.

The relative clause *Socks chased* modifies the noun *rat*; *rat* is the head noun of the whole complex NP *the rat Socks chased*. The relative clause means that Socks chased the rat, but the word *rat* doesn't actually appear as the object of the verb *chased*. The object of *chased* is missing. Since this is a verb that normally MUST have an object, we may assume that it does have an object in the relative clause but that the object is phonologically empty. Thus, the structure of (9) is as shown in (10).

(10)

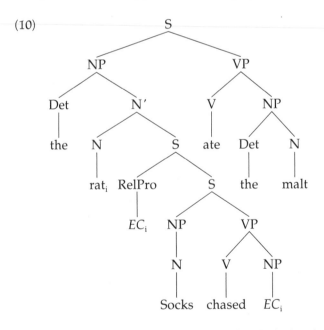

The empty object NP in (10) is coindexed with the head noun *rat*; this is to indicate the fact that the EC is interpreted as referring to the rat. Note also that another EC is shown in (10), in the pre-clause position where a relative pronoun (*who, whom, which*) often appears. In a sentence like *The*

rat which Socks chased ate the malt the relative pronoun is *which*, and it provides a link between the head noun and the EC in the relative clause. Sentence (9) is exactly similar except that its relative pronoun also happens to be an EC. Thus, the empty relative pronoun mediates the relation between *rat* and the empty object of *chased*. The fact that sentence (9) is easy to understand shows that this double linkage of ECs does not overload the human sentence processing routines.

Linguists have argued that the structure (10) is derived from an underlying structure in which the relative pronoun follows *chased*, in the "normal" position for the object of a verb. The underlying structure is transformed by moving the relative pronoun from the object position to the pre-clause position adjacent to the head noun that the clause modified. Whenever an element moves out of its underlying position, an EC coindexed with it is created in that position. An EC that is thus "left behind" by a movement operation is called a *trace* of the element that moved. Thus the EC after *chased* in (10) is the trace of the relative pronoun which moved leftward. This kind of trace is usually referred to as a WH-trace, since it results from the movement of a WH-phrase—an expression such as *who* or *which* or *with whom* or *how many of the elephants*, and so forth.

WH-phrases (which occur in many other languages though they do not typically start with *wh* except in English) appear in questions as well as in relative clauses. The question in (11) was formed by movement of the WH-phrase *which of the elephants* to the beginning of the question, leaving a WH-trace in its underlying position after the verb *tickling*.

(11)   [Which of the elephants]$_i$ was Bertram tickling *WH-trace$_i$*?

Note that, in a question, an auxiliary verb (the verb *was* in (11)) moves to the left of the subject NP; the usual order would be *Bertram was*, but here it is *was Bertram*. This is Subject-Auxiliary Inversion, discussed by Lasnik in chapter 10 of this volume. Though it is an important aspect of the syntax of questions in English, it is not germane to the concerns of the present chapter; we will sidestep it by focusing on relative clauses and embedded questions, where it does not apply. An embedded question is shown in (12).

(12)   The ringmaster asked [which of the elephants]$_i$ Bertram was tickling *WH-trace$_i$*.

The main clause of (12) is declarative, but it has a question embedded within it as the object of the verb *asked*. The WH-phrase *which of the elephants* has moved to the beginning of the question clause. In all cases of WH-movement, the semantic role of the removed phrase is determined by its underlying position. In (12), for instance, the WH-phrase originated in a position following the verb *tickling*, and the meaning is that the elephant was the object of the tickling action. The surface position of the WH-phrase itself cannot signal its semantic role, because the WH-phrase is always at the front of its clause regardless of the meaning. To comprehend a sentence that contains a WH-phrase, a perceiver therefore needs to know what its UNDERLYING position was. The underlying position is marked in the surface structure by a trace, but that is not very helpful; since a trace is an EC, it is inaudible and invisible to the perceiver. Let us consider how the perceiver (more precisely, the unconscious sentence processing routines in the perceiver's mind/brain) could set about locating the crucial EC position.

Consider first some simple strategies that WON'T work. The trace is not always at the end of the sentence, as is shown by (13). It is not always immediately following a verb, as is shown by (14), where it is the object of the preposition *with*. It is not always an object, as shown by (15), where it is the subject of the verb *were*. Example (16) shows that the trace may immediately follow its antecedent WH-phrase, and example (17) shows that it may be separated from the antecedent phrase by several intervening clauses.

(13)   You can always tell [which books]$_i$ Walter read *WH-trace*$_i$ in the bathtub.

(14)   I wonder [which of his books]$_i$ Walter lit the fire with *WH-trace*$_i$.

(15)   Do you recall [which books]$_i$ Walter proclaimed *WH-trace*$_i$ were unreadable?

(16)   Walter never did find out [which books]$_i$ *WH-trace*$_i$ were on the reading list.

(17)   It is remarkable [how many books]$_i$ Walter tried to bribe his roommate to inform the instructor that he had every intention of reading *WH-trace*$_i$ soon.

It seems the only way for the comprehension routines to locate a trace is to find a position in the sentence that "needs" a phrase of the kind that has been moved. In examples (13)–(17), an NP has moved, so somewhere in the sentence there must be a "gap" that is "NP-shaped"; that is, a position where an NP would normally occur. In example (18) the adverb *where* has moved, so the gap later in the sentences must be "adverb-shaped." In (19) the PP *to whom* has moved, so there is a gap later that is suited to a PP.

(18)   The waiter asked where$_i$ we would like to sit *WH-trace*$_i$.

(19)   Marsha is the person [to whom]$_i$ I am most indebted *WH-trace*$_i$ for my recent success on Broadway.

In each case the comprehension mechanism must be on the look-out for a gap of just the right type to fit the WH-phrase "filler" at the beginning of the clause. If it is lucky, the sentence contains just one gap of the appropriate category, and it is immediately recognizable AS a gap. If so, the processing mechanism can build the correct structure, with an EC in the right position, coindexed to the WH-phrase filler. Then, when semantic interpretation processes occur, the WH-phrase will be interpreted as having the sematic role normally associated with a phrase in the position that the EC is in.

However, in some cases the processing mechanism may not be able to tell, at least on the basis of neighboring words, whether there is a gap in some position or not. In (13) the verb *read* is missing an NP object, so that is where trace must be. But how could the processor establish that? It is not the case that *read* ALWAYS has an object; it can function as an intransitive verb in examples like (20) and (21).

(20)   Walter would never admit that he read in the bathtub.

(21)   You can always tell [which books]$_i$ Walter read about *WH-trace$_i$* in the *New York Review*.

In (20) there is no WH-phrase, no movement, and so no trace. In (21) there is WH-movement, but the trace is in a different position, following the preposition *about* rather than the verb *read*. Thus, the fact of the matter is that in (13) there MUST be a trace after *read*, but just looking at the position after *read* does not SHOW that there must be. Its presence there must be inferred. What entails that the trace is after *read* in (13) is that there is no other place in this sentence where it could be. When all impossible positions have been excluded, the only possible one must be the right one. In sentence (21) there are TWO possible positions for an empty NP: one after *read* and one after *about*. Only one of them can be the real trace site. And it is the position after *about* that wins, because it has the greater need: an NP object for *about* is obligatory, whereas *read* can do without one. (Note that English also contains a verbal particle *about* that does not need an object NP, as in *The children ran about all afternoon*; but the preposition *about* that occurs in *read about*, as in (21), MUST have an object.)

These examples illustrate the fact that locating an EC can involve a global inference over a whole sentence, finding and comparing candidate positions. But a sentence is not globally available to the perceiver; it is received one word at a time. This is obviously so in speech; and even in reading, the words are usually identified one after the other. Furthermore, it seems clear that normally we do not wait until we have heard or read an entire sentence before comprehending the beginning of it. This means that the processing routines will often be faced with a decision to make before they have enough information about the sentence to be able to make it. The first eight words of sentences (13) and (21) are identical. At the word *read* the question arises: Is there a trace next? If the processor guesses yes, it will be right about (13) but wrong about (21). If it guesses no, it will be right about (21) but wrong about (13). If it does not guess at all, it will fall behind in interpreting the sentence and may never recover. In some cases the information that resolves the issue arrives only much later. In (22), for example, there is a doubtful trace site after *was reading*, whose status is not resolved for another seven or eight words. In (22a) it is eventually shown to be the true trace position by the fact that the sentence ends without any other possible trace position; in (22b) it is shown NOT to be a real trace position by the fact that there is an undeniable trace after *about* seven words later.

(22)   This is the book that Walter was reading

  a. *WH-trace*$_i$ to his
     friends and fellow
     students on Friday.

  b. to his friends and
     fellow students about
     WH-trace$_i$ on Friday.

Thus, we see that the inference from grammatical constraints to sentence structure is often quite intricate, and the facts that should feed it are not always there when needed. How do the processing routines cope?

8.1.3   Ambiguity

The uncertainty that complicates the perceiver's task of detecting ECs is just one instance of a very common problem for the processing routines: ambiguity. There are fully ambiguous sentences such as Chomsky's example (Chomsky 1965) shown in (23).

(23)   Flying planes can be dangerous.

In cases of full ambiguity, the linguistic facts do not resolve the meaning; the perceiver must decide on some other basis (topic of conversation, plausibility, knowledge about the speaker) which of the two meanings the speaker intended. Full ambiguity sometimes arises with ECs, as in (24) where the WH-phrase is the PP *to whom* whose trace might be in the clause with *say* (to whom did she say it?) or in the clause with *mailed* (to whom did she mail them?). Nothing in the word string shows which analysis is intended.

(24)   To whom did Eloise say she had mailed three postcards?

More common than full ambiguity is temporary ambiguity. That is, for a processor receiving words over time, it may be that some early part of the word sequence is ambiguous but the ambiguity is then resolved by words that follow. The examples (13), (21), and (22) discussed above are temporarily ambiguous with respect to the trace position. Chomsky's example (23) can be turned into a case of temporary ambiguity if we change the verb so that it disambiguates one or the other of the two meanings. In (25), both sentences begin with the words *flying planes* whose structure is temporarily ambiguous (*flying* could be an adjective or a verb), but its structure is subsequently disambiguated by the singular or plural predicate.

(25) a. Flying planes is dangerous.
      b. Flying planes are dangerous.

In (25a) the disambiguator is the singular verb *is*, which requires the meaning that it is dangerous to fly planes; in (25b) the disambiguator is the plural verb *are*, which requires the meaning that planes which fly are dangerous.

Full ambiguity is an obvious threat to successful communication, but even temporary ambiguity can be troublesome for a system that is working at close to full capacity. Research on sentence comprehension has uncovered many varieties of temporary ambiguity. A handful of examples are shown in (26), with the disambiguating word underlined in each. (In some cases, such as f., what disambiguates is the fact that the sentence comes to an end without any more words.) Some of these examples involve ambiguities of trace position, and some involve other sources of ambiguity. In some cases the ambiguity is easy to spot, and in others it is very difficult.

(26) a. The cotton clothing is made of comes from Mississippi.

      b. Sally found the answer to the physics problem wasn't in the book.

      c. The package dropped from the airplane reached the ground safely.

      d. The commander of the army's bootlaces are broken.

      e. They told the boy that the girl shouted at in the playground to go home.

      f. Eloise put the book that she'd been reading all afternoon in the library.

      g. Have the soldiers given their medals by their sweethearts.

      h. He put the candy in his mouth on the table.

Where there is ambiguity, the sentence processing mechanism lacks guidance as to what structure to build. However, experimental data and perceivers' judgments on sentences like those in (26) suggest that the processor does not just grind to a halt when it encounters an ambiguity; rather, it makes a guess. The characteristic sign of a guessing system is that sometimes it wins and sometimes it loses. If the sentence happens to end in a way that fits the guess, processing will be easy—in fact, just as easy as if there had been no ambiguity at all. But if the sentence happens to end in a way that fits the other structure—the one the processor did not guess—then there will be trouble later on; at the disambiguation point the structural analysis of the sentence will be impossible to continue, and the processor will have to back up and try the other analysis instead. In psycholinguistic parlance this situation is called a "garden path": The processor makes a mistake and proceeds blithely on, not realizing there is any problem until later, when things take a sudden turn for the worse. The examples in (26) are all garden path sentences; that is, they all end in the unexpected direction, and the processing routines exhibit some distress (though in varying degrees) on encountering the disambiguating word. Consider (26a) (from Marcus 1980). The first six words are temporarily ambiguous. If followed by *expensive handwoven fabric from India*, the sentence is easy to process; there is no garden path. The sentence is about some cotton clothing and tells us that it is made of expensive stuff. In (26a) the same six words are followed by *comes from Mississippi*, and the sentence is extremely difficult to process—so much so that it may appear at first to be ungrammatical. The sentence is about cotton from which clothing is made, and tells us where it comes from. The fact that the first way of ending the sentence is easier to process than the second is our evidence that the processor makes a guess about the structure of the subject NP at the beginning, before it encounters the disambiguating information later on. It guesses that the structure is *[the cotton clothing]*, rather than *[the cotton]* plus a relative clause. Interestingly, this is true for virtually all perceivers, so it is not a matter of individual experience but reflects some basic fact about the way the human brain works.

One of the projects of psycholinguistic research is to map out the structural guesses that the sentence processor makes, by establishing which sentence completions are easy and which are difficult for all sorts of temporary ambiguity. From this we can hope to infer what kind of a machine this processor is. The basis for the inference is the plausible assumption that when there are no external restrictions, a mechanism will do what comes most naturally to it. By this logic, sentence (26a) could be very helpful in ruling out certain hypotheses about the design of the processor: it would rule out any kind of machine for which the analysis *[the cotton]* + relative clause would be easier to spot, or easier to build, than the analysis *[the cotton clothing]*. This empirical program has been under way for some years. Results show that the human sentence processor's guesses are far from random; they exhibit very consistent general tendencies. With regard to phrasal structure, what the human processor likes best is simple but compact structures, which have no more tree branches than are necessary, and the minimal tree-distance (walking up one branch and down another) between any pair of adjacent words.

With regard to ECs too, all the evidence suggests that in case of ambiguity the human sentence processor does not stop and wait until more information arrives. It makes a guess in order to be able to carry on parsing the sentence, and its guesses are not random. It appears to err systematically in the direction of overeagerness, anticipating ECs before they occur. Sometimes the remainder of the sentence confirms that guess, but sometimes it does not.

8.1.4   Anticipating ECs

Looking back at the examples in (22), test your own judgment about which is easier to parse. For most people the structure for (22a) is computed smoothly, while the analysis of (22b) hiccups at the *about on* sequence that shows the early gap to be wrong. It seems, then, that in processing both sentences, the processor notices the early gap position and likes it; it guesses that this is the real gap for the EC. By good fortune this turns out several words later to be correct for (22a). But in (22b), where a later gap position is correct, this guess causes a garden path.

A number of experimental results support this idea that the human sentence processor is inclined to be over-hasty in postulating traces. For instance, Frazier and Clifton (1989) tested sentences as illustrated in (27).[2] Like the examples above, these have an ambiguous trace site that is disambiguated in two different ways by the words that follow.

(27)   a.   What$_i$ did the cautious old man whisper *WH-trace$_i$* to his fiancée during the movie last night?

       b.   What$_i$ did the cautious old man whisper to his fiancée about *WH-trace$_i$* during the movie last night?

The correct trace positions are marked in (27). The doubtful trace position is after the verb *whisper*. The verb *whisper* (like the verb *read* in earlier

2. These are just examples of the sentences tested. In this experiment, and in all the others discussed in this chapter, many sentences of the same general type are tested, in order that statistical tests can be made, to distinguish chance performance from the phenomena of interest. Many other aspects of the linguistic materials and experimental procedure must also be carefully controlled. Details will not be discussed here but can be found in the original experimental reports in the articles referenced.

examples) sometimes has an object (*I whispered a message to my friend*) and sometimes has no object (*I whispered to my friend*). So when *whisper* appears without an overt NP following it, this might be because it has an EC as its object, or because it has no object at all. In (27a) it has an EC object; in (27b) it is intransitive, with no object at all. The problem for the processor is that word by word the two sentences in (27) are identical all the way up to *fiancée*; thus, when it encounters the word *whisper*, it has absolutely no way of knowing whether there is a trace after it or not. Frazier and Clifton's experiment was designed to tell us what the processor does in such a circumstance where the word string is not informative. If the processor guesses that *whisper* has a trace as its object, it should find the last part of sentence (27a) easier to cope with than the last part of sentence (27b). If it guesses that *whisper* has no object at all, it should find the rest of (27b) easier to parse than the rest of (27a). If it does nothing but just sits and waits for more information, it should find the two endings more or less equally easy.

The sentences were presented to subjects visually, on a CRT screen, one chunk (a few words) at a time, in what is called a "self-paced reading" paradigm; that is, the subject pushes a button after reading each segment of the sentence, to call up the next one. The subject can spend as long as is necessary to read each segment, but the amount of time taken is recorded by a computer and is used by the experimenter as a measure of how difficult that part of the sentence is to process. (The reading time is influenced, of course, by many properties of the words and the sentence structure, but this is no problem as long as other factors are held constant and only the factor of interest in the experiment is varied.) In Frazier and Clifton's experiment, subjects were faster at reading sequences like *to his fiancée during the movie* in (27a) than sequences like *to his fiancée about during the movie* in (27b). This is not very surprising since the former sequences are one word shorter; but the advantage for the (a) type was present even when the reading times were adjusted for the length difference. Thus, the experimental results provided confirmation of the intuitive judgment that early trace sentences like (27a) are easier to understand than are late trace sentences like (27b). It seems that if the processor has a filler on its hands, it is inclined to jump at the first gap it finds. Frazier and Clifton call this the Active Filler Hypothesis: "When a filler has been identified, rank the option of assigning it to a gap above all other options."

To sum up so far: We have seen that the human sentence processing system is capable of making mistakes about ECs. Because they are not signaled explicitly in the input, it can be difficult sometimes to distinguish between an EC and a nothing at all. The processor is at the mercy of each sentence to provide some cues from which it can deduce the difference between an EC and a nothing. If a sentence does not provide the information, or provides it too late, the processor has to resort to guessing. And, inevitably, roughly half the time it will guess wrong. It may recover itself later so that ultimately the sentence is understood correctly, but time and effort are wasted on the garden path; thus, processing is less than perfectly efficient. However, to be fair to this mental processing system that we are all equipped with, it should be noted that ANY system—except one with the leisure to sit back and wait for the needed information to arrive— would be bound to make mistakes on temporarily ambiguous sentences. Even a computer, with its vast memory and computational resources, has significant trouble with ambiguity. What is impressive about the human language processor is how FEW mistakes it makes in general. When relevant information IS available, we see over and over again that the processor makes extremely efficient use of it.

8.1.5   Using Linguistic Information

As an informal demonstration of how the processor takes advantage of information available, consider its performance on sentence (28).

(28)   What$_i$ are boxes$_j$ easy to store EC_j in WH-$trace_i$?

This is a very easy sentence to understand; yet, it contains two ECs only a word apart, each of which has to be assigned an antecedent. The indices in (28) show the correct antecedent–gap pairings. The WH-word *what* has moved from its underlying position as the object of the preposition *in*. There is also an understood object of the verb *store*, associated with the subject NP *boxes*. (Linguists analyze this association as involving WH-movement also, where what moves is a phonologically empty element, somewhat as in the case of the empty relative pronoun in (9)/(10) above. But the details are not important here.) Notice how clear it is that the question in (28) is about storing boxes in something, not about storing something in boxes: a good answer would be "closets," not "pencils." There seems to be no temptation at all to construe (28) the wrong way round, about storing things in boxes. This means that the processor has not only found the right fillers and gaps in (28) but has also matched them up the right way. In principle, either filler could go with either gap, but there is a constraint in the grammar that insists on one pairing and pro-hibits the other. This constraint requires two filler-gap relations in a sen-tence to be nested one within the other, not intersecting. Thus indices i j j i as in (28) are acceptable, but i j i j would not be. This Nested Dependency Constraint is the reason why (28) is NOT ambiguous but only refers to storing boxes in something else. Thus, this is a case where the word string and the grammar do determine, between them, a uniquely correct analysis. And the processor evidently knows it. It has no trouble working out the implications of the constraint for the analysis of this sentence, or in building a structure with two ECs at very close quarters. No wonder, then, that we see no sign of strain in the processor in its dealings with normal questions and relative clauses that have only one gap apiece.

Our informal assessment, then, is that as long as there is no ambiguity, sentence processing seems to be completely smooth and efficient. Experimental data support this impression. Whatever useful information a sentence provides, or the grammar of the language provides, the processing mechanism takes advantage of. Consider a very basic point. Since a WH-trace is created when a WH-phrase moves, there cannot be a WH-gap in a sentence if there isn't any WH-filler. This is potentially useful information; it could save the processor the trouble of going on a gap-hunt in sentences with no filler phrase. Does the processing device take account of it? If it did not, then regardless of whether a filler was present or not, it would process the rest of a sentence in exactly the same way. But, on the contrary, Crain and Fodor (1985) and Stowe (1986) have shown that the processor treats sentences with and without filler phrases differently. Crain and Fodor tested sentences like (29) and (30).

(29) Could the little child have forced us to sing those French songs for Cheryl last Christmas?

(30) Who$_i$ could the little child have forced us to sing those French songs for *WH-trace*$_i$ last Christmas?

In (29) there is no filler; in (30) there is a filler *who* at the beginning. Where is the trace associated with *who*? It must be in a position suitable for an NP. The correct NP position is after the preposition *for*, but as the processor works its way through the sentence, it will encounter various other potential NP positions along the way, and it needs to check each one in case it should turn out to be the right one. Consider the position after the verb *forced* in (30). What appears at that position is the pronoun *us*, and a pronoun constitutes an NP. The fact that this overt NP occurs at this point means that this is NOT the gap position. But for all that the processor knows, it MIGHT have been. This is clear from sentence (31), which is identical to (30) as far as the verb *forced*, but does have a gap right after it.

(31) Who$_i$ could the little child have forced *WH-trace*$_i$ to sing those French songs for Cheryl last Christmas?

As we know from the Active Filler Hypothesis, when the processor is in need of a gap it does not wait to see how things will turn out, but actively seeks out likely sites. The processor might thus ANTICIPATE a gap after *forced* in (30) and then be a little put out when it discovers *us* there, realizing that its hunt for the gap is not over after all. This phenomenon has been called the "filled gap effect." We would expect it to occur in (30). What we want to know is whether it ALSO occurs in (29), where there is no filler. If it does, this would mean that the processor is not taking full advantage of the grammar of the language, to reduce its workload on-line. But if there is NO filled gap effect in (29), this would show that the processor is smart enough to hypothesize a gap only when there is a filler. This is just what the experimental data reveal.

Subjects were presented with sentences like (29) and (30) in a self-paced reading task, as described earlier for the sentences in (27) except that each "chunk" was just one word; that is, as each word was read, the subject pushed the button to call up the next one. What is of interest here is the reading time for an overt NP such as the word *us* in (30), where a filled gap effect is expected, as compared with that same NP in a sentence like (29), where there is no filler. In fact, the reading time data showed that an overt NP after the verb is significantly more difficult to process in sentences like (30) than in sentences like (29). We can conclude that the processor seeks a gap only when it has a filler to go with it. In general, it seems that the human processing routines are highly sensitive to the grammar. By referring to the grammar, they can postulate ECs just where it is reasonable to do so, not unrestrainedly. A processor that concocted ECs without cause, simply at whim, could see ECs everywhere, between any two words in any sentence. A processor that didn't bother itself with ECs at all would misunderstand many sentences. But the sentence processor in the human brain apparently avoids both kinds of mistake, by paying close attention to the grammatical constraints on the language.

Being sensitive to grammatical constraints presumably exacts a cost in complexity of the computations the processor must perform. But it also confers real benefits in accuracy of comprehension, and all the more so in sentences where the correct structure is not transparently signaled by the overt word sequence. Stowe (1986) investigated the processor's sensitivity to other constraints on the grammatical transformation that creates WH-traces. WH-movement can move a phrase across many clauses in a sentence, as we saw in example (17) above. There is, in fact, no restriction at all on how far a WH-phrase may move between its original position in the underlying structure and its final position in the surface form of the sentence.[3] Nevertheless, a WH-phrase cannot move freely. It can move only "leftward," that is, closer to the beginning of the sentence. It can move

---

3. There is linguistic evidence which suggests that a phrase doesn't ever move across unbounded stretches of a sentence, but moves in short steps from one clause to the next one. (See Haegeman 1991, chapters 6 and 7, for more information.) This is called *successive cyclic movement*. It affects the linguistic description of the "island constraints" discussed below, but is not important to our present concerns.

only upward, from a more deeply embedded sentence position to a less deeply embedded one. And there are certain kinds of constructions within a sentence that a WH-phrase cannot move out of in any direction. Ross (1967) coined the term "island" for such constructions. The WH-phrase is marooned on the island; it can move within it but cannot escape from it. A subject phrase constitutes an island, as does an adverbial clause, and any complex noun phrase. In theoretical linguistics the important question is what it is about these constructions that makes them islands, when other constructions (for example, object complement clauses) are not islands. In psycholinguistics, our interest focuses on whether the processor KNOWS these island constraints and respects them in its search for traces.

Stowe tested sentences like (32), where the phrase that is bracketed is a subject island; *the silly story about Greg's older brother* is the subject of the verb *was* in the subordinate clause. Therefore, no WH-element is allowed to cross the borders of this phrase. This means there can be no trace INSIDE this phrase whose antecedent is OUTSIDE it.

(32)   The teacher asked what$_i$ [the silly story about Greg's older brother] was supposed to mean *WH-trace*$_i$.

In fact, sentence (32) does NOT violate the island constraint, since the WH-element *what* did not move out of the subject island; it started out as the object of the verb *mean* and moved to the top of the question clause introduced by *asked*. In doing so, it passed right over the subject island and was unaffected by it. But consider (32) from the processor's point of view. It proceeds through the words of the first clause, then encounters the filler *what*, and so it initiates a gap hunt. The fact that the subject phrase is an island means that it would be pointless for the processor to look for a gap inside the subject phrase; if the gap were there, the sentence wouldn't be well formed. But does the processing mechanism know that? And does it know it in the heat of the moment, on-line, or does it only catch up with the linguistic constraints later, when the sentence is over and it has had time to get its breath back? Stowe's experiment used the "filled gap effect" to show that the human sentence processor does exploit the island con-straint on-line to limit the scope of its gap search. Let's consider the logic behind the design of this experiment.

The island in (32) must not contain the trace associated with the word *what* outside the island; so the preposition *about* inside the island, which needs an NP object, must have an OVERT object. And indeed it does: *about* is followed by the the overt NP *Greg's older brother*. But a processor that did not know (or did not care) about island constraints might anticipate a gap after *about* and then show signs of distress when it encounters *Greg's older brother* there instead. In fact, Stowe did not find any filled gap effect in sentences like (32). She measured reading time for the word *Greg's* in (32) (that is, the first word after *about*, which shows that there is no gap there), and compared it with reading time for the same word in sentence (33). This sentence is exactly like (32) except that it has no WH-filler, so the processor should know that it could not contain a WH-trace.

(33)   The teacher asked if [the silly story about Greg's older brother] was supposed to mean anything.

The data showed no difference between (32) and (33). This contrasts with (30) and (29) above, where the findings did show a filled gap effect. Consider what can be inferred from this. We interpreted the filled gap effect in (30) as indication that when there is a filler, the processor contemplates the idea of a gap in any legitimate gap position. So now: the ABSENCE of a filled gap effect in (32) indicates that the processor is NOT prepared to contemplate the idea of a gap in a position that is illegitimate because it is inside an island.

Further experimental support for the precision with which the processor obeys the dictates of the grammar comes from the way in which the processor matches up fillers with gaps. Informally, we noted earlier that sentence (28) is easy to process even though it contains two fillers and two gaps. The fillers arrive first; therefore, when it finds the first gap, the processor has to choose which of the fillers to associate with it. As far as we can tell, it does so unerringly, with no temptation to pick the wrong one. Does the processor ever ignore grammatical constraints and consider an illegal antecedent for an EC? The experimental evidence suggests that it does not.

Consider a WH-trace in a relative clause construction. There is only one right answer as to where its filler is. The filler must be the the relative pronoun (overt or empty) that moved up from its underlying position to a position adjacent to the head noun that the relative clause modifies. This is the only kind of antecedent–trace relation that the grammar allows. For example, in the construction *the rat that Socks chased around the mat*, the trace is after *chased*, and the only legitimate antecedent for it is the relative pronoun *that* at the front of the relative clause. The antecedent cannot be any other NP inside the relative, nor any NP outside the relative. If we want to make a good test of how well the human sentence processor makes use of this grammatical information, we need to construct examples that contain a variety of other tempting NPs, to see whether the processor falls for them. Swinney et al. (1988) tested sentences like (34).

(34)   The policeman saw the boy$_i$ [that$_i$ the crowd at the party accused *WH-trace*$_i$ of the crime].

The bracketed phrase in (34) is a relative clause modifying the head noun *boy*. The relative pronoun *that* is coindexed with this head noun, and the trace is coindexed with the relative pronoun; as a result, the trace denotes the boy. Therefore the meaning of the clause is that the crowd at the party accused the boy. It cannot mean that the policeman was accused, or that the crowd was accused, because the trace cannot have *policeman* or *crowd* as its antecedent. But does the processor realize this? Swinney et al. used an experimental paradigm known as *cross-modal priming* to find out. They reasoned that when the processor finds a trace and assigns an antecedent to it, the meaning of the antecedent would be momentarily mentally activated. Thus, if sentence (34) is interpreted correctly, the meaning of *boy* should be active when the word *boy* is processed; then its activation would decline, but it would become activated again when the trace after *accused* is identified. All we need, then, is a method of detecting the mental activation of meaning, at specific points in a sentence.

Swinney et al. went fishing for the meaning of *boy* at the trace position, using a related word as bait. The sentence was spoken; and just as the word *accused* ended and the word *of* began, the word *girl* appeared briefly on a CRT screen. The subjects in the experiment had to respond to the word *girl* by reading it aloud; the time between when it appeared and when a subject began to pronounce it was recorded. Why test with the word *girl*? Because it is a close associate of the word *boy*, and words that are associated tend to "prime" each other. So, if the meaning of *boy* is active at the trace position, responses to *girl* should be facilitated at that position. That is, responses to *girl* should be faster there than responses to *girl* in other contexts, and faster than responses to other words that are unrelated to *boy* (though otherwise comparable to *girl* in length and inherent difficulty). Note that because the sentence is spoken and the word is presented visually, the word can be simultaneous with the relevant part of the sentence, without the two stimuli physically masking each other. This mix of auditory and visual presentation is the cross-modal aspect of cross-modal priming; it is important because it makes it possible to examine sentence processing right at the moment of interest, without having to stop or slow down the sentence in order to do so.

Using this method, Swinney et al. were able to determine how the sentence processing device interprets a trace on-line, that is, which of the NPs in the sentence it assigns as its antecedent. They tested not just the correct antecedent (*boy* in the case of (34)) but also incorrect antecedents (*policeman* and *crowd* in (34)). The results showed that the correct antecedent was activated at the trace position, but incorrect antecedents were not, indicating that in interpreting the trace the processor had respected the grammatical constraints on the language. Thus, once again, it appears that the human sentence processing routines make reliable use of grammatical facts and are speedy enough to be able to do so at the instant at which they become relevant to the sentence at hand.

Consider one final example of the impressive fine-tuning of the processing routines. In another experiment using the same cross-modal priming paradigm, Swinney et al. (1988) tested sentences like (35).

(35) The boxer$_i$ visited the doctor that the swimmer at the competition had advised him$_i$ to see about the injury.

Imagine that the processor has received just the beginning of this sentence so far, up to the verb *advised* as shown in (36). For all that the processor can tell at this point there might be a WH-trace after *advised*. If there were, its antecedent would be the relative pronoun that is associated with the head noun *doctor*, as in the example shown in (37).

(36) The boxer visited the doctor that the swimmer at the competition had advised....

(37) The boxer visited the doctor$_i$ that the swimmer at the competition had advised *WH-trace$_i$* to see an expert about the injury.

The Active Filler Strategy predicts that the processor will briefly anticipate a trace after *advised*, just until the next word arrives and shows that there is none. Since the trace would be coindexed with *doctor*, and the processor is good at getting its coindexings right, we could expect priming of an associated word such as *nurse* if it were visually presented right after the word *advised* in (35). But then, immediately after that, the pronoun *him* is heard, so the processor discovers that the object of *advised* is actually an overt pronoun, not a trace. And a pronoun is governed by different grammatical constraints than a trace is. Like a trace, a pronoun picks up its reference from a prior phrase. But for a pronoun the grammar stipulates that the antecedent cannot be the subject of the same clause, and it cannot be a relative pronoun. In (35), therefore, the antecedent of *him* cannot be *swimmer* and cannot be *doctor*. That leaves only *boxer* (or, less probably, the pronoun could refer to someone not mentioned in the sentence at all). Thus, once the processor encounters the word *him* in (35), there should be priming of a target word associated with *boxer*, but not of words associated with *doctor* or *swimmer*. The results of the experiment were almost as predicted. Immediately after the verb *advised*, only the meaning of *doctor* was activated. This suggests that the processor guessed (wrongly) that there was a trace at that position, and assigned it an antecedent, without waiting to see what actually came next. Immediately after the pronoun *him*, just a fraction of a second later, there was activation of both *doctor* and *boxer*, but not of *swimmer*. Activation of *doctor* there has no good linguistic explanation, but it is reasonable to suppose that this was leftover activation from the preceding position. The sudden onset of activation of *boxer* at this point suggests that the processor rapidly consulted its linguistic knowledge and computed that *boxer* is the right antecedent for the pronoun (though it was not for the trace). This is a particularly striking result because it shows that the parser's success on other sentences, such as (34), is not due merely to some simple-minded strategy such as "if you need an antecedent, find a relative pronoun." It seems that the processor knows very well that different kinds of dependent elements have different antecedents.

8.2   Are Empty Categories Real?

8.2.1   Linguistic Explanations

The conclusion we have arrived at is that the human sentence processing device is—except when ambiguity trips it up—very quick, very well informed, and very accurate. Because this is so, we can hope to use experimental results on the processing of ECs to answer some linguistic questions about the status and formal properties of ECs. They have been the focus of a great deal of theoretical attention in recent years, and a wealth of facts and interesting generalizations have been established. But there are still some unanswered questions and some conflicting theoretical proposals. Indeed, the very existence of ECs has been challenged. Since they are no more visible to linguists than to other language users, the claim that they exist rests on certain theoretical assumptions about how the OBSERV-ABLE facts are to be captured. Recall that the two essential properties of an EC are (a) that it has no phonological form and (b) that it is a constituent of a sentence structure with exactly the same syntactic status as any overt constituent. The justification for assuming, despite point (a), that something falls under point (b) is that once ECs are postulated, they are seen to obey the very same general principles that apply to overt constituents. Therefore, some properties of questions, relative clauses, and other constructions containing ECs do not have to be stipulated separately; they follow in large part from known properties of other constructions. This kind of consolidation of facts in two superficially different domains is what warms linguists' hearts.

The most striking similarities are between ECs and overt pronouns and reflexives. (Note: In linguistic discussions, reflexives may also be called *anaphors*.) Pronouns and reflexives share with ECs the property of being dependent for their content (their reference in the world) on their association with an antecedent phrase. The pronoun *her* in (38) is dependent for its content on the antecedent *Sarah*; the reflexive *themselves* in (39) is dependent on the antecedent *the children*.

(38) $Sarah_i$ bowed low when the audience applauded her_i.

(39)   The new au pair hopes that the children$_i$ won't tire themselves$_i$ out.

Included in the grammar of English (or in Universal Grammar, true of all human languages) are three *binding principles*, which regulate the relationship between a dependent element and its antecedent. And these principles have been argued to apply to ECs just as to non-empty pronouns and reflexives. Principle A applies to reflexives; Principle B applies to pronouns; and Principle C applies to full referential noun phrases (such as *Benjamin Franklin* or *this bathmat* or *the fastest kangaroo in Australia*). The evidence suggests that each of these principles also applies to one kind of EC.

Let's consider Principle C first. It says that a referential NP cannot be dependent for its reference on any other NP. More specifically, a referential NP may not corefer with any NP that stands in a potential antecedent position relative to it. We may think of a potential antecedent as a subject or object that is higher in the structure. (This is very approximate; for details, see Lasnik, 1989, 1990.) This is why in (40), the NP *Thomas* cannot refer to the same person as the higher subject NP *he*. (It can in certain special circumstances, such as if Thomas is unaware that he is Thomas, but we will set aside those cases.)

(40)   He$_i$ thinks you deliberately insulted Thomas$_j$.

Chomsky (1976) observed that if we were to assume that Principle C also applies to WH-trace, that would provide an explanation for an otherwise puzzling restriction on coreference in some WH-constructions. Consider the meaning of example (41).

(41)   Please tell us who$_i$ he$_j$ thinks you insulted *WH-trace$_i$*.

As one reads the pronoun *he* in (41), it is clear that it refers to someone who has not yet been mentioned in the sentence. And in particular, it is clear that *he* does not corefer with *who*. There's a very clear implication in (41) that one person thinks a different person was insulted. (Contrast this with *Tell me who thinks you insulted him* where the *who* and the *him* CAN refer to the same person.) This requirement of noncoreference in (41) does not follow from any other fact about WH-constructions that we have mentioned so far. But Principle C can explain it. Principle C prevents coreference between *he* and the WH-trace in (41). The structural relation between *he* and the WH-trace is just like the relation between *he* and *Thomas* in (40). The NP *he* stands in a potential antecedent position relative to the trace in (41) and relative to the referential noun phrase *Thomas* in (40). So if WH-trace is like a referential NP in falling under Principle C, coreference will be outlawed in both examples and for the same reason. There is one final step in explaining (41), which is that, as usual, the

WH-trace must corefer with its WH-antecedent, in this case *who*. Since *he* cannot corefer with the WH-trace, it follows that *he* cannot corefer with *who*, either. (Note: It might look as if Principle C would prevent the necessary coreference between the WH-phrase and its trace; in fact it does not, because the WH-phrase is not in a subject or object position but moved into the pre-clause position.)

Another kind of trace that linguists have postulated is known as NP-trace, and it seems to obey Principle A, the binding principle that applies to reflexives. NP-trace is the by-product of a transformational movement called NP-movement, which differs from WH-movement in certain ways: it applies to NPs only; it applies to any NP, not just to WH-phrases; and it moves the NP into subject position. (For more technical details, see Haegeman, chapters 3 and 6.) NP-trace occurs in passive sentences like (42), and in "raising" constructions like (43).

(42)   The pie$_i$ was eaten *NP-trace*$_i$ by the guests.

(43)   The pie$_i$ seems to me *NP-trace*$_i$ to have disappeared.

NP-trace marks the underlying position of the moved constituent and determines its semantic role in the sentence. Thus, the pie is understood as the object of the eating in (42), and as the subject of the disappearing in (43). In both examples the phrase *the pie* moved from its underlying position into the subject position of the sentence. But NP-movement is much more restricted than WH-movement. NP-movement must be quite local. An example such as (44) is ungrammatical because the moved NP is too far away from its underlying position. (An asterisk indicates an ungrammatical sentence.)

(44)   *The pie$_i$ was believed that the guests ate *NP-trace*$_i$.

This fact about NP-movement would be explained if NP-trace is like an overt reflexive and falls under Principle A. Principle A requires a reflexive to have a local (nearby) antecedent. (For the exact definition of "local," see Lasnik 1989, chapter 1). Principle A allows the reflexive *themselves* in (39), where its antecedent is *the children* in the same clause, but disallows it in (45), where *the children* is further away (and the nearer NP *the new au pair* is singular, not plural).

(39)   The new au pair hopes $_S$[that the children$_i$ won't tire themselves$_i$ out].

(45)   The children$_i$ hope $_S$[that the new au pair won't tire themselves$_i$ out].

Comparing the ungrammatical relationship in (44) and the ungrammatical relationship in (45), we see that they are similar: In both cases the subject of a higher clause is coindexed with the object of a lower clause. So Principle A can account for both examples in the same way. NP-trace and overt reflexives must have local antecedents, and in (44) and (45) the antecedents are not local enough. Here is another case where a fact about movement constructions receives a natural explanation as long as we make the assumption that when a phrase moves, it leaves a silent constituent behind. Without a trace in (44), there would be nothing for Principle A to apply to.

This is a clever form of argument and makes a strong case for the claim that sentences contain elements that cannot be heard or seen. It is not completely decisive evidence, however, as long as there are OTHER satisfactory explanations for the same range of facts. And, indeed, other linguists have proposed alternative explanations, which make no mention of ECs at all, or even of movement transformations. For instance, it has been argued that a passive sentence like (42) is generated just as it appears, with a subject and a passive verb and an optional PP. It is not derived by rearranging the subject and object. Instead, it is assigned a meaning in which the subject of the sentence denotes the patient, and the PP denotes the agent, so that (42) means just the same as the active sentence *The guests ate the pie*. The fact that a passive construction must be local can be explained without assuming that any NP moves from one place to another in the sentence structure, creating a trace. It follows simply from the fact that ALL relationships between a verb and its arguments (its subject and objects) are local. Example (44) is ungrammatical because *the pie* is supposed to be understood as the patient of the eating event, but it is too far from the verb *ate* for that to be so. Thus, this non-movement theory can account for the facts we attributed to NP-movement and Principle A a moment ago. It needs a little more elaboration for examples like (43), but we need not work through that here. (See Bresnan 1978 for the classic presentation, and chapter 1 of Bresnan 1982 for more details.) For our purposes what is important is that the linguistic facts lend themselves to more than one analysis, and it is not easy on purely linguistic grounds to determine which one is correct. Both cover the facts tolerably well, though in quite different ways. Because of this indeterminacy, it would be very satisfactory for the EC hypothesis if psycholinguistic research could offer independent confirmation of the existence of ECs, in just those positions in which linguists have postulated them. And it has been argued, by MacDonald (1989) and by McElree and Bever (1989), that experiments showing that traces activate their antecedents, such as we discussed in the previous section, provide strong support for the EC hypothesis. How could there be antecedent activation by traces if there were no traces?

Is it true that experimental evidence of antecedent activation settles the issue of ECs? Probably not, unfortunately, in any deep sense, though the experimental results may shed some welcome light nonetheless. To be decisive, the experimental evidence would have to reveal the presence of SYNTACTIC ENTITIES at the postulated trace positions. But the antecedent activation paradigms that psycholinguists rely on at present only reveal SEMANTIC INTERPRETATION. They show that perceivers are UNDERSTANDING the sentences correctly, that they are establishing the right relationships between verbs and their arguments, even though some of those arguments are not in their "canonical" positions but are elsewhere in the sentence. But this fact is compatible with any linguistic analysis that accurately associates form and meaning for sentences, whether the analysis involves ECs or not. Therefore, these experiments, however successful they are on their own terms, necessarily fall short of proving that ECs exist. They do not definitively establish that what we have been CALLING "antecedent activation" effects really ARE antecedent reactivation effects; that is, that they are the result of perceivers mentally computing a syntactic structure in which there is an EC that is coindexed with an antecedent. Perhaps one day we will find ways of achieving this more interesting goal. In the meantime, though, we may be able to make some progress toward it if we can establish some of the finer parameters of the comprehension process.

The experiment by MacDonald addressed NP-trace. Experimental data on NP-trace are particularly welcome, since NP-trace is more vulnerable to skepticism than WH-trace is. The linguistic arguments for ECs work best for WH-trace, but do not give much of a grip on NP-trace. Let's consider just two kinds of argument. First, there are facts which suggest that though an EC has no phonological content, it may nevertheless have phonological effects. It can get in the way of other phonological processes, such as the merging of *want* and *to* into *wanna*, in colloquial speech. In (46b) the two words have coalesced. This is known as *wanna*-contraction.

(46)   a.   Does Esther want to sing?

       b.   Does Esther wanna sing?

       c.   Who does Esther wanna sing "Hello, Dolly" with?
            (She wants to sing it with Martin.)

       d. Who_i does Esther want to sing "Hello, Dolly" with $WH\text{-}trace_i$?

       e.   *Who does Esther wanna sing "Hello, Dolly"?
            (She wants Martin to sing it.)

       f. Who_i does Esther want $WH\text{-}trace_i$ to sing "Hello, Dolly"?

       g.   There hafta be two student representatives on every
            committee.

h.   There$_i$ have $NP\text{-}trace_i$ to be two student representatives on every committee.

Contraction is also possible in the question (46c), whose structure is shown in (46d). But for most speakers *wanna* is not acceptable in (46e). The structure of (46e) is shown in (46f), and an interesting difference from the other examples is apparent. In (46e,f) the *want* and the *to* are not adjacent; they are separated by a WH-trace. This offers a good explanation for why contraction is blocked here; phonological merger can only occur when words are in close contact. But of course, this explanation is available only if WH-trace is assumed to exist as a genuine entity in linguistic structure. For NP-trace there is no such phonological evidence. Relevant examples are not plentiful, but what little evidence there is shows that words on either side of NP-trace CAN coalesce in colloquial speech. An example is shown in (46g). The *hafta* in (46g) is a reduction of *have* and *to*. Contraction occurs here despite the fact that an NP-trace intervenes. The structure of (46g) is shown in (46h); it is a raising construction in which the subject NP (the 'dummy' NP *there*) has moved up from the lower clause, leaving an NP-trace in between *have* and *to*. (Note: We have a terminological tangle here. Anyone who doubts the reality of NP-trace wouldn't want to describe (46g,h) in these terms anyway. But for convenience in discussing the experiments let's continue to talk AS IF sentences contain WH-trace and NP-trace even while we raise the question of whether or not they do.) Some interesting explanations have been proposed to account for why phonological contraction processes care about WH-trace but completely ignore NP-trace. But whatever the reason for it, this fact robs us of a potentially valuable form of evidence for NP-trace. For all that (46) shows, NP-trace might not exist.

Second: a WH-phrase often wears on its sleeve the fact that it started life in the position now occupied by its trace, but an NP-trace does not. For those English speakers (increasingly few) who make a *who* / *whom* distinction, a WH-pronoun is nominative or accusative in accord with its UNDERLYING position before movement. In (47a) it is nominative *who* because it started out as SUBJECT of *is clever* in the lower clause; in (47b) it is accusative *whom* because it started out as OBJECT of *consult* in the lower clause.

(47)   a.   I know who$_i$ Josephine thinks $WH\text{-}trace_i$ is clever.

       b.   I know whom$_i$ Josephine ought to consult $WH\text{-}trace_i$.

By contrast, the form of the moved NP in a passive or raising construction is always in accord with its SURFACE position. For instance, a pronoun subject of a passive sentence can be nominative *he* as in (48a), but it cannot be accusative *him* as in (48b), even though a pronoun in the underlying position would have been accusative, as shown by (48c).

(48)   a. He_i was greeted $NP\text{-}trace_i$ by the guests.

       b.   *Him_i was greeted $NP\text{-}trace_i$ by the guests.

       c.   The guests greeted him.

Thus, the positive evidence for NP-movement (and NP-trace) is considerably less compelling than the positive evidence for WH-movement (and WH-trace). Furthermore, the possibility of generating the sentence directly, without moving phrases around, is made easier for "NP-movement" constructions by the fact that the supposedly moved NP occupies a perfectly normal subject position, rather than the special before-the-clause position that a WH-phrase appears in, and also by the fact that NP-movement does not span great distances as WH-movement does. In view of this, there are three hypotheses worth considering about ECs: (1) that there are none; (2) that WH-trace exists, but not NP-trace; (3) that both WH-trace and NP-trace are real. Let us see what the experimental data can tell us.

8.2.2   Experimental Evidence

MacDonald (1989) tested "short" passive sentences (passives without an agent *by*-phrase) such as the second sentence in (49).

(49)   The terrorists wanted to disrupt the ceremonies.
       [The new mayor at the center podium]$_i$ was shot $NP\text{-}trace_i$.

MacDonald was looking for reactivation, at the NP-trace position, of its antecedent. In (49) the antecedent is the NP *The new mayor at the center podium*. For this purpose she used an experimental paradigm that had already been used to demonstrate antecedent reactivation for overt pronouns. Thus, if the passive sentences gave a similar result, that would be consistent with the hypothesis that a passive sentence contains an element similar to a pronoun, though not directly observable. The task MacDonald used is known as visual probe recognition (VPR). A sentence is presented on a screen; then a single word is presented which the subject must judge as having been, or not been, in that sentence. Many other sentences were presented in which the correct answer was "no," but in all the sentences of interest the correct answer was "yes." The probe word for the passive sentences was always the head noun of the antecedent NP. So for (49), the probe was *mayor*. The first sentence in (49) is there to provide some context and to suggest a plausible agent for the action in the passive sentence that follows. The logic behind this experimental design is much the same as for the cross-modal priming paradigm discussed earlier. The idea is that when the processor encounters an EC and assigns it its antecedent, the antecedent is mentally activated and so performance on it will be facilitated. Thus, "yes" responses to the probe word *mayor* after (49) should be faster than normal. How fast is normal? To establish that, MacDonald tested similar sentences that had an adjective in place of the passive verb, such as *furious* in (50).

(50)   The terrorists wanted to disrupt the ceremonies.
The new mayor at the center podium was furious.

Linguistic theories are all agreed that an adjective is not accompanied by an NP-trace, so (50) contains nothing that should trigger reactivation of the subject noun. The interesting comparison is between the response time for deciding whether *mayor* occurred in (49), where the hypothesis says there is an NP-trace, and the response time for deciding whether *mayor* occurred in (50), where there is no NP-trace. Any difference between them (after the difficulty of particular words is factored out) must be due to the facilitation of *mayor* in (49) due to its reactivation by the NP-trace.

As MacDonald had predicted, probe recognition was faster for the passive verb sentences than for the adjective sentences. McElree and Bever (1989) obtained similar results, for raising as well as passive constructions, using a similar visual probe recognition task. The evidence from VPR thus seems to offer solid support for the existence of NP-trace. Curiously, though, NP-trace has not shown such clear effects in the cross-modal priming (CMP) paradigm that provided evidence of antecedent reactivation for WH-trace in constructions like (34) and (35). Osterhout and Swinney (1993) tested passive sentences with CMP and did not observe significant reactivation until one second AFTER the NP-trace position. This contrasts with results for WH-trace, where the effect is standardly observed when the test word occurs right at the trace position. A second is a long time in sentence processing, so this discrepancy suggests that there is a serious delay in finding an NP-trace or in assigning it its antecedent. So here we have something of a mystery. WH-trace makes a strong showing in CMP. NP-trace does well in VPR but shows up only very weakly in CMP. (For no good reason, WH-trace has not yet been clearly tested with VPR.) Why might this be so? And, especially, what could be the explanation for the apparently contradictory NP-trace results? Do the VPR data overestimate the NP-trace phenomenon, or do the CMP data underestimate it?

This is a research issue still under study, but it seems likeliest that the CMP data provide the more realistic assessment. The CMP task is "online." Subjects respond during the processing of the sentence while they are computing the syntactic structure and meaning. By definition an EC is a syntactic entity. And this means that if we are going to see signs of its existence, the best time to observe them should be DURING processing. By the time processing is over, what perceivers retain of a sentence is mostly just its meaning; syntactic details are rapidly lost. (Test yourself: What can you recall of the meaning of the sentence prior to this one? How much of it can you repeat verbatim? That's much harder.) This fact about timing is important to our attempt to make sense of the apparently conflicting experimental results. The VPR task occurs after the sentence is over, and it is basically a memory task. The question "Was this word in the sentence?" taps a representation of the sentence that is the end-result of sentence processing and is now laid down in short-term memory. So, even if an EC had been computed along the way, it would have served its purpose by then and would have been discarded, once its effect on the meaning of the sentence had been established. Because of this, the VPR result for passive and raising sentences tells us only that the subject phrase is more strongly represented in memory when the predicate is a passive verb than when it is an adjective. And though that is evidence of SOME difference between passive verbs and adjectives, it might not be evidence of NP-trace.

Let us take stock here. Arguably, CMP is a better experimental para-digm than VPR for revealing the presence of ECs. But NP-trace does not show up robustly in CMP, especially by comparison with WH-trace, which gives immediate significant effects. This looks very much like evi-dence for hypothesis (2): that WH-trace exists but NP-trace does not. This is not an unreasonable inference to draw, at least as an interim conclusion pending more experiments in future. But if this is to be the verdict, we must find some other explanation for the memory enhancement that oc-curred in the experiments on passive and raising constructions. That must have some other source, if it is not due to the presence of NP-trace. If we cannot imagine any other explanation, perhaps we should think twice about giving up the idea of NP-trace.

In fact, a plausible account suggests itself. Passive sentences occur quite infrequently; certainly they are less common than sentences with adjectival predicates. In the processing of a sentence, then, a passive verb would be less expected than an adjective. And there is reason to believe that passive sentences are more effortful to process than active sentences are. (The evidence for this is murkier than one might expect. See Forster and Olbrei 1973 for a summary.) How could this make passive sentences EASIER than adjectival sentences in the VPR experiments? It sounds as if it would predict exactly the opposite. But this is not so, because there is known to be an INVERSE relation between VPR performance on a word, and its ex-pectability and ease of processing in the sentence. Earlier research (not all of it on language) had shown that the greater the effort that goes into processing a stimulus, the more distinctive its subsequent memory representation is. Cairns, Cowart, and Jablon (1981) applied this finding to sentences like those in (51).

(51)   a.   Kathy wanted a snapshot of my baby, but she unfortunately forgot her camera today.

       b.   Kathy finally arrived at my baby shower, but she unfortunately forgot her camera today.

In (51a) the word *camera* is more predictable than it is in (51b), because of the reference to a snapshot in the first clause of the sentence. On the basis of the prior research, we would expect that in the context in which it is less predictable, the word *camera* should be harder to process but easier to recall. Cairns, Cowart, and Jablon confirmed this for their test sentences by comparing three tasks: two measures of processing difficulty, and VPR as a measure of short-term memory. In one task, subjects listened to the sentence over headphones and pushed a button when they had understood the sentence well enough to be able to answer a comprehension question about it. Time of understanding was higher for sentences like (51b) with unpredictable words than for sentences like (51a). In another task, subjects listened to the sentences and pushed a button as soon as they heard a word beginning with a specified phoneme (speech sound), such as *t*. This is called *phoneme monitoring*. In (51a) and (51b), subjects told to monitor for *t* would push the button on hearing the beginning of *today*. The heavier the processing load at the point in the sentence at which the phoneme occurs, the slower the subject should be at detecting the phoneme; thus, slow monitoring reveals difficult sentence processing. Note that the *t* of *today* immediately follows the word *camera*, so the phoneme monitoring time should reflect how easy or difficult it is to integrate *camera* into the sentence. The results confirmed that sentences like (51b) were harder to process than sentences like (51a). However, when the same sentences were tested in VPR, with the word *camera* as the probe word for (51a,b), performance was significantly better for sentences like (51b) than for sentences like (51a).

Let us call this the *depth-of-processing effect*. It links three things: the less predictable an item is, the greater the effort of processing it, and the easier it is to recall. This provides a good explanation for why passive sentences fare better than adjectival sentences in VPR experiments. Because passive sentences are less common than adjectival sentences, they receive more attention during processing, so they are easier to probe in short-term memory. To pin this down more tightly, we would like to know if the passive sentences in McDonald's experiment were harder to process than the adjectival sentences were. In fact, no difference between them was observed. However, the only measure available is whole sentence reading time, and possibly this is not sensitive enough to show the difference we are looking for. A different way of checking up on the depth-of-processing explanation would be to confirm that a passive verb is indeed less expected by the processing routines than an adjective is. Wasow et al. (1994) tested the beginnings of MacDonald's sentences, up to the verb *be* (*was* in example (49)), in a sentence completion task. The beginning of the sentence appeared on a screen; the subject immediately read it aloud and continued speaking, completing the sentence in any way that came to mind. Fewer passive predicates were produced than adjectives, by a highly significant margin. If this production test is a good indicator of what perceivers are anticipating as they are reading a sentence, we can conclude that the passive verbs in MacDonald's experiment would have been less expected than the adjectives and hence more memorable. It seems quite likely, then, that the VPR facilitation for passive sentences is really a depth-of-processing effect, a matter of memory enhancement that has nothing to do with NP-trace or ECs at all.

To sum up: At very least, the experimental data seem to be telling us that NP-trace does not have the same status as WH-trace. And though caution is in order, since firm facts are still scarce, the data seem most compatible with hypothesis (2): that WH-trace appears in mental representations of sentence structure, but NP-trace does not. This is not the outcome that was anticipated by McElree and Bever or by MacDonald when they devised their experiments on NP-trace, but it is in keeping with their conception that sentence processing facts can illuminate linguistic issues on which standard linguistic methodology does not definitively pronounce (or has not yet).

Suppose this conclusion holds up as further evidence is gathered in future. How extensive would its impact be on current conceptions of linguistic structure? It could turn attention toward theories of language such as Lexical Functional Grammar and Phrase Structure Grammar, which are not committed to NP-trace and which account for the same language facts by different descriptive means, such as a lexicon that contains passive verbs on a par with active ones. Alternatively, it may be that even within Government and Binding theory, which makes the most extensive use of ECs, it is possible to reassess the need for NP-trace, or at least to reassess its supposed similarity to overt anaphors. In recent years it has been established that ECs (presupposing their existence) are subject to an additional constraint, the *Empty Category Principle* (Chomsky 1981). The ECP applies ONLY to phonologically empty elements; it does not apply to overt lexical pronouns and reflexives. Though motivated primarily by other facts, it turns out that the ECP can account for properties of passive and raising constructions that were previously attributed to the binding principles. This changes the internal dynamics within the theory in ways that have not yet been fully explored in psycholinguistics, and it may offer some interesting reconciliation of the apparent misfit between theory and experimental results. However, even if the ECP breaks the analogy between NP-trace and reflexives, it does not lessen the theory's commitment to NP-trace. Far from it—the ECP can apply to passives only if there is an EC in passives for it to apply to. And, in fact, the direction this theory is taking in general is toward more ECs rather than fewer. Current analyses assume many more movement operations than previously, such as movement of the verb and the subject in the derivation of every sentence; and every movement leaves a trace. Perhaps it might be argued, by way of defense against the experimental conclusions, that a single NP-trace in a passive sentence would naturally be undetectable amid this throng of other ECs. Such possibilities underline the need for psycholinguistics to keep on polishing up its premises and its methods, so that we can look more and more closely at how sentences are mentally represented. With new experimental techniques, or a new understanding of how theory and experiments should mesh, NP-trace might be banished once and for all, or it might bounce back stronger than ever. This is a lively field of research, so no one would want to bet now on which of these turns it will take over the next few years; it will be interesting to see.

Suggestions for Further Reading

Discussion of empty categories makes up a large part of the literature on syntactic theory for the last ten years and more, particularly within Government and Binding theory. To learn more about the linguistic motivation for ECs, and to see them at work in the syntactic derivations of sentences, it would be advisable to begin with textbook presentations such as Haegeman 1991 or Freidin 1992. These texts contain references to the original books and research articles on which they are based, such as Chomsky 1981, 1986a, 1986b, and they offer advice about how best to move on to reading this more technical literature.

Several linguistic theories do not employ movement transformations and assume either WH-trace only or no ECs at all. For Lexical Functional Grammar, the classic presentation is the paper by Bresnan 1978; a more recent discussion is Kaplan and Zaenen 1989; the most comprehensive collection of related papers is in the book edited by Bresnan 1982. For Head-driven Phrase Structure Grammar (HPSG) and its predecessor Generalized Phrase Structure Grammar (GPSG), a classic presentation is Gazdar 1981; a recent discussion is Sag and Fodor 1994; the most comprehensive presentation is in two volumes by Pollard and Sag 1987, 1994. For references on Categorial Grammar and its modern extensions see chapter 9 by Steedman in the present volume. Textbook level presentations of these and related theoretical positions can be found in Blake 1990, Horrocks 1987, and Sells 1985.

Experimental research on ECs is largely summarized in Foder 1989, which sets it in the context of earlier work on the same kinds of sentences before ECs were "invented." Fodor 1993 updates and extends this survey. Most of the material in the present chapter is drawn from these two papers. The most influential experimental studies have been those by MacDonald 1989, by McElree and Bever 1989, by Swinney, Nicol, and colleagues (reported in Nicol and Swinney 1989), and by Tanenhaus and colleagues (summarized in Tanenhaus, Garnsey, and Boland 1990 and in Boland et al. in press). An interesting recent debate starts with a challenge to empty categories by Pickering and Barry 1991 and continues with articles by Gorrell 1993 and by Gibson and Hickok 1993, and a reply by Pickering 1993. For evidence on the psychological status of ECs that derives from studies of aphasic subjects, see the references in question 8.10 below. A good source of discussion and references on garden-path sentences of many kinds is Gibson (in press).

Problems

8.1 Draw a tree diagram showing the structure of sentence (i). How many ECs does it contain (assuming both WH-trace and NP-trace exist)? What is the deep structure position of the phrase *which pie*?

(i) I have forgotten which pie Bertram said seemed to him to have been nibbled by mice.

8.2 State what category of constituent (NP, N, V, and so on) is "missing" in each of the following sentences:

(i) Pigs can play croquet but rabbits can't.
(ii) Bert was snappish to his mother but he wasn't to his father.
(iii) Tebaldi's recording of Tosca is terrific, but Melba's of Manon is more moving.
(iv) The cow's in the corn but I don't care.
(v) Enjoy!

8.3 For any or all examples (26b–h) in section 8.1.3:

(i) State where the temporary ambiguity begins.
(ii) Describe the two possible analyses of the word string.
(iii) Make up a sentence that starts the same but ends in a way compatible with the other analysis.
(iv) Decide which of the two analyses is easier to compute. (After noting your own intuitions of processing difficulty, try the sentences on some friends to see how uniform judgments are.)
(v) For each analysis, try to make up a sentence which has that analysis but is not even temporarily unambiguous.

Questions for Further Thought

8.1 For any language other than English that you know (or know someone who knows), find as many examples as you can of sentences containing ECs. What are the categories (NP, PP, VP, and so on) of these ECs? Are they traces of movement? Or are they deletions of repeated material (as in problem 8.2, (i)–(iv))? Or are they interpreted by reference to the discourse (as in (v) of problem 8.2)? Does English permit ECs in similar contexts? If not, do the ECs you have found have properties that would make them useful in testing psycholinguistic hypotheses not testable in English? (For example: Is NP-trace in passives more anticipatable on-line than it is in English? Does any EC appear in the same context as an overt pronoun, so that the two could be precisely compared in an experiment?)

8.2 The phonological argument for the existence of WH-trace, based on *wanna*-contraction, has been challenged by Schachter (1984). He observed that when a putative WH-trace is in subject position in a tensed clause, contraction is possible across it. In *Who do you think's clever?* the WH-trace is between *think* and *is*, but nevertheless the *is* can contract to *'s*. Read Schachter's article, and, if you wish, refer also to pp. 374–394 of Fodor (1993) and pp. 435–443 of Barss (1993). Does *think's*—contraction prove that WH-trace does not occur in subject position? that it doesn't exist at all? Is there any way to reconcile *think's*-contraction with the facts of *wanna*-contraction?

8.3 If there is a WH-trace in subject position in sentences like *Who do you think is clever?* (see question 8.2), it should reactivate its antecedent during sentence processing, just as WH-trace in object position has been shown to do. Construct a set of experimental sentences that could be used in a cross-modal lexical decision experiment to determine whether this is so. Design your sentences in matched pairs so that a comparison can be made between cases where there is verb contraction across the putative trace and cases where there is no contraction. Would you expect these to show the same amount of antecedent activation?

8.4 Pickering and Barry (1991) combine facts about center-embedding and facts about WH-constructions, to argue that WH-trace does not exist. (This is much more dramatic than claiming that experimental data DO NOT CONFIRM that WH-trace exists.) Pickering and Barry argue that IF there were WH-traces, a sentence like (i) should be as difficult to process as doubly center-embedded sentences like (4) in section 8.1.1.

(i) John found the saucer [on which]$_i$ Mary put the cup [into which]$_j$ I poured the tea WH-trace$_j$ WH-trace$_i$.

(4) The rat the cat the dog worried chased ate the malt.

But this is clearly not so. Sentence (i) is long but it is relatively easy to comprehend, while sentence (4), though shorter, is more difficult. Read the article by Pickering and Barry, and, if you wish, refer to the responses to it by Gorrell (1993) and by Gibson and Hickok (1993). Is this sentence processing argument against WH-trace valid? If not, why not? If so, can linguistic theory capture the facts of WH-constructions without WH-trace?

8.5 We have seen that the processor copes very efficiently (ambiguities aside) with ECs. So now it is not so clear, after all, that what pushes the processor beyond its limits is a heavy ratio of structural nodes to overt words (see section 8.1.1). So now it is not clear why the doubly center-embedded sentence (4) is so strikingly difficult to process. Can you explain this? Many ideas have been proposed over the years. Read Gibson (in press, chapter 3, and, if you wish, also chapter 4); look up some of the earlier works that Gibson cites. Is there any one explanation of the center-embedding effect that is convincing?

An interesting clue is that ungrammatical sentences with three NPs but only two VPs, such as (i), tend to be perceived (incorrectly) as more grammatical than sentences with three NPs and three VPs, such as (4).

(i) *The rat the cat the dog chased ate the malt.

(4) The rat the cat the dog worried chased ate the malt.

Does any account of the center-embedding effect explain this fact? If so, does it predict WHICH of the three NPs in (i) lacks a VP in (i)?

8.6 Visual probe recognition (VPR) experiments show facilitation for the head noun of the antecedent of an NP-trace (the noun *mayor* in (49) in section 8.2.2). It has been assumed that this is because the antecedent is reactivated at the trace position. If this explanation is correct, then a word that is in the sentence but NOT in the antecedent phrase should NOT be facilitated. The trace explanation would be undermined by across-the-board facilitation for the whole sentence. MacDonald (1989) checked for facilitation of a non-antecedent word (a word denoting the understood agent of the passive, such as *terrorists* in example (49)). She found a very slight effect that might have been due to facilitation but was not statistically significant. This is difficult to evaluate; perhaps facilitation occurred but was attenuated because the test word occurred far back in a previous sentence. Make up some sentences to put this issue to a more stringent test. This is more of a challenge than it may sound. One way to do it would be to compare responses to the same word when it occurs (a) in the antecedent phrase in a passive sentence and (b) in a non-antecedent constituent of a passive sentence. Ideally, the contexts in which the target word appears should otherwise be as similar as possible, the sentences should be equally plausible, and so forth. And the target word should be the same distance from the end of the sentence iny each case so that neither is nearer to the probe task than the other is. (Can all these criteria be satisfied at once?)

8.7   Evidence for the psychological reality of ECs may be provided by the pattern of deficits in aphasic speech, where brain damage has impaired the normal functioning of the grammar and/or the language processing systems (see chapter 13 of this volume). Read Caplan and Hildebrandt (1988) and Grodzinsky et al. (1993), and assess the evidence they provide for WH-trace, NP-trace, and other ECs. Read Zurif et al. (1993) to see how experimental methods outlined in this chapter can be adapted to the study of aphasic speech.

References

Barss, A. (1993). Transparency and visibility: Sentence processing and the grammar of anaphora. In G. Altmann and R. Shillcock, eds., *Cognitive models of speech processing: The second sperlonga meeting*. Hillsdale, NJ: Lawrence Erlbaum.

Blake, B. (1990). *Relational grammar*. London: Routledge.

Boland, J. E., M. K. Tanenhaus, S. M. Garnsey, and G. N. Carlson (in press). Verb argument structure in parsing and interpretation: Evidence from WH-questions. *Journal of Memory and Language*.

Bresnan, J. (1978). A realistic transformational grammar. In M. Halle, J. Bresnan, and G. A. Miller, eds., *Linguistic theory and psychological reality*. Cambridge, MA: MIT Press.

Bresnan, J., ed. (1982). *The mental representation of grammatical relations*. Cambridge, MA: MIT Press.

Cairns, H. S., W. Cowart, and A. D. Jablon (1981). Effects of prior context upon the integration of lexical information during sentence processing. *Journal of Verbal Learning and Verbal Behavior* 20, 445–453.

Caplan, D., and N. Hildebrandt (1988). Disorders affecting comprehension of syntactic form: Preliminary results and their implications for theories of syntax and parsing. *Canadian Journal of Linguistics* 33, 477–505.

Chomsky, N. (1965). *Aspects of the theory of syntax*. Cambridge, MA: MIT Press.

Chomsky, N. (1976). Conditions on rules of grammar. *Linguistic Analysis* 2, 303–351. Reprinted in N. Chomsky, *Essays on form and interpretation*. Amsterdam: North Holland.

Chomsky, N. (1981). *Lectures on government and binding*. Dordrecht, Netherlands: Foris.

Chomsky, N. (1986a). *Knowledge of language: Its nature, origin and use*. New York: Praeger.

Chomsky, N. (1986b). *Barriers*. Cambridge, MA: MIT Press.

Crain, S., and J. D. Fodor (1985). How can grammars help parsers? In D. Dowty, L. Karttunen, and A. Zwicky, eds., *Natural language parsing: Psychological, computational, and theoretical perspectives*. Cambridge: Cambridge University Press.

Fodor, J. D. (1989). Empty categories in sentence processing. *Language and Cognitive Processes* 4, 155–209.

Fodor, J. D. (1993). Processing empty categories: A question of visibility. In G. Altmann and R. Shillcock, eds., *Cognitive models of speech processing: The second sperlonga meeting*. Hillsdale, NJ: Erlbaum.

Forster, K. I., and I. Olbrei (1973). Semantic heuristics and syntactic analysis. *Cognition* 2, 3, 319–347.

Frazier, L. (1985). Syntactic complexity. In D. Dowty, L. Karttunen, and A. Zwicky, eds., *Natural language parsing: Psychological, computational, and theoretical perspectives*. Cambridge: Cambridge University Press.

Frazier, L., and C. Clifton (1989). Successive cyclicity in the grammar and the parser. *Language and Cognitive Processes* 4, 93–126.

Freidin, R. (1992). *Foundations of generative syntax*. Cambridge, MA: MIT Press.

Gazdar, G. (1981). Unbounded dependencies and coordinate structure. *Linguistic Inquiry* 12, 155–184.

Gibson, E. A. F. (in press). *Memory limitations and processing breakdown*. Cambridge, MA: MIT Press.

Gibson, E., and G. Hickok (1993). Sentence processing with empty categories. *Language and Cognitive Processes* 8, 147–161.

Gorrell, P. (1993). Evaluating the direct association hypothesis: A reply to Pickering and Barry (1991). *Language and Cognitive Processes* 8, 129–146.

Grodzinsky, Y., K. Wexler, Y. C. Chien, S. Marakovits, and J. Solomon (1993). The breakdown of binding relations. *Brain and Language* 45, 396–422.

Haegeman, L. (1991). *Introduction to government and binding theory*. Oxford: Blackwell.

Horrocks, G. C. (1987). *Generative grammar*. New York: Longman.

Kaplan, R. M., and A. Zaenen (1989). Long-distance dependencies, constituent structure, and functional uncertainty. In M. R. Baltin and A. S. Kroch, eds., *Alternative conceptions of phrase structure*. Chicago: University of Chicago Press.

Lasnik, H. (1989). *Essays on anaphora*. Dordrecht, Netherlands: Kluwer.

Lasnik, H. (1990). Syntax. In D. N. Osherson and H. Lasnik, eds., *Language: An invitation to cognitive science*. Vol. 1. 1st ed. Cambridge, MA: MIT Press.

MacDonald, M. C. (1989). Priming effects from gaps to antecedents. *Language and Cognitive Processes* 4, 1–72.

Marcus, Mitchell P. (1980). *A theory of syntactic recognition for natural language*. Cambridge, MA: MIT Press.

McElree, B., and T. G. Bever (1989). The psychological reality of linguistically defined gaps. *Journal of Psycholinguistic Research* 18, 21–35.

Miller, G. A., and N. Chomsky (1963). Finitary models of language users. In R. D. Luce, R. Bush, and E. Galanter, eds., *Handbook of mathematical psychology*. Vol. 2. New York: Wiley.

Nicol, J., and D. Swinney (1989). The role of structure in coreference assignment during sentence comprehension. *Journal of Psycholinguistic Research* 18, 5–19.

Osterhout, L., and D. Swinney (1993). On the temporal course of gap-filling during comprehension of verbal passives. *Journal of Psycholinguistic Research* 22, 273–286.

Pickering, M. (1993). Direct association and sentence processing: A reply to Gorrell and to Gibson and Hickok. *Language and Cognitive Processes* 8, 163–196.

Pickering, M., and G. Barry (1991). Sentence processing without empty categories. *Language and Cognitive Processes* 6, 229–259.

Pollard, C., and I. A. Sag (1987). *Information-based syntax and semantics*. Vol. 1, *Fundamentals*. CSLI Lecture Notes no. 13. Stanford: Center for the Study of Language and Information (distributed by the University of Chicago Press).

Pollard, C., and I. A. Sag (1994). *Head-driven phrase structure grammar*. Chicago: University of Chicago Press.

Sag, I. A., and J. D. Fodor (1994). Extraction without traces. In R. Aranovich, W. Byrne, S. Preuss, and M. Senturia, eds., *Proceedings of the West Coast Conference on Formal Linguistics* 13, 365–384. Published for Stanford Linguistics Association by CSLI Publications, Stanford, CA.

Schachter, P. (1984). Auxiliary reduction: An argument for GPSG. *Linguistic Inquiry* 15, 514–523.

Sells, P. (1985). *Lectures on contemporary syntactic theories*. Stanford, CA: CSLI.

Stowe, L. A. (1986). Evidence for on-line gap location. *Language and Cognitive Processes* 1, 227–245.

Swinney, D., M. Ford, U. Frauenfelder, and J. Bresnan (1988). On the temporal course of gap-filling and antecedent assignment during sentence comprehension. In B. Grosz, R. Kaplan, M. Macken, and I. Sag, eds., *Language structure and processing*. Stanford: Center for the Study of Language and Information.

Tanenhaus, M. K., S. M. Garnsey, and J. Boland (1990). Combinatory lexical information and language comprehension. In G. T. M. Altmann, ed., *Cognitive models of speech processing: Psycholinguistic and computational perspectives*. Cambridge, MA: MIT Press.

Wasow, T., K. Henniss, L. Re, and J. D. Fodor (1994). Thematic roles and expectations in processing passive sentences. Unpublished manuscript, Stanford University and Graduate Center, City University of New York.

Yngve, V. (1960). A model and an hypothesis for language structure. *Proceedings of the American Philosophical Society* 104, 444–466.

Zurif, E., D. Swinney, P. Prather, J. Solomon, and C. Bushell (1993). An on-line analysis of syntactic proceeding in Broca's and Wernicke's Aphasia. *Brain and Language* 45, 448–464.

Chapter 9
Computational Aspects of the Theory of Grammar
Mark Steedman

9.1 Introduction: Grammar and Computation

9.1.1 Competence and Performance

What relation would a cognitive scientist approaching the problem for the first time expect to hold between the syntax of human languages, their semantic interpretations, and the structures built by humans during processing? If they knew nothing specific about any of these modules, they would probably expect the rules and structures that they involve to be extremely closely related. They might reason as follows.

The function of rules of syntax in the artificial programming languages and the logical and mathematical calculi that we invent ourselves is purely and simply to identify the corresponding rules of semantics, so there seems every reason for these two modules, at least, to be as transparently related as possible in natural languages. Moreover, we know (for reasons discussed by Pinker in the present volume) that even finite state grammars cannot in general be induced from mere exposure to the strings of the language they generate (compare Gold 1967), and that more explicit guidance from adults to child language learners is minimal (compare Brown and Hanlon 1970 and much subsequent work). It is generally agreed as a consequence of these observations and others (discussed by Lasnik in this volume) that human language learners must bring something more to the task. The only remotely plausible candidate that has ever been offered as a basis for this innate capacity is access to the semantic or conceptual representations that the utterances convey. (In the context of modern linguistics, the suggestion goes back at least to Chomsky 1965, p. 59, and to Miller 1967, although the idea is much older.) Any divergence between

NOTE: I am grateful to Janet Fodor, Ed Stabler, and Mark Johnson for discussions on these questions at a number of stages. The work was supported in part by NSF grant nos. IRI90-18513, IRI91-17110, and CISE IIP, CDA 88-22719, DARPA grant no. N00014-90-J-1863, and ARO grant no. DAAL03-89-C0031.

syntax and semantics is therefore likely to be severely discriminated against in evolutionary terms, simply because it looks as if it would make the language unlearnable. (Of course, we have very little detailed knowledge of how this learning process works. See Pinker 1979 for a review of some proposed learning mechanisms; also see Gleitman 1990 for some cogent warnings against the assumption that such semantic representations have their origin solely in present perception and the material world in any simple sense of that term. The conceptual representations in question are likely to include at least such grammatically relevant notions as actual and potential participants and properties of events, and the attentional focus of other conversational participants, as well as the instantaneous sense-data of the physical environment.)

Such an investigator would probably also expect the rules and structures involved in processing to be similarly directly related, a version of what is usually called the *competence hypothesis*, a position that has been repeatedly endorsed within the generative tradition (compare Chomsky 1965, p. 9; 1975a, p. 7). While it is quite possible in principle for a processor to parse according to one grammar, and then to map the results via a string homomorphism onto the trees of another more semantically transparent competence grammar, it is hard to believe that such an arrangement could arise in natural processors. The rules of such "covering grammars" are not in general paired one-to-one with the rules of the semantically transparent grammar. Therefore, even if a child could, by virtue of access to a semantic interpretation, correctly identify a new rule to add to the competence grammar, the problem of deducing the appropriate changes to the covering grammar can in general be resolved only by recompiling the entire grammar. In the absence of any explanation for why an apparently unnecessary complexity should be endured, it too seems likely to be penalized by natural selection. This is the position advocated by Bresnan and Kaplan (Bresnan 1982) under the name of the *strong competence hypothesis*.

Of course, even if it is true (as seems highly likely) that syntax, semantics, and processing are entirely transparent to one another, it does not follow that each of these modules will be equally effective in helping us to understand the system as a whole. As Chomsky has always argued, it seems to be a matter of practical fact that syntactic form is the most testable and reliable source of information among the three. This insight has been so productive of generalizations and lasting results (of the kind discussed in the chapter by Lasnik in the present volume) that it is really inconceivable that we should abandon it now. It is perhaps worth pausing to ask why this should be.

The methodological priority of competence seems to follow from the exceedingly fortunate fact that the computation involved in mapping natural language strings onto their interpretations appears to be one for which a theory can be specified independently of the particular algorithm that is actually used to perform the computation. We know that for even quite simple grammars there are very many processing algorithms. Exactly how many there are, and the number of degrees of freedom that they offer us to account for performance data, depends upon what further assumptions we are willing to make. However, in the absence of an adequate formulation of exactly what it is that the corresponding algorithms for natural language compute, we have no clear grounds for limiting these assumptions. We are therefore unlikely to make progress in understanding the system as a whole on the basis of performance data.

The similar methodological priority of syntax over semantics seems to reflect the more melancholy fact that our intuitions about the level of meaning that is relevant to natural language sentence grammar seem not to be very reliable. This claim may seem surprising, since we arguably have fairly strong intuitions about meaning at the level of propositions, referring expressions, and relations among them, such as coreference and entailment. This level of meaning, though, seems to arise very high up in the hierarchy of levels of language understanding. It just turns out not to be very helpful in explaining the very diverse ways in which the same propositional meaning can be grammatically realized as an (active, passive topicalized, cleft, or whatever) sentence, in response to the demands of context. For that reason, this notion of meaning gives us very little help in understanding how sentences give rise to meanings. That process just seems to be very opaque to introspection. (Indeed, I suggest below that contemporary theories of syntax have not been nearly ruthless enough in avoiding the temptation to draw strong conclusions from certain compelling but deeply misleading intuitions about sentence meaning that confound two related but distinct levels of semantics, namely, function-argument structure and discourse information structure.)

Nevertheless, these harsh facts of life and brutal realities of research methodology should not lead us to forget that it remains highly likely that this very occult semantics and this needle-in-a-haystack of a processor stand, nevertheless, in the closest possible relation to natural language syntax. In particular, in the absence of strong arguments to the contrary, we would expect syntax and semantics to stand in what Bach (1976) has called a "rule-to-rule" relation, according to the following assumption:

(1)   *The rule-to-rule assumption.* Syntactic constituents and syntactic rules are paired with semantic interpretations.

This position is closely related to the by-now widely accepted requirement for "monotonicity" among modules of grammar, which says that commitments such as structure-building that are made at one stage of a derivation must not be undone by a later stage.

More controversially, I suggest below that we would expect the structures manipulated by the processor to be limited to *only* structures that are licensed by this monotonic competence grammar, an extreme version of the strong competence hypothesis that we might call *strict*. Before considering this claim, we must briefly consider the architecture of the processor in more detail.

9.1.2 The Anatomy of a Processor

All language processors can be viewed as comprising three elements. The first is a grammar, which defines the legal ways in which constituents may combine, both syntactically and semantically, to yield other constituents. The syntactic class to which the grammar belongs also determines a characteristic automaton, the minimal abstract computer that is capable of discriminating the sentences of the language in question from random strings of words and of assigning structural descriptions to sentences appropriate to their semantics. Under the strong competence hypothesis, this is assumed to be identical to the competence grammar.

The second component of a processor is a nondeterministic algorithm that uses the rules of the grammar to deliver such structural descriptions for a given sentence. Such an algorithm schema determines, for example, whether the rules are used "top-down" or predictively, or "bottom-up," or some mixture of the two, and whether the words of the sentence are examined in order from first to last or in some less obvious order. However, as the term "nondeterministic" suggests, this component does not in general determine what happens when more than one rule can apply in a given state of the processor.

This last responsibility devolves to the third component, the oracle, or mechanism for resolving such local processing ambiguities. The oracle decides *which* action should be taken at points in the analysis where the nondeterministic algorithm allows more than one.

Nondeterminism can arise from two distinct sources. The first source is lexical syntactic ambiguity, as in the English word "watch," which can be either noun, noun phrase, or verb. The second source is structural syntactic ambiguity, which arises when there is more than one way to combine the same lexical categories to yield a legal sentence. For example, a parser for English that has dealt with the words "put the book on the table..." is likely to be in a state in which the verb "put," the noun phrase "the book," and the prepositional phrase "on the table" could be combined to yield a complete verb phrase, but where the noun phrase and the prepositional phrase could also be combined to yield a noun phrase "the book on the table." If the sentence ends at that point, as in (2a), then this "local" parsing ambiguity is resolved in favor of the former analysis. However, if the sentence continues as in (2b), then the latter analysis, in which "on the table" modifies the noun phrase rather than the verb phrase, is available and is in fact preferred. (Another analysis is possible, so this sentence is said to be syntactically "globally" ambiguous.)

(2)   a.   Put the book on the table.

　　　b.   Put the book on the table in your pocket.

The extent of this nondeterminism in natural languages is quite astonishing and constitutes the central problem for the theory of performance. Nearly every noun in English can in a pinch function as a verb, and constructions such as the above give rise to exponentially proliferating numbers of syntactically legal analyses.

This nondeterminism is quite unlike anything that is permitted in the programming languages that we design ourselves. Such languages never permit global ambiguity. And while they do on occasion include symbols that are locally ambiguous, such ambiguities are always arranged so that the oracle can resolve them purely locally—usually by looking at the next symbol in the string.

Nondeterminism in human languages looks much less tidy. To take an example from Marcus (1980), consider the position a processor is in after having encountered the word "have" in either of the following pair of examples:

(3)   a.   Have the students who missed the exam taken the make-up?

　　　b.   Have the students who missed the exam take the make-up!

After the word "have," there is a nondeterminism between an analysis according to which it is an auxiliary followed by a subject "the students...," and one where it is a main verb followed by an object. This nondeterminism is eventually resolved by the word "take" or "taken." But because of the recursive or embedding property of English and all natural languages, the noun phrase may be indefinitely large—"the students," "the students who missed the exam," "students who missed the exam that I gave this morning," and so on. There is, therefore, no bound upon the number k of symbols that must be examined to resolve the nondeterminism. It follows that the psychological oracle must be extremely powerful and probably quite unlike the corresponding component of a compiler or interpreter for a programming language.

Perhaps the most important source of evidence for the nature of the psychological oracle arises from the fact that it is "incomplete"—that is, under certain circumstances it fails to deliver any analysis. (This is another property that is quite unlike the oracle of a compiler.) The most striking evidence of incompleteness arises from certain well-known "garden-path" sentences first noted by Bever and discussed in the chapter by Fodor in the present volume. Example (4a) includes a lexical ambiguity leading the processor so seriously astray that naïve subjects are typically unable to identify any analysis for a sentence with which they would otherwise have no trouble, as shown by the syntactically identical b:

(4)   a.   The horse raced past the barn fell.

      b.   The horse driven past the barn fell.

Despite this apparent complexity, the same considerations of evolutionary and developmental parsimony that led us to adopt the strong competence hypothesis suggest that the complexity of the nondeterministic algorithm and the oracle should be kept to a minimum, and in particular that their specification should be independent of any particular natural language.

9.2   Some Surprising Properties of Natural Grammars

9.2.1   Constituents, Interpretations, and Rules

A number of consequences follow from the rule-to-rule assumption and the architecture just outlined. The first, which follows from the expectation of transparency between syntax and semantics, is so strong and so utterly uncontentious that no theory of grammar has failed to observe it in spirit, though it is probably true to say that none have so far succeeded in following it to the letter. To say that syntax and semantics are rule-to-rule is to say no more than that every syntactic rule has a semantic interpretation. It immediately follows, however, that the syntactic entities that are combined by a syntactic rule must also be semantically interpretable. (Otherwise, they could not be combined by the semantic interpretation of the rule.) It follows that syntactic rules can only combine or yield *constituents*.

This condition, which has been called the *constituent condition on rules*, has been a central feature of Generative Grammar from its earliest moments. It frequently surfaces in that literature in the guise of the *structure-dependency* of grammatical rules, discussed in the chapter by Lasnik in the present volume. It is also the notion that is embodied in the *proper analysis* condition on transformations of Chomsky (1975a; chapters written in 1955). Perhaps the most illuminating and ambitious early endorsement of this principle is to be found in 1975a, 210−211 (chapters written in 1956), where the following four "criteria" are offered as tests for grammatical constituents and constituent boundaries (the scare quotes are Chomsky's own):

(5)   a.   The rule for conjunction.

      b.   Intrusion of parenthetical expressions.

c.   Ability to enter into transformations.

d.   Certain intonational features.

These criteria are very cautiously advanced, carefully surrounded with qualifications, and the subsequent discussion is deliberately designed to demonstrate that some of them at least raise as many questions as they answer. There is, though, an implicit claim of great boldness, however programmatically stated. If these operations are tests for constituency, it can only be because they are rules of grammar, subject to the constituent condition.

The bulk of Chomsky's *Logical Structure of Linguistic Theory*, and most work in Generative Grammar since, mainly bears on the claim relative to the third criterion, concerning transformational rules of movement (and their modern equivalents and alternatives), which it has overwhelmingly supported (as Lasnik's chapter in the present volume shows). It has, however, proved much more difficult to make good on the implicit claim with respect to the remaining three phenomena. Theories of coordination, intonation, and (inasfar as there are any) parentheticalization have generally been forced at some point to compromise the constituent condition.

A further consequence follows from the assumption of a rule-to-rule relation between syntax and semantics. It also implies that the *only* linguistic entities that have interpretations are constituents. This consequence is again entirely uncontentious, and virtually all theories of competence have adhered to it (inasfar as they have involved an explicit semantics at all). It will, though, be relevant to the discussion of performance and the strict competence hypothesis, below.

9.2.2   Well-behaved Constructions

To what extent do the facts of natural language competence and performance conform to the expectations set out above? The generative theoretical tradition, as was noted earlier, has had considerable success in accounting for many constructions involving discontiguities between elements that are semantically dependent upon one another. Many such constructions were originally brought within the fold of the constituent condition on rules by the introduction of transformational rules of "movement" of constituents. Such constructions fall naturally into two groups. The first group includes phenomena that can be accounted for entirely in terms of "bounded" dependencies—roughly, dependencies between items that occur within the same tensed clause as in examples (6b) and (c) below, which resemble (6a) in concerning the expectation that someone will win:

(6)   a.   Keats expects that Chapman will win.

b.   Keats expects Chapman to win.

c.   Keats expects to win.

d.   Chapman is expected to win by Keats.

As Brame (1978) and Bresnan (1978) were among the first to point out, the clause-bounded nature of these dependencies means that they can be base-generated, or (equivalently) specified in the lexicon, thus bringing them within the domain of the constituent condition without the use of movement as such.

The generative approach has also proved extremely successful in accounting for the phenomenon of unbounded dependency exhibited in relative clauses and topicalizations such as the following, again in terms of movement:

(7)   a.   That book, *I expect I shall find.*

b.   These articles, *I think that you must have read without understanding.*

In such constructions, elements that are related in the interpretation of the construction, such as the extraposed NPs and the verb(s) of which they are the objects, can be separated by arbitrarily long substrings and indefinitely much embedding. While the residue of topicalization or relativization clause at first glance looks like a nonconstituent fragment of a sentence, it can be rather satisfactorily regarded as a constituent of type S, with a special kind of invisible coindexed or "moved" argument, and thereby be brought within the constituent condition. While many of the theories discussed below entirely eschew movement or invisible categories of all kinds, the movement metaphor was so productive of generalizations concerning these constructions that it will be convenient in what follows to continue to describe them in terms of movement.

9.2.3   Coordination, Parentheticals and Intonation Structure

At first glance, there is a striking overlap between the kinds of fragments that result from relativization and the related topicalizing construction, and those that can coordinate. In particular, practically anything that can occur as the residue of leftward movement can be coordinated, as in examples like the following:

(8)   a.   A book which *I expect I shall find,*
            and *I think that you must have read without really understanding.*

b.   *I expect I shall find,*
            but *I think that you must have read without really understanding,*
            that novel about the secret life of legumes.

The second, (8b), involves rightward movement (again, the term is used descriptively). It is striking that there is a similarly overwhelming (though not quite so complete) conspiracy between the residues of leftward and rightward movement. That is, with a number of important lexically constrained exceptions such as subject extraction in English, virtually every residue that arises from leftward movement can also arise from rightward movement. Moreover (again with some important exceptions), both kinds of extraction are subject to broadly similar "island constraints" (asterisks indicate ungrammatiality or unacceptability of examples):

(9)   a.   *A book which *I hope that I shall meet the woman who wrote.*

      b.   *I hope that I shall meet the woman who wrote,*
           and *you expect to interview the consortium that published,*
           that novel about the secret life of legumes.

However, the fragments that result from coordination are much more diverse than those that result from (leftward and rightward) movement. For example:

(10) a.   I *want to try to commission,* and hope to see produced,
           a musical about the life of Sir Stafford Cripps.

      b.   Give Deadeye Dick a sugar-stick, and *Mexican Pete, a bun.*

      c.   I want to try to write a novel, and *you, a screenplay.*

While considerably less attention has been devoted to parenthetical utterances (but compare Emonds 1976, section II.9, and Levelt 1989), some similarly unconstrained fragments arise from their intrusion, as in:

(11) *Are you,* I ask myself, a member of the Friends of the Ukraine Film Society?

The result has been that, while linguistic theories have had some success in accounting for the relative clause construction in terms of devices that reinstate the constituent condition by deriving such fragments from traditional constituents such as S (or sentence) via devices like movement, (Chomsky 1965), indexed "traces" (Chomsky 1975b), or feature-passing, (Gazdar et al. 1985), they have been much less successful in showing that the same devices will account for coordination. Instead, coordination has led to the introduction of rules of deletion to supplement rules of movement. Such rules again attempt to reinstate the constituent condition to the grammar, by deriving the fragments from an underlying S; however, such rules have frequently not themselves adhered strictly to the constituent condition. For example, (10c) appears to require either the movement or the deletion of a nonconstituent, and (10d) appears to offer no alternative to the deletion of the nonconstituent *want to try to write.* More worrying still, this fragment looks suspiciously like the kind of fragment that is the surface structural *result* of deletion or movement, as in (10a).

Despite their apparent freedom from the constituent condition on rules, there can be no doubt that these constructions belong as centrally to the domain of grammar as Chomsky originally suggested. They are subject to some of the strongest cross-linguistic universal generalizations that we know of. Most importantly, there is an overwhelming tendency for these "fragmenting" constructions to remain consistent with the basic constituent order under the following two generalizations:

(12)   a.   If an "argument" such as a noun phrase or prepositional phrase is "missing" from the left-hand side of some fragment, then it will be found somewhere in the sentence to the left. If it is missing from the right-hand side of the fragment, then it will be found to the right.

       b.   If a "function" such as a verb is "missing" from the left-hand side of a fragment, then it will be found somewhere in the sentence to the left. If it is missing from the right-hand side of the fragment, then it will be found to the right.

The first of these regularities is illustrated for English in (10a) and the second in (10c). Both regularities are cross-linguistically robust: the following is an example of the "mirror image" of (10c) in Dutch, a basically SOV language:

(13)   Ze   heeft Dirk appels en   Piet peren gegeven
       She has   _Dirk apples and Pete pears given_
       "She has _given Dirk apples and Piet pears_"

Example (10d) exemplifies a further cross-linguistic universal: When the verb of an SVO language like English goes missing in a coordinated fragment, it invariably goes missing from the _rightmost_ conjunct. These important generalizations are due to Ross (1970).

Intuitively, all of these constructions appear to be related to the semantic notion of _abstraction,_ or definition of a _property._ Most obviously, a restrictive relative clause like (a) below seems to correspond to a predicate or property of _being preferred by Mary._ Formally, such properties, concepts, or abstractions can be conveniently and transparently represented by terms in the λ-calculus like (b):

(14)   a.   ...(which) Mary prefers

       b. λx [_PREFERS x MARY_]

For those who are unfamiliar with this notation, the operator λ declares the symbol x to be a variable local to the expression that follows. The expression can therefore be thought of as denoting the property of being "a thing such that Mary prefers it." The variable is thus in every way comparable to a parameter or formal variable of a subroutine or function in a computer programming language, and the operator λ can be thought of as defining a boolean function in such a language, mapping entities onto truth values according to whether Mary prefers them or not. (Here as elsewhere in the paper, constants like PREFERS are used to identify semantic interpretations whose details are not of immediate interest, and a convention of "left associativity" of function application is observed, so that the above formula is equivalent to λx [(PREFERS x) MARY]). When this function or concept is supplied with an argument CORDUROY, it *reduces* to give a proposition, with the same function argument relations as the canonical sentence:

(15)   PREFERS CORDUROY MARY

Most current theories of natural language grammar since "standard" transformational grammar (Chomsky 1965) more or less explicitly embody the analogy between relativization and abstraction over a variable. Thus, the *government-binding theory* explicitly identifies traces as bound variables, while GPSG and its descendants use explicit variable binding via the lambda calculus in the interpretation of the features that mediate long-range dependencies (compare Pollard and Sag 1983 and discussion below).

It has turned out to be extremely hard to identify a theory of coordination that is as satisfying as those that have been developed for the bounded constructions and relativization. As a consequence, and despite the apparently close relation between coordination and relativization, the responsibility for the former phenomenon, together with others including parentheticalization, and "scrambling" of free constituent order in other languages, these phenomena have tended to be relegated to a separate domain of "stylistic" rules, involving not only movement but deletion, operating at the level of *phonetic form*, a level that, despite its name, has come to bear more and more of a real syntactic burden.

Strikingly similar fragments to those found in coordinate constructions abound in spoken language, arising from phenomena associated with phrasal prosody and intonation, as well as less well-behaved phenomena like restarts, and the parentheticals discussed earlier. For example, one quite normal prosody for an answer to the following question (a), involving stress on the word *Mary* and a break and a rise in pitch at the end of the word *prefers*, intuitively imposes the intonational structure indicated in (b) by the brackets (stress, marked in this case by raised pitch, is indicated by capitals):

(16)   a.   I know that Alice prefers VELVET. But what does MARY prefer?

       b.   (MARY prefers) (CORDUROY).

Such a grouping is orthogonal to the traditional syntactic structure of the sentence.

Intonational structure nevertheless remains strongly constrained by meaning. For example, contours imposing bracketings like the following do not seem to be allowed, as Selkirk (1984) has pointed out:

(17)   #(Three cats)(in ten prefer corduroy)

Halliday (1967a) observed that this constraint, which Selkirk has called the *sense unit condition*, seems to follow from the meaning of phrasal intonation, which is to convey what will here be called "information structure"— that is, distinctions of focus, presupposition, and propositional attitude toward entities in the discourse model. These discourse entities are more diverse than mere noun phrase or propositional referents, but they do not seem to include such nonconcepts as "in ten prefer corduroy."

The categories that they *do* include are what Prince (1986) has termed "open propositions." One way of introducing an open proposition into the discourse context is by asking a Wh-question. For example, the question in (16), *What does Mary prefer?* introduces an open proposition, or topic of conversation, corresponding once again to the concept of *a thing such that Mary prefers it*. As Jackendoff (1972) pointed out, it is once again natural to think of this open proposition as a functional *abstraction*, and to express it in the notation of the λ-calculus, as in (14). It is the presence of the above open proposition rather than some other that makes the intonation contour in (16b) felicitous. (That is not to say that its presence uniquely *determines* this response, nor that its explicit mention is necessary for interpreting the response.)

These observations have led linguists such as Selkirk (1984) to postulate a level of "intonational structure," independent of syntactic structure and related to information structure. The involvement of two apparently uncoupled levels of structure in natural language grammar appears to complicate the path from speech to interpretation unreasonably and thereby to threaten the entire theory of grammar (not to mention its worrying implications for the feasibility of a number of applications in computational speech recognition and speech synthesis).

It is therefore interesting to observe that the constructions considered in the previous section—whose semantics also seems to be reminiscent of functional abstraction—are also subject to something like a "sense unit condition." For example, strings like "in ten prefer corduroy" seem to be as reluctant to take part in coordination as they are to be treated as intonational phrases:

(18)   *Three cats in twenty like velvet, and in ten prefer corduroy.

Since we have already noted that coordinate constructions constitute another major source of complexity for current theories of natural language grammar, and also offer serious obstacles to computational applications, it is tempting to suspect that this conspiracy between syntax and prosody might point to a unified notion of syntactic constituent structure that is somewhat different from the traditional one.

9.2.4 Constituency and Performance

The prevalence of apparent nonconstituents in the grammar of coordination, parentheticalization, and intonational phrasing is a problem in the domain of competence. It is striking that there is some evidence that some quite similar fragments are available to the processor.

In his first identification of the garden-path sentences, Bever noted that the effect was sensitive to content. Thus, while (19a) is a standard garden path, in (19b) the effect is greatly reduced:

(19) a. The doctor sent for the patient arrived.
      b. The flowers sent for the patient arrived.

The observation suggests that human processors can take into account the relative plausibility of doctors versus flowers as agents of the action of sending for something or someone. In fact, it suggests that they can take account of this plausibility information early on in the course of processing, *even before the spurious clause is complete*. (Otherwise, we would have no explanation for the persistence of the garden-path effect in case (19a)). While the effect has often been attributed to structural factors, this and a number of other experimental phenomena led Marslen-Wilson, Tyler, and Seidenberg (1978) to argue that the primary source of disambiguating information drawn upon by the oracle was semantic, a view that has support from much subsequent research (see, for example, Trueswell, Tanenhaus, and Garnsey 1994).

Something like the necessary mechanism was in fact embodied in the early natural language understanding program of Winograd (1972), which interpreted questions and commands in a simple simulated world of toy blocks on a table, using a dynamically changing discourse model. Winograd proposed not only that the parser should pay attention to semantic requirements such as animacy that verbs like "send for" imposed upon their subjects, but also that attachment ambiguities of the kind found in his domain (in instructions like the following) should be resolved simply by adopting whichever analysis successfully referred to an entity in the world:

(20) Put the block in the box on the table.

The program resolved this ambiguity on the basis of whether there was in the discourse model a block unique by virtue of being the only block or a recently mentioned block, plus a box similarly unique by virtue of being on the table, or whether instead there was a block unique by virtue of being in a unique box, plus a unique table. Thus Winograd's proposal was that the oracle worked by semantically "filtering" the alternatives proposed by the parser.

This definition of semantically interactive parsing is often called "weak" interaction, because it assumes that the grammar and the algorithm propose well-formed analyses entirely autonomously and that the oracle merely disposes among the alternatives, killing off or interrupting those analyses that are either semantically incoherent (flowers being unqualified to send for things) or referentially unsuccessful (there being no block in the box).

The weakly interactive or filtering processor should not be confused with alternative proposals for "strong" interaction, according to which an autonomously produced interpretation could supposedly manipulate the syntactic component itself, activating or suppressing rules, and thereby determining in advance which analysis was built. The sense in which it is possible to build semantic analyses independently of syntax, and the question of whether this is worth doing if the processor still has to build the syntactic analysis to check its predictions, were never very clearly resolved. It is not clear whether any truly strongly interactive processor was ever built. Such a model was strenuously (and in the view of the present author, correctly) opposed by J. A. Fodor (1983) on the grounds that it violated the modularity criterion—in effect, that it really did not qualify as an explanation at all. However, Fodor himself pointed out that the weak or filtering interaction was entirely modular (1983, see 78 and 135).

The fact that the anomaly is detected early enough in (19b) to prevent the garden path exhibited in (19a) suggests that an interpretation is available for the incomplete fragment *the flowers sent* ... or *the flowers sent for* .... Such fragments are strikingly similar to those that we encountered in connection with coordination and intonation.

The apparent conspiracy between competence grammar and performance that we see here should not tempt us to abandon our belief in the methodological priority of studying competence. *Any* grammar is compatible with incremental interpretations if we are prepared to abandon the strict version of the competence hypothesis and to allow the processor to build objects that do not correspond to constituents recognized by the grammar. (For example, Shieber and Johnson 1993 show how to do this by treating the state in an *LR* parser as encoding partial derivations.) It follows that until we have resolved the competence question, the psycholinguistic argument from incremental interpretation is at best suggestive. However, the family resemblance among the fragments that are involved across both systems suggests the possibility of a much simpler theory of competence under which such fragments are constituents in the fullest sense of the term. To explore this possibility we need a notation for grammars that is more directly compatible with computational applications that the standard ones.

9.3   Computational Theories of Grammar

9.3.1   The Context-Free Core

We will start with a computational notation for grammars called Definite Clause Grammars (DCG). This notation is convenient both because it is close to Phrase Structure Grammar and because it is directly compatible with a useful computational device called unification, which we can use to build derivations or even interpretations very simply indeed. A DCG for a fragment of English might begin with rules that we can write as follows:

(21)
$$S : vp\, np1 \rightarrow NP_{agr} : np1 \quad VP_{agr} : vp$$
$$VP_{agr} : iv \rightarrow V_{INTR,agr} : iv$$
$$VP_{agr} : tv\, np2 \rightarrow V_{TRAN,agr} : tv \quad NP : np2$$
$$NP_{SING} : pn\, e_1 \rightarrow PN_{SING} : pn$$
$$NP_{agr} : (q\, e_2)(n\, e_2) \rightarrow DET_{agr} : q \quad N_{agr} : n$$

In this notation, the familiar PS rules such as $S \rightarrow NP\, VP$ are expanded as in the first rule to include interpretations. Thus, an expression of the form $S : vp\, np1$ denotes a grammatical category of syntactic type S (a sentence) and semantic interpretation $vp\, np1$, in which the variable vp is a predicate that is applied to an argument $np1$. Whenever possible, we shall abbreviate such categories as S, and so on. In the first rule both vp and $np1$ also occur as the interpretations of two subconstituents of type NP and VP. Subscripts on symbols like V_{INTR} and V_{TRAN} are a convenient notation for categories that we want to think of as bundles of feature-value pairs, like $\pm transitive$. Features with lower case, as in NP_{agr}, are to be read as variables, or feature-value pairs with unbound values. Corresponding unsubscripted categories like NP are to be read as categories whose value on its features is irrelevant to the application of the rule.

We pass over the details of the actual semantic types of variables like iv, tv, pn, and q, except to note we are assuming that they range over higher-order types of the kind familiar from the work of Montague (1974) (and see the chapter by Partee in the present volume), so that the latter two are varieties of what are called "generalized quantifiers," binding the variables e_n which range over entities in the model or database, and that the former two are even higher types. The important thing to note about this semantics is that it is completely integrated into the syntactic rules, and that interpretations can therefore be assembled simultaneously with syntactic analysis.

Rules written as in (21) leave the string order of subconstituents on the right of a rule, such as *NP* and *VP* in the first rule, implicit under an obvious convention in the linear order of those symbols on the page. An alternative notation that makes linear order explicit—but which is in other respects very similar to DCG grammars—is that of Augmented Transition Network grammars (ATNs) (Woods 1970), which we can think of as replacing groups of one or more DCG rules by a finite automaton, where each automaton can "call" the others recursively. The earlier DCG rules might be written as in figure 9.1, although the notation used here differs considerably from Woods's own. (The original ATN grammars packed as many PS rules as possible into each network, so produced "flatter" grammars than this example suggests. In effect, they used a covering grammar, to make life easy for the algorithm.)

Like the PS rules that they resemble, the rules in either notation can be applied top-down ("To find a sentence meaning $S : vp\ np1$, find a noun phrase meaning $np1$ to the left of a verb phrase meaning vp") or bottom-up ("If you find a noun phrase meaning $np1$ to the left of a verb phrase

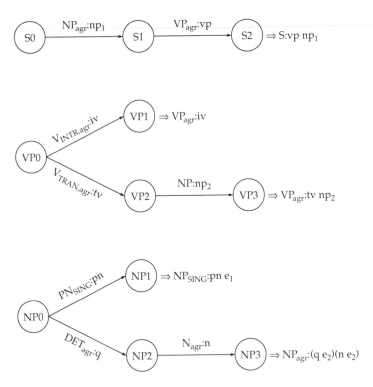

Figure 9.1
An ATN Grammar.

meaning vp, make them into a sentence meaning $vp\ np1$"). It is important, however, to remember that both DCGs and ATNs are *grammars*, not parsers, and can be fitted up with any algorithm/oracle combination we like.

Whichever notation we use and however the algorithm applies the rules, a mechanism called unification can be used to ensure that the S that results from a successful analysis of a given string is associated with the appropriate interpretation. (Again, the notation is nonstandard. The original ATN grammars associated explicit "register-changing" rules with transition networks to achieve the same effect of information-passing.)

Informally, unification can be regarded as merging or amalgamating terms that are "compatible," and as failing to amalgamate incompatible ones, via an algorithm that "instantiates" variables by substituting expressions for them in one or other of the expressions. More technically, the result of unifying two compatible terms is the most general term that is an instance of both the original terms. For example, the following pairs of terms unify, to yield the results shown. (Note that the unification of two variables is a "new" variable, distinct from either.)

(22) x A $\Rightarrow A$
      $F(GA)$ x $\Rightarrow F(GA)$
      Fx $F(Gy)$ $\Rightarrow F(Gz)$
      $(FA)x$ $(Fy)y$ $\Rightarrow (FA)A$

The following pairs of terms do not unify.

(23) A B $\Rightarrow fail$
      Fx Gy $\Rightarrow fail$
      $(FA)B$ $(Fy)y$ $\Rightarrow fail$

For example, suppose the lexicon tells us that the word "Harry" bears the category $NP: HARRY\ e_1$, and suppose that "walks" has the category $VP: WALKS$. (The "distinguished variable" e_1 ranges over individuals in the discourse model, which we can think of as a database of facts.) If we find the word "Harry" to the left of the word "walks," it follows that we can unify this sequence of categories with the right-hand side of the first rule in (21). This has the effect of replacing the variable vp by $WALKS$ and the variable $np1$ by $HARRY\ e_1$ throughout the rule. The resulting S is therefore associated with the expression $WALKS\ (HARRY\ e_1)$. The derivation, in which the unification does the work of a compositional semantics, can be represented by the usual sort of tree diagram, as in figure 9.2. In fact, there is a little more to it than this: the variable or undefined value agr on the syntactic categories NP_{agr} and VP_{agr} in the rule also got bound to the value $3SING$ by the unification. Had the subject and verb borne different values on the agreement feature, as in the following illegal string, the unification, and hence the whole derivation, would have failed:

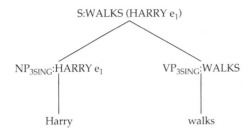

Figure 9.2
A DCG derivation.

(24) *Harry walk

Thus, we have the rudiments of an account of linguistic agreement. Of course, it is not a very *good* account. In a more complete fragment of English we would want to further unpack the feature *agr* and its values like 3*SING* into a bundle made up of a number of features like *num* (number) and *per* (person). (Linguists would probably point out that some phenomena of agreement appear to be most parsimoniously described in terms of *disjunction* of feature-value pairs, a fact suggesting that we need a more refined representation altogether.) These refinements are, though, of less interest for present purposes than is the observation that we have here the beginnings of a very simple account of a phenomenon that in the early days of generative grammar was thought to require transformational rules of the kind proposed in Chomsky's 1965 *Aspects of the Theory of Syntax*, a very powerful class of rule indeed.

The interpretation that is delivered by the above derivation is closely related to the derivation tree itself. The observation generalizes to other derivations that are permitted. This fact suggests that what we have so far developed is merely a computationally convenient form of context-free grammar, "slaved" via unification to a device that builds interpretation structures as derivation proceeds, an idea that seems to originate with Kuno in the 1960s. This is a helpful way to think about the processor, but some caution is in order. We have so far been quite vague about the unification mechanism and in particular about the types of values that features may bear. In particular, if we allow the values to be lists, then we change the automata-theoretic power of the grammar (which may, of course, be what we want). Completely unrestricted feature systems can also threaten the tractability of the parsing problem (compare Barton, Berwick, and Ristad 1987).

With this notation in place, we can begin to look at more complex constructions. It is convenient to collect these into three classes. The "bounded" constructions, which include many phenomena that were originally thought to require transformations, are those that relate argument positions *within a single tensed clause*. These constructions were earlier contrasted with "unbounded" constructions, such as relativization, which can relate elements of sentences across one or more clause boundaries. The unbounded constructions were divided into "well-behaved" constructions, like relativization itself, and "less-well-behaved" constructions, notably including coordination. The computational implications of this last class are a topic in their own right which we will defer until section 9.4 below. It is the first two classes that have received most attention, both from linguists and from computational linguists.

9.3.2 Bounded Constructions

As we noted earlier, the bounded constructions like passive and raising can naturally be handled *in the context-free base component of the grammar*, as proposed in the ATN framework by Woods (1970). Many modern theories of syntax make a related assumption, which goes by the name of the *base generation hypothesis* (compare Brame 1978). In the DCG notation we can capture the idea as follows. (As usual, the interpretation here is highly simplified, and all the real work is being done by the translation v of the object control verb. A linguist would foresee a problem for the binding theory in this particular representation, which we pass over here in the interests of brevity.)

(25) $VP : v(vp\ y)y \rightarrow V_{oc} : v \quad NP : y \quad VP_{to-inf} : vp$

Another very natural way to interpret base generation is to capture the bounded constructions *in the lexicon*—that is, in the subcategorization frames which specify the types of argument that a given verb can combine with. This is the tactic adopted in Categorial Grammar (CG) (Oehrle, Bach, and Wheeler 1988), Lexical-functional Grammar (LFG) (Bresnan 1982), certain versions of Tree-Adjoining Grammar (TAG) (Joshi, Vijay-Shanker, and Weir 1991), and Head-driven Phrase-structure Grammar (HPSG) (Pollard and Sag 1994).

A DCG grammar expanded in this way continues to be closely related to Woods's ATN analysis of the bounded constructions, with unification again doing the work of "register modification." The fact that both the ATN and the DCG work exclusively at the level of argument structure or the interpretations of immediate constituents goes a long way towards explaining the bounded character of these constructions. This benefit of the computational approaches has become standard and is implicit in nearly all linguistic theories of the constructions, including GPSG, HPSG, LFG, Lexicalized TAGs, and certain versions of Government-Binding Theory (GB) (Chomsky 1981). For this reason we say no more about the bounded constructions here, except to note that this is one place where computational linguistics has directly influenced mainstream linguistics and psycholinguistics (see Bresnan 1978 for further discussion of the relation between linguistic accounts and the ATN).

9.3.3   Unbounded Constructions

The unbounded constructions seem on the face of it to be quite different from those that we encountered in the last section. We cannot build the argument structures needed for semantic interpretation merely by identifying elements in translations of immediate constituents in a context-free rule, since in general the elements related by the dependency cannot be elements belonging to a single CF rule.

All approaches to the unbounded dependency exhibited by constructions like the relative take the form of a context-free core, augmented by some extra apparatus for handling the unbounded dependencies themselves. Many of the interesting contrasts between the theories concern the automata-theoretic power that such extensions implicate. Although we have no very clear information concerning an upper bound on the power of human grammar, mechanisms of lesser power than a Turing machine clearly have considerable theoretical interest, if only to show where they break down.

Linguistic and computational theories of this "weakly non-context-free" kind have broadly fallen into two categories. The first type can be characterized as using the context-free base to determine an argument structure for an entire complex sentence, then using additional apparatus to establish long-range dependencies in one fell swoop. An example is the transformational grammar of Chomsky's *Aspects of the Theory of Syntax*, which introduced tree-to-tree rules, including variables, in order to transform arbitrarily deeply embedded trees with *wh*-items *in situ* into trees with those items fronted. The other type of mechanism established long-range dependencies by "trickling" pointers or indices down a path through the derivation tree connecting the two dependent elements.

Aspects-style rules themselves were quickly identified as implicating full Turing machine power (Peters and Ritchie 1973). They also failed to explain a number of asymmetries in extractability of different arguments, of which a striking example is the *fixed subject constraint*, which describes the fact that in English and many other SVO languages, subjects cannot unboundedly extract, unlike other arguments, as illustrated in the following example. (Subjects of bare complements, as in "a man who(m) I think likes Ike" are exceptional in this respect.)

(26)   a.   A man who(m) I think that Ike likes.
        b.   *A man who(m) I think that likes Ike.

For both reasons, there was considerable interest in certain computational versions of the swoop mechanism that appeared to be more constrained. Following early work by Thorne and Bobrow, the idea was most elegantly formulated by Woods (1970) for the ATN.

Woods's ATN allowed certain kinds of register-changing *side-effects* to be associated with state-transitions. Most of Woods's register-changing operations have up until now been subsumed under the unification mechanism. However, to handle long-range dependency, we shall associate such actions with a number of transitions that we shall add to the NP and VP nets in figure 9.1. These actions will transfer special terms or markers into, and out of, a special globally accessible register or store called HOLD, extending the grammar as in figure 9.3. The actions concerning the HOLD register are enclosed in braces. They allow the grammar to achieve the same effect as a swoop transformational rule. To derive a relative clause, you simply use the ordinary rules of context-free grammar, except that whenever you encounter a relative pronoun, you make it one end of a potentially unbounded NP dependency, expressed as a note in the HOLD register; and whenever a verb needs an NP argument, it has the option of satisfying the need for that argument and making it the other end of an unbounded dependency by retrieving an NP from HOLD. A further check that the index has indeed been removed from HOLD is included on exit from the complex NP, in order to prevent accepting examples like *A man that I like Ike*.

Part of the attraction of the ATN HOLD mechanism is that it offers a way to think about constraints on long-range dependencies. For example, because we do not include the option of the subject being obtained from the HOLD register, we capture the fixed subject condition illustrated in (26). (A linguist would notice, however, that nothing in the present theory explains why this constraint appears to conspire with other aspects of word order, cross-linguistically. Nor have we revealed how bare complement subject extraction is allowed.)

Furthermore, the fact that sentences like (27a) involve more than one dependency and that those dependencies nest, as revealed by (27b), can be explained as arising from limitations on the HOLD store—perhaps that it is a push-down stack, as suggested by Woods (1973).

(27) a.   Which violin$_1$ is this sonata$_2$ easy to play$_2$ on$_1$
      b.   *Which sonata$_1$ is this violin$_2$ easy to play$_1$ on$_2$

The importance of this latter observation is considerable. When one sees a stack, one immediately thinks of a characteristic automaton, such as the push-down automaton (PDA) that is characteristic of context-free grammars. Since a push-down store is already implicit in the context-free

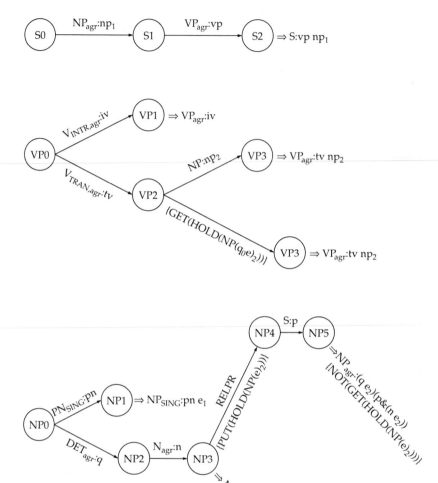

Figure 9.3
The ATN HOLD mechanism.

rules, and since adding a further stack to mediate long-range dependencies would in principle jump us up to full Turing machine power, the intriguing possibility is that the stack involved in long-range dependencies is in some sense the *same* stack involved in context-free rules, as proposed by Ades and Steedman (1982, 522) and as further specified in the work of Joshi, Vijay-Shanker, and Weir (1991) and the approach advocated below.

Of course, to claim this much is not the same as claiming that natural languages are context-free. We know from work by Aho (1969) that a "nested stack" automaton, equipped with a single stack whose contents may themselves be stacks, is of greater than context-free power (but of lesser power than context-sensitive grammars). It does suggest, however, that we should try to account for unbounded dependencies in much the same way we accounted for bounded ones, by putting as much of the work as possible into the base rules themselves. This insight can be seen as underlying the second group of mechanisms for unbounded dependencies, in which a similar kind of pointer or index is "trickled" down the sentence during derivation, as opposed to being established in one fell swoop.

Within mainstream linguistics this kind of explanation can be seen as surfacing in proposals by Bresnan and by Chomsky that resulted in the "comp-to-comp movement" account of unbounded dependencies, including relativization. According to this theory, unbounded dependencies were the sum of a series of local dependencies between argument positions and the complementizer position in individual clauses. Transformational "movement" was thus restricted to bounded movement.

Since we have seen that bounded dependencies can be captured within generalized PS rules, it should be clear that it is a comparatively short step to grammars that eliminate movement entirely and bring unbounded dependencies under the base generation hypothesis. The proposal takes an extreme form in the Generalised Phrase Structure Grammars (GPSG) of Gazdar et al. (1985). The GPSG treatment can be included in our DCG rules by associating a feature-value pair SLASH, equivalent to a local HOLD register. In the original version of the theory, the value of this feature was simply a pointer identifying a unique long-range dependency, and the theory was therefore weakly context-free. The original base set of rules for each category such as S are included again with an empty slash feature. It is convenient to write such categories simply as S, NP, VP, and so on, and to write the corresponding categories in which the SLASH pointer is of type NP as S/NP, NP/NP, VP/NP, and the like. For every old style rule defining "non-slash" categories, there may be one or more rules that specify how an S/NP with non-empty SLASH feature passes that feature to its offspring. For example, we might introduce the following additional rules, among others. (In the original version of the theory, such extra rules were induced via "metarules.")

(28) $S : vp\ np_1/NP : x \quad \rightarrow \quad NP_{agr} : np_1 \quad VP_{agr} : vp/NP : x$
$VP_{agr} : tv\ np_2/NP : x \quad \rightarrow \quad V_{TRAN,agr} : tv \quad NP : np_2/NP : x$
$NP_{agr} : (q\ e_2)(p\&(n\ e_2))$
$\rightarrow DET_{agr} : q \quad N_{agr} : n \quad RELPRO \quad S : p/NP : q_0\ e_2$

The category NP/NP corresponds to the linguist's notion of a trace or empty NP. We have again slyly captured the constraint upon extracting subjects by not including a rule of the form $S/NP \rightarrow NP/NP\ VP$. The multiple unbounded dependencies exhibited in sentences (27) could be handled within this type of GPSG, by a combination of the techniques we have seen for bounded and unbounded dependencies. However, the multiple intersecting unbounded dependencies that occur in Scandinavian languages and the arbitrarily many verb-argument dependencies that can intercalate in Germanic infinitival complements provide evidence that natural languages cannot be contained within the class of CF languages (see Gazdar 1988 for discussion). A number of other grammar formalisms with a computational orientation were developed in response to such observations, including Tree-Adjoining Grammars (TAG) (Joshi, Vijay-Shanker, and Weir 1991) and Combinatory Categorial Grammars (CCG) (Ades and Steedman 1982), and Gazdar's proposal to permit SLASH features to be stacks (compare Gazdar 1988; Pollard and Sag 1994). Joshi, Vijay-Shanker, and Weir (1991) showed that a number of these grammars were weakly equivalent to indexed grammars. They further showed that under certain limiting assumptions they were weakly equivalent to *linear* indexed grammars, in which only a single stack-valued feature is involved.

9.4   Turning the Problem Upside-down

9.4.1   Constituents and Fragments

The DCG and the ATN as presented above both embody the constituent condition on rules and, as such, seem to offer promising psychological models; however, it is far from obvious how they can be generalized to cope with coordination and the other phenomena discussed above without violating this condition. And, in fact, the interesting procedural mechanism proposed by Woods (1973), which makes coordination the responsibility of the parser rather than of the grammar, does abandon this condition with a consequent penalty in explanatory and psychological appeal.

When attempting to deal with an obstinate problem, it is sometimes necessary to consider scrapping cherished assumptions and starting afresh. The next section asks the reader to speculate concerning the form that grammars would take if we assumed that coordination and the like were the most basic phenomena of grammar, rather than the most exceptional.

In particular, we will consider how the world would look if we were to take the constituent condition at its face value and to assume that everything that can coordinate is actually a constituent in its own right.

9.4.2   A Lexical Grammar for a Fragment of English

Combinatory Categorial Grammar (CCG) (Steedman 1987) is one of a number of extensions of Categorial Grammar (CG) (Oehrle, Bach, and Wheeler 1988; Wood 1993) that have recently been proposed for this purpose. Elements like verbs are associated with a syntactic "category," which identifies them as *functions* and specifies the type and directionality of their arguments and the type of their result.

Categorial grammars use a notation in which a rightward-combining functor over a domain β into a range α is written α/β, while the corresponding leftward-combining functor is written $\alpha\backslash\beta$. This direction-specific slash notation should not be confused with the GPSG slash discussed in connection with example (28) (although there is a historical connection between the two). The domain and range α and β may themselves be function categories. For example, a transitive verb is a function from (object) NPs into predicates—that is, into functions from (subject) NPs into S (we ignore agreement here):

(29)   admires $:= (S\backslash NP)/NP$

This category expresses exactly the same syntactic information as the first and the third rule in the context-free DCG 21. Moreover, such categories can be regarded as encoding the semantic type of their translation. This translation can be made explicit in the following expanded notation, which associates a translation with each primitive category, via the colon operator, so that the category captures the semantic information in those rules as well:

(30)   admires $:= (S : ADMIRES\ yx\backslash NP : x)/NP : y.$

Such functions (in either notation) can combine, via the unification mechanism discussed earlier, with arguments of the appropriate type and position by the following rules of functional application, in which X, Y, and so on are variables ranging over categories:

(31)   *Forward Application:* ($>$)

   $X/Y \quad Y \Rightarrow X$

(32)   *Backward Application:* ($<$)

   $Y \quad X\backslash Y \Rightarrow X$

They yield derivations like the following:

(33)   Mary   admires   musicals

$NP:MARY$ $(S:ADMIRES\ x\ y \backslash NP:y)/NP:x$ $NP:MUSICALS$
$$\overline{\hspace{6cm}}>$$
$S:ADMIRES\ MUSICALS\ y \backslash NP:y$
$$\overline{\hspace{7cm}}<$$
$S:ADMIRES\ MUSICALS\ MARY$

The derivation yields an S with a compositional interpretation, equivalent under a convention of left associativity to (admire' musicals') mary', and, of course, such a "pure" categorial grammar is context free.

Coordination might be included in CG via the following rule, allowing constituents of like type to conjoin to yield a single constituent of the same type. (The semantics of this rule, or rather rule schema, is somewhat complex and is omitted here.)

(34) X $conj$ $X \Rightarrow X$

(35)   I   loathe   and   detest   operas

NP $(S \backslash NP)/NP$ $conj$ $(S \backslash NP)/NP$ NP
$$\overline{\hspace{6cm}}\&$$
$(S \backslash NP)/NP$
$$\overline{\hspace{5cm}}>$$
$S \backslash NP$
$$\overline{\hspace{4cm}}<$$
S

In order to allow coordination of contiguous strings that do not constitute constituents, CCG generalizes the grammar to allow certain operations on functions related to Curry's combinators (1958). For example, functions may nondeterministically *compose*, as well as apply, under the following rule:

(36)   *Forward Composition:* ($>$B)

X/Y $Y/Z \Rightarrow X/Z$

The most important single property of combinatory rules like this is that they have an invariant semantics. This one composes the interpretations of the functions that it applies to, as is apparent from the derivation of sentences like *I requested, and would prefer, musicals,* which involves the composition of two verbs (indexed as **B**, following Curry's nomenclature) to yield a composite of the same category as a transitive verb (the rest of the derivation is given in the simpler notation). Crucially, composition also yields the appropriate interpretation for the composite verb *would prefer:*

(37)

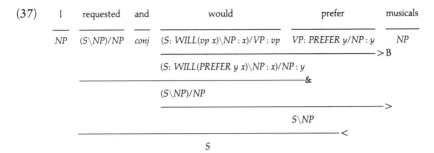

I	requested	and	would	prefer	musicals
NP	$(S\backslash NP)/NP$	$conj$	$(S: WILL(vp\ x)\backslash NP:x)/VP:vp$	$VP: PREFER\ y/NP:y$	NP

Combinatory grammars also include type-raising rules, which turn arguments into functions over functions-over-such-arguments. These rules allow arguments to compose and thereby take part in coordinations like *I dislike, and Mary admires, musicals*. For example, the following rule allows the conjuncts to form as below (again, the remainder of the derivation is given in the briefer notation):

(38) *Subject Type-raising:* $(>T)$

$$NP:y \Rightarrow S:s/(S:s\backslash NP:y)$$

(39)

I	dislike,	and	Mary	admires,	musicals
NP	$(S\backslash NP)/NP$	$conj$	NP	$(S:ADMIRES\ x\ y\backslash NP:y)/NP:x$	$S\backslash(S/NP)$

Like composition, type-raising rules have an invariant compositional semantics, ensuring that the result has an appropriate interpretation.

This apparatus has been applied to a wide variety of coordination phenomena, including "left node raising" and gapping in English, and "backward gapping" and verb-raising in Germanic languages. One example that is relevant to the following discussion is the following analysis for the first of these, first proposed by Dowty (1988).

(40)

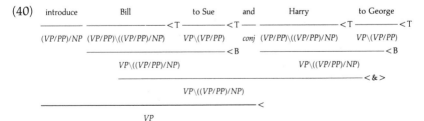

introduce	Bill	to Sue	and	Harry	to George
$(VP/PP)/NP$	$(VP/PP)\backslash((VP/PP)/NP)$	$VP\backslash(VP/PP)$	$conj$	$(VP/PP)\backslash((VP/PP)/NP)$	$VP\backslash(VP/PP)$

The important feature of this analysis is that it uses "backward" rules of type-raising $<T$ and composition $<B$ that are the exact mirror-image of the two "forward" versions introduced as examples (36) and (38). It is therefore a prediction of the theory that such a construction can exist in English, and its inclusion in the grammar requires no additional mechanism whatsoever. The earlier studies show that no *other* nonconstituent coordinations of dative-accusative NP sequences are allowed in any language with the English verb categories, because the type-raising rules preserve the left-right order of the verb and its complement. Thus, the following are ruled out in principle, rather than by stipulation.

(41)   a.   *Bill to Sue and introduce Harry to George

      b.   *Introduce to Sue Bill and to George Harry

A number of related well-known cross-linguistic generalizations concerning the dependency of so-called "gapping" upon lexical word order are also captured. For example, the parallel construction in Dutch, exemplified in the earlier example (13)—which obeys Ross's (1970) universal in having the verb go missing from the *left* conjunct rather than the right one—is immediately predicted simply from the fact that Dutch is a verb-final language, from which it follows that Dutch ditransitive verbs bear the category $(VP\backslash PP)\backslash NP$ (see questions at end of chapter).

Phenomena like the above immediately suggest that all argument categories such as NP should be *obligatorily* type-raised. One way to do this is by replacing categories like NP that are complements of verbs, and all functions into such categories, like determiners, by raised categories and functions into raised categories of the forms $T/(T\backslash NP)$ and $T\backslash(T/NP)$, at the level of the lexicon.

9.4.3   Implications for the Theory of Competence

It will be clear at this point that the combinatory approach implies a view of surface structure, according to which strings like *Mary admires* are constituents in the fullest sense of the term. It follows, according to this view, that they must also be possible constituents of noncoordinate sentences like *Mary admires musicals*, which must permit the following derivation (42a), as well as the traditional derivation (33), repeated here as (42b).

(42)   a. Mary   admires   musicals   b. Mary   admires   musicals

$$
\begin{array}{cccccc}
\underline{T/(T\backslash NP)} & \underline{(S\backslash NP)/NP} & \underline{T\backslash(T/NP)} & \quad & \underline{T/(T\backslash NP)} & \underline{(S\backslash NP)/NP} \quad \underline{T\backslash(T/NP)} \\
\multicolumn{2}{c}{\underline{\qquad\qquad\qquad}>B} & & & & \underline{\qquad\qquad\qquad}< \\
\multicolumn{2}{c}{S/NP} & & & & S\backslash NP \\
\multicolumn{3}{c}{\underline{\qquad\qquad\qquad\qquad}<} & \multicolumn{2}{c}{\underline{\qquad\qquad\qquad\qquad}>} \\
\multicolumn{3}{c}{S} & \multicolumn{2}{c}{S}
\end{array}
$$

The grammar outlined above guarantees that all such nonstandard derivations yield identical interpretations—equivalent in this case to $(ADMIRES\ MUSICALS)\ MARY$. In more complex sentences than the above, there will be many such semantically equivalent derivations for each distinct interpretation.

A linguist might well object at this point that such a claim flies in the face of well-established traditional accounts of surface constituency. However, it is a curious fact that none of the traditional linguistic tests for constituency—such as susceptibility to "movement" or representation in the lexicon—discriminates all and only the traditional constituents. Such tests are, in fact, confounded with the *semantic* notion of constituency that is here represented as argument structure, and it is arguable that intuitions about this level of structure have given rise to the traditional notion of constituency. Moreover, the generalized notion of constituency that is argued for here is entirely compatible with everything else that we know about grammar, as follows.

The interest of nonstandard structures like (42a) for the study of competence goes far beyond the study of coordination. While we do not go into the question further here, we may note that the nonstandard surface structures induced by the combinatory grammar subsume the intonational structures that are postulated by Selkirk (1984) to explain the possible intonation contours for sentences of English. In particular, the analysis immediately captures the following generalization within an entirely monotonic grammar.

(43)   Every string that can coordinate can be a phonological phrase, and vice versa.

What is more, if we abstract away from certain details in the effects of island constraints, the residual fragments that are created by relativization are simply a subset of the fragments that can coordinate. It follows that the account presented here can be made compatible with standard accounts of relativization, simply by assigning the following categories to nominative and accusative relative pronouns, which map the relevant categories into noun-modifiers $N\backslash N$:

(44)   a.   who $:= (N\backslash N)/(S\backslash NP)$

       b.   who(m) $:= (N\backslash N)/(S/NP)$

A number of famous constraints on WH-constructions follow immediately. For example, the fixed subject constraint (26), which forbids sentences like (45a), follows from the fact that such an extraction would require a different composition rule from (36), which allows (45b).

(45)   a.   (a man) *who(m) [I think that]$_{S/S}$ [likes Ike]$_{S \backslash NP}$

       b.   (a man) who(m) [I think that]$_{S/S}$ [Ike likes]$_{S/NP}$

Similarly, it follows immediately that extraction from coordinate structures is only allowed when it applies to *all* conjuncts "across the board" as in (46a) and is forbidden otherwise under the "coordinate structure constraint," as in (46b).

(46)   a.   (a man) who(m) [I like]$_{S/NP}$ and [you dislike]$_{S/NP}$

       b.   (a man) *who(m) [I like]$_{S/NP}$ and [you dislike him]$_S$

This follows from the fact that only like categories may conjoin.

As in the case of DCG and ATN grammars, the bounded constructions can be base-generated, in the lexical categories. For example, one might capture the generalizations that have been captured in GB, MG, LFG, TAG, GPSG, and HPSG concerning the argument structure of object control verbs by postulating the following category for verbs like *persuade*, parallel to the PS rule (25). (As in the earlier case, linguists will recognize a slight oversimplification here.)

(47)   persuade := $(S : PERSUADE(vp\ x)\ x\ y \backslash NP : y)/(VP : vp\ x))/NP : x$

Such links to the mainstream merely make the point that there is no obstacle to enjoying the benefits of both combinatory and traditional theories combined. They do not constitute a claim that all the problems are solved. In particular, the origin of island constraints and the conditions of the binding theory remain as much of a problem under the particular combinatory account presented here as they are in other theories.

9.4.4   Implications for the Theory of Performance

The above remarks are highly speculative, and it has been necessary to restrict drastically the set of grammatical phenomena under consideration and to pass over a considerable amount of further work in categorial framework. If, however, this theory can survive much closer scrutiny that we can give it here as a theory of competence, then (and only then) a further advantage may be available. The availability of nonstandard constituents of the kind exemplified in (42a)—made up of a subject and a transitive verb complete with a translation—also seems to provide exactly what the processor requires in order to detect the semantic anomaly of prefixes like *The flowers sent for . . .*, and thereby to avoid the garden path that lurks in example (19b), without compromising the strict competence hypothesis. While more traditional grammars, imputing a standard right-branching structure to English transitive clauses, can be made to assemble such partially complete interpretations incrementally (say, by treating the state of the parser's control stack as encoding partial derivations, as Shieber and Johnson 1993 do), such a stratagem is in violation of the strict competence hypothesis and therefore complicates the theory of performance.

9.5 Concluding Observations

The chapter began by stating some uncontroversial assumptions, in the form of the rule-to-rule assumption and the competence hypothesis, and by deducing the even more widely accepted constituent condition on rules of competence grammar. Having noted the difficulties presented by coordination and intonation vis-à-vis the constituent condition, it went on to advance an alternative view of competence grammar under which the paradoxical constructions could be seen to conform to that condition after all.

We noticed that a considerable amount of nondeterminism remains in the grammar, for both spoken and written language. The properties of the grammar are consistent with the suggestion that the basis for the oracle rendering the process as a whole deterministic is the incremental availability of semantic interpretations. The generalized notion of constituency that is engendered by the combinatory rules ensures that most leftmost substrings are potentially constituents with interpretations, subject, of course, to the limitations of the grammar and any further information that may be available from intonation. Such a theory of grammar may therefore have an added advantage of parsimony, in being compatible with such a processor without compromising the strict competence hypothesis.

Indeed, we can stand this argument on its head. If we believe that the parser has to know about interpretations corresponding to strings like *the flowers sent for . . .*, and we identify such interpretations with the notion of abstraction, then the advocates of traditional grammar must ask themselves why their grammar does *not* endorse such useful semantic concepts as grammatical constituents.

It is, of course, unlikely that we will ever know enough about the biological constraints to evaluate empirically with any certainty the assumptions on which the "strict" version of the competence hypothesis is based. In the absence of such certainty, we must beware of falling into the error of evolutionary Panglossism; however, it is interesting to speculate upon its implications for the theory as a whole, for the following reason.

Competence grammar and performance mechanism are in the end a package deal. Any claim about competence grammar is also a claim about the entire package. Any linguistic theory that survives the test of descriptive adequacy must ultimately be judged not merely on its purity and parsimony as a theory of competence, but also on its explanatory value as part of the package. We have already noted that all theories will require *something* more, in the form of an oracle for resolving grammatical nondeterminism, together with a language-independent algorithm and automaton. If a theory of competence requires much more than that, or if that mechanism in turn implicates additional structures that are not already covered by the competence grammar, then those assumptions will weigh against it. If there is another descriptively adequate theory that requires fewer such assumptions, perhaps even *no* further assumptions beyond the mechanism for resolving nondeterminism and the minimal bottom-up algorithm, by virtue of having a different notion of surface syntax, then the scales may tilt in its favor.

If it is true that the principal responsibility for local ambiguity resolution lies with incremental interpretation at extremely fine grain, then any theory that does not make similar assumptions to the grammar sketched above concerning constituency in the competence grammar will have to make some strikingly similar structures available to the processor, complete with interpretations. Such additional assumptions would not in any sense be inconsistent with the competence theory itself; nevertheless, they compromise the strict version of the competence hypothesis. To the extent that the combinatory theory achieves the same result without any additional assumptions, and to the extent that it is descriptively correct to include identical structures and interpretation in the competence grammar of coordination and intonation, it may point the way toward an explanatory account.

Suggestions for Further Reading

I have assumed familiarity above with the basic ideas of generative grammar, with formal semantics, and with the basic results of experimental psycholinguistics, all of which are presented elsewhere in this volume. I have also assumed a nodding aquaintance with formal language theory—in particular the Chomsky hierarchy. This and much other useful material is covered in the text by Partee, ter Meulen, and Wall 1990. The question of the automata-theoretic power characteristic of national languages is helpfully discussed by Gazdar 1988 and by Joshi, Vijay-Shanker, and Weir 1991. Allen 1987 is an excellent introductory text to the broader field of computational linguistics, and the indispensable collection edited by Grosz, Sparck Jones, and Webber 1986 gathers a number of key research papers in this broader area, including several of those cited above.

A trustworthy guide to the nature of parsers and parsing regimes is Kay 1980, from whom I have taken the general trimodular view of the processor, generalizing his notion of an "agenda" to the notion of the oracle presented in this chapter. The grammars, algorithms, and oracles described here are all designed to be very readily implementable in the programming language Prolog. The elegant text by Pereira and Shieber 1987 provides all the help that is needed. The "weakly interactive" semantically guided parsers that are briefly discussed in sections 9.2.4 and 9.4.4 are investigated at length by Hirst 1987, who provides an excellent review of the literature to that date. Some important more recent critiques of the psychological and computational assumptions implicit in the present paper are presented by Clifton and Ferreira 1989, Stabler 1991, and Shieber and Johnson 1993. A much broader class of "flexible" categorial grammars than it has been possible to present here—all of which engender similar generalized notions of surface structure to the one exploited here—are represented in the collection edited by Oehrle, Bach, and Wheeler 1988. They are helpfully surveyed by Wood 1993. The present chapter is a more speculative companion to my review paper "Natural Language Processing," in M. Boden, ed., *Handbook of Perception and Cognition, 14: Computational Psychology and Artificial Intelligence*, in which the computational nature of grammars, algorithms, and oracles is more impartially discussed, and much detail omitted here is fleshed out. The paper and this chapter are intended to be readable independently. As a consequence, certain sections concerning notation and the theory of natural language grammar are common to both.

Problem

9.1 Show via a CCG derivation and a lexical fragment for the words involved that the Dutch coordinate sentence in example (13) (repeated here) follows from the assumption that this construction in Dutch is exactly like the comparable construction of English illustrated in example (40), apart from the fact that Dutch non-tensed verbs look to the left for NP and PP arguments.

Ze heeft Dirk appels en Piet peren gegeven
She has *Dirk apples and Pete pears given*

"She has *given Dirk apples and Piet pears*"
If you make use of any assumptions that were not needed for English, say what they are and why they are necessary.

Question for Further Thought

9.1 A bottom-up or shift-reduce parser is one in which the algorithm nondeterministically "shifts"—that is, puts a category corresponding to a lexical entry for the next word onto the stack of a pushdown automaton—or "reduces"; that is, applies a rule of grammar to the topmost item(s) on the stack, replacing them by the result of the rule. Such an algorithm might for example parse the sentence *Gilbert walks* by shifting *NP : GILBERT*, shifting *VP : WALKS*, then reducing them via the PS rule $S : vp \; np \rightarrow NP : np \; VP : vp$, to yield $S : WALKS \; GILBERT$, then halting. Shift-reduce parsers can be written for any of the grammars described here.

Using any of the grammar formalisms described above and exploiting Prolog backtracking to (inefficiently) simulate the nondeterministic algorithm, and using Prolog lists and terms to represent the "rule-to-rule" syntactic/semantic categories and rules, write a shift-reduce parser in Prolog to cover as many examples in the chapter as possible. Leave coordination until last (or leave it out altogether). Use Prolog terms to represent interpretations, and investigate the possibility of evaluating these terms as prolog queries with respect to a simple database. Comment on the possibility of using the results to inform an "oracle" that might be used to replace the inefficient backtracking.

References

Ades, A., and M. Steedman (1982). On the order of words. *Linguistics & Philosophy* 4, 517–558.

Aho, A. (1969). Nested-stack automata. *Journal of the Association for Computing Machinery* 16, 383–406.

Allen, J. (1987). *Natural language understanding*. Menlo Park, CA: Benjamin Cummings.

Bach, E. (1976). An extension of classical transformational grammar. *Problems in linguistic metatheory, Proceedings of the 1976 Conference at Michigan State University*.

Barton, G. E, R. Berwick, and E. Ristad (1987). *Computational complexity and natural language*. Cambridge, MA: MIT Press.

Brame, M. (1978). *Base generated syntax*. Seattle: Noit Amrofer.

Bresnan, J. (1978). A realistic transformational grammar. In M. Halle, J. Bresnan, and G. Miller, eds., *Linguistic structure and psychological reality*. Cambridge, MA: MIT Press.

Bresnan, J., ed. (1982). *The mental representation of grammatical relations*. Cambridge, MA: MIT Press.

Brown, R., and C. Hanlon (1970). Derivational complexity and order of acquisition in child speech. In John Hayes, ed., *Cognition and the development of language*, 155–207. New York: Wiley.

Chomsky, N. (1965). *Aspects of the theory of syntax*. Cambridge, MA: MIT Press.

Chomsky, N. (1975a). *The logical structure of linguistic theory*. Chicago: University of Chicago Press.

Chomsky, N. (1975b). *Reflections on language*. New York: Pantheon.

Chomsky, N. (1981). *Lectures on government and binding*. Dordrecht, Netherlands: Foris.

Clifton, C., and F. Ferreira (1989). Ambiguity in context. *Language and Cognitive Processes* 4, 77–104.

Curry, H., and R. Feys (1958). *Combinatory logic*. Vol. 1. Amsterdam: North Holland.

Dowty, D. (1988). Type-raising, functional composition, and nonconstituent coordination. In Oehrle, Bach, and Wheeler (1988), 153–198.

Dowty, D., L. Kartunnen, and A. Zwicky, eds. (1985). *Natural language parsing: Psychological, computational and theoretical perspectives*. ACL Studies in Natural Language Processing. Cambridge: Cambridge University Press.

Emonds, J. (1976). *A transformational approach to English syntax*. New York: Academic Press.

Fodor, J. A. (1983). *The modularity of mind*. Cambridge, MA: MIT Press.

Gazdar, G. (1988). Applicability of indexed grammars to natural languages. In U. Reyle and C. Rohrer, eds., *Natural language parsing and linguistic theories*, 69–74. Dordrecht, Netherlands: Reidel.

Gazdar, G., E. Klein, G. Pullum, and I. Sag (1985). *Generalised phrase structure grammar*. Oxford: Blackwell.

Gleitman, L. (1990). The structural source of verb meanings. *Language Acquisition* 1, 3–55.

Gold, E. (1967). Language identification in the limit. *Information & Control* 16, 447–474.

Grosz, B., K. Sparck Jones, and B. Webber (1986). *Readings in natural language processing*. Palo Alto, CA: Morgan-Kaufmann.

Halliday, M. (1967). *Intonation and grammar in British English*. The Hague: Mouton.

Hirst, G. (1987). *Semantic interpretation and the resolution of ambiguity*. Cambridge: Cambridge University Press.

Jackendoff, R. (1972). *Semantic interpretation in generative grammar*. Cambridge, MA: MIT Press.

Joshi, A., K. Vijay-Shanker, and D. Weir (1991). The convergence of mildly context-sensitive formalisms. In P. Sells, S. Shieber and T. Wasow, eds., *Processing of linguistic structure*, 31–81. Cambridge, MA: MIT Press.

Kay, M. (1980). Algorithm schemata and data structures in syntactic processing. CSL-80-12, Xerox PARC. (Reprinted in Grosz, Sparck Jones, and Webber 1986).

Levelt, W. (1989). *Speaking*. Cambridge, MA: MIT Press.

Marcus, M. (1980). *A theory of syntactic recognition for natural language*. Cambridge, MA: MIT Press.

Marslen-Wilson, W, L. Tyler, and M. Seidenberg (1978). The semantic control of sentence segmentation. In W. J. M. Levelt and G. Flores d'Arcais, eds., *Studies in the perception of language*. New York: Wiley.

Miller, G. (1967). *The psychology of communication*. Harmondsworth, England: Penguin.

Montague, R. (1974). *Formal philosophy: Papers of Richard Montague*. Edited by R. H. Thomason. New Haven: Yale University Press.

Oehrle, R., E. Bach, and D. Wheeler, eds. (1988). *Categorial grammars and natural language structures*. Dordrecht, Netherlands: Reidel.

Partee, B., A. ter Meulen, and R. Wall (1990). *Mathematical methods in linguistics*. Dordrecht, Netherlands: Kluwer.

Pereira, F., and S. Shieber (1987). *Prolog and natural language understanding*. Chicago: CSLI/ University of Chicago Press.

Peters, S., and R. Ritchie (1973). On the generative power of transformational grammars. *Information Science* 6, 49–83.

Pinker, S . (1979). Formal models of language learning. *Cognition* 7, 217–283.

Pollard, C., and I. Sag (1983). Reflexives and reciprocals in English: An alternative to the binding theory. In M. Barlow et al., eds., *Proceedings of the 2nd west coast conference on formal linguistics*, 189–203, Stanford, CA.

Pollard, C., and I. Sag (1994). *Head-driven phrase structure grammar*. Chicago: CSLI/ University of Chicago Press.

Prince, E. (1986). On the syntactic marking of presupposed open propositions. *Papers from the parasession on pragmatics and grammatical theory at the 22nd regional meeting of the Chicago Linguistic Society*, 208–222.

Ross, J. (1970). Gapping and the order of constituents. In M. Bierwisch and M. Heidolph, eds., *Progress in linguistics*. The Hague, Netherlands: Mouton. 249–259.

Selkirk, L. (1984). *Phonology and syntax*. Cambridge, MA: MIT Press.

Shieber, S., and M. Johnson (1993). Variations on incremental interpretation. *Journal of Psycholinguistics* 22, 287–318.

Stabler, E. (1991). Avoid the pedestrian's paradox. In R. Berwick, S. Abney, and C. Tenny, eds., *Principle-based parsing*. Dordrecht, Netherlands: Kluwer. 199–238.

Steedman, M. (1987). Combinatory grammars and parasitic gaps. *Natural Language & Linguistic Theory* 5, 403–439.

Trueswell, J. C., M. K. Tanenhaus, and S. M. Garnsey (1994). Semantic influences on parsing: Use of thematic role information in syntactic ambiguity resolution. *Journal of Memory & Language*, in press.

Winograd, T. (1972). *Understanding natural language*. Edinburgh: Edinburgh University Press.

Wood, M. (1993). *Categorial grammars*. London: Routledge.

Woods, W. (1970). Transition network grammars for natural language analysis. *Communications of the Association for Computing Machinery* 3, 591–606. (Reprinted in Grosz, Sparck Jones, and Webber 1986.)

Woods, W. (1973). An experimental parsing system for transition network grammars. In R. Rustin, ed., *Natural language processing*. Courant Computer Science Symposium 8. 111–154. New York: Algorithmics Press.

Chapter 10
The Forms of Sentences
Howard Lasnik

When we speak, the utterances we produce are normally framed in a particular language, and we expect to understand an utterance only if we happen to know the language in which it is framed. Knowledge of a language is thus of paramount importance in every speech event and must be the primary target of the scientific study of language.

In fact, mature mastery of a human language involves knowledge of several different kinds. As speakers of English, we know facts about its *semantics* (chapters 11 and 12 of this volume), about its *phonology* or sound patterns (chapter 3), and—the subject of this chapter—about its *syntax* or sentence structure.

Most obviously, as speakers of a language, we know a large number of words. In addition, we evidently have command of a productive system for the appropriate arrangement of words into sentences, the syntax of the language. Given the creative use of language—the fact that new sentences are routinely used and understood—it could not be true that the syntax of a language consisted merely of a list of sentences that are memorized in the course of language acquisition. Something more complex, hence, more interesting, must be involved. In this chapter we will explore some central aspects of this complex and interesting system of knowledge.

10.1 Syntactic Structure

An initial assumption about syntactic structure might be that speech (like written English) is broken into sentences, and the sentences into words. This already involves a substantial degree of "abstractness," since in spoken language one word tends to run right into the next so that there are few, if any, direct physical correlates of these divisions. But, in fact, even further abstractness is required in a successful account of syntactic knowledge. Thus, a sentence cannot be analyzed as simply a sequence of words, but rather must be regarded as having a certain hierarchical structure as well. Consider a simple sentence such as (1):

(1) The man left.

Clearly, this is not simply a sequence of three autonomous words. *The* and *man* are closely associated in a way in which *man* and *left* are not. The former pair of words constitutes a sort of unit based on the noun *man*, as the following two syntactic tests demonstrate. First, a "pro-form" (in this case a pronoun) can substitute for *The man*:

(2)   He left.

No comparable substitution is possible for the sequence *man left* in (1). Second, an adverb modifying the sentence can easily be inserted between *man* and *left*, as in (3), but not between *the* and *man*, as in (4):

(3)   The man obviously left.

(4)   *The obviously man left. [* indicates an ungrammatical sentence, a sequence of words that is not a sentence of the language under investigation.]

This pattern of data strongly suggests that the sequence *The man* constitutes a unit, while the sequence *man left* does not. How can this fact be represented? Apparently, there is a division of sentence (1) into two major parts, or *constituents*. The first part is based on a noun, and the second part on a verb. Let us then designate the first part *noun phrase*, and the second *verb phrase* (henceforth NP and VP). We might now say that an English sentence (S) like (1) consists of an NP followed by a VP, roughly corresponding to the traditional subject-predicate division. (5) is a shorthand way of stating this property of English sentences:

(5)   S → NP VP

An NP, in turn, consists of a noun (N) possibly preceded by a "determiner," and a VP consists of a verb (V):

(6)   a.   NP → (det) N [Parentheses indicate an optional item.]

      b.   VP → V

There are many other types of NPs and VPs. In a moment we will look at some of the further possibilities for VPs.

The formulas in (5) and (6) are *phrase structure rules* governing the structure of English sentences. They can be thought of as part of the system of knowledge underlying the procedures for the analysis of structures and for the production of structures. By hypothesis, then, someone who knows English knows these rules, in some sense, though the knowledge is generally not conscious. The structure that the rules in (5) and (6) determine for (1) can be represented by the *phrase structure tree* in figure 10.1.

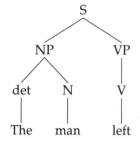

Figure 10.1
Phrase structure tree for sentence (1), "The man left."

Another way of representing the same information is the *labeled bracketing* in (7):

(7) $[_S [_{NP} [_{Det} \text{The}][_N \text{man}]] [_{VP} [_V \text{left}]]]$

In addition to very simple VPs containing only a verb, there are also VPs that contain NPs, as in (8):

(8) The man solved the problem.

This indicates that (6b) should be revised so as to allow an NP direct object for the verb:

(9) VP → V (NP)

As in (6a), the parentheses are to be understood as allowing, but not demanding, that the enclosed material occur in a structure. Taken together, (5) and (9) correctly assert that exactly the same kinds of sequences of words that can be subjects of sentences can be objects of sentences, since it is the constituent NP that occurs in both positions. Without analysis of sentences into constituents, this fact would remain entirely accidental.

We are now in a position to begin further exploration of the creative use of language. A major way of constructing longer and longer sentences is to embed one sentence inside another. We have already seen a VP consisting of just a V, and also one consisting of a V followed by an NP. Another extremely important possibility exists as well. The material following the V can be an entire sentence:

(10) The child thinks the man left.

In (10), the direct object of the verb is our original sentence, (1). The structure of (10) is represented in figure 10.2.

An additional VP phrase structure rule immediately allows for this possibility:

(11) VP → V S

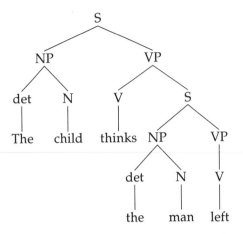

Figure 10.2
Phrase structure tree for sentence (10), "The child thinks the man left."

Now the structure in figure 10.2 can be produced by application of rule (5) followed by, among other things, application of rule (11), followed by *another* application of rule (5). Then, the usual rules for expanding NP and VP can apply. This process can be continued indefinitely, with rule (11) introducing an S which, by rule (5), introduces (in addition to another NP) another VP, and so on. Phrase structure rules with this property are called *recursive*. It is important to note that the simplest possible rule for generating the structure in figure 10.2—namely rule (11)—automatically gives the system of rules (the *grammar*) the recursive property, hence, the means for creating an unlimited number of sentences. Thus, with just the rules we already have, (10) can be further embedded to produce a still more complex sentence such as (12), with the structure given in figure 10.3.

(12)   The woman knows the child thinks the man left.

By providing finite means for generating an unlimited number of sentences, recursive rules supply a crucial part of the answer to the fundamental question of the creative use of language—of how the human brain, with its finite storage capacity, is nevertheless capable of producing and comprehending an infinite number of novel grammatical sentences of theoretically unbounded length.

10.2   Deep and Surface Structure

We have seen a number of reasons for assuming that sentences have phrase structure, even if this phrase structure generally has no direct physi-

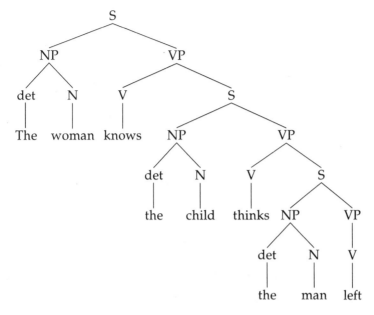

Figure 10.3
Phrase structure tree for sentence (12), "The woman knows the child thinks the man left."

cal manifestation. Thus, knowledge of language involves, in part, mental computation of abstract representations. In this section we will ultimately see evidence for an even further degree of abstractness.

In section 10.1 we examined some of the forms that the VP can take in English sentences, illustrated in (1), (8), and (10), repeated here as (13)–(15).

(13)   The man left. (VP → V)

(14)   The man solved the problem. (VP → V NP)

(15)   The child thinks the man left. (VP → V S)

So far, however, we cannot explain the fact that not just any verb can appear in any of these VP types. For example, the verb in (14) would be ungrammatical in the VP of (13):

(16)   *The man solved.

Similarly, the verb in (15) is incompatible with the VP in (14):

(17)   *The child thinks the problem.

Lexical properties, that is, properties of particular lexical items (words), thus play a major role in determining syntactic well-formedness. In traditional terms, there are transitive verbs, such as *solve*, which require a direct object to fill out their VP (a *complement* in the standard technical terminology). Alongside these are intransitive verbs, such as *sleep*, which do not tolerate a direct object:

(18)   *Harry slept the bed.

Further, some transitive verbs, such as *solve*, take an NP, but not an S, as their complement:

(19)   *Mary solved the man left.

Others, such as *think*, take an S, but not an NP, as complement.

The large lexical category V is thus divided into smaller lexical *subcategories*, each with its own special privileges of occurrence. We can express the properties of the subcategories in the mental lexicon (or dictionary) in the following way:

(20)   a.   sleep $\langle$___$\rangle$

        b.   solve $\langle$___NP$\rangle$

        c.   think $\langle$___S$\rangle$

(20a) is to be interpreted as the requirement that *sleep* can be inserted only into a VP that has no direct object, that is, a VP like the one shown in figure 10.4a. A verb with the requirement in (20b) could be inserted only into a VP like the one shown in figure 10.4b. And so on. These *subcategorization* requirements are linked to *thematic relations* (notions like understood subject, understood object).

With this much in mind, consider now an example such as (21), which is a variant of (22) and which is fully grammatical in some dialects of English, and at least marginally acceptable in virtually all dialects.

(21)   This problem, John solved.

(22)   John solved this problem.

Note that this is far better than the completely ungrammatical (23):

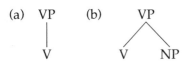

Figure 10.4
Phrase structure representation of the subcategorization requirement for (a) *sleep* and (b) *solve*.

(23) *John solved.

Now, we already know what is wrong with (23): *solve* belongs to the subcategory of verbs that must be inserted into VPs of the form in figure 10.4b. But then why is (21) acceptable? The VPs in the two examples appear to be identical. Even more curious is the fact that if an NP is introduced into the VP in (21) so as to satisfy (20b), the sentence becomes ungrammatical:

(24) *This problem, John solved that problem.

In (21) (but not in (24)), even though *This problem* is at the front of the sentence, it seems to function just as if it were in the VP. Notice that simply adding a new phrase structure rule such as S → NP NP VP to the system would not capture this fact, nor would it address the apparent subcategorization difficulty in (21). Suppose, then, that (21) really has *two* representations, one determining the *thematic relations* and the closely connected subcategorization properties of the sentence, and the other determining the order in which the parts of the sentences are actually pronounced. In the first representation, the so-called *deep structure* of the sentence, the understood direct object will actually be in the VP. In the second, the *surface structure*, that NP direct object will have been displaced leftward from the position that determines its thematic role. The deep structure of (21) will then be as shown in figure 10.5.

This deep structure representation neatly accounts for the interpretation of (21) and is consistent with all of the principles and lexical requirements we have discussed so far. It does not, however, account for the structure of the sentence as immediately perceived. For that we need an additional representation in which the direct object has been displaced to the front of the sentence, as shown in figure 10.6. The position from which movement

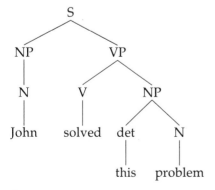

Figure 10.5
Deep structure representation for sentence (21), "This problem, John solved."

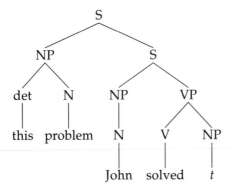

Figure 10.6
Surface structure representation for sentence (21), "This problem, John solved."

took place is marked by t (for "trace"; see chapter 8 for discussion of the role of traces in syntax and in the on-line processing of sentences).

An operation of this sort, relating one phrase structure representation to another phrase structure representation, is known as a *transformation* (hence, the name *transformational grammar* for this general theory of syntax). Transformational analysis, in addition to solving the descriptive problems we have been considering, provides a means for capturing the felt relatedness among sets of sentences. (21) and (22) feel related because they share the same deep structure.

A sequence of transformationally related phrase markers beginning with a deep structure and culminating in a surface structure is called a "(transformational) derivation." The transformation that relates the structure in figure 10.5 to the one in figure 10.6 is called *topicalization*. Topicalization displaces an item (in this case, an NP) and attaches it to another constituent (in this case an S) by creating a "higher" instance of the target category from which both the moved item and the target category hang. This particular sort of attachment is called *adjunction*. (Note that there is no possible topicalization analysis available for (24), since (24) has no vacant position from which *this problem* could have moved.)

One type of interrogative sentence exhibits a similar displacement phenomenon. In (25), *Which problem* is the understood direct object of *solve*, but as in the case of topicalization, it occurs in initial position in the sentence:

(25)   Which problem will John solve?

The major operative transformation in questions of this sort is called *wh-movement*, because interrogative words and phrases in English usually begin with the letters *wh* (*which, what, who, whose, when, where, why*). The order of words in the deep structure of (25) is presumably as in (26):

(26) John will solve which problem

Note that the relationship between (25) and (26) displays, in addition to *wh*-movement, one additional alteration. The order of *John* and the "auxiliary verb" *will* is reversed. This process of interrogative inversion will be the focus of the remainder of this chapter.

10.3   A Case Study: Interrogative Inversion

Interrogative inversion occurs not just in *wh*-questions like (25), but also in *yes-no* questions like (27). (Such questions, unlike *wh*-questions, lack a *wh*-word, and anticipate an answer of *yes* or *no*.)

(27) Will John solve the problem? [cf. John will solve the problem.]

(28) lists several further examples of declarative/interrogative pairs that are strongly felt as related in the way that topicalized sentences are felt as related to their nontopicalized variants. So once again, this suggests transformational derivation from a common deep structure for the two members of each pair.

(28) | | **Declarative** | **Interrogative** |
|---|---|---|
| a. | Susan must leave. | Must Susan leave? |
| b. | Harry can swim. | Can Harry swim? |
| c. | Mary has read the book. | Has Mary read the book? |
| d. | Bill is sleeping. | Is Bill sleeping? |

What is the correct description of this phenomenon? One hypothesis is stated in (29). This hypothesis is tempting for its simplicity and is consistent with all the data in (27)–(28), but it is ultimately incorrect.

(29) **Interrogative inversion process**—structure independent
    (first attempt)
    Beginning with a declarative deep structure, invert the first and
    second words to construct an interrogative.

What is appealing about (29) is that all it relies on is the surely necessary analysis of a sentence into words; it does not depend on hierarchical structure at all. A Martian scientist presented with the data in (28) would reasonably be expected to hypothesize (29). But (29) is not correct for English (nor, for that matter, for any other human language). Consider the pairings that (29) would predict for the examples in (30):

(30)   **Declarative**   **Interrogative**
a. The woman must leave.   *Woman the t must leave?

b. A sailor can swim.   *Sailor a t can swim?

c. Some student has read   *Student some t has read
the book.   the book?

d. My friend is sleeping.   *Friend my t is sleeping?

Compare these with the correct pairings:

(31)   **Declarative**   **Interrogative**
a. The woman must leave.   Must the woman t leave?

b. A sailor can swim.   Can a sailor t swim?

c. Some student has read   Has some student t read
the book.   the book?

d. My friend is sleeping.   Is my friend t sleeping?

Evidently, more than just division into words is implicated. Suppose, then, that the correct statement of the process involves, in addition to division into words, also categorization of the words. *Must, can* (and other *modal verbs,* such as *could, should, shall, may, might*), *has* (a form of the verb *have*), and *is* (a form of the verb *be*) could be assigned to the category of "auxiliary verbs" (verbs that are additional to the main verb of the sentence). With this additional information available, we might hypothesize the more adequate (32):

(32)   **Interrogative inversion process**—structure independent
(second attempt)
Beginning with a declarative deep structure, move the auxiliary
verb to the front to construct an interrogative.

(32) is consistent with all the data considered thus far and is very likely consistent with all the data many children learning English would be exposed to, but it is still inadequate in important respects. For one thing, it says nothing about structures containing more than one auxiliary verb. Such declaratives do, indeed, have corresponding interrogatives, and it is specifically the *first* auxiliary verb that is fronted:

(33)   **Declarative**   **Interrogative**
a. Bill could be sleeping.   Could Bill t be sleeping?
    *Be Bill could t sleeping?

b. Mary has been reading.   Has Mary t been reading?
    *Been Mary has t reading?

c.   Susan should have left.   Should Susan *t* have left?
                                    *Have Susan should *t* left?

Incorporating this property, we now have (34):

(34)   **Interrogative inversion process**—structure independent
       (third attempt)
       Beginning with a declarative deep structure, move the first auxiliary
       verb to the front to construct an interrogative.

(34) is almost certainly consistent with all the data the learner would
confront, but, surprisingly, it is still inaccurate. For slightly more complex
constructions, it gives wildly incorrect results:

(35)   **Declarative**   **Interrogative**
       a.   The man who is here   *Is the man who *t* here
            can swim.   can swim?

       b.   The woman who will sing   *Will the woman who *t* sing
            has arrived.   has arrived?

For these examples, we seem to have the reverse of the situation in (33).
Fronting the *second* auxiliary verb gives the correct form:

(36)   **Declarative**   **Interrogative**
       a.   The man who is here   Can the man who is here
            can swim.   *t* swim?

       b.   The woman who will sing   Has the woman who will sing
            has arrived.   *t* arrived?

Once again, we are not dealing with a peculiarity of English. No known
human language has a transformational process that would produce pairings like those in (35). Further, the incorrect forms in (35), like the incorrect
forms in (30) and (33), are not attested in any of the voluminous literature
documenting the errors that young children make in learning their language. In fact, experiments specifically designed to determine whether
such incorrect forms are possible for children have invariably shown that
they are not. The seemingly simple structure independent computational
operations in (29), (32), and (34) are evidently not available to the human
language faculty.

The right generalization is (a priori) much more complicated, relying
on structured hierarchical organization. Note that in the problematic (35)–
(36), the first auxiliary verb occurs within a "relative clause" (a sentence
used to modify a noun) contained in the subject of the sentence, and
the second auxiliary verb is actually the *first* auxiliary verb of the *main*
sentence. Reflecting this, the auxiliary inversion phenomenon could be
described as in (37):

(37)   **Interrogative inversion process**—structure dependent
Beginning with a declarative deep structure, move the first auxiliary
verb following the subject to the front to construct an
interrogative.

(38) shows the portion of the structural analysis relevant to (37):

(38)   **Declarative**   **Interrogative**
a. $[_{NP}$ The man $[_S$ who is   Can $[_{NP}$ the man $[_S$ who is
     here]] can swim.   here]] t swim?

b. $[_{NP}$ The woman $[_S$ who   Has $[_{NP}$ the woman
     will sing]] has arrived. $[_S$ who will sing]] t arrived?

Like the failed structure independent characterizations, (37) demands
analysis into words, and categorization of the words. But it additionally
requires abstract structural analysis, of the sort discussed earlier in this
chapter. While such operations seem complicated when viewed as purely
formal mathematical operations, as far as human language capacity is concerned, they are simple—so fundamental as to be the only options.

The process in (37), which we have concluded is simple as a human
language operation, so far says nothing about the interrogative counterparts of the simplest sorts of declarative sentences, those with no auxiliary
verbs at all, like (1), above, repeated as (39), or (40):

(39)   The man left.

(40)   Mary sleeps.

These do have interrogative counterparts, but ones that initially seem to
fall under entirely different mechanisms. Consider (41):

(41)   a.   Mary sleeps.   b.   Does Mary sleep?

This is actually felt by speakers of English as instantiating the same relation we have been investigating. The mystery is why. The superficial
differences between (41) and (42) are striking.

(42)   a.   Mary will sleep.   b.   Will Mary sleep?

Comparing (42a) and (42b), we see just the familiar inversion alternation.
But comparing (41a) and (41b), instead we see a change in the form of the
main verb (from *sleeps* to *sleep*) and the addition of a form of the auxiliary
verb *do* in presubject position. If the two processes truly have nothing in
common, how can we account for the strong intuition of parallelism?

Reconsidering (41), it is as if the inflectional ending (carrying present
tense and third person singular agreement information) that appears on the
main verb *sleeps* in (41a) has moved to the front of the sentence, much as
the auxiliary verb in the other examples (*will* in (42)) does. And in that

fronted position, it is realized as an inflectional ending on a sort of "dummy" verb *do*; that is, on a verb that makes no semantic contribution of its own to the sentence, but rather is present for some purely structural reason. The task now is to make these speculations more precise. To begin to do this, we must look at the relevant structures and processes in more detail.

Let us consider first the structure of S. Note that NP is *headed by* (based upon) N, and VP is headed by V. But S does not seem to be headed by anything. Suppose, though, that S does have a head, as other constituents do, and that in a sentence with a modal auxiliary, that modal auxiliary is the head. From this perspective, this type of S is really AuxP. The more articulated phrase structure rules for sentences are shown in (43), where Aux' is a constituent intermediate between Aux and the *maximal projection* of Aux, AuxP. Given these rules, the structure of (42a) is as in figure 10.7.

(43)   a.   AuxP → NP Aux'
       b.   Aux' → Aux VP

To derive (42b) from this underlying structure, Aux, the head of AuxP, is fronted. (We will put aside the precise specification of the derived structure resulting from the transformation.) Consider now (41). If Aux is indeed the head of S, then even a sentence without an auxiliary verb is expected to have an Aux. Further, if it is the inflectional ending that moves to the front in (41b) as conjectured above, and if the inversion process actually fronts Aux, then it is reasonable to conclude that in (41), the inflectional ending (*Infl*, for short) is the Aux. This is illustrated in figure 10.8.

As in (42), the Aux moves to the front of the sentence. This time, however, the Aux is not an independent word like *will*, but must be attached to a verb. An item like this, which cannot stand alone, is called an *affix*. The

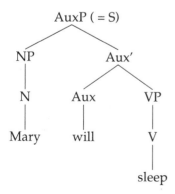

Figure 10.7
Deep structure of (42a,b): "Mary will sleep." "Will Mary sleep?"

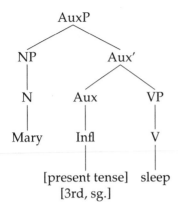

Figure 10.8
Deep structure of (41a,b): "Mary sleeps." "Does Mary sleep?"

semantically empty auxiliary verb *do* is inserted into the structure to support the now "stranded" affix, Infl. To derive the declarative (41a), Infl does not front, but rather attaches to the V, *sleep*. This analysis, designed to capture the felt similarity of process between (41) and (42), indicates that a deep structure can be quite abstract: figure 10.8 itself is not the superficial structure of any actual sentence. It is the underlying form of both (41a) and (41b), but to produce either of these, some transformation(s) must apply. Thus, while transformations play a crucial role in our explanation of felt relatedness between sentences, they are not actually operations changing sentences into other sentences.

The transformation attaching Infl to V (often called *affix hopping*) is standardly analyzed as an instance of adjunction (a type of operation we have seen before). Applying to the deep structure in figure 10.8, it yields figure 10.9 as the surface structure of (41a). This proposed structure follows the claim of traditional grammar that the verb *sleeps* is made up of two parts: a stem V plus an affix.

In the dialect we are considering, when the main verb of a sentence is *be*, the pattern diverges from that found with other verbs, such as *sleep*. Consider (44):

(44) a. John is the teacher.   b.   Is John the teacher?
                                          *Does John be the teacher?

Assuming that a sentence always contains a VP, and a VP always is headed by V, we should expect a deep structure as in figure 10.10, but the inversion process apparently gives us a result parallel to that obtained from the deep structure in figure 10.7.

If the Aux in figure 10.10 fronts, the Infl becomes stranded. *Do*-support then should apply, producing the ungrammatical *"Does John be the

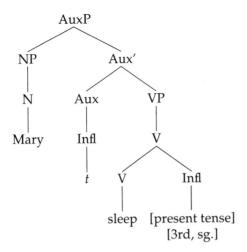

Figure 10.9
Surface structure of (41a): "Mary sleeps."

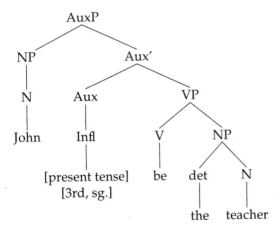

Figure 10.10
Deep structure of (44a,b): "John is the teacher." "Is John the teacher?"

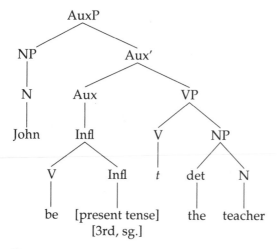

Figure 10.11
'Intermediate' structure of (44a,b): "John is the teacher." "Is John the teacher?" following raising of *be* to Infl.

teacher?" instead of the correct "Is John the teacher?" To produce the correct result, *be* must move to the front along with Infl when the Aux fronts. Since Infl and *be* must attach to each other eventually, we might kill two birds with one stone by moving *be* into Aux by attaching it to Infl. Assuming that this attachment is adjunction, the result will be as in figure 10.11.

Notice now that this possibility of raising a verb to Infl must not be general in English. If normal main verbs could undergo the process, we would derive (45), instead of the desired (46), via Aux fronting:

(45)   *Sleeps John?

(46)   Does John sleep?

We thus have the following generalization for modern standard English:

(47)   To instantiate the connection between Infl and V, if V is *be* it raises to Infl (V-raising). Otherwise, Infl lowers to V (affix hopping).

In certain constructions, main verb *have* also raises to Infl. Consider the following declarative-interrogative pair:

(48)   You have a dollar.   Have you a dollar?

The interrogative version is straightforwardly derived if *have* raises to Infl, and the Aux, now containing *have*, fronts in the usual fashion. Curiously, though, unlike the situation with *be*, there is an option in this instance.

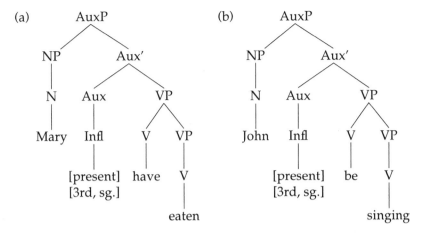

Figure 10.12
Deep structures of (50a,b): "Mary has eaten." "John is singing."

Instead of raising *have*, we could merely front Aux containing only Infl. The stranded Infl then triggers *do*-support, and we derive (49), contrasting with the situation with *be* seen in (44).

(49)   Do you have a dollar?

Significantly, *have* and *be*, the only main verbs that also function as auxiliary verbs (as in (50)), are the only main verbs that raise to Infl, thus moving into the Aux.

(50)   a.   Mary has eaten.

      b.   John is singing.

There is a question about examples like (50). Where is the auxiliary verb in deep structure? One possibility is that it is in Aux, as modal auxiliaries are. So far, however, we have seen no reason to posit a deep structure Aux with more than one item in it: either a modal or Infl. But *has* and *is* in (50a, b) seem to embody morphologically both V and Infl exactly as they do when they are main verbs. To capture this similarity while still preserving a simple Aux, we can posit the deep structures in figure 10.12, where *have* and *be* head their own VPs, and take additional VPs as their complements, via the phrase structure rule VP → V VP.

(47), extended to (51), thus covers a wide range of sentence types:

(51)   To instantiate the connection between Infl and V, if V is *be* or (certain instances of) *have* it raises to Infl (V-raising). Otherwise, Infl lowers to V (affix hopping).

10.4   Further Evidence: Negative Sentences

The conclusions we have arrived at so far—that S is AuxP, a constituent headed by Aux, and that Aux can be the affix Infl, standing alone in deep structure, but necessarily affixed to some verb by the time it reaches surface structure (via V-raising, affix hopping, or *do*-support)—allow for the treatment of a fascinating array of further phenomena. Consider, for example, the negative forms of simple sentences, as in (52):

(52)   **Affirmative**   **Negative**
    a. Susan must leave.   Susan must not leave.

    b. Harry can swim.   Harry can not swim.

    c. John is the teacher.   John is not the teacher.

    d. Mary has read the book.   Mary has not read the book.

    e. Bill is sleeping.   Bill is not sleeping.

The negative word *not* occurs in these examples immediately following the auxiliary verb. Further, a consideration of the several sentence types explored earlier as part of the investigation of interrogative sentences leads to a generalization quite reminiscent of the one used to characterize interrogative inversion:

(53)   In a negative sentence, *not* occurs immediately after the first auxiliary verb following the subject.

We must now try to determine more precisely where *not* appears in the structure so that we can explain (53). We have been assuming that structural constituents are all headed by a minimal element, the head of the constituent. Suppose that the converse is also true—that minimal elements always project phrasal constituents. *Not* would then project a phrase, which we will call *Neg(ative)P*. Further, assuming that *not* is present in deep structure, the relevant new phrase structure rules are stated in (54), and the deep structure of the negative version of (52a) is in figure 10.13.

(54)   a.   Aux' → Aux NegP
        b.   NegP → Neg VP

Consider now (52c), a negative sentence with *is*, a form of *be*, as its main verb. This time, as in the situations with *be* already discussed, *be* must raise to Infl. This is illustrated in the deep and surface structures of "John is not the teacher" in figure 10.14.

Parallel derivations obtain for (52d) and (52e) with *have* and *be* respectively raising across *not* to Infl.

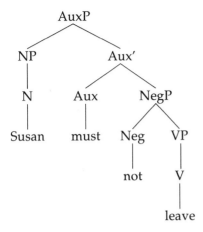

Figure 10.13
Deep structure (and surface structure) of "Susan must not leave."

As with interrogatives, negatives of very simple sentences, those lacking any auxiliary verbs, at first appear to wildly deviate from the standard pattern:

(55) a. John sleeps.   b. John does not sleep.

Here the difference is not just the presence versus absence of *not*. Additionally, in the affirmative sentence, the main verb is the present tense inflected form *sleeps*, while in the negative sentence it is the uninflected form *sleep*. Further, the dummy verb *do* appears in the negative sentence, and its form—present tense, third person singular—is just the form that the main verb had in the affirmative sentence. Clearly, this is the same abstract pattern we found with interrogatives. And, significantly, this patterning is automatically accounted for with no new mechanisms. Recall that we determined in our investigation of interrogatives that the tense-agreement inflectional ending showing up on a verb in superficial structure is initially generated as an autonomous item, Infl, in Aux. If we additionally continue to assume that *not* is the head of NegP, a phrasal constituent between AuxP and VP, we are led to postulate the deep structure in figure 10.15 for sentence (55b).

Beginning with this deep structure, some operation must take place so that Infl, an affix, winds up attached to a verb. If *sleep* could raise to Infl, (56) would be produced:

(56) *John sleeps not.

Thus, the ungrammaticality of (56) provides further evidence (in addition to that found in our investigation of interrogatives) that verbs other than

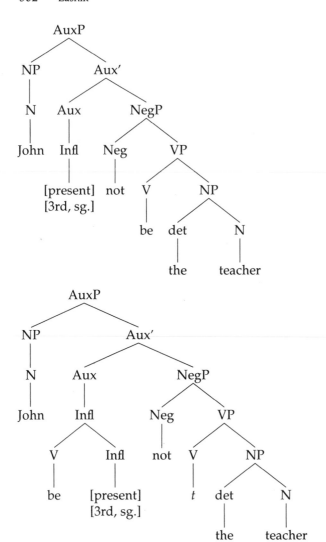

Figure 10.14
Deep and surface structures of "John is not the teacher."

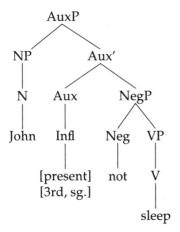

Figure 10.15
Deep structure of example (55b), "John does not sleep."

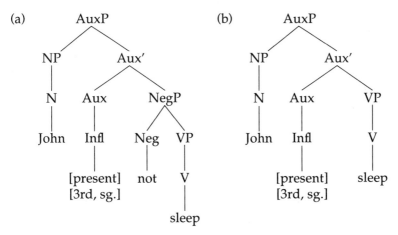

Figure 10.16
Deep structures of "John does not sleep." "John sleeps."

have and *be* do not raise in English. More specifically, this limitation holds in *modern* English. There was a different pattern found in earlier English, which, nonetheless, made use of the same syntactic elements.

Affix hopping provides another potential mechanism for connecting Infl with *sleep*. But if Infl could "hop" onto *sleep* in the deep structure in figure 10.15, (57) would incorrectly be generated:

(57) *John not sleeps.

There must be something preventing affix hopping in (57), while still allowing it in (55a), "John sleeps." Compare the deep structures of the two examples, presented in figure 10.16.

Observe that in figure 10.16b, the structure permitting affix hopping, Infl is adjacent to V, while in figure 10.16a, the structure not permitting affix hopping, *not* intervenes between Infl and V. Since there is no other evident difference, it is reasonable to take this difference to be the crucial one, as stated in (58):

(58) Affix hopping can hop Infl onto V only if Infl is adjacent to V.

With neither V-raising nor affix hopping available for the deep structure of (55b), *do*-support, which is a sort of "last resort" option, applies, rescuing what would otherwise be a stranded affix.

(58), the adjacency requirement on affix hopping, seems exceptional. None of the other transformations we have seen so far has such a restriction. Topicalization and wh-movement clearly do not. They can move an item a considerable distance, as evidenced by the examples in section 10.2. Similarly, interrogative inversion regularly moves Aux across the subject. Even V-raising, another transformation connecting an affix to a verb, is not constrained by adjacency. As exemplified in (59) repeated from (52), *have* and *be* can raise across *not*. A trace *t* marks the position from which movement of *have* or *be* took place:

(59) | | **Affirmative** | **Negative** |
|---|---|---|
| a. | John is the teacher. | John is not *t* the teacher. |
| b. | Mary has read the book. | Mary has not *t* read the book. |
| c. | Bill is sleeping. | Bill is not *t* sleeping. |

There is one further difference between affix hopping and all these other transformations: the former is a "lowering" operation, in that it moves an item to a lower position in the tree. The latter are all "raising" operations. It is the latter type that seem representative of transformations in the languages of the world. Lowering operations are decidedly atypical. We might speculate that the adjacency requirement on affix hopping is the penalty incurred by that transformation for deviating from the normal raising pattern.

10.5   VP Deletion

Let us turn now to a third phenomenon in English embodying the same abstract structures and processes we have found in interrogative and negative sentences. English has a variety of *ellipsis* operations whereby a portion of a sentence is not overtly expressed. One such operation involves the optional suppression of a VP when that VP can be interpreted by reference to an overt VP (the *antecedent* of the missing VP), as in (60):

(60)   Harry can not swim, but Susan can (swim).
        Harry can swim, and Susan can (swim) also.

The missing VP at the end of this example is understood as *swim*, the overt VP of the first half of the example. (61) is a similar example, but with a more complex VP:

(61)   Mary will not read the book, but Bill will (read the book).
        Mary will read the book, and Bill will (read the book) also.

An informal statement of this phenomenon is in (62):

(62)   **VP Deletion**
        Optionally delete a VP if it has an antecedent (that is, another VP to which it is identical).

Notice now that VP deletion is sensitive to the output of V-raising, in that only the material following a raised *have* or *be* deletes:

(63)   a.   John is not a teacher, but Mary is (a teacher).
        a'.   John is a teacher, and Mary is (a teacher) also.
        b.   Susan is not sleeping, but Bill is (sleeping).
        b'.   Susan is sleeping, and Bill is (sleeping) also.
        c.   Mary has not read the book, but Harry has (read the book).
        c'.   Mary has read the book, and Harry has (read the book) also.

Figure 10.17 shows how VP deletion operates in the derivation of the second half of sentence (63a, a').

We will now see that, as usual, sentences with no auxiliary verb superficially appear to deviate markedly from the normal pattern but, on deeper consideration, turn out to conform precisely. Consider (64):

(64)   John sleeps, and Bill does (sleep) also.

As with interrogation and negation, we wind up with a form of *do* in the target sentence. Why should this be? Recall that standard verbs (such as *sleep*) do not undergo V-raising in English; rather, they necessarily remain in the VP. This is why they cannot undergo interrogative inversion and cannot appear to the left of *not*, as we have seen. Given this, consider the

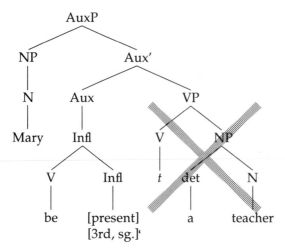

Figure 10.17
Structure of "Mary is (a teacher)."

structure of the second half of (64) just prior to VP deletion, illustrated in figure 10.18.

When the VP is deleted, we wind up with a familiar situation: a stranded Infl. The verb onto which that affix would have hopped is gone. The remedy is also familiar: *do*-support operates to rescue the stranded affix, yielding "Bill does." Thus, yet another set of facts fall under the same general analysis that we initially developed to handle the patterning of interrogative sentences.

So far, in trying to explain an array of phenomena involving the positions of verbs in simple English sentences, we have uncovered substantial evidence for abstract structure in sentences; for two different structural representations of sentences, a "deeper" one and a more superficial one, related by transformational processes; and for items that are independent syntactic heads in deep structure but are affixes necessarily attached to verbs in surface structure. These structures and processes were not accessible to direct inspection, but, as is common in scientific inquiry, were posited based on the role they played in accounts of facts that we were able to collect. These affixes are often discernible as relatively discrete parts of words, as in the examples in (65), which are clearly composed (phonologically, and, for that matter, orthographically) of a stem verb followed by an inflectional suffix:

(65)   a.   *looks* look + 3rd person, singular, present   *looked* look + past

      b.   *bats* bat + 3rd, sg., present   *batted* bat + past

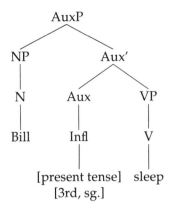

Figure 10.18
Structure of "Bill does (sleep)."

With certain verbs, the past tense form not only has an affix but exhibits an alteration of the stem as well:

(66) a. *sleeps* sleep + 3rd, sg., present   *slept* sleep + past

      b. *leaves* leave + 3rd, sg., present   *left* leave + past

And with still other forms, the alteration triggered by inflection is even more extreme:

(67) a. *has*   have + 3rd, sg., present   *had*   have + past

      b. *knows* know + 3rd, sg., present   *knew*   know + past

      c. *brings* bring + 3rd, sg., present   *brought* bring + past

This extreme sort of alteration is called "suppletion." (See chapter 5 of this volume for discussion of children's acquisition of such forms.) The forms of the verb *be* display a particularly striking pattern of suppletion:

(68) (I)   *am* be + 1st, sg., present

      (You)   *are* be + 2nd, sg. or plural, present

      (We)   1st, plural, present

      (They)   3rd, plural, present

      (She)   *is* be + 3rd, sg., present

In all these paradigms, the effects of the hypothesized Infl affix are directly observable, transparently so in the overt appearance of an affix in (65) and (66), and at least in the change in the form of the stem in the other examples. On the other hand, for present tense forms other than the third person singular, verbs other than *be* show no apparent difference at all from the uninflected form (for example, the one that shows up when the Aux contains a modal instead of Infl):

(69)   I   II
      a. You should look...   You look...

      b. We can bat...   We bat...

      c. They might sleep   They sleep

      d. I will leave   I leave (tomorrow)

      e. They might have...   They have...

A question immediately arises: is there no Infl at all in the sentences in column II of (69); or, alternatively, do these forms have an Infl, but one that has no phonological effect on the verb stem it attaches to? In fact, there is a wealth of evidence pointing toward the second of these two possibilities. Every syntactic phenomenon we have investigated that implicated Infl carries over to these apparently uninflected verb forms. (70) is representative:

(70) a. They sleep.

      b. Do they sleep?

      c. They do not sleep.

      d. We sleep, and they do too.

Do-support is triggered by interrogation (b), negation (c), and VP deletion (d) exactly as it was in the paradigms examined earlier. Considerations of simplicity lead us to conclude that the same abstract structures and processes are involved, thus, that (70a) has an Infl no less than (71) does, the only difference being the absence of phonological effects in the former case.

(71) He sleeps.

Evidently, it is not only possible, but indeed necessary, to assume the same basic sentence structure for all English sentences.

10.6   Conclusion

This brief exercise in syntactic analysis has led us to a seeming paradox. On the one hand, sentences are far more complicated than they at first appear. They have rich structure involving elements that begin in one position but end up in another—elements that begin as autonomous syntactic entities but wind up as affixes, and elements that are syntactically present but absent as far as pronunciation is concerned. On the other hand, the overall pattern must have a fundamental simplicity as far as learners and speakers of the language are concerned. Children acquire the system effortlessly with little or no explicit instruction, and speakers use it flawlessly. But if we assume that the child brings to the task of learning a language detailed knowledge of how a sentence could be structurally represented, and how a syntactic rule could operate, the paradox disappears. In place of the paradox, we have, instead, a set of specific hypotheses about the nature of one facet of the human mind.

Suggestions for Further Reading

For a detailed introduction to transformational grammar and some of the issues it raises for cognitive science, see Baker 1978. Freidin 1992 is another fine introduction, incorporating some more recent developments in syntactic theory. Chapter 4 of that book presents a detailed analysis of the English auxiliary verb system along similar lines to the one presented here. Crain and Nakayama 1987 lucidly report on an important series of experiments investigating structure dependence in children's acquisition of *yes-no* questions.

The general approach to syntax (and to the properties of the auxiliary verb system) outlined in this chapter was introduced in Chomsky 1957. This book had a revolutionary impact on the field of linguistics. The notion of deep structure was first presented in Chomsky 1965, which includes, in addition to a technical presentation of the transformational framework, an essential discussion of the philosophical and methodological foundations of linguistic theory, a discussion that is still as important for cognitive science as it was when it first appeared.

See Emonds 1978 for an illuminating account of differences between French and English in terms of properties of verb-raising in the two languages. Pollock 1989 and Chomsky 1991 are two very influential articles that further develop Emonds's ideas. These latter two articles presuppose more background in syntactic theory than this chapter has been able to provide—background that could be obtained from Freidin 1992, perhaps supplemented by Lasnik and Uriagereka 1988.

Problems

10.1 Imagine a language (L1) characterized by the following phrase structure grammar and with the lexicon of English (except that verbs are already inflected in the lexicon).

$$S \rightarrow NP\ VP \qquad NP \rightarrow N \qquad VP \rightarrow V\ (VP)$$

a. How many sentences does L1 have?
b. Give two sentences of L1, along with their phrase structure trees.
c. Present two sentences of English that are not sentences of L1.

10.2 Give the surface structure of example (10) in the text, assuming the more articulated phrase structure rules and transformations developed later in the chapter.

10.3 In English the form of a verb used in commands (the *imperative* form) sounds just like the bare form: "Eat your dinner"; "Leave"; and the like. Show that there is an affix on the verb, rather than nothing at all. (Hint: Consider negative imperative sentences.)

10.4   Imagine a language (L2) just like English except that *all* verbs undergo raising, not just *have* and *be*. Give the translations of the following English sentences into L2.

a. Does Mary like philosophy?
b. Bill did not solve the problem.
c. John is not a linguist.

10.5   For each of the following sentences, state whether it can be generated by the rules developed in this chapter. If it can, draw the deep structure tree. If it cannot, indicate just what the difficulty is.

a. Mary said the teacher has not presented this material.
b. Bill will give Susan a book.
c. Has the class not accepted the analysis?

References

Baker, C. L. (1978). *Introduction to generative transformational syntax*. Englewood Cliffs, NJ: Prentice-Hall.

Chomsky, N. (1957). *Syntactic structures*. The Hague: Mouton.

Chomsky, N. (1965). *Aspects of the theory of syntax*. Cambridge, MA: MIT Press.

Chomsky, N. (1991). Some notes on economy of derivation and representation. In R. Freidin, ed., *Principles and parameters in comparative grammar*. Cambridge, MA: MIT Press.

Crain, S., and M. Nakayama (1987). Structure dependence in grammar formation. *Language* 63, 522–543.

Emonds, J. (1978). The verbal complex V'-V in French. *Linguistic Inquiry* 8, 151–175.

Freidin, R. (1992). *Foundations of generative syntax*. Cambridge, MA: MIT Press.

Lasnik, H., and J. Uriagereka (1988). *A course in GB syntax*. Cambridge, MA: MIT Press.

Pollock, J.-Y. (1989). Verb movement, universal grammar, and the structure of IP. *Linguistic Inquiry* 20, 365–424.

Chapter 11

Lexical Semantics and Compositionality

Barbara H. Partee

Semantics is an inherently interdisciplinary subject, and one which benefits from the intrinsically interdisciplinary perspective of cognitive science. "Semantics" has meant different things in different disciplines: That situation is not just accidental but neither does it necessarily reflect "turf battles" or disagreements; mainly, it reflects the many different ways that different disciplines are concerned with meaning. And, even within a single discipline, "semantics" often means different things within different schools of thought. There it often reflects serious disagreement about the nature of the "best theory," disagreement about which kinds of data are most important, and even disagreements about such foundational issues as whether semantics is best viewed as a "branch of mathematics" or as a "branch of psychology" (see Partee 1979). In this latter kind of case, the arguments are between whole theories, not just between competing definitions of key terms (the arguments are not "merely semantic," to use an idiomatic expression that semanticists do not appreciate!). Everyone does agree, though, that semantics is the study of meaning. So the big question is: What is meaning?

It is not easy to tackle a question like that head-on; and while it is an important question to keep wrestling with, a total answer is not required in advance of doing fruitful work on semantics, any more than biologists wait for the answer to the still-difficult question "what is life?" before getting down to work. A scientific community just needs *some* clear examples to get started, and then empirical and theoretical advances proceed together, along with further sharpening of key concepts.

Semantics has roots in linguistics, psychology, anthropology, logic and philosophy of language, artificial intelligence, and more. Traditional differences in approaches to semantics in these fields reflect at least two factors. For one thing, the central questions concerning meaning may come out quite differently if one focuses on language and thought, on language and communication, on language and culture, on language and truth, on the design of natural language man-machine interfaces, or on language "structure" per se. A more accidental but no less profound source of differences

311

is the research methodology prevalent in the field within which one approaches questions of semantics. (This means, incidentally, that semantics is an area in which the student can get a good handle on historical differences among the fields that make up cognitive science, by reading articles on similar topics by scholars from the different disciplines.) To oversimplify a bit, one might say that when investigating meanings, some linguists have tended to look for feature structures (influenced by phonology and morphology); other linguists expect to find a level of tree structures, something like a more abstract syntaxlike representation; logicians tend to think in terms of formal systems and model structures; psychologists may be interested in studying concept discrimination, concept acquisition, and principles for scaling semantic fields; artificial intelligence researchers may approach meaning representations in terms of data bases and symbol manipulation; philosophers ask whether there are such things as meanings at all and, if so, what sorts of things they might be.

The perspective of the author of this chapter is that of "formal semantics" with roots in logic, philosophy of language, and linguistics, developed in an environment in which linguistic and cognitive science questions have been at the forefront, with logic and the philosophy of language providing important tools and foundations.

11.1   How Might One Approach the Question "What Are Meanings?"

Let's imagine that we are starting from scratch with this question. The plan of this chapter is to begin with a little philosophical reflection on broad methodological problems and foundational concerns and then to plunge into a series of case studies, all dealing with various aspects of the semantics of adjectives in English. The generalities in this section will be brief, since some of the same points will be covered in the next chapter. The case studies we will deal with in the following sections have been chosen to involve readily graspable empirical issues that have interesting theoretical ramifications; to compress into a chapter several decades of advances in semantic theorizing; and, last but not least, to help the novice to appreciate that there are always new questions opening up for new generations of researchers to work on, as well as old questions that need to be reexamined from new perspectives.

11.1.1   Compositionality

One of the starting points for thinking about what a semantic theory should be like is very similar to the main starting point of syntax: We need to account for a language user's ability to understand novel sentences, of which there are a potential infinity. Even before we have any handle on what sorts of things we should analyze meanings to be, this fundamental aspect of semantic competence provides an argument that they must be governed by some version of the Principle of Compositionality, or Frege's Principle.

Principle of Compositionality, first version: The meaning of a whole is a function of the meanings of the parts.

What are "parts"? Since one can form different, nonsynonymous sentences with the same smallest parts (words and morphemes), we can conclude that the Principle of Compositionality requires a notion of part–whole structure that is based on syntactic structure.

Principle of Compositionality: The meaning of a whole is a function of the meanings of the parts and of the way they are syntactically combined.

We will keep the Principle of Compositionality in the foreground as we work through our case studies, to see the powerful role it can play in helping to choose among alternative hypotheses about the meanings of words and phrases.

There are several key words in the Principle of Compositionality that, on closer examination, can be seen to stand for theory-dependent concepts. Sharpening the Principle of Compositionality requires a theory of syntax, to specify the nature of the relevant part–whole structure, and a theory of what meanings are and by what kinds of functions they are combined. (Here we might compare semantics with chemistry, looking at the history of theories of molecules and atoms. Clearly, it was both possible and necessary to investigate chemical structure and chemical processes without knowing the nature of the smallest parts or the fundamental forces—a clear example of "bootstrap" progress.) Let's assume that we have some syntax, while remembering that every hypothesis in syntax may have repercussions for semantics, and that the Principle of Compositionality may help choose among syntactic as well as semantic analyses, as we will see at several points below. Let us turn then to the key semantic concepts of meanings and functions that combine them. Given some commonsense ideas about meanings that all of us share pretheoretically, how might we identify a notion of meaning that will support fruitful theory-building?

11.1.2   Two Useful Strategies

Not surprisingly, it is philosophers who have provided two particularly useful strategies for thinking productively about the question of what meanings are. The first comes from David Lewis (1970).

Lewis's Advice: "In order to say what a meaning is, we may first ask what a meaning does, and then find something that does that." (p. 22)

So let's think about what meanings do besides combine in some way to make more meanings. For this, Max Cresswell (1982) has shown how a great deal of mileage can be gotten from a very minimal assumption. Cresswell notes that we have no good a priori conception of what meanings are, but we do know at least one thing about them, which he dubs his "Most Certain Principle."

Cresswell's "Most Certain Principle": "For two sentences α and β, if [in some possible situation—BHP] α is true and β is false, α and β must have different meanings." (p. 69)

If we follow these two strategic pieces of advice, they lead rather inevitably to the idea that truth-conditions are at least one fundamental part of what should go into the notion of the "meaning" of a sentence (not necessarily all, by any means). And while truth-conditions may at first look much too austere to make up a very large part of what meanings should be, it turns out to be surprisingly nontrivial to assign meanings to the lexical items and principles for combining meanings of syntactically structured parts so as to eventually arrive at relatively correct truth-conditions for sentences.

Let's just look informally at an example of the force of these strategic suggestions. It is normally accepted that "half full" and "half empty" are synonymous, just two different ways of describing the same property. But "almost half full" and "almost half empty" are clearly *not* synonymous, by Cresswell's principle. Then by Lewis's Advice, if one of the things meanings are supposed to do is combine to produce truth conditions of sentences, and if the expression "almost half full" has as its main syntactic parts "almost" and "half full," and similarly for "almost half empty," then we can argue that "half full" and "half empty" must have different meanings after all. How else could one and the same meaning (the meaning of "almost") combine with the meanings of those two expressions to give clearly different meanings as a result? (The second of the "if's" in the preceding sentence is a very big "if" involving syntax, and, in fact, I think that the hypothesis introduced about the structure in question may well be false; we'll come back to it below.)

Is this result really counterintuitive? Well, first we may note that with any other fraction than "half," there is not even apparent synonymy: "two-thirds full" and "two-thirds empty" have clearly different meanings. That may lead us to be more open to the possibility that "half full" and "half empty" are expressions that do not really have the same meaning, but rather have different meanings that happen to be applicable to the same state of affairs.

The same example can be used to show the importance of thinking about syntax and semantics together when evaluating proposals for compositional semantic analyses. Suppose that the correct syntactic bracketing is rather "almost half" plus "full" and "almost half" plus "empty." Then the argument above suddenly evaporates. All we need then is that "full" and "empty" have different meanings, which is uncontroversial, and that the relation between them is such that when they are modified by any fraction other than "half," the resulting meanings are different; but there is no longer any argument against saying that "half full" and "half empty" are synonymous.

What is the right syntax in this case? Let's leave that for a thought question. It is even possible that both syntactic analyses are correct, that the phrases are structurally ambiguous, synonymous when both have structure (1) and nonsynonymous when both have structure (2).

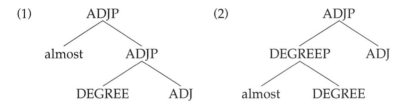

We have still not said very much about what sorts of things word meanings are. We have, though, begun to get a handle on how to do detective work to figure out some aspects of what we have to take word meanings to be in order to get them to combine compositionally to produce the truth-conditional aspects of sentence meanings.

11.1.3   Montague's Legacy

The truth-conditional perspective just discussed did not penetrate into linguistic work until the 1970s. One of the main forces was the work of the philosopher and logician Richard Montague, who startled the linguistic and philosophical communities with his famously titled paper "English as a

Formal Language" (Montague 1970), containing this famously provocative pronouncement: "I reject the contention that an important theoretical difference exists between formal and natural languages" (p. 189).

Well, of course, there are important differences; but taking a perspective from which one can analyze both with the same kinds of tools—many of them developed or deployed in novel ways by Montague himself—has proved to be immensely fruitful not only for providing good formal tools for the analysis of natural languages but also for elucidating the very differences between natural and formal languages and even for suggesting some fruitful innovations for logic, computer languages, and AI. The cooperative work between linguists, philosophers, and logicians taking off from Montague's seminal works was initially known as Montague Grammar; in more recent years, as that work has evolved and innovations have led to distinct theoretical frameworks variously related to Montague's original theory, Montague Grammar has gradually been replaced by the broader enterprise of "formal semantics." Montague is still recognized as having laid the foundations and set much of the agenda for the field, but the contributions of linguists and others have done much to enrich it into a productively interdisciplinary endeavor. The tensions between the antipsychologistic perspective on semantics of Frege, Montague, and most logicians on the one hand and the explicitly psychologistic perspective on all of linguistics of Chomsky and the bulk of the linguistic and cognitive science communities on the other hand have led to interesting foundational debates but, interestingly, have not prevented very fruitful interdisciplinary progress on substantive problems in semantics. (Compare progress in the development of the differential calculus invented by Newton and Leibniz and the accompanying stormy debates about the coherence or incoherence of the notion of infinitesimals.)

11.2   Case Study I. Adjective Meanings

11.2.1   Groundwork: Internal Structure of NPs: Syntax and Semantics

The next chapter includes syntactic and semantic rules for forming and interpreting NPs consisting of a DET and an N. Before we immerse ourselves in issues of adjective meanings, let's stand back a little and consider some of the other kinds of parts that can go into NPs, including adjectives (ADJ), prepositional phrases (PP), and relative clauses (REL).

In order to bring out the full range of kinds of semantic roles these parts can play in contributing to NP meanings, we need to add one more DET to our arsenal, namely "the," which has a broader range of distribution than any other DET. Whole books have been written about "the," and its semantics is much more controversial than that of "some," "every," or "no." For starters, let's work with the intuition that "the teacher," like "John," simply denotes an individual. (We could later convert our analysis to a "set of sets" analysis; see problem 12.3 in chapter 12. But, unlike a proper name like "John," a singular definite description like "the teacher" has meaningful parts, so the interpretation must be compositionally derived. What individual does "the teacher" denote? The individual that's a teacher. Well, that answer presupposes that there is such an individual, and furthermore that there's only one. If we postpone worrying about how to make it clear that we mean one and only one in the relevant context of our utterance, and not one and only one in the whole world, we have the core of the "individual-denoting" semantic analysis of NPs of the form "the N," and we can write a semantic rule as follows:

(3) $\|[_{NP}\ the\ N]\|$ = the individual a such that a is the one and only member of $\|N\|$, if $\|N\|$ has one and only one member; undefined otherwise.

This is by no means the last word about the semantics of *the*, but it is a reasonable first approximation and will do for now.

Armed with this much of the semantics of NPs consisting of DET + N and our general methodological principles, let's see what we can figure out about the semantic contributions of other parts of NPs. Consider examples (4)–(5).

(4)   (a)   the teacher from France

      (b)   the teacher of French

      (c)   the French teacher

(5)   (a)   the student who was curious

      (b)   the student, who was curious,

      (c)   the curious student

The PPs, ADJs, and RELs in these examples can all be loosely described as modifiers, adding greater specificity to the meaning of the NP, but on closer examination we can identify at least three semantic roles for these added parts; "arguments" (4b), "restrictive modifiers" (4a, 5a), and "nonrestrictive modifiers" (5b). Let's start with (4a) versus (4b) and examine the differences in inference patterns involving them, since that is one of the good ways to investigate systematic differences in truth conditions.

(6a) If Chris is the teacher from France, then
      (i)   Chris is a teacher? YES, Valid.
      (ii) Chris is from France? YES, Valid.

(6b) If Chris is the teacher of French, then
      (i)   Chris is a teacher? YES, Valid.
      (ii) Chris is of French? ??: Invalid; arguably not even well formed.

The pattern in (6a) is one diagnostic for the classification of the PP "from France" as a *modifier* of the noun "teacher"; the PP adds an additional property of the individual denoted by the NP. The PP "of French," by contrast, does not name a further property of the individual denoted by the NP—as illustrated in (6b); it does not even sound coherent to ask whether Chris is "of French." The relation of this PP to the noun "teacher" is more like that of the direct object to the verb in "teaches French." "Teacher," like "king," "summit," "destruction," "author," or "price," can be used as a *relational noun*, the analog in the noun domain of a transitive verb. When an NP or a PP fills in a slot in such a relation, it is called an *argument* of the head; so "of French" is an argument of "teacher" in (4b) (and the subject and object(s) of a verb are likewise called arguments of the verb). The line between modifiers and arguments is not always sharp, but there is general agreement about clear cases.

Within English NPs, "of"-PPs are mostly arguments rather than modifiers. PPs with "from" and other prepositions that express spatial or temporal or spatiotemporal relations are usually modifiers, since being "under the table" or "from France" express ordinary properties of individuals. This is one illustration of the distinction between "contentful" or "lexical" and "noncontentful" or "grammatical" prepositions. Prepositions in English are on the borderline between "open-class" and "closed-class" vocabulary, and this has interesting repercussions of several sorts. (Just to mention two: There are reports of differential responses of different kinds of aphasics to the two sorts of prepositions [see Friederici 1985]; and there are different optimal strategies for dealing with the notorious difficulty of translating PPs across languages. In particular, when translating a PP with a grammatical preposition, don't try to translate the preposition at all; rather, just see what preposition is "demanded" by the translation of rest of the construction.)

Example (4c) is ambiguous.[1] "French" here can be interpreted either as a modifier, analogous to (4a), or as an argument, analogous to (4b). This is

1. The spoken versions of this phrase are normally not ambiguous, being distinguished by two different stress and intonation patterns, the "modifier pattern" and the "compound pattern" discussed in section 11.3.3. In this section we will continue to speak of (4c) as a single phrase with two interpretations.

not a typical situation, however, as the reader can substantiate by asking whether "French" is an adjective on both readings. (If you know some other languages, try translating two readings of (4c); in many languages, it will be clear that the argument reading involves the *noun* "French," while the modifier reading is expressed with an adjective. And within English, you can test by substituting clear examples of adjectives and clear examples of nouns (such as "musical" and "music," "humorous" and "humor," to see what readings result.)

The added parts in (5a–c) are all modifiers; (5a) has a *restrictive* modifier, (5b) has a *nonrestrictive* modifier, and (5c) is ambiguous between a restrictive and a nonrestrictive reading. The clearest test for this distinction— easiest to apply when the determiner is *the* or another definite determiner —is to ask whether the modifier does or does not play a role in determining the reference of the NP; if it does, then the modifier is restrictive: it is helping to answer the question "which N?" The role of a nonrestrictive modifier is to add some further information about an independently established referent. So, (5a) would typically be used in a situation in which there was more than one student, but only one who was curious, and the NP is picking out that one. But (5b) would be used in a situation in which there was only one student, or one student who was already salient in the discourse, and the nonrestrictive relative clause adds an additional statement about that student. This time the ambiguity in (5c) is fully systematic and general; any adjective in that construction will produce the same ambiguity, an ambiguity that is usually readily resolved by context.

How might the distinctions among these different semantic roles, which so far we have just described informally, be captured in a compositional syntactic and semantic analysis? Let's ask what the relevant part–whole structure should be in each case. When the modifier or argument comes after the noun, we have to decide among various possible tree structures such as the following; these do not exhaust the possibilities but represent four serious contenders.[2] In these trees we have used PP/REL to mark the position where a PP or relative clause might go, and we have used the category N' to stand for "common noun phrase" (the "N-bar" in the X-bar theory of Jackendoff 1977, the CN or CNP of Montague grammar) under the hypothesis that there is a syntactic division between DET and the "rest of the NP."

---

2. When the modifier or argument comes before the noun, we have to choose among appropriately reordered versions of trees (7a, c, d); we defer adjective semantics to the next section.

(7) (a)

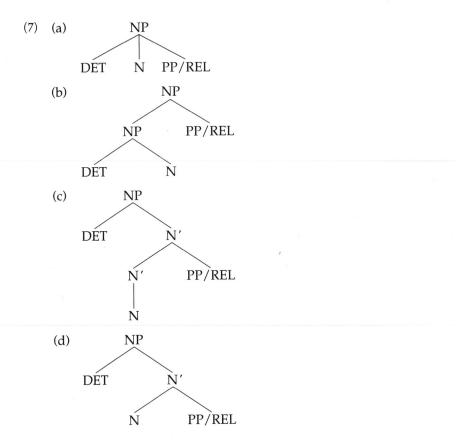

Let's begin by considering the semantics of restrictive modifiers as in (4a), (5a). The principal alternatives that have been advocated in the syntactic literature have been trees (7b) and (7c), and it is worthwhile to consider how the requirement of compositionality can help choose between them. First, let's eliminate trees (7a) and (7d). The simplest argument against trees (7a) and (7d) for restrictive modifiers is the fact that restrictive modifiers can be added *recursively*; that is, we can always add more of them. Trees (7b) and (7c) allow for such recursion because they involve *adjunction* structures of the form (8),

(8)

and such structures can be iterated to allow for multiple adjuncts, as in (9).

(9)

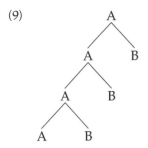

Now, which is the right kind of structure for restrictive modifiers in NPs—
(7b) or (7c)? We see that each analysis makes two binary subdivisions: in
(7b) the DET and the N combine to make an NP, which then combines
with the modifier to make a bigger NP, while in (7c) the N (by itself a
minimal N') and the modifier combine to make a bigger N'; then the DET
combines with that to make the NP. What we already know about the
semantics of *the* is that the interpretation of a phrase of the form *the* α
includes a presupposition that the set denoted by α has one and only one
member. The noun *teacher* denotes a set of individuals, and so does the PP
from France; similarly, for the noun *student* and the relative clause *who was
curious*. Under analysis (7c), the two set-denoting expressions are first
combined to form a complex set-denoting expression, which can be interpreted as denoting the intersection of the two sets; combining *the* with
the result leads to the correct presupposition that it is that class that has
one and only one member. On analysis (7b), on the other hand, *the* is first
combined with the noun alone, which would lead to the presupposition
that there is one and only one teacher in (4a), or one and only one student
in (5a), and that inner NP would denote that individual; if the modifier
combines with that already formed NP, there is no natural way for it to
play a restrictive role. The structure (7b) is thus a good basis for the nonrestrictive interpretation of the modifier in (5b) but not for the restrictive
interpretation of (4a) or (5a). (This is argued in Partee 1973 and in Rodman
1976, but see the alternative presented by Bach and Cooper 1978.) Put
another way, the problem with trying to use structure (7b) for the semantic analysis of restrictive modifiers is that the meaning of the phrase *the
student* is not a part of the meaning of the phrase *the student who was
curious*. Only by making the major subdivision between *the* and *student
who was curious* can a uniform semantic treatment of *the* be maintained.

We have argued that (7c) is the right structure for restrictive modifiers,
(7b) for nonrestrictive modifiers. (7d) can be argued to be the right structure for arguments; we will not go through detailed arguments here,
but note that (i) the nonrecursivity of (7d) is an advantage for arguments,
since unlike modifiers, arguments cannot be added ad infinitum; and (ii) the

close association ("sisterhood") of the noun and the argument in (7d) makes a good structural basis for the fact that the choice of noun governs whether and which arguments can occur. Baker (1978) also provides a nice argument to the effect that the "pro-form" *one(s)* that occurs in expressions like "a large green pencil and two small ones" acts as a "pro-common noun phrase," substituting for any well-formed N' expression, but not for a noun without its arguments. So the distribution and interpretation of that use of *one* can also be used to discriminate between modifiers and arguments, and its behavior is consistent with the correlation between structures and interpretations that we have argued for here (see problem 2 at the end of the chapter).

What about structure (7a)? It does not seem to be optimal for any of the constructions examined; and this, together with many other such cases, has led a number of researchers to propose that a great deal of syntactic and semantic structure is binary-branching. There is some suggestive evidence, but not unchallenged, that young children may have flatter structures like (7a), along with a corresponding lack of sensitivity to some of the semantic distinctions discussed in section 11.2.2, which can be made only with nested binary-branching structures; see Matthei (1979), but also see Hamburger and Crain (1984, 1987).

The example shows that the requirement that semantic interpretation rules correspond to syntactic structure can put very strong constraints on syntactic analyses. But caution is needed with this claim, since without independent constraints on permissible syntactic analyses and permissible means of semantic combination, the compositionality constraint by itself would have no teeth: it would be possible to construct a syntactic analysis to support virtually any desired semantic analysis. That is why many formal semanticists view compositionality as a methodological principle or a working hypothesis rather than as a testable empirical hypothesis (Janssen 1983; Gamut 1991). Compositional semantic analysis is typically a matter of working backward from intuitions about sentences' truth-conditions (the most concrete data we have, according to Cresswell's "Most Certain Principle"); and reasoning our way among alternative hypotheses concerning (a) lexical meanings, (b) syntactic structure, and (c) modes of semantic composition. Choices of any one of those constrain choices among the others; some choices lead to dead ends or at least make things much harder; others survive. "Solutions" are rarely unique and almost never final, since in any argument we are examining some particular set of alternative hypotheses with a great many assumptions explicitly or implicitly held constant. A new idea about any part of the syntax or semantics can affect the choices among existing alternatives or open up new alternatives for consideration.

11.2.2   The Semantics of Adjectives

For the rest of this case study, let us focus on the restrictive modifier uses of adjectives and inquire further about their semantics. In the preceding section, we took the semantics of restrictive modification to be just set intersection, and, in fact, that analysis works perfectly well for all restrictive modifier uses of PPs and all restrictive relative clauses. It is also a simple and appealing hypothesis about the semantics of restrictive modifier uses of adjectives, or adjective-noun semantics for short; but we can argue, based largely on work by Parsons (1972), Kamp (1975), and Siegel (1976a,b), that while it is adequate for many examples, it is not an adequate analysis for adjective-noun modification in general.

11.2.2.1   The Intersection Hypothesis

In most of what follows, our attention will be mainly on phrases containing one adjective and one noun; a simplification in terminology may therefore be in order. The recursive nature of the modifier structure requires that the explicit rules combine ADJ with N' to form a new N'; the "bottom" occurrence of N' will consist of an N alone, as in the following tree.

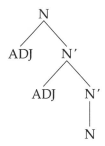

For simplicity, however, we may often speak of ADJ as combining with N, ignoring the intervening N' node. The explicit rule below is careful about using N', but subsequent informal references to it will often allude simply to intersecting the ADJ set with the N set.

Let us recast the intersection hypothesis in explicit rule form.

(10)   Given the syntactic configuration $[_{N'}$ ADJ N'], the semantic interpretation of the whole is $\|ADJ\| \cap \|N'\|$

We illustrate with the example *carnivorous mammal*, from Kamp and Partee (forthcoming):

(11) $\|$carnivorous$\|$ $= \{x \mid x \text{ is carnivorous}\}$
      $\|$mammal$\|$ $= \{x \mid x \text{ is a mammal}\}$
      $\|$carnivorous mammal$\|$ $= \|$carnivorous$\| \cap \|$mammal$\|$
      $= \{x \mid x \text{ is carnivorous and } x \text{ is a mammal}\}$

The cases to be considered in the next subsections show that the intersection hypothesis does not hold for ADJ + N combinations in general; the adjectives for which it does hold are often called "intersective adjective."

11.2.2.2 Nonintersective Adjectives

An adjective like *carnivorous* is intersective, in that (12) holds for any N.

(12) $\|$carnivorous N$\| = \|$carnivorous$\| \cap \|$N$\|$

But what about an adjective like *skillful*? At first it seems all right to think of it as intersective; after all, a skillful carpenter is skillful and is a carpenter. But, as Parsons (1968) pointed out, if the principle (12) were true with *skillful* substituted for *carnivorous*, then the inference shown in (13) should be valid, which it clearly is not.

(13) Francis is a skillful surgeon.
      Francis is a violinist.
      _____

      Therefore Francis is a skillful violinist.

So *skillful* isn't intersective; it does not simply pick out a set of individuals who are skillful—"period"—but rather carves out a subset of the set corresponding to the noun it combines with. We will say more about how this might be achieved in section 11.2.2.4.

Since *skillful* does obey the principle exemplified in (14), which says that the set of skillful surgeons is a subset of the set of surgeons, it is called a "subsective adjective." (Note that the intersective adjectives are all subsective; subsectivity is a weaker property than intersectivity.)

(14) *Subsectivity*: $\|$skillful N$\| \subseteq \|$N$\|$

Note that (14) does not give the meaning of *skillful* nor of the combination *skillful* + N; it merely specifies one property of the meaning of *skillful* (and of many other adjectives), a property that might be considered important enough to mark as a "semantic feature" in the lexicon. The principle in (14) can then be thought of as the semantic content, in model-theoretic terms, of such a semantic feature. Such principles or constraints are sometimes called *meaning postulates* in the philosophical and formal semantic literature. We will say more about meaning postulates in section 11.2.2.4.

11.2.2.3   Nonsubsective Adjectives

But are all adjectives at least subsective? The reader might start trying to think of some that are not. These should be adjectives that fail both the condition of intersectivity and the weaker condition of subsectivity; it should be possible for something to be an "ADJ N" without being an "N."

Here are some: The adjectives *former, alleged, counterfeit* are neither intersective nor subsective.

(15)   (a) $\|\text{former senator}\| \neq \|\text{former}\| \cap \|\text{senator}\|$

       (b) $\|\text{former senator}\| \nsubseteq \|\text{senator}\|$

That is, not only does the set of former senators fail to be the intersection of the set of former things (whatever that might mean) with the set of senators; moreover, as (15b) asserts, it is not even true that the set of former senators is a subset of the set of senators. Among the nonsubsective adjectives we might further distinguish a subclass of "privative" adjectives, those for which an instance of the ADJ + N combination is never an instance of the N alone. (See problem 4.) *Counterfeit* is of this sort, while *alleged* is not, since an alleged murderer, for instance, may or may not be a murderer. For some nonsubsective adjectives it is not completely clear whether they are privative or not; and the answer may be one that is dependent on the context and the domain of discourse. Is a *fake gun* a gun? Can it be? If a *fake gun* is necessarily not a gun, how can one make sense of a question like "Is that gun real or fake?" (See question 11.3.) Readers who have thought of some additional examples of possibly nonsubsective adjectives might compare notes to see if they agree about which of them indeed are nonsubsective, and about which of them are furthermore privative. (See problem 3.)

The semantic properties of adjectives that we have examined so far have been chosen because they provide increasingly strong counterexamples to the intersection hypothesis. They are by no means the only interesting semantic properties of adjectives, and we will consider some others in later sections. First, let's think about what kind of semantic interpretation of adjectives can do justice to the range of ADJ + N combinations we have just seen.

11.2.2.4   Adjectives as Functions

Parsons (1968), Montague (1970), and others argued that the simplest rule for the interpretation of ADJ + N combinations that is general enough to subsume all the cases considered so far involves interpreting adjectives as *functions* mapping the semantic value of any noun they combine with onto the value of the ADJ + N combination. And from the evidence of the nonintersective and nonsubsective cases they argued that the relevant semantic values must be *properties* rather than *sets*, that is, must be *intensions* rather than *extensions*. Let's look at some of the arguments for this analysis, introducing the key concepts as we need them.

First of all, we already have in (13) the germ of the argument that we cannot do justice to the semantics of ADJ + N if the semantic value of the N is just the set that it denotes (its "extension" in the given state of affairs). Let's just extend (13) a bit by considering a possible state of affairs in which every surgeon is a violinist and every violinist is a surgeon: that is, in which the set of surgeons IS the set of violinists. Then, no matter what function we were to take the adjective *skillful* to denote, if it has to apply to the set denoted by the noun, there is no way that we could get the semantic value of *skillful surgeon* to come out differently from the semantic value of *skillful violinist*. Why? Because we would have the same function applying to the same argument in both cases, necessarily giving us the same value. So we need to find semantic values for *surgeon* and *violinist* that can be different even when the sets denoted by those N's are the same.

The idea, which traces back to Frege (1892) and was further developed through the work of such philosophers as Carnap (1956), Hintikka (1969), Kripke (1963), and Montague (1970), is that every noun expresses a *property*, which we will call its *intension*; that property, together with the facts in a given state of affairs, determines what set the noun happens to denote (as its *extension*) in the given state of affairs. The *intension* comes much closer than the *extension* to what we ordinarily think of as the meaning of the noun; the intension is more like a characterization of what something would have to be like to count as instance of that noun. The nouns *unicorn* and *centaur* both have (presumably) the same extension in the actual world; namely, the empty set: there are not any of either. But they do not have the same meaning, and that correlates with the fact that there are fictional or mythical states of affairs where the two nouns have different extensions.

Intensions and extensions can be modeled using the notion of *possible world* (possible situation or state of affairs, possible way things might be), a notion that may be approached from various angles (see the collection in Allén 1989). Linguists working on formal semantics tend to view possible worlds as a formal tool for illuminating a certain kind of semantic structure, without necessarily taking a stand on the many deep philosophical issues that can be raised about them. It is worth noting, however, that some such notion is probably essential for an understanding of some very basic aspects of human cognition. Evidence for conceptualization of "other possible worlds" can be seen even at a prelinguistic level in any child or animal that can show surprise, since surprise signals mismatch between a perceived state of affairs and an expected state of affairs. The notion of alternative possible worlds should therefore be understood not as a matter of science fiction but as a fundamental part of the ability to think about past, future, and ways things might be or might have been.

To a first approximation, we can take the extension of the predicate *surgeon* at a time t in a possible world w to be the set of things that have the property of being a surgeon in w at t. More generally, the extension of a predicate in a given state of affairs is, by definition, the set of all those things of which the predicate is true in that state of affairs. This set is a reflection of what the predicate means; for, given the way things are, it is the meaning of the predicate that determines which things belong to the set and which do not. But the extension is also a reflection of the facts in the state of affairs or possible world; the meaning and the facts jointly determine what the extension happens to be. Two predicates may therefore differ in meaning and yet have the same extensions; but if they differ in meaning they should differ in intension. Or more accurately, if they differ in truth-conditional aspects of meaning, they should differ in intension. Frege (1892) notes that there are things like "tone" or "emotional affect" that might also be ingredients of meaning in the broadest sense that have no effect on determining extension and are therefore not reflected in intension. Two terms differing only in "tone" or "connotation" or the like might therefore have the same intension but not be considered to have quite the same meaning.

Limiting our attention to truth-conditional aspects of meaning, the reasoning we have gone through suggests that we want to assign *properties* as the semantic values of nouns and other simple predicates. And it is commonly (though not universally) accepted that the property a given predicate stands for is completely determined by the "spectrum" of actual and possible extensions it has in different possible worlds. In other words, the property is completely identified by the function that assigns to each possible world w the extension of the predicate in w. We therefore take such functions as our formal analysis of properties, and we assign them in the lexicon as the intensions of simple predicate expressions such as common nouns.

If properties are identified with predicate intensions, then we can see how adjective meanings can be understood as functions from intensions to intensions. The distinctions among the various subtypes we have looked at in the preceding subsections can be characterized in terms of restrictions on the kinds of functions that are expressed by the different classes of adjectives. Formally, these restrictions can be expressed as meaning postulates; informally, we can think of classifications like "subsective" and "intersective" as semantic features on adjectives like *skillful* and *carnivorous* respectively, cashed out as restrictions on the corresponding functions requiring them to obey restrictions analogous to the respective conditions (14) and (12) above.

The notion of meaning postulates is worth more discussion than we can give to it here. The central issue to which they are relevant is a long-standing debate concerning whether all lexical meanings can be fully analyzed via "lexical decomposition" into some sort of presumably universal semantic "atoms," representing basic or primitive concepts. That view, while appealing and recurrent, may well be too strong; and the notion of meaning postulates is offered as a technique for capturing significant generalizations about extractable regularities within lexical meanings without presupposing total decomposability. On both views, there are important regularities concerning semantic properties of lexical items that need to be captured; on the antidecomposition view, some lexical items have idiosyncratic "residue" parts of their meanings that cannot reasonably be analyzed further into compositions of simpler parts. Meaning postulates can then express whatever regularities there are to be found without entailing that what can be said about the meaning of a given item with meaning postulates should be supposed to exhaust its meaning. Another, perhaps related, problem in the field is whether and how we can draw a line between information that belongs in the lexicon and information that is part of our "world knowledge" or beliefs about the referents of our terms. This is an area where there are some clear cases and many unclear ones. Meaning postulates might be a helpful tool here as well, since they make the *form* of some kinds of lexical information no different in kind from the form of some kinds of general knowledge. That would make it possible to hypothesize that the very same "fact"—for example, whales are mammals—could be in either of two "places," a storehouse of lexical knowledge or a storehouse of empirical knowledge; whether it is part of the meaning of "whale" or not need not be fixed once and for all but could vary across different individuals or subpopulations or different historical times.

Now a further issue concerns generality. We seem to have two choices. We can, as suggested above, treat *all* adjectives as functions from intensions to intensions, with the subclasses like subsective and intersective defined by meaning postulates that are satisfied by the corresponding functions in those cases. Alternatively, could we perhaps say that different adjectives have different sorts of semantic values? The intersective ones are simply predicates whose extensions are sets and whose intensions are properties, and only the nonintersective ones have to be interpreted as functions from intensions to intensions. Compositionality in its strictest form requires a single semantic type for each syntactic category; therefore, this second strategy would require that adjectives also be divided into distinct syntactic subcategories corresponding to these different semantic types.

If we do want a single semantic type for all adjectives, that can be achieved only if all adjectives are treated as functions from intensions to intensions. It is possible, for instance, to treat an intersective adjective like *carnivorous* as a function from intensions to intensions of a highly restricted subtype (one that, in fact, ignores everything about the intension of the input except the extension it assigns in the given state of affairs). But the situation is not symmetrical; it is not possible to take adjectives like *carnivorous* as the general case. That is, we cannot treat adjectives in general as simple predicates and take the interpretation of the ADJ + N rule to be set intersection, because there is no comparable way to treat *former* or *skillful* as a restricted subcase of that.

Section 11.4 will introduce the concept of "type-shifting" and will explore the possibility of assigning to each category a family of types rather than a single type, with a slight weakening in the principle of compositionality. From that perspective we will be able to say that the interpretation of adjectives as functions from functions is the one type of interpretation that all adjectives can have, while some adjectives also have simpler meanings, such as interpretations as simple predicates expressing properties and denoting sets. We will appeal to that possibility at various points in what follows but will defer a fuller discussion to section 11.4.

The reader may be concerned that we have said nothing about the fact that adjectives also occur in predicate positions, typically after *be* or *become*; it turns out on examination that normally only the extensional, intersective adjectives occur in predicate position, where the simple interpretation of adjectives as denoting sets and expressing properties suffices. Siegel (1976a, b) discusses both this generalization and its apparent exceptions and argues for a corresponding syntactic distinction in subtypes of adjectives, noting that some languages, such as Russian, even have different morphological forms for predicate and function interpretations of adjectives. Of course, there is much more to say about the different uses of adjectives and the connections among them, but we will continue to restrict our attention principally to adjectives occurring as modifiers of nouns.

Let's sum up what we've concluded from this case study. We wanted to figure out what sorts of things adjective meanings might be. Following Lewis's Advice, we asked what we wanted adjective meanings to "do," what sorts of properties they needed to have. To get at that question, we focused on the principle of compositionality and on the truth-conditions of sentences containing adjective-noun combinations. Assuming that a common noun (phrase) (N or N') denotes a set (that is, has a set as its extension), we saw that the simplest case of restrictive modification could be analyzed as set intersection. But for the most general case we needed something more than sets and set intersection, and that motivated the notion of intensions: N's express properties (have properties as their intensions), restrictive modifiers are most generally interpreted as functions from properties to properties, and restrictive modification is most generally understood as function-argument application. Within that general analysis, the intersective adjectives can still be singled out as a natural simplest subclass, characterizable as such by meaning postulates (or on a type-shifting approach, as will be discussed in section 11.4, treated as having predicative interpretations as their simplest interpretations and as having derivative interpretations as functions via general type-shifting principles).

11.3   Case Study 2: Vagueness, Context-Dependence, and Point of View

11.3.1   Vagueness and Context-Dependence

In section 11.2.2.2 we indicated that the inference pattern (13) was a test of whether an adjective was intersective. By this test it looks as if vague adjectives like *tall* and *young* are nonintersective:

(16)   a.   Win is a tall 14-year-old.
       b.   Win is a basketball player.
       _____
       c.   ?? Therefore Win is a tall basketball player.

The inference in (16) seems to be invalid, just like that in (13), so by that test it would seem that *tall* is nonintersective. But *tall* is a vague adjective, and maybe it is interpreted differently in the premise (16a) and the conclusion (16c); if so, maybe this test is not conclusive. When an adjective is vague, like *tall* or *young* or *blue*, the lexical semantics is not simply a matter of classifying entities into those that are tall and those that are not. Intuitively, it seems that for vague adjectives, there may be some clear positive cases and/or some clear negative cases, and there are unclear cases, or a "range of indeterminacy," in between. For some vague adjectives, like *blue* and *round*, there are some "absolute" clear cases. This seems to correlate with the fact that these adjectives can sensibly occur with modifiers like *perfectly* and *absolutely*, whereas for others, like *big* and *old*, there may be no unequivocally clear cases and only relative to a given context can we identify any cases as clearly positive or negative. But for either kind of vague adjective, context clearly plays a major role in how we reduce or eliminate the range of indeterminacy. Context will lead us to draw the lines in particular ways for what will count as definite positive instances (the "positive extension") and what will count as definite negative cases (the "negative extension"); some contexts will eliminate indeterminacy, whereas others may leave a (smaller) range of indeterminacy.

So let's think about how vagueness and the influence of context might affect what we should conclude from our judgments about (16). Perhaps *tall* appears to fail the test of (16) simply by virtue of the influence of the noun on the context. As Kamp (1975) suggested and Siegel (1976b) argued at length, "relative" adjectives like *tall*, *heavy*, and *old* are context-dependent as well as vague, with the most relevant aspect of context a comparison class that is often, but not exclusively, provided by the noun of the ADJ + N construction. Why is this evidence against treating *tall* as a nonintersective adjective like *skillful* interpreted as a function applying to the noun's intension? Well, here is an argument. In (17) below, we see another example of the influence of contextual cues on the (partial) resolution of the vagueness of *tall*; only this time we have the same noun *snowman* in each case.

(17) a.   My 2-year-old son built a really tall snowman yesterday.

      b.   The D.U. fraternity brothers built a really tall snowman last weekend.

Further evidence that there is a difference between truly nonintersective subsective adjectives like *skillful* and intersective but vague and context-dependent adjectives like *tall* was noted by Siegel (1976b): the former occur with *as*-phrases, as in *skillful as a surgeon*, whereas the latter take *for*-phrases to indicate comparison class: *tall for an East coast mountain*. (An adjective can be nonintersective and also vague, and then one can use both an *as*-phrase and a *for*-phrase: *very good as a diagnostician for someone with so little experience*.)

It is both difficult and important to sort out the effects of context-dependence on the interpretation of different sorts of adjectives and nouns occurring alone or in combination. There are almost certainly some adjectives that are best analyzed as context-dependent intersective ones (probably including *tall*), and almost certainly some adjectives that are genuinely nonintersective (almost certainly including *former* and probably including *skillful*.) There may be many disputable or borderline case, and there may be cases that involve homonymous or polysemous doublets (as suggested by Siegel 1976b for *clever*, which she analyzes as having one vague but intersective reading meaning having to do with a general evaluation of persons and another nonintersective (also vague) reading that is a function applying to role-properties like *experimenter* or *magician* or *con artist*.)

Vagueness and context-dependence are in principle independent properties, although they often co-occur. There are adjectives like *left* and *right* that are context-dependent but not (very) vague—we will say more about context-dependence of that kind in section 11.3.2—and there are nouns like *vegetable* and *bush* that are vague but not (very) context-dependent.

Even the line between vague and nonvague predicates is vague; a concept may count as sharp for most purposes but vague relative to the demands of scientific or legal or philosophical argument. Probably almost every predicate is both vague and context-dependent to some degree.

Let's go back to our examples of vague adjectives and think about how to analyze their meanings. The existence of vague intersective adjectives like *tall* poses a puzzle for the semantic account we gave in section 11.2. We argued that for the intersective adjectives, the semantic interpretation of ADJ + N could be analyzed as set intersection; and we noted that there were various ways to maintain this claim even when we generalized ADJ + N semantics to function-argument application, either via meaning postulates or via the type-shifting analysis to be discussed in section 11.4. So, one way or another, we can still regard a simple intersective adjective as denoting a set that gets intersected with the noun set. But sets are sharply defined: any given element either is or is not an element of the set. How can we model the vagueness we have just been talking about? How can the intersective adjective *tall* denote a set?

We probably need to complicate our theory a little. Let's go back to Lewis's Advice to think about what the meaning of *tall* does, and to find something that does that. We have already seen some aspects of the behavior of *tall*, in thinking about tall 14-year-olds versus tall basketball players and in the examples about the tall snowmen. And we have noted that such adjectives generally have in any given context a positive extension, a negative extension, and often still some range of indeterminacy, and these vary from context to context somehow. Let's see if we can find out some more about how this variation works.

Here is an example in which we have a pair of words that can both be used either as nouns or as adjectives, with virtually the same meaning in either use; and we find a striking effect depending on which is which.

(18)   a.   Bobo is a giant and a midget.

      b.   Bobo is a midget giant.

      c.   Bobo is a giant midget.

It seems that these three sentences are most naturally understood as conveying propositions with mutually distinct truth-conditions, despite the fact that all three would appear to predicate of Bobo a compound concept with the same pair of constituent parts. So there seems to be some interesting effect of syntax here that affects how the resolution of the vagueness of these predicates is (partially) resolved.

In the case of (18a), with overt conjunction, the sentence is generally interpreted as contradictory, unless one can find grounds for imposing an interpretation that implicitly adds different "respects" to the two, for example, a mental giant and a physical midget. Note that both *midget* and *giant* are vague and context-dependent terms; one who counts as a midget on a college basketball team will probably be larger than one who counts as a giant on a basketball team of 10-year-olds. When the terms are directly conjoined as in (18a), it appears that the default case is for them to be interpreted relative to the same context; and it follows from their semantic content that whatever counts as a giant relative to a given context (and in a given respect) ipso facto does *not* count as a midget relative to that same context.

In (18b) and (18c), on the other hand, one predicate serves as head noun and the other as modifier, and the difference in interpretation is striking. Everyone seems to agree that a giant midget must be an unusually large midget, and a midget giant an unusually small giant. This tells us that the predicate serving as head noun is interpreted relative to the given "external" context (a boys' basketball team, a family of circus midgets, the fairy tale of Jack the giant-killer, or whatever), and the predicate serving as the modifier appears to be "recalibrated" in such a way as to make distinctions *within* the class of possible referents for the head noun. So whereas in (18a), *giant* and *midget* are normally construed as mutually exclusive categories, in both (18b) and (18c) the modifier-head construction virtually forces us to construe them as compatible if at all possible, apparently by adjusting the interpretation of the modifier in the light of the local context created by the head noun.

If we set up our theory so that it accommodates such adjustments to the interpretation of the modifier, then there will be no obstacle to maintaining the interpretation of the modifier-head construction as predicate conjunction (set intersection);[3] but without such an adjustment or "recalibration," a conjunction interpretation of the construction would lead to the false prediction that (18a–c) should all have the same interpretation. Combinations such as *tall tree* should presumably be handled similarly; *tall* is a vague term whose interpretation is affected by both the linguistic and the nonlinguistic context as illustrated above, but once the interpretation is specified—as something roughly like "at least d tall" for some degree of height d—the combination *tall tree* can be treated as simple set intersection.

Let's try to articulate some of the kinds of principles that may govern the dynamics of context effects with vague linguistic expressions. These tentative hypotheses, from Kamp and Partee (forthcoming), may be

---

3. To be safe, we need to question whether the semantics of the combination is indeed set intersection in this case, or whether *midget* and *giant* as modifiers have a nonintersective reading that explicitly builds in relativity to the noun they modify. Try the *snowman* test as in (17).

viewed as an invitation to more systematic exploration of a relatively undeveloped field of study that may cast light on both linguistic and nonlinguistic cognitive principles involved in the effects of context on the ways in which vague language is understood and vague concepts are applied.

Two principles suggested by the examples we have just considered are the following:

(19) *Parallel Structure Effect*: In a (syntactically) conjoined structure each conjunct is interpreted in a parallel way relative to its common context.

(20) *Head Primacy Principle*: In a modifier-head structure, the head is interpreted relative to the context of the whole constituent, and the modifier is interpreted relative to the local context created from the former context by the interpretation of the head.

In the simplest cases of the application of the Head Primacy Principle, the effect of the interpretation of the head noun will be to restrict the "local context" for the modifier to the positive extension of the head; so that one will, for instance, be interpreting the modifier "giant" in (18c) in a local context that consists only of midgets.

Both of those principles involve sensitivity to the choice of linguistic structure, but there are other principles that seem to be quite general, possibly universal, and not specifically linguistic. These may either cooperate or compete with principles like the Parallel Structure Effect and the Head Primacy Principle. For example:

(21) *Non-Vacuity Principle*: In any given context, try to interpret any predicate so that both its positive and negative extension are non-empty.

In the *midget giant* example, for instance, the Head Primacy Principle and the Non-Vacuity Principle cooperate to produce the observed results: we first interpret the head *giant* in the given context (such as the fairy-tale world of Jack and the Beanstalk) in such a way as to give *giant* both a positive and a negative extension in the domain of the context; then we interpret *midget* in such a way that it has both a positive and a negative extension within the positive extension of *giant*. This, of course, requires a very different "calibration" of *midget* than would be appropriate for the global context, since *midget* and *giant* are incompatible relative to one and the same context.

In the *giant and midget* example, (18a), on the other hand, we find a conflict between the Parallel Structure Effect, which will make the two predicates incompatible and their conjunction contradictory, and the Non-

Vacuity Principle, which bids us try to interpret the conjoined predicate as noncontradictory, perhaps leading us to search for "different respects," though this might in turn run counter to the Parallel Structure Effect again.

In the *giant midget* and *midget giant* cases, it is the positive extension of the modifier that has to be stretched to satisfy the *Non-Vacuity Principle*. In other cases the same principle may lead us to shrink the positive extension and to expand the negative extension: see problem 5.

In still other cases, the Non-Vacuity Principle seems to override the Head Primacy Principle. Consider the phrase *stone lion*: Is a stone lion a lion? With respect to the normal interpretation of the predicate *lion* the answer would seemingly have to be "no": stone lions fail both scientific and everyday tests for lionhood, would never get counted in a census of the world lion population, and so on. Yet, if we have to stick to normal interpretation, there cannot be any stone lions; lions are not made of stone, nor do we seem inclined to try to stretch the predicate *stone* to apply truly to lion-flesh. But *stone lion* is also not just an idiom; any name of a material can be substituted for *stone*, familiar or novel (glass, chocolate, velveteen), and just about any concrete noun can be substituted for *lion*. In this case it seems that the Non-Vacuity Principle overrides the Head Primacy Principle and leads us to reconstrue the head noun (as "representation of a lion" or something like that) so that the modifier can have a positive extension within the positive extension of the head noun. This is more like a case of meaning-shift (see section 11.4.1) than straight vagueness resolution, since we are moving things into the positive extension of *lion* that are ordinarily clear negative cases.

It may also be the Non-Vacuity Principle or some generalization of it that makes us so strongly inclined to reinterpret sentences that by their form and the Parallel Structure Effect should be tautologies and contradictions, like (22) and (23). It is likely that the hearer interprets (22) not as a tautology but as a denial of the existence of a range of indeterminacy for *new*, and interprets (23) not as a contradiction but with different "respects" implicitly filled in, much as one might do to make sense of the *midget and giant* case (see Kamp and Partee (forthcoming) for discussion).

(22)   Either it's new or it's not new.

(23)   Well, he's smart and he's not smart.

An explicit formalization of a compositional semantics of vague adjectives and their combinations with nouns is beyond the bounds of this chapter; there are several proposals in the recent literature, and this is still very much an open research area. The main point of this subsection has been to illustrate the strategy for working toward such an analysis and to show how there is constant interplay between hypotheses about the meanings of individual words and hypotheses about the compositional semantics of various syntactic constructions. A good analysis of vagueness may allow us to maintain the simple compositional rule of set intersection for many more modifiers than we could if we did not disentangle the context-dependent aspects of vagueness from the semantics of adjective-noun combination. Progress in semantics, as in many other fields, often depends on finding ways to understand complex phenomena as the result of interactions of several relatively simple principles.

As we close this discussion of vagueness, it is also worth noting that as one studies how vagueness works in more detail, one quickly overcomes the common prejudice that vagueness is always a bad thing, that it is some kind of "defect" of natural language. It is impossible for a natural language to get along without vague expressions (the reader is invited to argue this point in question 11.4); moreover, natural languages provide the means for reducing vagueness where needed, both by the implicit interactions with context discussed above, and by explicit stipulation. And as we have taken some initial steps towards showing, vagueness is no obstacle to formal modeling; a theory of the semantics of vague terms can be a perfectly precise theory. And as a practical goal, if we can understand vagueness better, we may be able to develop richer and more versatile computer languages and more user-friendly human-machine interfaces.

11.3.2   Context-Dependence and Point of View

In the previous section we saw one aspect of the context-dependence of natural language semantics, in the effect of context on vagueness reduction and vagueness resolution. In this section we will look at another dimension of context-dependence, one that shows up in clearest form when we think about the meanings of "demonstrative," or "deictic," expressions like *this*, *that*, and *there*, and "indexical" expressions, like *I*, *here*, *today*, and *now*.[4] Learning the meaning of a demonstrative or indexical is not like learning the reference of a proper name, since the reference of *that* or *I* changes from occurrence to occurrence; nor does it mean simply learning an associated property, as we do for the nouns and intersective adjectives we have looked at so far. Anything could be the referent of a use of the word *that*: a boiling teakettle, a number, a color we have no name for, the expression on a baby's face; what *that* refers to in a given utterance depends on the particular intentions of the speaker on that particular

4. The distinction between demonstratives and indexicals is not always sharp; the intended distinction is that demonstratives are typically accompanied by an explicit or implicit pointing or demonstration that fixes their reference (*deixis* is the Greek word for "pointing"), whereas indexicals have their reference fixed directly by the context of the utterance in which they occur: "I" must be the speaker of the utterance, and so on.

occasion of utterance. Few demonstratives and indexicals are quite as wide-ranging as *this* and *that*, but even more narrowly delimited ones like *yesterday* and *today* depend for their reference on the context of the given utterance, in this case on the time at which the utterance occurs.

Following Lewis's Advice again, it is generally agreed that the meanings of demonstratives and indexicals are best thought of as functions from contexts to referents.[5] So meanings have become more complex in another dimension. In general, whenever we discover that the reference of some expression depends on X, Y, and Z, we model meanings as functions from X's, Y's, and Z's to referents. (And then when working on case studies in which Y and Z play no role, we may simplify and treat meanings as just functions from X's.)

Now, an interesting phenomenon that linguists have studied is that there are quite a number of open-class lexical items like nouns, verbs, and adjectives that show mixed properties: their meanings involve a combination of ordinary properties with indexical or demonstrative-like behavior. Fillmore (1971, 1975) opened up this area with his classic studies of *come* and *go*, *take* and *bring*, and *in front of*, which involve interesting interplays of factors such as the position and orientation of the speaker and of the hearer, direction of motion, if any, and for the case of *in front of*, the question of whether the object in question has an intrinsic front or not: "in front of the car" is more ambiguous than "in front of the tree" (though even trees may derivatively acquire fronts and backs if closely associated with things like houses that have an intrinsic front). (See problem 6 and questions 11.5 and 11.6.) The difference between "Please come out to play!" and "Please go out to play!" is not a difference in the action being requested, but a difference in the point of view of the utterer—we know which of these is said by a neighbor kid on the doorstep and which by a parent in the house.

Let's continue looking at adjectives and see what sorts of demonstrative and indexical-like behavior we can find among them. Sample candidates include *right, left, nearby, far, ahead, behind, close, closest, local, foreign*, but the reader can surely find or think up many more (like vagueness, context-dependence of this kind seems to be almost everywhere once you look for it.) Let's look more closely at *right* and *left*, since they illustrate two different points about this family of words. (And more besides; we won't try to go into all the interestingly different properties these words show in their different uses such as "on the right," "to the right," "to my right," "turn right," "turn toward the right," and so on—we will just look at

---

5. Or more accurately as functions from contexts to intensions, that is, as functions from contexts to functions from possible situations to referents. But since, like names, demonstratives always have *constant* functions as their intensions, it is a benign simplification to think of them as functions from contexts to referents.

one tip of this particular iceberg.) In the first place, there is one kind of context-dependence that seems to be mere ellipsis for an *of*-phrase: the context-dependent (24a) may be viewed as elliptical for the (more nearly) context-independent (24b).

(24a)   Sew the team insignia to the right.

(24b)   Sew the team insignia to the right of the "A".

But, as the author realized when the instruction (24b) was received in a packet with her son's Little League baseball cap (the "A" was on the front, in the middle), (24b) still contains a crucial point-of-view ambiguity: to the right of the "A" as you look at it, or to the right of the "A" from the point of view of the person wearing the cap? That is, there is another context-dependent aspect of the meaning of *right* and *left*, much like that of *come* and *go*, which has to do with point of view and has no simple nonelliptical variant (although you may be able express the point of view with some added phrase like "from the point of view of so-and-so").

As words like *foreign* show, context-dependence and point of view are not limited to spatiotemporal aspects of the context. Who's foreign depends not simply on where you are but also on political boundaries and things like citizenship; when I'm in your country, it's me that's foreign (although a parochial tourist may not realize that and may remark on the experience of being surrounded by foreigners). And also worth noting is that the relevant context is not only the situation in which the utterance occurs: utterance-internal expressions can also affect the local context for the interpretation of successive expressions, much as we found the interpretation of vague adjectives to be affected by the local context established by their head nouns. How many interpretations can you think of for (25)?

(25)   Most foreigners speak a foreign language.

On one reading of (25), as spoken, say, by an American, (25) says that most people from countries other than America speak a language other than their own native language; this might be said by someone arguing for more teaching of foreign languages in the American schools. So on this reading, which is just one of several, the first occurrence of *foreigner* is "anchored" to the utterance context ("foreigner relative to this country"), while the later occurrence of *foreign* is anchored to that earlier occurrence of *foreigner*: "a language foreign to that foreigner."[6] (See problem 7.)

---

6. This last use illustrates that context-dependence interacts with quantification and variable-binding, which we are not going into here, but which provides one of the arguments for having to take account of this kind of context-dependence in an integrated account of the syntax and semantics of "sentence-grammar" rather than trying to leave it to a separate module of pragmatics where the use of language in context is the focus of attention.

So what are contexts? What does a theory have to look like to model the context-dependence of meaning? Some of the simplest examples might suggest that a context can be represented as an n-tuple of a speaker, a place of utterance, and a time of utterance. But we have already seen examples showing that there is no such simple enumeration, specifiable once and for all, of aspects of contexts that may play a role in context-dependence (see Cresswell 1973 for a classic discussion of this point). Trying to specify all the ingredients of "contexts" is as fruitless as trying to specify the ingredients of possible worlds or possible situations that go into the analysis of properties and propositions and intensions in general. In any particular discourse situation, or in any sample model or particular computational application, it may well be feasible and desirable to reduce possible worlds and possible contexts to "state-descriptions" in terms of values on some specified set of parameters. But for the workings of a natural language in an uncircumscribed context, all we can expect to do is to specify that an analysis must be in terms of a set of possible worlds or situations W and a set of possible contexts C, leaving the elements of W and C as primitives in the most general case.

So the extension of an adjective like *foreign* relative to a given context (providing a point of view) and a given state of affairs (a specification of "the facts") will be a set of individuals (persons and objects and languages and more—we must take the notion of "individual" very broadly). The intension of *foreign* relative to a given context is a function that maps each possible state of affairs onto the corresponding extension—two different states of affairs that differ in Vladya's citizenship may result in two different answers to whether Vladya is in the extension of *foreign*. And what we might optimistically call the "meaning" of *foreign* (until Lewis's Advice tells us to go searching for further ingredients) is a function from contexts to the relevant intension: the context has to tell us whose point of view establishes what is to count as foreign, and then the intension encodes how the extension depends on the facts.

Context-dependence of this sort, like vagueness, is one of the things that makes natural languages so versatile. User-friendly computer programs have learned to exploit context-dependence; the same short command may have different effects depending on the local context in which it is used. "Exit" and "Quit" are typically context-dependent (in fact "indexical") commands, meaning exit from "this," from whatever process you are currently in. By the same token, context-dependence can be a source of misunderstandings (both in human–human and human–computer communication) that may be hard to pin down because of the usually implicit nature of the relevant context-dependent aspects of meaning. (In the case of the Little League sewing assignment mentioned earlier, I was curious to see what other parents—well, back then, other mothers— would do. It turned out 50-50, but I suspect that relatively few people noticed that there was an ambiguity. You could do experiments to explore this kind of phenomenon.)

Context-dependence also provides us with an opportunity to think about the role of simplifying assumptions in ordinary uses of language as well as in science. We noted above that *right* and *left* are indeterminate without a point of view. In contrast, *up* and *down* are context-independent. Ah, but that's only because of gravity; what if you're in a gravity-free environment? Then *up* and *down* are just as much in need of a designated point of view as *right* and *left* are. Since gravity is a universal of terrestrial life, it is not surprising that languages evolved with gravity presupposed in the interpretation of some "vertical" prepositions and adverbs; this is a good example of a language universal that should probably not be attributed to the language faculty. (As a relevant side note, it reportedly turns out that astronauts prefer to have a "designated floor" and "designated ceiling" to prevent disorientation.)

11.3.3   Compounds Versus Modifiers and the Limits of Compositionality

The remarks made so far about ADJ + NOUN combinations are intended to apply to all cases of modifier-head constructions, including cases where a noun is converted into an adjective and used to modify another noun, as in *stone lion, oak table, cardboard box*. But they are not intended to apply to compounds, either of the noun-noun or adjective-noun variety. Compounds in English can generally be recognized by their heavier stress on the first word; see (26), in which heavier stress is indicated by capitalization.

(26)   *Modifier-head (compositional)*

   a.   black BOARD

   b.   brick FACTORY

   c.   toy STORE

   Compound (idiomatic)

   d.   BLACK board

   e.   BRICK factory

   f.   TOY store

The contrast in the case of adjective-noun combinations, as in (26a) versus (26d), is familiar. The similar contrast in noun-noun combinations is less familiar but perfectly analogous. *Brick* as an adjective means "made of brick" and is intersective; *toy* as an adjective means something like "a toy version of a ____" and is arguably nonsubsective, although this is debatable (see the discussions of *fake gun* in section 11.2.2.3 and *stone lion* in section 11.3.1). In compounds, on the other hand, there is no general rule for predicting the interpretation of the combination, intersective or otherwise.[7] A TOY store (in typical contexts) is a store that sells toys, a TOY box is a box that holds toys, and so on. Semanticists in general do not expect a semantic theory to provide a compositional semantics for compounds but do expect a compositional semantics for modifier-head construction. The reasoning is that a native speaker cannot generally interpret a novel compound on first hearing on the basis of knowledge of the language alone, but can do so for a novel modifier-noun construction.

It is an interesting question just what a semantic theory should say about compounds, but one that goes beyond the scope of this discussion. Presumably, the semantics for English must at least tell us that the syntactic head is also the semantic head in the sense that a BRICK factory is a kind of factory, not a kind of brick. One of the challenging parts of the problem is how to articulate the interface between linguistic and nonlinguistic contributions to interpretation so that the semantics specifies that this is a place where nonlinguistic knowledge has to fill in some "relevant" property "saliently" involving the first element of the compound to form a modifier or specifier of the second element. The semantic constraints are extremely weak and general; there seems to be no limit in principle on how that inferred property is related to that first word. This very absence of semantic constraints, however, results in a fairly strong pragmatic constraint: for a novel compound to be understood on first hearing, there must be a unique most salient or plausible interpretation; very far-fetched possibilities will be usable only in very "rich" contexts. (Silent exercise: construct three different possible interpretations for the compound "computer puzzle," and imagine scenarios in which each would be readily understood as the intended interpretation. See also problem 8.) The existence of compounds, like the existence of vagueness and context-dependence, appears to exploit the cognitive capacities of language users in ways that allow natural languages to be much more flexible than we can allow computer languages or other formal languages to be. In the past, it was commonplace for logicians and others to criticize natural languages for their "sloppiness" or "messiness" and to take pains to avoid properties like vagueness in the design of formal languages; but as these aspects of natural languages come to be better understood and appreciated, we are beginning to understand that this may be a little like criticizing living organisms for being messier than machines. Formal languages, like

7. This (non) generalization holds only for "free compounds," not for "argument compounds" like the earlier example of *French teacher* (section 11.2.1), where the first element is interpreted as an argument of a relational head noun.

machines, can be extremely useful tools, but natural languages, like people, do not have to apologize for not being more like them (respectively).

In this section we have seen several aspects of the interaction of meaning with context. Some word meanings—those we have characterized as being wholly or partly indexical or demonstrative—involve instructions for fixing aspects of their reference as a function of the context. The relevant context may be the situation in which the utterance occurs, or it may be a more abstractly constructed context, built up by the speaker and hearer together on the basis of the evolving discourse. We have seen examples in which we have to take into account very "local" contexts internal to sentences; the interpretation of one expression in a sentence can give rise to context-dependent effects in the interpretation of other expressions in the same sentence. The resolution (complete or partial) of vagueness is a very widespread case of context-dependence of meaning. We scratched the surface of what is still a wide-open domain of inquiry in posing some tentative hypotheses concerning the various linguistic and cognitive principles that interact in influencing how we "recalibrate" vague adjectives depending on the context in which they occur. And in this last subsection we have seen that compound constructions represent an extreme of context-dependence—the rules of language provide only some very general constraints on the interpretation of a compound, with inferences from context and plausibility bearing the bulk of the load, and with concomitant benefits and costs in flexibility of interpretation and potential for failure of interpretation.

11.4   Case Study 3: Meaning Shifts

We closed the previous section with some thoughts about constructions in which the semantics only constrains but does not completely determine the meaning, leaving a great deal to plausible inference from context. Another domain in which we can observe some tension between the drive for uniformity of principles of interpretation and the drive for flexibility of interpretation is the domain of "meaning-shifting" principles. We will look at some examples of such principles at work in the domain of adjectives, and use these examples as a basis for some speculations about more broadly cognitive notions of "natural" functions and relations of which these meaning-shifting principles might be linguistic instantiations.

11.4.1   Type-Shifting and Meaning-Shifting Principles

In the first part of this chapter we analyzed definite descriptions as denoting individuals, but remarked that we could reanalyze them as generalized quantifiers as in chapter 12. Compositionality seems to demand that for each syntactic category there be one and only one corresponding semantic type. And since the only type general enough to accommodate all kinds of NP meanings is the type of generalized quantifiers, uniform compositionality leads us to analyze all NPs as generalized quantifiers, including those that otherwise could have been analyzed in a simpler way, for example, as denoting an individual (see chapter 12, problem 12.3).

In section 11.2 we saw something similar with adjective meanings. The simplest adjectives could be adequately analyzed as denoting sets (and expressing properties), with set intersection for the semantics of adjective-noun combination. But we argued that this would not do in the general case because of the nonintersective and nonsubsective adjectives. For uniformity of adjective semantics we have to "generalize to the hardest case" and treat all adjectives as functions from intensions of common noun phrases to intensions of common noun phrases; nothing simpler will work for adjectives like *former* and *alleged*. This means that even the simple intersective adjectives also have to be analyzed as such functions; and we described how meaning postulates could be used to capture the fact that the corresponding functions in that case would be highly constrained ones, which in effect would mimic set intersection.

There is another approach to this situation, one that slightly weakens the form of the compositionality constraint but allows us to do more justice to the intuition that the "simpler" cases—like the proper names and the intersective adjectives—are indeed simpler. On this approach, known as "type-shifting," each syntactic category is associated with a set of semantic types rather than with a single uniform type. Each lexical item is entered in the lexicon in its simplest type, and there should be principles for assigning additional (predictable) interpretations of more complex types to those expressions that can have them. In the case of adjectives, this would mean that the intersective adjectives—which intuitively and formally can be argued to have as their "simplest type" an interpretation as simple one-place predicates (with a set as extension and a property as intension)—would indeed be interpreted that way in the lexicon. Type-shifting rules would then assign to them additional interpretations as functions from intensions to intensions in those constructions where meanings of that type are required. (See Partee (1987) and Partee and Rooth (1983) for details in the case of NPs and verbs; the discussion of adjectives here is modeled on those treatments but without developing formal details.)

In the case of adjectives, we can take this approach a step farther and let the syntactic rules themselves have a family of interpretation rules rather than a single uniform one; and, following what is called "type-driven translation" (Klein and Sag 1985), let the choice of combining rule itself depend on the semantic properties of the parts. Let's illustrate.

Consider again examples (11) and (15):

(11)   carnivorous mammal

(15)   former senator

We are still assuming that (ordinary) nouns are interpreted as one-place predicates, that their extension is a set of individuals, their intension a property. Now, since *carnivorous* is a simple intersective adjective, its simplest interpretation is also as a one-place predicate. And it turns out to be a general semantic principle that any modifier-head construction in which the modifier and head are both one-place predicates is interpreted as set intersection.[8] In that case, not only can we keep our first hypothesis about the semantics of the intersective adjectives, but we would not even need to formulate a type-shifting rule to turn them into functions when they occur prenominally; the simple intersection rule that we gave in section 11.2.2.1 would, in fact, be the applicable rule without having to be "stipulated" as such.

In the case of (15), we would have no such option. *Former*, as we remarked earlier, does not have any simple predicative interpretation: we cannot classify entities in a given domain into those that are former and those that are not. This correlates with the fact that *former* does not occur in predicate position; we cannot normally say sentences like (27) (except in poetry, advertising, and jokes, where creativity beyond the existing bounds of grammar may be welcome).

(27)   # # Some of my best friends are former.

So the only available meaning for *former* is as a function from intensions to intensions. Type-driven translation will predict in that case that the semantic principle by which the meaning of (15) is derived is application of the function denoted by *former* to the intension of the noun *senator*. Note that besides the different types of adjective meanings involved here, we are implicitly bringing in the assumption that sometimes a noun contributes its extension to the meaning of the whole, sometimes its intension. That is also all right as long as there are principles that predict which it is in any given case.

Going back to the case of (11), suppose instead that we wanted to say that modifier-head semantics was always function-argument application. (One reason for such a rejection of set-intersection interpretation of

---

8. Formally, one might suppose that set union should be just as natural an option as set intersection; in fact, possibly more natural insofar as "addition" is intuitively more natural than "subtraction." One would need to argue from more than purely formal principles that in a context in which one is trying to "add information," intersection, which narrows down the interpretation, is more natural than union, which broadens it.

ADJ + N combinations, even in the case of simple intersective adjectives, could be the evidence given in the discussion of vagueness in section 11.3.1 that there is an asymmetry in modifier-head constructions that is not present in conjoined constructions, and set intersection is basically a formalization of predicate conjunction.) Then what we might say about *carnivorous* could be as follows. Its simplest interpretation is still as a one-place predicate, and it gets that meaning when it occurs in predicate position, as in "is carnivorous." But when it occurs in prenominal position, as in (11), it is automatically reinterpreted by means of the following general principle:

(28) *Predicate-to-Prenominal Shift*: If an ADJ has an interpretation as denoting a set S_{ADJ}, then that ADJ also has a possible interpretation as a function applying to a set, namely as the function F_{ADJ} such that $F_{ADJ}(S_N) = S_N \cap S_{ADJ}$.

Note that when we pack set intersection into the shifted "function-type" meaning of the adjective itself, as we did in (28), the semantic interpretation principle for combining the shifted adjective and a noun must then be function-argument application. By distinguishing function from argument but defining the function in terms of set intersection, one can capture the modifier-head asymmetry needed for the Head Primacy Principle while still asserting that the interpretation involves set intersection.

The two choices we have illustrated with type-driven translation of (11) on the one hand and the meaning-shifting principle in (28) on the other hand represent two alternative strategies that are in principle available in this case and that would have the same effects except possibly for the issue of modifier-head asymmetries. Further investigation of such possibilities in a broader context of principles of grammar and processing should help to determine which of these accounts is closer to correct.

There are other kinds of meaning shifts that are common and familiar, some involving shifts in type (for example, from one-place predicate to two-place relation or function, from entity to generalized quantifier, and so on) and some not. Of course, individual lexical items can acquire shifted meanings through all sorts of idiosyncratic routes, and not all individual instances of meaning shifts reflect any general principles. But many do; we noted earlier that any English concrete noun X can turn into a modifier with the meaning "made of X" (this is not true in all languages; many languages require a prepositional phrase like "of N" to express material). Another common shift is a shift of a concrete count noun to a corresponding mass noun denoting the stuff that the count noun is made of: a potato, some potato on my plate; an egg, some egg on my plate. While not all count nouns have mass noun counterparts in common use, David Lewis (p.c.) has argued that that is just because we do not normally have occasion to use them all; he invites us to consider a "universal grinder": put a chair in one end, turn the crank, and there will be chair all over the floor. There are also familiar shifts of noun meanings to verb meanings of various sorts, illustrated by verbs like "to can," "to dust" (this one can mean either to put dust on or to take dust off; as in the case of compounds and in ambiguity resolution, plausibility in a given context plays a large role in selecting among available meanings), and "to staple." The reader is invited to explore the extent to which there are predictable subclasses of noun-to-verb meaning shifts and the extent to which they are predictable from properties of the subclasses of nouns involved. (Marchand 1960 is a classic source of data.)

A given kind of meaning shift may be productive or semiproductive in one language and not productive at all in another.[9] One minor pattern that seems to be semiproductive in English but not in any other language known to the author is the shift of a certain class of nouns we may call "attribute nouns" that allows NPs they head to be used as predicates or modifiers without having to be put into PPs or changed into adjectival phrases. This pattern is illustrated by the uses of the noun "color" in examples (29a–c) and the noun "length" in (30a–c), as discussed in Partee (1987).

(29) a.   Blue is a nice color.

  b.   This shirt is a nice color.

  c.   Sandy bought a shirt that color yesterday.

(30) a.   Is 6 feet 6 inches the same length as two meters?

  b.   Is your hair the same length as my hair?

  c.   A mahogany board that length would cost more than this table.

"Color" and "length" are abstract nouns that we may call "attribute" nouns, since the things that are most straightforwardly in their extensions are themselves properties, as in sentences (29a) and (30a), literal translations of which are well formed in many languages. Native English speakers do not notice anything odd about the (b) and (c) sentences, but speakers of other languages find them initially surprising, since shirts are not colors and hair and skirts are not lengths. (Other languages often express (29b)

---

9. "Productive" is a term used to characterize those patterns that can be freely applied to novel cases; "semiproductive" is a vague term that signals patterns that seem to be somewhat productive but not fully so. Semiproductivity has always been something of a problem for generative grammar and for theoretical accounts of linguistic competence more generally.

by the equivalent of "is of a nice color" or "has a nice color"; but in most languages it is nonsense to say that a shirt *is* itself a nice color, just as in English one does not say "Pat is an interesting occupation.") Of course, as English speakers we are not asserting with (29b) that shirts can be colors in the way that blue is a color. Rather, English seems to have an idiosyncratic rule that shifts NPs headed by nouns like *color, size, weight, length, shape,* and other "attribute" nouns into predicates with modifier-like meanings and quasi-adjectival syntactic distribution, thus allowing them to be used not only in postverbal predicate position, as in (29b) and (30b), but also in the kind of postnominal position normally reserved for adjectival phrases and prepositional phrases, as in (29c) and (30c).

The fact that there are differences in productivity among various meaning-shifting rules—and especially the fact that there are such language-particular rules as the one we have just seen—makes it clear that there is a complex relationship (one ripe for study) between the linguistic and the nonlinguistic aspects of our propensity to shift words from one meaning to another. What we do in English clearly is not all an inevitable result of more general cognitive principles, but neither does it seem to be wholly language-specific or independent of issues of "cognitive naturalness." As progress is made in the study of systematic shifts in lexical meanings, both synchronic and historical, and in the understanding of semiproductive processes, a rich area of research can be expected to open up with important implications for language acquisition, language change, and the relationship between linguistic and other cognitive processes.

11.4.2   Natural Functions

The examples of meaning-shifting in the previous section may be assumed to represent one way that natural languages deal with the tension between, on the one hand, the advantages of a very systematic correspondence between syntactic categories and semantic types and, on the other hand, the great flexibility and versatility that seem to be essential properties of natural languages.

They are also illustrative of the fact that words and phrases can easily shift their meanings—either temporarily, as in metaphorical or figurative uses of language, or permanently—leading to families of meanings that appear to have families of types. There are analogies in formal languages as well. If one thinks about the operation(s) denoted by "$+$" on integers and on the rationals, which we normally casually think of as the very same operation, it is clear that given those two different domains, it (they) cannot actually be exactly the same operation. But it is common for programming languages to allow the same symbol "$+$" for both operations (known as "overloading" the symbol), letting properties of the operands determine which interpretation is invoked (a process known as "coercion"; the general phenomenon of having single expressions interpreted with multiple semantic types is known as "polymorphism").

A broader and more speculative goal that we might try to approach from such examples is to take some steps toward sharpening up a notion of "natural" (those are scare quotes!) families of meanings, and, more broadly still, a notion of cognitively natural functions. We have clearly seen that multiple meanings of a single word are not always cases of accidental homonymy, and we have seen samples of reasonably "natural" rules for shifting from a given meaning of a word to some new meaning or meanings. Our examples have mainly been drawn from adjective and noun meanings, but this enterprise can be carried out in many sorts of domains. When we concentrate on semantic types and meaning-shifting principles that involve changes in types, this leads to the search for natural families of types and natural type-shifting principles, and for notions of natural functions shifting from meanings of one type to meanings of another.

Now, what is "natural"? This is a vague and loaded word, even a dangerous one to use in science, since it is easily subject to abuse and is often used as no more than a biased evaluation of one or another hypothesized principle or property or process. At the same time, if the object of our investigation is some aspect of human or animal mental functioning, then indeed we are trying to find out what sorts of principles are natural to the species. We therefore should not dismiss the notion; we should just be cautious about rushing to conclusions about it. Is formal elegance relevant? Well, it may be. The scientist's esthetic preference for formal elegance has itself evolved in nature, and our belief in a correlation between the beauty of a hypothesis and its approximation to truth may be a symptom, if we are lucky, of the survival value of a taste for beauty. If we can find analyses with a high degree of both formal elegance and empirical generality, we can suspect that we are on the right track. It will undoubtedly take the cooperation of linguists, mathematicians, and cognitive scientists to try to find some notion(s) of "natural functions" in this area that are satisfying in some degree from all those perspectives.

Let's broaden the context with an example from another domain. Suppose we were to ask, "What's the most natural function from the real numbers to the integers?" (The reader is invited to think about this before reading ahead.) One logician once volunteered the answer that obviously it is the function that maps every real number onto zero. To a logician, that might be the first thought of the most natural and maybe simplest function from the reals to the integers. And, indeed, it is undoubtedly a simplest such function, but not for most people a most natural one. Why not? Probably because it "ignores its input" and loses all the information about the argument in passing to the value. Most people seem to agree that the most natural function from the reals to the integers is some version of a rounding-off function—a function that maps a given real number to the nearest integer. So let's try to analyze why we all agree that such a function is the most natural one between those two domains. For one thing, it preserves order insofar as you can preserve order. When we are mapping from a larger domain to a smaller one we cannot, of course, preserve everything, but the rounding-off function preserves order insofar as it is preservable. In particular, "less than or equal to" is always preserved, even though "less than" is not always. That is, if $r_1 \leq r_2$, and r_1 rounds off to n_1 and r_2 to n_2, then it is always the case that $n_1 \leq n_2$, even though some instances of "less than" may be mapped into some instances of "equals." The rounding-off function also comes as close as is possible to preserving the various operations like addition and multiplication that are defined on both real numbers and integers. So, insofar as those two domains share a certain amount of structure, one can say that the most natural function, the most natural mapping from one to the other, is the one that preserves the most of the relevant structure that they share.

We can even take this example farther and ask what, if anything, we can say about the choice among the various different versions of rounding off functions, which differ as to how to round off a number that ends with .5. It is illuminating to see how the choice depends on one's purposes and goals. If you want simplicity and maximal replicability, then you choose some very simple rule like "always round down." Or, for instance, if you are a merchant and you want to maximize profits, then when you compute prices you always round up. But those are not the most natural rounding-off functions from the point of view of physics or other sciences, since always rounding up or always rounding down is bound to magnify errors when you multiply. So the one that is commonly taught in elementary physics is "If it's an even number, round down, and if it's an odd number, round up." Assuming that even and odd numbers are randomly distributed in the inputs, that will come as close as we can to minimizing the propagation of error and preserving the structure of the argument domain in applying operations that are defined on both domains. But we can pursue this example even further. The last-mentioned function was still replicable and still a very definite algorithm. If we really wanted to be physically "natural" and imagine that we are modeling something like balls falling down from a space that we imagine to have real-number distribution and being funneled into discrete containers, then the rule should be that to model a ball that is falling from a .5-type initial location, we should flip a coin to model which way it will go. That is, we should do something random to model the random part of the physical process; we should not make a deterministic algorithm out of it. The physics teachers do not suggest coin-flipping, probably because they need to be able to check our computations and want us to have the same answers. Besides, we have to stretch the notion of function even to be able to call that one a function, though if it is the most natural function for modeling a class of physical phenomena, the physicists should insist on being able to work with a notion of function that allows it. So, even in a simple example like this, the question of what is the "most natural" or the "best" function of a certain general type is interestingly nontrivial. On the one hand, we can often give strong arguments that converge on identifying certain properties of such functions (in the example above, that it must be a rounding-off function), but in some respects the choice of a most natural function may well depend on one's purposes and/or on empirical considerations.

The shift in proper noun interpretation discussed earlier can be argued to involve the formally most natural possible function from the domain of entities to the domain of generalized quantifiers; Lewis's "universal grinder" may represent the empirically most natural function from concrete count noun meanings to mass noun meanings. Studies focusing on type-shifting and other structurally based meaning shifts have also led to a better understanding of the English definite article and the variety of interrelated meanings of different types that can be attributed to it; the basis for the ability of numerals and many other weak determiners to function either as adjectives or as determiners; the analysis of the English copula verb "be"; and some explanation for the ease with which languages indicate definiteness and indefiniteness without explicit articles. The exploration of type-shifting and meaning-shifting functions might thus provide an opening wedge into a broader study of cognitively natural functions of various kinds.

One of the many domains in which language offers a "window on the mind" is the domain of metaphor. The investigation of metaphor may be at an opposite extreme in some ways from the investigation of most natural functions from real numbers to integers, but it can be seen as involving a particularly open-ended domain of meaning-shifting principles. While formal semantics has lagged behind more explicitly cognitively oriented approaches in contributing to the study of the extremely important and interesting area of metaphor, there is no obstacle in principle to the integration of the study of metaphor into the model-theoretic framework. There are also potential connections between work on type-shifting and meaning-shifting principles and investigations of what one might call structural metaphors. Lewis's universal grinder underlies one example of a kind of structural metaphor. Others can be found in the research area that Emmon Bach (1986) has dubbed "natural language metaphysics," where specific examples might include formal analogies that have been discovered between the mass-count distinction in the nominal domain and the process-event distinction in the domain of verbal aspect; shifts between viewing one and the same "thing" (such as a war or a thunderstorm or a random act of kindness) as an entity or an event with concomitant shifts in the use of nouns versus verbs in talking about them; and shifts between locative and temporal interpretations of adverbs, prepositions, and measure expressions. And there are shifts between frequency uses of adverbs like *often, seldom, usually,* and their use as "unselective quantifiers" over domains with no temporal dimensions but with formal properties that make notions like frequency distributions sensible (much as in the formal study of probability and sampling), as in a famous example of David Lewis's:

(31)   Quadratic equations usually have two distinct roots.

Further examples of structural metaphors include the imposition of spatio-temporal language and structure onto abstract domains; likewise, the extensions of so-called thematic roles (agent, patient, source, goal, and so on) from the frames of relatively concrete verbs to those of more abstract ones.

Metaphor has to do with the imposing of unfamiliar structures onto familiar domains, or describing one entity or event with language typically used for describing entities or events of a quite different sort. Understanding a metaphor as it was intended requires seeing a relevant pattern of similarity between two different domains—some structure they can be said to have in common in spite of other differences. Since any two domains have infinitely many properties in common and infinitely many differences, a successful metaphor cannot be based on just any similarity; it must be a sufficiently salient one so that the hearer will be able to identify it with some degree of confidence without the speaker having to "explain" it. It is no easy task to develop a theory of the kinds of similarities that are likely to be "salient" to creatures with our particular cognitive and perceptual propensities. The search for a characterization of "natural functions" can be seen as one part of such an effort.

While it is almost certainly impossible to define the notion of "natural function," such a notion may nevertheless be able to play a useful role in bringing formal techniques and cognitive insights closer together. It may provide one of the many potential bridges between semantics and other aspects of cognitive science.

11.5   Conclusion

Semantics is a field that goes back a couple of thousand years and is inherently interdisciplinary, with at least as many approaches to it as there are disciplinary entry points and reasons for being interested in meaning. Formal semantics is a young and dynamic field that is making exciting progress on some of the many questions that can be classified as semantic. Also inherently interdisciplinary, it is centered in linguistics, philosophy, and logic, with increasing connections to psycholinguistics and to computational linguistics, hence in principle close to the heart of cognitive science. One of the major foundational challenges facing the fuller integration of formal semantics into cognitive science is the tension that remains between the conceptualist foundations of generative grammar and the antipsychologism inherited by contemporary logic from its Fregean roots and transmitted from there to contemporary formal semantics through the work of Montague and other philosophers and logicians. In semantics, more than in other areas of grammar, there may well be good reason to distinguish between language and our knowledge of it; there may be an important distinction between "what's in the head" and "what's determined by what's in the head." There is so far, for instance, no good theory of what mental representations of possible worlds might be like; and, given that it is easy to argue that there must be nondenumerably many possible worlds and that they are therefore not finitely representable "one by one," this is a serious obstacle to the development of psycholinguistic models of intensionality and semantic processing. Possible worlds (or possible situations, of which there are even more) are a central notion in formal semantics, and possible worlds cannot be "in the head" in any straightforward way. But there is plenty of evidence that possible worlds and other notions explored by formal semanticists are at least indirectly cognitively robust; thus, it is to be hoped and expected that advances on these and the many other open problems in this rapidly developing field will be made by the next generation of researchers, especially those who have benefited from the interdisciplinary perspectives that are intrinsic to the field of cognitive science. And, lest any present student reader suffer from the same fear that this author had as a student—that the interesting problems will all be solved before she has a chance to start working on any of them—let me close with the assurance that every good solution opens up interesting new problems that perhaps could not even be posed before. There is little danger that a genuinely productive line of research will ever simply be "finished."

Suggestions for Further Reading

There are several good introductions to formal semantics. Chierchia and McConnell-Ginet 1990 is a good introductory textbook especially aimed at linguistics students; Bach 1989, based on a series of lectures given in China, is a good nontechnical introduction for the linguist or the interested general reader. Gamut 1991, translated from Dutch, is an excellent two-volume work that combines an introduction to logic with a solid introduction to formal semantics; it is the product of an interdisciplinary team of five Dutch coauthors whose fields are logic, philosophy, and linguistics, and the book shows the benefits of the long-standing Dutch tradition of interdisciplinary work among those fields. Dowty, Wall, and Peters 1981 is a classic introduction to Montague semantics; Cresswell 1973 is a comprehensible book-length introduction to an approach to semantics quite similar to Montague's, with discussion of both philosophical foundations and many particular English constructions.

Formal semantics traces its recent roots in considerable part to the seminal work of Richard Montague, collected in Montague 1974. Its development in linguistics and philosophy is traced in such works as Lewis 1970, Partee 1973, 1976, Dowty 1979, Partee 1989a, and in articles in the journal Linguistics and Philosophy since its inception in 1977, in volumes of proceedings of the biennial Amsterdam conferences held since the middle 1970s, and recently in many other books and journals. Three recent or forthcoming handbooks give good surveys of the current state of the art in formal semantics: Stechow and Wunderlich 1991, Lappin (to appear), and Van Benthem and ter Meulen (to appear). Lappin's handbook also includes some other contemporary approaches to semantics.

As noted at the beginning of this chapter, there are many approaches to semantics other than the formal semantic perspective adopted in this and the next chapter (and the boundaries of formal semantics are themselves somewhat vague.) The interested reader will find a good range of approaches to semantics presented or discussed in such works as the following: Jackendoff 1972, 1983, 1987, McCawley 1973, 1981, Lyons 1977, 1988, J. D. Fodor 1980, and May 1985. The earliest attempt to construct a theory of semantics to go with a Chomskyan theory of generative grammar was Katz and J. A. Fodor 1963.

Before Montague's work became known to linguists and the development of formal semantics in linguistics took root, the so-called "linguistic wars" between "generative semantics" and "interpretive semantics" dominated the semantic scene in linguistics. Central figures on the generative semantics side were Lakoff, McCawley, Ross, and Postal; central figures on the interpretive semantics side were Chomsky and Jackendoff. For original sources, see Lakoff 1972, McCawley 1973, Jackendoff 1972, and Chomsky 1971; for overviews of the dispute, see J. D. Fodor 1980 and Harris 1993.

There have been representative collections of articles published at various times that give a good snapshot of the state of the art, the interests of semanticists, and the development of interdisciplinary cooperative efforts among scholars working from different backgrounds. Steinberg and Jakobovits 1971 is an early interdisciplinary collection with contributions by philosophers, linguists, and psychologists; the articles are in the main written from a single disciplinary perspective; the volume therefore gives a good perspective on the disciplinary precursors of the current drive toward a more unified cognitive science. A sample of other important interdisciplinary collections would include Davidson and Harman 1972, and Keenan 1975.

Much of the foundation for work on lexical semantics in the context of Montague Grammar was laid in Dowty 1979, which is still an excellent point of entry for this research area. More about the semantics of adjectives in particular can be found in Kamp 1975, Siegel 1976a, Siegel 1976b, Klein 1980, and Kamp and Partee (forthcoming).

For more about the fascinating little word the, see Heim 1982 and Neale 1990.

Good starting points for a deeper understanding of the issue of intensionality and the role of possible worlds in its analysis are Carnap 1956, Lewis 1970, 1973, 1986, and Stalnaker 1984. For inquiries that attempt to bridge some of the gap between linguistic and philosophical work in formal semantics on the one hand and concerns for psychological representations on the other, see J. A. Fodor 1975, 1987, Cresswell 1978, Johnson-Laird 1983, and Stalnaker 1984.

There is some literature on the very interesting problems of vagueness touched on in section 11.3.1, some of it rather technical; see Pinkal 1983 for a good model of a formal semantics perspective on vagueness; and see Kamp and Partee (forthcoming) and references cited therein for some discussion linking formal semanticists' and psychologists' approaches to vagueness, particularly addressed to concerns raised about vagueness and compositionality by Osherson and Smith 1981. Problems of vagueness have gained some attention recently under the banner of "fuzzy logic," a term applied to a vaguely delimited family of approaches to the analysis of vagueness starting from the work of Zadeh 1965. A critique of Zadeh's classic version of fuzzy logic is included in Kamp and Partee (forthcoming).

For more on deictics, indexicals, and the interaction of point of view with semantic interpretation, discussed in section 11.3.2, see Fillmore 1971, 1975 (classic studies in this area), Weissenborn and Klein 1982 (a collection that offers a fascinating look at deictic expressions in a typologically diverse array of languages), and Partee 1989b and references cited therein.

With respect to the interpretation of compounds as discussed in section 11.3.3, see Gleitman and Gleitman 1971 for a most provocative study of how various groups of people interpret novel three-word combinations involving mixtures of compounding and modification and mixtures of adjectives and nouns.

For more on type-shifting and meaning-shifting (section 11.4) from a variety of perspectives, see Marchand 1960 (a classic philological work with a wealth of data), Dowty 1979 (which laid the foundations for work on lexical meaning in Montague Grammar), Partee 1987 (about type-shifting), Jackendoff 1976 (particularly about basic and metaphorically extended interpretations of thematic roles), and Lakoff and Johnson 1980 (a wide-ranging and illuminating study of metaphors, both lexical and structural, marred in the present author's view by the ill-founded claim that formal semantics is incapable of contributing to the study of metaphor).

There is an increasing amount of interesting work going on at the borderline of philosophy of language, formal semantics, and literary criticism, giving rise to a new field of literary semantics drawing in part on sources in formal semantics and philosophy. See Pavel 1986, which contains a good survey of the field and some of its central issues.

Problems

11.1   In section 11.2.1 it was noted that "the French teacher" is ambiguous, with possible paraphrases (a) "the teacher who is French" and (b) "the teacher of French." Translate "the French teacher," in both senses, into two other languages; if possible and perhaps with help from a native speaker, include translation into a non-Indo-European language. Identify nouns, adjectives, and PPs in the translations. Pool results in class, and see if the results might support or disconfirm the hypothesis that the English phrase has two different syntactic analyses, one in which the word "French" is used as an adjective modifying the head and the other a structure (perhaps a compound; see section 11.3.3) in which "French" is a noun that is interpreted as an argument of the head. (Some languages force you to choose a gender for "teacher"; if so, you may pick a gender at random, or include both.)

11.2 (section 11.2.1)   Although many postnominal of-PPs are arguments of the head, some are modifiers. Examples (a) and (b) below illustrate the one(s) test mentioned in section 11.2.1. Assume the correctness of the thesis that one(s) can only be substituted for an N'—and not for an N that is not also a complete N'. Then tell what conclusions can be drawn about the PPs in (a) and (b) below, and draw correspondingly different trees (selecting between tree types (7c) and (7d)) for the NPs *the owners of the shop* and *the owners of foreign origin.*

(a)   # # The owners of the shop cooperated with the ones of the used car lot. (Anomalous if *ones* is interpreted as *owners*.)

(b)   The owners of foreign origin cooperated with the ones of domestic origin.

11.3 (sections 11.2.2.1, 11.2.2.2, 11.2.2.3, and 11.3.1)

(a) Classify the following adjectives as (i) intersective, (ii) nonintersective but subsective, or (iii) nonsubsective; among the nonsubsective, classify further as (iiia) privative, (iiib) plain nonsubsective. There may be unclear or debatable cases; some unclear cases may have different answers for different readings of the adjective in question: if so, suggest readings and corresponding classification.

Adjectives: *red, strict, new, possible, wealthy, future, audible, poor, miniature, sick, typical, counterfeit.*

(b) Add two more adjectives to each category.

(c) Write a paragraph discussing one or two unclear cases, either from the list in (a) or from your list in (b).

11.4 (section 11.2.2.3)   Write a meaning postulate (analogous to (12) and (14) in sections 11.2.2.2 and 11.2.2.3) to characterize the privative meaning of an adjective like *counterfeit.*

11.5 (section 11.3.1)   Consider the following pair of sentences.

(a) Knives are sharp.

(b) This is a sharp knife.

If *sharp* is interpreted with the same positive extension in interpreting each sentence, then if (a) is true, (b) would have to be uninformative. Suggest a diagnosis of how we might adjust the positive extension of *sharp* differently in the two cases, making use of the Non-Vacuity Principle, the Head Primacy Principle, and whatever other hypotheses you need.

11.6 (section 11.3.2)   Illustrate—by means of diagrams that show position of speaker, position, and orientation (if relevant) of mentioned object, and possible intended "target" positions of hearer—how "Please stand in front of the car" can be ambiguous, whereas "Please stand in front of the tree" normally is not. Optionally, draw another diagram illustrating a situation in which the second sentence would also be ambiguous. Use descriptions if you find that easier or clearer than drawing diagrams.

11.7 (section 11.3.2)

(i) Consider example (25) again:

(25)   Most foreigners speak a foreign language.

Considering just the possible ways of "anchoring" the words *foreigner* and *foreign* to sentence-external or sentence-internal context, how many different readings does this sentence seem to have? (For simplicity, and to limit the number of relevant possibilities, imagine the sentence to be spoken in the United States by an English-speaking U.S. resident to another English-speaking U.S. resident, so that there is in effect only one relevant sentence-external context to anchor to, namely "the U.S.")

(ii) Do the possibilities you found show any differences with respect to the first and second NPs and their possible anchorings? (Question for further thought: make up a hypothesis about syntactic constraints on sentence-internal anchoring of context-dependent words like "foreign"; test it against three or four further examples with different syntactic structures. This is meant as just a sample first step in what could potentially be a much larger investigation.)

11.8 (section 11.3.3)   Think of three different possible interpretations for the compound "bear towel," and describe scenarios in which each would be readily understood by the hearer as the intended interpretation. Try to make at least one of them relatively "easy" and at least one of them quite improbable, so that a very specific context is required to evoke that interpretation in the hearer. (The relevant context may be either current perceived context or context of shared knowledge, beliefs, past conversations, or experiences.)

11.9 (section 11.4.2)

(a) Describe the nature of the productive meaning-shifting pattern by which temporal expressions come to be used in expressing distances, as in "I live just 10 minutes from

356 Partee

here." Describe the dependence of this particular meaning-shift on relevant nonlinguistic facts about the context.

(b) Give examples of two other kinds of meaning-shifting phenomena that show switches in one direction or the other between locative and temporal interpretations of expressions of some kind, such as adjectival phrases, adverbial phrases, or prepositional phrases, or shifts of phrases that are originally neither locative nor temporal into locative or temporal uses (for example, "two boyfriends ago" or "Now we're only about twelve logging trucks from New Aiyansh").

Questions for Further Thought

11.1 In section 11.1.2 we discussed two possible syntactic analyses for the expression *almost half full*. One possibility is that both analyses are correct and that they correspond to two subtly different semantic interpretations of the expression. Can you think of any arguments for or against such a possibility?

11.2 We discussed the ambiguity (in the written language) of the phrase *a French teacher* in section 11.2.1 and in problem 1. Consider the fact that the phrase "a French teacher and two German ones" unambiguously selects the modifier reading of *German* (and by parallel structure effects also selects strongly for the modifier reading of *French*); and explore whether that fact, together with the proposal about *one(s)* mentioned in section 11.2.1, might be used to argue that in addition to distinguishing *French* as an adjective and as a noun, there should be two different tree structures for *a French teacher* analogous to the two different trees (7c) and (7d) for NP's with postnominal PPs. Which tree would go with which interpretation, and why?

11.3 (sections 11.2.2.3, 11.3.1, and 11.4.1) Give arguments both for and against the classification of *fake* as a privative modifier. Do the same for *stone* as in *stone lion* (discussed in section 11.3.1). Which arguments do you find stronger in each case, and/or can you think of any resolution in either case that could show each side to be somehow correct?

11.4 (section 11.3.1) Suggest at least one argument for the need for, and usefulness of, vagueness in natural language. (Optional suggestion (just a sample): Consider the difficulty or perhaps impossibility of expressing generalizations like "Scarce things are usually more expensive than abundant things" if there were not vague words like *scarce* and *abundant*. (Note the apparent involvement of something like a Parallel Structure Effect in this example as well, although this is not a case of conjunction of the predicates.)

11.5 (section 11.3.2) Sketch the beginnings of a possible experiment designed to probe the degree to which objects are conceived as having "fronts," and by virtue of what sorts of properties (of the object and/or its location or motion, or of the structure of the setting in which it occurs, or the like); for example, look for relative prominence of different possible interpretations of expressions like "in front of X," "to the right of X," as noted in the text ("in front of the car" versus "in front of the tree" and the Little League anecdote) and in problem 6.

11.6 (section 11.3.2) If you know a language other than English very well or can tap the knowledge of someone who does, see if you can find examples of context-sensitive expressions similar to "in front of," "to the right of," "ahead of," and so on that work a little differently from the corresponding English expressions in how the interpretation is determined on the basis of the context.

11.7 (section 11.3.3) The following is a classic brain-teaser kind of question: "Why do mirrors reverse right and left but not up and down?" In the context of semantics and cognitive science, the interesting thing to try to puzzle out is what kind of a question this is: Is it a question about the semantics of "right" and "left" versus "up" and "down"; or about optics; or about conventions of reading and writing; or about gravity or some other domain of physics; or about the orientation of our eyes or how our visual system works, or what? If you lie down on your side and try to read your T-shirt then, then what? Are the presuppositions of the question correct? (Does gravity matter?) This question should be just for fun.

11.8 (section 11.4.1)   Consider various verbs derived from nouns, such as *hand, elbow, core, seed, can, dust* (the furniture), *dust* (the crops), and others. Explore the extent to which there are predictable subclasses of noun-to-verb meaning shifts and the extent to which they are predictable from properties of the subclasses of nouns involved.

11.9 (section 11.4.2)   This problem could be for the whole class together or could be the subject of an informal survey carried out by students. It is traditionally said that what makes an expression like "keep tabs on" an idiom is the fact that the meaning of the whole is not a function of the meanings of the parts, that is, that idioms are expressions whose meanings are not compositionally derived and which therefore must be treated like "phrasal lexical items." Write down your own (relatively unedited) understanding of what the "tabs" in "keep tabs on" are, and what (possibly metaphorical) action is involved in keeping them on somebody. Then compare responses with classmates, or survey a group of people and compare responses.[10]

References

Allén, S., ed. (1989). *Possible worlds in humanities, arts, and sciences: Proceedings of Nobel symposium 65.* Berlin and New York: Walter de Gruyter.

Bach, E. (1986). Natural language metaphysics. In Barcan Marcus et al., eds., *Logic, methodology and philosophy of science VII.* New York: Elsevier, 573–595.

Bach, E. (1989). *Informal lectures on formal semantics.* Albany, N.Y.: State University of New York Press.

Bach, E., and R. Cooper (1978). The NP-S analysis of relative clauses and compositional semantics. *Linguistics and Philosophy* 2, 145–150.

Baker, C. L. (1978). *Introduction to generative transformational syntax.* Englewood Cliffs, NJ: Prentice-Hall.

Carnap, R. (1952). Meaning postulates. *Philosophy Studies* 3, 65–73.

Carnap, R. (1956). *Meaning and necessity.* 2nd ed. supplements. Chicago: Chicago University Press.

Chierchia, G., and S. McConnell-Ginet (1990). *Meaning and grammar: An introduction to semantics.* Cambridge, MA: MIT Press, 1990.

Chomsky, N. (1971). Deep structure, surface structure, and semantic interpretation. In D. Steinberg and L. Jakobovits, eds., *Semantics: An interdisciplinary reader in philosophy, linguistics, and psychology.* 183–216. Cambridge: Cambridge University Press.

Cresswell, M. J. (1973). *Logics and languages.* London: Methuen.

Cresswell, M. J. (1978). Semantic competence. In M. Guenthner-Reutter and F. Guenthner, eds., *Meaning and translation: Philosophical and linguistic approaches.* London: Duckworth.

Cresswell, M. J. (1982). The autonomy of semantics. In S. Peters and E. Saarinen, eds., *Processes, beliefs, and questions,* 69–86. Dordrecht, Netherlands: Reidel.

10. This suggested project comes from the author's experience with an undergraduate semantics class in which virtually every student had a compositional, though metaphorical, interpretation for the expression and rejected the idea that "tabs" in that idiom is meaningless, but no two students had the same compositional interpretation. If this phenomenon is general, it provides interesting support for the robustness of the principle of compositionality.

Davidson, D., and G. Harman, eds. (1972). *Semantics of natural language*. Dordrecht, Netherlands: Reidel.

Dowty, D. (1979). *Word meaning and Montague grammar*. Dordrecht, Netherlands: Reidel.

Dowty, D., R. Wall, and S. Peters (1981). *Introduction to Montague semantics*. Dordrecht, Netherlands: Reidel.

Fillmore, C. (1971). Types of lexical information. In D. Steinberg and L. Jakobovits, eds., *Semantics: An interdisciplinary reader in philosophy, linguistics, and psychology*. Cambridge: Cambridge University Press. 370–392.

Fillmore, C. (1975). *Santa Cruz lectures on deixis*. Bloomington: Indiana University Linguistic Club.

Fodor, J. A. (1975). *The language of thought*. New York: Thomas Y. Crowell.

Fodor, J. A. (1987). *Psychosemantics: The problem of meaning in the philosophy of mind*. Cambridge, MA: MIT Press.

Fodor, J. D. (1980). *Semantics: Theories of meaning in generative grammar*. Cambridge, MA: Harvard University Press.

Frege, G. (1892). Ueber Sinn und Bedeutung. *Zeitschrift fuer Philosophie und philosophische Kritik* 100, 25–50. Translated as "On sense and reference," in P. T. Geach and M. Black, eds., *Translations from the philosophical writings of Gottlob Frege*, 56–78. Oxford: Blackwell, 1952.

Friederici, A. (1985). Levels of processing and vocabulary types: Evidence from on-line comprehension in normals and agrammatics. *Cognition* 19, 1–34.

Gamut, L. T. F. (1991). *Logic, language, and meaning. Vol I: Introduction to logic; Vol II: Intensional logic and logical grammar*. Chicago: University of Chicago Press.

Gleitman, L. R., and H. Gleitman (1971). *Phrase and paraphrase*. New York: Norton.

Hamburger, H., and S. Crain (1984). Acquisition of cognitive compiling. *Cognition* 17: 85–136.

Hamburger, H., and S. Crain (1987). Plans and semantics in human processing of language. *Cognitive Science* 11: 101–136.

Harris, R. A. (1993). *The linguistics wars*. New York and Oxford: Oxford University Press.

Heim, I. (1982). *The semantics of definite and indefinite NP's*. Ph.D. dissertation, University of Massachusetts, Amherst.

Hintikka, K. J. J. (1969). *Models for modalities*. Dordrecht, Netherlands: Reidel.

Jackendoff, R. S. (1972). *Semantic interpretation in generative grammar*. Cambridge, MA: MIT Press.

Jackendoff, R. S. (1976). Toward an explanatory semantic representation. *Linguistic Inquiry* 7, 89–150.

Jackendoff, R. S. (1977). *X-Bar syntax: A study of phrase structure*. Cambridge, MA: MIT Press.

Jackendoff, R. S. (1983). *Semantics and cognition*. Cambridge, MA: MIT Press.

Jackendoff, R. S. (1987). *Consciousness and the computational mind*. Cambridge, MA: MIT Press.

Janssen, T. M. V. (1983). *Foundations and applications of Montague grammar*. Amsterdam: Mathematisch Centrum.

Johnson-Laird, P. N. (1983). *Mental models: Towards a cognitive science of language, inference, and consciousness*. Cambridge, MA: Harvard University Press.

Kamp, J. A. W. (1975). Two theories about adjectives. In E. L. Keenan, ed., *Formal semantics for natural langauges*, 123–155. Cambridge: Cambridge University Press.

Kamp, H., and B. Partee (forthcoming). Prototype theory and compositionality. To appear in *Cognition*.

Katz, J. J., and J. A. Fodor (1963). The structure of a semantic theory. *Language* 39, 170–210.

Keenan, E. L. (1974). The functional principle: Generalizing the notion of "subject of." *CLS* 10, 298–309.

Keenan, E. L., ed. (1975). *Formal semantics for natural languages*. Cambridge: Cambridge University Press.

Klein, E. (1980). A semantics for positive and comparative adjectives. *Linguistics and Philosophy* 4, 1–45.

Klein, E., and I. Sag (1985). Type-driven translation. *Linguistics and Philosophy* 8, 163–201.

Kripke, S. (1963). Semantical considerations on modal logic. *Acta Philosophica Fennica* 16, 83–94.

Lakoff, G. (1972). Linguistics and natural logic. In D. Davidson and G. Harman, eds., *Semantics of natural language*, 545–665. Dordrecht, Netherlands: Reidel.

Lakoff, G., and M. Johnson (1980). *Metaphors we live by*. Chicago: University of Chicago Press.

Lappin, S., ed. (to appear). *Handbook of contemporary semantic theory*. Oxford: Blackwell.

Lewis, D. (1970). "General semantics" *Synthese* 22, 18–67; reprinted in D. Davidson and G. Harman, eds., *Semantics of natural language*. Dordrecht, Netherlands: Reidel (1972), 169–218; and in B. H. Partee (1976), 1–50.

Lewis, D. (1973). *Counterfactuals*. Cambridge, MA: Harvard University Press.

Lewis, D. (1975). Adverbs of quantification. In E. L. Keenan, ed., *Formal semantics of natural language*. Cambridge: Cambridge University Press.

Lewis, D. (1986). *On the plurality of worlds*. Oxford: Blackwell.

Lyons, J. (1977). *Semantics*, Vols. 1 and 2. Cambridge: Cambridge University Press.

Lyons, J. (1988). *Principles of linguistic semantics*. Cambridge: Cambridge University Press.

Marchand, H. (1960). *The categories and types of present-day English word-formation: A synchronic-diachronic approach*. Wiesbaden: Harrassowitz.

Matthei, E. H. (1979). The acquisition of prenominal modifier sequences: Stalking the second green ball. Unpublished Ph.D. dissertation, University of Massachusetts.

May, R. (1985). Logical form: Its structure and derivation. *Linguistic Inquiry Monograph* 12. Cambridge, MA: MIT Press.

McCawley, J. D. (1973). *Grammar and meaning: Papers on syntactic and semantic topics*. Tokyo: Taishukan. Reprinted (1976): New York: Academic Press.

McCawley, J. D. (1981). *Everything that linguists have always wanted to know about logic but were ashamed to ask*. Chicago: University of Chicago Press.

Montague, R. (1970). English as a formal language. In B. Visentini et al., eds., *Linguaggi nella Società e nella Tecnica*. Milan: Edizioni di Comunità; reprinted in Montague (1974) 188–221.

Montague, R. (1973). The proper treatment of quantification in ordinary English. In K. J. J. Hintikka, J. M. E. Moravcsik, and P. Suppes, eds., *Approaches to natural language*, 221–242. Dordrecht, Netherlands: Reidel. Reprinted in Montague (1974) 247–270.

Montague, R. (1974). *Formal philosophy: Selected papers of Richard Montague*, edited and with an introduction by Richmond Thomason. New Haven: Yale University Press.

Neale, S. (1990). *Descriptions*. Cambridge, MA: MIT Press.

Osherson, D. N., and E. E. Smith (1981). On the adequacy of prototype theory as a theory of concepts. *Cognition* 15, 237–262.

Parsons, T. (1972). Some problems concerning the logic of grammatical modifiers. In D. Davidson and G. Harman (1972), 127–141.

Partee, B. H. (1973). Some transformational extensions of Montague grammar. *Journal of Philosophical Logic* 2, 509–534; reprinted in B. Partee (1976), 51–76.

Partee, B. H., ed. (1976). *Montague grammar*. New York: Academic Press.

Partee, B. H. (1979). Semantics—mathematics or psychology? In R. Bäuerle, U. Egli, and A. von Stechow, eds., *Semantics from different points of view*, 1–14. Berlin: Springer-Verlag.

Partee, B. H. (1987). Noun phrase interpretation and type-shifting principles. In J. Groenendijk et al., eds., *Studies in discourse representation theory and the theory of generalized quantifiers*, 115–143. Dordrecht, Netherlands: Foris.

Partee, B. H. (1989a). Possible worlds in model-theoretic semantics: A linguistic perspective. In S. Allén, ed., *Possible worlds in humanities, arts, and sciences: Proceedings of Nobel Symposium 65*, 93–123. Berlin and New York: Walter de Gruyter.

Partee, B. H. (1989b). Binding implicit variables in quantified contexts. In C. Wiltshire, B. Music, and R. Graczyk, eds., *Papers from CLS 25*, 342–365. Chicago: Chicago Linguistic Society.

Partee, B. H., and M. Rooth (1983). Generalized conjunction and type ambiguity. In R. Bäuerle, C. Schwarze, and A. von Stechow, eds., *Meaning, use, and interpretation of language*, 361–383. Berlin: Walter de Gruyter.

Pavel, T. G. (1986). *Fictional worlds*. Cambridge, MA: Harvard University Press.

Pinkal, M. (1983). Towards a semantics of precization. In T. Ballmer and M. Pinkal, eds., *Approaching vagueness*, 13–57. Amsterdam: North-Holland.

Rodman, R. (1976). Scope phenomena, "movement transformations," and relative clauses. In B. H. Partee, ed., *Montague grammar*, 165–176. New York: Academic Press.

Siegel, E. A. (1976a). Capturing the adjective. Ph.D. dissertation, University of Massachusetts, Amherst.

Siegel, E. A. (1976b). Capturing the Russian adjecture. In B. H. Partee, ed., *Montague grammar*, 293–309. New York: Academic Press.

Stalnaker, R. C. (1984). *Inquiry*. Cambridge, MA: MIT Press.

Stechow, A. von, and D. Wunderlich, eds. (1991). *Semantik/semantics: An international handbook of contemporary research*. Berlin: Walter de Gruyter.

Steinberg, D., and L. Jakobovits, eds. (1971). *Semantics. An interdisciplinary reader in philosophy, linguistics, and psychology*. Cambridge: Cambridge University Press.

Van Benthem, J. F. A. K., and Alice ter Meulen, eds. (to appear). *Handbook of logic and language*. Amsterdam: Elsevier.

Weissenborn, J., and W. Klein, eds. (1982). *Here and there: Cross-linguistic studies on deixis and demonstration*. Amsterdam: John Benjamins.

Zadeh, L. (1965). Fuzzy sets. *Information and Control 8*, 338–353.

Chapter 12

Semantics

Richard Larson

We have seen that, as speakers of English, we know facts about its *syntax*: for example, that expressions divide into categories like verb, noun, preposition, and adjective, that verbs and prepositions typically precede their objects in English, that words in a sentence cluster into constituents. In addition, we know facts about the *semantics*, or meaning structure, of English: that sentences are related as synonymous or contradictory, that they are true under certain circumstances, that certain notions do or do not correspond to possible words.

12.1 Semantical Relations

Like other kinds of linguistic knowledge, knowledge of semantics reveals itself clearly in the form of certain abilities we possess. One such is the ability to judge that various relations hold among sentences. Consider the examples in (l) and (2):

(1) a. John believed that the Earth is round.

  b. John doubted that the Earth is round.

(2) a. John claimed that the Earth is round.

  b. John denied that the Earth is round.

As speakers of English, we know intuitively, and immediately, that a certain kind of relation holds within the pairs of (1) and (2)—the same one in both cases. Pretheoretically, we grasp it as a relation of "incompatibility" or "exclusion" of some kind.

This exclusion relation does not arise from the grammatical form of the sentences; we know this because other pairs with the same form (subject-verb-complement clause) fail to exhibit the relation:

(3) a. John knew that the Earth is round.

  b. John dreamed that the Earth is round.

Likewise, it does not arise from the particular phonetic shapes of the words; this is clear because other languages—for instance, German—express the same relation with quite different words ((4) corresponds to (1)):

(4)   a.   Hans glaubte, dass die Erde rund ist.

      b.   Hans bezweifelte, dass die Erde rund ist.

The relation we detect in (1) and (2) issues from another property of these sentences—their *meaning*. The members of the pairs "express contrary thoughts," "describe mutually exclusive situations," or "convey opposing information"; they "cannot both be true at the same time," and so on. It is in virtue of the meanings they have that the sentences in (1) and (2) exclude each other. And it is in virtue of knowing these meanings that we judge this relation to hold.

Exclusion is not the only kind of semantic relation we can recognize; (5)–(7) and (8)–(10) illustrate other, analogous forms:

(5)   a.   John sold a car to Mary.

      b.   Mary bought a car from John.

(6)   a.   John is in front of Mary.

      b.   Mary is behind John.

(7)   a.   John saw Mary.

      b.   Mary was seen by John.

(8)   a.   John is a human.

      b.   John is a mammal.

(9)   a.   Mary was laughing and dancing.

      b.   Mary was dancing.

(10) a.   Necessarily, apples are Nature's toothbrush.

      b.   Apples are Nature's toothbrush.

In (5)–(7) we grasp an identity relation of some kind holding between the members of each pair—a dimension in which the two are fundamentally the same. Likewise, in (8)–(10) we detect a relation of "inclusion" or subordination, a respect in which the first member in some sense "implies" the second member. Here again the relevant dimension is that of meaning. The pairs in (5)–(7) are all (largely) identical in meaning, or "synonymous," to use the common term. They "express the same thought," "convey the same information," "describe the same situation," and so on. Similarly, the meanings of the first members of (8)–(10) include those of the second members: the thought expressed by *Mary was laughing and dancing* includes that expressed by *Mary was dancing*, the meaning of *human* implies the meaning of *mammal*, and so on.

In each case we are able to judge a certain relation between sentences, one reducible to neither sound nor form. To account for this ability, we must assume a certain body of knowledge in our possession: knowledge of meaning.

Besides revealing itself in our capacity to judge various kinds of relatedness between sentences, knowledge of linguistic meaning is apparent in our ability to judge relations between language and the world. Consider the example in (11).

(11) The cat is on the mat.

As speakers of English, we recognize that a special relation holds between this sentence and the situation depicted in part (a) of figure 12.1—one that does not hold, for instance, between (11) and situation depicted in part (b). One way of describing this relation is through the familiar notion of *truth*; sentence (11) is true in the (a)-situation, but not in the (b)-situation:

What is it that effects this association between a sentence of English and the world? What is it that we as English speakers know about (11) that allows us to make judgments as to its truth or falsity? Surely not its grammatical form; many sentences with the same grammatical form as (11) (for instance, *the cows are in the corn*) fail to be true in (a)-situation. Not its phonetic properties; the German sentence *Die Katze ist auf der Matte* is also true in the (a)-situation, but it is pronounced quite differently. What links the sentence and the situation is meaning. It is in virtue of meaning what it does that (11) is true in the (a)-situation, but not in the (b)-situation. And it is in virtue of knowing this meaning that we can judge its truth or falsity.

12.2 Knowledge of Meaning as Knowledge of Truth-Conditions

These points make clear the reality of our semantical knowledge by showing various things that this knowledge enables us to do; however, they do not establish what knowledge of meaning actually *is*. They do not show precisely what it is we have internalized in acquiring English, German, or any other natural language, which grounds our judgments of semantic relatedness or of truth and falsity.

To get some insight into this question, consider a simple hypothetical situation. Suppose you are trying to discover whether a foreign friend X knows the meaning of a particular English sentence like (11). You possess a powerful video-display device capable of generating pictures of various

Figure 12.1
Situations in which sentence (11) is (a) true and (b) not true.

conceivable situations; by using it, you find that for any situation presented to X about which you can also make a judgment, X is able to say correctly whether or not sentence (11) is true. That is, for basically the same pictorial situations in which you can give a judgment, X is able to say "true" whenever the cat is on the mat, and "false" when it is not. What would you say about X? Does he or she know the meaning of *The cat is on the mat*? Does this kind of evidence settle the matter? Think about this question for a moment.

Intuitively, we are strongly inclined to answer "yes." If X can correctly judge whether the sentence is true or false whenever you can, then X knows the meaning. The evidence seems convincing in the sense that it is difficult to see what further proof we could require of X, or what stronger proof X could provide to show that he or she understood the meaning of *The cat is on the mat*. It is hard to see what X could be "missing" that, when combined with this knowledge, would "add up" to knowledge of what (11) means.

This little thought experiment suggests a simple idea about what it is we know when we know the meaning of a sentence, an idea extensively pursued in modern linguistic semantics. It suggests that knowledge of meaning might be fruitfully viewed as knowledge of *truth-conditions*, that is, knowledge of something of the form shown in (6), where p gives what the world must be like in order for the sentence in question to be true:

(12)   *The cat is on the mat* is true if and only if p

If X has internalized such a piece of knowledge (with p filled in), then X knows the conditions under which *The cat is on the mat* is true. With this knowledge X will be able to judge for any circumstance whether (11) is true or not. But we observed above that if able to do this, then, intuitively, X knows the meaning of (11). Thus, given our thought experiment, "knowing the meaning" seems to be largely captured in terms of "knowing the truth-conditions."

If knowledge of meaning amounts to knowledge of truth-conditions, then we can give a direct account of the semantic abilities discussed above. Recall the examples (1) and (2):

(1) a. John believed that the Earth is round.

     b. John doubted that the Earth is round.

(2) a. John claimed that the Earth is round.

     b. John denied that the Earth is round.

We said that in virtue of our knowing the semantics of English, we know that the two pairs in (1) and (2) bear a relation of "semantic incompatibility" or "meaning exclusion." Suppose we explicate this relation as follows: Two sentences are incompatible if their truth-conditions, together with our real-world knowledge, forbid them from being simultaneously true. Then this will predict incompatibility correctly. The first member of the pair in (1b), for instance, will be true if and only if (iff) John claimed the Earth is round, and the second will be true iff John denied the Earth is round. Assuming that we are talking about the same assertion by John, we know that the two cannot be simultaneously true. Any denial of p is a claim that not-p, and hence not a claim that p. Thus, the two exclude each other.

The pretheoretic notions of *synonymy* ("meaning identity") and *hyponymy* ("meaning inclusion") can be treated analogously. We can say that two sentences are synonymous if their truth-conditions, taken together with our real-world knowledge, entail that they are true in the same circumstances. Likewise, we can say that one sentence implies another if any situation in which the first is true is also one in which the second is true.

Under these proposals the sentence pairs in (5)–(7) will be correctly identified as synonymous. For example, (5a) is true iff John sold a car to Mary, and (5b) is true iff Mary bought a car from John. In virtue of how the world is, any circumstance of the former sort is also one of the latter sort. Hence, the two are synonymous. Similarly, the (a)-sentence of each example (8)–(10) will imply the (b)-sentence. Any situation making (9a) true will make (9b) true as well, since any situation in which Mary was laughing and dancing is one in which Mary was dancing. And so on.

Finally, knowledge of truth-conditions will clearly account for our ability to judge that a sentence S is true or false in a given situation. If we know the truth-conditions of S, then knowing whether S is true or false is just a matter of knowing whether these conditions are or are not met.

12.3 Compositionality

Truth-conditions appear to offer a promising approach to sentence meanings and the abilities that flow from knowing them. Let us now consider some facts bearing on the *form* in which that knowledge is encoded in us. In the exploration of syntax in chapter 10 we saw that the class of well-formed sentences in English—or any other natural language—is essentially boundless. With their grammatical knowledge, human language speakers are able to construct infinite collections of well-formed sentences, such as the following (from Platts (1979)):

(13)   a.   The horse behind Pegasus is bald.

       b.   The horse behind the horse behind Pegasus is bald.

       c.   The horse behind the horse behind the horse behind Pegasus is bald.

           .

           .

Given this *creative* aspect of syntactic ability, we know that our knowledge of the well-formed sentences of English cannot take the form of a simple list. Since the list is infinite, a finite object with finite storage capacity like our brain simply could not accommodate it. On the basis of this, we conclude that syntactic knowledge must be encoded within us in the form of a finite set of rules and principles allowing us to *generate* the sentences of English from smaller, subsentential elements such as words.

Similar issues arise with meaning and knowledge of truth-conditions. The expressions of (13) are not only well-formed sentences of English, they are all meaningful as well. More than that, (13a), (13b), (13c), and so on all have *different* meanings—or different truth-conditions, as we now say. The first is true only in situations containing at least two horses, the second only in situations containing at least three horses, the third only in situations containing at least four horses, and so on. Since the collection of interpretations associated with (13a–...) is infinite in number, it is clear that our knowledge of truth-conditions for the sentences of English cannot take the form of a simple list like (14). Once again, such a list could not be accommodated in our finite brains:

(14)   a.   *The horse behind Pegasus is bald* is true iff $p1$.

       b.   *The horse behind the horse behind Pegasus is bald* is true iff $p2$.

       c.   *The horse behind the horse behind the horse behind Pegasus is bald* is true iff $p3$.

           .

           .

Reasoning as above, it seems that our semantic knowledge must also take the form of a set of productive rules or principles that allow us to calculate truth-conditions for sentences from some "smaller" semantic contributions. That is, it appears that the truth-conditions matched with a given sentence of English must be *compositionally derived*.

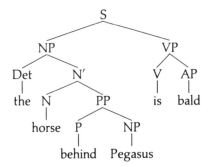

Figure 12.2
Phrase structure tree for sentence (13a), *The horse behind Pegasus is bald.*

How exactly might this go? How are the truth-conditions for a sentence composed, and from what? A plausible hypothesis is that they are calculated using internal syntactic structure. To illustrate, consider (13a), with syntax roughly as shown in figure 12.2, where N' is a nominal constituent intermediate between N and NP. (The phrase structure rules beyond those given in chapter 10 that are needed to generate this structure should be immediately clear.) Suppose we could assign some kind of semantic contribution or "value" to each of the "leaves" of this tree structure: a value to *bald*, a value to *Pegasus*, a value to *is*, and so on. Suppose further that we had a way of combining these values together for each of the branches in figure 12.2 so that, at the top, they yielded the truth-conditions for the sentence: a general way of combining the values of nouns and PPs in the configuration $[_{N'}$ N PP], a general way of combining verbs and adjectives in the configuration $[_{VP}$ V AP], a way of combining the values of NPs and VPs in the configuration $[_S$ NP VP] to yield the truth-conditions for S, and so on. Then we would in essence be using the syntactic skeleton of figure 12.2 as a guide to figuring out what it means. To borrow a phrase from Quine (1970), semantics would "chase truth up the tree of grammar."

If we could give such initial values and general combination schemes, then we could account very directly for our ability to assign truth-conditions to unbounded sequences of sentences like (13a–...). Consider the tree underlying (13b) depicted in figure 12.3. This tree differs from the one underlying (13a) in having extra $[_{NP}$ Det N'] and $[_{N'}$ N PP] branches involving the lexical items *the*, *behind*, and *horse*. But since all these elements already occur in (13a), it follows that if we have the semantic resources for computing the truth-conditions of (13a), we will "automatically" have the resources for computing the truth-conditions of (13b). Our semantic values and rules will deliver truth-conditions for (13a), (13b), and indeed *all* the sentences in the sequence.

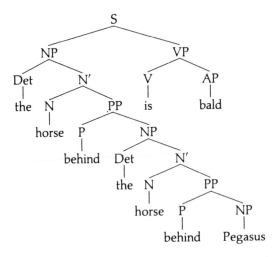

Figure 12.3
Phrase structure tree for sentence (13b). *The horse behind the horse behind Pegasus is bald.*

12.4   The Study of Meaning: Model-Theoretic Semantics

Let us now attempt to implement one version of the picture sketched above, giving elements of a theory that takes truth-conditions as the basis of our semantical knowledge and attempts to derive the truth-conditions for sentences in a compositional way. In doing this, we will adopt the basic perspective of *model theory*. As we have seen, truth-conditional theories take the view that meaning is fundamentally a relation between language and the world. Interpretation involves systematically correlating sentences with the world through the notion of truth. Model theory studies the relation between languages and worlds in a formal way. It does this by building mathematical models of worlds, using the devices of set theory, and by mapping expressions of language into them:

(15) *Language*   *Model (of a World)*
      Lexical items   →   Set-theoretic objects
      Syntactic rules for   →   Rules for combining
      building up phrases   set-theoretic objects

As (15) shows, constructing a model-theoretic semantics for a language L involves correlating the basic expressions with appropriate set-theoretic objects and giving rules that state how these constructs combine for each of the syntactic configurations of L. This yields an interpretation—an object in our model—for each of the subsentential expressions of L, and a set of truth-conditions for every sentence.

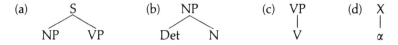

Figure 12.4
Syntactic configurations for Language L^*.

We can illustrate how a model-theoretic semantics operates by considering a small "sublanguage" of English, which we will call L^*. L^* contains the determiner elements *no*, *every*, and *some*, the common nouns *man* and *fish*, and the intransitive predicates *walks* and *drinks*. It also involves the syntactic configurations shown in figure 12.4 (where X is Det, N, or V, and where α is a lexical item). L^* thus includes phrases like *some fish, no man*, and sentences like *Every fish walks, Some man drinks*.

To construct our model-theoretic semantics for L^*, we start with some basic set A of individuals—intuitively, the set of entities in our model world M^*—and establish a general correlation between the syntactic categories of L^* and kinds of set-theoretic objects built out of A. We shall adopt the following mapping:

(16)   *Language*   *Model*
       Ns, Vs $\rightarrow$ Subsets of A
       Dets $\rightarrow$ Binary Relations on Subsets of A

The categories of common noun and intransitive verb are associated with subsets of A. Intuitively, the common noun *fish* is associated with the subset of A that contains the fishes, and the verb *walk* is associated with the subset of A containing the walkers, and so on.

Determiners are matched up with binary relations on sets of As. In particular, we will associate the determiners *no*, *every*, and *some* with the following specific relations (where '$[\![\alpha]\!]$' is to be read 'the interpretation of α'):

(17)   Dets: $[\![every]\!]$ = EVERY, where for any sets $X, Y \subseteq A$
                       EVERY $(X)\,(Y)$ iff $X \subseteq Y$

             $[\![some]\!]$ = SOME, where for any sets $X, Y \subseteq A$
                       SOME $(X)\,(Y)$ iff $X \cap Y \neq \varnothing$

             $[\![no]\!]$ =   NO, where for any sets $X, Y \subseteq A$
                       NO $(X)\,(Y)$ iff $X \cap Y = \varnothing$

The idea behind these assignments descends ultimately from the philosopher Frege, who suggested that determiners correspond to relations between properties or concepts. Thus, in examples like *Every whale is a mammal* or *Some whales are mammals*, the determiner serves to relate the properties of whalehood and mammalhood.

In the case of *every* the relation is one of subordination. Every whale is a mammal if whalehood is a "species" of mammalhood. We have captured the notion of subordination here using the subset relation. In the case of *some* the relation is one of nonexclusion; some whales are mammals if whalehood and mammalhood are not mutually exclusive properties. Again we capture this using a set-theoretic relation: that of non-empty intersection. The relation expressed by *no* is similar to the SOME relation. NO holds between two properties like whalehood and mammalhood if the two are mutually exclusive.

Having correlated the syntactic categories of L^* with set-theoretic "interpretation spaces," we can construct semantic rules of combination for each of the syntactic configurations in L^*. These are as follows:

(18)   a. $[\![[_X \alpha]]\!] = [\![\alpha]\!]$, where X is Det, N or V

      b. $[\![[_{VP} V]]\!] = [\![V]\!]$

      c. $[\![[_{NP} \text{Det N}]]\!] = \{ Y : [\![\text{Det}]\!] ([\![N]\!]) (Y) \}$

      d. $[\![[_S \text{NP VP}]]\!]$ is true if $[\![VP]\!] \in [\![NP]\!]$ and false otherwise

(18a,b) give the (essentially trivial) interpretation rules for lexical nodes and intransitive VPs. (18c) gives the interpretation of NPs as families of sets—the family of sets that stand in the "Det-relation" to the set associated with its common noun head. (18d) states that a sentence is true (in our model M^*) if, and only if, the set associated with the verb phrase falls in the family of sets associated with the subject NP.

The initial assignments plus the rules just given determine an interpretation (a set-theoretic counterpart) for every subsentential expression of L^*. These in turn determine a set of truth-conditions for every sentence with respect to M^*. To see a brief example of how this works, consider the sentence *Some man walks*. In L^*, the latter receives the syntax shown in figure 12.5. What will its truth-conditions be under our semantics? We compute them compositionally from the interpretations of the parts.

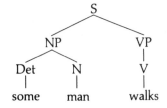

Figure 12.5
Phrase structure tree for the sentence *Some man walks* in language L^*.

By (18a), the lexical nodes in figure 12.5 all receive the same interpretations as the lexical items they dominate. *Some* corresponds to the binary relation between sets given above:

(19) $[\![_{\text{DET}} \text{ some}]\!] = [\![some]\!] = \text{SOME}$

The common noun *man* is interpreted as a set of individuals (intuitively, the set of men in our model):

(20) $[\![_{\text{N}} \text{ man}]\!] = [\![man]\!] = \{x : x \text{ is a man in } M^*\}$

Likewise, the intransitive verb *walks* is also mapped to a set of individuals, the set of runners in M^*. Taking this result together with (18b) we thus have:

(21) $[\![_{\text{VP}} \text{ walks}]\!] = [\![_{\text{V}} \text{ walks}]\!] = [\![walks]\!] = \{x : x \text{ is a walker in } M^*\}$

Rule (18c) allows us to combine the results in (19) and (20) and to compute the interpretation of NP. *Some man* will correspond to a family of sets—in particular, the family of sets bearing the SOME-relation to the set associated with *man*:

(22) $[\![_{\text{NP}} \text{ some man}]\!] = \{Y : \text{SOME} ([\![man]\!]) (Y)\}$

Given our earlier explication of the SOME-relation, this amounts to the following:

(23) $[\![_{\text{NP}} \text{ some man}]\!] = \{Y : \{x : x \text{ is a man in } M^*\} \cap Y \neq \varnothing\}$

That is, *some man* corresponds to the family of sets having a non-empty intersection with the set of men. Or, more informally, *some man* maps to the family of sets containing at least one man.

Finally, rule (18d) establishes the truth-conditions for the whole sentence. It says that *Some man walks* is true iff the family of sets corresponding to the subject NP contains the set corresponding to the VP. Given the results in (21) and (22), this comes to (24):

(24) $[_{\text{S}} \text{ Some man walks}]$ is true if $\{\text{walkers in } M^*\} \in$
      $\{Y : \{\text{men in } M^*\} \cap Y \neq \varnothing\}$,
      and false otherwise

which is just to say:

(25) $[_{\text{S}} \text{ Some man walks}]$ is true if $\{\text{men in } M^*\} \cap \{\text{walkers in } M^*\} \neq \varnothing$,
      and false otherwise

That is, *Some man walks* is true in M^* if, and only if, there is at least one individual who is both a man and a walker in M^*. This is intuitively the correct result.

The sample language L^* is a very simple one, but it shows how the model-theoretic approach attempts to formalize the basic line of thinking sketched in section 12.3. Using some resources from set theory, we can assign semantic values to basic lexical items and give rules for calculating the values of complex expressions on the basis of their syntax. This ultimately yields truth-conditions for each sentence. To carry this analysis further, we would expand the class of lexical items and syntactic configurations in our language L^*, but the basic procedure would remain the same.

12.5   Semantical Properties

Modeling of some domain by mathematical constructs has an important consequence, one that is exploited in all science; it allows us to study the properties of the domain through the mathematical properties of the constructs that model it. Since mathematical properties can be stated and manipulated precisely, our understanding gains depth and precision as a result.

These virtues hold in the domain of semantics as well. By modeling aspects of meaning formally, we can capture and study important linguistic properties in a precise way. We will illustrate this briefly with two semantical properties for the category of natural language determiners: *directional entailingness* and *conservativity*. For further exploration of the semantics of individual words, see chapter 11, "*Lexical Semantics and Compositionality*," by Barbara Partee.

12.5.1   Directional Entailingness

In the simple language L^* presented above, we modeled determiner meanings with relations between sets, and we associated English determiners with certain particular relations. These relations show a number of interesting differences. Consider the inference paradigms for *every* in (26) below (where '#' indicates an invalid inference):

(26)   a.   Every man runs.
              ⎯⎯⎯⎯⎯
              Every tall man runs.

       b.   Every tall man runs.
              ⎯⎯⎯⎯⎯
              # Every man runs.

       c.   Every man likes a green vegetable.
              ⎯⎯⎯⎯⎯
              # Every man likes spinach.

d.   Every man likes spinach.
        ―――――
     Every man likes a green vegetable.

With sentences involving *every*, we get a valid inference whenever we substitute a more specific common noun (*tall man*) for a less specific one (*man*), but not vice versa. On the other hand, we get a valid inference whenever we substitute a less specific VP (*likes a green vegetable*) for a more specific one (*likes spinach*), but again not vice versa.

Rather different patterns of inference emerge with the determiners *some* and *no*:

(27) a.   Some man runs.
           ―――――
        #Some tall man runs.

      b.   Some tall man runs.
           ―――――
           Some man runs.

      c.   Some man likes a green vegetable.
           ―――――
        #Some man likes spinach.

      d.   Some man likes spinach.
           ―――――
           Some man likes a green vegetable.

(28) a.   No man runs.
           ―――――
           No tall man runs.

      b.   No tall man runs.
           ―――――
        #No man runs.

      c.   No man likes a green vegetable.
           ―――――
           No man likes spinach.

      d.   No man likes spinach.
           ―――――
        #No man likes a green vegetable.

Evidently with *some* we must always infer from a more specific to a less specific phrase, whether it is the common noun or the VP. With *no* the situation is just the opposite: we must always infer from a less specific to a more specific phrase.

How can we state the semantical property behind these inference patterns? Taking determiners to correspond semantically to binary relations D between sets, where the common noun supplies the first argument (X) of the relation, and the VF supplies the second argument (Y), the relevant properties can captured as follows:

(29)   *Downward Entailingness*: A determiner relation D is
   a.   *downward entailing in its first argument* if for any X, Y, where $X' \subseteq X$, $D(X)(Y)$ only if $D(X')(Y)$

   b.   *downward entailing in its second argument* if for any X, Y, where $Y' \subseteq Y$, $D(X)(Y)$ only if $D(X)(Y')$

(30)   *Upward Entailingness*: A determiner relation D is
   a.   *upward entailing in its first argument* if for any X, Y, where $X \subseteq X'$, $D(X)(Y)$ only if $D(X')(Y)$

   b.   *upward entailing in its second argument* if for any X, Y, where $Y \subseteq Y'$, $D(X)(Y)$ only if $D(X)(Y')$

Thus, downwardly entailing environments are ones in which substitution of a set with a subset (from less specific to more specific) yields a valid inference, whereas upward entailing environments are ones in which substitution of a set with a superset (from more specific to less specific) yields a valid inference.

(26a–d) show that *every* is downward entailing in its first argument, the one corresponding to the common noun, but upward entailing in its second argument, the one corresponding to the VP. Similarly, (27a–d) and (28a–d) show (respectively) that *some* is upwardly entailing in both of its arguments whereas *no* is downwardly entailing in both its arguments.

Directional entailingness is a rather simple property of determiners, but one that holds considerable interest for linguists: it seems to shed light on certain puzzling facts of English grammar. Consider the distribution of words like *ever* and *anyone* and phrases like *give a damn*, *budge an inch*. These forms can occur smoothly only in certain rather restricted environments—typically the sort provided by a negative element (a word like *no*, *not*, or *never*):

(31)   a.   *John saw anything.

   b.   John didn't see anything.

(32)   a.   *I believe that she will budge an inch.

   b.   I don't believe that she will budge an inch.

(33)   a.   *Max said that he had ever been there.

　　　 b.   Max never said that he had ever been there.

　　　 c.   Max said that he hadn't ever been there.

Because of this property, expressions like *ever, anyone, anything, until, give a red cent,* and *lift a finger* are often referred to as *negative polarity items.*

One interesting question for the study of grammar is, What precisely are the environments in which negative polarity items are licensed? How are they to be characterized? The answer is not self-evident. Note that the licensing environments are not simply those involving negative words like *no, not,* or *nothing.* Negative polarity items are also sanctioned by *every* when they occur in its nominal term (the bracketed portion in (34a)). They are not, however, permitted in the VP (34b):

(34)   a.   Every [person who has *ever* visited Boston] has returned to it.

　　　 b.   *Every [person who has visited Boston] has *ever* returned to it.

This behavior contrasts with that of other determiners such as *no* and *some*:

(35)   a.   No [person who has *ever* visited Boston] has returned to it.

　　　 b.   No [person who has visited Boston] has *ever* returned to it.

(36)   a.   *Some [person who has *ever* visited Boston] has returned to it.

　　　 b.   *Some [person who has visited Boston] has ever returned to it.

The former licenses negative polarity items in both its nominal term and in the VP. The latter licenses negative polarity items in neither the nominal term nor the VP.

What is the generalization here? If we consider the directional entailingness properties discussed above, a simple answer suggests itself. Recall that *every* is downward entailing in its first argument but upward entailing in its second argument. *Some* is upwardly entailing in both arguments, and *no* is downwardly entailing in both:

(37)   EVERY (X) (Y) $\downarrow$ $\uparrow$
　　　 SOME　 (X) (Y) $\uparrow$ $\uparrow$
　　　 NO　　 (X) (Y) $\downarrow$ $\downarrow$

Recall also that in sentences like (34)–(36), the nominal term (the bracketed portion) corresponds to the X argument of Det and the VP corresponds to the Y argument. The generalization is clearly the following (from Ladusaw 1980):

(38)   A negative polarity item is licensed in a downward entailing
　　　 environment.

That is, whenever the phrase containing *anyone, budge an inch,* and so on corresponds to a downwardly entailed argument, the negative polarity item is licensed; otherwise it is not.

These facts argue strongly that the semantic property of directional entailingness has reality for speakers of English. It is the property to which we are "attuned" in judging the acceptability of sentences containing negative polarity items.

12.5.2   Conservativity

Directional entailingness is a semantical property that distinguishes determiners like *every, some,* and *no* in different argument positions. It is of interest because it appears to shed light on specific facts about the grammar of English. There are other semantical properties, however, that *every, some,* and *no* share; these are of interest because they seem to tell us something about human language generally. They appear to give insight into what constitute a "possible human determiner concept."

One such property that has been studied in some detail is that of *conservativity.* Consider our three determiner relations again:

(39)   a.   EVERY $(X)(Y)$ iff $X \subseteq Y$

      b.   SOME $(X)(Y)$ iff $X \cap Y \neq \varnothing$

      c.   NO $(X)(Y)$ iff $X \cap Y = \varnothing$

Given (39a), we can evaluate the truth of a sentence containing *every* by sorting through the set corresponding to the common noun (X), checking to see if all its members are in the set corresponding to the VP (Y). Similarly with *some* (39b), we can sort through the common noun set, checking to see that some of its members are in the VP set. Finally, with *no* (39c), we can sort through the common noun set, checking to see that none of its members is in the VP set. There is an important regularity here. Notice that in each case we can work always with members of the common noun set X in checking whether the given relation holds. The common noun uniformly "sets the scene"; it limits the collection of individuals over which we must range in making the evaluation.

This regularity observed with *every, some,* and *no* is not found in all quantifierlike relations. Consider the relations expressed by *all-but* and *everyone-except* as they occur in examples like (40a, b):

(40)   a.   *All but* boys received a prize.

      b.   *Everyone except* mothers attended.

Intuitively, to evaluate whether (40a) is true, we do not sort through the set of boys to see if some quantity of them are prize recipients; rather, we must look precisely at non-boys. Similarly, we do not look at mothers but rather at non-mothers in evaluating (40b).

This notion of "setting the scene" or "fixing the collection over which we quantify," which characterizes *every, some,* and *no* but not *all-but* and *everyone-except,* is, in essence, the property of conservativity. We may define it more precisely as follows:

(41) A determiner relation D is *conservative* if for any X, Y $D(X)(Y)$ iff $D(X)(X \cap Y)$.

A conservative determiner relation is one that holds between two sets X, Y just in case it holds between the first and the intersection of the first with the second. Since X and $X \cap Y$ are both subsets of X, this means that we always range over members of the common noun denotation in evaluating whether a conservative determiner relation holds. X sets the scene.

Conservativity is a property that appears to characterize all human language determiner concepts—not just *every, some,* and *no,* but also *few, many, most, two, three, several,* and so on, and their many counterparts in world languages. It is what might be called a *semantic universal.* This result is quite surprising on reflection, since there is no clear a priori reason why things should be so. There is no sense in which nonconservative determiner relations are "conceptually inaccessible"; nor are they somehow "unnatural" or "unuseful." We have noted informally that *all-but* and *everyone-except* do not share the conservativity property because their common noun does not specify the range of quantification. Notice now that although these expressions are not themselves determiners in English (indeed they are not even syntactic constituents), there is no difficulty in defining a hypothetical determiner relation NALL having exactly their semantics:

(42) $NALL(X)(Y)$ iff $(A - X) \subseteq Y$

(where X and Y are subsets of A, our model's universe of things). Under this definition a sentence like *Nall squares are striped* would be true, and presumably useful, in exactly the same situations as the sentences *All but squares are striped* or *Everything except squares is striped* (see figure 12.6). *Nall* is thus a perfectly reasonable candidate for a natural language determiner relation on general grounds. Nonetheless, no such relation occurs in English or in any other human language as far as we know. Nonconservative determiners like *nall* simply seem to be disallowed.

Why conservative determiners should be singled out by natural language is an interesting question that we cannot pursue in detail here. Results by Keenan and Stavi (1986), however, suggest that this may arise from natural language determiner meanings being typically composed out

Figure 12.6
Situation in which the sentence *Nall squares are striped* is true, where NALL $(X)(Y)$ iff $(A - X) \subseteq Y$.

of certain basic, "atomic" meanings. It can be shown formally that if one begins with elementary determiner concepts such as *EVERY, THE (ONE)* and *POSS*(essor) and augments this set with more complex determiner meanings constructed by elementary operations like intersection and complementation, then the result will include only conservative determiners. This is because the "atomic" determiners are all conservative, and elementary set-theoretic operations preserve conservativity. The ubiquity of conservative determiners may thus reflect a deep fact about the way our space of determiner concepts is structured: that it forms a so-called Boolean algebra over certain elementary determiner meanings.

Suggestions for Further Reading

The truth-conditional approach to semantics has been developed along a number of different lines. An excellent, extended introduction to the general model-theoretic framework discussed in this chapter is Chierchia and McConnell-Ginet 1990. A good follow-up volume in the same framework, but at a slightly higher level of technical complexity, is Dowty, Wall, and Peters 1992.

A classic paper setting out a somewhat different approach to truth-conditions and their relation to meaning is Davidson 1967. Davidson's views are united with Chomskian theory (which emphasizes knowledge of language as the object of linguistic theory) in Larson and Segal (1995). The latter is a textbook that extends Davidson's truth-conditional analysis to many natural language constructions.

A clear nontechnical introduction to the relational analysis of natural language determiners is Bach 1989, lectures III and IV. See also the chapter on "Generalized Quantifiers" in Partee, ter Meulen, and Wall 1990 for an extended introductory discussion of quantifiers and quantifier properties. Technical works in the relational analysis of determiners include Barwise and Cooper 1981; Higginbotham and May 1981; and Keenan and Stavi 1986. For a conceptual, philosophical discussion of the relational account see Wiggins 1980.

The phenomenon of negative polarity is discussed in more detail in Ladusaw 1980 and in Linebarger 1987. The first argues for the analysis given in this chapter, and the second argues against it.

The truth-conditional approach to natural language meaning is not universally accepted. For criticisms and an alternative line of investigation see Jackendoff (1983, 1991).

Problems

12.1 Show how the appropriate truth-conditions *Every fish drinks* are derived using our semantic interpretation rules for L^*.

12.2 The language L^* contains *every*, *some*, and *no*. Consider extending it to include the determiners *two* and *most*. What determiner relations should be associated with these elements?

12.3 Extending L^* to include proper names like *John* and *Eunice* raises an interesting question. In our semantic theory for L^*, NPs are interpreted as sets of sets. But, intuitively, it seems that the semantic value of *John* should be an individual j (a person). Can you see a way to interpret proper names that reconciles the view that NPs denote sets of sets with our intuition that *John* ought to be associated with an individual?

12.4 Examine the determiners *all*, *at least two*, *few*, and *not many* with respect to upward and downward entailingness, and check whether the distribution of negative polarity items conforms to these results.

12.5 Do the rules in (17) determine that *every* is downwardly entailing in its first argument position and upwardly entailing in its second argument position? Similarly, do the interpretation rules for *some* and *no* allow us to predict their directional entailingness properties?

12.6 In view of the definition of conservativity, one simple way to check whether a given determiner Det is conservative is to consider the validity of sentences of the following general form, for any nominal A and VP B:

Det A B iff Det A is an A that B
are As

(For instance, *Both men run iff both men are men that run*.) If the scheme always yields a true sentence for any substitution of A and B, then the determiner is conservative. If the scheme yields a false sentence, then the determiner is not conservative. Using this scheme, investigate the conservativity of *every*, *some*, and *exactly two*.

12.7 The expression *only* appears determinerlike in sentences like *Only cats meow*. Consider, however, the following simple instance of the scheme in question 12.6:

Only men run iff only men are men who run

Is this sentence always true, or are there situations in which it is false? If the latter, does this overthrow the claim that natural language determiners are conservative, or can you think of a way of defending the latter claim?

12.8 In the chapter it was claimed that natural language determiners are uniformly conservative, but consider this sentence (due to Westerstahl):

Many Scandinavians have won the Nobel Prize.

On reflection this example is ambiguous. What are its readings? Do any of them raise problems for conservativity?

References

Bach, E. (1989). *Informal lectures on formal semantics*. Albany, NY: SUNY Press.

Barwise, J., and R. Cooper (1981). Generalized quantifiers and natural language. *Linguistics and Philosophy* 4, 159–219.

Chierchia, G., and S. McConnell-Ginet (1990). *Meaning and grammar*. Cambridge, MA: MIT Press.

Davidson, D. (1967) Truth and meaning. In *Inquiries into truth and interpretation*. Oxford: Oxford University Press.

Dowty, D., R. Wall, and S. Peters (1992). *An introduction to Montague's semantic theory.* 2nd ed. Dordrecht, Netherlands: Kluwer.

Higginbotham, J., and R. May (1981). Questions, quantifiers and crossing. *The Linguistic Review* 1, 41–79.

Jackendoff, R. (1983). *Semantics and cognition.* Cambridge, MA: MIT Press.

Jackendoff, R. (1991). *Semantic structures.* Cambridge, MA: MIT Press.

Keenan, E., and Y. Stavi (1986). A semantic characterization of natural language determiners. *Linguistics and Philosophy* 9, 253–326.

Ladusaw, W. (1980). On the notion "affective" in the analysis of negative polarity items. *Journal of Linguistic Research* 1.

Larson, R., and G. Segal (1995). *Knowledge of meaning.* Cambridge, MA: MIT Press.

Linebarger, M. (1987). Negative polarity and grammatical representation. *Linguistics and Philosophy* 10, 325–387.

Partee, B., A. ter Meulen, and R. Wall (1990). *Mathematical methods in linguistics.* Dordrecht, Netherlands: Kluwer.

Platts, M. (1979). *Ways of meaning.* London: Routledge and Kegan Paul.

Quine, W. V. O. (1970). *Philosophy of logic.* Englewood Cliffs, NJ: Prentice-Hall.

Wiggins, D. (1980). "Most" and "all": Some comments on a familiar program, and on the logical form of quantified sentences. In M. Platts, ed., *Reference, truth and reality,* 318–346. London: Routledge and Kegan Paul.

Chapter 13

Brain Regions of Relevance to Syntactic Processing

Edgar B. Zurif

This chapter discusses aphasia research, that is, research on language disorders resulting from focal brain damage. The aim is to provide a view of how parts of the sentence comprehension system are neurologically organized. To this end, a description will be offered of how the failure to represent particular forms of syntactic information can be traced to processing disruptions that can be localized in the brain. This will provide a basis for inferring how different brain regions normally serve syntactic analysis during comprehension.

13.1 The Clinical Material

The studies that illuminate this neurologically based functional architecture build upon clinical descriptions first provided in the 1870s, at the start of the modern era of aphasia research (e.g., Wernicke 1874/1977). These "classical" descriptions have it that there are two kinds of language failure and that each can be related to a specific region of brain damage.

One kind, now called Broca's aphasia, clinically appears as an output problem. That is, comprehension is relatively normal; but speech is nonfluent, syntactically limited, and "agrammatic" such that grammatical morphemes, both bound and free, tend to be omitted. This aphasia is generally associated with damage to the left frontal lobe of the brain. And this includes a region in the third frontal convolution referred to as Broca's area—namely, that portion of the cortex in front of the primary motor zone for the muscles serving speech (Goodglass and Kaplan 1972).

The second kind of aphasia, now termed Wernicke's aphasia, is characterized by fluent and effortless speech, with phrasal construction appearing to be largely intact. But speech in this syndrome tends to be empty,

The writing of the manuscript and some of the research reported in it were supported by NIH Grants AG 10496 and DC 00081. I am very grateful to Yosef Grodzinsky and Marnie Naeser for their help.

381

marked by the use of vague filler words ("thing" and "this" and "that"). Also, comprehension is usually noticeably impaired. This aphasia results from damage to the posterior region of the left hemisphere—particularly to Wernicke's area, an area in the superior temporal gyrus adjacent to the cortical region involved in hearing (e.g., Goodglass and Kaplan 1972).

It will be noted that these descriptions emphasize the distinction between speaking and comprehension and that this emphasis has commonsense force and a certain clinical reality. But these classical descriptions have turned out to be seriously incomplete. As will be shown in this chapter, a fuller understanding of the aphasias—indeed of brain-language relations generally—requires reference not only to the observable activities of speaking and listening, but also to abstract linguistic structures and processes.

Before elaborating on this claim, however, a neurological update is in order: The brain area involved in Broca's aphasia now seems to have greater extent than initially proposed. Broca's area in the third frontal convolution is no longer considered to be singularly important; rather, adjacent and deeper areas have also been implicated (e.g., Naeser et al. 1989). Still, the fact remains that the modal lesion site for Broca's aphasia is clearly distinguishable from that for Wernicke's aphasia, where, in line with early descriptions, the greatest involvement is still considered to be in the superior temporal gyrus. In brief, each of these two aphasias still has brain localizing value—a fact that must be borne in mind throughout the remainder of this chapter.

13.2   Sentences That Aphasic Patients Have Difficulty Understanding

13.2.1   Some Initial Characterizations

Although for many years, descriptions of Broca's aphasia emphasized the output disorder, it was, nonetheless, recognized that comprehension, too, was not entirely normal. As earlier noted, the working phrase was always "*relatively* normal" comprehension; however, the results of a series of experiments in the 1970s and 1980s belied even this characterization (e.g., Caplan and Futter 1986; Caramazza and Zurif 1976; Zurif, Caramazza, and Myerson 1972; and see Grodzinsky 1990 for a review). By assessing comprehension via sentence-picture matching tests (the patient hears a sentence and chooses its correct depiction), comprehension in Broca's aphasia was observed to be relatively limited, not relatively normal.

Two general patterns emerged from this work in the 1970s and 1980s. The first had to do with word-order relations within a sentence. This pattern can be illustrated by the contrasting sentence: "It was the girl who chased the boy" and "It was the boy whom the girl chased." In both sentences the girl is causing the event to unfold and is thereby assigned the role of agent of the action. The boy is the person affected by the action in both sentences; he is assigned in each case what is termed the role of theme. What differentiates the two sentences is the order of mention of the participants involved in the activity. In the first sentence—referred to as a subject-cleft construction—the first participant encountered is the agent; in the second sentence—referred to as an object-cleft construction —the theme is the first encountered. This difference is crucial. In English sentences it is much more usual for agents to appear in first position, and themes in second. In other words, the agent-first position is the canonical position in English syntax. And, directly to the point of this chapter, Broca's patients showed good comprehension for sentences containing this order—for sentences such as subject-clefts. By contrast, when canonical order was violated, as in object-cleft sentences, the Broca's patients performed poorly on the sentence-picture matching tests.

The second comprehension pattern turned on whether or not semantic and/or plausibility cues were present in sentences. By systematically manipulating the availability of such cues, the studies in the 1970s and 1980s documented that Broca's patients could understand sentences even with complicated (noncanonical) syntax when plausibility considerations supported "educated guesses." So, they could understand "It was the mouse that the cat chased;" but, as mentioned earlier, they could not understand "It was the boy whom the girl chased." Both are noncanonical (object-cleft) sentences; the first, however, constrains guessing in a way that the second does not—mice rarely chase cats, but boys are as likely to chase girls, as girls, boys.

These result patterns have held up reasonably well over the years. Although exceptions have been observed, it remains a fairly solid generalization that in the absence of plausibility constraints, Broca's patients show better comprehension for canonical, agent-first sequences than for noncanonical sequences (e.g., Caplan and Hildebrandt 1988; Grodzinsky 1990).

Comparable analyses have not appeared for Wernicke's patients—and probably not by chance. Although Wernicke's patients also seem to have considerable difficulty understanding noncanonical constructions, their comprehension problem seems less syntactically focused than it is for Broca's patients; it seems to require also a consideration of semantic factors. For example, faced with "It was the boy whom the girl chased," Wernicke's patients are as likely to point incorrectly to the depiction of a girl hitting, as opposed to chasing, a boy as they are to confuse agent and theme (in the manner of Broca's patients).

As it happens, this difference between Wernicke's and Broca's has lately figured importantly in thinking about brain-language relations from a real-time processing perspective. To make sense of this perspective, however, we first need to consider the Broca's syntactic limitation on its own. This follows.

13.2.2   The Extent of the Syntactic Breakdown in Broca's Aphasia

The initial accounts held that no syntactic capacities at all are retained in Broca's aphasia, other, that is, than the ability to identify lexical categories (nouns and verbs) (e.g., Caramazza and Zurif 1976). In this view, in the absence of any semantic and/or plausibility constraints, the patients were seen to rely solely on the nongrammatical strategy of assigning thematic roles—agent, theme, goal, and the like—to linear strings of nouns and verbs. More specifically, it was hypothesized that the Broca's patients could bank only on the usual, or canonical, agent-first position—that is, they could rely only on the strategy of assigning agency to the first encountered noun in a sentence. This worked in most cases, but not always—not, for instance, for object-cleft sentences in which the first noun is the theme, not the agent. (Again, in "It was the boy whom the girl chased," the first N ("boy") is the person chased, not the person chasing.)

This characterization of Broca's having no syntactic capacity at all now, however, seems too harsh. The argument against it turns on error patterns. Specifically, it turns on the fact that Broca's patients are very rarely 100 percent wrong—or even significantly below chance—for sentences such as object-clefts, where the first noun is not an agent (Caplan and Futter 1986; Caramazza and Zurif 1976; Grodzinsky 1986; Wulfeck 1988). But with no syntax available to the patient, with thematic assignment rooted to the agent-first strategy, the Broca's patient would be expected *always* to interpret object-clefts backwards (regarding who chased whom); they would not be expected ever to perform at the roughly chance level that is most typically observed. In effect, the agent-first strategy does not seem to be the only determinant of sentence comprehension; there seems to be some opposing force.

13.2.3   The Trace Deletion Hypothesis

This notion of competing forces is at the heart of a descriptive generalization formulated by Yosef Grodzinsky (1986, 1990) and much discussed in the recent literature. His account is grounded in *government-binding theory* (Chomsky 1981), wherein movement of a constituent leaves a trace (an abstract, phonetically empty marker) in the position it vacated. As described elsewhere in this volume, traces are deemed crucial for the assignment of thematic roles in sentences, since these roles are assigned to hierarchically structured positions regardless of the assignee. If a thematic position is filled with a lexical NP, then it receives its thematic role directly. But if a thematic position contains a trace, then the trace is assigned the thematic role and the moved constituent (the antecedent) that left the trace gets its role only indirectly, by being coindexed to the trace.

Grodzinsky's characterization of the comprehension limitation in Broca's aphasia is that, although patients of this type appreciate hierarchical syntactic organization, they cannot represent traces and, therefore, cannot grammatically assign thematic roles to moved constituents. Faced with a thematically unassigned noun phrase, the Broca's patient applies the above-mentioned agent-first strategy. But in contrast to the earlier accounts, Grodzinsky's claim is that this strategy is applied in the context of an otherwise normally elaborated syntactic representation.

How Grodzinsky's analysis works can be illustrated by referring again to the cleft sentences, this time to their abstract linguistic representations. Consider first the object-cleft construction. Its representation can be approximated as follows: "It was the boy$_i$ whom the girl chased $(t)_i$." (The vacated slot, or gap, in the object position of the verb "chased" is indicated by the trace (t); and the coindexation of the moved constituent and the trace is shown by the subscript (i).) Normally, the moved constituent "the boy" is assigned the role of theme via coindexation. But Broca's patients cannot represent the trace and cannot, therefore, grammatically assign any role to "the boy." Accordingly, the patients adopt the agent-first default strategy, but by Grodzinsky's reasoning this sets in motion competing thematic assignments: Specifically, the incorrect strategic assignment of agency to the moved constituent ("the boy") is countered by the normal grammatical assignment of agency to the constituent that has not undergone movement ("the girl"). Faced with two agents (on a sentence-picture matching task), the patient is forced into a guessing situation that leads to random performance, as opposed to a systematic inversion of thematic roles.

Consider now the linguistic representation of the subject-cleft: "It was the girl$_i$ who $(t)_i$ chased the boy." Here "the boy" has not undergone movement, and movement of "the girl" is from the subject position. The agent-first strategy works; were grammatical capacity normal, it would yield the same solution—"girl" as agent.

Grodzinsky's theoretical analysis applies, as might be expected, to more than just cleft sentences. Generally, Broca's patients understand sentences in which constituents have been moved from subject position (for which the agent-first strategy works), and they show poor comprehension for sentences involving movement from object position (for which the agent-first strategy does not work). This generalization includes subject-relative sentences (good comprehension) and object-relative sentences (poor comprehension)—two sentence types that will figure importantly in studies of real-time processing to be presented in a later section of this chapter.

13.2.4 Trace-Deletion-Hypothesis Updates

Syntactic theory is under vigorous development, and current work suggests that syntactic representations are richer in traces than previously thought—richer in traces than is suggested in government-binding theory, the theory informing Grodzinsky's trace deletion hypothesis. A recent development in this respect is that termed the verb phrase (VP)-internal-subject hypothesis (Kitagawa 1986; McNally 1992). The suggestion here is that the grammatical subject (even in simple active sentences) does not receive its thematic role directly from the verb. Rather the subject NP is claimed to originate within the VP and to occupy its surface position only by undergoing movement and leaving a trace behind. The assignment of a thematic role to the moved subject NP is, therefore, mediated by the trace. Only unmoved object NPs are directly assigned thematic roles.

Making use of the VP-internal-subject hypothesis, Mauner, Fromkin, and Cornell (1993) and Hickok (1992; also Hickok, Zurif, and Canseco-Gonzalez 1993) have independently reformulated Grodzinsky's trace deletion hypothesis. Both criticize Grodzinsky for his use of the agent-first strategy (they consider it an unnecessary theoretical encumbrance), and both offer the same alternative. For both, it is a matter of how many traces—or trace-antecedent chains—appear in any one sentence. If there is only one, all the Broca's patient need do is "fill-in" a thematic role by the process of elimination. But if there are two traces or chains, there are too many unknowns and the patient must guess.

This can all be illustrated by some examples provided in Hickok's (1992) analysis. The representations are for subject-cleft and object-cleft sentences —that is, for the same constructions considered earlier, but this time as specified by the VP-internal-subject hypothesis: respectively, "It was the girl$_i$ who [$_{VP}$ (t)$_i$ chased the boy]" and "It was the boy$_i$ [whom the girl$_j$ [$_{VP}$ (t)$_j$ chased (t)$_i$]]." As in the earlier illustrations of the linguistic representations of subject- and object-cleft sentences, vacated positions are indexed by traces (t) and coindexation is shown by matching subscripts (either i or j). What has been added to the representations here is that the VPs have been set out in brackets. This has been done in order to show the movement of the subject NP from within the VP. And, of course, it is this movement and its resultant trace that distinguish the present set of representations from those entered earlier when describing Grodzinsky's work. For the subject-cleft construction, the NP "the boy" is in object position of the verb "chased"; it has not undergone movement (this is the same as in Grodzinsky's analysis), and therefore it receives its thematic role—theme (the person being chased)—directly from the verb. Accordingly, the thematic role for the NP "the girl" (which has been moved from the subject position of "chased" within the VP) can be filled in. It can be assigned the role of agent, the one remaining role that fits in with a depiction of the sentence. By contrast, for the object-cleft sentence, both of the NPs have undergone movement. As in Grodzinsky's formulations, the NP "the boy" has been moved from its position as object of the verb "chased" (as indicated by subscript i); and, as now dictated by the VP-internal-subject hypothesis, the NP "the girl," this time being in subject position of the verb "chased," has also been moved (as indicated by subscript j). Both thematic role assignments must thus be mediated by traces. And since Broca's patients cannot capture antecedent-trace links for the purpose of comprehension, they cannot narrow their options—they cannot fill in. So they guess. In this manner, chance performance results from completely unspecified thematic assignment; unlike Grodzinsky's original formulation, there is no need to pit grammatical and nongrammatical (strategic) forces against each other.

The matter does not rest here, however. Grodzinsky (1993) has lately challenged the Mauner et al. and Hickok accounts. He bases his challenge on the demonstration that a different pattern of comprehension breakdown occurs for sentences featuring so-called "psych" verbs—verbs that do not take agents, but rather experiencers (as in, "It is the young man that Mary desires" where "Mary" is to be considered the experiencer of "desires," not its agent). In such sentences the nongrammatical strategic assignment of agent to the moved constituent "the young man" is not met by a like grammatical assignment of agent to "Mary"; rather, it is agent versus experiencer.

The consequences of this mismatch are taken up in the problems section. For the present, however, the similarity of these accounts must be emphasized, not their few differences. It should be apparent that Mauner, Fromkin, and Cornell, and Hickok, and Grodzinsky, before them, all agree on what is particularly problematic for Broca's patients; namely, the inability of these patients to represent intrasentence dependency relations involving traces and their resultant inability to understand noncanonical sentences in which constituents have been extracted from object position.

What is next considered is the source of this problem. The question here is whether the problem reflects a fundamental loss of syntactic competence or whether it reflects a processing disruption, according to which, knowledge of syntactic dependencies is still present but cannot be implemented during the act of comprehension. As forecast at the outset of this chapter, the evidence will suggest the processing explanation to be the more likely.

13.3　Processing Disruptions in Aphasic Comprehension

13.3.1　Dissociations between Comprehension and Grammatical Judgment

The idea that comprehension limitations of the sort described above are to be linked to processing disruptions turns on a discrepancy between judgment and comprehension data (Linebarger, Schwartz, and Saffran 1983)—not so much of a discrepancy as originally claimed (see Mauner, Fromkin, and Cornell 1993; Zurif and Grodzinsky 1983), but enough to be dramatic and surprising. Specifically, Linebarger, Schwartz and Saffran found that Broca's patients, with noticeable syntactic limitations in comprehension, were, nonetheless, able to detect a variety of grammatical deformations, including some that required an awareness of syntactic dependencies involving traces. So, for example, they could detect the ungrammaticality of "Mary ate the bread that I baked a cake," where there is no empty position—no trace—to associate with "bread" (as there is in "Mary ate the bread$_i$ that I baked $(t)_i$").

What emerges from this is a picture of Broca's patients in which they can be seen to carry out quite complex judgments, yet lack the ability to exploit this sensitivity for comprehension. And this seems to call for a processing account—for recognition that the limitation is NOT due to some unalterable loss of knowledge that would be revealed on all tasks, judgment as well as comprehension. (See Shankweiler et al. 1989, and Wulfeck and Bates 1991, for different variations on this idea.)

The goal, then, is to specify the nature of the processing disruption: to determine where the defect is in the system that converts the input stream into an interpreted structure.

Linebarger, Schwartz, and Saffran (1983) suggest that the problem is one of thematic mapping, an operation that can be placed somewhere between syntax and meaning. In this view the problem arises, not from a failure to parse sentences for their grammatical functions, but rather from a difficulty in assigning those functions the appropriate thematic roles (that is, agent, theme, and the like).

Upon reflection, however, the connection between grammatical judgment data and this mapping hypothesis seems to be very indirect and not particularly compelling. After all, the task of making a grammatical judgment about a sentence need not depend upon the normal construction of a syntactic representation. Consider again the example "Mary ate the bread that I baked a cake." As pointed out above, there is no trace after "baked" to associate with "bread." In effect, "baked" has too many arguments in this ungrammatical sentence. But noticing this need not require a fully elaborated syntactic analysis. Rather, all that need be done is to check the number of arguments that "bake" can take and the number of arguments locally present. And this is a very different matter from filling an empty position in a nondeformed sentence in real time—from establishing a dependency relation between a trace and its moved constituent during the strict time constraints imposed upon the initial structure-building process.

Moreover, even if it is a mapping problem, it is clearly not an undifferentiated one—one that arises for all syntactic types. Schwartz and her colleagues acknowledge this by pointing to what they term a "thematic transparency effect"; namely, that Broca's patients have noticeably more difficulty in mapping NPs that have moved and left traces than in mapping NPs that have not moved (Schwartz et al. 1987). But since this distinction is also at the heart of the various versions of the trace-deletion hypothesis (Grodzinsky 1986; Hickok 1992; Mauner et al. 1993), the "transparency" notion does not help us to decide whether the problem is one of mapping or of initially establishing the link between a trace and its antecedent. In order to make this decision, we must observe what happens as comprehension unfolds in real-time.

13.3.2   Priming and Gap-Filling

Techniques are now available with which to measure real-time operating characteristics of processes involved in syntactic analysis. The reference here is to the on-line techniques described by Fodor elsewhere in this volume; specifically, the priming techniques that enable us to detect the role of traces *during* sentence comprehension—that enable us to observe the real-time formation of a dependency relation between a trace and its antecedent.

Before discussing how these techniques have been applied to the study of aphasia, it will be helpful to review what priming is and how it has been used to examine normal syntactic processing.

Priming has to do with how lexical processing is facilitated under certain conditions. The measure used is either word naming time or lexical decision time—the time it takes to determine whether or not a string of letters forms a word. We will focus here on "semantic" priming, which refers to the finding that a lexical decision is faster for a target word when that word is immediately preceded by a meaningfully related word than when preceded by an unrelated word (Meyer, Schvaneveldt, and Ruddy 1975; Neely 1977). This result is taken to indicate that the first word—the prime word—has been present to aid the recognition of the subsequent, or target, word. And this, in turn, connects to the assumption of an automatic propagation of activation within a network of mental representations in which word meaning is enmeshed—a spread of activation from the mental representation of the prime word to representations of semantically related words including the target (Collins and Loftus 1975; Neely 1977).

So, with respect to the detection of traces, if a target word related to the moved constituent is primed at the trace site (or gap)—that is, if at the gap, a lexical decision for such a target is faster than for a word unrelated to the moved constituent—if this happens, then it can reasonably be assumed that the moved constituent has been *re*activated at the gap to provide the prime for the target. (See Fodor in this volume and Swinney and Fodor 1989 for reviews of this work.) This phenomenon is referred to as gap-filling. And such reactivation reliably occurs for certain forms of constituent movement as in cleft and relative sentences of the sort mentioned earlier. In effect, in these constructions, the trace appears to have a real-time processing consequence—one that can be defined in terms of a finely grained pattern of lexical reactivation.

13.3.3   Gap-Filling in Aphasia

The effects of focal brain damage on gap-filling are also now being examined. This work widens the perspective to include Wernicke's aphasic patients as well as Broca's. And it builds upon the rather consistent finding that Wernicke's patients, but not Broca's patients, show roughly normal lexical activation characteristics in circumstances that foster automatic processing—that is, in circumstances in which the processing is mandatory and not under the control of statistical bias or indeed any conscious strategy (e.g., Milberg and Blumstein 1981; Prather, Zurif, and Love 1992; Prather, Zurif, Stern, and Rosen 1992). In these circumstances Wernicke's patients, but not Broca's, show the normal pattern of facilitated word recognition (lexical decision) for targets preceded by semantically related primes.

Of course, the Wernicke's patients' data can be taken only to indicate initial lexical activation and the spread of this activation to semantically associated nodes. It does not necessarily signal a normally nuanced pattern of activation—a pattern by which only the correct node, the precise word meaning, remains active. Contrariwise, the Broca's patients' failure to show normal priming should not be taken to indicate complete insensitivity to prime-target relations. These patients are not, after all, disbarred from activating word meanings. Rather, on the evidence available, automatic priming in Broca's aphasia seems to be temporally protracted; or, more to the point, lexical meaning activation as revealed by priming seems to have a slower-than-normal time course (Prather, Zurif, and Love 1992; Prather, Zurif, Stern, and Rosen 1992).

The effects of the Broca's aberrant lexical activation might reasonably be supposed to ramify throughout the comprehension system. Gap-filling should be especially vulnerable. This is an operation that is implemented under strict time constraints. And, this being so, the inability of Broca's patients to represent antecedent-trace relations can be viewed in real-time terms as the inability to reactivate the moved lexical item at the normal time in the processing sequence—in time, that is, to fill the gap left by its movement.

It is this scenario that has lately been put to the test in two separate experiments (Zurif et al. 1993; Swinney et al. 1993).

The first experiment (Zurif et al. 1993) used subject-relative constructions of the sort, "The man liked the tailor$_i$ with the British accent who $(t)_i$ claimed to know the queen." As shown by this example, movement from subject position is hypothesized. And in this respect the subject-relative construction is equivalent to the subject-cleft construction that has been used to illustrate both Grodzinsky's and Hickok's work. The shift from cleft to relative is motivated here only by the fact that normal gap-filling experiments have made greater use of the latter.

The subject-relative construction also offered the possibility of revealing whether the brain areas implicated in Broca's and Wernicke's aphasia are distinguishable in terms of the way in which each serves syntactic analysis. The relevant point in this respect is that Broca's and Wernicke's patients differ, not only with respect to lexical activation, but also in their ability to understand the subject-relative construction. Broca's patients, as already indicated, show relatively normal comprehension for this construction. But Wernicke's patients are unpredictable, more often than not showing chance comprehension (e.g., Grodzinsky 1984). So, do Broca's patients show normal syntactic analysis as suggested by Linebarger, Schwartz, and Saffran (1983)? Or does their aberrant lexical activation pattern disallow normal gap-filling, requiring, instead, a reliance on one or another non-grammatical strategy for thematic assignment? And, to consider a reverse situation, do Wernicke's patients show normal gap-filling even though they often ultimately fail to achieve a normal level of comprehension for this sentence type?

The assessment of gap-filling and the range of possibilities just outlined, turned on the use of the on-line task termed cross-modal lexical priming (CMLP) (Swinney, Onifer, Prather, and Hirshkowitz 1979; see also the Fodor chapter, this volume). The features of the task are these: Subjects listen to a sentence over earphones (delivered uninterruptedly and at a normal speaking rate) and at one point, while listening to the sentence, are required to make a lexical decision for a visually presented letter string— the target probe—flashed on a screen in front of them.

To discover whether the moved constituent was reactivated, or filled, at the gap (thus providing the prime), lexical decision times were recorded for antecedent-related target probes and for letter string probes that formed semantically unrelated control words—that is, formed words that the antecedent could not prime. For the example given earlier, "The man liked the tailor$_i$ with the British accent^1 who^2 $(t)_i$ claimed to know the queen," the visual probes were "clothes" (the probe for the antecedent, "tailor") and "weight" (the control probe).

As indicated by the superscripts 1 and 2, priming was examined at two points—at the gap indexed by the trace (superscript 2) and at a pregap position (superscript 1). The latter served as a baseline; it allowed the experimenters to distinguish structurally governed *re*activation at the gap site from any residual activation due simply to the earlier appearance of the antecedent ("the tailor"). The inclusion of this pregap baseline was of particular importance when testing Broca's aphasic patients; in the face of their slower-than-normal lexical activation, residual priming was clearly a possibility. At any rate, at each point—pregap and gap—priming was determined by comparing the lexical decision time for the related visual probe to that for the unrelated visual probe.

The data that were obtained are straightforward. A control group of elderly, neurologically intact subjects and the Wernicke's patients showed gap-filling; the Broca's patients did not. Specifically, the neurologically intact and the Wernicke's aphasic subjects showed priming (relative facilitation in lexical decision for words related to antecedents) at gap sites but not at pregap sites. The Broca's patients did not show priming at either position.

The data clearly point to the different roles played by the brain areas implicated in Broca's and Wernicke's aphasia, respectively. The first-mentioned area is crucial for the real-time formation of intrasentence dependency relations—for gap-filling—in a way that the second is not. Indeed, the data show that the Broca's patients cannot normally establish such relations even for subject-relative sentences that they interpret at a level significantly above chance.

As earlier noted, a second experiment was also carried out (Swinney et al. 1993). In this one, object-relative sentences were used, these being equivalent to object-clefts in terms of constituent movement and trace location (just as subject-relatives are equivalent to subject-clefts). Actually, the object relatives were either plausibly or semantically constrained, since the intention was to have the patients actively listening for meaning. Even so, given the Broca's failure to fill gaps for subject-relatives, there was little expectation that they would normally form dependency relations for object-relatives. In fact, the interest in using object-relatives had mostly to do with Wernicke's patients. The aim was to broaden the base of observations of this group's gap-filling capacity, particularly because reactivation in subject-relatives might have been affected by the relativizer "who" in that construction and also because movement within subject-relatives has the special property of being "string vacuous"—such movement does not reorder any of the elements in the sequence.

Accordingly, the second study featured object-relatives of the sort, "The priest enjoyed the drink$_i$ that the caterer was^1 serving^2 $(t)_i$ to the guests." Again, the CMLP task was used; and again, priming was assessed in two locations—at the gap indexed by the trace (superscript 2) and at a baseline, pregap position (superscript 1). At each location the experimenters recorded lexical decision times for visual probes related to the moved constituent and for visual probes forming unrelated control words. For the example given, "wine" was the probe for "drink" and "boat," the control probe. And once more, Wernicke's patients, like normal controls, filled the gap (and only the gap), whereas the Broca's patients did not. Again, regardless of ultimate sentence understanding, Wernicke's carried out the syntactic business of linking antecedents and traces, and Broca's could not.

13.4   Concluding Remarks

13.4.1   Wernicke's Aphasia and Functional Localization

The line of research that has been described here is clearly only just beginning. Experimenters have yet to determine, for example, whether Wernicke's patients reactivate only appropriate antecedents at gaps. Still, even now, experiments that have been done using two different sentence types point rather convincingly to the Wernicke's patient's sensitivity to structurally licensed gaps and to their ability to fill these gaps—to form dependency relations involving traces at either subject or object positions—as sentences unfold in real time.

What does this reactivation at the gap signify, however? Does it indicate that the Wernicke's patient is assigning a thematic role to the antecedent, whether agent or theme? Or does it reflect the consequences of an earlier processing stage—a stage at which the antecedent and trace are coindexed prior to such thematic assignment? In the light of work by Shapiro and his colleagues, the latter possibility seems more likely (Shapiro et al. 1993). These investigators have shown that Wernicke's patients are not normally sensitive during comprehension to the argument-taking properties of verbs. Unlike neurologically intact subjects, the patients are unable to access momentarily all the possible argument structure configurations within a verb's lexical entry—to access, for example, the information that a dative verb like "send" can allow both an agent-theme configuration ("He sent the book") and an agent-theme-goal configuration ("He sent the book to Mary"). In effect, the Wernicke's patients appear unable to generate thematic information in real-time in the normal manner. It seems reasonable, therefore, to view gap-filling for these patients as being the reflection of processing that occurs at a stage prior to thematic assignment or mapping. The fact that they were capable of filling gaps in sentences for which they show uncertain comprehension strengthens this conclusion.

Whatever its precise role, however, it is clear that the brain region implicated in Wernicke's aphasia is not crucially involved in the reflexive syntactic activity of recognizing and filling gaps left by constituent movement as the sentence unfolds in real time.

13.4.2 Broca's Aphasia and Functional Localization

By contrast, the cortical region usually associated with Broca's aphasia does appear to be necessary for the operation of gap-filling. The data reviewed here show that Broca's patients are unable to form dependency relations involving traces—whether for object-relatives that they have difficulty understanding or even for subject-relatives that do not pose difficulty for them.

The consequences of this problem seem relatively straightforward. Since they do not have the processing resources to establish dependency relations normally—to fill the gap at exactly the right time in the processing sequence—they cannot provide the syntactic information necessary for thematic assignment to moved constituents. Presumably, therefore, the Broca's patients rely abnormally on some nongrammatical strategy to achieve thematic mapping for moved constituents—on a fill-in strategy (Hickok 1992) or an agent-first strategy (Grodzinsky 1986). And when such strategies do not work, their comprehension fails.

Accordingly, the structural limitations in Broca's aphasia described by Grodzinsky; by Mauner, Fromkin, and Cornell; and by Hickok can be linked to disruptions of automatic lexical reactivation. Thus, the brain region implicated in Broca's aphasia need not be the locus of syntactic representations per se. Rather, in the view developed here, this region seems to provide the processing resources that sustain lexical (re)activation and its syntactic ramifications. Possibly, as already suggested, these resources sustain the normal *speed* of activation and reactivation. This would be in line with independent evidence of slowed lexical processing in Broca's aphasia (Prather, Zurif, and Love 1992), and it is a possibility that is currently being explored.

There are, however, other possibilities concerning the responsibility of the brain area implicated in Broca's aphasia. For example, several investigators have suggested that it accommodates the memory storage demands that arise during comprehension (Kolk and van Grunsven 1985). And, certainly, a prima facie case can be made that long-distance dependency relations of the sort described here are especially reliant upon some form of working memory capacity.

Another possibility is that the broad cortical area associated with Broca's aphasia sustains multiple functions, including both speed of input activation and working memory. And yet another possibility is that memory capacity is diminished only as a consequence of slower-than-normal lexical activation—only because of the increased cost of such activation.

The point that is common to all of these accounts, however—and indeed, the moral of this chapter—is that structural limitations statable in the abstract terms of linguistic theory can be traced to changes in cortically localizable processing resources. Thus, descriptions of language localization in the brain can be offered in terms of speed of activation and storage capacity—in terms, that is, of processes and processing resources that intuitively appear biologically fixed or "wired in." And this reduces the distance between cognitive science and neuroscience.

Suggestions for Further Reading

A detailed consideration of the trace-deletion hypothesis is to be found in Grodzinsky's book *Theoretical perspectives on language deficits* 1990. The updates of this hypothesis provided by Mauner, Fromkin, and Cornell and by Hickok figure as part of two special issues of the journal *Brain and Language* 45:3 (October 1993 and in press). All the papers in these issues, including several that provide cross-linguistic perspectives, are characterized by detailed linguistic analyses, a practice that is, unfortunately, not that common in aphasia research.

The processing issues treated here—gap-filling and the real-time access of argument structure configurations in aphasia—are also described in considerable detail in these issues of *Brain and Language*.

It ought to be apparent that the representational and processing matters covered in this chapter form only a very small part of aphasia research. For much wider coverage of current work—including studies of production, repetition, and other activities, marked by varying degrees of theoretical focus—see Goodglass's book *Understanding aphasia* 1993.

Problems

13.1 Although not mentioned in the text of this chapter, Broca's patients also have difficulty interpreting pronouns in sentences. Faced with "The boy kicked him," it is not uncommon for Broca's patients to take "him" to refer incorrectly to "the boy." As it happens, Hickok's (1992) version of the trace deletion hypothesis—framed within the VP-internal-subject hypothesis—tries to account for this difficulty. The question here is how Hickok's account works.

To answer this question, two additional notions must be entered. The first is in the form of a principle stating that a pronoun must be free (not corefer with a NP) in its governing category; and the second is the hypothesis that the relevant governing category is the VP (Kitagawa 1986). The answer can be formulated by applying these two notions to representations that show subject NP movement from inside the VP; that is, to representations that accommodate the VP-internal-subject hypothesis. For the example given above, the representation is "The boy [$_{VP}$(t) kicked him]."

13.2 Grodzinsky (1990, 1993) has assessed Broca's patients' comprehension for sentences containing "psych" verbs. As noted in the text, verbs of this type replace the theta role of agent with that of experiencer. In "The man was hated by the woman," "the man" is the theme and "the woman" can best be described as the experiencer of the emotion, not its agent. Granting this characterization, what finding would vindicate Grodzinsky's use of the agent-first strategy? Recall that this strategy figures crucially in his original trace-deletion hypothesis and that it has been abandoned in the Mauner Fromkin, and Cornell (1993) and Hickok (1992) revisions.

Question for Further Thought

13.1   The major point in this chapter is that representational limitations can be linked to rather elementary processing disruptions—in particular to alterations in the speed of lexical activation. To state the matter more generally, language localization in the brain appears to reflect, not a distribution of knowledge types, but the anatomical allocation of processing resources. But, if so, should these resources be considered linguistically specific or domain general? This question has yet to be answered.

References

Caplan, D., and C. Futter (1986). Assignment of thematic roles by an agrammatic aphasic patient. *Brain and Language* 27, 117–135.

Caplan, D., and N. Hildebrandt (1988). *Disorders of syntactic comprehension*. Cambridge, MA: MIT Press.

Caramazza, A., and E. B. Zurif (1976). Dissociation of algorithmic and heuristic processes in language comprehension: Evidence from aphasia. *Brain and Language* 3, 572–582.

Chomsky, N. (1981). *Lectures on government and binding*. Dordrecht, Netherlands: Foris.

Collins, A., and E. Loftus (1975). A spreading-activation theory of semantic processing. *Psychological Review* 82, 407–428.

Goodglass, H. (1993). *Understanding aphasia*. San Diego, CA: Academic Press.

Goodglass, H., and E. Kaplan (1972). *The assessment of aphasia and related disorders*. Philadelphia: Lea and Febiger.

Grodzinsky, Y. (1984). Language deficits and linguistic theory. Unpublished doctoral dissertation, Brandeis University.

Grodzinsky, Y. (1986). Language deficits and the theory of syntax. *Brain and Language* 27, 135–159.

Grodzinsky, Y. (1990). *Theoretical perspectives on language deficits*. Cambridge, MA: MIT Press.

Grodzinsky, Y. (1993). Trace-deletion, theta-roles, and cognitive strategies. Manuscript, Aphasia Research Center, Boston V.A. Medical Center.

Hickok, G. (1992). Agrammatic comprehension, VP-internal subjects, and the trace-deletion hypothesis. Occasional Paper #45, Center for Cognitive Neuroscience, MIT.

Hickok, G., E. Zurif, and E. Canseco-Gonzalez (1993). Structural description of agrammatic comprehension. *Brain and Language* 45, 371–395.

Jackendoff, R. (1972). *Semantic interpretation in generative grammar*. Cambridge, MA: MIT Press.

Kitagawa, Y. (1986). Subjects in Japanese and English. Unpublished doctoral dissertation, University of Massachusetts, Amherst.

Kolk, H., and M. van Grunsven (1985). Agrammatism as a variable phenomenon. *Cognitive Neuropsychology* 2, 347–384.

Linebarger, M., M. Schwartz, and E. Saffran (1983). Sensitivity to grammatical structure in so-called agrammatic aphasics. *Cognition* 13, 361–393.

Mauner, G., V. Fromkin, and T. Cornell (1993). Comprehension and acceptability judgments in agrammatism: Disruptions in the syntax of referential dependency. *Brain and Language* 45, 340–370.

McNally, L. (1992). VP coordination and the VP-internal subject hypothesis. *Linguistic Inquiry* 23, 336–341.

Meyer, D., R. Schvaneveldt, and M. Ruddy (1975). Loci of contextual effects on visual word recognition. In P. Rabbit and S. Dornic, eds., *Attention and performance*. Vol. 5. New York: Academic Press.

Milberg, W., and S. Blumstein (1981). Lexical decision and aphasia: Evidence for semantic processing. *Brain and Language* 14, 371–385.

Naeser, M. A., C. Palumbo, N. Helm-Estabrooks, D. Stiassny-Eder, and M. L. Albert (1989). Severe nonfluency in aphasia: Role of the medial subcallosal fasciculus and other white matter pathways in recovery of spontaneous speech. *Brain* 112, 1–38.

Neely, J. H. (1977). Semantic priming and retrieval from lexical memory: Roles of inhibitionless spreading activation and limited-capacity attention. *Journal of Experimental Psychology: General* 106, 226–254.

Prather, P., E. B. Zurif, and T. Love (1992). The time course of lexical access in aphasia. Paper presented to the Academy of Aphasia, Toronto, Ontario.

Prather, P., E. B. Zurif, C. Stern, and J. Rosen (1992). Slowed lexical access in non-fluent aphasia: A case study. *Brain and Language* 43, 336–348.

Schwartz, M., M. Linebarger, E. Saffran, and D. Pate (1987). Syntactic transparency and sentence interpretation in aphasia. *Language and Cognitive Processes* 2, 85–113.

Shankweiler, D., S. Crain, P. Gorrell, and B. Tuller (1989). Reception of language in Broca's aphasia. *Language and Cognitive Processes* 4, 1–33.

Shapiro, L., B. Gordon, N. Hack, and J. Killackey (1993). Verb-argument structure processing in complex sentences in Broca's and Wernicke's aphasia. *Brain and Language* 45, 423–447.

Swinney, D., and J. D. Fodor, eds. (1989). *Journal of Psycholinguistic Research* (Special Issue on Sentence Processing) 18, (1).

Swinney, D., W. Onifer, P. Prather, and M. Hirshkowitz (1979). Semantic facilitation across sensory modalities in the processing of individual words and sentences. *Memory and Cognition* 7, 159–165.

Swinney, D., E. Zurif, P. Prather, and T. Love (1993). The neurological distribution of processing operations underlying language comprehension. Manuscript, Department of Psychology, University of California, San Diego.

Wernicke, C. (1874). The aphasia symptom complex: A psychological study on an anatomical basis. Reprinted in G. Eggert (1977), *Wernicke's works on aphasia*. The Hague: Mouton.

Wulfeck, B. (1988). Grammaticality judgments and sentence comprehension in agrammatic aphasia. *Journal of Speech and Hearing Research* 31, 72–81.

Wulfeck, B., and E. Bates (1991). Differential sensitivity to errors of agreement and word order in Broca's aphasia. *Journal of Cognitive Neuroscience* 3, 258–272.

Zurif, E. B., A. Caramazza, and R. Myerson (1972). Grammatical judgments of agrammatic aphasics. *Neuropsychologia* 10, 405–417.

Zurif, E. B., and Y. Grodzinsky (1983). Sensitivity to grammatical structure in agrammatic aphasics: A reply. *Cognition* 15, 207–213.

Zurif, E. B., D. Swinney, P. Prather, J. Solomon, and C. Bushell (1993). An on-line analysis of syntactic processing in Broca's and Wernicke's aphasia. *Brain and Language* 45, 448–464.

Chapter 14

Some Philosophy of Language

James Higginbotham

Syntactician, Semanticist, Logician, and Philosopher occasionally meet over coffee in the common room. They are disciplinary personae, only occasionally correlated with actual persons; so, even when they are all together it is not always clear how many of them there are. Their concerns may interact and then separate again, and they may be united in a single person. The significant point is that on these occasions they are all present and speak in their several voices.

The Cast: SYN, SEM, LOG, and PHIL

The First Day

PHIL: Well, Syn, is the project rolling along? Morphemes coming out in the right order?

SYN: Of course not, or else what would we be investigating? Besides, even if we could describe everything adequately (which we can't), there would remain problems of explanation and of understanding the new phenomena that come into view as we proceed. Just now I'm worried about a certain syntactic creature that doesn't fit comfortably with our scheme of classification, and it seems to raise semantic and logical problems as well.

SEM: Say on; Log and I have some time before our seminar.

SYN: Well, as you know, whole sentences can function as the objects of verbs. The simplest type in English is that of the finite or tensed complement, consisting of a complete clause preceded by the word "that" (which may be omitted). That gives Phil's favorite constructions, as in

John believes (that) [snow is white]

and generally, "believes that S," "wishes that S," and so forth. There is also the nonfinite complement or infinitive, as in

Mary wants [John to go to the store]

You and Phil keep telling me that there's only a grammatical difference between the two types, finite and nonfinite; that both finite and nonfinite

399

complements designate propositions; and so that the verbs "believe" and "want," among others, express what you call propositional attitudes.

SEM: Yes, and there are also the epistemic verbs, as in

John knows (that) [snow is white]

Knowledge is not just an attitude, since what one knows has to be true.

SYN: OK, but there's no immediate grammatical distinction between these and the attitude verbs. And if we really want to be complete, we have to add the gerundive complements as in

Mary regrets [their writing letters to the editor]

where the meaning is, as you would put it, that the proposition, or the truth of the proposition, that they wrote letters to the editor is something that Mary regrets.

LOG: The general syntactic form is then

NP — V — Sentence

where NP is the subject, and Sentence is the direct object, designating a proposition. The verb expresses a relation between these, so that the general logical form is

$R(a, b)$

The syntactic differences between the sentence types, as

Mary — believes — that they wrote letters to the editor

Mary — wants — them to write letters to the editor

Mary — resents — their writing letters to the editor

all wash out, logically speaking.

SYN: Shows you logic isn't everything, doesn't it? Actually, there are subtle differences among all the types, but right now I wanted to get on to another type of complement, where there is no "that" (in fact, there cannot be) and where the verb of the complement is neither gerundive nor infinitival. The type is exemplified by

Mary saw John leave

You can see that the complement "John leave" isn't tensed at all; for if it were present tense it would be "John leaves," and if it were past it would be "John left." But it isn't infinitival either, because there's no "to," and, of course, it isn't gerundive because the verb is "leave" and not "leaving."

PHIL: Hold on, though, isn't it just that "see" has an extended sense where it means "know by using one's eyes" or something of the sort? After all, you can say

Mary saw that John left

so your example is a stripped-down version of that. Oh, but that's wrong! You might see that John left by noticing that his chair is empty, but then you didn't see him leave. Conversely, you might see John leave while thinking you were seeing Fred leave, and then you wouldn't believe that John left, let alone know it.

LOG: Don't get ahead of yourself, Phil. Doesn't the truth of the complement follow in both cases? If Mary saw that John left, he left; and if Mary saw John leave, he left.

SEM: Yes, it follows, but for different reasons. Can't we say

Mary watched John leave?

But it would be nonsense to say

*Mary watched that John left

SYN: I was coming to that. The sentences in question have the structure

NP — V — NP — VP

as in

Mary — saw — John — leave

and it turns out that the verbs that fit are verbs of perception: so we have

Mary — saw/watched/heard — John — leave

PHIL: Don't you have the same thing in

Mary demanded John leave?

SYN: No, that's just a subjunctive (pretty rare in modern English).

PHIL: Well, I reserve the point. But what did you have in mind, Sem, by saying that the truth of the complement follows for different reasons in these cases?

Mary saw John leave
Mary saw that John left

SEM: My thought was that in the second case, where, as you put it, the verb "see" means "know by using one's eyes," the complement refers to a proposition. The proposition can be true or false; but, since seeing in this sense is a species of knowledge, and knowledge involves truth, the complement must be a true proposition if the sentence as a whole is to be true. In the first case, however, what Mary is said to have seen isn't a proposition at all, but a sort of perceptual object. So the fact that John left if Mary saw him leave isn't the same sort of fact as the fact that John left if Mary saw that he left. Then if you choose instead of "see" a verb of perception that doesn't have an extended sense involving knowledge—say the word "watch"—then it would be all right to follow it with "John leave" because that gives a perceptual object, but not with "John left," which gives only a proposition.

PHIL: You'll have to tell me more about the "perceptual objects" of yours.

SEM: I knew you would be skeptical. But I think we're getting ahead of Syn's story.

SYN: Yes, let me arrange some of the data for you. For certain verbs of perception, including "see," "watch," "hear," and "feel," we have a bare or—as it has been called—*naked infinitive* complement NP–VP, as in

> We saw John leave
> We heard everybody sing
> We watched a student solve a problem
> We felt the walls shake

My question as a syntactician is, first of all, what the syntactic structure of these complements is, and in particular whether the subject and predicate form a constituent or not; that is, whether the structure is the flat

> see — NP — VP

or the more complex

> see — [NP — VP]

with NP and VP together forming a constituent phrase. Suppose, for instance, that we replace the subject "John" above by a pronoun. Then we get

> We saw him/*he leave

so we know that accusative case is assigned by the verb "see." The same phenomenon occurs with the infinitival complements, since we have

> We expected John to leave
> We expected him/*he to leave

On the other hand, at least if Phil and Sem are right, we want the infinitival complement to designate a proposition, so it ought to have the complex structure rather than the simple flat one. So the fact that the subject of the naked infinitive is accusative doesn't show anything conclusive by itself. We encounter a real difference between the infinitival and the naked infinitive, in that the first generally allows the passive, but the second does not. We have

John/He was expected to leave

but never

*John/He was seen/watched/heard/felt leave

Log: In fact you can construct what you people call a minimal pair, can't you? You can have

Mary was seen to be qualified for the job

which would be the passive of

We saw Mary to be qualified for the job

but if you drop the infinitival "to" the result is

*Mary was seen be qualified for the job

and that's not on.

Syn: Very good, Log; that is a minimal pair. The fact that the passive is completely unavailable is evidence that the subject and predicate of a naked infinitive do form a constituent; for if they did not, then we would expect the passive. If you can say

Mary was seen

there would be no reason you can't say

*Mary was seen be qualified

Phil: Suppose then that 'John leave' is a constituent of 'We saw John leave'. Then why doesn't it just indicate a proposition that we "saw", or saw to be true, or something like that?

Sem: I see that you're eager to get back to my perceptual objects. I have no answer to Syn's problem, but here is the thought. Suppose that besides seeing, watching, or hearing ordinary physical objects we can stand in the same perceptual relations to things that happen to them (in fact, "We saw John leave" might be a reasonable answer to the question "What did you see happen?"). These things are somehow indicated by subject-predicate complexes (but not when the predicate is tensed, or marked with an infinitive, as Syn has shown). Then, if I see one of these things—such as John leave or everybody sing—happen, of course it does happen, so the proposition—that John left or that everybody sang—has to be true. In fact, Fred Dretske pointed out some time ago that there were cases of perception whose objects were events, not things. He gave examples like

We saw John's departure

John's departure is an event: it takes place, it comes before and after other events, and so on. And if we did see John's departure, then he departed (how else could we have seen it?). So I'm conjecturing that there is no semantic difference between Dretske's examples and, say,

We saw John depart

LOG: Let me bring in another kind of consideration. You were worried, Syn, about whether the naked infinitive was a constituent, like an ordinary complement sentence. In complement sentences, as you know, it's possible for expressions to take narrow scope, being understood within the complement alone, or wide scope, understood with respect to the whole sentence . . .

SYN: Stop! Give me something more intuitive than this scope-distinction stuff.

LOG: Right. Consider the sentence

Mary saw that one of the students left

We can understand it in such a way that we can ask "Who was it?" But it need not be so understood. Take a scenario similar to Phil's: Mary looks around the seminar room and notices that one of the chairs that used to have someone in it (she doesn't know who) is now unoccupied; and she concludes, correctly, that one of the students has left. Then my example is true, but it's not on to ask "Who was it that Mary saw left?" The ambiguity is explained if we say with Quine that the sentence can be understood either as

One of the students is an x such that Mary saw that x left

or as

Mary saw that one of the students is an x such that x left

In the first case there is some student x or other such that Mary saw that x left; so we can ask "Who was it?" In the second case there need be no student at all with this property. The first is the case where the expression "one of the students" has wide scope, the second where it has narrow scope. Clear enough?

SYN: I can see the ambiguity anyway. It becomes clearer with other examples. I know that I'll die from something or other, but there is no particular thing I expect to die from, so I understand the sentence

I know I'll die from something

with the word "something" having narrow scope in your sense.

LOG: That's right, and anyone who asked you "What is it?" when you said that would have misunderstood you. But now consider my example with one of your "naked infinitives":

Mary saw one of the students leave

In this case it must be in order to ask "Who was it?" The implication is that there is no ambiguity, and narrow scope is impossible

PHIL: But there was no ambiguity in Syn's example, either.

LOG: Only because Syn meant it one way rather than another. The sentence

I know I'll die from something

is ambiguous, considered as a sentence. The different meanings are

(For some x) I know [I'll die from x]

—false, in Syn's case—and

I know that [(for some x) I'll die from x]

—unfortunately true for all of us. Or remember Quine's example:

Witold wishes someone were President

Quine says that we may understand this either as

(For some x) Witold wishes [x were President]

the interpretation according to which "Witold has his candidate" or as

Witold wishes that [(for some x) (x were President)]

where he merely wishes "that the appropriate form of government were in force." The sentence can have either meaning, the second one being that where the expression "someone" has narrow scope. What I'm suggesting is that this kind of meaning is missing from the naked infinitive complements.   ·

PHIL: I see now. Your claim is that whereas

Mary saw that one of the students left

is ambiguous in the usual way, the trivially different sentence

Mary saw one of the students leave

is not. But doesn't that imply that we have full substitutivity of identity as well? But that's right! The inference

Mary saw that the man across the street waved to her
The man across the street was John; therefore,
Mary saw that John waved to her

doesn't go through, but the inference

> Mary saw the man across the street wave to her
> The man across the street was John; therefore,
> Mary saw John wave to her

does, I believe.

SYN: Slow down, Phil.

PHIL: OK, from the top: in some linguistic contexts you can always put equals for equals. So it's trivial, for instance, that if

> Mary saw a

and

> a is b

then

> Mary saw b

Mary herself might know that she saw a, but not that she saw b, even though a is b; but if she did see a, and a is b, then she saw b, whether she knows it or not. In the case at hand, if she saw the man across the street, and that man was John, then she saw John (even if she doesn't know it was John she saw). A context like that, namely

> see _____

is said to admit substitutivity of identity. But it's notorious that substitutivity of identity doesn't work in contexts like

> knows that _____ is so-and-so

and it doesn't work with

> sees that _____ waved to her

That is why putting "John" for "the man across the street" can lead you from a truth

> Mary saw that the man across the street waved to her

to a falsehood

> Mary saw that John waved to her

even if in fact the man across the street is John. Now what is funny is that if we drop the "that" and the past tense—so we get one of your naked infinitives—it does go through: if

> Mary saw the man across the street wave to her

and that man is John, then even if she doesn't recognize him it's true that

> Mary saw John wave to her

SEM: Let me try to put this together. I see that Syn's original question is in danger of receding into the background, but I want to hold on to it as well as the other observations. Our sentences are, as Syn put it

$$NP_1 - V - NP_2 - VP$$

where V is a verb of perception, and the VP is "bare" or "naked." In these cases (i) NP_2 is accusative (and that shows up if it is a pronoun); but (ii) the construction may not undergo the passive. On the semantic side, we have (iii) the fact that if such a sentence is true (with V in the past tense), then so is

$$NP_2 - VP$$

with VP in the past tense, and (iv) that there appears to be substitutivity of identity, and no ambiguities of scope. Taken together, these properties contrast with those of the minimally different infinitival construction

$$NP_1 - V - NP_2 - to - VP$$

which has properties (i) and (iii), but neither (ii) nor (iv), and where V are not limited to verbs of perception.

SYN: Thank you, Sem; but there is more.

PHIL: Hold on, though. Can't we explain everything by supposing that with the V of perception the object is just NP_2? So in

Mary saw John leave

we just have the meaning that Mary saw John, and he was leaving at the time. I can paraphrase it by

For some time t in the past, Mary saw John at t & John left at t

So property (iii), the truth of NP_2–VP, follows trivially. You can put equals for equals in the subject position NP_2, and, of course, there won't be any ambiguities of scope. In

Mary saw one of the students leave

for instance, we get

For some time t in the past, one of the students is an x such that
Mary saw x at t & x left at t

To use Log's terminology it must be "in order" to ask "Who was it?" in response to "Mary saw one of the students leave," just as it is to ask "Who was it?" in response to "Mary saw one of the students."

SYN: Well, Phil, with your usual enthusiasm you have taken the contrary of what I was going to say right out of my mouth. Renaat DeClerk has observed that if what you say were true it would allow us to infer from

> I felt the tank approach

that

> I felt the tank

or from

> I heard the door open

that

> I heard the door

Both of these seem wrong. Also, how would your suggestion apply to this?

> I saw it rain

You wouldn't paraphrase that as

> For some time t in the past, I saw it at t and it rained at t

PHIL: Well, probably not. . . .
SYN: Definitely not. And how about idioms like these?

> We watched all hell break loose
> We saw advantage taken of John

You're not going to say that you watched all hell when it broke loose, or you saw advantage when it was taken of John.

PHIL: So conjecture meets refutation. A mark of progress.
SYN: As you say. Anyway, the conclusion is that the NP–VP that follows a perception verb forms some kind of unit; otherwise, you wouldn't get pleonastic "it" for a subject, or idioms like "all hell," or "take advantage of." But it must be a peculiar sort of unit if it doesn't designate a proposition.

SEM: I think that Syn has given strong evidence that these naked infinitive complements designate perceptual objects. Take DeClerk's example

> I felt the tank approach

Suppose this is just like

> I felt the approach of the tank

that is, I perceived something happening. And similarly for the other cases: if I heard the door open, then I heard the opening of the door, and so forth. The naked infinitive is a kind of nominalization, I think, as I originally suggested.

SYN: But you wouldn't say that you saw

the raining of it
the breaking loose of all hell
the being taken of John of advantage

PHIL: You are ahead of me. Why is this relevant?

SYN: Well, there are systematic processes that convert sentences into NPs. One of these is the gerundive, where you add -*ing* to the verb, and what would have been the subject (and object, if there was one) show up with prepositions, or as possessives. So if you start from

the door — open

you get

the opening — of the door

(Sem's example), or

the door's — opening

or from

Mary — solve — the problem

you get

the solving — of the problem — by Mary

The other is the *derived* form, where you put some suffix on the verb (you have to know which one), as you get

Mary's departure/the departure of Mary

from

Mary — depart

or

the examination of the tooth by the dentist

from

the dentist — examine — the tooth

Sem is suggesting that the naked infinitives are nominalizations like these, and I was pointing out that, if so, then they are pretty peculiar, because they are around even when nominalizations of the gerundive or derived kinds don't exist. There is no nominalization of

all hell — break loose

because it is an idiom.

SEM: But that isn't an objection, is it? Why can't we have a nominalization where nothing happens syntactically?

LOG: Something has to happen. I mean, where does the nominalization get its meaning? And what meaning does it have anyway?

SEM: I wanted it to designate the perceptual object.

LOG: Right; but how does it do that? Take Syn's example

the examination of the tooth by the dentist

This nominalization, one is told, comes from the sentence

the dentist examine(s) the tooth

but the logical form of that sentence is just

$R(a,b)$

with R the examining relation, a the dentist, and b the tooth. How do you get a perceptual object out of that? I see two ways, and only two. The first is to take the perceptual object as coming somehow from the proposition $R(a,b)$, and the second is to nominalize over some structure that the $R(a,b)$ form doesn't reveal.

PHIL: But what are these perceptual objects?

LOG: Let's worry about that when the time comes. Perhaps they are like what Jon Barwise calls situations, complexes of objects and relations. If we said that, then the proposal for the meaning of, say,

We watched the dentist examine the tooth

would be

We watched a situation s, and s bears relation F to the proposition that the dentist examined the tooth

Our problem would be to fill in F.

SEM: And to fill it in so that you get the right consequences: you can put equals for equals; there's no ambiguity of scope; and the truth of the complement "the dentist examined the tooth" is guaranteed.

LOG: Yes, those would be constraints on F. But there is also the method of hidden structure....

SYN: Of what sort? We know the syntax, except for the question whether the naked infinitive NP–VP is a constituent.

LOG: The structure would lie in the words, not the syntax. You might put these situations inside the verbs themselves. So, suppose we said that we don't simply have the form $R(a,b)$ but rather

$R(a,b,s)$

where s is the situation. The nominalization then picks out s.

PHIL: Donald Davidson has suggested something like this for ordinary sentences. On his view, if you take any ordinary action sentence, say,

the boy threw the ball

then it really has a logical form

For some situation s, throw(the boy, the ball, s)

He supports this with a number of arguments.

LOG: Very well, adopting this view let us suppose that in

I saw the boy throw the ball

you get this

I saw the situation s such that throw(the boy, the ball, s)

But it's a trivial consequence of this that the boy did throw the ball. Also, you can put equals for equals because the context of the subject "the boy" is just as it is in the simple sentence "the boy threw the ball." And if we take our earlier example

Mary saw one of the students leave

we won't have any possibility of ambiguity such as we find in

Mary saw that one of the students left

Thus, we deduce all three of the semantic points that Syn and Sem have raised.

PHIL: Then the nominalization is that business of constructing a term "the situation s such that ..." out of the sentence?

SEM: Exactly. It is just like some other nominalizations in that respect. English has the affix -er, for example, which attaches to a verb and nominalizes it in such a way that what would normally be the subject is referred to. So

the drinker of coffee

for example comes from

drink(x, coffee)

or "x drinks coffee", and putting on -er gives the meaning

the x such that x drinks coffee

We even have the suffix -ee, which picks out the object, so that

the employee of the chocolate factory

comes from

employ(the chocolate factory,x)

and yields

the x such that the chocolate factory employs x

what we have in these nominalizations is just a way of picking out the position for situations. Log's suggestion even fits with the fact that we get idioms and such. There is no difficulty in having

We saw it rain

for that is just

We saw the situation s such that rain(s)

The situation is a perceptual object, even if there is no real subject of the sentence.

PHIL: I have several objections.

SYN: Remember, Phil, this is an empirical inquiry.

SYN: And mine are empirical objections. First of all, why do you say that in

Mary saw John leave

what she saw was the situation in which John left? Couldn't there have been several? Davidson argued that in

John left

the meaning was

There is *some* s such that leave(John,s)

One of his reasons was that you couldn't otherwise make sense of

John left twice

because that requires that there be two "leavings" by John, not just one. But can't you say

Mary saw John leave twice

meaning that she saw two different departures?

LOG: I take the point. I was hasty. For "I saw the boy throw the ball" we should have

There is a situation s such that throw(the boy,the ball,s) and I saw s

SEM: Good, Phil. We now get a difference between

Mary saw John leave (or: depart)

and

Mary saw John's departure

The first one is general: she saw some departure or another. But the second is specific, and to get something general we would say instead

Mary saw one of John's departures

But this is a minor modification.

PHIL: Second objection: what do you do with negation? Can't you say this?

Mary saw John not leave

On Log's proposal this comes out

There is a situation s such that not(leave(John,s)) & Mary saw s

but then it follows that if she saw John smile she saw him not leave; for smiling isn't leaving. But that's absurd.

LOG: That is a problem.

SYN: But think of when you would say that Mary saw John not leave. You would say that, for instance, if she saw him pointedly refrain from leaving the boring meeting he was itching to get out of. It's as if you were to say

Mary saw John stay

PHIL: Very well, maybe you have something. Can you hear the audience not clap? When you do, do you hear their silence?

SEM: Enough with the metaphysics. You had another objection?

PHIL: Yes. The scope problem resurfaces, I think. Suppose I'm at the ball game and I am the last to leave. Then I might say

I saw everybody else leave

But it wouldn't be right to say that everybody else is a person I saw leave: I just saw the crowd.

LOG: We have room for that, if we recognize that we can have situations with plural subjects. You must have looked at this, Sem. Isn't it recognized that you can say

Everybody carried the piano upstairs

where you mean they all did it as a group?

SEM: Sure. Phil's example would be like that. You're saying

There is a situation s such that everybody else left in s & I saw s

and you're not saying

Everybody else is an x such that there is a situation s such that x left in s & I saw s

The second way of putting it gives a different situation for each person; the first gives just one situation in which everybody was involved.

SYN: Can I get back to the syntax? Why should naked infinitives behave in this strange way? And why can't you get the passive? Actually, your discussion reminds me of what I now realize is a prescient remark that James Gee made in 1977. He wrote that the semantics may correlate with the absence of tense from the naked infinitive. Put it this way: if the tense is there, as in

Mary heard John left

the subject and predicate form a proposition (she might have heard a rumor to the effect that John left); if it isn't there, as in

Mary heard John leave

we can't get a proposition, but one of these nominalizations. Tense is a member of the inflectional elements of syntax, like the infinitival "to." So I have a new problem: why the correlation between the presence of an inflectional element and a propositional interpretation, or the absence of such an element and the—what shall I call it—situational interpretation?

SEM: Log and I would love to sort this out for you, but it's time for our seminar.

SYN: There are other parts of the syntactic story I haven't explained yet. You got some time tomorrow?

SEM: OK.

[*Sem* and *Log* dash off; *Syn* takes notes; *Phil* stares at the ceiling.]

The Second Day

PHIL: More coffee, Syn? Got a fresh pot.

SYN: Thanks. Over there please, not on my notes.

SEM: Can I sum up? The theory so far says that sentences

$$NP_1 - V - NP_2 - VP$$

where V is a perception verb, express relations, signaled by V, between NP_1 and a situation designated by the complex NP_2–VP. These contrast with superficially similar sentences

$$NP_1 - V - NP_2 - tense/to - VP$$

which express relations between NP_1 and the proposition given by NP_2–VP. The difference is correlated somehow with the presence of the infinitive in the latter and its absence in the former; but we don't know how, and we don't know whether NP_2 VP always forms a phrase. But we do have a hypothesis for the semantic difference. In the second, infinitival case, assuming with Davidson that sentences have a special place for situations, the object of the verb is

the proposition that (for some situation s) $VP(NP_2,s)$

Call this proposition p. Then the whole sentence expresses

$V(NP_1,p)$

So, for example

Mary saw that John left

is

Saw(Mary, the proposition that (for some s) leave(John,s))

But in the first case the object of the verb is a situation itself so that the whole sentence expresses

(For some situation s) $V(NP_2,s)$ & $VP(NP_1,s)$

So that

Mary saw John leave

is

(For some situation s) (leave(John,s) & saw(Mary,s))

SYN: Thanks, Sem. Let me put some more of the syntax before you. Adrian Akmajian [1977] discussed, besides the naked infinitive cases, also the case where the VP is gerundive. An example would be

Mary saw John leaving

He noticed also that there was very good evidence that the complement "John leaving" really is a phrase. You can get it, for example, as a whole subject, as in

[John leaving] — is a distressing sight

but not

*[John leave] — is a distressing sight

He also noticed that the gerundive complement is much more productive than the naked infinitive. For example, there is a contrast between

Mary observed John leaving

and

*Mary observed John leave

PHIL: I thought gerundive complements with *-ing* designated propositions. Didn't you give this example?

Mary resents their writing letters to the editor

SYN: There's a difference, Phil: in this case the subject is possessive
"their," not accusative "them."
PHIL: You mean that matters?
SYN: Sure. Notice that you get

Mary saw him/*his leaving
Mary resents *him/his leaving

PHIL: I see. So the case of the element really is important to you.
SYN: More than that, it's a diagnostic, so we know what we're dealing
with.
LOG: This latter type of example does not appear to affect the hypothesis just outlined by Sem, however. Could we not say that for

Mary saw John leaving

we have this?

(For some situation s) (leaving(John,s) & saw(Mary,s))

I should think that we could.
SEM: Yes, why not? There is a contrast in meaning between

Mary saw John leave
Mary saw John leaving

in that in the first case John must have really left, and the action is
completed, whereas in the second it is incomplete. But that is the same as
the contrast between

John left
John was leaving

But before you go farther, Syn, assuming this is all right, a problem did
occur to me. I considered sentences

Mary saw John VP

and tried to see what VP would comfortably go there. Let me show you
some of the examples:

Mary saw John: buy a house
                  pray for rain
                  own a house
                  hope for rain

I also looked at cases that aren't naked infinitives in your sense, but where in place of VP you just have an adjective, like "Mary saw John unhappy." Consider this list:

Mary saw John: happy
                  drunk
                  stupid
                  six feet tall

What do you think?

SYN: The first two examples in each list are fine; the others are strange.

SEM: That's what I think. And the result reminded me of Gregory Carlson's and Angelika Kratzer's work on stage-level and individual-level predicates.

LOG: What is the distinction?

SEM: An individual-level predicate is one expressing a state that applies to its subject for a long period or essentially; a stage-level predicate applies only temporarily. We know that sentences beginning "there is ..." are sensitive to this distinction. So, for instance, contrast

There's a man drunk in the next room (stage-level)

with

*There's a man stupid in the next room (individual-level)

Also, simple present-tense sentences in English are acceptable with individual-level VPs, but not stage-level. So

John owns a house (individual-level)

just means: that's the way things are right now. But

John buys a house (stage-level)

doesn't mean that, at least not taken all by itself. Now, this same distinction seems to be at work in the case of naked infinitives. You can say

Mary saw John buy a house (stage-level)

but not

Mary saw John own a house (individual-level)

PHIL: What if John were playing Monopoly? Couldn't you say

Mary saw John own a house on Park Place?

SEM: I like that, Phil! What you've done is come up with a context where the predicate "own a house" has been made stage-level, because we know that in Monopoly houses get owned for possibly short periods.

PHIL: And the same would go for the other examples. Suppose that John is stupid on the afternoons he takes stupid pills, but not on other afternoons. Then you could say

Mary saw John stupid (on Wednesday afternoon)

Or suppose you could vary your height at will, as you can vary your hair color. Then you could say

Mary saw John six feet tall

SYN: Your thought experiments are as outrageous as ever, Phil; but I think you have a point in this case.

LOG: Before we go further with the science fiction, may I observe that we have no way to express the distinction Sem has noticed? There is, one assumes, a situation of John's being six feet tall, and so the sentence

John is six feet tall

has the logical form

for some situation s (six feet tall(John,s)

and then nothing precludes the nominalization that will assign to "Mary saw John six feet tall" the meaning

for some situation s (six feet tall(John,s) & saw(Mary,s)

SYN: Perhaps John's being six feet tall is a situation you can't see?
PHIL: But you can say

Mary saw John unhappy

What makes John's being unhappy a situation you *can* see?

SYN: I think I have an explanation.... But I have to begin farther back.

PHIL: I see Syn caffeineless. I'll get the coffee.

SYN: Yesterday Phil brought up Davidson's views about action sentences, which are very interesting and all that but leave me puzzled how this position for situations ever gets noticed in the syntax. I mean, if you say that

John left

is

(For some situation s) (left(John,s))

where does that "for some situation s" come from? You certainly don't hear it. But if some current views of syntax are correct, then besides the core NP "John" and VP "leave" we have the tense (in this case Past), and it belongs to its own inflectional category INFL. So really the structure is

NP — INFL — VP

where the INFL contains the feature for tense that surfaces as an affix on the verb. Now what if this category INFL was what gave us the "for some situation s" bit? If it did, then the category could give us something else, too; namely, a way of distinguishing the individual-level from the stage-level predicates. The reason is that besides the neutral "for some situation s" we might have in INFL something that, in the present tense anyway, requires an individual-level predicate, call it I. Then in

John owns a house

we have

(For some I-situation s) owns(John,a house,s)

But this kind of INFL would be incompatible with a stage-level predicate. Inversely, for cases where you get stage-level predicates but not individual-level ones, like

There is a man drunk/*stupid in the next room

we might suppose that you have an INFL that requires a stage-level predicate, call it S. Now Sem has observed that individual-level predicates aren't acceptable in naked infinitives. But maybe they do have a kind of INFL (which you never hear) of the same sort as in the simple present tense in English. If that were so, then you would get exactly Sem's distinction. You could say

Mary saw John buy a house

because that would be

For some S-situation s ...

but not

Mary saw John own a house

because owning a house isn't normally an S-situation.

Log: That would mean recognizing some further structure in your naked infinitives.

Syn: Yes, but it correlates with a real distinction. It also answers, in a roundabout way, my question about whether naked infinitives are constituents; if they have a kind of INFL, then they must be.

Phil: That went by me.

Syn: OK, here's the reasoning. There's a lot of support for the hypothesis that a simple sentence consisting of a subject NP, a VP, and a tense actually starts out as a structure like this:

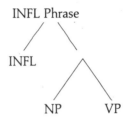

where the NP moves to the left past INFL, and INFL moves down to become an affix on the VP (the tense). The NP couldn't fail to be there, because the VP would then lack a subject. And the INFL gets together with NP–VP under a higher point INFL Phrase; so, if INFL is there, then NP–VP must be a phrase.

PHIL: Very well. Suppose that the complements to perception verbs do generalize over S-situations, and for some reason only over these. Yesterday I was skeptical about Sem's perceptual objects, but on thinking it over I've become less so. Even though I stand ready to be corrected at any moment by Syn, I think there's another class of naked infinitives that haven't been considered yet. What about the example

Mary made John leave?

I can repeat Syn's diagnostics, I think: the verb "leave" has no tense, and there's no infinitival "to." And if Mary made John leave, then surely he left; so the consequences are the same as for "Mary saw John leave."

SYN: I agree: in fact Akmajian gives this case. But he adds examples like

Mary had John bring the car

and you can also include

Mary helped John pack
Mary let John bring the car

PHIL: Just what I wanted to see. All these verbs—"help," "make," "have" (in this sense), and "let"—have this in common, that they all involve causation. They fit perfectly Sem's remarks about "happenings" because you can make, or let, or have, or help something happen. So suppose the objects are situations, things that happen, and that we analyze them the same way as the perception verbs. For "Mary helped John pack" that would give

(For some situation s) (pack(John,s) & helped(Mary,s))

You can translate back from the formal notation into (rather stilted but intelligible) English as Davidson does; and that would give

There was a packing by John and it was helped by Mary

LOG: May we check the matter out with respect to the phenomena that we brought to bear on perception verbs? There was the problem of negation, for instance . . . .

SYN: I was just wondering about that. It checks out, doesn't it, because you can say

Mary had John not bring the car

and the meaning is that she had him stay put, or something like that. Also, you do get idioms, and pleonastic "it":

They made it rain/all hell break loose

So I'm ready to accept that these cases go along with the perception verbs syntactically as well as semantically. But why does all this make you happier about perceptual objects, Phil?

PHIL: Because situations in the sense in which we are now speaking of them aren't *intrinsically* perceptual at all. They are just things, some of which can be perceived, and different ones by different sensory modalities. As Sem put it yesterday, citing Dretske, they are things that happen, and so things that are or can be the causes and effects of other things. From this, it's true, we don't know very much about their nature; but at least we know that they show up in other contexts than just perception.

SYN: Actually, Phil, I found myself beginning to think that your skepticism had a point (I know I pick up bad habits from you). According to the view we're now taking, when you see a situation you don't have to know what you're seeing, or know what the things are that you're seeing. I remember I once told my mother

I see a star moving through the sky

and she said

What you see is an airplane landing

I did see something; I was just wrong in describing what I saw.

PHIL: This is a point in favor of the analysis in terms of situations. They can be misdescribed, just like anything else.

SYN: But I already had the concepts to see what I did. Could I see those things without the concepts? I mean, I paid my taxes this morning by writing a check, and my dog was watching me the whole time. Did the dog see me pay my taxes?

PHIL: If I were where the dog was, I would have seen you pay your taxes?

SYN: Yes. But if I made a list of "things my dog saw me do" I don't know if I would put "paying my taxes" on the list.

PHIL: What a thing for you to be worried about, Syn! I don't really know the answer to your question, but I can make a distinction. It may be that you have to have concepts of certain kinds to be able to see certain situations. But to the extent that's true it's not true only of seeing situations. Suppose you took your dog driving around Oxford. Would you put on your list of "things my dog saw today" all the things that you yourself saw? Even if the dog is exposed to the same images as you, there may be limits on what it can take in. Would you feel happy saying it saw a three-way intersection, for example?

SYN: I'm not yet satisfied, but I get the idea.

LOG: I think I see a problem with the causal verbs you've been discussing. Perception verbs admitted both

Mary V John leave
Mary V John leaving

but these causal verbs do not. You cannot have

*Mary made John leaving
*Mary let John bringing the car

SYN: You're right. But we can have

Mary had John bringing the car

I don't know why there should be a difference.

SEM: There's another thing, too. For the perception verbs you had to have stage-level predicates, what Syn calls S-situations. But for these later cases you don't. You can say, for example

Vitamins made John six feet tall

SYN: Right again.

PHIL: What do you do when these odd things pop up, Syn? It always seems that when you have nice generalizations you also have exceptions.

SYN: Sometimes you just have to put up with that. But I can say anyway how these differences among the verbs can be stated in the theory. Verbs are said to *select* for the nature of their objects or complements. Going back to the case of ordinary propositional complements, we have to say that "believe" selects for *that*-clauses and infinitives, but not gerunds, because we have

Mary believes — that they wrote letters to the editor
Mary believes — them to have written letters to the editor
*Mary believes — their writing letters to the editor

and we have to say that "regret" selects for *that*-clauses and gerunds, but not infinitives:

Mary regrets — that they wrote letters to the editor
*Mary regrets — them to have written letters to the editor
Mary regrets — their writing letters to the editor

and, finally, that "want" selects infinitives only:

*Mary wants — that they write letters to the editor
Mary wants — them to have written letters to the editor
*Mary wants — their writing letters to the editor

In the cases at hand we have to say:

"make" and "let," but not "have," do not select for gerunds
"see" selects for S-situations, "make" does not

and so forth. There may be deep reasons for these facts, but they are not easy to find.

SEM: In the same vein, I wondered if you were going to bring up the fact that the causal verbs can't take for their objects ordinary nominalizations that refer to situations, like "John's departure." Although you can have

Mary saw John depart/John's departure

you can't have

*Mary made John's departure

in the sense that she made him depart (but only in the irrelevant sense that she made it go well). The resistance of the causal verbs to NP objects for situations extends to pronouns and again contrasts with the perception verbs. So you can say

Mary saw John depart, but Bill didn't see it

where the "it" refers back to the thing that Mary saw, but not

Mary made John depart, but Bill didn't make it

In fact the sentence

Bill made it

besides the idiomatic meaning "Bill succeeded," only means something like "Bill made the cake" and never means that he made some situation.

LOG: Such are the vagaries of ordinary language.

SEM: You're right, Log, and you're wrong, too. In these cases, I was going to say, there is a way of getting around the requirements of the formal syntax. You can say

Mary made John depart, but Bill didn't make it happen

It's just that, to use Syn's terminology, the causal verb selects for an NP–VP complement when situations are to be referred to. But before you lament the vagaries of language, consider this. We have examined lots of sentences of our (no doubt slightly different) varieties of English, and we've substantially agreed about what they mean and whether they are grammatical. The facts that we've been trying to systematize were already known to us before the subject ever came up. How did we know these facts? Mother (or whoever) never told you, "Now, Log, when you want to refer to a situation with a pronominal object to 'make' or 'let,' you must always remember that formal syntax requires you to put in the verb 'happen'." The facts you know constitute your linguistic competence, which takes in syntactic and semantic elements in complex ways. The clean lines of your suggestion for the logic of perception verbs (and now for these causal verbs as well) were immensely helpful, just because they abstracted away from many details of linguistic organization. Likewise for Phil's thought-experiments and metaphysical remarks. But the details of language aren't exhausted in the logic and philosophy.

LOG: I was being ironic, Sem. But I take the point. Let me think some more about the logic of perception (and causation).

PHIL: The nature of situations still puzzles me. Syn's problem about the dog, for instance . . . .

SYN: Oh, there are plenty of problems outstanding. I haven't even given you some of the facts from languages other than English. And I still don't know why you can't say

*John was seen/made leave

SEM: Still, we've made progress. The distinction between situational reference and propositional reference is worth exploring further. Let me again sum up. What is peculiar about naked infinitives is that they refer to situations rather than to propositions. They do this by a kind of hidden nominalization, which picks out the position for situations already found in the verb. Following Syn's suggestion the structure for a naked infinitive sentence is

$$NP - V - [_{\text{INFL Phrase}}INFL [NP - VP]]$$

where the INFL acts so as to generalize over situations, giving

(For some (S- or I-) situation s) (VP(NP,s) & V(NP,s))

where perception V always pick S-situations, and the causal V are neutral. From this proposal the semantics, and some of the syntax, follows.

[*Phil* rises to prepare the coffee.]

Suggestions for Further Reading

Phil's discussion of situations relies on Davidson 1967, who spoke more narrowly of events. This work is reprinted with further remarks in Davidson 1980. Davidson's work forms the background of the study by Parsons 1990, which considers perception verbs in passing and causal constructions rather extensively. Different ways of thinking about reference to events are surveyed in Bennett 1988, especially chapters 1 and 2.

Syn draws on the discussion of the syntax of perception verb complements in Akmajian 1977, with comments in Gee 1977. Gee, in turn, builds on the seminal discussion in Dretske 1969, reprinted 1988.

Dretske's account of the sort of seeing that is involved in naked infinitive complements was extended by the logical and semantic study by Barwise 1981, reprinted in Barwise 1989. Barwise took the view that Log alludes to but then does not pursue, that situational reference is mediated by some relation to the proposition; but his account of propositions is one that is itself based on situations in his sense (see at length Barwise and Perry 1983). The semantic peculiarities of naked infinitives in allowing substitutivity of identity and not permitting (under ordinary circumstances) scope ambiguity of quantifiers are due to Barwise, who provides other logical points and puzzles for reflection. The *locus classicus* of problems of scopal ambiguity and substitutivity of identity is Quine 1956, reprinted in Linsky 1971 and in several other collections on the philosophy of language. Further development is due among others to Hintikka 1969, also reprinted in Linsky. Hintikka's discussion in terms of possible-worlds semantics is the chief critical target of Barwise 1981; for a further development of Hintikka's point of view, see Niiniluoto 1982.

Higginbotham 1983 and Vlach 1983 respond to Barwise, Higginbotham taking the view that Log ultimately suggests. Articles critical of this view include Asher and Bonevac 1985a and 1985b, and Neale 1988. Recent syntactic discussion of both perception verbs and causatives includes Mittwoch 1990 and Ritter and Rosen 1993. Both these papers consider the problems of selection that Syn discusses in the text.

The distinction between stage-level and individual-level predicates is explored in Kratzer 1994, who demonstrates its grammatical and semantic significance; the question of the exact nature of the distinction remains largely open at this time. Nominalizations have been discussed from several points of view; a good source for the types in English is Grimshaw 1990.

Problems

14.1   In response to Phil's question about the example

Mary demanded John leave

Syn replied that the complement "John leave" was in this case a subjunctive rather than a naked infinitive. How do the following data support Syn's response?

Mary demanded that John leave
*Mary saw that John leave
Mary demanded he/*him leave
Mary saw *he/him leave

14.2   Sem argues that the reason you can say

I saw everybody else leave

where you wouldn't be prepared to say that there is any particular person you saw leave is that the subject is plural, as in the interpretation of

Everybody carried the piano upstairs

where they all worked together to lift the piano. Characterize, and then use Sem's distinction to explain, the difference between these:

I saw everybody walk down the street
I saw every single person walk down the street

14.3   The fact that seeing as reported by a naked infinitive complement is independent of knowledge is exemplified by the difference between these two sentences (noted by Barwise):

Ralph saw that a spy was hiding a letter under a rock, but thought she was tying her
shoe
Ralph saw a spy hiding a letter under a rock, but thought she was tying her shoe

Explain why.

14.4   Log concedes that in order to allow a sentence like

Mary saw John leave twice

we have to allow that the complement "John leave" doesn't refer to a unique situation. Fill in the reasoning. How would we give a logical form to this sentence?

14.5   Determine, using the tests above, which of these predicates are stage-level and which are individual-level. Do they all fit neatly as judged by all the tests?

have blue eyes
unconscious
know the answer
wear glasses
witty

14.6   The discussants are quick to agree that the causal verbs and the perception verbs fit the same semantic pattern. Check the cases

Mary had the man across the street wave to her
Mary helped a boy read a book

to see that the first satisfies substitutivity of identity, and the second shows no scope ambiguity. Do you find an ambiguity in

Mary made a boy read a book?

If so, what problem does this create for the account given in the text?

14.7   When Phil raised the question what to say about negation inside naked infinitive complements as in

John saw Mary not leave

Syn suggested that the function of negation in these cases was to give, not the contradictory of the predicate, but a contrary one, such as

John saw Mary refrain from leaving

Is Syn right? Think of some examples to test the hypothesis.

References

Akmajian, A. (1977). The complement structure of perception verbs in an autonomous syntactic framework. In P. Culicover, T. Wasow, and A. Akmajian, eds., *Formal syntax*, 427–460. New York: Academic Press.

Asher, N., and D. Bonevac (1985a). Situations and events. *Philosophical Studies* 47, 57–77.

Asher, N., and D. Bonevac (1985b). How extensional is extensional perception? *Linguistics and Philosophy* 8, 203–228.

Barwise, J. (1981). Scenes and other situations. *The Journal of Philosophy* 78. Reprinted with an Appendix in Barwise (1989), 5–36.

Barwise, J. (1989). *The situation in logic*. Stanford: Center for the Study of Language and Information Lecture Notes, no. 17.

Barwise, J., and J. Perry (1983). *Situations and attitudes*. Cambridge, MA: MIT Press.

Bennett, J. (1988). *Events and their names*. Indianapolis: Hackett Publishing Co.

Carlson, G. (1977). *Reference to kinds in English*. Doctoral dissertation, University of Massachusetts, Amherst. New York: Garland Press.

Davidson, D. (1967). The logical form of action sentences. In N. Rescher, ed., *The logic of decision and action*. Pittsburgh: University of Pittsburgh Press. Reprinted in Davidson (1980), 105–148.

Davidson, D. (1980). *Essays on actions and events*. Oxford: Clarendon Press.

DeClerk, R. (1982). On the derivation of Dutch bare infinitives after perception verbs. *Theoretical Linguistics* 9, 161–179.

Dretske, F. (1969). *Seeing and knowing*. Chicago: University of Chicago Press.

Gee, J. (1977). Comments on the paper by Akmajian. In P. Culicover, T. Wasow, and A. Akmajian, eds., *Formal syntax*, 461–481. New York: Academic Press.

Grimshaw, J. (1990). *Argument structure*. Cambridge, MA: MIT Press.

Higginbotham, J. (1983). The logic of perceptual reports: An extensional alternative to situation semantics. *The Journal of Philosophy* 80, 100–127.

Hintikka, J. (1969). Semantics for propositional attitudes. In J. Davis et al., eds., *Philosophical logic*. Reprinted in Linsky (1971), 145–167.

Kratzer, A. (1988). Stage level and Individual level predicates. In M. Krifka, ed., *Genericity in natural language*, University of Tuebingen technical report.

Linsky, L., ed. (1971). *Reference and modality*. Oxford: Oxford University Press.

Mittwoch, A. (1990). On the distribution of bare infinitive complements in English. *Journal of Linguistics* 26, 103–131.

Neale, S. (1988). Events and "logical form." *Linguistics and Philosophy* 11, 303–321.

Niiniluoto, I. (1982). Remarks on the logic of perception. In I. Niiniluoto and E. Saarinen, eds., *Acta Philosophica Fennica 35: Intensional Logic: Theory and Applications*, 116–129.

Parsons, T. (1990). *Events in the semantics of English*. Cambridge, MA: MIT Press.

Quine, W. (1956). Quantifiers and propositional attitudes. *The Journal of Philosophy* 53. Reprinted in Linsky (1971), 101–111.

Ritter, E. and S. T. Rosen (1993). Deriving causation. *Natural Language and Linguistic Theory* 11, 519–556.

Vlach, F. (1983). On situation semantics for perception. *Synthese* 54, 129–152.

Index

429

Interrogatives, syntactic structure for, 18–19
Intersection of adjectives, 323–324
Intonation structure in grammar computation, 258–259
Intransitive verbs
  argument structures for, 170–172
  lexical properties of, 288
Invention of languages by isolated deaf children, 6–8
Inversion, interrogative, see Interrogative inversion
Irregular verbs
  Blocking principle in, 115–122, 116, 169–170
  connectionist modeling of, 122–128
  frequency of, 121–122
  overregularization of, 109–114
Island constructions, 226–227, 255
Isolation in language learning, 10–20

Jablon, A. D., 239
Jackendoff, R. S., 22, 258, 319, 353–354, 378
Jakobovits, L., 353
Janowsky, J. S., 140
Janssen, T. M. V., 322
Jenkins, J., 89
Johnson, J. S., 13
Johnson, M., 260, 279, 354
Johnson-Laird, P. N., 353
Johnston, J., 22
Joshi, A., 265, 269–270, 278
Judgment tasks, 141
Juliano, C., 205
Jusczyk, P. W., 101, 104

Kamp, H., 333
Kamp, J. A. W., 323, 331, 353–354
Kaplan, E., 381–382
Kaplan, R. M., 241
Katz, J. J., 353
Kay, M., 278
Kay, P., 22
Kearnes, M. J., 176
Keenan, E. L., 353, 377–378
Kegl, J., 152
Kenstowicz, M., 84
Kim, J. J., 127, 130
Kiparsky, Paul, 158
Kitagawa, Y., 386
Klein, E., 343, 353

Klein, W., 354
Klima, E. S., 6
Kolk, H., 394
Krasnegor, N. A., 176
Kratzer, Angelika, 417, 425
Kripke, S., 326
Kuczaj, Stan, 119
Kuhl, P. K., 104, 142

Labeled bracketing, 285
LaBerge, S., 15–16
Labial consonants, 63
Labiovelar consonants, 64–65
Labov, W., 52, 153
Ladusaw, W., 375, 378
Lakoff, G., 353–354
Lalonde, C. E., 92, 101
Landau, B., 9, 22, 157
Language acquisition, 1–2, 99–100, 149–151
  abstract nouns, 169
  biology in, 137–141
  bootstrapping in, 162, 165–169
  by children, 157–161
  context in, 156–157
  course of, 141–145
  creativity in, 107–109
  environment in, 4–10, 137
  explanation of, 146–149
  exposure deprivation in, 10–15
  grammar in, 145, 161–162, 168–172
  innateness of, 108, 136–137, 150–151, 158
  input in, 151–157
  isolation in, 10–20
  language-exposure deprivation in, 10–15
  language-learning algorithm in, 161–165
  learning in, 149–151
  maturation in, 140–141
  milestones in, 2–3
  modularity in, 135–137
  Motherese in, 154–156
  negative evidence in, 153–154
  overregularization in, 109–114, 116
  parameter-setting in, 172–174
  pidgins and creoles, 15–16
  positive evidence in, 151–153
  prosody in, 156
  rules in, 108, 146
  second language, 13–14, 100, 140
  Subset Principle in, 174–175
  words in, 99, 102